QUANTITATIVE MODELS
FOR
PRODUCTION MANAGEMENT

PRENTICE-HALL INTERNATIONAL SERIES IN MANAGEMENT

QUANTITATIVE MODELS
FOR
PRODUCTION MANAGEMENT

Hans-Jürgen Zimmermann
Technische Hochschule
Aachen, Western Germany

Michael G. Sovereign
Naval Postgraduate School
Monterey, California

Prentice-Hall, Inc., Englewood Cliffs, New Jersey

Library of Congress Cataloging in Publication Data

ZIMMERMANN, HANS JÜRGEN.
 Quantitative models for production management.

 (Prentice-Hall international series in management)
 Includes bibliographical references.
 1. Production management—Mathematical models.
2. Decision-making. I. Sovereign, Michael G.,
joint author. II. Title.
TS155.Z513 1974   658.5   73–1870
ISBN 0-13-746966-7

Printed in the United States of America

10 9 8 7 6 5 4 3 2 1

PRENTICE-HALL INTERNATIONAL, INC., *London*
PRENTICE-HALL OF AUSTRALIA, PTY. LTD., *Sydney*
PRENTICE-HALL OF CANADA, LTD., *Toronto*
PRENTICE-HALL OF INDIA PRIVATE LIMITED, *New Delhi*
PRENTICE-HALL OF JAPAN, INC., *Tokyo*

PRENTICE-HALL, INC.
PRENTICE-HALL INTERNATIONAL, INC., *United Kingdom and Eire*
PRENTICE-HALL OF CANADA, LTD., *Canada*
DUNOD PRESS, *France*
MARUZEN COMPANY, LTD., *Far East*
HERRERO HERMANOS, SUCS., *Spain and Latin America*
R. OLDENBOURG VERLAG, *Germany*
ULRICO HOEPLI EDITORS, *Italy*

Contents

Foreword

A. Who Should Read This Book—and Why

I. INTRODUCTION

The title *Quantitative Models for Production Management* should not discourage the reader who is not currently either a manager or a "quantitative type." We intend most of this book to be readable by anyone seriously interested in the decisions which must be made in modern enterprises producing goods or services. The enterprises may range from factories and shops to government agencies. We feel that production decisions are important enough that the topic should be brought within the reach of a wide range of backgrounds. Most of our daily lives are concerned with the production and consumption of economic quantities. The decisions regarding how, when, and where production occurs are therefore important to all of us who hope to understand our economic organization and to improve it through intelligent management.

II. OBJECTIVE OF THE BOOK

In reading this book you should be aware that our objective is much more than to show you a bag of tricks for some special situations. We seek the development of your ability to take any problem in the broadly defined production area and set up your own conceptional model of your own decisions. In addition, we show you the way toward implementation of these decisions through models already developed for the common general problems in the production area: the size, location, design, cost, planning, scheduling, and maintenance of production processes.

III. THE TYPICAL READER OF THE BOOK

We anticipate that most readers will be students in undergraduate or graduate curricula in business or industrial engineering. These readers will probably have a background in mathematics through calculus, a course in microeconomics, and course in statistics; also, some exposure to linear programming via matrix algebra and computers is desirable. We believe that everyone has participated in some production efforts—such as schools, voluntary organizations, etc.—and that no other experience is necessary.

B. Approach of the Book

The reader will find in Chap. 1 that the book examines a comprehensive sequence of decisions required in the implementation of a production process. We emphasize the modeling of the decision maker's choices and then the selection of the best of these alternatives. In general, the decision maker must "manage" the resources available to him to accomplish a task most economically. This makes optimization of resource allocation the basic theory of the book. It is not surprising then that mathematical programming is present in every chapter. An additional technique, the comparison of the results of descriptive simulations of probabilistic situations, is also common. Naturally, economic theory is useful in establishing criteria, determining costs, and finding rules for optimal resource decisions.

The production decision areas which are discussed are

Chap. 2: The size or capacity of the production process.
Chap. 3: The location of the production facility.
Chap. 4: The design or layout of the production facility.
Chap. 5: The question of replacement or selection of equipment, i.e., capital budgeting.
Chap. 6: The aggregate planning of production.
Chap. 7: The size and timing of inventory ordering.
Chap. 8: The scheduling of production manpower and machines.
Chap. 9: The maintenance of production processes.

Obviously these areas are not exhaustive, nor are they always addressed in this order, but we believe that this is a rational sequence for a large new firm.

For each decision the important factors are identified, their interrelationships are described, criteria are selected, and the techniques for selection of the best alternatives are specified. Often this procedure results in a specification of optimality conditions or rules which can be applied with generality. Or the result may be a mathematical program which must be solved. The information requirements for application of the rules or determination of the coefficients of the program are discussed.

This approach to the decisions emphasizes the managerial viewpoint rather than the mathematical technique involved in solution. We believe that it is important to develop the model from this viewpoint for two reasons: Many problems can become intractable in their full development, but the information requirements are usually not sufficient to support a model at that level of detail and much effort may be wasted. Second, even an approximate solution to the right problem is better than the exact optimum for an irrelevant statement of the problem. Unfortunately, that tends to happen when technique is emphasized. We have supplied appendices and references for the techniques which we believe are adequate to give the manager a confidence in the method. Although techniques are not emphasized, a wide range of them is applied to the decisions. Mathematical programming, including the simplex method, transportation methods, Kuhn-Tucker conditions, branch and bound, dynamic programming, and decomposition techniques are presented. However, they are presented with an example emphasis which will enable anyone with a previous knowledge of matrix algebra and the simplex method to understand them. Appendices and references supply an additional source of information in these areas.

C. Format of the Book

I. INTRODUCTION AND SUMMARY

Chapter 1 is an introduction to the decisions in production management and a detailed discussion of the steps toward providing solutions to the problems. Chapter 10 is a review of the previous chapters with some examples which integrate the total problem. Somewhat similarly, each chapter begins with an introduction and ends with a summary.

II. NUMBERING SYSTEM

Within each chapter, the topics are separated by subheads which indicate the topic and its level within the chapter as follows:

A. Part.
  I. Section.
    a. Paragraph.
      1. Subparagraph.

III. PROBLEMS

Some of the problems are exercises calling for use of the solution techniques discussed in the chapter. Many of the problems present additional material or provide an extension of the previously discussed models. They are therefore more difficult and more rewarding in terms of finding out whether the reader can proceed toward building his models of his own situation.

IV. REFERENCES

Each chapter concludes with a list of the references cited in the chapter. In some cases additional readings in the area are noted. Of course, new references to problems and techniques are occurring daily. We recommend that the serious student of the area begin to develop a system for noting the relevant references in the journals such as:

1. Operations Research.
2. Management Science.
3. Journal of Industrial Engineering.
4. Naval Logistics Research Quarterly.
5. Harvard Business Review.

V. APPENDICES

At the end of the book are appendices on microeconomics, forecasting with moving averages and exponential smoothing, duality (including Lagrange multipliers and Kuhn-Tucker conditions and the decomposition technique), and queuing, as well as standard statistical and discounting tables. These appendices are referred to in the text when the topic first appears.

VI. STYLE

Within each chapter we first describe the general decision, build a simple model or models of parts of the decision, and then proceed to means of solution and more advanced models. In each area the first model is usually explained in some detail, whereas later discussions will assume that the reader has gained familiarity with the problem and the general technique.

Thus there may be a deliberate difference in style as the reader concludes one chapter and begins another. We believe that this will be helpful.

D. Required Background for the Book

A minimal background would be equivalent to that presented in most courses in operations research or quantitative methods. In more detail, the minimal topics required are some exposure to methods of linear programming and a knowledge of simple probability theory and statistics. Calculus and some familiarity with matrix operations are also required. A well-prepared student might have had a course in the following areas:

1. Microeconomics.
2. Computer programming.
3. Statistics and probability.
4. Linear programming.
5. Accounting or finance.

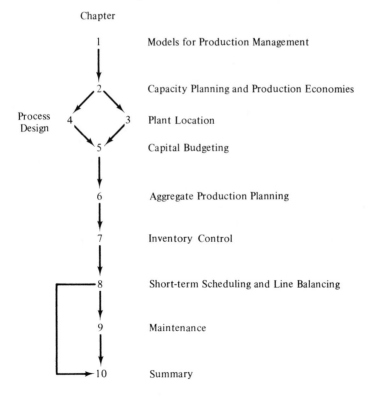

Chapter

1   Models for Production Management

2   Capacity Planning and Production Economies

Process Design   4   3   Plant Location

5   Capital Budgeting

6   Aggregate Production Planning

7   Inventory Control

8   Short-term Scheduling and Line Balancing

9   Maintenance

10   Summary

Of course, more courses in these areas and any others in business or mathematics would be helpful. We believe that most business or industrial engineering curricula now specify the list. The practitioner who has not had calculus or matrix algebra or statistics will still find many sections of the book quite readable.

E. Interrelationship of the Chapters

The flow diagram shows the interrelationship of the chapters of the book. In summary, Chaps. 3 and/or 4 and 9 could be deleted without destroying the reader's comprehension of other chapters. Well-prepared students can probably cover all but the advanced material in one semester.

F. Acknowledgments

We would like to collectively thank our students for serving as experimental subjects for parts of this material. We appreciated the comments of reviewers W. K. Holstein, State University of New York at Albany; L. Joseph Thomas, Cornell University; and Charles H. Kriebel, Carnegie-Mellon University. Special thanks to our colleagues, employers, and teachers for the opportunities to learn what little we know. Finally, we acknowledge the support and sacrifice of our wives and children.

This book was conceived of by Professor H. J. Zimmermann while the authors were teaching at the University of Illinois, Urbana. The work has continued while the authors have moved over many thousands of miles, eventually to their present positions. We hope that the flavor of our diverse experience in academia, industry, and government on two continents has not been entirely filtered out of the manuscript. Although the book was largely an integrated effort, the first drafts of Chaps. 2, 3, and 4 were prepared by Professor Sovereign, while Professor Zimmermann first prepared Chaps. 5, 7, 8, and 9. Chapter 6 was split—networks by Professor Zimmermann and repetitive models by Professor Sovereign. Nevertheless, the authors bear full joint responsibility for the results. We encourage any reader with comments or questions to contact one of the authors.

H. J. Zimmermann
Aachen, Germany

M. G. Sovereign
Monterey, California

QUANTITATIVE MODELS
FOR
PRODUCTION MANAGEMENT

chapter 1

Models for
Production Management

A. Introduction

The objective of this book is to introduce the reader to a series of models of production problems. The authors believe that these models or mathematical abstractions of production problems can serve as (1) a conceptual basis for a detailed understanding of the factors involved in production management decisions and (2) an introduction to the degree to which some of the problems in production management can be solved by analytical techniques.

Before discussing these goals further, the necessity for abstraction will be justified. Real production processes, by their nature, involve complex systems of physical equipment and material in addition to personnel. These elements have many detailed characteristics which can affect the output of the production process, from the microanalytic composition of a crude oil to Joe's toothache. The production manager faces decisions requiring difficult analysis of the large quantities of information constantly before him. Most production is subject to the harsh criteria of profitability. Thus production managers must deal with real and pressing physical, human, and monetary constraints, often while under severe time pressure. Therefore it is almost useless to discuss production management in vague generalities. However, on the other hand, the complexity and variety of production processes and the pace of technological change make it virtually impossible to deal with specific processes. We are forced to deal with abstractions, but we hope to maintain consideration of the criteria and constraints of real decisions as we build the abstract models.

The first purpose is probably more important both to the reader and to the authors. Our major goal is that the reader develop organized methods for the abstraction of a real production problem in its massive complexity into a form which is tractable for analysis. This is the reason we have organized the material in a decision-oriented fashion. We have related techniques to a progression or refinement of the steps in the production process rather than presenting the techniques as a grab bag of tricks. Production problems are the focus, rather than the techniques.

These production problems, to be further introduced in the next few pages, are

1. Capacity of the production process.
2. Location of the production process.
3. Layout of the production process.
4. Capital budgeting.
5. Aggregate planning.
6. Inventories.
7. Scheduling and assembly line balancing.
8. Maintenance of the production facility.

As each problem is examined, this book presents a consistent approach through the framework of resource allocation techniques of economics. That is, we shall identify an objective such as cost minimization and specify the measurement of the objective. Then we shall proceed to build a model of the production process and find a technique to optimize the attainment of the objective; as we shall point out, this is only a basic framework which *must* be linked with consideration of the behavioral aspects of the situation and the technical and information requirements of the process as well as modified by the manager's own style. We believe this framework will allow the production manager to conceptualize problems in a way which

1. Is consistent with the underlying economic framework in which he must function.
2. Allows him most ready access to the models of the production process which have been and are being developed.

Of course the models described here are constantly being improved by researchers and practitioners. New and better models can and will be built before the print on these pages is dry, but they will undoubtedly deal with the same sorts of problems and require the same optimization techniques as described in our discussion.

The second objective is to bring the reader as nearly as possible to the state-of-the-art in the application of these techniques so that he has a firm basis on which to further explore those areas in which he becomes engaged. We hope our work can serve as a guide to the major works in the areas covered. In the end the reader should be able to discuss existing models and the problems of formulation with those specialists in operations research and computation who can assist in the actual implementation of most of these applications.

In the next section of this chapter we shall outline our feeling of what the production system is. We think that production is an extremely important and, unfortunately, misunderstood function. In the last section we shall discuss the general principles of model building.

B. The Production System

I. INTRODUCTION: WHAT IS A PRODUCTION SYSTEM?

A system is often defined as a set of interrelated elements. However, the reader may object that everything is interrelated to some extent. To answer this objection, the definition must be made more precise. In this book a system will consist of men and/or machines and material which is organized to transform some *input* elements into other *output* elements. The inputs may be the materials and the output may be consumer goods or the inputs may be skilled labor and the output services. The boundary or level of a system shifts with each question or problem at hand. The president's production system is much larger than the foreman's. By virtue of authorship we choose to discuss the portion of the economic system concerned with the production of goods and services.

A production system is any organization of men, machines, and material that engages in the provision of goods or services within the economy. Such activity usually is conducted in a *firm*—a business enterprise in the capitalistic societies—but it may also occur in a school, governmental agency, nonprofit organization, or any other economic entity. Production systems might therefore range in size from single persons to vast industrial complexes. Each of these offers something to the society and in turn receives goods and services with which to maintain itself. We shall examine these diverse groups only as they participate in the production activities, in keeping with the idea that the selection of the elements of a system must be motivated by some problem or decision. Thus, although individuals are elements of the production system, we shall not, for example, worry about the recreational problems of individuals unless they impinge on the plant location problem, for instance, or unless the production process with which we are concerned is the manufacture of recreational equipment or the management of a ski lodge. Another group, the board of directors, makes some production policy decisions with which we shall be concerned, but it also makes many other types of decisions which we shall not address.

As mentioned above, the size of the relevant system shifts with the problem. Often we shall focus on some very small portion of a production system and may yet refer to that portion as a system rather than a subsystem. The justification for the switching of levels is that particular production problems are concerned with particular subsystems of the entire process. Thus the application of the concept of a system rests upon some motivation for the examination of the system—a problem or decision. We shall define these problems and decisions in the chapters that follow.

We have specified that the economic system contains the production system. As an aid to gross classification we shall define that the nonproduction portion is the marketing system. Man has institutions which enable him and his organizations to exchange their goods and services for those produced by others. This marketing process will be excluded from the production system. The line of demarcation between production and marketing becomes blurred at the interfaces. Both must consider inventory and delivery, product design and selection, and capacity problems, to name only a few of the overlapping areas. The logistical aspects of marketing, both shipment and storage, are sometimes included in production. However, in general the division of business activity into two major systems, production and marketing, is not difficult to comprehend. Production naturally centers its attention on activities within a producing organization, *the firm*. Marketing centers much of its attention outside the firm since it deals with customers and with other firms in the industry. A similar "inside-outside" distinction is sometimes made for the procurement system, which obtains raw materials, the labor force, and capital for both the marketing and production systems; the capital procurement function is often called *finance*. Here we shall not specify the procurement aspect as a separate system but shall treat it as a functional subsystem of production or marketing as necessary.

II. THE FUNCTIONAL SUBSYSTEMS OF PRODUCTION

Next we shall describe some of the functional or apparent subsystems of the production system. In this book these functional subsystems, such as finance, are to be distinguished from the problem or decision subsystems, which will be developed later. These functional subsystems reflect departmental organization or specialization of labor. Decision or problem subsystems often cross organizational lines, such as the location decision.

The distinction between production and the functional subsystems of finance, engineering, accounting, purchasing, personnel, operations research, data processing, and supervision of the operating departments is that the production system includes these subsystems when they are performing production-related activities. They also perform or support marketing activities. An organizational chart of this structure appears in Fig. 1-1. These departmental functions will be specified as services to production or marketing, as

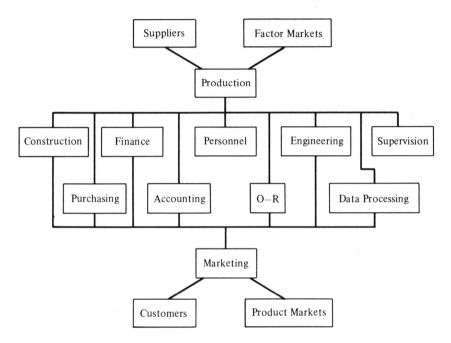

Figure 1-1. The firm's marketing and production systems and their functional subsystems.

shown, even though they may each have activities for which they alone are responsible, i.e., the preparation of financial reports for governmental agencies by the accounting functional subsystem.

It should be clear that the production system as viewed here does not correspond to any one management area. For too long the production system was associated only with supervision, industrial engineering, or plant design groups. The *system concept*, as applied here, means that consideration is to be given to all aspects of the production of goods and services by the firm. The fact that there may be no one management group responsible for all these areas does not negate the necessity that the overall picture be kept in view by the student and the practitioner, be he manager or specialist. The firm will live or die by the results of its production which become available for sale. The results of purchasing, personnel, accounting, etc., are not sold, and so they must be judged by what they contribute to production or to marketing.

With the focus fixed on the production portion of the activities of the firm, a more detailed examination of the production system is in order. In the most concrete terms, a typical factory is a production system. Visualize the mass of buildings and rows of machines, the truckloads of raw materials and supplies, the myriads of workers performing the tasks to turn the raw materials into finished goods. Notice the scurrying of all those in the functional subsystems who aid in the transformation—the personnel department and safety staff, the maintenance crew, the engineering and testing staff, cafeteria workers, union stewards, data-processing clerks, and all the other specialists, as well as the remainder of the staff. All these people and their equipment, from janitor to president and from ball-point pens to gigantic metal stamping machines, are essential parts of the production process. The number and complexity of the elements of the modern production process are amazing. The daily output of each element may be one adjustment of a machine tool or 500,000 molded plastic parts. As many as 100,000 people work in one location for some firms. It is not enough that they go about their jobs on their own. Constant coordination is required between people in different jobs. The raw materials and supplies must arrive at the right locations at the time that the workers are ready. The output rates of one group must match the capabilities of the workers at the next stage in the transformation of finished goods. Machine breakdowns must be fixed immediately. Quality is tested at each stage in the transformations. Provisions for pickup and storage between stages must be made. The whistle blows, workers pour through the gate, boxcars are unloaded, conveyors whir, assembly lines crawl forward with workers attaching and adjusting parts. The finished products are continuously rolled away to waiting trucks. Behind the scenes skilled machinists create equipment that will make products faster. Engineers draw up new processes. Chemists test batches of raw materials. Clerks wade through piles of orders and requisitions. Managers huff and puff through another day.

If the effort to visualize one factory as a production process has been successful, now try to let your mind roam over all existing production processes at firms in just one city. Refineries, mills, packaging plants, warehouses, mines, airline and rail terminals, service stations, barber shops, stores, the post office, the schools, all can be thought of as firms with production processes. Look at the different inputs, outputs, and transformation processes involved in each one. The range is almost incredible.

Instead of reviewing the details of all the various production processes or of the functional subsystems or departments, we shall proceed by identifying a structure which is common to all production processes and which is essential to the managers of the process. The common structure is the framework of decisions involved in all production processes. A description of actual processes only reflects past decisions; it does not describe the kinds of decisions or tools that help to make new ones that a future manager will face. We select the following decisions for definition and prescription of quantitative techniques in this book:

1. Capacity or level of the production process. What should be the planned output of the production process? This decision is critical to plant design and size, employee selection and recruitment, transportation connections—virtually all the planning that goes into establishing a production process.

2. Location of the production process. Where should the plant be placed with regard to raw materials and markets? A poor location may permanently handicap a firm.

3. Plant layout. How should each element of the production process be brought together? The upper limit on efficiency of the production process is decided at this early and important stage.

4. Capital budgeting. What equipment should be purchased when a limited number of dollars are available? The continued competitiveness of the facilities depends on these answers.

5. Aggregate planning or master scheduling. When should employees be fired or products placed in cyclical inventories? Despite new concepts and computerization, these remain difficult questions.

6. Inventory. How many of each item should be in inventory and when should they be purchased or produced? Large investments are determined by these policies.

7. Scheduling and assembly line balancing. How should an assembly line be designed and operated? When should parts be produced? These have become prime questions in the modern, mass-production society.

8. Maintenance. How many men are needed to keep a machine in running order? What about preventive replacement? A smoothly running production process depends upon these questions.

These decisions are examined in detail in the following chapters. Techniques are applied as appropriate for the decision. In one decision we may focus on a subsystem of the firm because only these elements are directly related to the decision. We must recall that the interrelationship of all the subsystems may require coordination or integration of the decision in one problem area.

Systems are treated differently by different disciplines. Since management is a melding of various disciplines, it may be useful to briefly sketch the concepts of a production system as it might appear when examined from the separate viewpoints of engineering, economics, and behavioral science. Some of these concepts will be used as we discuss the decision framework of the production system in the following chapters.

To the engineer, a production process is chiefly a design problem. It is a collection of pieces of equipment each of which presents interesting challenges in design or operation at their highest efficiencies. The engineer is usually concerned with minimizing the amount of raw materials, minimizing heat or other energy loss, or increasing the quality of the output. Usually these are individual problems and are attacked piecemeal in a suboptimizing manner since not everything can be changed at once. We shall make some use of the basic engineering tools but shall attempt to take an overall, or systems, viewpoint.

The economist is likely to treat the production process only as an abstraction. A production process can be viewed as a "black box" for transforming inputs to outputs. The transformation may involve a service rather than a good. Obviously the ouputs must represent some improvement over the inputs if the firm is to be of social value or to be able to pay for the inputs. The economist explains that the prices of the inputs and outputs are translated into potential profits which attract producers. The economist would, of course, urge the manager to *optimize* the production process so that resources are used efficiently.

The economist represents the production process by a production function which is a statement of the relationship of the inputs to the outputs. The statement may be in the form of an input-output table, graphs of output versus input, or an equation for output as a function of input. Unfortunately, not all problems can be placed in this framework, although we shall show many examples which can.

The behavioral scientist views the production process as an organizational problem. How should the people in the system be assigned to the necessary tasks of making the process a viable cooperative venture, a progressive goal-seeking entity? The manager must constantly face this difficult task. Most of the time he will be dealing with particular individuals and with the problems in their relationships with others. Or he may be helping them to strengthen their ability to adapt, plan, and change. The study of behavioral science can help him.

The production manager should be able to use the concepts, techniques, and viewpoints of each of these disciplines when necessary. The manager must be skilled in combining the various outlooks of several other specialists as well as the accountant, political scientist, operations researcher, etc.

Perhaps the most relevant outlook for this text is that of the economist. Because of the complexity and variety of modern production technology, we are forced to treat the production process in a somewhat abstract way. Abstraction leads to the use of the economist's relationship of inputs to outputs. Indeed, this is less an engineering text than an applied economics text because the manager is primarily concerned with economic results. He needs strength in the behavioral sciences and arts as well, but unfortunately quantitative techniques in that area are still in a very early stage of development, and so we have few models of this type to discuss.

The emphasis in this book will primarily be on the physical aspects of the production system. Personnel will be treated as having a capability to produce at certain rates. We shall seldom deal with the problems of motivating them to produce, to reach quality standards, etc. Although there are beginning to be some quantitative models in these areas, we do not feel qualified to discuss them. One reference is [1].

III. DESIGN, PLANNING, AND CONTROL IN PRODUCTION SYSTEMS

The structure of eight separate production decisions described in Sec. B.II can be broken into segments. There is a well-established, three-pronged description of all management as consisting of design, planning, and control. In a sense these three activities can be thought of as a systematic method for accomplishing any task. Thus they can be used at many levels, just as can the systems concept.

This division of management activities can be applied to the list of production decisions above as follows:

Design: capacity, location, and process design decisions.
Planning: aggregate planning and capital budgeting decisions.
Control: scheduling, inventory, and maintenance decisions.

The three activities of design, planning, and control are carried out within departmental levels of the firm as well as overall for the firm and also within the functional subsystems of production and marketing. Design includes the

1. Specification of the objectives of the system.
2. Definition of the characteristics of the elements of the system.
3. Organization of the elements into a feasible system for accomplishing the objectives.

Design decisions in production systems are made on an infrequent basis. They tend to be major long-term decisions of a top-level policy nature. Planning takes over after design and specifies the amounts of the inputs of the process and how they will interact. Planning decisions are generally made on a recurring cyclical basis, with longer than a daily period between decisions. They determine the basic operational pattern. Only marginal changes in equipment are possible within the planning cycle.

Finally, the control of the process is exercised through precise specification of the time phasing of the inputs and exactly how the system will be operated. The control of the process must be adjusted in real time when necessary to allow for variations imposed by a changing environment, and so frequent decisions are necessary. It is therefore one of the most difficult tasks. We shall now discuss production decisions in terms of these three activities.

The design activity certainly carries with it the location not only of the entire plant or production process but also of each of the elements of the process. In turn the number of elements roughly determines the productive capacity and vice versa. Therefore we believe that capacity determination is clearly part of the design activity. Once capacities and processes are set, management tries to get the best out of them by planning how to use them.

The planning activity is distinguished from the design and the control phases primarily by the time frame. Intermediate-term actions concerning types and quantities of inputs and outputs are predominate in planning. Aggregate planning or master scheduling is usually done on a quarterly to yearly basis and would fit the description above. The capital budgeting process is merely the intermediate planning device for equipment. The planning decisions are often made by staff agencies at an intermediate level between the policy decisions of design, which are made at the top level of management, and the control decisions, which are made by line management.

Control has, of course, the shortest time frame. Control is usually thought of as a closed loop with feedback. We shall largely describe planning or open systems even in the control portion of the book, but open-loop control becomes essentially a closed loop if (1) the time period is short enough for perception of the current status of important variables and (2) delays in translating decisions concerning response to the variables are avoided. Detailed scheduling is thus a control activity because it completely specifies timing and because rescheduling upon receipt of new information is usually a possible and even necessary part of the procedure. Inventory control is complementary to scheduling since either inventory or production can be used as a source of finished goods. It is therefore also a control activity. Finally, maintenance policies can be given for the long term but short-term maintenance depends closely on the operating schedule and vice versa. Therefore it can be classified as a control decision.

An additional control activity discussed in production books is the quality control system. We have not included this activity primarily because of the requirement for additional probability background on the part of the reader and because of the length and complexity of the book. Secondarily, we believe that the integration of quality control with the overall economic objectives of the firm has not been as fully developed as other areas. A good short reference on this topic is Fetter [2].

There is, of course, a fine line between the classification of production decisions into the three levels of design, planning, and control. As noted in the plant design chapter, planning must be done in order to get a good design. Similarly, a certain amount of control is necessary for successful activity in design or planning. In other words, the concept of breaking an activity into these three phases can be done at various levels of definition of an activity. Although we could address the design, planning, and control within each decision area, we shall do so only on occasions when particular difficulties are present.

While demonstrating the classification, we want to note the typical division of these types of production activities within the firm. Typically, the organization of the major groups within a firm that are responsible for production is as shown in Fig. 1-2. The decisions which each group would make appears in the following list:

1. The upper-level management chiefly participates in the design decisions and in setting operational policy.
2. The corporate staff is chiefly concerned with detailed design and overall or aggregate planning.
3. The plant manager is responsible for control and implementation of designs and planning.
4. The engineering staff of the plant has the following duties:
   a. Plant engineers are primarily concerned with changes in physical facilities.
   b. Process engineers improve the production process, chiefly the equipment.
   c. Industrial engineers have responsibilities in work methods improvement as well as in control of the labor force.
   d. Product engineers test current products and design new ones.
5. The operations staff is often divided into groups with the following titles and responsibilities:
   a. Production control department for scheduling.
   b. Quality control department for inspection of incoming materials and products.
   c. Inventory control department for keeping track of both raw materials and finished goods.
   d. Maintenance department for keeping the process in operational condition.
6. The line management below the plant manager, i.e., division heads and foremen, is responsible for the day-to-day control of

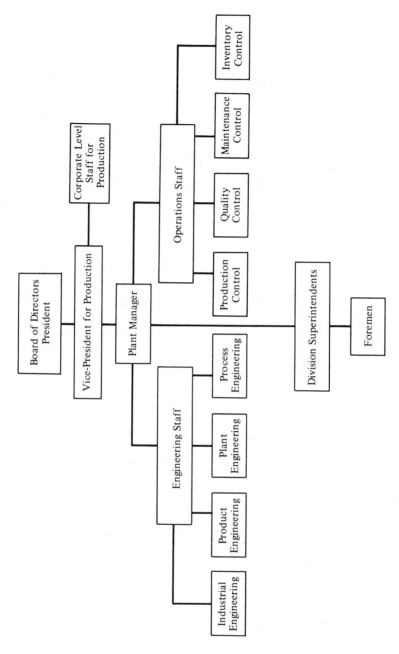

Figure 1-2. Typical production management organization structure.

12

the operation as indicated by policy and plans and an understanding of how to accomplish them.

Although these groups may have primary responsibility for only one of the three types of decisions, they may, and, in fact, should, participate in all levels. Otherwise there will be inadequate coordination between design, planning and control. The following chapters are arranged in the order of design, planning, and control in the interest of enabling the student to see the importance of a systematic method of viewing any problem area using the design, operation, and control sequences.

C. Decision Making and Models

I. DECISION MAKING

Miller and Starr [3] assert that the production executive is primarily paid his salary for making decisions. A manager is primarily a problem solver. Decisions are necessary to solve problems. In a large firm the production executive may do little else but consider decisions, if we include finding information and communicating the decision as part of the decision. In a small firm the manager's job may be much less specialized, and many additional functions may be required. Decision making is one aspect of management which can be aided by off-the-job education, which is one reason we shall concentrate on it here.

One way to study decision making is to review historical decisions. However, knowledge of past decisions is not all that the executive needs if the firm is going to adapt to the changes in the environment and to avoid the mistakes of the past in the uncertain future. He must have an understanding of the decision process and knowledge of concepts and techniques for his area of decisions.

The decision process in any system starts with the definition of the decision in terms of the relevant level of the system. This requires that the manager or his staff thoroughly investigate the problem to find out what it is. Often what looks like a short-term problem is only a symptom of a higher-level and longer-term planning problem. Another pitfall in problem definition is that too much of an abstraction of the problem is made because solution techniques are already in the minds of the decision maker. We often look where the information is rather than where the problem is, like the man looking for his wallet under the street light even though it was lost down the block in the dark. The problem definition should not be slanted to "pet" alternatives or techniques for solution. Once the problem is defined, its solution consists of three steps.

Step 1. *Development of physically and chronologically feasible alternative solutions.* This step requires not only a formidable collection of data but much creative effort as well. The alternatives must be realistic alternatives and should be tempered with the problem analyst's best judgment as to what each alternative would require in implementation. Too often the analyst's favorite alternative is the only one sufficiently developed and therefore the only one that seems reasonable when the selection is presented.

Step 2. *Identification of the more economically attractive alternatives from among those produced in step 1.* Here the importance of the complete fulfillment of the first step becomes clear. The methods used in this step must be understood by those performing the first step or the right information will not be available. A wide variety of methods for economic analysis is in use, but the relationships of the methods are not always kept clear by those who use them.

Step 3. *Selection of an alternative for implementation from those identified in step 2,* based on consideration of the behavioral effects of the alternatives. Here the judgment of the manager must be relied on more heavily than ever because our models are generally not adequate for this final screening.

There are, of course, feedback relations between these steps. Each is dependent on adequate completion of the previous step. These steps can also be identified with a particular discipline which most directly applies to each step:

Step 1: Physical development—engineering.
Step 2: Monetary considerations—economics and operations research.
Step 3: Human considerations—behavioral science and judgment.

The major focus in this book is on step 2 and on applied microeconomics. This may not be the most important step of the three; however, we feel that the engineering education must come primarily from engineering courses and experience. Production managers certainly need training in the behavioral sciences and practice in applying them to production. The training can come from behavioral science courses or on the job. The application of behavioral science is very difficult to learn in a text or in a course. The behavioral considerations follow the physical and economic screening steps because humans are the most adaptable resource.

Even with excellent engineering and a flexible production organization with skilled leaders the execution of step 2 is far from trivial in the complex production systems of today. Thus the focus on step 2, identification of the more economical alternatives, is necessary for this book but certainly not sufficient for a total understanding of production management. Good alternatives require good engineering, the first step. And the third step of examining any decision from a behavioral viewpoint must never be overlooked.

Another reason for the focus on step 2 is the uniformity of methodology available, as will be discussed in the next section concerning models. Of necessity, the focus in modern production system analysis is quantitative. Production inputs, outputs, and facilities and their costs can usually be measured quantitatively. Profit is a very quantitative measure. Therefore scientific methods are available for this phase of decision making. The final step of decisions relies much more heavily on qualitative judgments, which are most difficult to present in a book directed toward step 2.

II. MODELS

a. Introduction

The purpose of examining models, particularly quantitative models, in this text is that they are of great aid in production decision making. We have stated that decision making is an important phase of production management, and so quantitative models are worth examining in detail.

We have already identified certain decisions such as location as central to the management of the production process in Section B.II. For each decision we have tentatively defined the relevant system. These definitions will be further developed as each decision is discussed in the following chapters. Moreover, the problem or motivation for the definition of the system, which determines the relevant level of the system, will be refined into an objective or criterion for the decision. The criterion will usually be profit, but there may also be constraints on the dominance of profit or there may be alternative criteria. For example, the capacity decision implies an objective of finding a maximum profit level of planned output, but this is subject to marketing and other considerations.

After the problem is defined and a criterion developed, what is needed is a model which will generate and/or evaluate solutions to the problems in terms of the criterion. A model is simply an abstraction of the actual system. To be useful, the model must include the elements and relationships which have important effects on the criterion. Once the model is specified, an acceptable decision can usually be determined.

b. Type of Models

The following types of models can be distinguished:

1. Iconic.
2. Qualitative.

3. Quantitative.
   a. Exact analytical.
   b. Statistical.
   c. Simulation.

Iconic models are those which faithfully reproduce the original physical system except for size or scale, at least outwardly. For example, a minature refinery is an iconic model which can be very useful for the design of piping.

A qualitative model is a description of at least the major elements of a system and some definition of the relationships between the elements. It may be as crude as a verbal description of how a process works, or it may be a written historical description such as a business school case. In each case the author must abstract from the real situation and presumably identify major elements and relationships. Considerable refinment of the qualitative model may result in a functional mathematical statement of the set of elements and their relationships, such as "inventory is a function of sales and production." If the relationships can be expressed as direct or inverse and if such statements as "A increases more rapidly than B" are specified, then the model is ready to be developed into a quantitative one.

Quantitative models require measurement scales for the inputs and outputs. With the form of the relationships and data from experimentation, we can predict a measured output to be achieved from the inputs. If we understand the function and objectives of the system, we can even identify a criterion which the decision maker may be trying to optimize. Often some simplification of the system is necessary in order to accomplish this sophistication. We shall be primarily concerned with such quantitative models in this book.

Analytical models are those quantitative models in which the relationship between inputs and outputs is expressed as a mathematical function. For example, the total production may be defined as an integral of the production rate over the operating time.

Statistical models are those in which the relationship has been established through examination of empirical data or observations. A least-squares regression may be used to relate output and carbon content of coke in a steel furnace, for example.

Simulation models are quantitative models in which digital or analog computers provide the equivalent of observations from real systems. Many relationships within subsystems can be included in these detailed simulation models. The relationships may be of the analytic or statistical type in a simulation model. The relationships between the subsystems are also specified. The simulation model combines the outputs of the subsystems into an output for the entire system. The simulation can be repeated for many different combinations of inputs for the subsystems. These pseudo-observations from the simulation can be treated statistically. The advantage is that the physical system need not be built to get observations. Alternative production systems can be simulated and evaluated without large investments in the actual equipment.

The use of models in business has greatly increased in recent years. Not all models are successful, but modeling has become an accepted technique. This acceptance of modeling is partly attributable to the fact that it is a primary step in the scientific method. Science has enjoyed convincing success in certain areas and many people are eager to develop a science of management.

c. Quantitative Production Models and Management Science

Modeling is an essential step in the process of developing theories which will explain and ultimately predict the relationships between particular sets of elements of the real world. That is exactly what is being attempted with the production system as analyzed in this text. We would like to develop a science of optimization models for production decision making, realizing that it will always be necessary to adapt models to particular situations and to evaluate decisions in additional ways beyond these models. For example, behavioral and political considerations are probably not adequately handled with the types of models developed to date. It may be argued that a good production manager can take an incomplete plan based on a bad alternative, designed to accomplish an ambiguous objective, and still carry it out with success because of his ability to work with the people below him. But imagine how well the same manager would do with a complete plan for the best alternative to reach a demonstrable goal.

We should always remember the full range of the steps in the decision making process, which is even broader than the scientific method. Unfortunately, management science has sometimes seemed to concentrate only on the modeling effort. Since the title of this book is *Quantitative Models*, we may legitimately overlook some of the additional steps, but we encourage the reader to keep in mind the entire decision-making process as we describe the modeling.

The application of science to management is probably older than we might think. Moses was told to install leaders of 1000, leaders of 100, and leaders of 10, apparently demonstrating an early rule for span of control. However, by most accounts management science is a relative new science, even if we begin with Adam Smith, an early economist whose account of the manufacture of pins in the *Wealth of Nations* in 1760 is fascinating in its prediction of later work in specialization of labor and development of methods and tooling.

The Industrial Revolution brought production from an agricultural craft basis to a stage where uniformity of product and training of workers became a real management problem. Eli Whitney's contribution of interchangeability of parts helped solve this problem, but many more had to be dealt with in an ad hoc manner by thousands of individual managers and early engineers of whom we have little record.

Frederick Taylor was the first scientific manager to be called by this name. His pioneering work in time and motion study, training, industrial relations, and planning around the turn of the century foretold future developments in four major areas. His slogan "a science of each man's work" grew to be the practice of time and motion study as well as ergonomics and human engineering. His emphasis on training and selection of workers led to the development of the personnel field. Despite rumors to the contrary, he preached cooperation and fair play between labor and management at a time long before the modern concepts of labor relations were accepted. Finally, he charged management with doing a much better job of planning and control, indirectly pointing to the development of many techniques in common use today.

Taylor's efforts in work measurement were quickly picked up by the Gilbreths and many others who became known as industrial engineers. In 1917 Henry Gantt developed the Gantt chart for scheduling production. This simple chart is the forerunner of a long line of scheduling techniques, including line of balance, the critical path method (CPM), and machine loading.

The economic lot size model developed by Ford Harris in 1915 was the first of a long line of economic models for decisions in production. Economists and operations researchers have a long tradition of abstraction and mathematical representation of the behavior of firms. Recently, as their mathematical tools have become more powerful with the development of the computer, they have made many large contributions to management science, including Dantzig and linear programming and Modigliani and Simon and the linear decision rule, to name only two major contributions.

Additional techniques in the field of quality control were developed in the period between the world wars. Shewhart in 1920s and later H.F. Dodge and H.G. Romig at Bell Laboratories and many others developed means for scientifically selecting pieces for inspection and rules for interpreting the results. These techniques became a necessity with the development of high-speed tools and the demands of the assembly line for a constant flow of standard material.

World War II had a large effect on the development of management science, particularly the branch called operations research. In Great Britain and the United States, many scientists were diverted from their usual tasks to those of warfare and the supply of war materials. Quality control techniques were further developed by the statisticians for munitions. Large-scale scheduling and inventory control systems became necessary. Linear programming was developed from an Air Force-sponsored research project. N. Wiener and others brought control theory out of its infancy to track aircraft.

By the end of the war, digital computers were becoming available. The use of computers for data processing in business made a precise understanding of methods for making business decisions essential and indirectly gave a large boost to the field of management science. Computer manufacturers turned to the management scientists to formulate large-scale systems using the computer. In turn, computers made possible calculations and data gathering on a previously unheard of scale.

By 1954 both the Operations Research Society of America and the Institute of Management Science had been formed. Their journals and those of the American Institute of Industrial Engineers, as well as the journals of mathematical economics and computer organizations, are a major source of new research in the field. Throughout this book there are references to these works.

The field of management science contains several areas in addition to production management problems, for example, marketing, but we believe that the majority of the literature deals with what we have defined as production problems or techniques which are applicable to production problems, in their largest sense. We shall now describe the steps in modeling as they would be applied by a management scientist along with a particular example of a large-scale transportation model.

D. Steps in Model Building

The steps in building a satisfactory quantitative model are actually the same as those of the scientific method except that they are problem-oriented. That is, the model is designed for a specific problem rather than simply as an attempt to develop and prove a theory.

Step 1. Definition of the level of the actual system, its relevant elements and relationships.

Step 2. Abstraction of the important elements and relationships into an *optimizing* or problem-solving framework.

Step 3. Collection of data concerning the quantitative variables as a preliminary to steps 4 and 5.

Step 4. Identifying the structure of the relationships of the variables— finding the relevant group of functions.

Step 5. Estimating the values of relevant cost and physical structural parameters.

Step 6. Designing experiments for testing the model with base levels and ranges of variables and specifying the sets of parameters to be controlled.

Step 7. Testing and verification of the model.

Step 8. Generation of solutions and selection of an *optimal* solution.

Step 9. Performing sensitivity analyses and improving the model.

The student should realize that the following chapters will emphasize the first two, the fourth, and the eighth steps, primarily because of size. It would take many more pages to deal with the other steps; they are equally essential to successful use of the techniques, but their subtleties may best be learned in practice. Moreover, procedures for the other steps are not unique to production problems. Data collection and reduction techniques, estimation techniques, and verification techniques are about the same for models of any problem. The structure of production problems is more specialized, as are some of the techniques.

We shall devote a few pages to a brief description of all the steps at this time. In many of the following pages of this book it will seem that models spring full-blown as from the forehead of that modern Zeus, the operations researcher. These next pages will try to dispel that feeling. Most models have a long historical development both in theory and practice. Most useful models have undergone many changes and will continue to be improved. It is hard to convey this evolutionary progress in the following description, but it should not be forgotten. We shall describe the building and evolution of one model with which we are familiar as a concrete example of each step.

The first step in model building coincides with the first step of decision making discussed earlier. The model builder or the decision maker must first find out what the problem is, without preconceived notions of solutions. One of the virtues of model building is that it forces the decision maker to be much more explicit about the definition of the problem and to avoid dealing with only portions of the problem or of dealing with the problem at too low a level, thereby missing the real problem entirely.

Our example concerns a model for determining the strategic mobility assets required for the Department of Defense for use in deploying U.S. forces world-wide. Military transport planes and ships, commercial aircraft, and the merchant marine are some of the obvious elements in this problem. However, prior to 1964 only the military assets were considered and each was considered entirely separately by the armed service involved. That is, the Air Force decided how many transport aircraft it needed to buy, and the Navy decided how many transport ships it would maintain. In 1964 a group was established to look at the entire problem of strategic mobility. The importance of the commercial airlift and sealift became apparent. When the requirements for material to be moved were considered, it became obvious that the Army was to be the major user of these vehicles, not the services that operated the military airlift and sealift. It became apparent that forward-basing of troops overseas and even the readiness of the troops in the United States were actually important elements of strategic mobility. Not until these observations were made was the problem adequately defined.

The second step is that of abstraction of the real system into a model with a driving force or criterion or objective. The assembling of the elements must be structured around the output of the system or the function of the system. The output must be stated in a problem-solving manner. A measurement standard for judging the relationship of output to the inputs and establishing some idea of efficiency must be found. In other words, we cannot be content with only description or history. For operational modeling this step is not hard because the operating managers usually know what their objectives are. When the system being analyzed is something like the U.S. educational system, this step is virtually impossible. Most problems fall somewhere in the middle.

In our example the problem was stated as that of determining the amounts of the various strategic mobility assets required to handle several wartime contingencies simultaneously at least cost during peacetime. The vehicles or other assets are directly applied against the movement requirements in what is essentially a transportation model of linear programming. Although this statement of the problem sounds straightforward, it was not easy to win acceptance for it. Major points such as looking at cost only in peacetime were not easily accepted by everyone concerned. Minor points such as the number of contingencies had apparently never before been explicitly treated.

Finally, it should be noted that this formulation continues to be challenged and changed. Few problems really stand still. For example, it has recently become necessary to add to *least cost* the phrase "and politically feasible."

The third step is the collection of data concerning the quantifiable elements. Unfortunately, few variables appear quantifiable when closely examined. Most data require considerable manipulation before they become information. Volumes could be written on this subject but only experience is of much value in dealing with it. The best instruction is to "immerse oneself in the data." Hopefully both the structure of the data and the ways of estimating the parameters, steps 4 and 5, will emerge from this data collection step.

In our example, many exploratory studies were commissioned and many man-years of both experienced operating personnel and model builders were required in this phase. Moreover, the process is continuing. Each new person brings to the problem his own collection of data acquired through the years. Finally, there is a feedback from the conceptual steps and the estimation steps as the data base grows. In fact, management of the data base and avoidance of "reinventing the wheel" is an important task after several years of data are built up. This is particularly true when the data base is frequently changed and yet never based on truly definitive information, which was the case in our example with data such as payloads of aircraft. Although this seems like an easily established figure, it depends critically on what the load is, since the "weight versus cubic load" problem arises.

The fourth step is the determination of the type of functional relationships between elements of the problem. The first assumption is usually that the relationships are deterministic (nonprobablistic) and linear (additive).

Whether this is innate human logic or based on model availability is a question of some debate. Needless to say, all relationships are not of this type, but model makers have devised several ways of making them so, as well as models for probabilistic and nonlinear relationships.

The linearity assumptions which are basic to the linear programming transportation model were made in our example model. However, the consequences are mitigated by studying in separate simulation models the elements that may be nonlinear, such as the effectiveness of additional aircraft on one route, or nondeterministic, such as the queuing behavior of ports or integer variable problems [4, 5]. The nonlinearities in cost in one now infamous aircraft, the C-5A, were dealt with by a piecewise linear approximation in our example model.

The fifth step is the estimation of the relevant parameters. This may range from merely extracting a few relevant factors from the data base to sophisticated statistical estimation procedures applied on a continuing basis. These problems are part of a major field, which we cannot deal with at length in this book.

In our example model there were about 30,000 nonzero coefficients. Behind each of these are several pieces of data. Large-scale models have been built merely to obtain some of these coefficients. Several preparatory routines and one to generate the coefficients are required—something like an hour's run of large-scale computer time. Still, many of the data elements are questionable, resting mainly on an analyst's judgment. How many ships are required to move a division? This question sounds easy enough—an answer should be readily available—but you find that it is hard to say what either a ship or a division looks like in physical dimensions unless you are willing to describe every ship and each existing military unit, which is impractical. Even the complete list would not be relevant because of the necessity of planning for 5 years in the future.

The sixth step is the establishment of the variables to be controlled and the ranges of the variables to be tested. Essentially this is a problem of experimental design. Most complex systems can be manipulated in many ways. The model builder must determine the most relevant variables and control values for his problem so that a meaningful set of answers can be obtained. Real problems change so often that one single answer is not really what is desired. A model should be flexible enough to answer a range of questions.

In our example the question is to determine which strategic mobility variables are fixed by either policy of past actions and which can be adjusted through some range. Since several variables are adjustable, different combinations of limits on the uncontrolled variables must be put together in a reasonable fashion. Thus we determine what can be deployed with up to six squadrons of C-5A aircraft and up to so many ships plus not more than a limited number of troops in Southeast Asia under a range of conditions from full to partial mobilization. The model can be run either to determine what vehicles are required or what a given set of vehicles can do.

The next step is the testing and verification of the model. Often when first constructed a model will simply not behave logically. Important variables may have been neglected or relationships of the wrong type specified. Often just plain mistakes are made. Sooner or later these errors and logical inconsistencies are eliminated. As a next step it is usual to compare the results of the model with the past. We shall discuss how this was done for several aggregate planning models in Chap. 6. It is difficult to statistically validate a model against past data, but at least a general feel for similarity can be obtained. Another method is comparison with the results from other models. Often both the new and old models or systems are run concurrently for a period of time to establish the consistency, if not the validity, of the new model.

For testing our example model, little actual data were available that were not already used as input. Several other models of more limited scope were available for comparisons and were run under conditions as close as possible to those for the new model and the results compared, but it is difficult to put the same inputs in a simulation and linear programming model.

The next to last step is the actual generation of solutions and/or the optimal solution. The experimental design which was set up in the sixth step should be followed to assure that answers are obtained. Usually the results suggest additional variations in the experimental design as well as new additional variables that it would be desirable to include and the need for more verification. This is often a feedback step to start the whole process again. However, management usually wants some tentative answers after investing this much work in the model. The interpretation of the entire process and its results to those who have not participated must now be attempted. This is one of the most difficult tasks. If poorly done, it can result in charges of wastefulness by management because so little has been accomplished or, on the other hand, dishonesty by the model makers as to how solid and general the answer is.

The actual solutions developed by the example mobility model take several hours of computer time but many more hours and considerable judgment in interpretation into policy recommendations. At this point all the weaknesses of the model and data come screaming back at the model builder and he is likely to get cold feet and ask for another 6 months. However, decisions must be made and recommendations put forward, with appropriate limitations noted. In many cases this process will shed enough light on the structure of the problem that management will be able to use the recommendations, the model, and the insight and experience gained by the model builder to make significantly better decisions.

We hope that the reader is now ready to get on with looking at specific production models.

SUMMARY

In this chapter we have established our framework for analyzing the production management function. The system has been defined as any part which provides goods or services of the economic system. Its subsystems were examined. In so doing we have emphasized the importance of the systems approach and the role of modeling as part of the approach. Eight basic decision areas have been identified for consideration.

1. Capacity.
2. Location.
3. Plant design.
4. Capital budgeting.
5. Aggregate planning.
6. Inventories.
7. Scheduling.
8. Maintenance.

Finally, we explored and illustrated the steps in modeling. At this stage the reader should have an orientation to the area and our methods and a desire to examine the models in each decision area.

REFERENCES

1. LEONARD R. BURGESS, *Wage and Salary Administration in a Dynamic Economy*, Harcourt Brace, New York, 1968.
2. ROBERT B. FETTER, *The Quality Control System*, Irwin, Homewood, Ill., 1967.
3. D. W. MILLER and M. K. STARR, *Executive Decisions and Operations Research*, Prentice-Hall, Englewood Cliffs, N.J., 1960. An additional reference for this general area is H.L. Timms, *The Production Function in Business*, Irwin, Homewood, Ill., 1966.
4. ARTHUR MIHRAM, "A Cost-Effectiveness Study for Strategic Airlift," *Transportation Science*, 4, No. 1 (Feb. 1970), 79.

5. RICHARD L. NOLAN and M. G. SOVEREIGN, "A Recursive Optimization and Simulation Approach to Analysis with an Application to Transportation Systems," *Management Science*, 18, No. 12 (August 1972), B676.

PROBLEM

1. Suppose that you have decided to open a shoe repair shop. What decisions must you make?

Part I

DESIGN
OF
PRODUCTION SYSTEMS

The following three chapters describe the design problems of production systems: the size, location, and organization or layout of the personnel and equipment of the system. In general, design includes

1. The specification of the objectives of the system.
2. The definition of the characteristics of the elements of the system.
3. The organization of the elements into a feasible system for accomplishing the objectives.

These steps must be accomplished in answering the problems above. In Chapter 2, which deals with size or capacity, we shall deal with the economics of the overall production process. This is the central criterion for the entire system. Later, in Chapter 5, we shall discuss capital budgeting procedures for investment in portions of the process. The economic principles developed in this chapter will also be of use in later chapters.

In the chapter on location (Chapter 3) we shall discuss the geographical location of the entire production system, which includes the distribution system for reaching markets. This requires consideration of the definition and selection of market areas. A great variety of operations research models is applicable here.

In Chapter 4, on design of the facilities, we shall first introduce the important distinction between product-oriented and process-oriented systems. Next, basic data from time studies and process charting are introduced. The number of machines and layout are established for both types of processes. Finally, information- and material-handling systems are addressed.

The physical production system is designed in the steps determined by these three chapters. These decisions have far-reaching effects on all other problems.

chapter 2

Capacity Planning and Production Economics

A. Introduction

Capacity planning is the first and perhaps most fundamental problem of production management. It is not the most obvious problem, which in most operational systems is usually scheduling. Scheduling problems, however, are often the result of poor capacity planning. Scheduling problems are often caused by shortages of capacity. Because of its fundamental nature, its difficulty, and its strong relationship to other areas of the firm such as overall policy and strategy and the marketing activities of the firm, most of the discussion of capacity planning will be of a general nature. Economic techneques are emphasized because they have the desired generality and validity. In addition, the education of the production manager is generally weak in this area. The development of this economic base will be of use in future chapters. A review of Appendix A may be helpful for some readers.

In this chapter we shall define capacity as the level of production of a process operating under normal conditions. Because we are considering long-run capacity planning, we are free of any limitations on inputs and so capacity can be chosen to minimize costs, i.e., no overtime or the like. Identification of the capacity of an actual operating industry is a more general and more difficult question, which we shall not attack. Once capacity is built, the actual utilization level is determined by short-run cost considerations, which will be discussed in Chapter 6 on aggregate planning. Changes in capacity are discussed in Chapter 5 on capital budgeting.

B. Production Economics

I. MANAGERIAL IMPLICATIONS OF PRODUCTION ECONOMICS

The production manager must have a detailed knowledge of the actual production process, its raw materials, technology, and equipment and the required skills and even the personalities of many of those who participate in the process of producing the output. In addition he needs an overall concept or abstraction of the process, a systems viewpoint of what happens. In Chapter 1 we discussed several black box or abstract ways of representing the production process. In this chapter we shall concentrate on the economist's method, the production function, because economics is particularly suited to answering overall questions such as the decision on capacity. After all, the most basic decision of the firm is whether to produce a product or not, which is a capacity decision. We generally assume that such decisions are approached on a primarily economic basis in our society.† We therefore need to develop economic tools to determine the best capacity for the plant. Many of the

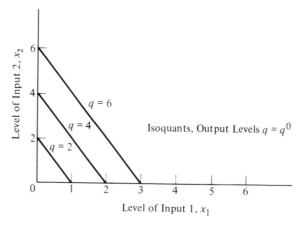

Figure 2-1.   Isoquant representation of a production function.

---

†Consideration of capacity planning for public goods, e.g., roads, is primarily of an economic nature but requires additional theory.

economic concepts are simple ones which you have no doubt acquired in elementary economics. A short review is contained in Appendix A. We shall make use of some of the mathematical properties of the definitions of these tools, which also appear in Appendix A. We shall start by examining the production function in some detail.

In economics the production side of the firm is usually represented by a functional relationship of output and the inputs. Considering first the case of one output and two inputs, the production function $q = f(x_1, x_2)$ expresses a general relation of quantity of output and quantities of inputs, for example, amounts of capital and labor, two inputs or factors of production. The maximum output for these inputs is represented by q. In a particular case, say a mixing operation, the expression can be presented as shown in Table 2-1. The same production function can be represented graphically, as in Fig. 2-1, or as a particular equation, such as

$$q = 2x_1 + x_2 \tag{2-1}$$

for Fig. 2-1 and Table 2-1 or

$$q_1 = \tfrac{1}{5} x_1^{1/2} x_2^{1/2}, \tag{2-2}$$

$$q_2 = 24 x_1 x_2 - 10 x_1^2 - 8 x_2^2, \tag{2-3}$$

Table 2-1   Tabular Representation of a Production Function

		Level of Input 1, x_1			
		0	1	2	3
	0	0	2	4	6
	1	1	3	5	7
Level of Input 2, x_2	2	2	4	6	8
	3	3	5	7	9

Output

which we shall use later. In any case, the production function serves as a handy shorthand for a production process without losing the important relationships between output and inputs.

A capacity decision should in part depend on how much you get out of the plant compared to what is put into it. In addition, it depends on the prices of outputs and inputs, which we shall address later. The specific economic relationships which measure the change in output when one input is changed are the average and marginal productivities (AP and MP). You may wish to review these in Appendix A. The AP is simply the common measure of average output per unit of input. The MP focuses measurement on the *margin* where decisions should be made concerning changes. This makes the economist's concept particularly valuable to the manager, since he is usually making marginal changes as he manages.

For any input or factor the ratio of MP over AP is defined as the marginal elasticity, E_i, of the factor X_i or the percentage change in output per percentage change in input of the factor. All other inputs are held constant. The marginal elasticity is useful not only in measurement of short-term change but in long-range planning, as will be discussed in Sec. B.II. The ratio of the MP for two inputs is the rate of technical substitution, RTS, between the two input factors.

To see how the RTS gets its name, envision the following situation. As production manager you are told that one of a particular type of machine will be under repair today. Additional machines of another type can be used to replace it. If you know the marginal productivities, that is, the change in total output as a machine is added or dropped, you can decide the number of replacements that will be needed. If the RTS or ratio of MPs for the two types of machines is two to one, you need two machines to replace one of the first type and maintain production at the current level.

If we have an equation for the production function, the RTS can be calculated for the particular output. More likely we do not have the equation but have sufficient experience to estimate the marginal productivities and choose the proper number of machines to maintain production.

In general, the decision relationships derived in this chapter are similar to the marginal productivity decisions above. Rules for adjustment of the production process will be obtained. They can be applied either rigorously if the production function can be specified, or roughly by experienced estimation of marginal quantities or ratios by the production manager. Many times the rules will be little more than common sense but the techniques can be extended to more complex situations where the common-sense solution may be less obvious.

II. RETURNS TO SCALE

Up to this point all relationships have varied one factor of production while holding the others constant. This situation is often encountered in short-run production planning. It is also desirable to explore the relationships of output to the factors when all inputs are increased, as would be possible in long-range planning. *Scale* questions are what we usually call those pertaining to increasing the factors of production but holding all in the same proportion. The scale coefficient, E, is the ratio of percentage change in total output to percentage change in all factors. As shown in Appendix A, it is equal to the sum of the marginal elasticities of each factor. If the sum is equal to 1 we say there are constant returns to scale, and if greater than 1, increasing returns. The scale concept is essential in deciding on the capacity for production plants since it relates output and input levels. For example, increasing returns to scale in a production process could be expected to encourage larger plant size, since each additional unit of output requires less input.

Homogeneous production functions are those which have scale coefficients which are constants. The functions are often taken to be of the form $ax_1^b x_2^c = q$. In Eq. (2-2) the sum of the elasticities is unity. These functions are called linearly homogeneous production functions, a type assumed in the linear programming model of the production process. Some economists argue that all production processes are linearly homogeneous since if all inputs are increased, certainly the output must increase proportionally. If this were true, it would make the capacity design question easier, but unfortunately it is true only in a very limited sense. Let us consider a rather specific capacity design problem. It is quite common in business to refer to certain processes as having economies of scale. For example, a common rule of chemical engineers is the six-tenths exponential formula used to scale up the cost of a piece of equipment. Given equipment of one known capacity, A, and its cost, the rule states that cost at capacity B is

$$\text{cost at } B = \text{cost at } A \times \left(\frac{\text{cap. } B}{\text{cap. } A}\right)^{.6}. \tag{2-4}$$

At first glance this appears to be a contradiction of the linearly homogeneous production function. However, it should be noted that the measurement above is in terms of costs rather than physical inputs. If the choice of inputs is restricted to multiple pieces of equipment of a small capacity, there will be no conflict with constant returns to scale. The process is then linearly homogeneous. But rather than employ additional pieces of equipment to obtain the larger capacity, the chemical engineer will usually design a single larger unit such as a reactor, a distillation tower, a mixer, or a heat exchanger. This large piece of equipment will cost less per unit of output than the smaller piece, following the six-tenths rule. Again the distinction of input quantities rather than costs becomes important. The major inputs to make the equipment are pounds of metal and labor for fabrication. The capacity of equipment of the above types must physically contain the output. The input of metal is a function of the surface of the equipment. Capacity is proportional to r^3, while surface is proportional to $4r^2$, where r is the radius. Suppose that capacity is to be multiplied by k. Then the radius must be multiplied by $(\sqrt[3]{k})^2$ or $k^{.66}$, which is reasonably close to the six-tenths rule.

The six-tenths rule is only relevant to enlarging single pieces of equipment. In many cases a chemical plant will consist of parallel streams of a product, each with a fraction of the full capacity because the size of distillation towers, mixers, and other equipment has certain practical limits. In such a case the rule is not applicable to the cost of capacity of the plant.

For example, the overall coefficient for ethylene plants is .58 to .60 but the coefficient for the pyrolysis furnaces, which must be installed in multiples, is .8 or .9. [1]. The rule does not apply to labor costs, although increasing returns might be suspected. Moreover, it does not contain any reference to overhead, communication, and other activites which may show decreasing returns.

This example establishes the necessity for careful use of the concept of scale as a strictly technological phenomenon. We shall bring in costs at a later point.

C. The Possibility of Technical Optimization

It might seem intuitively desirable to design the process with capacity to produce at a level that would maximize average productivity for each production factor. By this "efficient"-sounding criterion, the level of output would be chosen where MP equals AP, since this is a condition for maximization of AP (see Appendix A). If this rule were applied, no economic theory would be needed because optimal plant size would be strictly a function of the technology that establishes the production function. However, this condition can rarely hold for more than one input at a time. Furthermore, there is no guarantee in the condition above that the process is producing anything of social benefit or of use to the economy. Ultimately some measure of value is needed, as we shall see in the section on optimization. However, even performing the purely technical optimization in the sense of maximizing productivity for all factors is not possible for many production functions.

Consider the case of linearly homogeneous production. (See Table 2-2.) One

Table 2-2   Calculations for the Linearly Homogeneous Production Function[a]

Marginal Products	Average Products	Elasticities
$MP_{x_1} = \frac{1}{10}x_1^{-1/2}x_2^{1/2}$	$AP_{x_1} = \frac{1}{10}x_1^{-1/2}x_2^{1/2}$	$E_{x_1} = \frac{1}{2}$
$MP_{x_2} = \frac{1}{10}x_1^{1/2}x_2^{-1/2}$	$AP_{x_2} = \frac{1}{10}x_1^{1/2}x_2^{-1/2}$	$E_{x_2} = \frac{1}{2}$

[a] Scale coefficient $E = \frac{1}{2} + \frac{1}{2} = 1$.

example is the Cobb-Douglas function: $q = \frac{1}{5}x_1^{1/2}x_2^{1/2}$. Note that the APs are hyperbolic functions. There is no maximal AP for a hyperbolic function. This can also be seen by the fact that the marginal elasticities are $\frac{1}{2}$ and constant. Maximal AP occurs when MP equals AP, which means that E_i is 1. However, for the two-factor Cobb-Douglas production functions, the E_is are never 1, since the sum of the E_is is 1. Therefore technical optimization is impossible for Cobb-Douglas functions.

The economic optimization problem will be explored after a brief discussion of the derivation of production functions.

D. The Derivation of Production Functions

Up to this point the production function has been freely used. Particular mathematical examples of production functions have been suggested without substantiation for their existence in the "real world." A brief report on the state of measurement of production functions is in order. It should be remembered that the rules derived do not depend solely on our ability to measure the production function because experience will often allow the production manager to estimate marginal relationships without knowing the full form of the production function.

A production function assumes, as stated earlier, that the output has been maximized for the amounts of inputs. In economic terms the production function output is achieved by "efficient" combinations of inputs. An efficient point in a factor diagram such as Fig. 2-1 is a technologically feasible combination of quantities of inputs such that output cannot be increased without increasing the quantity of at least one input. Two general methods have been applied to derive production functions. The first is to examine the engineering aspects of the process where mass and energy conservation equations can be applied so that maximization is assured. Vernon L. Smith provides many examples of this technique in Chap. II of *Investment and Production* (Harvard University Press, Cambridge, Mass., 1956). The transportation of electrical energy through a cable is an example of a production function derived from engineering principles. If P_o is the power output required, P_i is the input, and P_L is the power loss, then

$$P_o = P_i - P_L. \tag{2-5}$$

$P_L = I^2R$ for transmission of current I through resistance R and $P_o = E_oI$, where E_o is the required voltage. The power factor is assumed to be unity. The resistance is $(2Lp)/A$, where L is length, A is cross-sectional area, and p is a physical coefficient. Then output is

$$P_o = P_i - \left(\frac{P_o}{E_o}\right)^2 \frac{2Lp}{A}. \tag{2-6}$$

Substituting and transforming to the standard notation for the implicit form $F(q, x_1, x_2)$ of the explicit function $q = f(x_1, x_2)$, where d is the density of the conductor and x_1 is the power input or P_i, $x_2 = 2dLA$ is the weight of conductor which we consider the second input, and q is power output, P_o:

$$F(q, x_1, x_2) = x_2(x_1 - q) - \frac{4L^2q^2pd}{E_o^2} = 0 \qquad (2\text{-}7)$$

or

$$0 = x_2(x_1 - q) - kq^2, \qquad (2\text{-}8)$$

where

$$k = \frac{4L^2pd}{E_o^2}. \qquad (2\text{-}9)$$

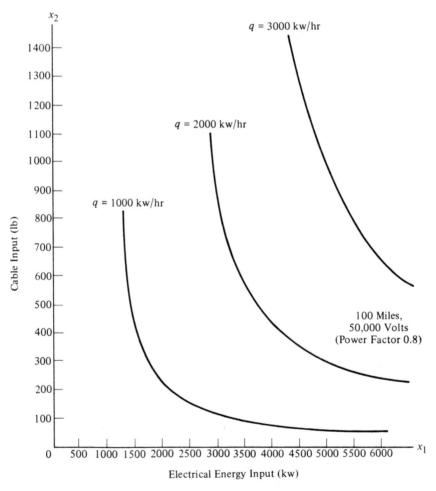

Figure 2-2.   Isoquants of transmission production function.

This is an implicit form of the production function whose usefulness will be demonstrated in the next section. Graphically the production function appears as in Fig. 2-2. Another example of a simple production function, but with stochastic inputs, was derived by Levhari and Sheshinski [2].

Another method for avoiding suboptimization in the derivation of production functions is to reduce the analysis to a level on which all factors appear to be additive, i.e.,

$$q = a_1 x_1 + a_2 x_2, \tag{2-10}$$

so that maximization is reduced to addition. Usually some input levels are fixed. This then requires the linear programming or activity analysis approach, which will be demonstrated later as an optimization technique at the higher state of analysis, that of determining the rules for optimization.

The other approach to the derivation of production functions has been the estimation of aggregate production functions by economic methods from aggregate economic data, where it can be assumed that managers have applied optimization. Usually these studies are based on aggregate industry data and make use of the Cobb-Douglas relationship, or its generalizations. It is at the industry level that the argument that all production functions are linearly homogeneous makes the most sense, and so the choice of the Cobb-Douglas function is justified. However, the two- or three-factor aggregate production functions obtained to date would not be of much use to the production manager except for very long-range planning because they specify gross inputs such as labor or capital. Nor are new versions such as the constant elasticity of substitution model of much more use to the manager [3] except perhaps in dealing with aggregate trends such as technological change.

E. Economic Optimization

I. INTRODUCTION AND SURVEY

This section introduces prices and costs which must be combined with the production function for optimization. The production manager can choose optimal levels of inputs and outputs for the production process by comparing prices and marginal properties of the production function. Section E.II sets up the mathematical conditions for optimization, either profit maximization or cost minimization, or output maximization. Section E.III shows the conditions for constrained optimization when some variables are not under the complete control of the production manager. Section E.IV applies the optimization technique to the electrical transmission production function derived in Sec. D. Section E.V gives examples of a modified optimization. Section E.VI looks at the optimization of linearly homogeneous production functions which present special difficulties, particularly for capacity planning. Section E.VII explores optimization of multiproduct production functions.

Since technical optimization is not possible for some production functions, as we found in Sec. C, and because both society and the firm are concerned not only with quantities but values of inputs and outputs, optimization must consider additional information. This information is usually taken to be the market prices of inputs and outputs. The U.S. economy treats prices as the standard of value. Here prices will be considered to be independent of the level of inputs or the level of output. In other words, the firm buys in competitive markets and also sells in a competitive market. Although these assumptions do not hold for all companies, we cannot examine all the models of industry structure which may exist. The reader is referred to [4] for an introduction to this area.

An additional assumption is that the production manager and the firm have the goal of maximizing profits or at least of minimizing total costs. There are, of course, considerations which sometimes override these criteria. There is also a considerable problem in defining the time period of long-run or short-run profits. The assumption of profit maximization provides a base from which to measure the impact of other considerations and will be carried forward in this analysis.

It might be argued that these goals are not ideal for society. We previously examined the possibility of maximizing average productivity of each factor because it had some intuitive desirability. Choosing the production level and inputs to minimize average cost would also seem to be an intuitive, socially desirable criterion. The framework chosen for this material, that of the firm, rather than society, could conceivably conflict with this desirable minimization. It would be profitable for the firm to produce at a level above that which has minimum average cost if the price is higher than that cost. The saving grace for our focus on the firm, besides the fact that our economy is so structured, is that economic theory has shown that if markets are competitive, the maximization of profits by the firm will result in minimization of costs for production. In addition, the results of such a system are Pareto optimal, that is, no one can be made better off economically without making someone worse off. Noncompetitive markets can destroy the validity of these statements, however. A reference to this topic is [5].

Assume that the production manager is given a price p for the output and is free to set output and choose inputs so as to maximize profit. His problem can be formulated for two inputs and one output as

$$\text{maximize profit } \pi = \text{revenue} - \text{cost,}$$

where revenue is pq and the cost, C, for production of output level q is

$$C = w_1 x_1 + w_2 x_2 = \sum_{i=1}^{n} w_i x_i \qquad \text{for } n \text{ inputs} \qquad (2\text{-}11)$$

The x_i are the input levels from the production function $f(x_1, x_2)$ and the w_i are prices of the inputs. The problem of measuring the level and prices of capital equipment inputs can be handled by multiplying the capital cost, W_i, by an interest rate, r, to given an equivalent annual cost for an indestructible asset. We shall present more sophisticated capital equipment models later.

II. CONDITIONS FOR OPTIMIZATION

The goal of the production manager is to maximize profit

$$\pi = pq - w_1 x_1 - w_2 x_2 \qquad \text{for two inputs} \qquad (2\text{-}12)$$

or to maximize

$$\pi = pf(x_1, x_2) - w_1 x_1 - w_2 x_2, \qquad (2\text{-}13)$$

where $f(x_1, x_2)$ is the production function. Standard calculus maximization techniques are applied to obtain the first-order conditions for a maximum by taking the partial derivatives of profit with respect to the decision variables x_1 and x_2:

$$\frac{\partial \pi}{\partial x_1} = p \frac{\partial q}{\partial x_1} - w_1 = 0 \qquad (2\text{-}14)$$

$$\frac{\partial \pi}{\partial x_2} = p \frac{\partial q}{\partial x_2} - w_2 = 0 \qquad (2\text{-}15)$$

or

$$p\text{MP}_{x_1} = w_1 \quad \text{and} \quad p\text{MP}_{x_2} = w_2. \qquad (2\text{-}16)$$

The product $p\text{MP}_{x_1}$ can be interpreted as the value of adding one more unit of input x_1 or, as it is sometime called, the marginal value product, MVP, of input 1. The optimality rule is to use inputs until the value of their output is just equal to their cost. This is a reasonable rule, since up to that point each unit is profitable. This rule also determines the output level. The cost of capital or reward to management and stockholders is included in the economist's concept of cost. The output is expanded until revenue just meets cost.

We can also obtain, by division of Eq. (2-14) by Eq. (2-15), the rule

$$\frac{w_1}{w_2} = \frac{\text{MP}_{x_1}}{\text{MP}_{x_2}}, \qquad (2\text{-}17)$$

which determines the relative level of each input to be used. Second-order conditions for the optimization can be found in standard texts on economic analysis such as Henderson and Quandt [6]. In practice these are seldom necessary because the manager has a feel for whether a solution will be a maximum or minimum or saddle point.

III. CONSTRAINED OPTIMIZATION

Perhaps a more common decision for the production manager is the minimization of costs for a given output level. The projected output level is often determined by the marketing side of the firm. More will be said concerning this division of decisions later. The production manager's decision, then, is to minimize cost, C.

$$\text{minimize } C = w_1 x_1 + w_2 x_2 \qquad (2\text{-}18)$$

while producing output q^0, a fixed level, or we can say to perform the optimization subject to $q^0 = f(x_1, x_2)$. The Lagrangian function

$$L = w_1 x_1 + w_2 x_2 + \lambda[q^0 - f(x_1, x_2)] \qquad (2\text{-}19)$$

must be minimized with respect to x_1, x_2, and λ. Any such minimum point will have $q^0 = f(x_1, x_2)$ because this expression is the partial derivative of L with respect to λ and is equated to zero. As a result, the cost function is minimized at the same values of x_1 and x_2 as the Lagrangian function. The distinguishing last term of L becomes zero when $q^0 = f(x_1, x_2)$. Appendix C contains a more detailed description of the Lagrangian technique. The optimality conditions can be written as

(1)
$$\frac{\partial L}{\partial x_1} = w_1 - \lambda \frac{\partial f(x_1, x_2)}{\partial x_1} = w_1 - \lambda MP_{x_1} = 0 \qquad (2\text{-}20)$$

(2)
$$\frac{\partial L}{\partial x_2} = w_2 - \lambda \frac{\partial f(x_1, x_2)}{\partial x_2} = w_2 - \lambda MP_{x_2} = 0 \qquad (2\text{-}21)$$

(3)
$$\frac{\partial L}{\partial \lambda} = -q^0 + f(x_1, x_2) = 0. \qquad (2\text{-}22)$$

The constraint equation is always the $\partial L/\partial \lambda$ and often has an important interpretation as the cost of the constraint. Dividing (1) by (2) gives

$$\frac{w_1}{w_2} = \frac{MP_{x_1}}{MP_{x_2}} \equiv RTS. \qquad (2\text{-}23)$$

This rule establishes that the inputs should be chosen so that their MPs at q^0, the given output level, are in the same ratio as their prices, an intuitively sensible condition equivalent to the rate of technical substitution.

Another very similar but perhaps less common question for the production manager is how to maximize production given a budget or cost constraint or

$$\text{maximize } q = f(x_1, x_2) \qquad (2\text{-}24)$$

$$\text{subject to } C^0 = w_1 x_1 + w_2 x_2. \qquad (2\text{-}25)$$

Forming a Lagrangian function

$$\max L = f(x_1, x_2) + \lambda(C^0 - w_1 x_1 - w_2 x_2) \tag{2-26}$$

and setting the derivative to zero results in the same decision rule as Eq. (2-23):

$$\frac{w_1}{w_2} = \frac{MP_{x_1}}{MP_{x_2}} \equiv RTS. \tag{2-27}$$

The λ in Eq. (2-26) is the change in output with respect to cost, the inverse of the λ for the cost minimization decision.

IV. APPLICATION OF OPTIMIZATION TO THE CABLE DECISION

Recall that the production function for the transmission of electrical energy in implicit form was Eq. (2-8):

$$x_2(x_1 - q) - kq^2 = 0 \tag{2-28}$$

For a cost minimization our problem would be

$$\text{minimize } C = w_1 x_1 + w_2 x_2 \tag{2-29}$$
$$\text{subject to } x_2 x_1 - q^0 x_2 - k(q^0)^2 = 0, \tag{2-30}$$

where $w_1 =$ price of electrical input in dollars per kilowatt hour
 $w_2 =$ price of copper wire
  $i =$ interest rate on investment in copper wire
 $w_2 = iW_2$, the annual equivalent of investment cost

The Lagrangian function is

$$L = w_1 x_1 + w_2 x_2 + \lambda[x_2 x_1 - q^0 x_2 - k(q^0)^2] \tag{2-31}$$

and the derivatives give conditions

$$\frac{\partial L}{\partial x_1} = w_1 + \lambda x_2 = 0 \tag{2-32}$$

$$\frac{\partial L}{\partial x_2} = w_2 - \lambda(q^0 - x_1) = 0 \tag{2-33}$$

$$\frac{\partial L}{\partial \lambda} = -x_2 q^0 + x_1 x_2 - k(q^0)^2 = 0. \tag{2-34}$$

We can divide Eq. (2-32) into Eq. (2-33) and substitute $x_1 - q^0 = x_L$ since input of energy minus output of energy equals energy lost in transmission.

This gives

$$\frac{x_2}{x_1 - q^0} = \frac{w_1}{w_2} = \frac{x_2}{x_L} \quad \text{or} \quad x_2 w_2 = w_1 x_L. \tag{2-35}$$

This is Kelvin's balance equation; the investment cost of copper is equal to the cost of energy lost in transmission. We shall follow Kelvin's derivation in a later paragraph.

The answer above follows the general rule that the marginal product ratio equals the price ratio since

$$\text{MP}_1 = \frac{x_2}{-2kq - x_2} \quad \text{and} \quad \text{MP}_2 = \frac{x_1 - q}{-2kq - x_2}. \tag{2-36}$$

Their ratio is obviously the same as in Eq. (2-35). Since the production function is known, an explicit solution can be found as

$$x_2 = q \frac{\sqrt{w_1 k}}{iW_2} \quad \text{and} \quad x_1 = q\left(1 + \frac{\sqrt{iW_2 k}}{w_1}\right). \tag{2-37}$$

These results were known to Kelvin in 1881, who attacked the problem by the usual engineering approach—the balance method. This method finds some design variable, not an input or output (here area), for which some costs increase (those associated with a variable input) and some costs decrease (the cost per unit for the fixed input). Then for the given output level, the design variable (here A, the cross-sectional area) is varied until total cost is minimized. See Fig. 2-3. The total cost, C, per unit length as a function of cross-

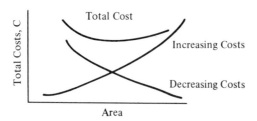

Figure 2-3. Cost balance.

sectional area equals the increasing capital cost plus the decreasing cost of the power lost. Algebraically,

$$C = iC_e A + \frac{KI^2 C_e}{A}, \tag{2-38}$$

where C_c = cost of copper per cubic unit = w_2
     C_e = cost of energy lost per unit = w_1
     K = twice the coefficient of resistivity

The minimum is obtained for A such that

$$\frac{\partial C}{\partial A} = iC_c - \frac{KI^2C_e}{A^2} = 0 \qquad (2\text{-}39)$$

or

$$iC_c A = \frac{KI^2C_e}{A}. \qquad (2\text{-}40)$$

In more general terms, the equation above can be written as $w_2 x_2 = (q - x_1)w_1$, which is the same as Eq. (2-35). This is just

$$\frac{w_1}{w_2} = \frac{x_2}{q - x_1} = \frac{\mathrm{MP}_{x_1}}{\mathrm{MP}_{x_2}} \qquad (2\text{-}41)$$

after transforming from area to pounds of copper, x_2, and power, x_1. Explicitly, we can solve for the area:

$$A = \frac{KI^2C_e}{iC_c} = \frac{K(q - x_1)w_1}{iW_2} \qquad (2\text{-}42)$$

The engineering balance approach and the economic optimization are equivalent when correctly done. Note that the condition for minimum cost using the balance approach is that the slopes of the costs of the fixed and variable inputs be equal, *not* that the costs be equal or at the point of intersection of the cost curves.

    An advantage of the economic approach is that λ, a shadow price, is also available. It is the change in cost if the constraint is relaxed one unit. Since λ measures the cost of the restriction, it can be useful in price or output decisions. In this example it measures $\partial C/\partial q^0$ or the marginal cost of transporting more electricity. If the price paid for transmission is greater than λ, it would be profitable to increase output.

    It should be noted that we have only considered optimizing the conductor size. Voltage level and other factors might also be explored.

V. EXAMPLES OF OPTIMIZATION WITH A MODIFIED PRODUCTION FUNCTION TECHNIQUE

    There is an alternative to either the engineer's exploration of the sensitivity of the total cost curve to the design parameter or the economist's separation of the costs and the technological production function. The cost equation can be written directly as a function of the output and minimized. This is, of course, the equivalent of the economist's procedure. The economist writes the cost equation as a sum of amounts of inputs times prices and uses the production function to determine the amounts of inputs. The more direct method is to write the cost equation as a function of inputs. Two examples which are taken from the June 1968 issue of *Management Science* will be briefly discussed.

A study was undertaken by Jen et al. [7] of the optimal capacities for three parts of an oxygen production facility: the capacity of the production plant itself, P; a compressor with capacity H for preparation for storage; and a storage capacity, V. The total cost equation was found from engineering relationships. Demand was given with two known levels, D_0 from time t_0 to t_1 and D_1 from time t_1 to t_2.

This demand cycle repeats indefinitely and so the capacity of the oxygen plant must be at least the time average of D or D_{av}. The decision variables can be reduced from P, H, and V to P, the production capacity, and a maximum pressure for storage, p, since this pressure determines the compressor pressure and the amount of gas that can be stored. The cost function is

$$\min C = a_1 + a_2 P + b_1 b_2 \left[(D_1 - P) \frac{t_2 - t_1}{t_1} \frac{RT}{k_2 k_1} \ln \left(\frac{p}{p_0} \right) \right]^{b_3}$$

$$+ b_4 (D_1 - P)(t_2 - t_1) \frac{RT}{k_2 k_1} \ln \left(\frac{p}{p_0} \right) + c_1 c_2 \left[t_1 (D_{av} - D_0) \frac{K}{p} T \right]^{c_3}$$

$$\tag{2-43}$$

$$\text{subject to} \quad P \geq D_{av} \tag{2-44}$$

$$p \geq p_0 \qquad \text{the minimum production pressure} \tag{2-45}$$

where
K = product of gas constant and the gas compressibility factor
T = temperature in degrees Rankine
a, b, c = cost and physical constant parameters

The total cost function was explored by gradient methods for optimal values of P and p which determine the capacity of the oxygen plant and the storage size. Note that although the demand was given, it could have been treated as a variable since it was explicitly defined. The cost function above is therefore an implied production function with cost parameters attached to each input.

The second example is the choice of number of capacity of fertilizer plants in India, as determined by Erlenkotter and Manne [8]. For this purpose a less detailed model is both necessary and desirable. Demand is increasing and can be met by construction of increments of capacity. Rather than express the cost as a continuous function of demand, the costs were determined only for the largest- and smallest-sized practical plants. A shipping penalty cost c is added for the cases when fewer, larger plants are added. The cost equation is

$$C = f(X \cdot D) \cdot \text{capital recovery factor} + cXD + G, \qquad (2\text{-}46)$$

where G is the discounted summation of annual operating costs. See Chap. 5 for discounting. Here the yearly demand, $X \cdot D$, is expressed in increments of the annual increase in demand, D. The cost was minimized for several values of D by inspection, since only two plant sizes and up to six possible locations were considered.

Table 2-3 gives the calculations for optimal selection of the larger or smaller plant under varying conditions of D and r.

Table 2-3   Unit Cost Comparison for Nitrogenous Fertilizer Plants (Rupees/ton of nitrogen)[a]

| Interest Rate, r (%/yr) | Yearly Increment of Demand, D | | | | |
	10	30	50	70	100
5	734/699	713/667	708/661	707/658	705/656
	(4.8)	(6.4)	(6.6)	(6.9)	(7.0)
10	847/823	797/747	787/733	783/727	780/722
	(2.8)	(6.3)	(6.9)	(7.2)	(7.4)
15	982/974	895/843	878/818	870/807	865/799
	(0.8)	(5.8)	(6.8)	(7.3)	(7.6)
20	1140/1155	1004/952	978/912	967/896	959/884
	(−1.3)	(5.2)	(6.7)	(7.3)	(7.8)

[a] For each parameter combination, this table first lists the unit costs for the smaller plant and then those for the larger one. Below the costs, the percentage advantage of the larger plant over the smaller is given in parentheses.

VI. LONG-RUN ECONOMIC OPTIMIZATION OF LINEARLY HOMOGENEOUS PRODUCTION FUNCTIONS

For the linear homogeneous production function $q = f(x_1, x_2)$ the profit maximization equation

$$\pi = pq - w_1 x_1 - w_2 x_2 = pf(x_1, x_2) - w_1 x_1 - w_2 x_2 \qquad (2\text{-}47)$$

is also linearly homogeneous since

$$pf(tx_1, tx_2) - w_1 tx_1 - w_2 tx_2 = t[pf(x_1, x_2) - w_1 x_1 - w_2 x_2]. \qquad (2\text{-}48)$$

The previously derived rule for output level under profit maximization was to produce at the point where $p\text{MP} = w$; however, for the linearly homogeneous production function, MP is constant for proportional increases of inputs (constant returns to scale). Therefore pMP does not change with the design level of output. It is either equal to w_i, in which case any output meets the optimality criterion, or it is not equal to w_i, in which case there is no optimal output level and profit or loss increases without bound. Although this appears to produce problems for analyzing the size of the plant, it merely points out that in very long-run considerations, when production functions can more safely be considered linearly homogeneous, it is not safe to say that p is constant. Over the long run, when capacities can be changed considerably, price varies with the level of output. More will be said about this problem once some way of representing price changes is introduced in Sec. H.

The linear homogeneous production function occurs in some perhaps unsuspected cases. If a fixed factor is divisible in either time or space or is used in a batch process, the production function becomes linearly homogeneous. There is automatic proportional variation of the fixed factor because of the possibility of varying the utilization rate. An example of spatial divisibility is using less than all the land available for a farm or shutting down units of a plant when producing at a lower level. Time divisibility occurs when the fixed inputs can be utilized for varying amounts of machine hours in a period. The productivity of the variable factor is constant since the proportion of fixed to variable factor is constant. The cost of the fixed factor is usually assumed to be zero. Therefore the cost curve is also linear. As noted in the paragraph above, no optimal output level can be reached unless price varies. This explains the fluctuations in price observed in batch-type production processes.

VII. MULTIPRODUCT PRODUCTION FUNCTIONS

If a firm produces more than one product, there are three major ways the production processes and outputs can be related:

1. The processes may be entirely separate with no relationship between the inputs of the various processes or between the outputs of the processes.

2. The processes may be unrelated except that they use some of the same fixed facilities, i.e., metal products using the same press. In this situation the processes can be called *alternative*. Figure 2-4 represents an alternative relationship between processes. It is essential to the definition that x_1 be a fixed input once the process is in use.

3. Some processes may produce several products which are either more closely related than above either in terms of inputs or else

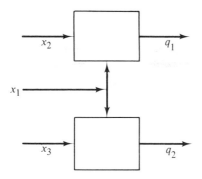

Figure 2-4. Multiproduct process.

the products are the result of one process and cannot be produced separately. These are joint processes. Examples range from mutton and wool to multiproduct industrial plants such as refineries.

The multiproduct process of type 1 can be treated by the same rules as the single-product production function. The alternative process, type 2, involving a fixed capacity is a short-run situation and will be dealt with under the heading of planning for aggregate production in Chap. 6 and scheduling in Chap. 8, since in the design stage, the capacity is not yet fixed. The case of joint production will be dealt with in the following paragraphs.

In the joint production case the production function can be written implicitly as

$$F(x_1, x_2, \ldots, x_n, q_1, q_2, \ldots, q_n) = 0 \qquad (2\text{-}49)$$

or explicitly

$$q_1 = f(x_1, \ldots, x_n, q_2, \ldots, q_n). \qquad (2\text{-}50)$$

Any other single variable may be selected to be moved to the left instead of q_1. A continuous range of input and output combinations is assumed possible. This is similar to the continuity condition on inputs for the single-product case. Given one factor and two products, for profit maximization,

$$\text{maximize } \pi = p_1 q_1 + p_2 q_2 - wx \qquad (2\text{-}51)$$

where the explicit production function is

$$x = g(q_1, q_2) \qquad (2\text{-}52)$$

or

$$\text{max } \pi = p_1 q_2 + p_2 q_2 - wg(q_1, q_2). \qquad (2\text{-}53)$$

Taking partial derivatives and equating them to zero gives the decision rules:

$$p_1 - w\frac{\partial g(q_1, q_2)}{\partial q_1} = 0$$

$$p_2 - w\frac{\partial g(q_1, q_2)}{\partial q_2} = 0$$

(2-54)

or

$$\frac{p_1}{p_2} = \frac{\partial q_2}{\partial q_1}.$$

(2-55)

The ratio $\partial q_1/\partial q_2$ is defined to be the rate of product transformation, RPT, or marginal rate of substitution of product 1 for product 2. The decision rule is to produce levels of products 1 and 2 so that the RPT is equal to the ratio of prices received for the products. This is not unexpected since it merely asserts that it should not be possible to make a higher profit by switching to production of more of one of the products.

By moving the product price terms to the right in Eq. (2-54) and (2-55), the cost of the input is given by

$$w = p_1 \frac{\partial q_1}{\partial g(q_1, q_2)} = p_2 \frac{\partial q_2}{\partial g(q_1, q_2)} = p_1 \frac{\partial q_1}{\partial x} = p_2 \frac{\partial q_2}{\partial x}$$

(2-56)

since

$$x = g(q_1, q_2).$$

(2-57)

This condition says that the value of marginal product of each input in producing each product must be equal to the cost of the input for the profit-maximizing level of input.

Perhaps a more usual task is producing the most profitable mixture of products with given resources, which is particularly common for service concerns. The first condition, RPT equal to the ratio for each pair of products, holds. The level of input resources is fixed so that the second condition, Eq. (2-56), is not necessary.

F. Effect of Technology on the Production Function—Limitational Production Functions

I. INTRODUCTION

Up to this point we have assumed that inputs are continuously substitutable. In the very long run this seems to be a good assumption. For example, in agriculture less manpower and less acreage are being used to produce the same output as was needed years ago. The automation of industry is another example. For the period between the short run where productive facilities are fixed and the very long run in which technology changes substantially, there may be a horizon in which the input proportions are essentially fixed. This time horizon corresponds roughly to the planning for construction of new processes. If a production manager is planning a new plant, he has no limitations placed by previous choices of equipment, but the range of substitutability of factors is somewhat restricted by the present level of the technology of his industry and of the industries which supply his equipment. Equipment manufacturers, for example, must standardize to a large extent. Their decisions limit the choice of input for the production manager, who may have a rather different situation with regard to prices of inputs and outputs than those the equipment manufacturer had in mind when designing the line of equipment. Similarly, the availability, skills, and degree of job classification and specialization of the labor force at any time is approximately fixed. All these influences reduce the substitutability of factors, as discussed below.

II. DEFINITION OF LIMITATIONAL PRODUCTION FUNCTIONS

Because fixed factor proportions, sometimes called fixed coefficients of production, restrict the choices of the production manager, we shall examine the production function and optimization in this case. The production function with fixed coefficients can be written as

$$x_1 = a_1 q \quad \text{and} \quad x_2 = a_2 q. \tag{2-58}$$

In other words, for each unit of an output, we need a_1 units of x_1. These two relationships can be written in the usual production function form $q = f(x_1, x_2)$ only if each term on the right-hand side of the equation is understood to be a limit on q or

$$q = \min \left(\frac{x_1}{a_1}, \frac{x_2}{a_2} \right). \tag{2-59}$$

This case is often referred to as having limitational production coefficients. Since there is no substitution of one input for another, the quantity of any one input available may limit the output. This is the assumption for all linear programming models of scheduling, for example. It is therefore important for the production manager to understand this type of production function.

Since each input is limitational, by the previous definition of marginal product, the MP of any input is zero. That is, $\partial q / \partial x_1$ is zero, where x_2 is held constant as in any partial derivative. This presents no immediate problem for choice of inputs because the ratio of the inputs is fixed. The problem of choosing between processes with different input ratios will be considered later.

III. OPTIMIZATION OF LIMITATIONAL PRODUCTION FUNCTIONS WITH VARIABLE COEFFICIENTS

If long-run optimization of limitational production functions is considered, the variation of the production coefficients must be examined. Although by definition there is no substitution of one input for another, that is, the factor proportions are fixed for any output level q, it is still true that the coefficients may vary as a function of output. We shall therefore refer to limitational coefficients rather than fixed coefficients to describe the production functions above. Since factor proportions are held constant, this is a scale question. The question is whether the coefficients are constant, which simply means a linearly homogeneous production function, or whether they vary and have increasing or decreasing returns to scale. To illustrate, first assume that the a_i are constant. The production decision is to maximize profit given a price p,

$$\text{maximize } \pi = qp - \sum w_i x_i, \tag{2-60}$$

substituting for x_i with $x_i = a_i q$,

$$\pi = qp - \sum w_i a_i q = q(p - \sum w_i a_i). \tag{2-61}$$

Taking the derivatives with respect to the only variable, q,

$$\frac{d\pi}{dq} = p - \sum w_i a_i = 0. \tag{2-62}$$

However, p was assumed to be a given constant and the prices, w_i, are given. There is no output level decision possible since the constants cannot be forced to obey the rule. The case of constant limitational coefficients is again that of a linearly homogeneous production function where no optimization of output level is possible unless p is considered variable. The rule becomes either produce or do not depending on whether $p - \sum w_i a_i$ is positive (profit) or negative (loss). If there are increasing returns, $\sum \partial a_i / \partial q < 0$, or decreasing returns, $\sum \partial a_i / \partial q > 0$, differentiating the equation for profit yields

$$q \sum w_i \frac{\partial a_i}{\partial q_i} = p - \sum w_i a_i \tag{2-63}$$

or choose q so that marginal cost equals marginal revenue. Explicitly solved for q^*, the optimal output level,

$$q^* = \frac{p - \sum w_i a_i}{\sum w_i (\partial a_i / \partial q)}. \tag{2-64}$$

The formula for optimal output level given above does not necessarily exclude negative quantities of output or inputs. If the usual constraints that q and the x_i are positive are added, the result is a mathematical programming problem which may be nonlinear. It is perhaps easier to watch for boundary solutions than to resort to programming.

As an example, we shall take

$$a_1 = 30 + 2q \quad \text{and so} \quad \frac{\partial a_i}{\partial q} = 2 \tag{2-65}$$

$$a_2 = 30 - q \quad \text{and} \quad \frac{\partial a_2}{\partial q} = -1 \tag{2-66}$$

for

$$q = \min\left[\frac{x_1}{a_1}, \frac{x_2}{a_2}\right], \quad p = \$100, \quad \text{and} \quad w_1 = w_2 = \$1. \tag{2-67}$$

Substituting in Eq. (2-64),

$$q^* = \frac{100 - (30 + 2q^* + 30 - q^*)}{2 \cdot 1 - 1 \cdot 1} = 20. \tag{2-68}$$

This is a profit-maximizing output level for q.

The input levels are

$$x_1 = a_1 q = (30 + 2 \cdot 20)20 = 1400 \tag{2-69}$$

$$x_2 = a_2 q = (30 - 20)20 = 250 \tag{2-70}$$

$$\pi = 20 \cdot 100 - 1650 = \$350, \tag{2-71}$$

but if

$$a_2 = 30 - 3q, \quad \text{then } q^* = -20, \tag{2-72}$$

which is a minimization point. For x_2 and a_2 to be positive, q must be ≤ 10.

This boundary point is the profit-maximizing position and could be obtained by linear programming, which we shall discuss in the next few paragraphs, or the Kuhn-Tucker conditions for inequality constrainted optimization could be applied as discussed in Problem 3 at the end of this chapter and in Appendix C.

IV. MULTIPROCESS PRODUCTION FUNCTIONS WITH LIMITATIONAL INPUTS

a. Choice of Technology with One Product

Rather than being faced with only one *technology* or process for accomplishing production with fixed factor proportions, a more realistic or common situation is a selection from some limited number of processes, each having different fixed factor proportions. This is the situation, for example, when the degree of automation is being decided. A large number of workers with hand tools, a smaller number with multipurpose machines, or a few with automatic equipment are the choices available.

Graphically the processes appear as rays from the origin on the factor diagram in Fig. 2-5, which shows the expansion path rather than the isoquants,

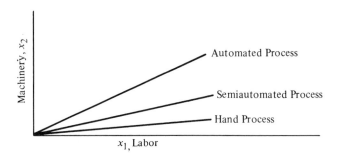

Figure 2-5. Expansion paths. Limitational production functions with fixed coefficients.

which appear in Fig. 2-6. In Fig. 2-5 the slope represents the ratio of a_2 to a_1 for each process. Here it is assumed that the coefficients a_i are not a function of output but are constants. The rays are therefore similar to isoclines, points with a constant ratio of MP of the factors for continuously substitutable production functions. Recall that straight-line isoclines are characteristic of linear homogeneous production functions, a condition fulfilled by limitational production functions with constant coefficients.

Despite the apparent difference between the factor diagram for choice of limitational input processes and the earlier diagram for the continuous substitution of inputs, the isoquants are quite similar. Suppose that three points d_1, d_2, and d_3 each produce the same amount of product, q^0. Three points of the isoquant, q^0, have been established, but since no factors are fixed and since each function is linearly homogeneous, the product q^0 can also be obtained by using combinations of the three processes. Thus the isoquants actually are straight-line segments joining points on the process isoclines so as to form a polygon convex to the origin. Budget lines giving the price ratios of the inputs can be established to find a least-cost ratio of inputs and processes given any fixed output level or optimum output given a fixed total cost. For example, consider Fig. 2-6. With equal prices the semiautomatic process is the least-cost choice to produce q^0.

It is not possible to establish the long-run optimum scale or level of output for these production functions without changing p, output price, to a variable

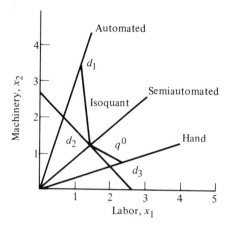

Figure 2-6. Optimization of processes.

or considering some input factor or input cost to be fixed. The long-run planning usually need not consider that any inputs are fixed. If some factors are fixed, the decision can be considered the same as short-run or scheduling problems using linear programming, as will be demonstrated in Chap. 8. A horizontal or vertical line in the diagram would represent the fixed input constraint.

b. Long-Run Choice of Multiproduct Technologies

If multiple outputs are produced by a process, the isoquant analysis above will not be adequate. The type of analysis used for determining the best combinations of technologies is often called activity analysis [9]. Activities correspond to processes or combinations of inputs and outputs operated at an arbitrary *unit* level. The technologies or possible processes can be arranged in a technology matrix listing the outputs (positive sign) and inputs (negative sign) of all commodities. Table 2-4 is a technology matrix for four processes

Table 2-4   Technology Matrix

	Process			
	1	*2*	*3*	*4*
Output 1	1	1	1	0
Output 2	0	b_1	b_2	1
Input 1	$-a_{11}$	$-a_{12}$	$-a_{13}$	$-a_{14}$
Input 2	$-a_{21}$	$-a_{22}$	$-a_{23}$	$-a_{24}$

which can be used to produce two outputs with two inputs. Processes 2 and 3 are joint processes which produce b_1 or b_2 units of output 2 per unit of output 1. It is assumed that intermediate products have been eliminated, that each product is desired as an output, and that each input is a scarce, not fixed, commodity. We can eliminate some processes quickly because they are "inefficient." An efficient process of the four is one such that no output of any other process is higher while requiring less inputs and keeping at least the same other output. In decision theory terms, any efficient process is an undominated strategy. For example, the matrix may be as shown in Table 2-5.

Table 2-5   Example Technology Matrix

	Process				
	1	*2*	*3*	*4*	*5*
Output 1	1	1	1	1	1
Output 2	0	2	2	0	1
Input 1	−2	−3	−4	−2	−2
Input 2	−3	−5	−3	−2	−2

Process 4 is efficient compared to process 1 but it is not efficient compared to process 5. Both 1 and 4 are therefore inefficient compared to the other processes. Process 5 is efficient compared to all the processes since it requires less inputs than either process 2 or 3. The other efficient processes are 2 and 3, neither of which dominates the other since each requires more of an input.

The technique of finding the efficient processes is a commonsense procedure that will give the production manager some guidance in selection of processes for long-range planning, but often more than one process is "efficient." When more than one process is efficient, the analysis above is not sufficient for selection of one technological process. In fact, it is not necessarily true that only one process should be chosen. For long-run optimization, where no inputs are fixed, a corner solution will always result such as in the example Fig. 2-6 when only one output is specified. After the process is installed, there will be input restrictions. Having two or more processes available may make it possible to obtain better use of a fluctuating restricted resource such as manpower. In Fig. 2-6 this would mean operating on the isoquant between processes. In general terms this is operational flexibility. One good procedure would be to make assumptions about demand, as is done in the next few paragraphs, and test whether one process in the planned amounts will better meet these assumed operational conditions.

The now familiar problem of undefined long-term optimization with linearly homogeneous production functions is still with us. Either prices must be considered variable or some input must be considered fixed if we are to select an optimal output level when confronted with several limitational technologies. If only the price of the output changes, all processes are affected equally. If the price of one input factor changes with amount used, processes which use more of that factor will be handicapped if the price increases and favored if the price decreases. We shall explore a methodology for this analysis in Sec. H.

c. Choice of Technology When Demand Is Fixed

The analysis of Sec. H will make the assumption that there is one primary product or that all products can be aggregated for capacity planning. If we look carefully at the multiproduct technology matrix, we can see that this assumption is necessary to avoid the situation we shall now discuss. Suppose that demand for each of several products has been established. The planning situation is intermediate in that demand is fixed but selection of resources or a technology has not been determined. This is equivalent to submitting bids on a multiproduct contract without having facilities. This is probably an unusual situation, but in this case it would not be possible to simply choose a single least-cost technology because it is not likely that any one technology would have exactly the right product mix. This problem can be solved by a simple linear programming calculation. For the example technology matrix of Table 2-5 we shall add that input prices are $1 each. Then efficient process 2 drops out of the running because its cost, $8, is more than that of process 3 and its output is the same. The demand is assumed to be 10 units of output 1 and 12 units of output 2. The optimal combination of processes to meet demand is solved in the graphical linear program shown in Fig. 2-7. It can be stated as

$$\text{minimize cost } Z = 7x_3 + 4x_5 \tag{2-73}$$
$$\text{subject to } x_3 + x_5 \geq 10 \tag{2-74}$$
$$2x_3 + x_5 \geq 12. \tag{2-75}$$

The optimal levels are to produce 2 units of output 1 and 4 units of output 2 by an activity level of 2 for process 3 and 8 units of each by process 5. An activity model of a cement plant is discussed in [10]. Also see [11].

It should be obvious that choice of technology for a multiproduct case but with no joint products is simply a matter of costing out each process and selecting the least-cost process for each product rather than the LP model for joint products. There have been some elaborate attempts to justify a complex transfer price programming approach to this problem; see Wietzman [12]. In a long-range planning problem, transfer prices are entirely superfluous. For an operational problem where transfer prices become important, the technology is already fixed in capacity.

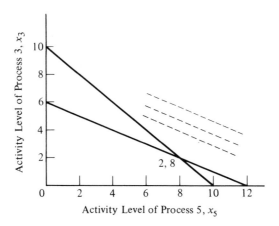

Figure 2-7.   Graphical solution of process selection.

G. Mixed Production Functions

Two types of production functions have been considered, those with continuous substitution between inputs and those with limitational inputs. There can, of course, be production functions where both types of input relations are present. For example, consider as a production function the two equations $q = f(x_1, x_2)$ and $x_3 = a_3 q$. Here, by assumption, there is continuous substitution between x_1 and x_2 but x_3 is in a fixed relationship with output. Frisch [13] calls x_3 a product shadow since it follows production like a shadow. The cost minimization with no fixed factors can proceed as a Lagrange constrained maximization or by substitution of $a_3 f(x_1, x_2)$ for x_3.

Suppose that we want to maximize profit for this mixed production function.

$$\pi = pq - w_1 x_1 - w_2 x_2 - w_3 x_3. \tag{2-76}$$

Substituting for q and rearranging,

$$\pi = (p - w_3 a_3) f(x_1, x_2) - w_1 x_1 - w_2 x_2 \tag{2-77}$$

$$\frac{\partial \pi}{\partial x_1} = (p - w_3 a_3)\mathrm{MP}_{x_1} - w_1 = 0 \tag{2-78}$$

$$\frac{\partial \pi}{\partial x_2} = (p - w_3 a_3)\mathrm{MP}_{x_2} - w_2 = 0. \tag{2-79}$$

The rule for continuous substitution was that the input price ratio equals the marginal value product ratio. From the conditions above it can be seen that the only change is that the cost of the limitational factor per unit of output is subtracted from the price of the output since the other inputs require that much additional expense in production. It is obvious that production should not be expanded as far as with the product shadow since the *gross margin* has been decreased. The rule of equating the ratio of input prices to marginal products is unchanged except that MP is not defined for the third factor.

As an example of a production function with both continuous inputs and a product shadow, Danø [14] analyzed a chocolate molding process where the percentage of defective castings depended on the percentage of cocoa fat in the batch of product. Defectives must be remolded, so the total cost is a complex function of the fat content. An optimal amount of fat must be determined, where

$$x_1 = \text{quantity of chocolate paste excluding fat}$$
$$x_2 = \text{quantity of fat input} \qquad\qquad (2\text{-}80)$$
$$x_3 = \text{molding labor input.}$$

The maximum q equals $x_1 + x_2$ if there are no defectives and

$$x_3 = \frac{q}{1-d}, \qquad\qquad (2\text{-}81)$$

where d is the percent defective, and

$$d = f\left(\frac{x_2}{x_1}\right), \qquad\qquad (2\text{-}82)$$

an empirically derived function. In this example the third input, labor, is not only a product shadow, $x_3 = a_3 q$, but it is also related to the other inputs, fat, x_1, and paste, x_2, because

$$a_3 = \frac{1}{1-d}, \qquad\qquad (2\text{-}83)$$

where d is a function of x_1 and x_2. The derivation of the optimal rules must now treat a_3 as a variable.

Another example of the mixed production function occurs when one input must be present in a fixed relationship with one of the substitutional inputs

$$q = f(x_1, x_2) \qquad\qquad (2\text{-}84)$$
$$g(x_1, x_2) = 0. \qquad\qquad (2\text{-}85)$$

The second function may represent a quality specification, for example. Here again optimization may be carried out by Lagrangian analysis.

Finally, the production function for subassemblies of the same unit, the case Frisch calls disconnected factor rings, is

$$q = \min [f(x_1, x_2), g(x_1, x_2)]. \qquad (2\text{-}86)$$

When optimized by Lagrangian analysis, this production function will yield the usual MP ratio = price ratio for each of the subassembly functions; $\lambda_1 + \lambda_2$ is the marginal cost at the optimum and $p = \lambda_1 + \lambda_2$.

H. Optimal Long-Run Capacity Planning with Variable Price

I. INTRODUCTION

The optimal capacity decision rule derived in Secs. C and D was to set output at the level where $p\text{MP}$ equals w for all inputs. This rule obviously depends on the market price of the product. The rule avoids consideration of uncertainty in price or amount which can be sold at that price. Even the prediction of a stable average price versus quantity relationship over the period necessary for capacity planning is exceedingly difficult. The need for price versus quantity prediction becomes more crucial as capacity decisions reach further into the long term.

In shorter-range planning the effective production function will tend to be nonhomogeneous because of the necessity of considering some inputs as fixed, such as managerial talents. Recall that a linearly homogeneous function shows decreasing returns if all but one factor is varied proportionately. The optimum output level for the shorter-range conditions can be set strictly from the supply side ($p\text{MP} = w$) even if the price is assumed constant, i.e., the product is sold in a competitive market, but when a long-run capacity decision must be made, the following conditions are more likely to hold:

1. The production function is most likely linear or shows increasing returns to scale up to some point.
2. As a result, the rule $p\text{MP} = w$ leads to an unlimited increase in production if any at all.
3. Finally, the price cannot be considered constant because the firm will logically expand until its production does influence market price or other limits are reached.

In this case price and quantity relationship must be considered. We assume that the production manager obtains information from the marketing side of the firm concerning the price versus quantity relationship.

Most firms dealing in established products have only incremental capacity or price decisions to make. These are incremental changes essentially based on aggregate planning and capital budgeting decisions—increasing one of several inputs which has become a bottleneck. The framework presented here is best viewed in terms of planning capacity for a new production process. Locational factors are to be considered explicitly in the next chapter. Here they may be assumed to be merely another input in the production process.

The criterion remains maximization of profit rather than sales or rate of return on investment. For most real firms, this is probably the most reasonable compromise. It is assumed that equipment costs can be converted to annual equivalents at a standard interest rate as the cost of capital.

II. CAPACITY PLANNING AS AN ITERATIVE PROCEDURE

In reality the firm is liable to be between the two extremes of short-run and long-run planning in capacity planning. Therefore the manager will generally perform analysis of both production and market conditions to make sure that they are relevant at the level selected. First the production manager may assume that price p will be constant up to a certain level and that the production function is homogeneous. He establishes the levels of inputs needed at the output level where price would begin to decrease. He then constructs a model of the production process, a preliminary design (see Chap. 4), at that output. It can be used to determine if

1. There are increasing or decreasing returns to scale because of changes in MPs.
2. There are changes in prices of inputs because of the increased demand for them.

If either MPs or factor prices (w) would change at that plant scale or output level, he must adjust the model to make input ratios equal to the ratio of factor prices. Then he would test the model for $p\mathrm{MP} = w$. It may be that output is now too high, because price is lower or MP has decreased or w has increased. If so, he would pick a lower output and repeat the process outlined above.

If the production function is still homogeneous or shows increasing returns at the projected level, he should repeat the process for a slightly higher output level with decreasing p until the $p\mathrm{MP} = w$ rule holds. Output cannot profitably be increased at that level. The total revenue and cost slopes are equal.

III. GRAPHICAL ILLUSTRATION OF THE ITERATIVE PROCEDURE

The following steps outline the procedure above graphically:

1. Estimate the output where price must be decreased in order to increase sales.
2. Prepare a preliminary design of the plant and determine the costs in order to test for homogeneity of the production function. Also check for changes in input prices because of the required level. See Fig. 2-8.
3(a). If the production function is still homogeneous or shows increasing returns, establish the increase in output under decreas-

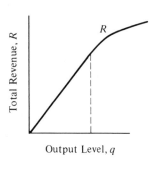

(a) Estimating Price Break

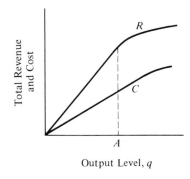

(b) Check for Homogeniety

Figure 2-8.

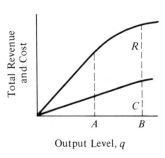

(a) Optimality for Increasing Returns

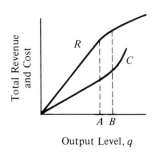

(b) Optimality for Decreasing Returns

Figure 2-9.

ing price conditions which will make the two curves parallel [marginal revenue (MR) = marginal cost (MC)]. See Fig. 2-9(a).

3(b). If the production function shows decreasing returns, i.e., the cost curve turns upward, backtrack to the point where the curves are parallel. See Fig. 2-9(b).

4. Recheck the design for equality of the input MP and price ratios at the point selected in step 3(a) or 3(b).

IV. EXAMPLE OF THE FIRST STEP IN THE ITERATIVE PROCESS

Assume that the firm is investigating the manufacture of aluminum in India, to follow the data contained in Manne [15]. The demand in 1970–1971 is forecasted at 240 million metric tons. Above this output level the sale price would drop, presumably. The variable costs of manufacture—bauxite, electricity, coal, labor, caustic soda, etc.—come to 1720 rupees per ton for one particular process. The plant costs have a scale coefficient of .77 because of higher-amperage smelting pots at higher volumes.

Investment as a function of output q is $197q^{.77}$ million rupees. The production manager first considers an output level of 240 million tons and picks the process which is least cost (including the equivalent annual cost of facilities). The requirements for coal, bauxite, and electricity should be checked to see if they are limiting or if adjustment of the factor prices would be needed. If prices of the factors would rise because of the strain on limited supplies, a lower output should be considered.

A profit can be made at the 240-million-ton level if input prices do not increase. Therefore an increase in production should be considered since even a reduced price may yield added revenue above cost. The output should be expanded until the MC equals the MR. These prices versus volume data are not available in Manne [15], as it often would not be in a company. Often the production manager is given a price and a market level which can support the price. This may be the total extent of the price versus quantity information. Despite the lack of market data, Manne should point out that increased capacity is possible and demonstrate the profit involved if the price can be held constant and output expanded.

V. CAPACITY PLANNING FOR EXPANDING MARKETS

The discussion in Sec. H.IV assumes static market conditions for a new product. Such an occasion is rare, since most markets for new products are expanding. If demand is increasing, the manager faces a decision. He can save construction cost by building large plants which have the advantages of economies of scale but which have idle capacity for some period. Alternatively, he can build a series of smaller plants to meet additional growth as it occurs.

These will have higher costs, unfortunately. It is assumed that the small plants cannot be enlarged at a cost less than that of new construction, nor would an enlarged plant be more efficient than the smaller. Total discounted costs at the discount rate r for the optimal addition of plants every x years with increased capacity of xD must obey the following recursive relationship:

$$C(x) = f(xD) + e^{-rx}C(x) + e^{-2rx}C(x) + \cdots, \qquad (2\text{-}87)$$

where $f(xD)$ is the cost as a function of capacity. We can sum this infinite series of terms as follows:

$$C(x) = \frac{f(xD)}{1 - e^{-rx}}. \qquad (2\text{-}88)$$

If we assume a linear increase in demand which must be met and the usual exponential relationship of cost of capacity,

$$C(x) = \frac{k(xD)^a}{1 - e^{-rx}}. \qquad (2\text{-}89)$$

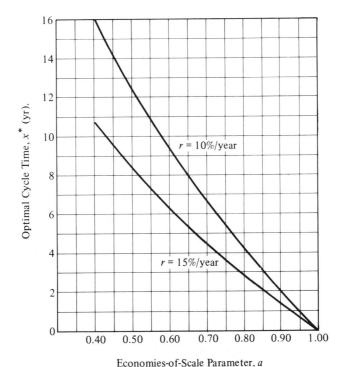

Figure 2-10.   Solution to Eq. (2-90).

Source: Alan A. Manne, Investments for Capacity Expansion, *M.I.T. Press, Cambridge, Mass., 1967, p. 37. Courtesy of M.I.T. Press.*

For optimal x, we take the logarithms, differentiate, and set the derivative equal to zero:

$$rx = a(e^{rx} - 1). \tag{2-90}$$

This is not easy to solve for x, and so we include the graphical solution from Manne, Fig. 2-10.

For the example of investment above, the table can be entered at $r = 10\%$ and $q = .77$ for an optimal x of 4.5 years. Note that D and k do not affect the answer. The analysis above assumes that there is an optimal cycle of building with a constant number of years between new plants. The use of dynamic programming on the recursive relation could eliminate the need for the constant cycle assumption, but Manne's analysis indicated that the data are much more uncertain than the inaccuracies introduced by the assumption of a constant cycle.

For a dynamic programming solution to the problem under a variety of constraints see Howard and Nemhauser [16]. For a solution under conditions of technological change, see [17]. For a solution under uncertainty, see [18] and Problem 10 in Chap. 6.

I. The Multifacility Firm

Up to this point we have dealt with medium to long-range capacity planning. We introduce a short-range capacity planning program simply because of its similarity to the analysis above and to set the stage for Chap. 8.

Many firms have more than one plant or more than one facility within a plant which can be used to produce a particular product. If total capacity is not required, a decision must be made as to which facility should be used. Examples are generator loading in a utility and shift work in an industrial plant. In Chap. 8 somewhat similar scheduling situations will be examined by linear programming analysis under assumptions of constant marginal productivity. In many cases, such as generator loading, marginal productivity is not constant and is an important consideration. The problem can be stated as follows: Given a total cost function C for two facilities as a function of output Y_i,

$$\min C = C_1(Y_1) + C_2(Y_2) \tag{2-91}$$
$$\text{subject to } Y_1 + Y_2 - Y^0 \geq 0$$

where Y^0 is the required supply, or

$$\min L = C_1(Y_1) + C_2(X_2) - \lambda(Y_1 + Y_2 - Y_0). \tag{2-92}$$

The Kuhn-Tucker† conditions for the derivatives are

$$\text{MC}_1 - \lambda \geq 0 \qquad \text{if} > 0, \; Y_1 = 0, \qquad \text{where } \text{MC}_1 = \frac{\partial C}{\partial Y_1}$$

$$\text{MC}_2 - \lambda \geq 0 \qquad \text{if} > 0, \; Y_2 = 0 \tag{2-93}$$

$$Y_1 + Y_2 - Y^0 \geq 0 \qquad \text{if} > 0, \; \lambda = 0.$$

If the boundary conditions are not operable, the solution is to produce so that $\text{MC}_1 = \text{MC}_2$. The second-order condition for a minimum is that the determinant

$$\begin{vmatrix} 0 & g_1 & g_2 \\ g_1 & L_{11} & L_{12} \\ g_2 & L_{21} & L_{22} \end{vmatrix} < 0. \tag{2-94}$$

Here g is the function $Y^0 = Y_1 + Y_2$ and so $g_1 = \partial g/\partial Y_1 = 1 = \partial g/\partial Y_2 = g_2$ and

$$L_1 = \frac{\partial C_1(Y_1)}{\partial Y_1}, \qquad L_{12} = 0,$$

$$L_{11} = \frac{\partial^2 C_1(Y_1)}{\partial Y_1^2}, \qquad L_{21} = 0,$$

and so the second order condition is

$$\begin{vmatrix} 1 & 1 & 1 \\ 1 & \dfrac{\partial^2 C_1(Y_1)}{\partial Y_1^2} & 0 \\ 1 & 0 & \dfrac{\partial^2 C_2(Y_2)}{\partial Y_2^2} \end{vmatrix} < 0$$

or

$$\frac{\partial^2 C_1(Y_1)}{\partial Y_1^2} + \frac{\partial^2 C_2(Y_2)}{\partial Y_2^2} > 0 \quad \text{or} \quad C_1'' + C_2'' > 0, \tag{2-95}$$

where C_i'' is the second partial derivative. This condition says that either the marginal cost is increasing in both facilities or that the rate of change in the increasing one is larger than in the decreasing MC facility. This suggests the graphical representation of Fig. 2-11.

The nonboundary solution (more than one plant producing) is given by the points of equal MC and which obey the second-order conditions $C_1'' + C_2''$ > 0. The two total cost curves can be converted to one set of isocost curves for convenience. The convexity or concavity of the isocosts depends on the convexity or concavity of the total cost curves or C''.

---

†See Appendix C for a description of the Kuhn-Tucker conditions.

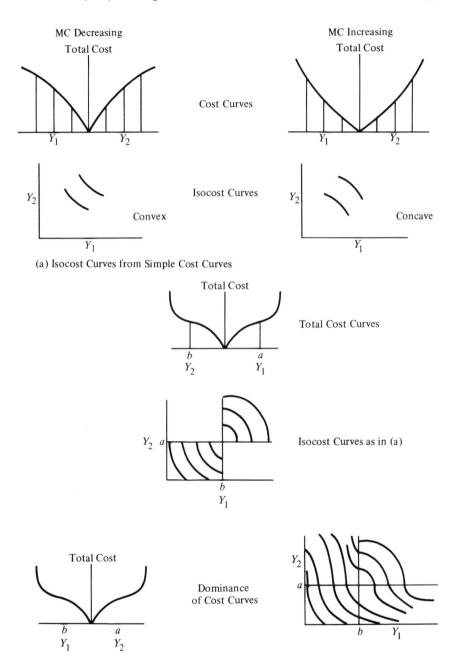

Figure 2-11. Graphical illustrations of capacity scheduling for two facilities.

If the MC decreases, the isocost curves are convex to the origin. If the MC increases, the curves are concave. If the MC is decreasing, the isocost curves are convex. If the MC is increasing, the isocost curves are concave. For the general cost curve, which is first decreasing in MC and then increasing with inflection points a and b, the isocost curves are convex and concave in quadrants I and III, respectively. The curvature in the other two quadrants is dependent on which curvature dominates.

A numerical example of assignment of production to the facilities is given below.

A firm has two plants, 1 and 2, with total cost curves

$$C_1 = \frac{Y_1^3}{3} - 3Y_1^2 + 9Y_1$$
$$C_2 = \frac{Y_2^3}{3} - 4Y_2^2 + 16Y_2.$$

(2-96)

See Fig. 2-12.

$$MC_1 = Y_1^2 - 6Y_1 + 9 \qquad C_{11}'' = 2Y_1 - 6$$
$$MC_2 = Y_2^2 - 8Y_2 + 16 \qquad C_{22}'' = 2Y_2 - 8.$$

(2-97)

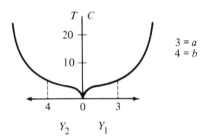

Figure 2-12.   Cost curves for example facilities.

Assume that desired production is $10 \leq Y = Y_1 + Y_2$.
    The Kuhn-Tucker conditions are

(1) $\qquad\qquad MC_1 - \lambda \geq 0 \qquad$ if > 0, $Y_1 = 0$

(2) $\qquad\qquad MC_2 - \lambda \geq 0 \qquad$ if > 0, $Y_2 = 0$ $\qquad$ (2-98)

(3) $\qquad\qquad Y_1 + Y_2 \geq 10 \qquad$ if > 10, $\lambda = 0$

We can deduce what the plants produce by examining the possible cases for $Y_1 = Y_2 = 0$ or the nonboundary solution from these conditions.

Case 1. $(1) = 0$, $(2) > 0$, and $(3) = 0$, production in plant 1 only:

$$\lambda = MC_1 = Y_1^2 - 6Y_1 + 9 \qquad \text{from (1)}$$
$$Y_1 = 10 - Y_2 \qquad\qquad\quad \text{from (3)} \qquad \text{(2-99)}$$
$$Y_2 = 0 \qquad\qquad\qquad\qquad \text{from (2)},$$

and so

$$\lambda = 100 - 60 + 9 = 49.$$

Checking assumptions for this case,

$$MC_2 - \lambda \geq 0, \qquad Y_2 = 0,$$

but

$$MC_2 = 16, \qquad 16 - 49 \not> 0,$$

and so case 1 is not applicable.

Case 2. $(1) > 0$, $(2) = 0$, and $(3) = 0$, production in plant 2 only:

$$\lambda = Y_2^2 - 8Y_2 + 16 = 36 \qquad \text{from (2) and (3)} \qquad \text{(2-100)}$$

but

$$9 - 36 \not> 0 \qquad\qquad\qquad \text{from (1)},$$

and so case 2 is not applicable.

Case 3. $(1) = 0$, $(2) = 0$, and $(3) = 0$, both plants producing:

$$\lambda = MC_1 = MC_2$$
$$Y_1^2 - 6Y_1 + 9 = Y_2^2 - 8Y_2 + 16 \qquad\qquad \text{(2-101)}$$

Substituting $Y_1 + Y_2 = 10$,

$$Y_1 = 4.5$$
$$Y_2 = 5.5$$

Checking the second-order conditions $C_{11}'' + C_{22}'' > 0$,

$$3 + 3 > 0,$$

and so this case obeys all the conditions for a minimum.

In contrast, we lower the production requirement to $Y_1 + Y_2 \geq 3$. Taking a hint from the best case above, case 3 $[(1) = 0$, $(2) = 0$, and $(3) = 0]$,

$$Y_1 = 1, \qquad Y_2 = 2, \qquad\qquad\qquad \text{(2-102)}$$

but second-order conditions are not fulfilled:

$$-4 - 4 \not> 0.$$

Both marginal costs are declining and so it would be foolish to produce in both plants.

In case 1 [(1) = 0, (2) > 0, and (3) = 0],

$$\lambda = MC_1 = 9$$
$$MC_2 - \lambda > 0 \tag{2-103}$$
$$16 - 9 > 0$$

and so this is the solution, to produce all three units in facility 1.

The expansion path for the two facilities is as shown in Fig. 2-13. The expansion path is $OSTUV$. From O to S, produce in plant 1 only. Above a

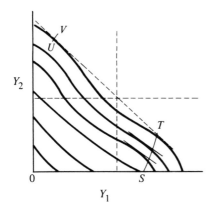

Figure 2-13.   Isocost diagram for two facilities.

rate of S the optimal schedule includes both plants with a predominance in plant 1 at first and then a discontinuity along the 45° dashed line from T to U, where the predominance is in plant 2.

J. Capacity Planning under Risk

I. INTRODUCTION

Up to this point we have assumed that the information available to the production decision maker was known with certainty. There is some question whether the cost information is known with high certainty for investments in new technological developments, but the information on price as a function of quantity is almost never known with certainty. Therefore we shall briefly examine several ways of dealing with uncertainty or risk in capacity decisions. One method is the use of the break-even chart. Another is the examination of the utility of a decision under risk. Both will be discussed in this section.

II. THE BREAK-EVEN CHART

The break-even chart is a common tool in the marketing function, where it is usually used in pricing decisions. It can also be used to explore the feelings of top management concerning the uncertain price-quantity relationship and the resulting decision for capacity [19].

The break-even chart is simply a projection of revenue and expense as a function of volume or quantity, such as appears in Fig. 2-14. Total revenue is

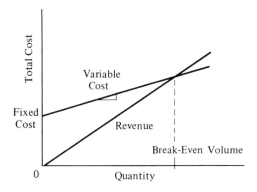

Figure 2-14. Break-even chart.

taken as a linear function of price through the origin. The cost curve has an intercept representing "fixed" costs and a constant slope representing "variable" costs. The distinction is based on the time dimension. Capital investment and perhaps salaried personnel costs are considered fixed and raw material and labor are usually treated as variable costs. The intersection of these curves gives the *break-even* volume for that price and cost structure. Obviously, at the break-even point there is no profit or return on investment. Since management is clearly not interested in only zero profit, the purpose of the break-even chart is to examine uncertainty through a sensitivity analysis of several break-even charts.

The introduction of the time dimension can be very important in cost analysis. Unfortunately most economic models are static or timeless. Often this is a serious defect which can lead to substantial errors in practice. The break-even charts' distinction between fixed and variable costs can be very important in capacity decisions when marketing information is not perfect.

A basic assumption made at the beginning of this chapter was that the firm operates in a perfectly competitive market. If this is put aside, the time dimension and fixed and variable costs become very important. The perfect competition model assumes that price will adjust to clear markets of the goods supplied at some price. Also, it does not address cyclical variations in demand and price. However, in reality, demand does vary and prices are definitely sticky in a downward direction. Therefore capacity planners must examine the effects of variation in quantity sold in making the capacity decision. This is only one reason for uncertainty in price-quantity relationships, but an important one.

Another source of time variation of cost is the learning or start-up effect [20]. In some industries it has been observed that if the quantity produced per time period is kept constant, the unit production cost decreases because of "learning." Additionally, or conversely, it has been observed that in starting up a new plant, unit costs are higher than planned and production is less than the design capacity [21]. Finally, although we earlier discussed capacity planning for growing markets, there may be a short-term delay in reaching the designed sales volume, which contributes to uncertainty in the initial volume of operation.

Although there are methods for dealing with these problems by estimation of their particular effect (see Problem 9 at the end of this chapter), we shall lump them into the effect of uncertainty and address them through the break-even chart and more sophisticated methods.

Let us examine the capacity decision as aided by the break-even chart. Suppose that a new plant is being designed for a new product to be sold at $10 per unit. Earlier we discussed the fact that alternative technologies may be available, but without considering the time dimension. In Fig. 2-15 we have three technologies, again ranging from automated to hand labor. Because of the high investment and high overhead in skilled maintenance men and parts, the automated process has the highest "fixed" cost and the lowest "variable" cost per unit produced. We can see that its break-even point is higher than the other technologies. It is therefore more appropriate for higher production quantities. If there is either cyclical fluctuation in volume or uncertainty about volume, we might say that the automated technology has more "risk" of incurring a loss. Instead of automating, the decision maker might install the same capacity but with the more flexible semiautomated technology.

For the moment let us neglect the choice of technology and merely specify that there are three different capacities of the plant, each of which has a

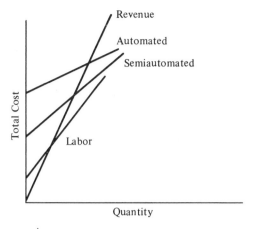

Figure 2-15. Break-even chart with three technologies.

slightly different cost curve because of economies of scale. How does the break-even chart help the decision maker? It identifies

1. The minimum sales quantity per time period required to avoid a loss.
2. The amount of profit (loss) generated at other sales volumes by looking at the vertical distance between the curves.

These estimates along with top management's feeling for the accuracy and variability of the sales projections may enable them to select a "good" capacity. Then additional consideration is required for the technology decision. In the next Sec. J.III we shall present a more sophisticated means of dealing with this problem in which management's feelings about sales are translated into a probability distribution and the break-even charts, profits, and losses are translated into *payoffs*.

III.   UTILITY THEORY APPROACH

A more complete examination of the problem involves an examination of the decision maker's feeling about consequences of a decision, its utility, and the probabilities of the outcomes of the results.

The simplest approach to decisions under risk is to assume that there is no risk and essentially treat the "best estimate" as a certain result. This is what we have done in this chapter up to now. Perhaps the next easiest treatment is to admit that some estimates have a probability distribution and calculate the expected value of the various alternatives. A simple example appears in Table

Table 2-6   Expected Value and Risk of Alternative Investments

Distribution of Demand

Demand D, units/day	10	20	30
Probability of demand, $P(D)$	$\frac{1}{4}$	$\frac{1}{4}$	$\frac{1}{2}$

Revenue = \$2/unit, cost = \$1·installed capacity plus \$10

Profit = \$2·min (demand, capacity) − \$1·installed capacity − \$10

Profit or Payoff Matrix (\$/day)

Capacity	Demand 10	20	30
10	\$0	\$0	\$0
20	−\$10	\$10	\$10
30	−\$20	\$0	\$20

Expected Value of Profit of Alternative Capacities, E(cap.)

$E(\text{cap. }10) = 0$

$E(\text{cap. }20) = -10 \cdot \frac{1}{4} + 10(\frac{1}{4} + \frac{1}{2}) = \$5$

$E(\text{cap. }30) = -20 \cdot \frac{1}{4} + 0 + 20(\frac{1}{2}) = \$5$

Variance of Profit of Alternative Capacities, V(cap.) = risk

$V(\text{cap. }10) = 0$

$V(\text{cap. }20) = -15^2 \cdot \frac{1}{4} + 5^2 \cdot \frac{1}{4} + 5^2 \cdot \frac{1}{2} = 75$

$V(\text{cap. }30) = -25^2 \cdot \frac{1}{4} + 5^2 \cdot \frac{1}{4} + 15^2 \cdot \frac{1}{2} = 275$

2-6, where a price has been established and estimated quantity sold at that price has a three-valued discrete probability distribution. Capacity must be installed in multiples of 10 units per day. The results of each capacity decision under each possible sales level is calculated and presented in a payoff matrix, a handy way of presenting alternatives and their outcomes. Note that the linear revenue and cost functions are similar but not identical to the usual break-even chart in this case, since cost is a function of capacity rather than sales. Any appropriate payoff structure can be represented in this manner. The expected payoffs for the three alternatives are calculated by summing the product of payoff times the probability of the sales resulting in that payoff across each row or capacity decision.

In our example the capacities of 20 and 30 have the same expected payoff.

This leads to some interesting alternatives to decision making in addition to selection of the alternative with highest expected value. We return to the payoff matrix and note that with the capacity of 30 we have some chance of both gaining or losing more money than with a capacity of 20. In common terminology, the higher capacity is *riskier*. Attitudes of decision makers toward risk varies, particularly when survival is not involved and sometimes even then. In our example some readers might prefer the chance to make $20. They would be taking the optimistic view of maximizing the maximum payoff in choosing the larger capacity. Others might be more pessimistic and minimize the maximum loss, thereby choosing the lower capacity. We call this a minimax decision strategy or criterion, versus a maximax or optimistic strategy.

Part of the explanation of opposing reactions to situations such as these is the outlook toward the situation: Is it really a probabilistic event depending on random events or is this a game against someone else who will "choose" the sales level in such a way as to minimize your profit? If there is an opponent, we should abandon the probabilistic interpretation and resort to game theory, the study of decision making in competitive environments, which is an area of high complexity except for the two-person zero-sum game (see the Problems). However, our basic assumption in this book was of non-influence in the market place, and so we shall return to the probabilistic world of our example.

Although other decision criteria are available [22], we return to the expected value criterion and the concept of risk. By now it should be obvious that both of these are important. One way of quantifying risk is to associate it with the variance of the probability distribution. Variance is the second moment about the mean or the probability weighted sum of the squares of the difference between the values of the variable and the mean. There are higher moments which may also be associated with risk but it is difficult enough to deal with variance.

In our example the variances are quite different, 75 and 275, as shown in Table 2-6, which points out that the higher capacity decision has higher risk. Although attitude toward risk does vary, it is usually assumed that important business decisions are made by risk-averse decision makers, who would therefore choose the lower capacity decision in our example. This raises the interesting question of how much decrease in expected value should be given up to get a specified decrease in risk. Since our example had equal expected values, this difficult trade-off of risk and expected value was not required, but it is often a necessary decision.

In practice the trade-off between risk and expected value is usually accomplished by presentation of alternatives including their expected value and risk to top management for their direct choice. However, there are quantitative techniques for dealing with this trade-off which are receiving considerable attention in the literature. With such techniques it may become practical to delegate some less important decisions to lower levels. In addition they illustrate one way of thinking about the trade-off of risk and expected value which can be useful in making decisions without quantification.

If we can accept the following three fairly reasonable assumptions or postulates, it can be shown that a utility curve for probabalistic decisions must exist for the decision maker following the postulates [22]. We define a prospect as the chance to win a positive integer amount X with discrete probabilities represented by $f(X)$. For example, if we can win \$1, \$2, or \$3 with probability $\frac{1}{4}, \frac{1}{2}, \frac{1}{2}$, respectively, the prospect is $f(1) = \frac{1}{4}, f(2) = \frac{1}{2}, f_3 = (\frac{1}{4})$. A finite limit M is assumed on the size of the largest reward. The postulates are:

1. For any prospect there is an amount we would trade for the prospect if the amount was exchanged with certainty, i.e., a certainty equivalent exists for each prospect. In the example above someone who believes in expected value would have a certainty equivalent of \$2. For anyone, some certainty equivalent exists.

2. As the probability of reward increases, the certainty equivalent increases. In the example, if we raise the probability of winning \$3, the certainty equivalent should increase.

3. Any prospect can be replaced by another prospect composed of either a chance of winning zero or one minus that chance of winning M. This binary prospect is denoted (p_b, M). If M is \$4, a person who believes in expected value would say that the prospect $(\frac{1}{2}, 4)$ has the same certainty equivalent, \$2, as the original prospect in the example. To compute this binary prospect, we simply examine each reward X and treat it for the moment as a certainty. We select the probability p_r with which we would feel indifferent between that chance of winning M and the certainty of X. Having obtained p_r for each X, or $p_r(X)$, we now recall $f(X)$, the probability of getting X in the prospect. We replace $f(X)$ with $f'(X) = 0$, $f'(M) = p_r f(X)$, and $f'(0) = (1 - p_r) f(X)$. We repeat this process for each X. If we sum the product of the probability $f(X)$ times the p_r for each X, we shall obtain the binary prospect's probability (p_b, M). An example calculation is given in Table 2-7. Here we do *not* assume that the person giving binary prospects is a believer in expected value. In fact, this person likes to gamble since he rates $\frac{1}{2}$ a chance of 4 as equivalent to 3 with certainty.

From Table 2-7 we can see that for the decision maker who found the equivalents p_r in the third column, the original prospect would be exchanged

**Table 2-7　Example Calculation of Binary Prospect Equivalent
to Multioutcome Prospect**

X	$f(X)$	$(p_r(X), M)$, Binary Prospect so that M with p_r is Equivalent to X with Certainty	Replace $X = 2$	Replace $X = 1, 3$
0	0	$(0, 4)$	$f'(0) = \frac{3}{4} \cdot \frac{1}{2}$	$f''(0) = \frac{3}{4} \cdot \frac{1}{2} + \frac{1}{2} \cdot \frac{1}{4} + \frac{4}{5} \cdot \frac{1}{4} = \frac{7}{10}$
1	$\frac{1}{4}$	$(\frac{1}{5}, 4)$		$f''(1) = 0$
2	$\frac{1}{2}$	$(\frac{1}{4}, 4)$	$f'(2) = 0$	$f''(2) = 0$
3	$\frac{1}{4}$	$(\frac{1}{2}, 4)$		$f''(3) = 0$
$M = 4$	0	$(1, 4)$	$f'(4) = \frac{1}{4} \cdot \frac{1}{2}$	$f''(4) = \frac{1}{2} \cdot \frac{1}{4} + \frac{1}{4} \cdot \frac{1}{2} + \frac{1}{5} \cdot \frac{1}{4} = \frac{3}{10}$

$$p_b = \tfrac{3}{10}; \quad (p_b, M) = (\tfrac{3}{10}, 4)$$

for a binary prospect $(\frac{3}{10}, 4)$. The formula for this computation can be written as $p_b = \sum_X p_r(X) f(X)$. In fact, we can call the p_r values in the third column the utility of the rewards X, or we can use any linear transformation of them rather than the probabilities. Then we have a utility function, $U[f(X)] = \sum_{X=0}^{M} p_r(X) f(X)$, which transforms the utilities of the rewards into the utility of the prospect. This is often called the expected utility hypothesis. Once the decision maker has given his p_r values, they can be represented by utility curves as in Fig. 2-16.

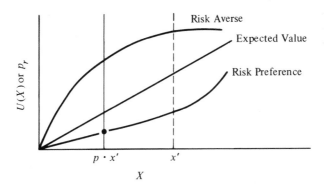

Figure 2-16.　Types of utility curves.

The particular curve depends on the decision maker's feeling established by his certainty equivalents. If he is risk-averse, the utility of pX, $U(p \cdot X)$ is greater than $pU(X) + (1 - p)U(0)$.

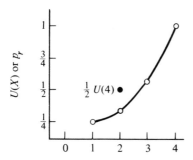

Figure 2-17.

For our example the plot of p_r or $U(X)$ versus X is as shown in Fig. 2-17. Since $U(2) = U(\frac{1}{2} \cdot 4) < \frac{1}{2}U(4)$, this decision maker has a risk preference in this range of prospects. Once this curve is established, we can compute the utility of any prospects in this range of payoff without further questioning of the decision maker. For convenience we convert the curve to mathematical form, assuming a parabolic function. In general this curve can be represented by $U(X) = X - aX^2$. If we have a prospect $f(X)$, $U[f(X)] = \sum_X (X - aX^2)f(X)$ or

$$U[f(X)] = \sum_X Xf(X) - a \sum_X X^2 f(X)$$

$$U[f(X)] = \sum_X Xf(X) - a[\sum_X Xf(X)]^2$$

$$\qquad - a \sum [X - \sum Xf(X)]^2 f(X) \qquad (2\text{-}104)$$

$$U[f(X)] = E - aE^2 - aV,$$

where E is the expected value and V is the variance of $f(X)$.

We can determine the value of the parameter a by statistically fitting a parabola to the decision maker's certainty equivalent plot such as above. Then given any prospect, the utility can be determined by first computing the mean and variance and then using Eq. (2-104).

The example has only positive payoffs and so any prospects in this range should be undertaken, in the order of their utility if choice is required. For prospects with negative payoff the certainty equivalents must also be established for the negative payoffs. Then a positive utility of the prospect is the criterion for acceptance or the greatest positive utility if a choice must be made. Measurement of the certainty equivalents is discussed in [23]. Applications in capital budgeting are described in [24].

We shall make a final comment on capacity planning under risk in a problem in Chap. 7 where we shall examine a technique for finding optimal inventory policies under certainty.

SUMMARY

This chapter has initiated the reader into our style of economic analysis of production problems. Simple economic rules have been developed for optimization of a variety of general models of production processes. The capacity decisions have been emphasized in our examples but many of these techniques will reoccur, particularly

1. Marginal analysis, such as the rule for the equality ratios of marginal products and prices.
2. The Lagrange multiplier technique for equality-constrained optimization and interpretation of opportunity cost.
3. Use of cost functions and their minimization.
4. Economies of scale and constant returns to scale.
5. Linear activity analysis of production processes.
6. Kuhn-Tucker conditions for inequality-constrained optimization.
7. Expected value and other decision criteria.
8. Utility theory and the trade-off of expected value and risk.

These concepts will be useful for production managers in many areas as well as in the case of capacity decision problems.

The capacity decision is, as we have said, one of the most basic decisions of the firm; therefore it requires a total analysis of the proposed operation. Indeed, all the topics of this book, and others, must be investigated before that decision can finally be made. It is not surprising in recalling the variety of production processes from Chap. 1, then, that our models have been somewhat general. We trust the reader now has a sufficient understanding of the problem to be able to proceed to the more detailed problems of organizing the plant for a given capacity.

REFERENCES

1. John W. Hackney, "Capital Cost Estimates for Process Industries," *Chemical Engineering* (March 7, 1960), 116.
2. David Levhari and Etyan Sheshinski, "A Micro-economic Production Function," *Econometrica*, 38, No. 3 (May 1970), 559.
3. Ryuzo Sato, "The Estimation of Biased Technical Progress and the Production Function," *International Economic Review*, 11, No. 2 (June 1970), 179.

4. W. F. COWHER, W. B. WIDHELM, and T. W. CADMAN, "Optimal Design in Dynamic Competitive Environments," *Industrial and Engineering Chemistry*, forthcoming.

5. K. J. ARROW and TIBOR SCITOVSKY, eds., *Readings in Welfare Economics*, Irwin, Homewood, Ill., 1969.

6. JAMES M. HENDERSON and R. E. QUANDT, *Microeconomic Theory*, McGraw-Hill, New York, 1958, p. 274.

7. FRANK C. JEN, C. C. PEGELS, and T. M. DU PUIS, "Optimal Capacities of Production Facilities," *Management Science*, 14, No. 10 (June 1968), 573.

8. DONALD ERLENKOTTER and A. S. MANNE, "Capacity Expansion for India's Nitrogenous Fertilizer Industry," *Management Science*, 14, No. 10 (June 1968), 533.

9. R. G. D. ALLEN, *Mathematical Economics*, St. Martin's, New York 1963, p. 568.

10. DAVID A. WISMER, "On the Uses of Industrial Dynamics Models," *Operations Research*, 15, No. 4 (July–Aug. 1962), 752.

11. C. F. FLORE and R. T. ROZWADOWSKI, "The Implementation of Process Models," *Management Science*, 14, No. 6 (Feb. 1968), 360.

12. MARTIN WEITZMAN, "On Choosing an Optimal Technology," *Management Science*, 13, No. 5 (Jan. 1967), 413.

13. RAGNAR FRISCH, *Theory of Production*, Rand McNally, Skokie, Ill., 1965.

14. SVEN DANØ, *Industrial Production Models*, Springer Verlag, New York, Inc., New York, 1966.

15. ALAN S. MANNE, *Investments for Capacity Expansion*, M.I.T. Press, Cambridge, Mass., 1967, p. 37.

16. GILBERT HOWARD and G. NEMHAUSER, "Optimal Capacity," *NLRQ*, 15, No. 4 (Dec. 1968), 535.

17. HIDE HINOMOTO, "Capacity Expansion with Facilities Under Technological Improvement," *Management Science*, 1, No. 5 (March 1955), 581.

18. RICHARD J. GIGLIO, "Stochastic Capacity Models," *Management Science*, 17, No. 3 (Nov. 1970), 174.

19. JOHN Y. D. TSE, *Profit Planning Through Volume Cost Analysis*, Macmillan, New York, 1960, p. 5.

20. GENE FISHER, *Cost Considerations in Systems Analysis*, American Elsevier, New York, 1970.

21. N. BALOFF and R. MCKENSIE, "Motivating Startup," *Journal of Business*, 39, No. 4 (Oct. 1966), 473.

22. KARL BORCH, *The Economics of Uncertainty*, Princeton University Press, Princeton, N. J., 1968, p. 34.

23. Robert Schlaifer, *Analysis of Decisions Under Uncertainty*, McGraw-Hill, New York, 1969.

24. R. F. Byrne, A. Charnes, W. W. Cooper, O. A. Davis, and D. Gilford, *Studies in Budgeting*, American Elsevier, New York, 1971.

PROBLEMS

1. Given the production function for a firm, $q = ax_1^b x_2^{2-b}$,
   a. Find all the marginal products.
   b. What important economic law does this production function violate?
   c. Find all the average products.
   d. Sketch the relationship between MP and AP for this production function.
   e. Find all the marginal elasticities.
   f. Find the elasticity of production, E.
   g. Is this a homogeneous production function?
   h. Are there increasing, decreasing, or constant returns to scale?
   i. What would the cost minimization levels of inputs be if the prices of x_1 and x_2 are \$1 and \$2 and the amount of output desired is d?
   j. What is the problem in determining the profit maximization level of output with this production function?
   k. What capacity plant would you build?
   l. Write the second-order conditions for the cost-minimizing solution above.

2. Maximize earning, E, subject to a capital constraint W,

$$\frac{X}{2} - y \leq W,$$

   where X is investment in inventory and y is investment in floor space and earnings are

$$E = 4X + 5y + Xy - X^2 - y^2 + 5.$$

3. Using the Kuhn-Tucker conditions, find the complete solution to

$$\text{maximize } f(X_1, X_2) = -a_1 e^{-b_1 X_1} - a_2 e^{-b_2 X_2}$$
$$\text{subject to } 1 - X_1 - X_2 \geq 0, \qquad X_1, X_2 \geq 0.$$

4. Derive the production function for a power plant having two kinds of capital, a turbine generator and a boiler using gas as an input and producing electrical power as output and operating according to the flow diagram in Fig. P-4. Notation: y = output; x_1 = current input; X_2, X_3 = successive applications of capital; x_2 = intermediate output − input to X_3; α = conversion factor for gas ($\alpha = 1$ in this problem); k_2 and k_3 = positive constants. Energy losses:

$$B_L = k_2 \frac{p_2}{X_2} \qquad T_L = k_3 \frac{y}{X_3}.$$

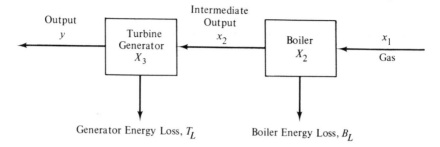

Figure P-4.

In other words, find y as a function of the inputs; you will have to eliminate X_2.

5. Cost curves for a two-facility firm as a function of output y are

$$C_1(y_1) = 1000y_1 + 100y_1^2, \qquad C_2(y_2) = 2000y_2 + 50y_2^2.$$

Minimize $C = C_1(y_1) + C_2(y_2)$ with respect to y_1 and y_2 subject to $y = y_1 + y_2$.

6. Construct a production function for an idealized trucking firm where the function is in implicit form, $F(y, x_1, X_2) = 0$, the parameters being α, β, m. y = truck miles per unit time (output); x_1 = man-hours of repair labor per unit time; X_2 = stock of trucks (number); The queuing formula is

$$\bar{n} = \frac{\lambda/\mu}{1 - (\lambda/\mu)},$$

where $\lambda/\mu < 1$; $\bar{n}$ = average number of trucks awaiting repair; λ = truck failures per unit time (repair station input rate); and μ = trucks repaired per unit time (repair station output rate).

Assume that $\lambda = \alpha y$, where α is a constant > 0 (failures as a function of miles); $\mu = \beta x_1$, where β is a constant > 0 (repairs as a function of repair labor); $\bar{N} = X_2 - \bar{n}$, the mean number of trucks in service; and $y = m\bar{N}$, where m = miles per unit time. Leave the production function in implicit form.

7. If a set of process technologies are efficient, there exists some vector of "prices" which will yield zero profit for all the technologies. Find the prices for the efficient technologies of the following production set:

$$\begin{bmatrix} 2 & 2 & 1 \\ 2 & 1 & \frac{3}{2} \\ -1 & -1 & -1 \end{bmatrix}.$$

8. Assume that the production function for a firm is $f(q_1, q_2, x_1, x_2, x_3) = 0$. This firm wants to *minimize profits*. Carefully state all first-order conditions.

The first-order condition should be stated in the ratio form and described in economic terms as well as in mathematical symbols.

9. A particular cost function of use in many industries is the so-called learning curve which can be expressed as $y = ax^b$, where y is either the cost of the xth unit or the average cost of the first x units. The parameter b is related to how fast costs decrease as the quantity produced increases. The parameter a is the first unit's cost. We shall deal only with the relationship of the xth unit's cost. Then if S is the fraction by which unit cost decreases as the quantity produced doubles,

$$S = \frac{y_{2x}}{y_x} = \frac{a(2x)^b}{ax^b} = 2^b$$

or

$$b = \frac{\log S}{\log 2}.$$

If $S = 75\%$, for example, $b = -.415$. Since these calculations are clumsy, if $a = 1$, a linear log-log plot is available as shown in Fig. P-9 for 80%.

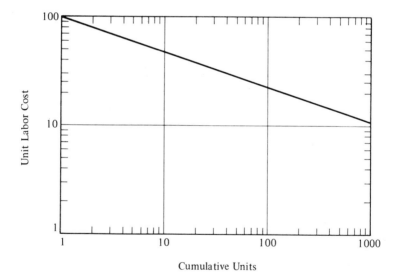

Figure P-9.

a. If the unit cost of the first item is $100 and an 80% learning curves applies, how much will the fiftieth unit cost?

b. If the cost of the first item is $2500, what will the tenth unit cost?

10. a. Suppose that the multiple prospect shown in Fig. P-10 is offered to an

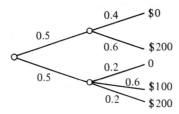

Figure P-10.

expected value maximizer (EVM). What would he be willing to pay for the prospect?

b. Write the formula for the above computation.
c. Suppose that the EVM could purchase a perfect forecast of which branch which will obtain at the first junction before paying for the prospect. How much should he be willing to pay for this perfect information?

11. Suppose that you are not an EVM and are faced with Problem 10.
   a. If you were offered either $100 with certainty or $200 with probability p_r, what would p_r have to be before you would take the chance at $200?
   b. Can we replace the lower half of the tree with the prospect shown in Fig. P-11?

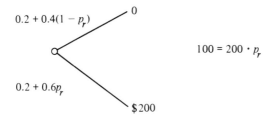

Figure P-11.

c. What would you pay for the entire prospect?
d. Draw a utility curve from zero to $200 using other values in addition to $100.

12. The break-even chart in Fig. P-12 is for a clay processing plant with a yield of 60% product from a ton of clay.
   a. Where does the $29,195 loss figure come from?
   b. Should the company continue this operation in 1956 if sales are estimated to be up 10%?
   c. Assume that the variable expense of mining and processing is inversely proportional to yield and that all other costs are fixed. Next year the yield will be 60 or 70% with 70% being three times as likely as 60%. Should the company continue this operation?

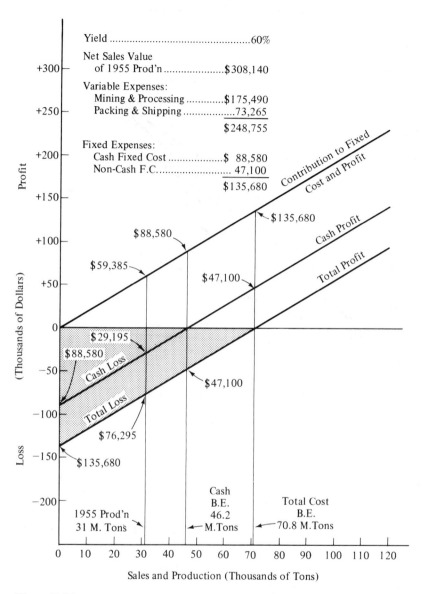

Figure P-12.

Source: John Y. D. Tse, Profit Planning through Volume-Cost Analysis, *The Macmillan Company, New York,* © *1960 by John Y. D. Tse. Courtesy of The Macmillan Company.*

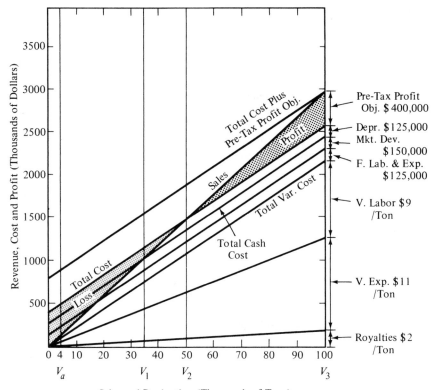

Figure P-13.

Source: John Y. D. Tse, Profit Planning through Volume-Cost Analysis, *The Macmillan Company, New York*, © 1960 by John Y. D. Tse. Courtesy of The Macmillan Company.

13. Figure P-13 is a break-even chart for a paint pigment manufacturer.
   a. What are total fixed costs?
   b. What are total variable costs per ton?
   c. Calculate V_1, V_2, and V_3.
   d. What would you say about the prospects of this company?
   e. Would it change your mind to know that sales have doubled each year?

14. You have a utility function $u(x) = x^{2.3}$, where x is in dollars. You are offered the following choices: (1) $8.00 with certainty and (2) A lottery with a one-half chance for $0 and a one-half chance for $64.

a. Which lottery should you choose?

b. Does this match your feelings?

15. The Iota Engineering Company does subcontracting on government contracts. Iota is a small company with limited capital. The utility function is described as follows:

$$u(x) = -\frac{x}{100} - \frac{x^2}{5000}, \qquad x < -1000$$

$$u(x) = \frac{x}{100} - 170, \qquad -1000 < x < 10,000$$

$$u(x) = \sqrt{x}, \qquad x > 10,000.$$

a. Suppose that Iota is considering bidding on a given contract. It will cost $2000 to prepare the bid. If the bid is lost, the $2000 cost is also lost. If Iota wins the bid, it will make $40,000 and recover the $2000 bid preparation cost. If Iota feels that the odds are 50-50 of winning the contract if a bid is submitted, what should it do?

b. What would the probability of winning have to be before Iota would submit a bid?

16. Sometimes the uncertainty in a situation comes from the possibility that a competitor will be able to react to the decision maker's action. In such a "game" situation the decision maker must consider the choices available to his competitor. Assume that one "player's" winnings are the other "player's" losses—a zero-sum game is to be played. We might expect each player to use a minimax strategy which minimizes his maximum loss regardless of the other players choice. If a competitive situation exists where the payoffs are described by the matrix given below, what course of action will be followed by each participant? Assume a zero-sum, two-person game.

	B_1	B_2	B_3	B_4
A_1	Fair	Good	Excellent	Poor
A_2	Terrible	Poor	Poor	Fair
A_3	Terrible	Good	Fair	Terrible
A_4	Good	Fair	Excellent	Fair

(The matrix is written for A.) This game has an easy solution. Other such games, in which there is no saddle point or outcome which is minimum in its row and maximum in its column, must be played with a randomized strategy in which the players choose certain actions a calculated percentage of the time. Multiple-person, non-zero-sum games are often insoluble. A good reference in this area is *Games and Decisions* by R.D. Luce and H. Raiffa, John Wiley & Sons, Inc., 1957.

chapter 3

Plant Location

A. Introduction and Survey of the Chapter

The choice of a location for a plant or distribution facility, like the choice of capacity, is a major decision of long-term importance to the firm. As with capacity decisions, poor choice of location can drastically affect the short-run operational problems of the firm. Moreover, locational changes are even more difficult than capacity changes because they cannot be made incrementally. Because of their extreme importance and their long-run nature, the final decisions require top-level management's judgment. However, theoretical analysis can contribute substantially to determining how to formulate location decisions. A great amount of quantitative information can be brought to bear on the decision. Location theory has been an established field of economics for over 100 years. It provides the framework on which quantitative data can be applied.

We shall first briefly list the factors which should be considered in location decisions. Because our ability to measure these factors is not at all uniform and comparison is difficult, a subjective rating method is presented and its shortcomings are pointed out.

We shall discuss classic location theory in Sec. C. Sec. D presents modern least-cost location analysis. Section D concludes with a note on the more general problem of regional development.

B. Location Problems and Decision Making

As we mentioned in the introduction to this chapter, the choice of a location for a plant or distribution facility is a major decision of long-term importance to the firm. The location decision is usually made with heavy applications of top-level-management judgment because of its extreme importance and its long-run nature. This is true because many of the factors influencing the decision are intangible or not easily measured and so top-level management must directly examine them. Some means of presenting the myriad of factors concerning each location and comparing them is necessary. One method that has found considerable favor is the calculation of the weighted sum of scaled factors. Instead of absolute measurements such as profit or revenue and cost, this method is based on relative measurements, as we shall show in the following sections concerning the factors and the rating method.

I. CONSIDERATIONS IN THE LOCATION DECISION

In Chap. 1 we described the complexities of production processes for multiple-product firms. In Chap. 2 we addressed the economics of inputs and outputs. We found that prices and limitations on inputs were vital. Every input and output and the production process itself are subject to the environment around it, i.e., its location. Wage rates and consumer demand certainly vary according to location. Availability of clean water does also. Many other effects are less obvious, but it is true that location can affect the entire production process, including what happens to its outputs.

The astute reader of Chap. 2 will undoubtedly reply, "Yes, but I can sum up all those effects by looking at the profit which can be obtained in that location and choosing the location by that one simple measure, highest profit." Indeed, we shall model the decision in this fashion, but in reality few location decisions are that easy. The difficulty with profit as the only measure arises from two sources:

1. Our ability to model or predict long-run profit in the location decision is greatly reduced because the decision itself can greatly change the environment. Short-run profit is almost irrelevant to long-term decisions such as location. Wage rates in a small town may change if a manufacturing firm moves in. Sales near an old plant may decrease if production is centralized in another location.

2. There may well be factors in location in addition to profit. We shall return to this aspect in Sec. D.

Because of the uncertainties in many of these long-term location considerations, it is useful to examine them individually rather than through a measurement of profit alone. We shall divide them into two categories, cost factors and market factors or considerations.

Some of the cost factors for any particular location are

1. Labor costs: unionization, supply, skill, education, productivity.
2. Transportation of raw materials: availability, reliability, convenience, governmental regulation, expansion.
3. Management: availability, educational facilities, living conditions, salary level.
4. Power and fuel: expansion capacity, ability to negotiate rates, convenience.
5. Water and waste disposal: expansion capability, regulation.
6. Financial and other services: banking, supplies, special skills, legal, insurance.
7. Government and legislation: taxes, zoning, services.

Some of the market factors which must be considered are

1. Transportation cost to markets: zone, basing point and delivered price systems, rate negotiation.
2. Delivery time and reliability to markets: special facilities, railroad, switching, terminal availability.
3. Customer communications costs: mail, telephone and travel connections, sales results of close contact.
4. Special sales generation potential of location: traffic, presence of special customers, community contacts.
5. Recognized center of production for a particular item.
6. Export potentialities of location: transportation, expertise and contacts.
7. Access to distribution system of warehouses, wholesalers, jobbers.
8. Availability of marketing services: advertising, press, TV, regional image.
9. Retention of specialized personnel that uniquely contribute to market acceptance: sales, research, management.

There have been books written on each of these factors alone. The proper consideration of each is a difficult task. Often a company prepares voluminous studies on each factor. What, then, should be done with this information, particularly if more than one man is involved in the decision process? We shall examine this question in the next subsection.

II. RATING OR INDEX METHODS FOR LOCATION DECISIONS

One method of dealing with the vast amount of information concerned in the location decision is the rating or index method for scoring each alternative location. The factors relevant to the decision are listed and each location is given a score on that factor. These scores are subjectively weighted and added together to give an index for each location. The advantages are that all factors can be considered and a quantitative measure obtained. Before discussing the disadvantages, we shall discuss an example. In Table 3-1

Table 3-1   Rating or Index Method

Factor (1)	% Weighting (2)	Location 1 Rating (3)	Weighted Rating (4)	Location 2 Rating (5)	Weighted Rating (6)
1	10	2	.2	8	.8
2	20	6	1.2	7	1.4
3	20	7	1.4	6	1.2
4	10	6	.6	5	.5
5	5	6	.3	6	.3
6	5	8	.4	6	.3
7	30	10	3.0	8	2.4
		45	7.1	46	6.9

two locations are considered with seven different factors such as those in the previous list. Ranking the locations with respect to one factor is not difficult since only two different locations are being compared. That is, the ordering of locations on each factor is relatively easy. Mathematicians refer to a mere ranking of alternatives as an ordinal measure. But in Table 3-1 each of the factors is rated on a scale from 1 to 10, with a rating of 10 representing perfection. This is necessary because the rating for different factors must be combined and a cardinal measure is required for the aggregation into one measure.

The rating of each alternative location from 1 to 10 requires an absolute measure called a cardinal measure. In a cardinal measure we must not only say that a location is better than another but how much better. Estimating the difference on the scale for each pair of locations is more difficult than ordering, so often the best and worst locations are spread over the scale from 1 to 10. Then the intermediate ranking can be obtained with a little judgment, but this introduces a difficulty that we shall address later.

These rankings for all factors can sometimes be performed by one executive who can supply the required judgment and maintain a uniform scale. This one executive may have to review a great deal of data in this method. If several persons perform the rankings, they must be careful to maintain the same standards, which is quite difficult.

The scores for each factor can be totaled to get an overall score or index for each location, as shown in columns (3) and (5) of Table 3-1. This procedure makes it very important to control the number and composition of factors. That is, if the majority of the factors are sales-related, the locations with good market potential will be favored over those with good cost characteristics. The best procedure is to weight each factor. For example, we might multiply each score by a percentage which reflects the relative importance of that factor in the total decision, as shown in columns (2), (4), and (6) of Table 3-1. Ideally, these weights would reflect the contribution of each factor to a criterion such as long-term profit. Note that the weighted ratings reverse the overall rating of the two locations in Table 3-1.

Other decisions can be analyzed with this same framework. This technique is essentially a crude model. It identifies elements in the decision and the direction of their effect on the decision but does not define the measurement scales or precise relationships between factors or their effect on the overall criterion, except to ask for the intuitive feelings of managers. The method above may be valuable for judgmental problems when factors are difficult to quantify, but we shall now consider some of the difficulties of the technique.

As we noted earlier, one difficulty is the absolute rating of the locations with respect to a factor. Spreading the locations out over an arbitrary range, such as 1 to 10, while making the rating easier, actually distorts the overall measure or total score. For some factors the locations may all be very close and so the decision should not be affected by their small differences. However, the spreading technique suggested makes all differences between the best and the worst equal to 9 units. On the other hand, if the spreading technique is not used, we must rely on the executive's ability to absolutely place each location relative to each other *and* the right distance from the origin of zero for all factors. It would seem that he could do this only if he knows fairly precisely how in each location each factor will affect some criterion such as profit. If so, it would clearly be better just to estimate that profit. A good reference on the scaling problem is [1].

Even after rating each factor for each location, the factors must be weighted. Again it would seem that if enough information and judgment are available to reasonably estimate how important a market factor is to the ultimate criterion such as profit, then this should be enough information to actually estimate the revenue effect. Finally we note that scaling and weighting interact.

We prefer the more direct examination of the factors by assessing their contribution to revenue and cost. Such a technique is probably more reproducible and it is more easily explained to others. More important, we believe that the models of revenue and cost will lead the decision maker to the detailed analysis of his problem, while the index method may merely present a way of rationalizing his prejudices. The rating method may be a good first step which will show the executive that more explicit analysis of costs and revenue is required.

In the following sections we shall examine some models of cost revenue and profit.

C. Review of Classic Location Models

I. SURVEY OF THE SECTION

Classic economic theory of location can be divided into two segments, a demand or market viewpoint and a cost or supply viewpoint. Of course, all real location problems must be considered from both viewpoints. However, these viewpoints have been developed separately and are of varying importance for any particular product. We shall develop them separately in Sec C. II and III. Section C. IV deals with both revenue and cost in an overall analysis.

II. COST MODELS

a. Minimization of Transportation Cost

1. Thünen's model. Johann Heinrich von Thünen, a German economist of the early nineteenth century, explained the location of agricultural producers around a consumption center [2]. His analysis assumed that labor and land are of uniform productivity. Either freight rates per ton-mile or the value of the product per ton were assumed to differ according to the particular product or crop grown. He assumed that the price of the product did not affect the amount sold, a usual assumption by those who consider only the cost aspect of location theory. He showed that the sources of the different crops would be located in concentric rings around the city.

The reason for the locational pattern of rings of crops around the city is that the product which has the higher transport cost has a higher opportunity cost for location near the city versus the remote area. The producer with the higher opportunity cost will be willing to pay a higher rent for land closer to the city. For example, suppose that A and a competitor B both produce the same product under different brand names. It sells for $10 per ton and costs $8 per ton to produce. Assume that B has a bargaining advantage so that his freight cost is $1 per ton-mile, while for A it is $2 per ton-mile. Only A or B can be located in any one region. For convenience three regions are considered: up to $\frac{1}{2}$ mile from town, $\frac{1}{2}$–1 mile from town, and 1–2 miles from town. All points in one region have the same shipping cost, which is computed to the outer border of the region. Table 3-2 demonstrates that A should locate in region 1. The key to Table 3-2 is that the opportunity costs are obtained by

Table 3-2   Opportunity Costs for Agricultural Producers

Location	Production ($8) & Transportation Cost ($/ton)		Profit ($/ton)		Opportunity Cost ($/ton)	
Region	B	A	B	A	B	A
1	8.50	9.00	1.50	1.00	Up to .50	Up to 1.00
2	9.00	10.00	1.00	0	Up to 1.00	Up to 2.00
3	10.00	12.00	0	−2.00	0	0

looking *down* the Profit column. Even though B makes more profit than A in region 1, A is willing to pay more rent because his change in profit is greater if he produces in region 2. He should therefore locate in region 1 and should outbid A for that location.

2. Lösch's model. August Lösch, a German economist of this century, relaxed the assumptions of equal productivities, prices, and costs but specified the same freight rate per ton for all products [3]. Instead of relying on the difference in freight rates or value per ton to produce the locational rings, he made the more natural specification of differing abilities to produce the crops. The results are the same configurations for location. Lösch details 27 cases which can result from different assumptions concerning price, costs, and yields. He found that ring formation occurs in most but by no means all cases. The width of the rings can be found from equating marginal revenue and marginal cost.

The effect of the early work referred to above was to establish the importance of transportation cost in determining the location of economic activity. It is now clear that location of industrial activity does not merely depend on natural resources, labor costs, and skills or other natural factors. Technology alone does not determine location decisions. Moreover, many of the seemingly technological factors are actually economic. For example, why do workers' skills tend to develop in certain areas? Why are labor costs low in some areas? Why do populations (markets) concentrate at certain points? Why are many different grades of ore mined if one is highest in metal content? All these are at least partially economic questions.

3. Weber's model. In 1904 Alfred Weber, another German economist, published his study of the location of industries [4]. This study moved from the assumption of uniform availability of the necessities for production, i.e., crop land, to the question of the location of industries which depend on

certain raw materials available only in certain specific locations. It is not clear whether industrial activity will take place at the raw material site or at the market or perhaps at some point in between. This was the question Weber tried to answer. He found that, assuming equal labor costs, location of an industry depends on how the weight of the raw materials is reflected in the weight of the product. As a first step, Weber distinguished between two types of raw materials:

1. Localized materials available only in specific locations, such as iron ore, which often lose weight in processing.
2. Ubiquities which are generally available, such as water.

The second step concerns whether the raw material lost weight in being transformed into the product. Weber defined the material index as the ratio of the weight of localized raw material over the weight of the product. All industries with a material index less than 1 are located at the point of consumption. This is obvious because a material index of less than 1 means that ubiquities predominate in the manufacture. It would be uneconomic to transport ubiquities, or, in Weber's terms, pure materials can never bind production to the location of their deposit. *Pure* materials are those which do not lose weight in being processed into the product, such as oil. Weber assumed that the cost of transporting the finished product per ton is at least as high as the cost of transporting the raw material, which is not always true. We shall study methods which make use of actual transportation costs in Sec. D.

The material index can also be calculated separately for each raw material. If the material index for any one raw material is greater than the sum of the material index of each of the other materials plus the integer 1 (1 is the material index of the product), then the location of production is at the origin of that raw material.

As an example of the use of Weber's material index, assume that two localized raw materials and one ubiquity are used and that their sources are A and B while the market is at C. These products are examined in Table 3-3.

Finding the exact location of the manufacturing point with the least transport cost by the above method is not always possible. For example, the material index for the third product does not indicate where the location would be. More powerful methods for the solution of the least-cost location will be discussed in Sec. D and in the following graphical presentation.

b. Minimization of Transportation and Other Costs

A more realistic problem is that of locating the plant when labor or other input costs do vary. Relaxing the assumption of constant labor and material costs transforms the problem above into a general cost minimization problem.

Table 3-3   Calculation of Material Indices and Location

Product	Lb of Product	Lb of A used	Lb of B Used	Lb of Ubiquity Added at C	Material Indices	Location
I	10	1	1	9	Total $=$ .2	C because .2 $<$ 1
II	10	20	2	2	A $=$ 2.0	
					B $=$ .2	A because
					C $=$ .0	2 $>$ 1.2
					Total $=$ 2.2	
III	10	10	10	5	A $=$ 1.0	Unknown
					B $=$ 1.0	because
					C $=$ .0	2 $>$ 1 and
					Total $=$ 2.0	1 $<$ 2

One approach to this problem is Weber's isodapane construction. First, the transport costs are considered. Assume that two raw materials sources, A and B, and one market, C, are located as in Fig. 3-1. The cost contours for transporting the amount of each raw material per unit weight of product are drawn around each raw material source. The cost contours for transporting the unit weight of the product are drawn around the market. The intersection of the three cost contours represents the total transport cost for a manufacturing location at that particular point. For example, point D is at the intersection of cost contours of $8 per ton of product from C, $12 per amount of raw material needed per ton from B, and $16 from C. Therefore point D is on the $36 isodapane and so is point E, which is $4 closer to A but $4 farther from C. A line joining all intersections with the same total cost is called an isodapane. Assuming that transport costs are proportional to distance, there will be one minimum transport cost point or minimum isodapane represented by the peak in the center of the figure.

Now additional costs can be considered. Suppose, for example, that some locations have labor savings relative to the least-transport-cost location (minimum isodapane). If the labor savings at any point are greater than the difference between that point's isodapane and the minimum isodapane, then that point is a location of lower total cost. For example, if labor is $2 per ton cheaper at point D, the least-cost location would be point D because its transportation cost is only $1 higher than the minimum of $35 per ton. The method can be used for additional raw material sources and for additional markets if the split of shipments to the markets is known. Unfortunately, locally optimal points are quite possible for the total cost solution, and, of course, the best of the locally optimal points is desired. In the three-location problem a geometric construction is also available; see [4], p. 230.

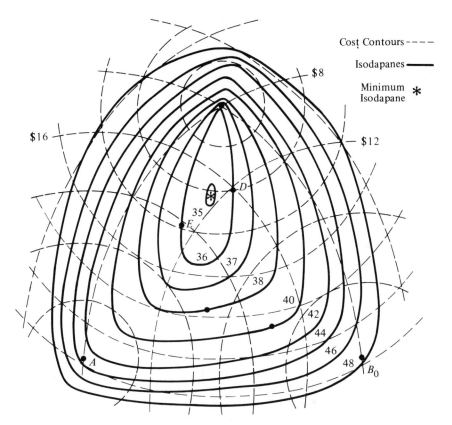

Figure 3-1.   Isodapanes for total cost minimization.

In theory, the point of minimum total cost can be determined by other classic methods. One method is the isoquant technique of microeconomics, which is very clumsy for more than two inputs. The other is the classic mathematical optimization. A production function including transportation inputs ($y_1 \cdots y_n$) could be written as we did in Chap. 2 with current inputs x_i and capital inputs X_i:

$$\text{output } q = f(x_1 \cdots x_n, X_1 \cdots X_n, y_1 \cdots y_n). \qquad (3\text{-}1)$$

The Lagrangian equation for constrained maximization of profit could be written and optimality rules could be derived for ratios of prices of locational inputs to prices of nonlocational inputs and their marginal productivities. These rules would be similar to the ones obtained in Chap. 2 and could be used if either (1) the production function could be written explicitly in terms of transportation inputs or (2) intuitive feelings for marginal rates of substitution between transport and nontransport inputs were available as they are for the usual relations between nontransport inputs. Unfortunately, neither of these conditions can be met. It is difficult enough to derive production functions without transport inputs. It is also hard to find people with good judgment of the marginal location substitutions because plants are not moved to different locations within the experience of any one man.

As a final word on costs, there are some costs which are often neglected in classic location theory. It should be noted that the least-cost location may be affected by

1. Prices of inputs, including the price of transportation, which may vary with location.
2. Varying ratios of inputs or technologies may be available at different locations because of the presence of raw materials or labor skills.
3. The optimal scale of size of plant may change because of different market sizes at various locations.

Ideally, all three variations should be considered at once. A theoretical technique for doing so will be discussed later. It is easier to see the problem if these aspects are considered independently. For example, if transport costs vary, the isocost lines in Weber's isodapane construction in Fig. 3-1 have varying instead of constant spacing around the alternative locations. If advantageous technologies or plant sizes are available, the savings can be treated the same way as labor savings were treated in the isodapane diagram. It is always wise to check a least-cost model to see if these effects have been neglected when they are actually considerable.

III. PROFIT MODELS

a. Optimization of Market Size without Spatial Competition

1. Introduction. The other important consideration in location is the effect of location on revenue. An extreme least-cost solution is to locate where nothing can be sold, giving zero cost but also zero profit. We shall eventually assume that profit is the variable which should be maximized, but here let us consider revenue, unless it affects profit directly, as when the cost of freight is absorbed by the seller. We shall usually assume that transportation cost is added to price. Transportation costs increase the price to the consumer. Higher price means lower sales unless the demand curve is perfectly vertical which we assume is rare.

The concept of a locational area rather than location at a point is important in treating the revenue side of location. We consider market areas with customers assumed to be distributed in a constant or decreasing density around a point. It is assumed that the product is undifferentiated, so that only one price for the product can exist at any consumer's location. Under these assumptions, the market area can be established if the individual consumer's demand curve is known. Suppose that the individual demand curve is as shown in Fig. 3-2. For any given commodity price, P, the extent of the market

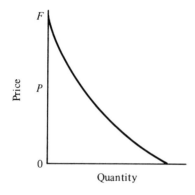

Figure 3-2.   Individual customer demand curve.

is limited by the potential delivery transportation cost, PF, which would raise total price including transportation to the point that all individual customers would be forced out of the market; i.e., the quantity purchased becomes zero. It is obvious that a firm cannot make a pricing decision independent of the consideration of market area. Market size is in turn determined by transportation costs. Therefore transportation cost affects pricing.

2. The demand cone. The classic approach to an optimal location considering the effect of transportation is to generate the total demand curve for each location and pick the location which maximizes profit. As stated above, the total demand curve uses the individual demand curve, the cost of transportation, and the location of each individual customer to obtain the total demand at a plant location as a function of price at the manufacturing site or *mill* price. For example, if

D_i = total demand for a location with a mill price p_i

S = population density (assumed constant)

r = maximum radius of sales with transport cost (t) a linear function of distance (m) from the mill location (r varies with p_i)

$f(\cdot)$ = demand function for an individual customer (assumed identical for each customer)

then

$$D_i = S \int_0^{2\pi} \left[\int_0^{m=r} f(p_i + mt)m\ dm \right] d\theta, \qquad (3\text{-}2)$$

where $d\theta$ is a sector swung around the location. Determination of D_i with various p_i gives a total demand curve such as that shown in Fig. 3-3. The demand cone for a price p_i is first determined in Fig. 3-3(a), and the D_i and

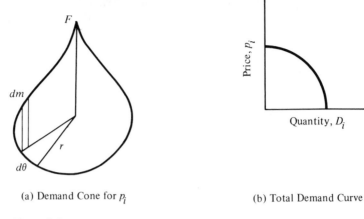

(a) Demand Cone for p_i (b) Total Demand Curve

Figure 3-3.

p_i pairs are plotted as in Fig. 3-3(b). The total demand curve supplies marginal revenue information. For optimization, cost information is also needed. If the long-run average production cost curve is known, the price with maximum profit can be determined for the location from the equality of marginal revenue and marginal cost. Then the profits at various locations can be determined and compared.

3. Freight absorbtion: an example. The profit-maximizing transportation and price policy for the firm at a location is generally to absorb some of the transport cost in order to widen the firm's market area. The firm widens its market area and increases total revenue by quoting a lower price than the total of average production cost plus transportation cost. Freight absorbtion is a common practice in some industries.

As an example of the effect of location on price with absorbtion, assume two buyers, one at the manufacturing site and one at a distance. The demand curve for each customer is as shown in Fig. 3-4. MR is the marginal revenue curve for the demand curve and b is the highest price either customer will pay. The quantity is measured for convenience in units such that b is also the maximum amount purchased by either. The profit-maximizing price considering only the customer close to the plant is $b/2$, assuming for simplicity that MC is zero, since MC equals MR at $b/2$. However, if both customers are considered, the optimal price is lower, as shown in Fig. 3-5 and the following calculation. If $k < b$ is the freight to the distant market, $m + k$ is the price to the distant customer, where m is the mill price and $b - (m + k)$ is the amount purchased by the distant customer. The amount purchased by the customer at the plant location is $b - m$ and so total revenue, TR, is $m[b -$

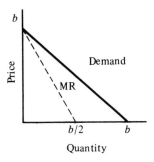

Figure 3-4.   Individual demand curve.

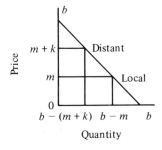

Figure 3-5.   Demand for the example customers.

$m + b - (m + k)$]. The revenue-maximizing price is obtained as follows:

$$\frac{dTR}{dm} = \frac{d(2mb - 2m^2 - km)}{dm} = 2b - 4m - k = 0 \qquad (3\text{-}3)$$

$$m = \frac{b}{2} - \frac{k}{4}. \qquad (3\text{-}4)$$

If marginal cost is zero, this is also the profit-maximizing price. Note that it is less than the profit-maximizing price with only one customer, so freight is absorbed. This is a simple case, but in the more complicated cases treated by Greenhut [5] there continues to be absorption of transport cost by the profit-maximizing firm.

b. Maximization of Revenue Including Spatial Competition

So far we have looked only at the behavior of the firm with regard to the market. If the possibility of competition is added, the problem becomes much more interesting. Gamelike choices must then be considered. Suppose that two wineries are thinking of moving into a finite uniform linear market with uniform density, for example, the Weser River Valley. Customers are responsive to transport costs. In other words, total sales are not independent of location, which merely requires a sloping demand curve. The maximum profit location for the two wineries is one at each quarter along the river, as shown in Fig. 3-6(a). Each will then have half the market and total sales of

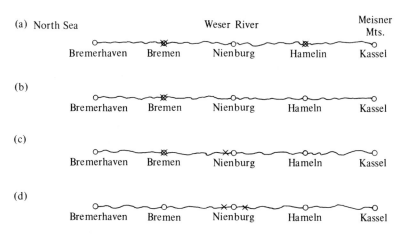

Figure 3-6.   Winery location.

the two wineries will be maximized. However, suppose that the first winery locates at the quarter-point, as shown in Fig. 3-6(b). The location of the first is not easily changed, and so another winery coming into the market would want to locate close to the first rather than at the opposite quarter-point, as shown in Fig. 3-6(c). With the closer location it would take away part of the other's market and still be protected in its own market upstream. Then, however, the first winery would try to move closer to the center to protect more market downstream. The end result could be the location of both at the center, as in Fig. 3-6(d). Total sales would then be smaller because higher transportation costs to the ends of the market would decrease demand. Also, promotional costs of the wineries would be high because they would tend to compete for the market close to the center point.

The case above assumes natural boundaries on the market. If there is no natural boundary on the market area, there will still be a boundary due to transport costs.

Because this is a production book, we shall not proceed further with these market models. Good references for the competitive markets are [6, 7].

Several factors which influence the development of areas of concentration or agglomeration should now be mentioned:

1. Natural transport advantages such as harbors.
2. Location of raw materials in particular spots.

3. The tapered structure of transport rates, which encourages location at either the raw material site or the market but not in between.

4. Competitive strategy, such as the example above.

All these reasons and other agglomerating forces such as existing communications, police, fire, utilities, financial services, and labor supply and training have played an important role in the development of certain areas as centers of a particular type of production. However, these factors are generally becoming less important. Improvements in transportation, availability of services, and labor mobility have made it less imperative today that a particular industry locate in one of a few areas.

IV. OVERALL ANALYSIS OF REVENUE AND COST

a. An Iterative Approach to Overall Analysis

It should now be clear that revenue and cost interact. It is conceptually possible to find the optimal location considering both cost and revenue if only a finite number of possible sites are evaluated. Churchill has developed the theory in a recent article [8], but the necessary data for the theory, production functions and demand curves, are seldom known to the manager or location analyst. However, a location analysis can follow the same general procedure without the specific forms of these functions in the following steps.

1. Evaluate, for a "good" price and the resultant total market size, the sales picture including competition for locating at each possible plant site; i.e., use a crude demand cone approach to assess sales at each market, given the plant location.

2. For the good sales pictures find the least-transport-cost location, and check if the least-transport-cost location is "close" to the plant location picked. Repeat steps 1 and 2 until it is nearly the same. List all the different good locations for which the convergence of market and cost location is met. For these sites, continue with step 3.

3. Examine the various sites for labor cost savings, special production technologies available, and other special factors.

4. Select the site with the largest difference between revenue and transportation cost including labor savings and other special factors.

5. Reevaluate steps 1–4 for different prices. Of course, the iterative solution above is not optimal but it is likely to match the available

information. The least-transport-cost location(s) in step 2 can be found as described in Sec. D, where modern methods are discussed.

b. An Example of Revenue and Cost Analysis

We shall briefly describe an example by Shenoy and Sifferd [9] of the analysis of both revenue and cost as an introduction to modern methods which depend heavily on computers. The problem was to locate a set of warehouses to service agricultural chemical demands at 127 demand points. A substitute for revenue, market share, was taken as a step function of distance from the warehouse, as shown in Table 3-4. The transportation costs

Table 3-4   Revenue Information

Distance (miles):	0–10	11–25	26–40	41–50	51–60	61–70
Percentage of market share:	40	30	25	18	15	5

were linear at 2.25 cents per ton-mile from the plant (location 15) to the warehouses and 5 cents per ton-mile from the warehouse to the demand point. A mileage chart for an example with 15 demand points is given in Table 3-5. The total potential demand within each demand area is given in the last row. The cost per ton of operating the warehouses is a decreasing step function because of economies of scale, as shown in Table 3-6. If we start with a policy of just one warehouse located at location 1, total sales would be

$$5030 \times 40\% + 3075 \times 18\% + 7510 \times 25\% + 850 \times 18\% = 4595 \text{ tons.}$$
$$(3\text{-}5)$$

Only four market areas would have sales because the others are beyond the 70-mile limit of Table 3-4. The cost of transportation to the warehouse is $4.05 per ton ($.0225 × 180 from Table 3-5). The transshipment cost at the warehouse is $.45 per ton from Table 3-6, and the transportation costs from the warehouse are $2.50, $1.50, $3.75, and $2.50 per ton to the four-market areas served, Table 3-5. With a net revenue contribution per ton (not revealed), the profit from a policy of one warehouse located at area 1 could now be obtained since costs and sales are known. The remaining possibilities are numerous, i.e., one warehouse at area 2, 3, . . . or two warehouses at various locations, etc. Over 8 million other combinations of warehouse locations for the 127 demand areas were examined. The final version included multiple time periods with growing demands. The set of locations which had the greatest profit potential over the five time periods was chosen.

Table 3-5 Mileage between Each Area and Demand

Area	1	2	3	4	5	6	7	8	9	10	11	12	13	14	15
1	0	50	30	75	105	100	50	85	75	110	100	115	165	170	190
2	50	0	80	40	75	140	90	55	25	80	95	155	135	140	175
3	30	80	0	45	80	130	80	110	80	135	130	145	140	195	180
4	75	40	45	0	35	140	90	95	65	120	135	155	95	170	135
5	105	75	80	35	0	105	55	90	100	115	105	120	60	135	100
6	100	140	130	140	105	0	50	85	115	110	100	30	145	140	105
7	50	90	80	90	55	50	0	35	65	60	50	65	115	120	140
8	85	55	110	95	90	85	35	0	30	25	40	100	110	85	120
9	75	25	80	65	100	115	65	30	0	55	70	130	140	115	150
10	110	80	135	120	115	110	60	25	55	0	15	125	85	60	95
11	100	95	130	135	105	100	50	40	70	15	0	115	70	70	105
12	115	155	145	155	120	30	65	100	130	125	115	0	115	110	75
13	165	135	140	95	60	145	115	110	140	85	70	115	0	75	40
14	170	140	195	170	135	140	120	85	115	60	70	110	75	0	35
Plant	190	175	180	135	100	105	140	120	150	95	105	75	40	35	0
Demand tons	5030	3075	7510	500	1450	1000	850	1800	8000	2550	4050	3500	3070	2800	700

103

Table 3-6   **Warehouse Transshipment Costs**

Quantity demanded:	1000–1999	2000–2999	3000–3999	4000–up
Cost ($/ton):	0.85	0.70	0.60	0.45

D. Modern Location Theory

I. INTRODUCTION AND SURVEY OF THE SECTION

Both modern and classic location theory divide the revenue from the cost considerations. Classic theory dealt with only a few location alternatives at a time. The major improvement of modern theory is the ability to handle larger numbers of locations and factors. This increased ability stems from the development of new mathematical techniques which are closely related to the development of computers. We have already seen one example of modern techniques which utilized a computer to handle both cost and revenue factors. Most modern models that we shall consider deal only with cost. The revenue models can be described as data-oriented with the objective of statistically measuring and relating demographic characteristics to buying habits. Empirical demand estimates, demand cones, are then prepared for various sales locations. Because of the production emphasis in this book, we shall not further explore these models. The cost models of modern location theory focus on the location of plants and warehouses, both of which we shall call distribution centers, to serve a given set of markets.

This focus has usually neglected the possible strategy of not serving some markets. This simplification may be justified by the emergence of a national market not only for goods but for labor, capital, and many of the other production inputs and outputs. Improved transportation and communication have brought about vastly enlarged market areas. Merger and consolidation of companies have resulted in coordinated networks of plants across the country under the control of one corporate organization.

We should make a few general remarks concerning the formulation of modern location problems:

1. Location decisions are usually long-range decisions, of the same time span as capacity decisions. In location decisions, the assumption is made that plant or warehouse capacity is yet to be determined.

2. The following discussion considers only one product. A final note discusses the extension to multiproduct distribution systems.

In this section we shall first investigate an introductory problem of locating one distribution point. Then the problem of locating several distribution points will be discussed. Finally, the problem of location of both warehouses and plants will be discussed.

II. OPTIMAL LOCATION OF THE SINGLE DISTRIBUTION CENTER

a. Introduction

The introductory problem, problem 1, can be phrased in either of the following forms:

> Problem 1a. Optimal location of one plant serving given markets and drawing from given raw material locations.
>
> Problem 1b. Optimal location of one warehouse to serve given markets and supplied from a given plant location.

These problems are mathematically the same. The solution is dependent on the following: for problem 1a, the relative cost of transportation of the raw materials versus the cost of the product, i.e., Weber's classic solution; for problem 1b, the relative cost of transportation from the plant to the warehouse versus the generally higher transportation cost from the warehouse to the markets. If the cost per ton-mile from the plant to the warehouse equals the transportation cost from the warehouse to the market, the obvious solution is to locate the warehouse at the plant, because a straight line is the shortest distance between two points. Thus we usually assume that the cost is higher from warehouse to market, typically because of smaller size of shipment. There can be no question of a problem of economics of scale of production or operation in a single distribution center. Therefore minimum transportation cost will be the criterion.

The most obvious method of solution is to write the total transportation cost as a function of location at a point x, y in the Cartesian plane. In this formulation a continuous expression for cost is derived. Here x_L, y_L represent the known locations of the sources and markets.

$$\text{TTC} = \sum_{L=1}^{I+K} W_L C_L [(x - x_L)^2 + (y - y_L)^2]^{1/2} \qquad (3\text{-}6)$$

where $\text{TTC} = $ total transportation cost. Transportation is considered as moving in a straight line between the markets and the distribution points. W_L is the tonnage to be shipped either to one of the K markets or from the I raw material locations to the plant in problem 1a. In problem 1b, the product is shipped from plant I to the warehouse and then to the K markets. C_L is the transportation cost per ton.

Unfortunately, finding the minimum cost location, x, y, from this equation is not easy. Some of the classic methods which were mentioned in Sec. C have been used or extended to solve this problem.

b. Six Methods for Solution

Method 1. Weber's isodapane construction of the transportation cost surface is a feasible but lengthy procedure, as described in Sec. C.

Method 2. Another method is the mechanical model used by Varigon to demonstrate the parallelogram of forces. It happens that if the physical model shown in Fig. 3-7 is devised, a point is observed that is equivalent to

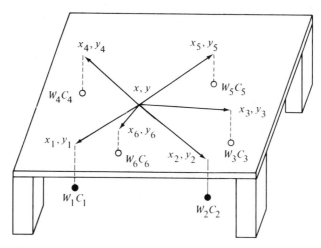

Figure 3-7. Physical model for minimum transportation cost location of a single distribution point.

the minimization of Eq. (3-6). Suspend strings with weights equal to $W_L C_L$ through holes in a fixed surface at the L locations scaled to the markets and plants. Tie all strings and observe the equilibrium location of the knot if it does not go through a hole.

If the knot goes through a hole, no equilibrium is possible within the convex hull of the location. Weber's material index method would be a shortcut way to indicate the solution in that case. If the knot does not go through a hole, the system must be in a state of minimal potential energy when the knot stops moving. The potential energy of the system can be written as

$$PE = \sum_{L=1}^{I+K} W_L C_L [h_L - (s_L - D)], \qquad (3\text{-}7)$$

where h_L equals the height of the surface which can be set to zero, s_L is the length of the string, and D is the distance from the hole to the knot. Equation (3-7) can be arranged into

$$\text{PE} = -\sum_{L=1}^{I+K} W_L C_L s_L + \sum_{L=1}^{I+K} W_L C_L D, \tag{3-8}$$

which is equivalent to the right-hand side of Eq. (3-6) plus a constant $W_L C_L s_L$. Since Eq. (3-8) has been minimized by the location of the knot, so has Eq. (3-6) been minimized. Haley [10] and others have resurrected this model for one stage of a method to solve problem 1.

Method 3. There is a widely suggested but incorrect folk method for this problem. It is to find the center of gravity of the weights $W_L C_L$ at the L locations. Perhaps this method arose because of some similarity to Varigon's method. There is no reason to assume that the center of gravity and equilibrium of forces described by the knot in method 2 are at all the same. The center of gravity assumes forces acting perpendicular to the locational plane with a torque due to the distance. There is no such torque present in Varigon's model since the surface is statically determined by other forces, the table legs. The edge of the hole translates the weight into a force in the plane equal to the weight, not the product of weight times distance, as in the torque or center of gravity. Table 3-7 shows the computation for the example of Fig. 3-7, which we shall use further. For the center of gravity, the sum of the torques is divided by the sum of the weights to give an x of 2.3 and a y of 2.

Table 3-7   Center of Gravity Calculation

General Coordinates	Type	Location Coordinate	Cost × Weight $W_L C_L$	X-Axis Torque	Y-Axis Torque
x_1, y_1	Market 1	1, 1	5	5	5
x_2, y_2	Market 2	3, 1	1	3	1
x_3, y_3	Market 3	4, 2	3	12	6
x_4, y_4	Market 4	2, 3	3	6	9
x_5, y_5	Raw mat. 1	5, 3	2	10	6
x_6, y_6	Raw mat. 2	2, 2	10	20	20
			24	56	47

Method 4. Equating the partial derivatives of Eq. (3-6) to zero gives

$$\frac{\partial TTC}{\partial y} = \sum_{L=1}^{I+K} \frac{W_L C_L (x - x_L)}{D} = 0 \tag{3-9}$$

$$\frac{\partial TTC}{\partial x} = \sum_{L=1}^{I+K} \frac{W_L C_L (y - y_L)}{D} = 0, \tag{3-10}$$

```
1                    DIMENSION XD(7), YD(7), ALPH(7,2), COST(63), XJ(2), YJ(2),X(2),
                   1 Y(2), X1(63), X2(63), Y1(63), Y2(63), SUX1(2), SUX2(2),
                   2 SUY1(2), SUY2(2)
2                    DO 5 I=1,7
3                  5 READ 10,  XD(I), YD(I)
4                 10 FORMAT (2F2.0)
5                    PRINT 15
6                 15 FORMAT (1H1,54H              OPTIMUM VALUE FOR EACH ALTERNATIVE
                   1   /// 2H N, 5X, 10H  COST   , 5X, 32H            COORDINATES
                   2      // 20X, 6H  X1 , 2X, 6H  Y1 , 4X, 6H  X2 , 2X, 6H  Y2  ///)
7                    DO 170 N=1,63
8                    READ 20,  ALPH
9                 20 FORMAT (14F1.)
10                   DO 62  J=1,2
11                   AL=0.0
12                   DO 30  I=1,7
13                30 AL=AL+ALPH(I,J)
14                   ALS=0.0
15                   DO 40   I=1,7
16                40 ALS=ALS+ALPH(I,J)*XD(I)
17                   XJ(J)=ALS/AL
18                   AL=0.0
19                   DO 50  I=1,7
20                50 AL=AL+ALPH(I,J)
21                   ALS=0.0
22                   DO 60   I=1,7
23                60 ALS=ALS+ALPH(I,J)*YD(I)
24                62 YJ(J)=ALS/AL
25                65 DO 70   J=1,2
26                   SUX1(J)=0.0
27                   SUX2(J)=0.0
28                   SUY1(J)=0.0
29                   SUY2(J)=0.0
30                   DO 70   I=1,7
31                   SQ=SQRTF((XD(I)-XJ(J))**2+(YD(I)-YJ(J))**2)
32                   SUX1(J)=SUX1(J)+ALPH(I,J)*XD(I)/SQ
33                   SUX2(J)=SUX2(J)+ALPH(I,J)/SQ
34                   SUY1(J)=SUY1(J)+ALPH(I,J)*YD(I)/SQ
35                70 SUY2(J)=SUY2(J)+ALPH(I,J)/SQ
36                   DO 80   J=1,2
37                   X(J)=SUX1(J)/SUX2(J)
38                80 Y(J)=SUY1(J)/SUY2(J)
39                   PRINT 85,   X(1), Y(1), X(2), Y(2)
40                85 FORMAT (20X, F6.2, 2X, F6.2, 4X, F6.2, 2X, F6.2)
41                   IF (ABSF(X(1)-XJ(1))-1.E-03)       90, 90,120
42                90 IF (ABSF(X(2)-XJ(2))-1.E-03)     100,100,120
43               100 IF (ABSF(Y(1)-YJ(1))-1.E-03)     110,110,120
44               110 IF (ABSF(Y(2)-YJ(2))-1.E-03)     140,140,120
45               120 DO 130   J=1,2
46                   XJ(J)=X(J)
47               130 YJ(J)=Y(J)
48                   GO TO 65
49               140 PHI=0.0
50                   DO 150   J=1,2
51                   DO 150   I=1,7
52               150 PHI=PHI+SQRTF((XD(I)-X(J))**2+(YD(I)-Y(J))**2)
53                   COST(N)=PHI
54                   X1(N)=X(1)
55                   X2(N)=X(2)
56                   Y1(N)=Y(1)
57                   Y2(N)=Y(2)
58                   PRINT 160,  N, COST(N), X1(N), X2(N), Y1(N), Y2(N)
59               160 FORMAT (1X,I2,5X,F10.2,5X,F6.2,2X,F6.2,4X,F6.2,2X,F6.2)
60               170 CONTINUE
61                   DO 210   N=2,63
62                   IF (COST(1)-COST(N))    210,210,200
63               200 COST(1)=COST(N)
64                   X1(1)=X1(N)
65                   X2(1)=X2(N)
66                   Y1(1)=Y1(N)
67                   Y2(1)=Y2(N)
68               210 CONTINUE
69                   PRINT 215
70               215 FORMAT(1H1, 29HTHE MINIMUM COST ALTERNATIVE , 35HAND ITS NUMBER
                   1AND COORDINATES IS   ///)
71                   PRINT 217
72               217 FORMAT(1X,2H N,5X,10H  COST   ,5X,32H            COORDINATES
                   1   // 20X,6H  X1 ,2X,6H  Y1 ,4X,6H  X2 ,2X,6H  Y2  ///)
73                   PRINT 220,  N, COST(N), X1(N), Y1(N), X2(N), Y2(N)
74               220 FORMAT (1X,I2,5X,F10.2,5X,F6.2,2X,F6.2,4X,F6.2,2X,F6.2)
75                   END
```

Figure 3-8. Program for cost-minimizing location.

OPTIMUM VALUE FOR EACH ALTERNATIVE

COORDINATES

X1	Y1,	X2	Y2
19.51	24.22	18.95	17.53
19.63	24.56	19.77	17.48
19.75	24.75	20.20	17.40
19.84	24.86	20.42	17.31
19.90	24.93	20.54	17.23
19.94	24.98	20.62	17.18
19.97	25.01	20.67	17.14
19.99	25.04	20.70	17.11
20.01	25.05	20.72	17.09
20.02	25.06	20.73	17.08
20.02	25.07	20.74	17.07
20.03	25.07	20.75	17.07
20.03	25.07	20.76	17.06
20.03	25.08	20.76	17.06
20.04	25.08	20.76	17.06
20.04	25.08	20.76	17.06
20.04	25.08	20.76	17.06
20.04	20.76	25.08	17.06

where

$$D = [(x - x_L)^2 + (y - y_L)^2]^{1/2}. \tag{3-11}$$

Unfortunately, these conditions cannot be solved simultaneously for x and y because of the form of the equations. However, Cooper [11, 12] has suggested an iterative solution which merely rearranges Eq. (3-9), solving for x and subscripting the x with the number of the iteration:

$$x_{m+1} = \sum_{L=1}^{I+K} \frac{W_L C_L x_L}{D_m} \div \sum_{L=1}^{I+K} \frac{W_L C_L}{D_m} \tag{3-12}$$
$$D_m = [(x_m - x_L)^2 + (y_m - y_L)^2]^{1/2}.$$

Also, y_{m+1} is the similar rearrangement of Eq. (3-10).

Initial values for x and y, say x_1, y_1 are chosen, perhaps by method 3, and a new x and y, say x_2, y_2, are calculated with Eq. (3-12) iteratively until x_{m+1} approximates x_m. Figure 3-8 gives the computer program and the converging results for the example problem. If a computer is available, this is the preferred method of the six methods.

Method 5. The fact that Eq. (3-6) is convex can be used to exploit gradient search methods based on the derivatives of Eq. (3-6). Vergin and Rogers [13] have used a digital computer gradient search method to find the solution. Eilon and Deziel [14] have used analog computer techniques for the same purpose. An advantage of the latter method is that the isodapanes are obtained so that differences in production cost can then be taken into account, as discussed in Sec. C.

Method 6. Another approach for minimization of Eq. (3-6) is a dynamic programming approach suggested by Bellman [15], which involves a numerical L-stage computation, which is computationally difficult.

In summary, it can be seen that several methods for solving the problem of locating one warehouse or plant are available. However, none are particularly convenient. The iterative technique has been programmed and is efficient for reasonably large problems of 50–100 locations.

III. OPTIMAL NUMBER AND LOCATION OF DISTRIBUTION CENTERS

a. Introduction

It may not, of course, be optimal to have only a single distribution center. A more general problem is to find the locations of the unknown number of distribution points that will minimize total costs. Since more than one facility is included, the question of economies of scale will arise. Problem 2 can be stated as follows:

> Problem 2a. Select the optimal number and location of plants to serve the given markets from given raw material sources.
>
> Problem 2b. Select the optimal number and location of warehouses to serve the given markets from the given plant(s).

First we shall assume one plant in problem 2b and one set of raw material sources in problem 2a. Problem 2 is much more difficult to solve than problem 1.

The introduction of a variable number of distribution points means that costs other than transport cost must be included. If only transportation costs are considered, the answer is obviously to locate a distribution point for each market. In problem 2b a distribution point would be at each and every market and would be supplied by the nearest plant. In problem 2a each plant would be located optimally for each market and the closest raw material locations, considering each market individually. There must be some cost assigned to opening additional distribution points because without this cost the number of distribution points is intuitively unappealing.

The costs of additional centers can be brought in as either fixed charges associated with each distribution center or as economies of scale of operation, or both. Let us consider the fixed charge. The fixed charge will be taken to be independent of the volume of material handled by the distribution center.

Total cost is then

$$TC = nF + \sum_{L=1}^{I+K} W_L C_L [(x - x_L)^2 + (y - y_L)^2]^{1/2}, \qquad (3\text{-}13)$$

where F is the fixed cost and n is the number of centers. An attempt to optimize this equation by classic calculus (integer values would be a problem here) would give

$$F = -\frac{dW_L C_L D_L}{dn},$$ (3-14)

which suggests that an additional warehouse in problem 2b or plant in problem 2a would be opened only if the transportation savings equal the fixed charge. Transportation costs will be decreasing at a decreasing rate with larger n because the radius decreases slower than the area. Therefore an optimum will exist. A convenient procedure to find the optimal number of centers is to first find the optimal location for one plant or warehouse by any of the six methods in Sec. D.II.b and compute total costs. Then compute the optimal location for 2, 3, 4, . . . plants or warehouses by the methods below, adding another warehouse or plant only when the transportation savings are greater than the fixed cost. The first time that the savings are not enough to offset the fixed cost, the procedure can be terminated. If the fixed charge varies with the volume of material, only a little more effort is required.

b. Locational Plane Method

The recommended method of solving problem 1 was the iterative solution of the derivatives. We can attempt to solve the problem of locating two distribution points the same way. At first there seems to be no problem. An additional two equations, the partial derivatives with respect to the additional x, y locations of the second distribution points, would have to be added. However, unfortunately the transport cost depends on what combinations are made of markets and plants in problem 2a or markets and warehouses in problem 2b. There are seven ways to assign four markets to two plants. There are

$$S(L, M) = \frac{1}{M!} \sum_{k=0}^{M} \binom{M}{k}(-1)^k (M - k)^L$$ (3-15)

ways of assigning L markets to M plants. When economies of scale are not large, each plant or warehouse should ship to the nearest market, but until the locations of the plants or warehouses are chosen, the nearest markets cannot be determined. The only recourse is to assign markets to the distributional points in all possible combinations and see which allocation has the lowest transportation cost. For example, let us consider the four markets and two raw material sources of Fig. 3-7 and Table 3-7 reproduced as Fig. 3-9. If we are to locate two plants, we might first assign the top two markets to one plant and solve a single distribution center problem for the top two markets and the two raw material sources. This would give a location for one

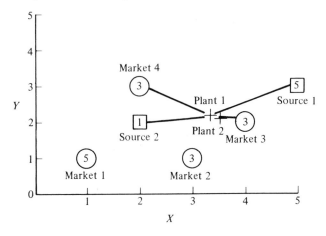

Figure 3-9. Optimal locations for two plants, top markets assigned to plant 1.

plant at about (3.3, 2.2), as shown in Fig. 3-9. The transportation cost for this plant could then be found as the sum of $D_L W_L C_L$ or about 22 total cost units.

The other plant would serve the lower two plants from the two raw material sources. The optimal location for the second plant can be found to be (3.5, 2.1). The total transport cost for the two plants can be obtained as 22 plus 21. Note that the raw material movements must reflect the production at the particular plant. Next, all the six other assignments of four markets to two plants must be made and the transport cost computed. For example, we might assign the two right-hand markets to one plant. Finally, the total transportation costs are compared for all seven combinations and the pair of locations that has the lowest transportation cost is chosen. The savings in transportation cost over the cost of the one plant solution can then be compared to the additional cost of the second plant.

To summarize, the procedure calls for use of one of the six methods of Sec. D.II.b on a set of single location problems to solve for the optimal locations of multiple distribution centers. The procedure can be given in two steps:

1. For a given number of distribution points, take every possible combination of each distribution point with the market locations. Then solve the single distribution center problem for each center and pick the combination with the least transportation cost.

2. Do step 1 for 1, 2, 3, . . . distribution points until the transportation savings from an additional center are less than the fixed cost of the additional center.

The computational procedure for the optimal single location is itself iterative in nature, so there is roughly a twofold combinatorial increase in the number of computations as the number of locations increases. That is, the iterative single-point solution must be done not once but a number of times, which increases combinatorially. The implications for computation are extremely bad if the number of locations is at all large. For this reason another formulation of the problem has been introduced by several researchers.

c. Finite Set of Locations Method

1. Introduction. The major feature of the other formulation is to consider only a finite set of locations as candidates for the distribution centers instead of the infinite number of points in the locational plane. This method has several advantages besides the computational one:

1. In actuality, not all locations make sense as warehouse locations. In practice a number of feasible alternatives must be evaluated to find the best actual location after using the methods discussed above.

2. The choice of actual location allows the use of the particular cost coefficient C_L which would apply to each particular route. In the previous model, the mode of transportation could not be specified, because the location of the center was not known. Actual freight rates for the best modes available can be used in this method of solving the problem. Straight-line distances need not be assumed.

3. Because convexity is no longer required, costs other than transportation can be included. Operating costs with economies of scale, locational differences in production costs, and fixed charges for having warehouses can all be handled, although not without effort.

One disadvantage of this formulation of the problem is that the optimum location may not be among the finite number of points evaluated. However, if a large number of likely locations are included, this objection can be overcome. For the example of Figs. 3-7 and 3-9, we might consider only three potential locations for the distribution centers, which in this case are plants. We consider potential plants at 3, 3 and/or 3, 2 and/or 4, 3, as shown in Fig. 3-10. We can compute the transportation and operating cost for supplying all markets with each market supplied from the nearest of the one, two, or three plants. In the example, there would be eight (2^3) total costs. We can then choose the least-cost number and location of plants from among the

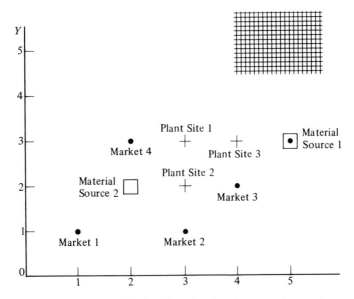

Figure 3-10. Potential plant location for the example problem.

eight. However, none of these combinations has exactly the same locations as the optimum as derived by the method of Sec. D.III.b. On the other hand, we could specify a grid of potential plants spaced every tenth of a distance unit as shown in the corner of Fig. 3-10. We could then select locations close to the optimal set of locations, although at great computational cost. Another disadvantage of this method is that the differential calculus can no longer be used on this discrete formulation.

The pioneering work on this problem was done by Baumol and Wolfe [16]. In their example they considered five possible warehouse sites for supplying eight customers from two factories. They attempted to interject a nonlinear cost into the problem by an iterative minimization of costs using the transportation method of linear programming. A typical transportation LP tableau for assigning customers to the closest warehouse was obtained as the first step. A marginal cost for the operating level at each warehouse was added to the transportation cost in each cell of the transportation tableau before the second solution of the assignment was begun. Repetition of these steps tends to reduce the number of warehouses. This method has been shown to be nonoptimal, but the efforts of Baumol and Wolfe in formulating the problem pioneered an entire series of approaches to this problem.

Most of the recent work follows the same principle of assuming a set of possible locations for the distribution centers and then performing a search through the possible combinations of centers and markets. In attempting such a search, various investigators have tried a variety of methods which demonstrate the breadth of operations research techniques available. The problem of searching for the best subset of locations among the finite set involves two steps. The first is the formulation of a cost function. The second is the evaluation of the cost of each or a subset of the locations to be considered. Most of the investigators have assumed a cost structure with economies of scale in the operation of the distribution structures and/or fixed charges for opening additional centers. Their methods of search have varied quite widely. Of course, all possible combinations could be evaluated for a solution by complete enumeration.† For any substantial number of customers and possible locations for distribution centers, this would be impossible. The following paragraphs briefly describe several methods that have been used for the search.

2. Six methods for solution

Method 1: the linear programming search technique. Because formulations with only linear transportation costs would result in too many warehouses, Baumol and Wolfe adapted the transportation method by an iterative approach which included a marginal cost for each particular warehouse volume. However, this effort has been shown to be nonoptimal.

Method 2: the integer programming search technique. Balinski [18] has formulated an integer fixed-charge problem which minimizes transport cost plus a fixed cost for each warehouse. The integer linear program requires the generation of a series of additional linear constraints in the usual Gomory integer programming fashion. To the author's knowledge, no computational results from this method have become available. The fixed-charge formulation has been solved by Gray [19] with a branch and bound procedure but at the cost of considerable computation; see method 3.

Balinski's model is as follows:

$$\text{minimize transportation and fixed cost} = \sum_{j=1}^{n} \sum_{k=1}^{m} a_{jk} c_{jk} d_k Y_{jk} + \sum_{j=1}^{m} f_j Z_j,$$

$$(3\text{-}16)$$

where subscripts k are for markets and j are for distribution centers, with the following constants:

$a = $ distance from distribution center to market

$c = $ cost per ton-mile

$d = $ demand at market

$f = $ fixed cost at distribution center.

---

†For an actual small problem, see Stollsteimer [17].

The variables are

$$Y_{jk} = 0 \quad \text{if the route from center } j \text{ to market } k \text{ is not used}$$
$$Y_{jk} = 1 \quad \text{if the route from center } j \text{ to market } k \text{ is used}$$
$$Z_j = 0 \quad \text{if } \sum_k Y_{jk} = 0 \text{ for } k = 1, \ldots, m$$
$$Z_j = 1 \quad \text{if } \sum_k Y_{jk} \neq 0 \text{ for } k = 1, \ldots, m$$

all subject to the constraint

$$\sum_{j=1}^{n} Y_{jk} = 1 \qquad \text{for } k = 1, \ldots, m. \qquad (3\text{-}17)$$

We shall return to this type of formulation in the last method. The method can be extended to nonlinear costs by use of piecewise linear functions, as shown in Fig. 3-11, but at the expense of greatly increased computations.

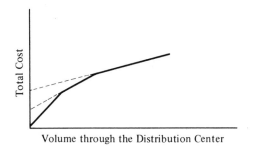

Figure 3-11.   Piecewise linear cost function for distribution centers.

Method 3: the branch and bound technique of implicit enumeration. Efromyson and Ray [20] attempted to validate one of the heuristic methods of search listed below by this method. The branch and bound technique analyzes the possible combinations by a tree search or branching. The bound is available owing to the fact that an optimal integer solution cannot have lower cost than the linear programming solution, which is easy to compute. In branching, the route variables Y_{jk} are sequentially set to 0 or 1 and a linear programming solution found for both the 0 and 1 values of the variable creating the branches of a decision tree. The branch with value 0 or 1 which has the lowest bound is used from that point on. The search continually discards branches when it can be seen from the LP solution that the branch will have higher cost than the current lower bound. The lower bound is determined by progressively moving through the tree. It is not necessary to evaluate the entire tree because many branches are eliminated from further search because of the size of their lower bound. Branch and bound methods are discussed further in Chap. 6.

The branch and bound method reported by Efromyson and Ray was used with only a two-piece linear approximation to convex cost. The purpose was a general verification of a heuristic method rather than as a method of solving large problems. However, Kurt Spielberg of IBM [21, 22] has reported an improved version which has good computational ability for the one-piece cost function or nonconcave cost function.

Method 4: the heuristic approach to search. Kuehn and Hamburger [23] presented the first heuristic model for choosing a good subset of locations. By definition, a heuristic uses reasonable rules of thumb to arrive at a good or nearly optimal solution. The Kuehn and Hamburger approach is to put customers into "natural" local groups and then attempt to reduce or increase the number of warehouses serving the locality. The heuristic rules are

1. Most geographical locations are not promising sites for regional warehouses. Locations with promise will be at or near a concentration of demand.
2. Near-optimum warehousing systems can be developed by locating warehouses one at a time, adding at each stage of the analysis that warehouse which produced the greatest cost savings for the entire system.
3. Only a small subset of all possible warehouse locations need be evaluated in detail at each state of the analysis to determine the next warehouse site to be added.

Thix model was extended from a fixed-charge formulation to a piecewise (two-piece) approximation to continuous economics of scale by Feldman et al. of Esso [24]. In this case the assignment of customers to warehouses is no longer trivial because lower operating cost may offset longer transportation routes. Therefore an approximation for both selection of locations for warehouses and assignment of markets to the warehouses selected was necessary. In general these approximations were the consideration of a "local" set of markets for each warehouse, picking the best warehouse by the local measure for possible incorporation into the location plan. Somewhat similarly, the assignment was solved using reference levels of volume through each warehouse which were determined by the sum of demand for a set of local markets, a procedure similar to the first and second steps of Baumol and Wolfe. The problem with these steps is twofold: (1) computation time for versions with nonlinear, volume-related costs and (2) the fact that the results for the algorithms may be considerably nonoptimal with no way to approach optimality since much of the problem revolves around a definition of "local" areas.

Method 5: the simulation approach. In this approach, the search technique is performed by judgment of a relatively small number of subsets of possible locations. However, these subsets are evaluated in far greater detail than by the other methods. The inclusion of size and frequency of orders, breakdown by individual product, freight rate break-points, and other considerations are major features. Shycon and Maffei [25] have used this method for a large number of industrial clients. It would be possible to combine this method with a heuristic or other type of search for a particular location which could then be evaluated by the more complete simulation approach.

Method 6: the discrete optimizing search approach. Manne [24] has used an early form of the discrete optimizing technique suggested by Reiter and Sherman in his study of location of facilities with economies of scale. The discrete optimizing technique developed by Reiter and Sherman [27] is a probabilistic search method. It guarantees finding an optimal solution only as the number of trials reaches the total of all combinations of subsets of the finite set of possible locations. On the other hand, if the cost surface is reasonably shaped, it will give a close-to-optimal result in a short time. In some cases, the distribution of results can be derived and a confidence interval placed on the answer obtained after any number of trials. Manne makes use of the steepest ascent one-point move algorithm (SAOPMA) generally applied in discrete optimization, but he uses it oniy once rather than making use of the computational features of the technique.

d. Discussion of the Discrete Optimizing Model

The example model that we shall discuss is a minimization of three costs, including variable, fixed, and volume-related costs. The resulting cost function is concave. A matrix of zeros and ones representing assignment of each market to warehouse is searched for a combination with minimal cost.

$$\text{minimize cost} = \underbrace{\sum_{j=1}^{n} \sum_{k=1}^{m} a_{jk} c_{jk} d_k Y_{jk}}_{\text{variable costs}} + \underbrace{f \sum_{j=1}^{n} Z_j}_{\text{fixed costs}} + \underbrace{b \sum_{j=1}^{n} (d_k Y_{jk})^{1/2}}_{\text{volume-related costs}} \qquad (3\text{-}18)$$

$$\text{subject to } \sum_{j} Y_{jk} = 1 \qquad \text{for } k = 1, \ldots, m, \qquad (3\text{-}19)$$

where, as before, subscripts j are for distribution centers and k are for markets, with constants

$a =$ distance from distribution center to market

$c =$ cost per ton-mile

$d =$ demand at market

$f =$ fixed cost at distribution center

$b =$ volume-related cost coefficient

and variables

$$Y_{jk} = 0, 1 \quad \text{for closed or open routes from a center to a market}$$
$$Z_j = 0, 1 \quad \text{for } \sum_k Y_{jk} = 0 \text{ or } > 0.$$

This model assumes that fixed and volume-related costs are the same at each center, but this assumption could be relaxed by moving f within the summation. A square root function of volume is used by tradition for warehouse handling cost but other exponents could be appropriate, particularly for scale of plant in the plant location version of the problem, which can also be handled by this method. More than one source, plant or raw material location, can be handled with a preliminary computation of the cost to serve each distribution center from each source. The selection of the source for each plant or warehouse can be made on the basis of this cost alone since only transport cost is involved.

The solution procedure starts with a binary matrix of Y_{jk}s such as Table 3-8, which has only one in a column because each market is served by one distribution center. Three procedures have been used to generate the matrices, one based strictly on random generation of binary matrices, one which is biased to take advantage of possible economies of scale, and one which picks the least-transportation-cost solution as a starting point.

Procedure 1: random generation. This random localized search procedure takes a random binary matrix with columns representing the markets and rows representing the centers for the assignment of a warehouse to each market. It evaluates the cost of that assignment. Then the first column, which has only one 1, is changed so that the 1 is in a different row. This represents a change of the warehouse supplying market 1. Each warehouse is in turn assigned to the first market and evaluated. The least-cost warehouse to serve market 1 is selected. The same procedure is applied independently to the remaining columns. The entire procedure is repeated for a new random matrix until a near-optimal point is reached. "Near optimality" is estimated by observation of the total cost function. Alternatively, a fixed number of iterations may be performed.

Procedure 2: economies of scale. Procedure 1 would take advantage of the economies of scale with only small probability since (1) only rarely would the same warehouse be best for more than a few of the locations and (2) a randomly selected assignment would rarely specify use of only a few warehouses because it would rarely have a majority of a row filled by the 1s. Therefore in this procedure the search is conducted with the starting positions utilizing the economies of scale. Specifically, the initial matrix assigns all markets to one warehouse, as in Table 3-8, and in turn evaluates each column to see whether it is best to assign all markets to one warehouse.

Table 3-8   Binary Matrix for Economies of Scale

		Markets					
		1	2	3	4	5	6
	1	0	0	0	0	0	0
Distribution centers	2	1	1	1	1	1	1
	3	0	0	0	0	0	0

$y_{jk} = 0$ if center j does not serve market k
$y_{jk} = 1$ if center j serves market k

Procedure 3: least transport cost. This procedure searches the columns of the cost matrix for the least-cost route and assigns each market to that center that has the least transportation cost to serve that market. Then each distribution center in turn has its service area extended to additional markets, and other centers are closed if it is shown to be less costly.

Computational results. The methods above are able to solve the 50-market, 50-warehouse problems of Kuehn and Hamburger in a relatively short but not inconsequential computing time. The methods are sufficiently simple that they can be programmed for more complex problems with minimal investment in programming. Special constraints and cost of revenue structures can be handled. The authors have solved an actual problem involving choice of 1 or more of 10 plant locations to serve 40 markets with 4 products obtained from 1 raw material which can be purchased in any of the 40 markets in less than an hour of 360–75 computer time using a combination of the three procedures. Although this may sound like a long time, the decision is major and infrequent, with large potential savings.

IV. OPTIMAL LOCATION OF BOTH WAREHOUSE AND PLANTS

In setting up a production *and* distribution system, both plants and warehouses must be located, a more complicated problem. If there are no economies of scale either in construction or operation for the plants or warehouses, the solution is to treat each market separately, optimally locating a plant and warehouse as a unit by the method for determining one distribution point. There would be no reason to separate the plants and warehouses in this case.

If there are economies of scale for the plants or warehouses, the problem becomes one of considerable enumeration. Fortunately it appears that there are usually no trade-offs between warehouses and plants. Subsequently, it is possible to start with one plant, determine the optimal number and location of warehouses by the method above (problem 2b), and proceed to two plants, etc., stopping when transport savings no longer make up for additional plant costs.

V. FIXED CAPACITY AND THE TRANSPORTATION METHOD OF LINEAR PROGRAMMING

Up to this point we have discussed location problems within a design framework where capacities of the distribution centers can be set by the decision maker after location. This leads to the condition that each market can be serviced from one distribution center with the volume of each center equal to the sum of demands of the markets in its area.

Two circumstances might negate this condition:

1. Adding a distribution center to an already existing system.
2. When market demands change, it may be necessary to split the requirements between several distribution centers if one distribution center becomes temporarily overloaded.

The presence of inventories at the distribution centers and the design flexibility to handle a fairly wide range of volume will often overcome both of these circumstances. It is usually administratively desirable to maintain the assignment of each market to a certain one of the distribution centers, although if many products are involved, this may not be feasible. Transportation costs will be minimized when each market is served by only one distribution center.

A means of testing a proposed location for an additional distribution center is the transportation method of linear programming. The capacities of the current distribution centers and one of the proposed locations along with the variable costs to supply each of the markets are placed in a transportation tableau along with the demands as shown in Table 3-9. The transportation method of linear programming is used to find the optimum allocation of capacity to the demand points. Total relevant costs can be determined by adding the fixed costs of the new center, for comparison with other alternatives. Examination of the shadow price on the capacity of the new center when compared to fixed costs of the new center indicates whether the amount of planned capacity is optimal. This procedure can be repeated

**Table 3-9   Transportation LP Tableau for
Additional Capacity Center**

Markets

Existing distribution centers	Variable production and transportation cost to supply each market from each distribution center	Capacity of each center
New distribution center location	— — — — — — — —	—
	Demands	Total of demands and capacities

for several proposed locations including no new location, and the least-cost solution can be selected.

It is important to carefully define the capacities and demands and costs in this problem with reference to the earlier point concerning variability of demand and the desirability of serving one market from one distribution center. For example, a case appearing in a recent text explores the location of a new bakery in a chain [28]. Capacities are given that total to the average demand including a new bakery and location which replaces a considerable amount of current baking capacity. The transportation model of linear programming is used to allocate all capacity to demand. What will happen to this new system in a period when demand is above average? Also, the new system will require daily scheduling of deliveries by a centralized facility which can distribute the capacity to demand. Many markets will be supplied by two bakeries. This will be considerably more complicated than the present system which assigns each store to one bakery. Finally, since the transportation method does not handle fixed charges and the authors did not add the fixed cost of the new bakery separately to variable costs but used average costs including depreciation for all bakeries, they implicitly assumed that the displaced capacity could be sold at book value, a rather dubious assumption.

VI. MULTIPRODUCT MODELS

Most of the models discussed have been single-product models. This is usually not a bad assumption for the long-range planning necessary in location analysis. Products can usually be aggregated into a single measure of weight or volume. The cost can be a weighted average of the costs of transporting each product.

Sometimes not all products are to be made or handled at all centers. Then the analysis must proceed separately for each group that is common to certain centers. This becomes difficult only when the costs at the centers are not independent between groups of products. Often this would be the case since cost is a function of total volume, as in warehouse operation.

The method of discrete optimizing search can explicitly handle multiple products with the types of constraints above. An addition summation and subscript is needed along with a matrix of allowable locations. Of course, this increases computational time.

E. Other Factors in Location

Up to this point the discussion of location has primarily dealt with theory of maximizing profit or minimizing transport cost. It would be desirable to conclude with a discussion summarizing how location choices are actually made. Unfortunately, this is not a feasible task. Greenhut [5] has prepared a considerable list of all the transport, processing cost, and demand factors which should enter a location decision in the fashion described above. He also includes another category of factors which are not nearly so easy to analyze. These include advantages from agglomeration such as capital, availability of insurance, or repair facilities; from nearness to customers such as personal selling relationships and extra fast delivery; and from purely personal considerations on the part of the decision maker such as climate and educational or cultural advantages. In his study of actual location decisions by small firms, Greenhut found the last set of factors to be of more importance than an analyst might have guessed. Even Lösch [3] admits that

> The mathematical derivation of the optimum transport location is infinitely more impressive but also incomparably less accurate than the statement that the entrepreneur will establish his enterprise at a place he likes best.

Even as the entrepreneur and his preference tend to disappear from the current economic scene and from the significant location decisions, the considerable effect of the giant corporations' decisions with regard to the economy of the country introduces new factors into the location decision. As Galbraith [29] points out:

> The corporate planner becomes almost indistinguishable from the socialist state's economic planner. There is now a distinct possibility that a new auto plant will be located in Louisiana to appease the chairman of the Congressional auto-safety investigation or in the slums of New York to help answer another of the nation's problems.

The location decision, because of its long-range and substantial nature, is inevitably tied into the major problems of the economy, which are described in the fashion shown in Fig. 3-12 by Lösch.

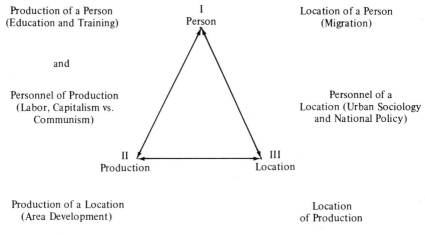

Figure 3-12.

With this framework it is easy to see that while location decisions should be made with knowledge of costs and sales, they will rarely be made on this basis alone. For this reason, each important location decision must be subjected not only to the types of analysis we have suggested but also more subjective assessment such as that referred to in Sec. B.

SUMMARY

Location decisions are not routine. They require large amounts of information and analysis. Revenue and cost projections for alternative locations are necessary but not sufficient determinants in the decision. Computation of optimal profit, cost, or revenue is a lengthy and difficult task, but since location decisions are seldom made and not easily changed, considerable investment in aiding the decision maker is worthwhile.

Methods for finding the revenue-maximizing and cost-minimizing locations have been presented. Discussion of several models indicates how to fit them together for a good, if not optimal, overall solution.

The mathematical programming techniques discussed in this chapter will be useful in later chapters.

REFERENCES

1. Peter C. Fishburn, "Utility Theory," *Management Science*, 14, No. 5 (Jan. 1968), 335.

2. JOHANN HEINRICH VON THÜNEN, *Der Isolirte Staat in Beziehung auf Landwirtschaft und Nationalö Konomie*, S. Fischer Verlag, Frankfurt am Main, 1966.

3. AUGUST LÖSCH, *The Economics of Location*, Yale University Press, New Haven, Conn., 1954.

4. C. J. FRIEDRICH, ed., *Alfred Weber's Theory of Location of Industries*, University of Chicago Press, Chicago, 1929.

5. MELVIN L. GREENHUT, *Plant Location in Theory and Practice*, The University of North Carolina Press, Chapel Hill, 1956, p. 145.

6. FRITZ MACHLUP, *The Economics of Seller's Competition*, The Johns Hopkins Press, Baltimore, 1952.

7. E. H. CHAMBERLIN, *The Theory of Monopolistic Competition*, Harvard University Press, Cambridge, Mass., 1962.

8. GILBERT CHURCHILL, "Production Technology, Imperfect Competition and the Theory of Location: A Theoretical Approach," *Southern Economic Journal*, XXXIV, No. 1 (July 1967), 86.

9. B. V. SHENOY and D. W. SIFFERD, "A Heuristic Simulation Approach for Locating Warehouses and Plant Facilities," TIMS/ORSA Joint Meeting, San Francisco (May 1–3, 1968).

10. K. B. HALEY, "The Siting of Depots," *International Journal of Production Research*, 2, No. 1 (March–May 1963), 41.

11. LEON COOPER, "Solutions of Generalized Locationed Equilibrium Models," *Journal of Regional Science*, 7, No. 1 (1967), 1.

12. LEON COOPER, "Location Allocation Problems," *Operations Research*, II. No. 3 (May–June 1963), 331.

13. ROGER C. VERGIN and JACK C. ROGERS, "An Algorithm and Computational Procedure for Locating Economic Facilities," *Management Science*, 13, No. 6 (Feb. 1967), B-240.

14. SAMUEL EILON and D. P. DEZIEL, "Siting a Distribution Centre, An Analogue Computer Application," *Management Science*, 12, No. 6 (Feb. 1966), B-245.

15. RICHARD BELLMAN, *An Application of Dynamic Programming to Location-Allocation Problems*, RM-4115-PR, RAND Corp., Santa Monica, June 1964.

16. W. J. BAUMOL and P. WOLFE, "A Warehouse Location Problem," *Operations Research*, 6 (March–April 1958), 252.

17. JOHN F. STOLLSTEIMER, "A Working Model for Plant Numbers and Locations," *Journal of Farm Economics*, 45 (Aug. 1963), 631.

18. M. L. BALINSKI, *On Some Decompostion Approaches in Linear Programming*, Mathematica, Princeton, N.J.

19. PAUL GRAY, *Mixed Integer Programming Algorithm for Site Selection*

and Other Fixed Charge Problems Having Capacity Constraints, Technical Report No. 6, Department of Operations Research, Stanford, Calif.

20. M. A. EFROYMSON and T. L. RAY, "A Branch and Bound Algorithm for Plant Location," *Operations Research,* 14, No. 3 (May–June 1966), 361.

21. KURT SPIELBURG, "An Algorithm for the Simple Plant Location Problem with Some Side Conditions," 322.0900, IBM New York Scientific Center, New York, May 1967.

22. KURT SPIELBERG, "Plant Location with Generalized Search Origin," *Management Science,* 16, No. 3 (Nov. 1969), 165.

23. A. A. KUEHN and M. J. HAMBURGER, "A Heuristic Program for Locating Warehouses," *Management Science,* 9, No. 4 (July 1963), 41.

24. E. FELDMAN, F. A. LEHNER, and T. L. RAY, "Warehouse Location Under Continuous Economies of Scale," *Management Science,* 12, No. 9 (May 1966), 670.

25. H. N. SHYCON and R. B. MAFFEI, "Simulation-Tool for Distribution," *Harvard Business Review,* 41, No. 6 (Nov.–Dec. 1960), 65.

26. ALAN S. MANNE, "Plant Location Under Economies of Scale–Decentralization and Computation," *Management Science,* 11, No. 2 (Nov. 1964), 213.

27. STANLEY RIETER and G. SHERMAN, "Discrete Optimizing," *Journal of the Society for Industrial Applied Mathematics,* 13, No. 3 (Sept. 1965), 864.

28. J. L. HESKETT, R. M. IVIE, and N. A. GLASKOWSKY, *Business Logistics,* Ronald, New York, 1964. Student Supplement, p. 118.

29. J. K. GALBRAITH, *The New Industrial State,* Houghton Mifflin, Boston, 1969.

30. PHILLIP E. HICKS and ARUN M. KLUMTHA, "One Way To Tighten Up Plant Location Decisions," *Industrial Engineering* (Apr. 1971), 19.

31. STEPHEN KONZ, "Where Does One More Machine Go," *Industrial Engineering* (May 1970), 18.

32. PAUL LIPTO and JOHN CABRERA "Plant Location and Integer Programming Application," *Production and Inventory Management,* 12, No. 1 (1972), 32.

PROBLEMS

1. Tables P-1(a) and (b) give the ratings of each of 10 locations on 6 factors [30]. The ratings were obtained by estimating the dollar result of the factor on the firm in each of the extreme locations for each factor. For example, transportation costs at Franklin are $760,000 per year lower than at Hobbsonville. The

Table P-1(a) Point Aggregates for All Locations

Location / Factor	Adamsville level	Adamsville pts	Backwater level	Backwater pts	Casper Junction level	Casper Junction pts	Davidson level	Davidson pts	Edgewater level	Edgewater pts	Franklin level	Franklin pts	Granny Forks level	Granny Forks pts	Hobbsonville level	Hobbsonville pts	Immerson level	Immerson pts	Jagged Forks level	Jagged Forks pts
TANGIBLES																				
Transportation cost	350	127	715	258	625	226	150	54	75	27	0	0	550	199	760	275	95	35	275	100
Labor cost	510	166	0	0	320	104	70	23	475	155	210	68	165	54	350	114	580	189	195	64
Building cost	240	82	100	33	0	0	400	137	340	116	150	51	15	5	295	101	85	29	305	104
Cost of utilities	75	23	320	111	255	78	0	0	235	72	120	37	270	83	160	49	50	15	310	96
INTANGIBLES																				
Community attitude	3	63	1	0	2	29	2	29	2	29	5	157	1	0	2	29	3	63	4	90
Labor attitude	2	31	4	100	1	0	3	66	3	66	4	100	5	131	3	66	4	100	2	31
AGGREGATE		492		502		437		309		465		413		472		634		431		485

Courtesy American Institute of Industrial Engineers, Inc.

ratings for the other locations were obtained by comparison with the extremes.

a. Add up the unweighted dollar differences over the least-cost location for each factor. Compare this total to the decision based on the "points" in Tables P-1(b) and (c).

Table P-1(b) Four Tangible and Two Intangible Factors Considered in the Plant Location Problem

Factor	Maximum Difference in Cost Effect in $1000	Standard Deviation	Weight $= \dfrac{SD}{\sum SD}$	Maximum Point Assignment
Tangible factors				
Transportation cost	760	283.7	.275	275
Labor cost	580	195.1	.189	189
Building cost	400	141.4	.137	137
Cost of utilities	120	114.3	.111	111
Intangible factors				
Community attitude	540	162.5	.157	157
Labor attitude	450	134.4	.131	131
Total	1031.4		1.000	

Table P-1(c) Final Point-Rating Plan

Factor	Point Assignment				
	Level 1	Level 2	Level 3	Level 4	Level 5
Community attitude and service	0	29	63	90	157
Labor attitude	0	31	66	100	131
Transportation	←		275		→
Labor cost	←		189		→
Building cost	←		137		→
Cost of utilities	←		111		→

b. The points were obtained by weighting each factor by its variability, an important step in most such comparisons. Why use standard deviation? What does this imply about loss functions, and is this appropriate?

2. A lawn fertilizer is made up of the materials from the locations shown in Table P-2 and sold in city A. Where should the manufacturing plant be located if all materials and the product are shipped by truck?

a. Does it matter where A, B, and C are?

b. What assumption is made about transportation costs? What if it does not hold?

Table P-2

Ingredient	Lb/Ton of Product	Source
Nitrogen	100	Ubiquitous
Phosphate[a]	1800	B
Potassium compound	600	B
Lime	200	C
Inert (soil)	100	Ubiquitous
	2800	

[a]Reduced to 1000 pounds per ton by separation of impurities during mixing.

c. What if there are two markets?

3. Individual customers for beer have the following linear demand function per period:

$$D = 10 - 2 \cdot \text{price (in six packs)}.$$

Freight along this river valley market is a $1 terminal charge plus $1 per mile. Population along the river bank is concentrated toward the middle in the fashion shown in Fig. P-3. Price is f.o.b.

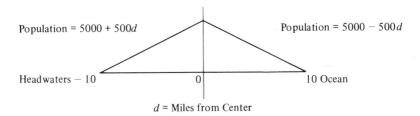

Population = 5000 + 500d   Population = 5000 − 500d

Headwaters − 10   0   10 Ocean

d = Miles from Center

Figure P-3.

a. Find at least two points on the total demand curve for the firm located at the obviously optimal point. How would the curve be used?
b. One important factor in revenue has been neglected. What is it, and what effects would it have in this case?

4. A company distributes varieties of soap on a national basis from two plants, each of which makes the entire line. Public warehouses are used for storage of the soap in major market areas. Formulate a model to locate the warehouses. The cost for public warehouse rental includes $1 per case in average inventory per month except for a discount on volumes over 5000 cases per month plus a charge of $10,000 for each month the warehouse is used. Describe the following:
a. Model type.
b. Allocation of warehouses to plants (no economy of scale in plants).
c. Setup for allocation of markets to warehouses.
d. Total cost equation.

e. Additional data needed.
f. Optimization technique or method to be used.
5. You have prepared Fig. P-5 and Table P-5 showing raw material sources and markets for a new product.

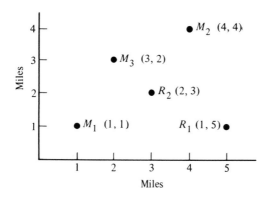

Figure P-5.

Table P-5

Symbol	Designation	Yearly Demand or Amount of Material	Coordinates	Freight ($/ton-mile)
M_1	Market 1	100	1, 1	.03
M_2	Market 2	200	4, 4	.03
M_3	Market 3	300	3, 2	.03
R_1	Raw material 1	300	1, 5	.04
R_2	Raw material 2	400	2, 3	.01

a. Where should the factory be located to minimize transport costs?
b. What question should you have in mind concerning R_1?
c. Assume that labor costs are less at (2, 3). What should you do?
d. Suppose that you are a potential competitor of the company whose plant you located in part a. You have the same production costs. Where should you locate, approximately?
e. You are now back in the company of part a and are faced with the competitor of part d. What pricing terms or policies would you consider as effective weapons against your competitor?
6. Two firms 10 miles apart each produce a product which has price p f.o.b. at the plants. The transportation costs from firm 1 are three times as much as from firm 2.
a. On a two-dimensional surface or map, what shape will the market area for firm 1 be if customers consider the products equivalent except for price?
b. Where will the boundary of the market areas be between the plants? What are the radius and center of the figure in part a?

7. Table P-7 shows the location of six customers.

**Table P-7   Customers 1–6 and Their Coordinate Locations
so that Transportation Costs to Sites A or B
Can Be Calculated**

Customer	X Coordinate	Y Coordinate	Weight
1	40	70	156
2	60	70	179
3	80	70	143
4	30	30	296
5	90	10	94
6	0	60	225

a. Draw the isodapanes for the location of a plant shipping the indicated amounts per month by finding costs at grid points spaced 20 units apart.
b. Suppose that only locations (30, 20) and (90, 30) are being evaluated but that all travel is by rectangular movement. What is the best site?
c. Suppose that we are trying to find the site for an air raid siren and that the *detectable* sound level drops with the square of distance. Revise the optimality criterion accordingly and solve [31].

8. In the problem of Sec. C. IV. b, evaluate the revenue and cost of two warehouses at locations 4 and 10.

9. The data of Table P-9 are available on transport cost between potential warehouse facility locations and demand outlets, as well as demands and fixed costs

**Table P-9   Transportation, Demand, and Fixed Cost Data,
Transportation Cost Matrix**

Outlet	Facility						Demand (000)
	1	2	3	4	5	6	
1	.00	.05				.06	3.5
2		.07	.08		.07	.07	10
3	.04	.03		.07	.09	.19	4
4			.20	.16	.10	.13	16
5	.08	.09	.10	.50	.30	.19	18
6		.10	.07			.10	25
7	.09					.05	20
8	.12		.13			.14	7
9		.12		.10	.25	.03	10
10					.04	.11	12
Fixed cost to open a facility:	670	420	435	0	500	410	

of the facilities. There is only one plant and no variable cost other than transportation.

a. Set up and solve by LP for the optimal set of warehouse facilities *after* attempting the solution by giving a good hard look at the transportation cost tableau.

b. Find the optimal integer solution without solving by integer programming. It is reported that the linear and the integer solutions are within a penny but that they cannot be obtained simply by rounding [32].

10. A company has six sales territories served from three plants in Philadelphia, Chicago, and San Francisco. Three additional territories are served by warehouses in Atlanta, Houston, and New York, which must be supplied by the closest plant. Freight from plant to warehouse is 4 cents per ton-mile, and from warehouse to customer it is 15 cents per ton-mile. Table P-10 gives the mileage between these cities. The customers are widely distributed.

Table P-10

	Atlanta	Chicago	Houston	New York	Phila.	S.F.
Atlanta	0					
Chicago	690	0				
Houston	810	1080	0			
New York	860	820	1650	0		
Philadelphia	760	740	1550	100	0	
San Francisco	2520	2170	1950	2990	2990	0

a. Where should the boundary between the Chicago and Atlanta sales territories be?

b. Where should the boundary between the Atlanta and Houston territories be?

c. Why six territories? How would you determine the optimal number?

d. What is the relationship between this problem and Problem 9?

11. a. Your company has 2 plants, 1 product, and 150 customers each with predictable sales. You wish to locate one central product warehouse. What model might you use to locate the warehouse? Describe in detail your method and the assumptions involved.

b. Your company has 10 plants, 50,000 customers, and several products. Describe in detail one method by which you could determine the best locations for warehouses.

c. In which instance, part a or b, might market considerations of location be more important? Why, and what effect would this have on planning locations for your warehouse?

12. A product is produced in batches of size q_1 at a rate k at location 1. There are two demand points 2 and 3 which have deterministic demands of r_2 and r_3 and holding costs of c_2 and c_3 per unit per time period. There is also a holding cost C_1 at location 1 and a fixed setup cost C_f for production. Finally, there is a fixed-charge portion of the transportation cost from 1 to 2 or 3, C_{12} and C_{13}.

Think of this cost as a minimum transport charge, for example. Shipment is therefore in batches of size q_2 and q_3. See Fig. P-12.

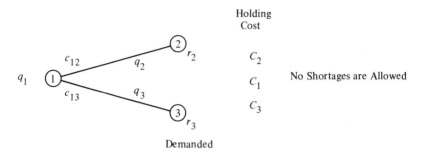

Figure P-12.

a. Give procedures for the optimal decision values for q_1, q_2, and q_3. Do not forget the fact that there are to be no shortages.
b. Suppose that you had a real multiechelon system like that of part a but larger and in addition that demand was not known for certain. What changes would be necessary in the system? You may wish to discuss (1) transshipment, (2) buffer inventories, and (3) information flows.

chapter 4

Process Design

A. Introduction

In process design, an idea for a new product or a new way to make a product is transformed into a complete model or set of instructions for the production of the product. The design must be so complete that the physical facilities can be built and workers trained on the basis of the design. Process design often contains a substantial amount of scientific research since often there is no known method of production when the design is begun. In addition, process design always calls for a large amount of engineering because no two production systems are exactly the same. Often equipment must be specially designed for the process. In every case, detailed production methods must be investigated for the particular conditions under which the plant will operate.

There is also a large component of creative art to the research and engineering phases of process design. It is valuable for the production manager to have experience in research and development since the top level of production management must oversee and approve the final results of process design as well as accept responsibility for operating the resulting system. However, much of the responsibility for the innovative end of process design must rest with the research and engineering groups. In this book we cannot say a great deal about production management's task in the area of research and design because there are very few quantitative models in it. But we shall note that production management should be responsible for the application of the tools of scheduling and control, such as the critical path methods of Chap. 6, to all phases of process design. They must assure the timely, thorough completion of an economical process design.

In the implementation of a process design, the model or instructions for making the product must be transformed into an existing, functioning process. Usually, the designer turns this phase over to construction and operating personnel, but the process designer must be concerned with how the process will be constructed and operated because he must design a facility which will be economically sound in operation, as described in Chap. 2. For example, a chemical plant designed for batch operation must include analysis of scheduling and inventory policies in order to determine the capacity of the equipment. Therefore there is a great need for feedback and exchange of information between the process designer and operating and construction management.

Process design is a task which continues even after the initial design and construction of a plant because of the need for process improvement. In an existing organization it is usually easy to obtain the cooperation of process design, construction, and operating personnel as these improvements are made, but ensuring that an entirely new plant is properly designed from an operational view is much harder because operating management may not yet be on hand. This is a strong reason for careful control and monitoring of the design of the process by production management.

This chapter will describe some procedures which may be incorporated into process design in order to minimize costs and allow operating flexibility. As noted in the paragraphs above, these procedures are not nearly the whole of process design, but they will affect the operation of the plant. Production management should be sure that they are applied, along with good design, research, and engineering, whenever new processes are developed.

The major topics to be discussed in this chapter are process charting, time studies, machine and capacity requirements, shop layout, assembly line design, and information and control systems. The first two sections give only a brief outline of two types of descriptive models, charting and time studies. These models provide much of the basic data for the optimization models which follow.

B. Process Charting of Product-Oriented and Functionally-Oriented Systems

I. INTRODUCTION

The reduction of an idea for a product to a feasible, economically sound, completely detailed process design is made easier through the use of a series of charts. The first is a process flow chart usually consisting of only about a page of very general steps outlined in logical sequence. An example is Fig. 4-1, which is for the separation of starch and gluten in a corn milling

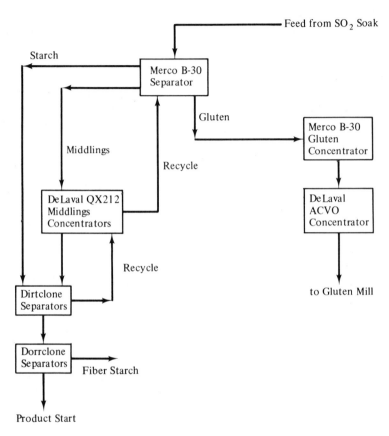

Figure 4-1.   Flow sheet of cornstarch-gluten separation.

plant. Often a detailed flow chart employing standard symbols and specifying the exact type of facility is prepared. Sometimes only a blueprint of the final product is available and the chart is derived from the blueprint by an experienced engineer. At this point it is worthwhile to categorize the types of production systems and describe how they affect the preparation of detailed process charts.

There are two basic types of production systems, the functional, job-shop, or machine-oriented type and the product, continuous, or assembly line type. See Table 4-1. As can be seen by the large number of names for each of the two types, there are differences within these categories. Basically the func-

Table 4-1

| Feature | Orientation | |
	Functional (*machine shop*)	Product (*assembly line*)
Subdivisions of firm	Process	Product
Operational decision making	Decentralized	Centralized
Equipment	Flexible, general-purpose	Specialized, often automated
Labor	Flexible, high-level skills	Specialized, low-skill
Supervision	High skill, expert	Manager
Storage between stages	Storerooms, on floor around machines	Conveyors, bins
Materials handling	Batches in boxes, pallets, etc.	Continuous line or piping
Production control	Dispatching, high information requirement	Permanent design of routing
Cost accounting	Job-order system	Process cost

tional systems consist of equipment of facilities that are physically grouped by their inherent function, while the product-oriented system arranges equipment in the order required by the series of steps in making the product, i.e., an assembly line.

These systems often occur in a mixed form. Several product lines may pass through functional areas, such as in a painting shop. One stage of a plant may be of a functional nature, such as fabrication of parts. Another stage may be a product-oriented assembly line to put the parts together. In a particular stage however, most systems can be identified as either one or the other of these two types. Different models can be applied to the different types, and so we shall examine them individually.

II. FUNCTIONALLY-ORIENTED SYSTEMS

In a functionally-oriented system, such as a machine shop, the first step in detailed process charting depends on whether the product will be produced in an existing or a new facility. If a new facility is planned, several methods can be used for laying out the facility, as will be discussed in Sec. E. If an existing facility is available, each of the individual operations in making the product is examined in detail on the flow sheet to determine what equipment should be used. The materials-handling equipment between operations is usually not sophisticated in a functionally-oriented system. The activity of men and machines at each stage may be developed in a man-machine chart unless the operation is so standard that it need not be explained to the worker.

One page of a simplified man-machine chart for the starch-gluten separation is shown in Table 4-2. In many companies a method and time study will be prepared for each operation. Method and time studies are described briefly in Sec. C. Finally, procedures for materials handling between operations and the paper work for control of movement and proper performance of operations must be developed. We shall comment further on these in Secs. E and F.

Table 4-2   Man-Machine Chart, ABC Company:
Centrifugal Operator

| | | Work Minutes Per | | | |
| | | 1st Pass (machine hr) | Midd. Conc. (machine hr) | Machine-Bushels Dry Substance | Operation (hr) |
Elements of Operation	Symbol				
Walk to QX212 middlings concentrators, inspect discharge to funnel, regulate feed setting as necessary, flush strainers, walk between machines	A		.491		
Take individual sample from each QX212 machine in spin tube with dye added, deliver to sink area; pick up 1 tube from clip at machine, dump to sink; place spin tube samples in centrifuge, remove after spin, return to machine, and place in clip	B		.503		
Start up or shut down QX212 machines as necessary	C			.104	
Walk from B-30 Merco to B-30 Merco, check Be' and adjust setting as necessary; wipe off hygrometer with damp rag	D			.850	
Walk from Merco to Merco, take starch and gluten sample, deliver to sink area; rinse off and wipe spin tubes, place in centrifuge, run spin test; remove tubes to carrying rack, deliver to machines, place in clip, remove previous sample to sink	E	.617			

Table 4-2 (cont.)

Elements of Operation	Symbol	Work Minutes Per			
		1st Pass (machine hr)	*Midd. Conc. (machine hr)*	*Machine-Bushels Dry Substance*	*Operation (hr)*
Walk from Merco to Merco, reset feed rate, check and set Be' as necessary	F			.755	
Walk from Merco to Merco, flush rotary strainers; open and close valve	G			.518	
Walk from Merco to Merco, inspect foam box; rod out pipe when plugged	H				1.81
Start up or shut down B-30 Mercos at direction of head operator; open and close necessary valves, set Be' instrument, check foam box, set flow rate	I			.224	
Walk to 8 Dorrclone strainers, flush same; open and close each valve, walk between units	J				

III. PRODUCT-ORIENTED SYSTEMS

It is not as easy to prepare the man-machine chart for product-oriented systems because the layout is not as easily envisioned. If a product-oriented system is to be developed, the step after the detailed flow chart is usually an estimate of the capacity of each unit of the equipment. The type and number of machines determine, to a large degree, the form of the physical layout. The layout and capacity determine the grouping of operations into work stations. We shall know the desired output capacity of the system before process layout is carried into this stage of refinement on the basis of considerations such as those described in Chap. 2. At this point it is the capacity of each particular machine that must be established. The capacity of each machine influences the layout, which in turn influences the man-machine chart. For example, for large capacities it will pay to design machines to perform the operations and most of the materials handling with only minimal manual labor.

Another example is the influence on the size of the work station. If 6 items are to be produced per hour with each item requiring 3 man-hours of labor,

18 men will be required on the assembly line and each man will work on each item for 10 minutes. Each man's station must be designed for 10 minutes of work. However, if 60 units are produced per hour on the assembly line, each of 180 men will do only 1 minute of work on each item, and each station will be designed for only 1 minute of work. Thus capacity greatly affects how the work is to be arranged and performed at each station.

Once the capacity of the machine or station is estimated, as discussed in Sec. D, the number of workers per machine can be obtained and each operation can be investigated through a method and time study. Again we refer to Table 4-2, the man-machine chart which would be developed for each station. At this point a tentative sequence of the operations and the equipment needed for an assembly line has been accomplished. Precise groupings and daily fluctuations are handled by line-balancing techniques, discussed in Chap. 8.

C. Method and Time Studies

An important step in process design is determining the best method by which each operation can be performed and the standard time for performance. The standard time can be obtained by observation with a stop watch or from predetermined data, once the proper method has been devised. A very brief discussion of method and time studies is given here. For a more complete reference, see Barnes, *Time and Motion Study*, John Wiley and Sons, 1937 or its revisions. Standard times are indispensable for planning purposes in process design.

A method study requires a careful arrangement of the flow of raw materials and the work place with provision for easy access to tools and equipment. A work station is often made up as a life-size paper drawing. Although there are certain principles which are applicable, the best method for performing an operation can be found only by a creative, experienced methods engineer or worker. The predetermined time data described below is often useful in evaluating method changes. Alternative methods can be broken into elements which have standard times and the total time for each alternative compared.

Stop-watch studies consist of observations of the timed length and pace of the elements of an operation as performed by a trained worker. Sampling theory can be used to establish the proper number of observations to assure a statistically valid estimate of the mean time for an operation. Unfortunately we have to assume that the worker is not affected by the observations. Tables of sample size (number of observations) are available in [1]. There is no similar way to establish statistically the validity of the pace or performance rating, which is usually given as a percentage of "normal" working pace. A percentage allowance for fatigue, material delays, and personal time is set by policy and negotiation. The allowance is added to the mean time to perform each operation and the total is multiplied by the performance rating to give the standard time of the operation.

Time standards set by predetermined data break the operation into small elements of motion. Standard times for these elements are available in tables such as those in [1], e.g., p. 12.65. No performance rating is necessary. If there are difficulties in performing the operation, such as heavy weight or extreme accuracy, an adjustment factor is applied. Allowances are also applied. Table 4-3 on p. 142 shows results of the stop-watch method and two predetermined time methods.

The results of Table 4-3 may indicate that time study methods are still not an exact science, since there are significant differences in the times estimated. However, it is probably true that consistency in setting standards is more desirable than accuracy. Within any given class of jobs in any one production plant, only one method is applied by only a limited number of observers. These observers can probably come up with consistent measurements. These measurements can then be relied on for relatively rational and fair decisions on productivity standards, incentives, and scheduling in the plant despite the fact that they might not be applicable in another plant. On the other hand, a poorly maintained or loose system of methods and time standards may be worse than none at all. Loose standards sometimes retard improvement in productivity by workers and may result in endless labor difficulties and the filing of many formal grievances protesting the accuracy of standards.

The number of machines required can be determined after a detailed process chart, the system capacity, individual machine capacities, and a set of time standards are known. Again, the determination differs somewhat for the functional or product-oriented processes and so we shall examine them separately.

D. Design of Product-Oriented Processes

Our discussion of the design of product-oriented processes will be described in three parts, the determination of the number of machines, the layout, and the specification of the amount of inventory space to provide between stages.

I. CAPACITY AND NUMBER OF MACHINES FOR A PRODUCT-ORIENTED SYSTEM

a. Introduction

In a product-oriented system, the total capacity quite closely specifies the number of machines, given the size of each machine. For most equipment, only certain capacities are available in standard models. The largest model is

Table 4-3 Task Performance Times (in minutes)[a]

Task	Predetermined Motion, Time System A			Predetermined Motion, Time System B			Stopwatch Time Study		
	Normal Time	Allowance Factor (%)	Standard Time	Normal Time	Allowance Factor (%)	Standard Time	Normal Time	Allowance Factor (%)	Standard Time
1	.0569	122	.0694	.0456	122	.0511	.0499	117	.0584
2	.0618	129	.0797	.0622	113	.0703	.0620	126	.0781
3	.0615	122	.0750	.0538	114	.0613	.0576	120	.0691
4	.0744	129	.0960	.0622	115	.0715	.0688	128	.0881
5	.0347	117	.0406	.0447	112	.0501	.0513	117	.0600
6	.0476	126	.0600	.0602	113	.0680	.0584	126	.0736

[a]From Nicholas J. Aquilano, "A Physiological Evaluation of Time Standard for Strenuous Work as Set by Stopwatch Time Study and Two Predetermined Motion Time Data Systems," *The Journal of Industrial Engineering*, XIX, No. 9 (Sept. 1968), 427. Courtesy of the American Institute of Industrial Engineers, Inc.

usually cheapest per unit of capacity. Obviously, about 10 separators with a capacity of 10,000 gallons per hour are needed to process 100,000 gallons per hour. However, there are a few additional points to be considered. In most systems the capacity in the early stages of the process must be higher than the output capacity because of losses in processing. Even on an assembly line, defectives are produced and taken off the line. An increased capacity is needed at the front end to achieve the 100,000 gallons per hour of finished product.

In addition, there will undoubtedly be short-run fluctuations in the rate at which the process is operated due to breakdowns of equipment along the line. If more than just enough capacity is available at each stage, it may be possible to operate the remaining equipment faster and cancel out the effect of the breakdowns. Alternatively, spare equipment is often installed in parallel in case of breakdowns. In the preceding example, 11 separators might be installed so that a breakdown can be handled merely be switching some of the flow to the spare separator.

Finally, there are almost always long-run fluctuations in demand around the designed capacity. For example, there may be seasonal variation in demand. An inventory of the finished product could be accumulated during the slow season, as discussed in Chap. 6, but often it will be more economical to provide extra capacity so that the output can be enlarged during periods of heavy demand. This trade-off can be determined by comparing the investment in equipment with the investment in inventory, as discussed in Chap. 6 and 7, or the total cost comparison of Chap. 2 can be applied.

Solution techniques for each of the first two of these problems will be discussed briefly in the following paragraphs, since these problems are more related to production management than to the engineering design of the equipment.

b. Estimation of the Effect of Process Losses

Sometimes the capacity of each stage in the entire process is designed to exactly match the output capacity. In some instances this practice has a severe effect on actual output because it turns out that there are losses in the process. If these unforeseen losses do occur, the capacity at the front end of the process has to be increased at great cost in order to reach planned output. A similar problem occurs in chemical plant design when a distillation tower, which is a separation device, is designed to run at a given reflux or recirculation rate in a manner similar to the recycle streams of Fig. 4-1. Sometimes it turns out that the required purity of separation cannot be achieved without increasing the reflux stream or the amount of recirculation. The increasing of the recirculation drastically cuts the output capacity.

Of course, any process should be designed to operate with a minimum of losses, but even these minimal losses must be accounted for in the design of

Stage

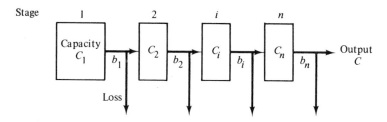

Figure 4-2.   Multistage process with losses.

capacity at each stage. The method described in Fig. 4-2 is simply a stagewise application of algebra. If the losses, b_i, as a percentage at each of the n stages are known, the capacity at each stage must be equal to the final output divided by the product of $1 - b_i$ for all stages downstream from that stage.

If the process can be represented by Fig. 4-2, the capacity at each stage, C_i, can be represented as

$$C_i = C \div \prod_{j=i+1}^{n} (1 - b_j). \tag{4-1}$$

c. Estimation of the Effect of Short-Run Fluctuations

Suppose that a multistage process such as that shown in Fig. 4-3 is to be operated at output capacity C. Then if the failure probabilities of the operating equipment units, y_i, are low and if adequate inventory storage is maintained between operating units, how much operating capacity is needed in each unit? The answer can easily be seen for the last unit. Installed capacity, C_3, must be $C/1 - y_3$ to make up for the period when the equipment has failed. The inventory between stages and the low rate of failure keep each unit independent so that the same formula would hold for each piece of equipment and its failure probability. If there were no inventory, it would be necessary for the downstream units to increase their production rate to compensate for

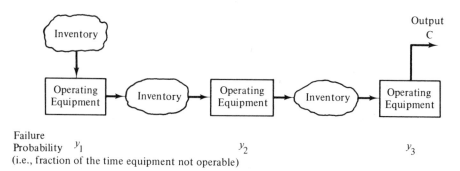

Figure 4-3.   Multistage process with inventories.

all interruptions in units, or

$$C_i = \frac{C}{1 - \prod_{j=1}^{n} y_j}.$$ (4-2)

We shall discuss design and operation of inventory between stages in Sec. V. Since inventory space is usually much cheaper than equipment capacity, the general policy is to provide enough inventory to keep the stages largely independent.

In the calculation above we have assumed that the capacity of one stage is infinitely variable and is one piece of equipment. If a parallel arrangement of n pieces of equipment is necessary to reach the desired capacity, it may be more economical to have an extra equipment unit held as a backup for the others. One alternative is to have each unit have its capacity increased to $C/1 - y$ to provide extra capacity in the event that one unit fails. Total equipment cost will be less with one unit as a backup if $y \div 1 - y$ is greater than $1/n$. If, on the other hand both y and n are small, it may not be necessary to assume that each machine will make up for its own failures but that all machines can contribute to handling the flow when a failure occurs. Then the best way to handle anticipated failure is merely to increase the capacity of each unit to

$$C_i = \frac{1}{n} \frac{C}{1 - y}.$$

Later we shall address reliability and queuing as probabalistic processes, but often their treatment will give simple solutions within the accuracy of the data, as described by Newell in his chapter on fluid approximations [2].

II. BUDGET-CONSTRAINED DESIGN

As described in the previous section, the usual sequence of decisions is to determine the required number of units of equipment from the designed capacity, allowing for losses. Sometimes, however, the designer is given a budget constraint, say a limit on capital expenditures, and told to design a plant which has the largest possible output. In addition, a given level of technology must be specified. In this case it is not obvious what capacity is required at each stage. We shall discuss a simple example and introduce a dynamic programming technique of Howard [3], which will also be useful in a later section.

The four-stage production system with two inputs is outlined in Fig. 4-4 and Table 4-4, in which we ignore losses. Note that although stages 1 and 2 both modify input B, process 2 uses some existing equipment which can be

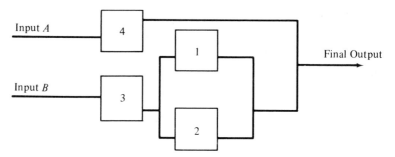

Figure 4-4.   Flow diagram for example and output for each stage.

Table 4-4   Processing Capability of Stages as a Function of Investment, K_i (units/day)

Stage	Investment in Stage Capacity (millions of $)							
	$1	$2	$3	$4	$5	$6	$7	$8
1	1	2	3	4	5	6	7	8
2	0	5	5	5	10	10	10	10
3	5	8	10	11	12	12	12	12
4	2	4	8	10	11	12	12	12

modified at a cost of $2 million for 5 units of output and $5 million for 10 units. Note that quite different cost functions are represented.

To solve the problem of maximizing output for our budget of $8 million of investment, we could guess at an output and cost it out and then juggle the numbers around attempting to find the maximum. By simple observation we can see right away that it cannot be more than 10 and that it is more than 4.

A more efficient way of examining the combinations is dynamic programming. We define X_i, the amount spent on all stages up to the ith stage as the state variable and $f_i(X_i)$ as the output of the system up through stage i.

The capacity of a stage is $k_i(d_i)$. We look at the alternatives at each stage, starting with stage 1, and identify the best decision d_i^*. It gives the highest capacity for the system up through that stage and must be determined for each spending level within the budget. As we move to the next stage, we need only consider d_i^* for each spending level.

The only trick is to observe the effect of the series and parallel arrangement of facilities. If the facilities are in parallel for an input, the capacity is the sum of the two facilities. If facilities are in series for an input, the capacity is the minimum of the two capacities, which is also the effect at the junction of the two inputs. Mathematically we maximize the total output capacity for each stage, with the form depending on the flow diagram. The maximum output for each stage is

$$f_1(X_1) = \max_{0 \le d_1 \le X_1} k_1(d_1) = k_1(X_1),$$

which is simple, but

$$f_2(X_2) = \max_{0 \le d_2 \le X_2} [k_2(d_2) + f_1(X_1)]$$

because of the parallel position of 1 and 2 and

$$f_3(X_3) = \max_{0 \le d_3 \le X_3} \min [k_3(d_3), f_2(X_2)]$$

because of series position and finally

$$f_4(X_4) = \max \min [k_4(d_4), f_3(X_3)]$$

because the inputs come together for final output.

The solution of these equations can be found as follows: First, consider facility 1, which has the simple linear investment function. At this point we could spend any of the $8 million on this facility and receive 1 unit per day for each million, which gives us d_i^* as a function of X_i. Next consider facility 2. We consider each possible spending level on the two stages and compare the *sum* of their outputs because of the parallel processes. We can limit computation by observing that capacities of 5 and 10 costing $2 and $6 million are the only nonzero choices. We can check the zero choice merely be comparing the sum against $f_1(X_2)$, i.e., making all the investment for the first two stages in facility 1. See Table 4-5. It is also necessary to check that spending the $6 million all on facility 2 would have higher capacity than spending some on facility 1. The last column in Table 4-5 performs this check. Making the calculation of X_2 in facility 1, the last row, and comparing the last two rows, we see that d_2^*, the optimal decision for the investment of up to $8 million as

Table 4-5 $f_2(X_2) = \max k_2(d_2) + f_1(X_1)$

	1	*2*	*3*	*4*	*5*	*6*	*7*	*Check*
				Alternatives				
Investment in facility 2, d_2	2	2	2	2	6	6	6	2
Total investment, X_2	2	3	4	5	6	7	8	6
Investment in facility 1, $X_1 = X_2 - d_2$	0	1	2	3	0	1	2	4
Capacity of facility 1, $f_1(X_1)$	0	1	2	3	0	1	2	4
Capacity of facility 2, $k_2(d_2)$	5	5	5	5	10	10	10	5
Sum of capacity, $f_2(x_2) = k_2(d_2) + f_1(X_1)$	5	6	7	8	10	11	12	9
Capacity if X_2 in facility 1, $f_1(X_2)$	2	3	4	5	6	7	8	6

per second row, is given in the top row of Table 4-5. The optimal capacity $f_2(X_2)$ is the second to last row. We next move to stage 3 and put down the decisions for investment in facility 3 that are possible with up to \$8. See Table 4-6. We now determine system capacity by picking the minimum of $f_2(X_2)$ or

Table 4-6 $f_3(X_3) = \max(\min[k_3(d_3), f_2(X_2)])$

							Alternatives								
d_3	1	1	1	1	2	2	2	2	2	2	3	3	3	3	3	3
X_3	1	2	3	4	2	3	4	5	6	7	3	4	5	6	7	8
$X_2 = d_2^*$	0	1	2	3	0	1	2	3	4	5	0	1	2	3	4	4
$f_2(X_2)$	0	1	5	6	0	1	5	6	7	8	0	1	5	6	7	8
$k_3(d_3)$	5	5	5	5	8	8	8	8	8	8	10	10	10	10	10	10
$\min[f_2(X_2), k_3(d_3)]$	0*	1*	5*	5a*	0	1	5a*	6*	7*	8*	0	1	5	6	7	8*

aTie.

$k_3(d_3)$. In the first row we end each sequence of d_3 values when X_3 reaches 8 or when $f_2(X_2)$ equals or exceeds $k_3(d_3)$. A final step of this stage is to note the maximum value of the minimum for each value of X_3. These minimums are marked with a star and are d_3^* for X_3.

The final stage is to consider facility 4. We can safely assume that $X_4 = 8$ because capacity is a monotone increasing function of investment. We list in Table 4-7 the possible d_4 and the corresponding value of X_3. The maximum

Table 4-7 $f_4(X_4) = \max(\min[f_3(X_3), k_4(X_4)])$

				Alternatives					
d_4	0	1	2	3	4	5	6	7	8
$X_3 = d_3^*$	8	7	6	5	4	3	2	1	0
$f_3(X_3)$	8	8	7	6	5	5	1	0	0
$k_4(X_4)$	0	2	4	8	10	11	12	12	12
$\min[f_3(X_3), k_4(X_4)]$	0	2	4	6*	5	5	1	0	0

value is starred and the optimal solution is $d_4 = 3$, $d_3 = 2$, $d_2 = 2$, $d_1 = 1$, tracing back through the previous computations. The capacity is 6 units. It is interesting to note that the restriction on buying integer million dollars' worth of equipment prevents us from reaching a higher capacity, since facilities 3 and 4 have a higher capacity than facilities 1 and 2 combined. A finer breakdown of investment alternatives would allow a capacity of somewhat more than 6 units per day.

This technique will be used again later in our discussion of reliability.

III. RELIABILITY OF A PRODUCT-ORIENTED SYSTEM

Many product-oriented systems have a real-time function; that is, their output can be measured as percentage time available rather than, or in addition to, some volume of work performed or output level. Defense systems, communications systems, and safety systems have this property. We can call this the reliability of the system. If the system is made up of components which fail independently and if failures are Poisson-distributed, it follows that the reliability of a series system is the product of 1 minus the individual component failure probability for each factor. Systems can be made more reliable by decreasing component failure probability or by installing additional components in parallel.

Finding the optimal reliability of a system is almost impossible because the cost of failure is very hard to estimate. Consequently the reliability is usually specified as a design constraint, such as 90% reliability. Of course, higher reliability increases total cost since it will cost money to either add additional components or achieve a lower failure rate. If a given dollar amount is to be spent on a system, the optimal amount of reliability to purchase in each component and the number of components can be found by a stagewise dynamic programming maximization of reliability in a fashion very similar to that of the investment problem just considered. The only difference is in the $f_i(X_i)$ functions, the reliabilities of the system up to the ith stage, which for series components are

$$f_i(X_i) = 1 - (1 - P_i)[1 - f_{i-1}(X_{i-1})].$$

Otherwise the problem proceeds like the capacity investment problem under a budget constraint [4].

IV. LAYOUT FOR A PRODUCT-ORIENTED SYSTEM

Once the number of machines is determined, some overall considerations such as work flow and management of the facilities are in order. Here the basic idea is to design a general layout which will provide for a logical series of work stations linked by materials-handling equipment that will make use of building space efficiently. In general, buildings have the lowest cost per square foot when they are rectangular but are not extremely narrow. Consequently, the flow must attempt to conform to this shape. Several basic arrangements are the comb and fishback arrangements with machines feeding a central assembly line (backbone). Similarly, certain arrangements of machines at individual work centers make particular sense for space utilization or worker production, such as diagonal placement of machines next to the conveyor line or a circular pattern around a worker. This stage of the

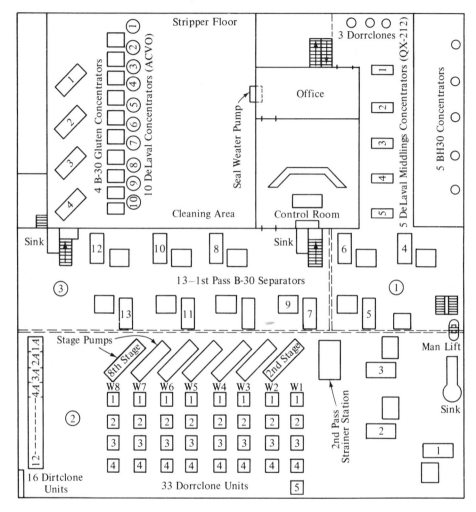

Figure 4-5. Layout for starch-gluten separation.

layout design is particularly subject to judgment and experience. As an example, the layout for the starch-gluten separation is shown in Fig. 4-5.

V. INVENTORY SPACE FOR PRODUCT-ORIENTED PRODUCTION PROCESSES

In an assembly line the placement of machines must be accompanied by determination of the inventory storage space between stages of the line. A queuing situation will develop at each work station unless the time to perform work elements is perfectly regular and there is no variation in speed of transfer along the line. It is desirable to have sufficient space to store the resulting queue most of the time. Of course, if the space required is too large, an alternative is to redesign the work elements so that the variability of flow is reduced. The reader who is not familiar with queuing theory should refer to queuing in Appendix E. We merely make two warnings at this point:

1. If a facility is utilized or busy more than 80% of the time, the queues may become quite long.
2. With utilizations of 80% or more, the queuing systems can require a very long time to come to the equilibrium for which results are computed in the standard formulas.

For these reasons production processes are often designed to be deterministic so that queuing is controlled.

The usual queuing assumption of exponential distribution of service time is not often directly applicable to assembly line operations, but the alternative is probably a simulation or physical model. As a protective factor against errors in the assumption of the form of the distribution, we have the ability of personnel on the line to work at an increased speed when the queue builds up. If an exponential distribution of service time can be assumed for each station and arrivals at the first station are Poisson-distributed with an average rate, p, the queues at each stage are independent. By setting up the differential equations for changes in the number of units in the system and solving, as demonstrated in Appendix E, we find that the probability of having n units in the queue at any stage, see Figure 4-3, is

$$P(n) = p^n(1 - p). \tag{4-3}$$

Suppose that only a 5% chance of exceeding the capacity is desired. Then the required number N of units for capacity of the inventory storage between stages is, by Eq. (4-3),

$$.05 = \sum_{n=N}^{\infty} P(n) = p^N(1 - p) + p^{N+1}(1 - p) + p^{N+2}(1 - p) + \cdots \tag{4-4}$$

$$.05 = p^N(1 - p)[1 + p + p^2 + \cdots] = p^N. \tag{4-5}$$

If the unit in service is subtracted and the equation is solved for N, the number of units of capacity needed between stages is

$$N = \frac{\log .05}{\log p} - 1. \tag{4-6}$$

The analysis above assumes that each inventory stage in the assembly line is independent. A phenomenon called blocking may occur when the inventory space fills up. The machine producing the items going to the inventory may have to stop operation if the inventory is full. The machine must then stop accepting items. Then the inventory space feeding it will fill up and block the previous machine. This chain will continue until all machines have to stop. Obviously the probability of being blocked is highest for the first machine and increases with the size of the line. Blocking can shut down the entire line and reduce the production capacity.

Hatcher [5] has examined the increase in blocking going from a two- to three-stage production line. The added differential equations complicate the analysis of higher numbers of stages, but Hatcher believes that his general results are substantiated by simulation results for larger numbers of stages. For two stages the limiting production rate as a fraction of the capacity of the second stage is $N + 1/N + 2$, where N is the capacity of the inventory space between the machines. For three stages of equal capacity the fraction is down to

$$\frac{R}{U_3} = 1 - \frac{N + 3(\frac{1}{2})^N}{N^2 + 4N + \frac{5}{2}} \tag{4-7}$$

where R is the production output rate and U_3 is the service capacity of the third stage. Figure 4-6 gives the fraction as a function of N. It appears from these results that inventory space for 10 items between stages will provide 90% of rated capacity for a three-stage line under the exponential assumptions.

An important assumption in the analysis above is that the design problem can be considered separately from the operational policy. Unfortunately this general assumption is often made in design of facilities and often results in

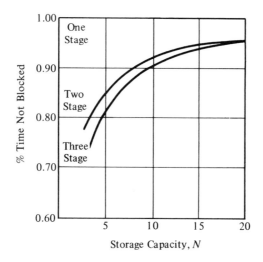

Figure 4-6. Blocking as a function of stages.

Source: J. Hatcher, "The Effect of Internal Storage on the Production Rate of a Series of Stages Having Exponential Service Times," AIIE Transactions, I, No. 2 (June 1969), 155. Copyright American Institute of Industrial Engineers, Inc. Courtesy of AIIE.

difficulties when the system becomes operational. Scheduling problems often prevent the full design capacity from being realized, for example. In this particular case of inventory capacity between stages, the designer has to assume that the system will be in statistical equilibrium and that steady-state probabilities will accurately estimate the number in storage between stages during operation. However, from an operational viewpoint there are additional considerations which will probably assure that equilibrium will not be a usual configuration. Both the foreman of the line and the operators like to have a large inventory available between stages to ensure that the following stages can operate despite a breakdown or the momentary absence of the operator at the previous stage. This is one reason for the observation of large piles of inventory between fixed positions in an assembly line. Similarly, if an assembly line worker is free to move, he tries to work as far forward on the line as he can, so that he has an "inventory" of completed work.

The operational inventories are built-up by keeping a worker on his station when the line is shut down or simply by the operator working at a faster than normal pace. The problem the designer faces is either to disregard the operational policies or to try to allow extra capacity. This is a fairly general problem. In this particular case it would appear likely that if operations are flexible enough to permit the build-up of inventories, they may also be flexible enough to avoid creation of overflow of the storage. This assumption is not always true in the more general case of design versus operation. For example, inflexibilities in scheduling may not be so easily overcome in general.

E. Design of Functionally-Oriented Systems

We shall discuss the calculation of the number of machines and their layout in Secs. E.I and E.II. Space for in-process inventory for the functionally oriented system is exceedingly hard to estimate. It will almost certainly be necessary to provide space for one day's inputs and outputs at each machine. Additional requirements are a function of the responsiveness of the control system and materials-handling systems, as will be described in Sec. F. In addition, the aggregate planning system may even affect the in-process storage requirements. The best procedure for planning the inventory space would be simulation, as discussed in Sec. F.

I. NUMBER OF MACHINES FOR A FUNCTIONALLY-ORIENTED SYSTEM

For the functionally oriented system such as a machine shop, it is somewhat harder to get good estimates of the capacity and number of machines needed because there is not just one product with one flow and output. Instead there are many different products, some of which may not even be designed yet. We must estimate the work load for a planning period by product and size of order. The number of parts for the estimated work load can be computed from the bill of materials which lists the name of every part and the number required. The required operations and times for each part have to be obtained from the process charts and man-machine chart. With this information we can estimate the number of each type of specialized machine from

$$N = \frac{TP}{HC},\tag{4-8}$$

where N = number of machines

T = time required to perform the operation on the machine per unit of output

P = total production required, including defectives (quantity started)

H = hours worked per year

C = a utilization factor.

Fractions of machines are rounded upward unless the fraction can be covered by a previous rounding up of the same general type of machine.

The most difficult part of using the formula is the estimation of the utilization factor. This depends on such factors as (1) the degree of labor limitation rather than machine limitation on production and (2) the efficiency of materials-handling and job information systems. A full-scale simulation is one desirable but expensive way of checking this estimate.

One certainty is that utilization and other production factors are stochastic variables rather than constants. A probabilistic model, which is given in Reed [6], explicitly recognizes this fact in adapting Eq. (4-8) for determining the number of machines under uncertainty. The essence of Reed's model is to estimate the variance of each of the factors, the time standard T, the production quantity P, the hours H and utilization C. For example, C depends on the schedule of preventive maintenance and a random factor for the variation in the time for maintenance.

According to Reed, the distribution of the total variable N can be determined to be approximately normal with an expected value of essentially TP/HC. The variance can be estimated by combining the variances of the factors which contribute to the distribution; we estimate it as follows:

$$\operatorname{var} N = \left(\frac{1}{H_a}\right)^2 \left\{ E(m+1)^2 \cdot \operatorname{var} \sum_{j=1}^{n} \bar{t}_{aj} P_j + E(\sum_j \bar{t}_{aj} P_j)^2 \operatorname{var}(m) \right.$$

$$+ \sum_j \frac{E(N_j)^2}{Q_j} \cdot \operatorname{var}(P_j \bar{t}_{sj}) + \sum_{i=1}^{v} (M_i)^2$$

$$\left. \cdot \operatorname{var}(\bar{t}_{mi})[\sum E(N_j)]^2 \right\}.\tag{4-9}$$

The first two terms are the variances for operation time. The last two terms are for setup and maintenance. The subscript a signifies average value.

The explanation of the notation and a set of values from Reed's example are given in Table 4-8. The subscripts s and m are mnemonics.

Table 4-8   Notation and Input Values for Reed's Example

Variable	Value
$\bar{t}_{a1}$, average operating time for operation 1	0.0185 hour
t_{a2}, average operating time for operation 2	0.0314 hour
t_{a3}, average operating time for operation 3	0.0129 hour
$E(t_{sj})$, expected setup time for operation j	2.145 hours
$E(t_{m1})$, lubrication time	0.034 hour
$E(t_{m2})$, electrical inspection time	1.308 hours
$E(t_{m3})$, mechanical inspection time	2.262 hours
M_1, number of lubrications per year	250
M_2, number of electrical inspections per year	4
M_3, number of mechanical inspections per year	4
m, ratio of maintenance to operation hours	0.14
var(m), variance of M	0.04
var $\sum_{j=1}^{n} (\bar{t}_{aj}P_j) = 344{,}379 + 886{,}485 + 146{,}012$	1,376,876
$\text{var}(P_1\bar{t}_{s1})$	416,576,670
$\text{var}(P_2\bar{t}_{s2})$	383,968,305
$\text{var}(P_3\bar{t}_{s3})$	365,052,970
$\text{var}(\bar{t}_{m1})$	0.00000196
$\text{var}(\bar{t}_{m2})$	0.0015
$\text{var}(\bar{t}_{m3})$	0.0046
var $(\bar{t}_{sj})$	0.00414
Q_1, economic order quantity of part 1	9,000
Q_2, economic order quantity of part 2	8,640
Q_3, economic order quantity of part 3	8,420
$\text{var}(\bar{t}_{a1})$	0.0000034225
$\text{var}(\bar{t}_{a2})$	0.95596
$\text{var}(P_2)$	12,180.86
$\text{var}(\bar{t}_{a3})$	0.0000016641
$\text{var}(P_3)$	19,278.438

The expected number of machines is estimated by Reed's formula (with the addition of a factor for the number of machines in the maintenance term, which Reed seems to have overlooked) as

$$E(N) = \left\{ \sum_{j=1}^{n} \frac{E(N_j)}{Q_j} E(P_j \bar{t}_{sj}) + \sum_{i=1}^{v} M_i E(\bar{t}_{mi}) \sum_{j=1}^{n} E(N_j) \right.$$
$$\left. + E(m+1) \sum_{j=1}^{n} E(\bar{t}_{aj}P_j) \right\} \frac{1}{H_a}. \tag{4-10}$$

The three terms are just setup time, maintenance time, and operation time. The example involves three sequential operations performed on one machine in batches. Operators are assumed to be 70% efficient on a schedule of 2000 hours. See Table 4-9. The deterministic formula with utilization of .85 would

Table 4-9 Reed's Example Calculation of Quantities
To Be Started through the Process

Operation	Standard Time (hr)	Expected Fraction Detective, p	Annual Requirement	Starting Quantity
1	.013	.04	—	317,210
2	.022	.025	—	304,520
3	.009	.03	288,000	296,910

estimate N as the sum of the requirements for each operation

$$N_1 = \frac{TP}{HC} = \frac{.013(317,210)}{1400 \times .85} = 3.465$$

$$N_2 = \qquad\qquad 5.630$$

$$N_3 = \qquad\qquad \underline{2.246}$$

$$N = 11.341 \text{ machines.}$$

For the probabilistic estimate we need estimates of variances. In Reed's example, a coefficient of variation, the ratio of the standard deviation to the mean, was estimated at .03 for maintenance and setup times and .1 for operation times. The number of pieces to be started into the first operation was assumed to be known with certainty. The estimates of N and its variance are calculated in Table 4-10 using Eqs. (4-9) and (4-10) and the data above.

With the estimated values for N and its variance, we can make decisions concerning the number of machines to install. Suppose that overtime will have to be used every day on which the number of machines required is greater than 12, since 12 is the number indicated to buy by the deterministic formula. Assume a machine life of 10 years and $8 per hour for overtime. At least 1 hour of overtime must be paid if any is required. The average number of machines required, 11.518, is .482 machine or .482/2.04 or about .25 standard deviation less than 12. Therefore slightly more than 12 machines will be needed on 40% of the days, using the fact that requirements are normally distributed with a mean of 11.518 and a standard deviation of 2.04. The overtime costs over 10 years would be $8000, perhaps enough to pay for an additional $5000 machine. This would indicate that another machine

**Table 4-10   Computations for N and Variance of N
for Reed's Example**

$$N = \frac{1}{2000}\left\{\frac{3.465}{9000}(2.145 \times 317{,}210) + \frac{5.63}{8420}(2.145 \times 304{,}520)\right.$$

$$+ \frac{2.246}{8420}(2.145 \times 296{,}910) + [250 \times (.034) + 4(1 \times 308)$$

$$+ 4(2.262)]11.341 + 1.14[(0.0185 \times 317{,}210) + 0.0314$$

$$\left. \times 304{,}520 + .0129 \times 296{,}910)]\right\}$$

$$N = 11.518$$

$$\text{var } N = \frac{1}{(2000)^2}\left\{(1.14)^2 \times 1{,}376{,}876 + (19{,}260.46) \times 0.04\right.$$

$$+ \left(\frac{3.465}{9000}\right)^2 \times 416{,}576.670 + \left(\frac{5.63}{8640}\right)^2 \times 383{,}968{,}305$$

$$+ \left(\frac{2.246}{8420}\right)^2 \times 365{,}052{,}970 + (11.341)^2[250^2(0.00000196)$$

$$\left. + 4^2(.0015) + 4^2(.0046)]\right\}$$

$$\text{var } N = 4.16 \qquad \text{Standard deviation} = 2.04$$

should be added, although one more machine would not result in zero over-time.

As another example, suppose that the facility ran three shifts per day, all year long. Overtime would be of little help in this situation. Management might specify that they want to be 95% sure of being able to meet the 288,000 units demanded. Two standard deviations or four extra machines should be obtained to meet this criterion. Of course, this simple example is somewhat misleading. It would often be true that the variance of demand would be larger than the variance of utilizing four machines.

Suppose that demand can be assumed to be normally distributed around 288,000 with a standard deviation of 5000. We could use the machine equivalence, 288,000/11.518 or about 2500 items per machine, to convert this standard deviation to two machines and add that to the 2.04 standard deviations of utilization and perform the same analysis as above to get a rough idea of the total variation and machines required. Essentially we have an expected value versus risk trade-off, as discussed in Chap. 2.

Once the number of machines is decided, only the detailed placement of the machines remains. In the product-oriented production system this is a question of arranging the machines within the flow process as discussed above. For the functionally-oriented system the decisions are not restricted by flow considerations and are therefore more complicated. We shall examine them next.

II. LAYOUT FOR FUNCTIONALLY-ORIENTED SYSTEMS

a. Formulation of the Quadratic Assignment Problem

The final step in the design of a plant layout is to specify the placement of machines or work centers within a general flow pattern or arrangement. Although many factors enter the decision, the basic idea is to locate together the machines which interact. That is, when there is a large volume of work that moves between the machines, as indicated in the flow charts, they should be close together. A wheel for deburring should be near the drill. For a functionally-oriented system many different flow patterns may occur for the different jobs. The layout should consider the predominant or typical flows. A good reference on measurement of flows is [7].

The minimization of the product of the distance times the amount of work flow is the basic criterion. This criterion is most easily dealt with in the form of a distance-amount matrix, which can be determined as follows. Divide the entire building, which is usually almost rectangular, into locations of about the size of the smallest work station to be considered. The distance between each location can then be specified using actual distance to be traveled or a distance weighted by costs. We shall discuss materials-handling considerations later. Consider the distance matrix in Table 4-11 as an example. A similar flow matrix can also be set up for the amount of flow between work stations. See Table 4-12. These figures come from the estimated work load and the operations sheet. These two matrices can be combined into a matrix of distance times amount of flow for each pair of machines located in any

Table 4-11   Distance between Locations (yards)

		Location			
		1	2	3	4
	1	0	2	6	1
	2	2	0	4	2
Location	3	6	4	0	3
	4	1	2	3	0

Table 4-12   Flows between Work Stations (tons/day)

		Next work station			
		A	B	C	D
	A	0	10	36	9
	B	19	0	4	4
Work station	C	6	2	0	6
	D	70	26	1	0

two locations. This is accomplished by multiplying each distance times the sum of the two flows between the two stations. This operation is repeated for all possible combinations of locations for the centers as shown in Table 4-13. Note that to keep the matrix small, we arbitrarily made the matrix

Table 4-13 Distance Times Amount of Work Flow (yard-tons/day)

Work Centers	*Location Pairs*						*Path Flow*
	1–2	*1–3*	*1–4*	*2–3*	*2–4*	*3–4*	
A–B	58	174	29	116	58	87	29
A–C	84	252	42	168	84	126	42
A–D	158	474	79	316	158	237	79
B–C	12	36	6	24	12	18	6
B–D	64	192	32	128	64	96	32
C–D	14	42	7	28	14	21	7
Path length	2	6	1	4	2	3	

symmetric. We shall refer to this matrix as the $a_{ij,kr}$ matrix, with work centers i and j first and locations k and r second.

The matrix would have four times as many entries if the distance matrix was not symmetric, since rows such as B-A and columns such as 2-1 would be needed.

The number of locations is determined by the size required for the smallest work center. The number of work centers is usually less than the number of locations unless all centers are of the same size. Dummy work centers can be added so that there are n locations and n work centers. For example, if only three work centers were to be located, the entries for any pair labeled D would be zeros.

The matrix above allows the problem of minimizing distance times flow to be formulated as a problem, called the quadratic assignment problem by Lawler [8], which is to minimize

$$\sum_{ij=\text{A-B}}^{\text{C-D}} \sum_{kr=1-2}^{3-4} a_{ij,kr} x_{ij,kr} \tag{4-11}$$

$$\text{subject to } \sum_{kr} x_{ij,kr} = 1 \quad \text{for } ij = \text{A–B}, \dots, \text{C–D} \tag{4-12}$$

$$\sum_{ij} x_{ij,kr} = 1 \quad \text{for } kr = 1\text{–}2, \dots, 3\text{–}4. \tag{4-13}$$

The $a_{ij,kr}$ are the distance flow matrix entries. The $x_{ij,kr}$ form a decision matrix of zeros and 1s, as shown in Table 4-14. It is in the same format as the distance work matrix above. Also, it implicitly gives the assignments for the

Table 4-14 Assignment Matrix $x_{ij,kr}$

Work Centers	Locations					
	1-2	*1-3*	*1-4*	*2-3*	*2-4*	*3-4*
A–B	1	0	0	0	0	0
A–C	0	1	0	0	0	0
A–D	0	0	1	0	0	0
B–C	0	0	0	1	0	0
B–D	0	0	0	0	1	0
C–D	0	0	0	0	0	1

work centers to locations because it indicates the paths. The constraints on the matrix are (1) only one 1 is allowed each row and each column; and (2) pairs of locations and pairs of facilities must be chosen so that the location of each facility is uniquely determined. The $x_{ij,kr}$ used here are a disguised quadratic variable $x_{ij}x_{kr}$. Although an undisguised formulation would be more powerful in that the second constraint would be more clearly stated, the $a_{ij,kr}$ and $x_{ij,kr}$ matrices are easier to explain. The matrix of Table 4-14 is a feasible solution with a value of 498, the sum of the diagonal elements of $a_{ij,kr}$. The quadratic assignment problem can be solved for an optimal solution by certain enumerative methods, but the computation of optimal solutions for large problems is currently impractical.

Two nonoptimal but "good" or heuristic methods are available as computer programs for solving the quadratic assignment problem and will be described next.

b. The CRAFT Solution

The CRAFT model, devised by Buffa et al. [9], is of interest for two reasons. First, it uses an interesting heuristic for solving the quadratic layout problem and then interchanges pairs or triples of work centers. The algorithm terminates when no such changes result in savings. Of course, the nonexistence of reductions in cost by pair and triple exchanges is not a gurarantee that changes involving the simultaneous shift of more work centers would not reduce costs even further.

Second, CRAFT has been fully implemented and is readily available for computers as a system for facility planning. It deals directly with the problems of unequal size and shape of departments. Figure 4-7 shows an example of the necessary inputs and outputs for the system. Note that CRAFT converts the distance between work centers (departments in CRAFT notation) and the movement volume (flow) into a dollar cost by multiplying by a matrix of costs per 100 feet per unit load. In some instances the meaning of the total

161

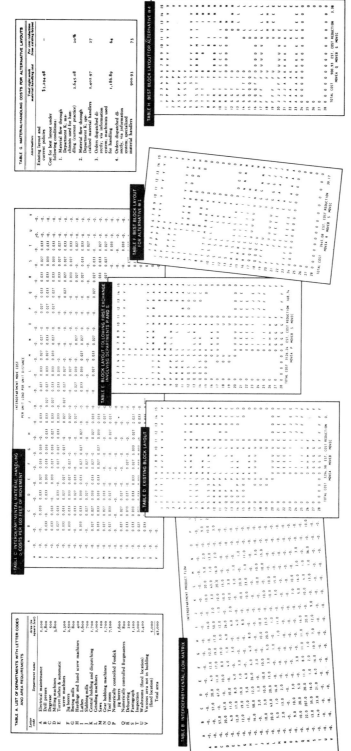

Figure 4-7. CRAFT data and output.

Source: Elwood S. Buffa, Gordon C. Armour, and Thomas E. Vollmann, "Allocating Facilities with CRAFT," Harvard Business Review (March–April 1964), p. 141. Courtesy of Harvard Business Review.

cost obtained by this method is not clear, as we shall discuss in paragraph d. Department V in Fig. 4-7, with a fixed location at the top, converts the actual shape of the building to a rectangle.

c. The Hillier-Connors Solution

We shall demonstrate a modified Hillier-Connors heuristic applied to the example given above [10]. We shall first determine a lower bound on the cost of the solution assuming that the first work center is placed in the first location. The same computation is performed for each work center in each location. The results are displayed in a matrix, and by a version of Vogel's approximation method, we choose the best center to be located first. The procedure is repeated until all centers have been located. The data for the problem previously described can more conveniently be displayed for this technique in Table 4-15. A method for minimizing the sum of the product of distance times flow *without regard to constraints* is to multiply the third and sixth columns in Table 4-15 element by element. This would be a minimum because the path lengths are arranged by increasing value and the flows by decreasing value. By a theorem from antiquity, this procedure results in a minimum sum of products. We use this approach in finding a lower bound for every possible first assignment, which may not be feasible.

**Table 4-15 Minimizing Order for
Example Quadratic Assignment Problem**

Paths			Flows		
Path Number	*Location*	*Path Length*	*Flow Number*	*Work Center*	*Two-way Flow*
1	1–4	1	1	A–D	79
2	1–2	2	2	A–C	42
3	4–2	2	3	B–D	32
4	3–4	3	4	A–B	29
5	3–2	4	5	C–D	7
6	3–1	5	6	B–C	6

Assume first that work center A is placed in location 1. Three paths are now partially specified. Flows A–D, A–C, and A–B will certainly have to be selected from paths 1–4, 1–2, and 3–1. Let us minimize the distance times flow by assigning them, respectively, in the order above, which is the same as given in Table 4-15. These three locations specify the fourth location in our simple problem, but this would not be true for larger problems. Moreover, as we look at the other paths, we can no longer be sure that the three locations already chosen have not restricted us to a nonminimizing set of locations overall. We therefore simply again assign the remaining paths and flows in their order from Table 4-15, disregarding any infeasibilities such as conflicting assignments for one work center. We are interested in a lower bound in this step, not in a "good" solution. The calculation is shown in Table 4-16.

Table 4-16 Lower Bound Calculation[a]

Path	Distance	Flow	Center	Product	Status
1–4	1	79	A–D	79	Partially specified
1–2	2	42	A–C	84	Partially specified
3–1	6	29	A–B	174	Partially specified
4–2	2	32	B–D	64	Not specified
3–4	3	7	D–C	21	Not specified
3–2	4	6	B–C	24	Not specified
			Lower bound	446	

[a]Assume that center A is in location 1.

Products can be obtained from the $a_{ij,kr}$ matrix, Table 4-13. The status column indicates whether or not the flow is partially specified in location. The calculation for A in location 2 would have paths with a 2 in each of the first three rows of the table instead of a 1. The calculation for B in location 1 would have locations with a B in each of the first three rows. Table 4-17 gives the results

Table 4-17 Lower Bounds for First and Second Decision

		Location			
		1	2	3	4	Opportunity Cost
	A	446	447	635	376	70
	B	438	393	425	476	32
Center	C	467	471	391*	534	71*
	D	380	415	519	400	20
Opp. cost		58	22	34	24	20

		Location			
		1	2	4	Opp. Cost
	A	499	473	391*	82*
Center	B	438	393	476	45
	D	393	441	426	33
Opp. cost		45	48	35	

of the 16 bound calculations. Optimum results are starred. The best choice for the first assignment is obtained by looking at the immediate opportunity loss or cost of not making a particular assignment. This is the difference between the least and next-to-least entry in each row and column. The "best" choice is to assign the element with the least cost in the row or column with the greatest opportunity cost. In the example, center C is placed in location 3. The bound calculations are now performed for the second decision. See Table 4-18. The

Table 4-18   Lower Bound Calculation[a]

Path	Distance	Flow	Center	Product	Status
1–3	6	40	A–C	252	Totally specified
1–4	1	79	A–D	79	Partially specified
1–2	2	29	A–B	58	Partially specified
3–2	4	7	D–C	28	Partially specified
1–3	3	6	B–C	18	Partially specified
3–4	2	32	B–D	64	Not specified
			Lower bound	499	

[a]Assume that A is in location 1 and that C is in location 3.

bounds are again collected in a decision table, Table 4-17. The best choice is to put A in location 4. One more set of bounds (only two) is calculated. The resulting assignment is C in location 3, A in location 4, B in location 2, and D in location 1 with a total distance times flow of 393, a considerable improvement over the diagonal value of 498. Nugent et al. [11] have compared CRAFT, Hillier-Connors, and their own algorithms. All appear useful for problems of at least up to 30 centers. The availability of CRAFT and its capability for irregular work centers are considerable advantages. Recently a good heuristic for initial solutions has been proposed [12]. Another algorithm is given in [13].

d. Integration of Layout and Materials-Handling Decisions

The formulation of the job-shop or functionally oriented facility design as a quadratic assignment problem is sometimes only a suboptimization. Modern practice has been to mechanize materials handling with equipment such as conveyors and fork-lift trucks. The quadratic assignment problem requires a uniform measure of effectiveness, such as amount of movement times distance or a dollar cost. We have worked with volume times distance above. This can be converted to dollar cost, as is done in CRAFT, by the use of some measure of cost per foot per unit moved. However, the cost for some materials-handling systems such as conveyors is not easy to put in that unit of measurement. The cost is often not linear since there are significant economies of scale with distance. Some of the equipment exists only in large discrete units, such as fork-lift trucks. One fork-lift truck and operator can serve many work centers. Moreover, changes in the location of work centers may affect different materials-handling systems in different ways.

A model which attempts to resolve this suboptimization formulation of the facility design problem is LACH, *L*ocation *A*ssignment by *C*ost of *H*andling, originated by Willoughby [14]. Since the costs of materials-handling systems are "lumpy" and nonlinear, a sequential evaluation is necessary to determine costs so that we can consider incremental costs. The technique of dynamic programming involves stagewise optimization. LACH uses dynamic programming to integrate the materials-handling and location decisions.

The integrative dynamic programming model must have two state variables, the locations left to be determined and a measure of the materials-handling systems chosen. Dynamic programming problems with two state variables can be attacked by Lagrangian methods, but Willoughby chose to avoid the enlargement of the problem by separating the decisions to some extent. He selected the highest-volume work center and examined the various materials-handling costs for that work center's flows between it and all fixed locations. The least-cost materials-handling systems for each flow from every possible location for the highest-volume center can then be established. Additional work centers are added and a least-cost materials-handling system is selected for each possible location of each additional work center. At this stage the incremental costs of materials-handling systems can be included. Finally, the combinations of work centers and locations are optimized by dynamic programming.

An example from Reed [6] for the addition of three facilities at four possible locations is shown in Fig. 4-8. Facility A can be located at L_1 or L_3; B at L_2, L_3, or L_4; and C at any of the locations. Five materials-handling systems

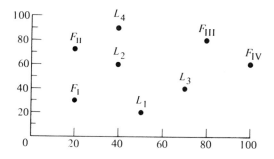

Figure 4-8. Location of existing facilities and available locations.

are specified: P, fork truck; Q, hand truck; R, electric truck; S, belt conveyor; and T, trolley conveyor. A method for calculating the costs of the systems on each possible route between departments is assumed. Not all systems are applicable between all work centers, nor do all work centers have flows to others. Table 4-19 shows the first-stage calculation for the selection of a

**Table 4-19   Materials-Handling Costs for
Work Center A in Locations L_1 and L_3[a]**

	\multicolumn{7}{c}{*Interdepartmental Flow Paths*}
Available Locations and Cost	\multicolumn{3}{c}{*A to F_{III}*}	*A to F_I,*	*A to F_{II}*	
	Hand Truck	*Electric Truck*	*Trolley*	*Fork Truck*	*Fork Truck*	*Trolley*
L_1						
Investment	1200	2000	2800	5000	5000	2440
Operating	2270	810	378*	100*	114	110*
L_3						
Investment	900	2000	1760	5000	5000	2440
Operating	1300	527	238*	150*	114	110*

[a]Operating cost includes depreciation. Optimal choices starred.

materials-handling system for the work center with the highest volume, center A. Each of the two possible locations, L_1 and L_3, is considered. The least-operating-cost combinations of trolley, fork truck, and trolley for locations L_1 to F_{III}, F_I, and F_{II}, respectively, cost $378 + 100 + 110 = 588$. Coincidentally, the same combination costs 498 for L_2 and is the best. These systems are starred and saved. They are one input to the next stage, the selection of the least-cost systems for each location for facility C. Note in Table 4-20 that facility A is treated as fixed and that its flows enter the choice of systems for C. The total investment cost is accumulated for later use in a measure of optimality. Note that no additional investment cost is specified for the fork truck because the fork truck decided upon in the previous stage for A to F_I can handle this work as well. This is the way in which a skilled analyst of materials-handling systems and costs can make the analysis integrative of both materials handling and location. If this analysis is done in a mechanical fashion without noting savings such as these, no real advantage will be gained by the dynamic program over separate analysis of materials handling and location. In Table 4-20 the least-cost systems have again been selected and starred. They are not the same in all cases this time. The similar calculation for facility B requires a three-way breakdown and becomes quite large with 178 entries. It introduces no new concepts. We shall present instead Table 4-21, which merely selects the least-cost system for B and adds up the

Table 4-20 Materials-Handling Costs for Work Center C in Locations L_2, L_3, and L_4[a]

Available Locations and Costs, A in / C in		C to F_{II}			C to F_{IV}		C to A	
		Fork Truck	Electric Truck	Hand Truck	Electric Truck	Hand Truck	Electric Truck	Belt Conveyor
L_1	L_2 Investment	0	2000	600	2000	300	2000	1025
	Operating	128*	288	890	315*	576	176	82*
	L_3 Investment	0	2000	600	2000	300	2000	700
	Operating	304*	683	720	293*	432	144	56*
	L_4 Investment	0	2000	600	2000	500	2000	1775
	Operating	176*	359*	1200	450*	864	288	142*
L_3	L_1 Investment	0	2000	600	2000	300	2000	700
	Operating	304*	612	1260	450	432*	144	56*
	L_2 Investment	0	2000	600	2000	300	2000	900
	Operating	128*	288	840	315*	480	160	72*
	L_4 Investment	0	2000	600	2000	600	2000	1450
	Operating	176*	359	1200	450*	864	288	116*

[a]Operating cost includes depreciation.

Reproduced with permission from R. Reed, *Plant Location Layout and Maintenance* (Homewood, Ill.: Richard D. Irwin, Inc., 1967).

**Table 4-21   Summary Table for Facility B
and Decision Table for Solution**

Location			System from B to			Total Op. Cost	Total Investment
A in	C in	B in	A	F_I	F_{II}		
L_1	L_2	L_3	Trolley	Belt*	Belt*	1290*	16,480
L_1	L_2	L_4	Fork	Belt	Belt	1438	16,515
L_1	L_3	L_2	Fork	Belt	Belt	1451	15,340
L_1	L_3	L_4	Fork	Belt	Belt	1566	16,190
L_1	L_4	L_2	Fork	Belt	Belt	1566	16,415
L_1	L_4	L_3	Trolley	Belt	Belt	1533	17,230
L_3	L_1	L_2	Trolley	Belt	Belt	1511	15,860
L_3	L_1	L_4	Trolley	Belt	Belt	1675	17,590
L_3	L_2	L_1	—	—	—	—	—
L_3	L_2	L_4	Trolley	Belt	Belt	1330	17,790
L_3	L_4	L_1	—	—	—	—	—
L_3	L_4	L_3	Trolley	Belt	Belt	1443	16,610

operating costs and incremental investment costs for each combination of locations.

From Table 4-21 a final decision on location can be made on the basis of operating cost including depreciation or by other criteria. If operating cost is critical, the location assignment is A to L_1, C to L_2, and B to L_3. The best materials-handling systems for each flow are among those checked in the previous tables.

A reminder that this method departs from strict optimality may be in order. The sequential treatment of the work centers is somewhat arbitrary and might well affect the results, particularly in a new design with no initial fixed facilities. All in all, it provides one of the most thorough structures for examining the problem to date.

F. Information and Control Systems in Design

I. CONTROL THEORY AS A BASIS FOR AN INFORMATION SYSTEM

The last but very important element of process design, which is often neglected, is the provision for adequate collection of information about the operation of the process so that it can be adequately controlled. The basic requirements are the provision of information sources (sensors) and the design of sufficient flexibility into the system that the errors detected can be controlled by manipulation of the system. Information is useless unless it can be transformed into control. Too many systems have been designed and constructed which would produce quite well if all inputs were exactly correct. In our imperfect world this perfection of conditions is rarely the case. Provision for measurement of speed, position, temperature, pressure, quality, quantity, and other variables must be available to assess the present operating conditions. Experience and automatic or computer control can then indicate changes in the control variables which will maintain the system or move the system to a desired specification. However, this can be done only if the system is flexible enough, that is, if some variables can be manipulated through an appropriately large range of variation. We shall first investigate control processes in order to provide a framework for the information discussion.

The general control problem can be stated as

$$\text{optimize } Z = \int_0^T F(u_1, \ldots, u_n, v_1, \ldots, v_m)\, dt \qquad (4\text{-}14)$$

$$\text{subject to } v_i \leq a_i, \qquad (4\text{-}15)$$

where the u_i are the state variables describing the system and the v_i are the controllable variables with control limits a_i. Often the control variables are simply rates of change of state variables, and a control limit merely indicates the limit on rapidity of change. The integral may be simply a total cost function over time. Once the state variables are measured, the problem is to indicate settings for the control variables which will optimize the functional Z. This may be done simply by providing an experienced control operator or by use of automatic feedback controllers in the process. The feedback controller may respond automatically with simple proportional control when it has been shown that a proportional change gives acceptable response in terms of stability. Linear control system analysis [15] is used to show such stability under proportional control or a slight variation, proportional control with reset. Alternatively analog computer analysis and selection of control settings can provide adequate changes to keep the systems stable, or digital computer programs using calculus of variations, dynamic programming, or Pontryagin's maximum principle may be in constant control of the process through sensors and control elements. In any case the designer must provide one of these means of establishing new settings for the control variables.

Finally, there must be physical means of changing the control variables of the process within the control limits, for example, increasing the fuel rate by manipulating a remotely controlled valve. The provision of the necessary sensor, computer, and control elements may add considerably to the cost of a system, but if they are designed into the system, the cost is much less than if they have to be added later when it is found that the system cannot handle the minor variations which occur in daily operation.

As a crude example of a control system of interest to production management, consider a production and inventory system where I^* is the ideal or lowest-cost inventory considering both holding and shortage costs and P^* is the optimal production level. Then

$$\text{minimize } Z = \int_0^T C_p[P(t) - P^*]^2 + C_I[I(t) - I^*]^2 \, dt \qquad (4\text{-}16)$$

$$\text{subject to the inventory constraint } \frac{dI}{dt} = P(t) - S(t), \qquad (4\text{-}17)$$

where C_p and C_I are incremental production and inventory costs. Production, $P(t)$, and inventory, $I(t)$, are the control variables, and sales, $S(t)$, is a state variable. The means for measuring and reporting these variables continuously must be provided, say a computerized perpetual inventory system and a production monitor. Euler's necessary condition for a solution to this calculus of variations problem is [16]

$$\frac{dL}{dx_j(t)} - \frac{d}{dt}\left[\frac{dL}{dx'_j(t)}\right] = 0,$$

where L is the Lagrangian function, $Z - \lambda(t)[P(t) - S(t) - (dI/dt)]$, $x'_j(t)$ is dx_j/dt, λ is the undetermined Lagrangian multiplier, and the x_j are the control variables. For $x_1 = I(t)$, Euler's condition gives

$$2C_I I(t) - \frac{d}{dt}\lambda(t) = 0.$$

For $x_2 = P(t)$,

$$2C_p P(t) - \lambda(t) = 0.$$

For $x_3 = \lambda$,

$$I'(t) - P(t) - S(t) = 0,$$

where $I' = dI/dt$. Solving these three equations simultaneously results in the following second-order differential equation:

$$\frac{C_p}{C_I}P''(t) = -S(t),$$

which can be solved easily for the optimal production as a function of sales. The same problem can be attacked by the maximum principle [17].

The example above dealt with a unified, continuous single-product system of few variables. Unfortunately most production systems are considerably more complex. They require far more measurements, which usually can be collected only at discrete time intervals. There are usually stochastic inputs and elements in measurement. Control of such a process is more likely to be based on experience or generalizations from a static situation. This may be appropriate for most systems, which are still slow-moving, but some sophisticated production systems now require almost instantaneous or real-time control.

II. INFORMATION SYSTEMS FOR CONTROL

a. Introduction

We shall discuss information systems on several different levels:

1. As an abstract portion of a control system.
2. As a physical system for transmission of data within a production process to facilitate decisions.
3. As an abstract system for organizing data and producing information.

Some of the great amount of confusion in both practice and the literature is caused by these radically different viewpoints of the same system. Mathematicians interested in the first viewpoint do not communicate well with managers interested in the second. The managers in turn have difficulty understanding the computer specialists who deal with the problems of the last viewpoint.

We have already discussed the basic control problem. Control problems exist through time. A control system must have the following information in the required time frame:

1. The status of the state variables, temperature and the like.
2. The value of the control variables, whether valves are open or shut, etc.
3. The output of the control computations or directions for changing the control variables.

One of the primary limitations on the control of many systems is the lack of ability of the information system to sense the environmental data, process it, and relay it to the control devices in time to have the desired effect. If the information system's speed is not fast in comparison to the change in the environmental variables, control simply cannot exist. For example, if the control system adjusts for an increasing temperature when the temperature has already started to decrease, someone is going to get cold. However, timely information for production systems is a difficult problem, as it is in the rest of society. There are, of course, as many information systems as there are production systems, but let us try to classify them and limit our discussion somewhat. The classification from earlier in the chapter, product-oriented versus functionally oriented systems, may again be useful.

b. Information Systems for Product-Oriented Production Systems

The product-oriented system is basically a flow system. The flow is generally either along conveyors or enclosed in vessels and pipes. Some of the information required concerns the nonflow portion before and after the main flow processing. For example, a refinery needs data describing the chemical content and quantities of crude oil which will be arriving or is on hand. Also needed are the amounts of inventory space in the storage tanks and the amount of the tank car and truck capacity to take the output away. The major cost of the information system in the product-oriented system is the elements monitoring the system flows and their characteristics. The refinery must have adequate fluid-flow measurement devices and temperature, pressure, and composition sensors. It must relay these measurements to the computers on a real-time basis so that control valves, input rates of catalyst, and heater settings can be changed. The entire rationale of a product-oriented flow system is to reduce inventory by achieving coordinated rapid throughput of a high volume. The information system must be designed so that it does not become the limiting factor. This may be expensive. The information system for a refinery can easily cost 20% of the total.

The fact that a product-oriented system is specialized is an advantage in the design of the information system. Positions and characteristics of the items in the system are well defined and limited in number. Major difficulties in the design, besides getting a production rate that is high enough, usually occur when flexibility of the product line is necessary. For example, the ability to make 40,000 slightly different automobiles on the same assembly line puts a tremendous strain on the information system. The system must provide a means of instructing every worker on the line exactly what variations are needed. This in turn means changes in the parts requirements sent out to subcontractors and a vast multiplication of the number of items in the inventory listings. Of course, the inventory system has major information demands in assembly line operation because of the rapid input and output of items. An accurate account of these flows is necessary or the line will have to be shut down.

c. Information Systems for Functionally-Oriented Production Systems

The functionally-oriented production system has different information requirements. First, the pace is usually much slower. There is more decentralization of routine decisions and so there is less relaying of information. Batch processing of the information is usually possible rather than real-time processing. On the other hand, there are at least two disadvantages or difficulties. Because the production process is much more flexible rather than specialized, it is much harder to say what range of characteristics the information system will encounter. Indeed, the information system must be flexible enough to deal constantly with new products, new raw materials and processes, new customers and suppliers, and new machines and skills.

Second, the control procedures and algorithms themselves are less well established, as we shall see in Chap. 8. New control problems keep arising because of the above changes. Scheduling is difficult, decentralized, and lacking in overall algorithmic approaches. When decision systems are not clearly defined, which is often the case in job shops, information systems are deprived of their real basis, the control framework. Then it becomes extremely hard to say what are data, what is information, and what is garbage.

A description of an information system for a functionally-oriented system, or job shop, is given in Figs. 4-9 and 4-10. Figure 4-9 shows conversion of the

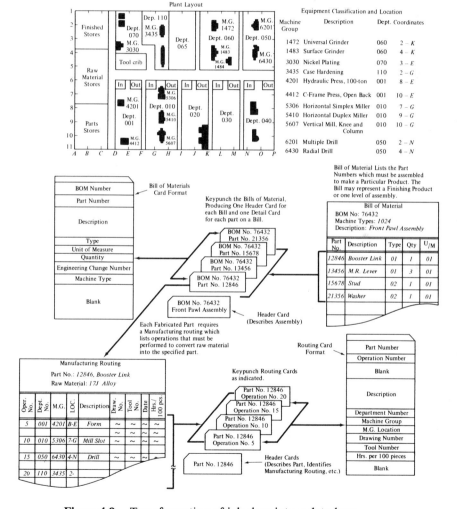

Figure 4-9. Transformation of job shop into a data base.

Source: D. B. Thompson, "Transaction-Oriented Information Handling Systems," Control Engineering *(Jan. 1964). Courtesy Dun-Donnelley Publishing Corporation.*

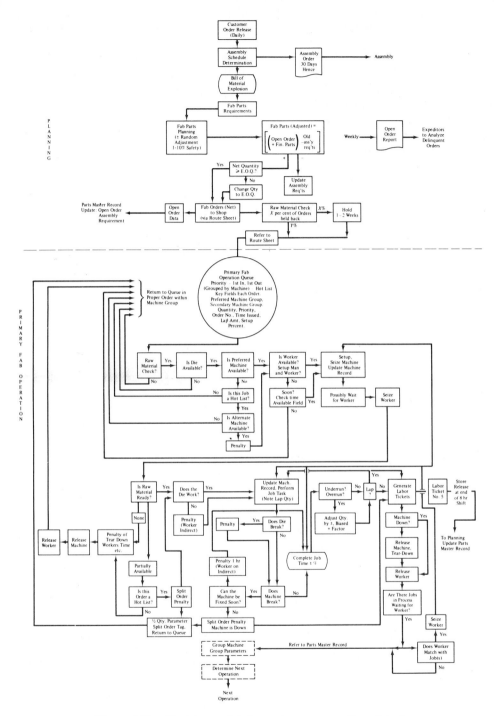

Figure 4-10. Decision and information structure for a job shop.

Source: D. B. Thompson, "Transaction-Oriented Information Handling Systems," Control Engineering (*Jan. 1964*). *Courtesy Dun-Donnelley Publishing Corporation.*

elements of the shop into data and an information structure. Figure 4-10 shows how the information flow would be used in the decisions for scheduling the work in the shop. A more complete discussion can be found in [18] and in Chap. 6.

Analysis of information systems has generally been approached through experience, intuition, and trial and error. Figure 4-10 suggests that simulation would be an appropriate tool for analysis because of the sequential nature of the decisions. Some theoretical analysis of desirable structures for information systems has been done, but only a minor amount has been implemented. We shall discuss this topic further in other chapters, particularly Chap. 6.

SUMMARY

This chapter has introduced the charting and time study procedures which serve as the data base for may of the quantitative models which follow. The important distinction between product-oriented and functionally oriented processes has been followed in the steps in design. These steps include charting, time study, number of machines required, and layout. In addition, the general topics of design control and information systems have been introduced. The models for many of these areas are well developed, but it is clear that these models do not cover all the creative aspects of design.

The models do illustrate the way the various problems of design interact, from the data base problem right through control.

REFERENCES

1. GORDON B. CARSON, *Production Handbook*, Ronald, New York, 1958, p. 12.27.

2. G. F. NEWELL, *Applications of Queueing Theory*, Chapman & Hall, London, 1971.

3. G. T. HOWARD, "Designing for Maximum Production in a Series and Parallel Network," unpublished working paper, Naval Postgraduate School, Monterey, Calif.

4. R. M. BURTON and G. T. HOWARD, "Optimal System Reliability for a Mixed Series and Parallel Structure," *Journal of Mathematical Analysis and Applications*, 28, No. 2 (Nov. 1969), 370.

5. JEROME HATCHER, "The Effect of Internal Storage on the Production Rate of a Series of Stages Having Exponential Service Times," *AIIE Transactions*, 1, No. 2 (June 1969), 150.

6. RUDDELL REED, *Plant Location Layout and Maintenance*, Irwin, Homewood, Ill. 1967.

7. WILLIAM K. HOLSTEIN and W. L. BERRY, "Work Flow Structure: An Analysis for Planning and Control," *Management Science*, 16, No. 6 (Feb. 1970), 324.

8. EUGENE L. LAWLOR, "The Quadratic Assignment Problem," *Management Science*, 9, No. 4 (July 1963), 586.

9. ELWOOD S. BUFFA, G. C. ARMOUR, and T. E. VOLLMANN, "Allocating Facilities with CRAFT," *Harvard Business Review* (March–April 1964), 136.

10. FREDERICK S. HILLIER and MICHAEL M. CONNORS, "Quadratic Assignment Problem Algorithms and the Location of Indivisible Facilities," *Management Science*, 13, No. 1 (Sept. 1966), 42.

11. C. E. NUGENT, T. E. VOLLMANN, and JOHN RUML, "An Experimental Comparison of Techniques for the Assignment of Facilities to Locations," *Operations Research*, 16, No. 1 (Jan.–Feb. 1968), 150.

12. HARRY K. EDWARDS, B. E. GILLETT, and M. E. HALE, "Modular Allocation Technique (MAT)," *Management Science*, 17, No. 3 (Nov. 1970), 161.

13. G. W. GRAVES and A. B. WHINSTON, "An Algorithm for the Quadratic Assignment Problem," *Management Science*, 17, No. 7 (March 1970), 453.

14. DAVID W. WILLOUGHBY, "A Technique for Integrating Location and Materials Handling Equipment Selection," unpublished thesis, Purdue University, Lafayette, Ind., 1967.

15. B. M. BROWN, *The Mathematical Theory of Linear Systems*, Associated Book Publishers, Ltd., London.

16. MICHAEL M. CONNORS and D. TEICHROEW, *Optimal Control of Dynamic Operations Research Models*, International Textbook Company, Scranton, Pa., 1967, p. 14.

17. C. L. HWANG, L. T. FAN, and L. E. ERICKSON, "Optimum Production Planning by the Maximum Principle," *Management Science*, 13, No. 9. (May 1967), 751.

18. D. B. THOMPSON, "Transaction-Oriented Information-Handling Systems," *Control Engineering* (Jan. 1964), 87.

19. BUREAU of NAVAL WEAPONS, *Reliability Engineering*, Handbook NAVWEPS 00-65-502, GPO, Washington, D.C., 1964.

20. IGOR BAZOVSKY, *Reliability Theory and Practice*, Prentice-Hall, Englewood Cliffs, N.J., 1961.

PROBLEMS

1. Suppose that your firm has bid on a batch of 4000 parts and that there is time to produce only one batch. If the process produces 10% defectives, how many parts should be started? The answer to this question affects capacity and design problems. If the number of defective parts is Poisson-distributed, Table 1 in Appendix G can be used to find the probability of any number of nondefective parts given the number of parts started. In addition you need the relative costs of (1) the penalty for not delivering exactly 4000 parts and (2) the cost of excess nondefective parts. This is similar to the inventory problems considered in Chap. 7. As an exercise, suppose that 20 parts are ordered, that the defectives are Poisson with $pn = .1$, and that it costs twice as much to be short a part as to have one in excess.
   a. What is the optimal number of parts to start?
   b. Derive a formula for the answer to part a.

2. Prepare a flow chart of the operations required to register at your institution. Note particularly any feedback of information between steps or as checking procedures. Obtain 10 pairs of bolts and nuts. Suppose that one operation of an assembly is to place the nuts on the bolts.
   a. Lay out a work station for performing the operation. Test the layout and modify.
   b. What accessories or jigs can you devise to help in this work?
   c. Time the rate at which you can assemble the batch of nuts and bolts, keeping track of the total number of times you have assembled them, and see if the improvement follows a learning curve, referred to in Problem 9 in Chap. 2.

3. By use of the formulas in this chapter, the number of machines required has a mean of 12 units and a variance of 16 units² in a functional shop.
   a. What number of machines are required for 90% protection against lack of sufficient capacity? How should this protection be defined?
   b. Suppose that if capacity is not available as computed above, the alternative is to subcontract, which results in the loss of a profit of $20 per hour of capacity lost. How many machines should be purchased if the hourly cost of a machine allocated over the appropriate period is $1? Assume that a machine has 2000 available hours per year. See Chap. 7 for a similar inventory problem.

4. Reliability theory is the study of the probability distribution of no failure during a given period of operation of a piece of equipment. For some electronic components the failure rate during their useful life can be assumed to be Poisson with mean time between failures (MTBF) of $1/\lambda$, where λ is the Poisson parameter. For a part the reliability is therefore $R = e^{-\lambda t}$.
   a. What is the formula for a group of parts in series if failures are independent?
   b. What is the reliability of 100 parts in series for 1 hour if the components each have a MTBF of 1000 hours?
   c. Can you derive the formula for parallel components?
   For references to this material, see [19, 20].

5. The bill of materials gives "the part that goes into" each subassembly and final product. It is therefore called a Gozinto graph or matrix as follows. An element of a triangular matrix a_{ij} gives the number of part or subassembly i that is included in subassembly or final product j. The parts are numbered such that if i is a part of j, $i < j$. See Fig. P-5.

		j					
		1	2	3	4	5	6	7
i, Part, Subassembly or Final Product	1	0	3	1	0	3	1	0
	2		0	2	0	0	0	0
	3			0	0	0	2	1
	4				0	2	1	2
	5					0	1	0
	6						0	1
	7							0

Figure P-5.   Part, subassembly, or final product.

a. Draw the Gozinto graph with nodes for each part.

b. Suppose that 8 of number 6 and 12 of final product number 7 are needed as output. How many of each part and subassembly are needed?

c. Show that if T_{ij} is the total number of part i needed for a unit of j, $T_{ij} = \sum_k a_{ik} T_{kj}$, where $T_{ij} = 1$, or $T = (I - A)^{-1}$, where the inverse is simple because of the triangular matrix.

d. This is a special case of the input-output matrix of linear activity analysis, Chap. 2. If there is a cycle in the Gozinto graph, the matrix is no longer triangular. This is quite possible over a longer time span since it may take ball bearings to keep the ball-bearing machine running.

6. An assembly line is being set up with an output to be 100 items per hour. There are five stations each with an expected rate of defectives of 5%.

a. Suppose that the service rate is exponentially distributed. What should the average capacity of each station be if intensity is kept at .9?

b. How would a decision on intensity be made?

c. If storage capacity (length of conveyor) between stations is to be determined so that there is only a 10% chance of not having enough space for the queue which develops because of the exponential service rate and the Poisson arrival rate at each of the elements in a series of stations, what should be the length between the first and second stations in units?

d. What assumption is made concerning operation of the system here? What would a good designer do to minimize the affect of this assumption?

7. A buffer inventory is desired between two production stations.
   a. Why?
   b. Suppose that management wants a level of confidence of continuous operation of the second machine of 5%. How should they have obtained this level?
   c. What should the buffer be if breakdowns occur randomly (exponentially) with a mean time to failure of 50 hours and if the length of breakdown is normally distributed with a mean of 4 hours and a deviation of 2 hours?

$$\text{Buffer } B = r \ G^{-1}\left(1 - r\mu\frac{h}{c}\right),$$

$G(1)$ is the cumulative distribution function
where r = production rate of first machine
h = holding cost of buffer
c = cost of idle time per machine hour
μ = average time between breakdowns for first machine

8. A model very similar to that in Problem 7 was studied for which the optimal length of the conveyor between two work stations was sought. What differences in assumptions were there and what differences in results? Assume no defectives.

9. Fork trucks move material on demand in a job shop. The mean number of demands for fork trucks is 1000 per shift, and the standard deviation is 100. A fork truck can perform 200 jobs per shift with a standard deviation of 15 jobs. The cost of having a truck available is $40 per hour and the cost of jobs not accomplished on regular time is the overtime cost of $10 per hour additional. How many trucks should be obtained?

10. A two-stage system is shown in Fig. P-10. Units arrive at a Poisson rate of 6 per hour. Station 1 has a normally distributed service time with a mean of 10 minutes and a standard deviation of 1 minute. Station 2 has a normally distributed service time with a mean of 11 minutes and a standard deviation of 1 minute. Queue 2 has space for only two units. If the two spaces are filled when station 1 finished the unit, station 2 blocks station 1.

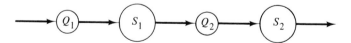

Figure P-10.

a. What is the average total waiting time?
b. What is the average fraction of time that station 1 is blocked?
c. What fraction of time are the stations idle?
d. What is the average number of units in queue 1?

11. An engineer has designed the assembly line shown in Fig. P-11 which has a special repair treatment for a random one-fourth of the items at stage 3. No defects are expected, and the arrival of items is nondeterministic. Naturally the engineer designed the capacity of stage 3 to be one fourth of the capacity of stage 1. What will happen?

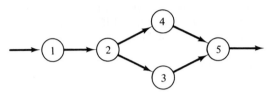

Figure P-11.

Part II

PLANNING
FOR THE
PRODUCTION PROCESS

In the following two chapters we shall discuss the planning system for operating the production process. The raw materials, personnel, and facilities of the firm must be matched in time over a fairly long range in order to achieve low-cost production of the best set of outputs. Cyclical planning lays the groundwork by providing the aggregate resources for the detailed scheduling which takes place in the control phase.

First, in Chap. 5 the equipment portion is considered since it is the least flexible of the resources. Methods for selecting from the alternative ways to produce a given output are discussed, as well as problems involving both the mix of products and the equipment to be used.

In Chap. 6 planning for the medium-range use of manpower and material resources is addressed. For nonrepetitive production processes or projects, some important new special techniques for the matching of manpower and resources to the sequence of tasks in a project are introduced. The aggregate planning function is the central direction of the production process and requires inputs from all areas. Through examination of the trade-off of fluctuations in labor or in cyclical inventories, we can match the output and inputs of the production process with the aid of mathematical programming.

chapter 5

Capital Budgeting

A. Conceptual Problems

I. IMPORTANCE AND CLASSIFICATION OF INVESTMENT DECISIONS

When we considered facilities and capital equipment in Chaps. 2, 3, and 4, we were often concerned with their technical capabilities. We studied their suitability for certain manufacturing processes, we studied their best location with respect to other facilities, we studied their optimal capacities, and we investigated their interface with the human part of our total production system.

It is easy to mistake these subjects as being concerned with the engineering efficiency of our productive facilities. The achievement of engineering or technical efficiency is not the prime goal of managerial decision making, as we discussed in Chap. 2. More important than engineering efficiency is the economic efficiency of the total invested capital. The economic or financial efficiency or return on capital is the main concern of capital budgeting decisions.

The important role that capital budgeting decisions play in the area of managerial decision making can easily be seen by looking at companies' balance sheets or profit and loss statements. The size of the fixed assets account, which is a direct result of previous investment decisions, will often be nearly three fourths of the net worth. In the profit and loss statements, the proportions of expenses for labor, materials, power, and depreciation are in large part direct results of previous captial budgeting decisions.

It is impossible for an enterprise or for the production manager to avoid capital budgeting decisions. Even if he postpones the decision to purchase a new machine and keeps using an old machine, this is a capital budgeting decision with the consequence of preserving inefficiencies for another year.

A firm may maintain the present status of its productive capacity by postponing all new investments, but if its competitiors improve the efficiency of their manufacturing facilities, its relative profit position will soon deteriorate because of its poor capital budgeting decisions. The company which passes up an opportunity for savings from a new machine must pay for the consequences of not buying it.

In Chap. 2 we studied the economic considerations connected with the selection of capital equipment and the degree of automation in the decision on productive capacity. We assumed that the costs of using capital equipment could be represented by multiplying the original price of the equipment by an interest rate that the firm would have to pay. The assumption was made that the capital equipment would last forever and taxes were not considered. In this chapter we shall relax these assumptions and provide formulas which could have been used in Chap. 2 under realistic conditions, instead of merely an interest rate. Also in this chapter we shall focus on the capital equipment decisions which are made on a continuing basis rather than decisions for a new plant or process.

Decisions on capital expenditures can be considered a two-step process. First is the selection of the best alternative from among those available. Second, we decide whether even the best alternative should be implemented or at what level it should be implemented. Actually our best models will identify both the relative ranking and whether the alternative should be implemented, but for those which only give the ranking, we must rely on the analysis of Chap. 2 to tell us whether the project should be undertaken.

In this chapter we are mainly concerned with the decision of how to allocate the available funds to different projects. In other words, how do we select from the number of potential investment opportunities those projects to which funds should be allocated in order to maximize the company's financial efficiency or return?

Most of these potential projects can be found in one of the following three classes:

1. Investments for the purpose of mechanization or modernization of production facilities, i.e., to increase technical efficiency.

2. Investments to replace or repair obsolete or worn-out facilities.

3. Investments to expand the existing production capacity.

It should be realized that many investment projects are combinations of two or three of these classes. We might, for instance, want to modernize and to expand a facility while we are replacing an old and obsolete machine by a new and more efficient one.

Discussion of investment decisions is interesting only if there are at least two alternatives from which to choose. In some cases these alternatives might be to buy or not to buy a specific facility. In other cases we might have the choice between numerous machines which could perform a certain task. In any case, three conditions must be satisfied if the decision is to be reasonable:

1. For each alternative, all costs, cost savings, additional income streams, and other consequences have to be considered. That means that we have to consider the future as well as the present.
2. The evaluation criteria and techniques or models have to be economically sound.
3. All relevant alternatives have to be considered.

In Sec. B of this chapter we shall study some of the major models that can be used for the evaluation of alternative investment projects. We shall see that there is no single "correct" method but that the decision maker has to make the choice between different techniques as appropriate. These models can be modified to suit specific criteria and situations.

II. COST OF CAPITAL AND THE TIME VALUE OF MONEY

The operation of a productive facility in which we have invested our capital usually costs money. We have to pay wages to the operators of the machines, we have to provide raw materials and power, and we have to maintain the facility in good working condition. This kind of cost, usually called *operating cost*, is not the only cost consequence of an investment decision. If we have to raise money from outside the company, we shall have to pay a certain charge to the provider of the money. This fee can take the form of an interest charge for a loan or for bonds or it can be the promise of dividend payments to buyers of corporate shares.

At first glance it might seem that the use of money that is invested from within the company is free. This, however, is not correct. If we do not use the capital for the specific investment, then we can lend it to other investors who would pay us a fee. In investing our money in one of our own investment projects we forego this income. Even if we decided not to give our money to investors outside our company, we could probably invest it in some of our other investment opportunities and earn a profit.

Because we always forego other opportunities of investing our money if we decide to invest it in one specific project, this kind of cost is usually called an *opportunity cost*. It can be estimated as the highest of the profits we could earn in investing our money in other projects.

In contrast to operating costs, which depend on the level of operation of the facility, the opportunity cost or *cost of capital* depends only on the ownership of productive facilities. It occurs even if we do not operate or use our facilities. The three factors which determine the total cost of capital for a project in units of dollars are

1. The rate of cost of capital or opportunity cost per time period.
2. The amount of capital invested.
3. The length of the time period for which we are using the capital.

The fact that invested money can earn profit over time is known as the *time value of money*. A simple example will clarify these relationships.

Example 5-1

Let us assume that we loan $1000.00 to someone who pays us 10% interest per year. In other words our rate of return on this thousand dollars is 10%. At the end of the first year our initial investment will have grown to $1000.00 plus $100.00, or to $1100.00. At the end of the second year our debtor will owe us $1100.00 plus the additional cost of using that amount for another year, or $110.00. Thus he will owe us $1210.00 at the end of the second year, $1331.00 at the end of the third year, $1464.00 at the end of the fourth year, and eventually $1610.51 at the end of the fifth year.

Our capital of $1000.00 has grown to $1610.51 within 5 years. Any investment in productive facilities would therefore have to earn at least this $610.51 profit, taking into consideration all operating costs during the period of operation, in order to be profitable in comparison to this outside investment. We assume here that no other investments depend on the approval of this investment project.

There is one other implication of the time value of money. If we want to compare different amounts of money, such as costs, profits, and investments, all the values should have a common reference point in time. We shall have to *discount* future payments, i.e., determine their value at the present or any other convenient time.

III. RISK AND UNCERTAINTY

Up to this point, it was implicitly assumed that all the relevant data required to conduct the analysis were known with certainty. However, everyone realizes that the returns, the costs, and even the economic life of very few investments are known with certainty for the next year, much less for the next 10 or 20 years. Therefore we count on the results of many investments *averaging out* to give us the planned return.

The chance that estimation errors average out for different investments is much smaller for estimation errors concerning the economic life of facilties than they are for errors in the estimation of costs or returns. Assuming that the overestimations of costs and returns are of the same magnitudes as the underestimations, we can expect that they offset each other to a large extent. This is not the case for errors in estimation of the economic life of an investment. If the economic life of some projects in a group of investments is 1 year less than their estimated life, they will lower the average discounted rate of return more than projects with the same dollar value would raise the average if they have a longer than estimated life by 1 year.

Solomon [1] prepared the following example to illustrate this fact.

Example 5-2

If the returns of a particular estimated 7-year, $1000.00 per year investment are subject to an error of plus or minus 2.5% and plus or minus 1 year, the maximum and minimum rates of return are 15.6 and 6.5%.

If we extend the possible error to plus or minus 2 years, the maximum and minimum rates are 16.8 and 2.8%. Errors of this magnitude do not appear at all unlikely.

If all capital budgeting decisions could be handled effectively without considerations of risk, the determination of optimal decisions would merely be a matter of mathematical calculation. Since we do not have perfect knowledge of the future, we have to employ approximations and "educated guesses." They will never be completely dependable, but we can make them more consistent by using formalized estimation methods.

Before further using the terms *risk*, *uncertainty*, and *certainty*, which are often used very loosely, let us define their exact meaning.

Certainty: Each decision alternative results in exactly one outcome. The decision criterion is unique. Under certainty we choose that course of action whose outcome maximizes the criterion.

Risk: More than one outcome is possible for each decision alternative. Both the outcomes and the probability distributions for their occurrences are known to the decision maker. As we shall see, there are different decision criteria that can be chosen. One way would be to choose that course of action which maximizes the expected value of possible outcomes. One might, however, in addition to the expected value, want to take into consideration additional criteria for the risk of the investment, such as the variance of their probability functions, the range as an indication of best and most possible outcomes, etc. [2].

Uncertainty: Each decision alternative can result in different outcomes, the probabilities of which are unknown to the decision maker. This is a difficult albeit a very common decision situation. Recommended procedures to solve this problem are still rarely powerful enough to aid the decision maker.

We shall pretend in the following two sections that all relevant data are known with certainty. After we have developed and studied evaluation techniques applicable to certainty situations, in Sec. D we shall investigate how these techniques and criteria can be modified in situations of risk and uncertainty.

B. Common Evaluation Criteria and Techniques for Investment Decisions

I. CRITERIA WHICH NEGLECT THE TIME VALUE OF MONEY

a. Nonquantitative Methods

Many of the methods still used by executives to evaluate investment alternatives are "fast" methods which are very easy to handle and give quick results by ignoring many of the relevant data and the time value of money. In many cases they even have logical errors.

The most popular of these methods is probably the *intuitive* method. This method substitutes management's hunches for mathematical and economic analyses. This method might be justified in some cases, for instance, in situations of uncertainty or if relevant quantitative data cannot be found. It can only be considered as a very weak substitute for quantitative, formalized evaluation methods because it eliminates completely the consideration for gathering all relevant data, formulating explicit criteria, and comparing different decision alternatives objectively.

Another way of selecting investment projects for approval is the very common *squeaky wheel* method. Here the investment projects are judged according to the urgency with which they are supported and according to the "noise" that accompanies them. The squeaky wheel gets the grease! Management neither requires a quantitative justification nor is it in a position to refuse the request, because of lack of sufficient data.

To the same group of "techniques" belongs the *necessity method*. One waits until the equipment is completely worn out and has to be replaced if the production is to be continued. This saves the analyst the trouble of gathering data for justification of a new investment. A threatened shutdown is normally persuasive enough to force approval of any replacement project. It should, however, be realized that the company very likely has foregone possible advantages over several years prior to the replacement.

Although it is obvious that these techniques are not adequate for proper evaluations of investment projects, there are other methods where this is not quite as obvious but still true.

b. Simple Rate of Return

The simple rate of return is defined as the ratio of net operating advantage to investment:

$$\text{simple rate of return} = \frac{\text{net operating advantage}}{\text{investment}},$$

where *net operating advantage* is taken to be the difference in operating costs corrected for depreciation and taxes for a certain period. This period can be a year, a period of some years, the useful life of the equipment, or any other time span. *Investment* is the initial or average investment, new or gross, over the same period. None of the elements are discounted. Correct comparison of two alternative investment projects can be carried out with this criterion only if

1. The useful life of all potential facilities is equal and the operating advantages and investments during these total operating lives are considered.
2. These operating advantages and investments are distributed in exactly the same way over the time span of consideration.

Even then the simple rate of return tells nothing about the *profitability* or financial efficiency of the two alternatives.

c. Payback Period

Another criterion is the *payback period* or *payout period*. It is the reciprocal of the simple rate of return:

$$\text{payoff period} = \frac{\text{net investment}}{\text{net operating advantage}}.$$

We are in a time of development in which machines may be technologically obsolete after a very short time because better machines have been developed. The products which we are selling now may be outdated within the next few months. In this situation many executives strive for greater flexibility of their productive capacity. For them it seems to be important that a machine has "paid off" after a relatively short time and can be replaced by another, newer, or more advanced machine without suffering a loss from having to sell or to scrap a machine which has not yet earned its investment. For this purpose the payoff period can certainly be used as an indicator of the liquidity of the investment.

For purposes of evaluating different machines as to their profitability, however, the payoff period can be used only if the two assumptions above mentioned hold. Example 5-3 shows why the payoff period cannot be used as an investment criterion in any other situation.

Example 5-3

Let us assume that we have to evaluate the two investment proposals shown in Table 5-1 and decide which of the two we should approve. Figure

Table 5-1

	Machine A	Machine B
Initial investment	$2000.00	$2000.00
Operating advantage		
Year 1	300.00	200.00
Year 2	300.00	200.00
Year 3	400.00	200.00
Year 4	400.00	300.00
Year 5	400.00	300.00
Year 6	300.00	400.00
Year 7	200.00	400.00
Year 8	150.00	400.00
Year 9	100.00	300.00
Year 10	—	300.00
Total operating advantage	$2500.00	$3000.00

5-1 shows graphically the cumulative payoffs of the two machines as a function of time.

We see that we reach the break-even point after $5\frac{2}{3}$ years in the case of machine A and after 7 years with machine B. The payoff periods are therefore $5\frac{2}{3}$ and 7 years, respectively, and we would decide to approve machine A because it has the shorter payoff period.

We would, however, completely disregard all payoffs that occur *after* the break-even point, i.e., that part of our operating advantages which makes our investment "profitable." In our example, the alternative with the shorter payoff period is the less profitable one, even if we do not consider the time value of money, since it "earns" only $550.00 after its break-even point, compared to $1000.00 in the case of machine B.

Summarizing, it can be said that the payoff period cannot, in general, be considered as an appropriate investment criterion because

1. It disregards all data after the payout period.
2. It disregards the time value of money.
3. It disregards differences in the economic lives of different investment projects.

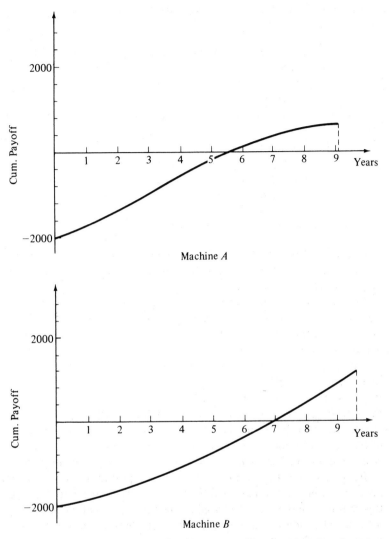

Figure 5-1. Cumulative payoffs of investments.

II. APPROACHES CONSIDERING THE TIME VALUE
   OF MONEY

Although we have seen the importance of taking into account the time value of money, it has not yet been shown how this can be done. We shall study this question in the following paragraphs. We shall arrive at a number of formulas which will be of great help to us in the subsequent analysis of investment decisions.

In accordance with commonly used notation we shall use the following symbols:

P = present sum of money at point 0 on the time scale, i.e., at the beginning of year 1

S = future sum of money at the *end* of the last period under consideration

R = uniform series of payments made at the *end* of the respective periods

i = interest rate, rate of return, or rate of profit earned or charged for 1 year's use of capital

n = number of time periods (years) contained in the time interval under consideration.

a. Discounting Factors

One indication of the time value of money is that a certain amount of money put into a bank account or invested into other projects will earn interest, return, or profit. If we do not withdraw the premiums earned at the end of the first year, then in the second year one's initial investment *and* the first year's premium will earn interest. This process is called *compounding of interest*. Contrast this with the situation where the first year's interest is withdrawn at the end of the first year. In that case we would only earn exactly as much interest in the second year as we earned in the first year and so we then speak of *simple interest*.

It is important *when* the earned interest is added to the initial deposit. If the interest earned after half a year is added to the initial capital after 6 months, then in the second half of the year the initial capital *plus* the interest of half a year would earn interest rather than *only* the initial capital. In this case we would talk of *compound interest, compounded semiannually*.

Because of the time value of money, compound-interest mathematics is normally used in comparing different investment alternatives. The rest of this chapter will therefore be based on the assumption of *annually compounded interest*. The factors can be used for other compounding periods if time is measured in these periods.

1. Single-payment compound amount factor. Our first problem is to answer the question, Given that we invest a certain amount P today, what will be its future worth S_n after n years at a compound rate of return of $i\%$? See Fig. 5-2. S at the end of the first year will be

$$S_1 = P + Pi = P(1 + i).$$

At the end of the second period,

$$S_2 = (P + Pi) + (P + Pi)i$$
$$= P(1 + i) + P(1 + i) = P(1 + i)^2.$$

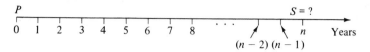

Figure 5-2. Single-payment compound amount factor.

At the end of the nth period,

$$S_n = P(1 + i)^n. \qquad (5\text{-}1)$$

The factor $(1 + i)^n$ is called the single-payment compound amount factor. There exist tables of these factors for wide ranges of i and n which can be used to simplify the computations. Appendix F contains such tables. If we abbreviate the single-payment compound amount factor by (pcaf), we can write

$$S_n = P(\text{pcaf})_{i,n}. \qquad (5\text{-}1a)$$

Example 5-4

To what amount S_n will \$1000.00 have grown after 7 years at a compound interest rate of 8%?

$$P = 1000, \qquad n = 7, \qquad i = 8, \qquad S_7 = ?$$

In a table of compound amount factors we shall find for $i = 8$ and $n = 7$ the factor $(\text{pcaf})_{8,7} = 1.714$. Thus

$$S_7 = P(\text{pcaf})_{8,7}$$
$$S_7 = 1000 \times 1.714 = \$1714.$$

\$1000.00 invested at an annually compounded interest rate of 8% will have grown to \$1714.00 after 7 years.

2. Single-payment present worth factor. If we know the value of a certain capital n years from now, we might want to know the present value or the present worth of that amount. In other words, we know S_n and we want to know P. Rearranging our compound amount formula, we get

$$P = S_n \frac{1}{(1 + i)^n} = S_n \frac{1}{(\text{pcaf})}. \qquad (5\text{-}2)$$

To avoid division by (pcaf), we define the single-payment present worth factor as

$$(\text{ppwf}) = \frac{1}{(1 + i)^n} = \frac{1}{(\text{pcaf})}.$$

3. Uniform series compound amount factor. In contrast to the last two

cases let us now assume that we are not interested in the present worth or compound amount of single payments but of a uniform series of payments. Figure 5-3 presents the situation graphically.

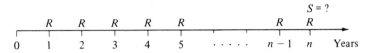

Figure 5-3.   Uniform series compound amount factor.

S_n is now the sum of the compound amounts of n payments R. Each payment R, however, earns interest for a different period.

The last payment R will earn no interest at all, since it is deposited at the time for which we want to compute S. The next to last payment will grow to $R(1 + i)$, the R deposited at the end of year $n - 2$ will grow to $R(1 + i)^2$, etc. The first payment, finally, deposited at the end of the first year, will grow to $R(1 + i)^{n-1}$. Thus

$$S_n = R + R(1 + i) + R(1 + i)^2 + \cdots + R(1 + i)^{n-1}.$$

Multiplying this equation by $1 + i$ gives

$$S_n(1 + i) = R(1 + i) + R(1 + i)^2 + R(1 + i)^3 + \cdots + R(1 + i)^n.$$

Subtracting the first equation from the second,

$$S_n(1 + i) - S_n = -R + R(1 + i)^n$$
$$S_n i = R[(1 + i)^n - 1]$$

or

$$S_n = R\left[\frac{(1 + i)^n - 1}{i/n}\right]. \tag{5-3}$$

The last factor is called the uniform series compound amount factor, abbreviated (scaf), and there exist tables for various ranges of i and n. The compound amount of a series of uniform payments can then be written as

$$S_n = R(\text{scaf})_{i,n}. \tag{5-3a}$$

4. Sinking fund factor. It may be that we are interested in the size of a series of uniform payments the sum of which will have grown to a certain amount S_n after n years. For this purpose we transform our uniform series compound amount formula correspondingly:

$$R = S_n\left[\frac{i}{(1 + i)^{n-1}}\right]. \tag{5-4}$$

The bracketed factor is now called the sinking fund factor, which is abbreviated (sff) and can also be found in standard tables.

We observe that

$$R = S_n \frac{1}{(\text{scaf})} = S_n(\text{sff}).$$ (5-4a)

5. Uniform series present worth factor. It is, of course, possible to compute the present worth of a uniform series of payments. Since we already know the compound amount of a series of uniform payments and how to discount a single amount, we can use a two-step procedure:

$$S_n = R\left[\frac{(1 + i)^{n-1}}{i}\right]$$

and

$$S_n = P(1 + i)^n.$$

Substituting,

$$P(1 + i)^n = R\left[\frac{(1 + i)^{n-1}}{i}\right]$$

or

$$P = R\left[\frac{(1 + i)^n - 1}{i(1 + i)^n}\right].$$ (5-5)

If we call the bracketed factor uniform series present worth factor, abbreviated (spwf), we can write

$$P = R(\text{spwf})_{i,n}.$$ (5-5a)

6. Capital recovery factor. Finally, if we are interested in the size of the yearly amount which we have to deposit in order to recover an amount P over n years, we can transform the above formula appropriately:

$$R = P\left[\frac{i(1 + i)^n}{(1 + i)^n - 1}\right].$$ (5-6)

The factor is now called the capital recovery factor and is abbreviated (crf).

By means of these six formulas we can now analyze any alternatives. They will all be one of the above-described situations or a combination of not more than two. It should be realized, however, that a series has to consist of *uniform* payments if we want to apply the uniform series formulas.

b. Economic Evaluation Models and Techniques

1. Uniform annual cost approach. The first evaluation approach which we shall consider has probably been the most widely used in the past, the annual cost comparison. It is based on the conversion of the cost of different

investment alternatives into an equivalent uniform series of annual costs using the miminum required rate of return as the interest rate.

There are three main reasons for the popularity of this approech:

1. In the past, most people concerned with the evaluation of investment alternatives were engineers, who are normally more familiar with and conscious of cost rather than revenues.

2. In many cases revenues are hard to determine or estimate for single facilities, or they might be the same for alternative machines; i.e., the type of investment in many cases does not influence the expected revenues.

3. The approach is easier to understand and to apply than some of the other, newer methods.

We shall illustrate the approach using the following example.

Example 5-5

Machine A costs $5000.00 and has a salvage value of $1000.00 at the end of 6 years. The operating cost for this machine is estimated at $800.00 for the first 3 years and $1000.00 for the last 3 years. Machine B costs $7000.00 and has a salvage value of $500.00 at the end of 10 years. The operating costs are expected to be $600.00 a year for the first 5 years and $700.00 a year for the last 5 years. The minimum required rate of return, i.e., the opportunity cost of the company at the present time, is 10%. Figure 5-4 represents the problem on two time scales.

We shall use the following symbols:

AC = annual cost: a uniform end-of-year series of costs equivalent to all costs over the economic life of the equipment

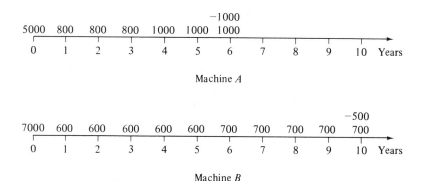

Figure 5-4. Annual cost approach.

P = initial investment
R = annual amount of a uniform series of payments
L = salvage value at the end of the economic life
n = number of years of the economic life
i = minimum required rate of return.

It should be observed that in Fig. 5-4 the salvage values have negative signs. They represent incomes and can be treated as negative costs.

Using the factors derived in the first section of this chapter, we could approach our problem as follows: The uniform series of end-of-year payments equivalent to initial investment minus salvage value is

$$R = P(\text{crf})_{1,n} - L(\text{sff})_{1,n}.$$

The present value of a uniform series of payments is

$$P = R(\text{spwf})_{i,n}.$$

Multiplying P by $(\text{crf})_{1,n}$, we obtain the uniform series of payments equivalent to P. Observe that the present values of the second uniform series of payments have to be discounted another 3 and 5 years, respectively, to be comparable with the present values of the first series.

Machine A:

$$\text{AC} = P(\text{crf})_{10,6} - L(\text{sff})_{10,6} + [R_1(\text{spwf})_{10,3}$$
$$+ R_2(\text{spwf})_{10,3} \cdot (\text{ppwf})_{10,3}](\text{sff})_{10,6}$$
$$\text{AC} = 5000(.2296) - 1000(.1296) + [800(2.487) + 1000(2.487)$$
$$\times (.7513)] \times (.1296) = \$1777.60.$$

Machine B: Proceeding accordingly, we obtain

$$\text{AC} = 7000(.1627) - 500(.0627) + [600(3.791)$$
$$+ 700 \times (3.791) \times (.6209)](.1627) = \$1818.50.$$

According to our calculations, machine A, the machine with the lower annual cost, should be bought if the revenues are not affected by the type of equipment used for production. From Fig. 5-4 we can observe, however, that the annual cost for machine A represents the expected annual cost for the next 6 years, while the annual cost for machine B represents the expected annual cost for the next 10 years. Strictly speaking, we therefore could not compare the two. Depending on the annual cost of equipment bought 5 years hence, the annual cost of machine A could be lower or higher than it is, considering the first 6-year period only.

To correct this shortcoming of our method, we have to make certain assumptions about future developments:

1. We could assume that at the end of the economic life of machine A we would substitute an identical facility for the equipment. This would leave the computed annual costs unchanged but would increase the total study period to 12 years. Now we would have to apply the same considerations to machine B, which has a 10-year economic life, i.e., does not extend into year 11 and 12. It is obvious that we would have to consider a 60-year period (the smallest common multiple of the economic lives of machines A and B) in order to achieve comparable economic lives of the two types of equipment. It seems almost impossible to estimate costs of alternatives so far in the future. We know, however, that the annual cost computed under the above assumption would be the same as our previously computed annual cost. If we assume that we can and will always substitute our worn-out machines by identical units, we imply that the annual cost computed on the bases of unequal economic lives of alternative projects will remain constant indefinitely. They could then be used as a proper basis for comparisons.

2. Another way to "correct" unequal economic lives of machines is to consider a *study period* which is smaller or equal to the shorter of the two economic lives. In Example 5-5 we could have chosen, for instance, a study period of 6 years. We should include in our considerations only those costs that can fairly be charged to this 6-year period. For machine A all costs mentioned concern the first 6-year period and should be included in the study. The annual cost will therefore be equal to the annual cost over its lifetime, or $1777.60. For machine B this is not the case; first we would have to reallocate the investment costs which pertain to the entire life of the machine:

$$R_6 = [P(\text{crf})_{10,10} - L(\text{sff})_{10,10}] \cdot (\text{spwf})_{10,6} \cdot (\text{crf})_{10,6}$$
$$R_6 = [7000 \times (.1627) - 500(.0627)](4.355) \times (.2296) = \$1138.90$$

As we would have expected, the part of the annual cost due to net investment cost (i.e., initial investment minus salvage value) did not change with a change of period under consideration. This implies, however, that machine B has a higher salvage value at the end of 6 years than it has at the end of 10 years, which can be found by

$$L_6 = [P(\text{crf})_{10,10} - L(\text{sff})_{10,10}] \cdot (\text{spwf})_{10,4}$$
$$L_6 = 1138.90 \times (3.170) = \$3610.00.$$

We would have reached the same result if we had predicted the salvage value of machine B after 6 years to be $3610.

Turning to that part of our annual cost which is due to operating cost and considering only the first 6 years for machine B, we obtain

$$R = 600 + 100(\text{sff})_{10,6} = 600 + 100(.1296) = \$612.96$$

This is lower than our original amount of $680.50, reflecting the fact that we consider only the "better" part of the economic life of machine B. This would lead to the lower annual cost of $1741.86 for machine B, which would seem to make machine B more favorable than machine A.

Our conclusion is that the study period approach is appropriate only if the operating costs are uniformly (or linearly decreasing or increasing) distributed over the economic life of the machine with the longer economic life.

There is one other feature of the annual cost model which we should observe: We neglected all revenues, assuming that they are not affected by the type of machine used. In this same fashion we could have neglected any costs which are equal for both machines. Looking at it from a slightly different point of view, we considered only elements which were different for the two machines. Common cost or revenue streams would add only a constant to the annual cost of both machines and would not change our result. This leads to two conclusions concerning the annual cost approach:

1. Only *differences* between the alternatives matter.
2. Annual cost can only indicate which of two or more alternative investments is more favorable in terms of the factors taken into consideration. There is *no* indication for the absolute profitability of an investment, i.e., for its return on investment.

If we want to know whether or not we should invest our funds in a single investment, we have to apply one of the methods studied in the following sections or compute the annual net revenue rather than annual cost.

2. Present worth or present value approach. Techniques based on the present worth compute the present worth of all future cost and of all streams for each alternative, or the present worth of the difference between the cost and the income streams of several projects.

Given that the annual cost of a project has been computed, including all elements which would have to be included in the present worth of that investment, we can easily convert the annual cost into the present worth. In some cases it will even be easier to compute the annual cost first and then to convert it into the present worth. This implies that

1. If we use the present worth approach for the purpose of comparing alternative investments, then only differences between the costs and the incomes of the projects are important.
2. The present worth comparisons have to be made over comparable time periods.
3. If the economic lives of investment alternatives are different, we have the same ways of "converting" them as we had using the annual cost approach. The only difference between the annual cost and present worth approaches, with respect to unequal economic lives, is that in the former we would correct by a uniform series of payments while in the latter we would correct the present value by one lump sum only.

Example 5-6 illustrates the present worth approach for two alternatives of equal economic life.

Example 5-6

Two types of equipment are expected to have economic lives of 5 years. Machine A costs $1000 initially, and it will have annual operating costs of $200. The salvage value is expected to be $200. Revenues of $400 annually are expected from the sales of the products of this equipment. Machine B requires an initial investment of $1500, incurs annual operating costs of $180, and has no salvage value at the end of 5 years. Due to superior quality of the manufactured products, revenues will amount to $600 yearly. The minimum required rate of return is again 10%. Figure 5-5 illustrates the problem

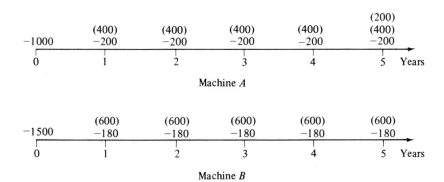

Figure 5-5. Present worth approach.

graphically. Numbers in parentheses indicate revenues, others are costs:

$$PW_A = 400 \cdot (spwf)_{10,5} + 200(ppwf)_{10,5} - 200(spwf)_{10,5} - 1000$$
$$PW_A = 400 \cdot (3.791) + 200(.6209) - 200(3.791) - 1000 = -\$117.62$$
$$PW_B = 600(3.791) - 180(3.791) - 1500 = \$92.22.$$

the advantage of B over A is $117.62 + 92.22 = $209.84.

In contrast to our annual cost example, we treated costs as negative amounts and revenues as positive amounts. A present worth of $-$117.62 for machine A indicates therefore that the expected revenues are not sufficient to recover our initial investment and the operating costs at a required rate of return of 10%. For machine B, however, the revenues exceed the cost by a present sum of $92.22.

A present worth of zero would indicate that the cost of a certain investment is recovered at exactly the required rate of return.

Because of the treatment of cost as negative and revenues as positive, the more favorable alternative is indicated by a *higher* present worth, in contrast to the annual cost approach where *lower* annual cost indicated the favorable project.

The main advantages of present worth computations as compared to annual cost are that

1. Single numbers express the differences between alternatives rather than series of numbers.
2. The present worth can be used to evaluate single-investment projects.

As an example of the second advantage, let us assume that you are offered the opportunity to invest money in a certain project which guarantees a yearly income of $500.00 for the next 20 years. How much would you be willing to pay for it? Certainly not more than the present value of that project, computed at the rate of return which you can achieve elsewhere (opportunity cost). In this case this would be $P = 500/(spwf)_{20,10} = 500(8.514) = $4257.00 if your opportunity cost were 10%.

3. Rate of return approach. The annual cost and present worth approaches used the required rate of return to compute either a uniform series of annual cost or annual operation advantages or to discount all future cost or income streams to one present value. We observed that zero annual cost or a zero present worth indicated that the respective investments recovered the initial investment over its lifetime at exactly the rate of return which was used to compute annual costs or present worth.

Rate of return methods are based on the following principle: They try to find the rate of return at which operating advantages and revenues recover all costs over the economic life of the equipment; i.e., these methods try to find the rate of return at which annual cost or present worth is exactly zero. This is then the rate of return achieved by the respective investment projects. If there is no salvage value at the end of economic life and if incomes and costs are distributed uniformly, we can solve the annual cost or present worth formula directly for the rate of return (i). If, however, the situations are more complex, the rate of return can be found only by trial and error.

Example 5-7. Rate of Return for Total Investment

The initial investment in a certain machine is \$4510. No salvage value is expected at the end of its economic life of 5 years. Annual operating cost are \$400 and annual revenues are \$1500. Let us compute the annual cost and the present worth of this project at minimum required rates of return of 6 and 8%, respectively.

1. At a 6% rate of return,

$$AC = [4510 + (400 - 1500)(\text{spwf})_{5,6}](\text{crf})_{5,6}$$
$$AC = -123.20 \times (.2374) = -\$29.20$$
$$PW = (1500 - 400)(\text{spwf})_{5,6} - 4510 - \$123.20.$$

2. At an 8% rate of return,

$$AC = [4510 + (400 - 1500)(\text{spwf})_{5,8}](\text{crf})_{5,8} = \$119.20$$
$$PW = (1500 - 400)(\text{spwf})_{5,8} - 4510 = \$117.70.$$

At a 6% rate of return the ACs are negative and the present worth of the project is positive, both indications that we are achieving a higher rate of return than 6%. The AC computed at 8% is positive and the respective present worth is negative. Recall that this is an indication that we do not realize a rate of return of 8% by investing in this project. The rate of return actually achieved for the suggested project will therefore be somewhere between 6 and 8%.

In this simple case we could find the rate of return which makes the present worth and the annual cost of the project equal to zero by rearranging, for instance, our present worth formula as follows and determining the series present worth factor which results in a zero present worth of the project:

$$PW = (1500 - 400)(\text{spwf})_{5,?} - 4510 = 0$$

or

$$(\text{spwf})_{5,?} = \frac{4510}{(1500 - 400)} = 4.100.$$

Looking for this (spwf) in a series present worth table in the row for 5 years, we would find that 4.100 is the (spwf) for a 5-year period and a rate of return of 7%. Thus the actually achieved rate of return is 7%. In more complex cases this direct solution is not readily available and we would have to use trial and error to find our rate of return.

Example 5-8

A project which requires an initial investment of $10,044 is expected to have an annual operating advantage of $1000 and a salvage value of $5000 at the end of its economic life of 7 years. What rate of return could we achieve by investing in this project?

$$PW = 1000(spwf)_{7,?} - 10,044 + 5000(pwf)_{7,?} = 0.$$

Let us, tentatively, use a rate of return of 4%:

$$PW = 1000(6.002) - 10.044 + 5000(.7599) = -\$242.50.$$

Since the present worth is negative, we have to use a lower rate of return, say 3%:

$$PW = 1000(6.230) - 10.044 + 5000(.8131) = \$250.00.$$

The present worth is positive and our actual rate of return will be between 3 and 4%, and so we shall try $3\frac{1}{2}$%:

$$PW = 1000(6.1145) - 10.044 + 5000(.7859) = \$0.$$

Since the present worth of this project is zero at a rate of return of $3\frac{1}{2}$%, this is the rate of return which we would achieve by investing in this project.

4. Alternative levels of investment. In all our previous discussions and examples we have considered the *total* investment of a project. In many cases, however, the amount to be invested in a certain project can be varied within some range. For example, attachments to a machine may give it certain additional capabilities.

In general, increasing the amount of money invested in a certain facility will not increase the benefits from that equipment proportionally. According to the law of diminishing returns, the additional return per additional dollar will decrease and perhaps eventually become negative. If we consider only the total investment project, at a specified level, we are able to compute only an average rate of return over all the incremental investments which could be identified. This average rate of return can be larger or smaller than the rate of return which we achieved on the last increment of investment.

To ensure a minimum required rate of return for *all* levels of the investment, we have to compute the rate of returns for the basic investment and for each addition to it. Only additional investments which achieve a higher rate of return than the minimum required rate of return are justified and should be undertaken.

Example 5-9. Additional Investments [3]

There are certain attachments available for a certain machine which produces a consumer good. They make the machine more efficient and add additional features to the product. The optional attachments can be added only in a certain sequence; i.e., the existence of attachment 1 is a prerequisite for the use of attachment 2, the use of attachments 1 and 2 is a prerequisite for the use of attachment 3, etc.

Table 5-2 shows the relevant data for the machine and all attachments. Table 5-3 shows the rates of return of the total investments at possible levels

Table 5-2   Incremental Investments

Object	Total Investment ($)	Extra Investment ($)	Annual Operating Advantage ($)	Extra Annual Operating Advantage ($)
Machine	2000.00	2000.00	400.00	400.00
Att. 1	3000.00	1000.00	620.00	220.00
Att. 2	4600.00	1600.00	940.00	320.00
Att. 3	6600.00	2000.00	1240.00	300.00
Att. 4	9000.00	2400.00	1500.00	260.00

Table 5-3   Incremental Investments

Object	Total Investment ($)	Total Annual Operating Advantage ($)	Rate of Return on Total Investment (%)	Rate of Return on Additional Investment (%)
Machine	2000.00	400.00	15.1	15.1
Att. 1	3000.00	620.00	16.0	17.6
Att. 2	4600.00	940.00	15.7	15.9
Att. 3	6600.00	1240.00	13.5	8.8
Att. 4	9000.00	1500.00	10.5	2.5

and the rates of return of the respective additional investments (attachments) only.

The economic life of the machine and each of the attachments is 10 years and there is no salvage value expected at the end of the economic life. The minimum required rate of return is 10%. Should the machine be bought, and if so, what attachments?

It is obvious that only the two first attachments should be bought since attachment 3 and attachment 4 do not achieve the minimum required rate of return of 10%. If there were an attachment b which earned enough to bring the rate of return on attachments 3 and 4 up to 10%, then and only then should they be purchased.

c. Difficulties in Using the Present Worth or Rate of Return Approach

Before discussing some methods which are commonly used in industry, we should point to some weaknesses of the approaches described above:

1. Allocation of costs and revenue to single machines. To use any of the above-mentioned methods, we have to know the costs of the machine and the revenue achieved by that machine. In many cases it will be possible to determine the costs caused by the machines. However, if these machines are part of productive capacity which consists of many machines and possibly even of many stages, it will be extremely difficult to determine revenues. These problems can be avoided only if the revenue of the capacity as a whole is considered, as is done when using linear programming methods in the last section of this chapter.

2. Nonuniform economic lives. Often machines which we want to compare using present worth, rate of return, or average cost techniques have the same *economic* life because they are performing the same function. Otherwise we have to make certain assumptions concerning the cash flows during the time in which one machine has to be replaced while the other is still running. This problem is discussed in more detail in Example 5-5.

3. Ambiguity of present worth and rate of return. In general an investment is "favorable" if the present worth of all its cash flows is positive. Let us consider a machine which costs $3000, has a return of $9000 during the first year, and incurs costs of $6300 at the end of the third year (demontage, etc.). The present value computed at different interest rates are

Interest Rate (%)	Present Worth ($)
$i = 0$	-300
$i = 20$	125
$i = 100$	-75

Whether the project is favorable or not obviously depends on the interest rate used for discounting future cash flows.

Let us now compute the rate of return for a machine with an economic life of 2 years. The cash flow at the beginning (initial investment) is Q_0, the cash flow at the end of the first year is Q_1, and the cash flow at the end of the second year is Q_2. The present worth is

$$PW = +Q_0 + Q_1(1 + i)^{-1} + Q_2(1 + i)^{-2} = 0$$

$$i = -1 - \frac{Q_1}{2Q_0} \pm \sqrt{\frac{Q_1^2}{4Q_0^2} - \frac{Q_2}{Q_0}}.$$

It is obvious that for

$$\left(-1 - \frac{Q_1}{2Q_0}\right) > \sqrt{\frac{Q_1^2}{4Q_0^2} - \frac{Q_2}{Q_0}}$$

and for

$$\frac{Q_1^2}{4Q_0^2} > \frac{Q_2}{Q_0}$$

two rates of return will exist. For

$$\frac{Q_1^2}{4Q_0^2} < \frac{Q_2}{Q_0}$$

the rate of return is a complex number. Example:

$$Q_0 = -1000, \qquad Q_1 = 2090, \qquad Q_2 = -1092$$
$$i_1 = 4\%, \qquad i_2 = 5\%$$
$$Q_0 = -100, \qquad Q_1 = 100, \qquad Q_2 = -100$$
$$i = -.5 \pm \sqrt{-.75}.$$

In practice, however, computed rates of return are in most cases real numbers and are predominantly unique.

d. Rate of Return Methods Applied in Industry

Several methods have been developed which are in common use in industry and are based on the rate of return approach. We shall consider two of the most commonly used: the discounted cash flow method and the MAPI method.

1. Discounted cash flow method. The discounted cash flow method is a rate of return method using the present worth approach.

The achieved rate of return for a certain investment is normally arrived at by

1. The use of single-payment present worth factor.
2. Equating the necessary extra investment to the present worth of all expected savings (cash flow).

In a majority of applications, continuous rather than discrete interest and continuous rather than end-of-year cash flow is assumed. This does, however, not change the basic approach of the rate of return technique such as outlined in the previous paragraphs. Tax and depreciation considerations are commonly included in the analysis.

Let us illustrate the technique by a rather simple example.

Example 5-10. Discounted Cash-flow Method [4]

There are two ways to perform a certain operation. We can use machine A with a purchase price of $1000 and annual operating cost of $600 or machine B with a purchase price of $2000 and annual operating cost of $1000.

Either machine has an economic life of 5 years. Let us assume an income tax of 50% and straight-line depreciation.

Table 5-4 shows a work sheet which can be used for the computation of

Table 5-4   Determination of the Cash Flow

Year	Investment B	Investment A	Operating Cost B	Operating Cost A	Depreciation B	Depreciation A	Gross Adv. of B	Tax Due to B	Net Adv. of B	Cash Flow
0	2000	1000								
1			100	600	400	200	300	150	150	350
2			100	600	400	200	300	150	150	350
3			100	600	400	200	300	150	150	350
4			100	600	400	200	300	150	150	350
5			100	600	400	200	300	150	150	350

cash flows. The gross advantage of B is the operating advantage, including depreciation, of B over A. The net advantage is the gross advantage minus taxes due to additional income by B. The cash flow is then the net advantage of B plus the difference of depreciation between A and B. The true rate of return is that rate which makes the present worth of cash flows minus the initial investment equal to zero. In other words, it makes the present value of the cash flows equal to the initial investment. The ratio of present value of of cash flows over initial investment is then equal to 1.

Table 5-5 shows a second work sheet which can be used to find the range in which the true rate of return can be found. In Table 5-5 we have used interest rates and present worth factors for discrete end-of-year cash flows.

Observe that only the additional investment due to B is taken into consideration in order to correspond to the additional depreciation of B in the determination of the cash flows. In our example the true rate of return of this additional investment lies between 15 and 25%, as indicated by the ratio row

Table 5-5 Determination of the True Rate of Return

Rate of Return		0%		10%		15%		25%		40%	
Year	Cash Flow	(pwf), 0	PW, 0	(pwf), 0	PW, 0	(pwf), 0	PW, 0	(pwf), 0	PW, 0	(pwf), 0	PW, 0
1	350	0	350	.909	318	.869	304	.800	280	.714	250
2	350		350	.826	289	.756	265	.640	224	.510	178
3	350		350	.751	263	.657	230	.512	179	.364	127
4	350		350	.683	229	.571	200	.409	143	.260	91
5	350		350	.620	217	.497	174	.328	115	.186	65
I: Total			1750		1316		1173		941		711
II: Investment, 1000			1000		1000		1000		1000		1000
Ratio: I/II			1.75		1.31		1.17		.94		.71

at the bottom of Table 5-5. To find its exact value, we could interpolate and find that $i = 22.4\%$.

2. MAPI method. The MAPI method was developed in the mid-1950s by George Terborgh in cooperation with the Machinery and Allied Products Institute (MAPI) [5]. The MAPI method arrives at a very special rate of return using the annual cost approach.

It computes a one-more-year rate of return taking into account the disadvantages of installing the proposed machine now rather than waiting for one more year and investing *then* in a probably better machine. These disadvantages are capitalized at 8.25% interest after taxes. The rate of return computed by the MAPI method is therefore not the true rate of return, even for the first year, on the total additional investment. It is rather a special ranking indicator which is appropriately called *urgency rating* by George Terborgh. The MAPI method is particularly suited for the evaluation of *replacement* investments and should not be used in a number of situations in which the underlying assumptions, which we shall discuss, are not satisfied.

It is not intended to explore the MAPI method in detail in this book. If the reader wants to apply MAPI, he is urged to consult Terborgh's book carefully before doing so. We shall merely outline the main features and discuss the applicability of this method.

The following five factors are taken into account:

1. Net investment. Net investment is the installed cost of the new equipment less the salvage value of the old equipment at the present time less any major repairs or capital addition to the old equipment which would be necessary if the new equipment is not installed.

2. Next-year operating advantage. This is the total of all next year's decreases in operating cost or increases in revenues due to the new equipment, except capital cost and income tax adjustments. The last two are taken into account in elements 3, 4, and 5.

3. Next-year capital consumption avoided. This is the difference between the salvage value of the equipment at present and 1 year hence. It takes account of the fact that the present equipment will depreciate further if used for one more year.

4. Next-year capital consumption incurred. This is the capital consumption of the investment project itself. It is the amount by which the salvage value of the project at the end of the year is below its installation cost. In other words, it is the amount by which the resale value decreases during the year, or it is the annual accumulation of *inferiority*. The inferiority of the equipment is presumed to increase over the service life according to predicted patterns or models. This allows a simplified calculation of the

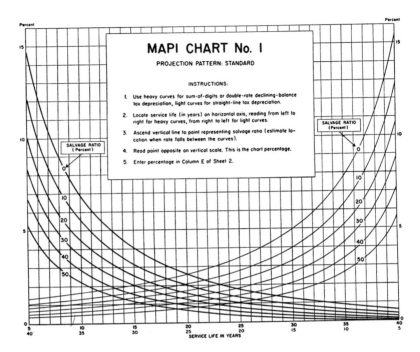

Figure 5-6. MAPI chart.

Source: George Terborgh, Business Investment Policy. *Courtesy of Machinery and Allied Products Institute.*

next-year capital consumption incurred by the use of charts. These charts (see Fig. 5-6) have been developed for three patterns of accumulation of inferiority:

a. Standard projection. The rate of depreciation and obsolescence stays constant over the economic life of the equipment (use of straight-line depreciation).

b. Variant A. Here the accumulation of inferiority is slower in the early life of the equipment than it is in the later part of it. It corresponds to a geometric series, $g + ag + a^2g$, in which $a^n = 4$ for variant A and n is the number of years of the economic life of the equipment.

c. Variant B. Variant B represents cases in which the rate of accumulation of inferiority is rather high at the beginning and decreases with time. This, again, corresponds to a geometric series—this time, however, with $a^n = \frac{1}{4}$.

The graphs for the next-year capital consumption incurred are based on rather complicated mathematical expressions which we do not want to discuss in detail. To illustrate the time saving which is achieved by using prepared charts, the following formula for the standard variant is given as stated in Terborgh [5], p. 43 and Appendix D:

$$C = \frac{n(Q^n - w^n)(Q - 1)^2 - (1 - b)P[(Q^n - 1) - n(Q - 1)]}{nQ^n(Q - 1) - (Q^n - 1)}$$
$$- (Q - 1) \tag{5-7}$$

where C = first-year capital consumption as a ratio to the cost of the asset

n = service life in years

b = rate of income tax (in decimals)

w = rate of relative decline required to write down the capital cost to the terminal salvage value over the period n (w^n equals the terminal salvage ratio)

$P = w^n[1 - w + py + (1 - p)z/(1 - b)]$

$Q = 1 + (1 - b)py + (1 - p)z$; the symbols p, y, and z standing for, respectively, the ratio of borrowed to total capital, the rate of interest (in decimals) paid on borrowed capital, and the rate (in decimals) of after-tax return on equity capital.

These variables are combined into the composites P and Q in order to avoid making the formula even more involved.

5. Next-year income tax adjustment. This is the net change in income tax that is expected as a result of the investment. The MAPI methods provides *tax-adjustment factors* for a future income tax rate of 50%.

The MAPI urgency rating is computed, using the above-mentioned five factors, as follows:

$$\text{urgency rating} = \frac{(2) + (3) - (4) - (5)}{(1)} \times 100. \tag{5-8}$$

Before pointing to some non-MAPI situations, let us summarize the important elements of the MAPI-method as follows:

1. The time interval considered is 1 year; i.e., the analysis is a one-more-year test and is therefore designed mainly as a test of replacement investments.

2. Future sums beyond the first year are capitalized at 8.25%. This rate is derived from a 10% after-tax return on equity and a 25% debt ratio with a 3% interest rate on debt. The rate of 8.25% is

kept fixed; i.e., for the purpose of a MAPI analysis the above-mentioned situation with respect to debt ration, rate of return, etc., is assumed to apply.

3. The accumulation of inferiority is assumed to follow one out of three patterns, standard, A, or B.

4. The resulting urgency rating is a percentage annual return on the extra equipment after recovery of all costs. Included is an allowance for the cost disadvantage, capitalized at 8.25%, of buying the suggested equipment now rather than 1 year hence. Different dollar values in the formula therefore apply to different times.

The obvious advantages of the MAPI method, which are the relative simplicitly in applying it and the higher structured form of its computational aids, which do not require a mathematical background of the analyst, do result in some limitations.

Terborgh [5] refers to some of them in his book on p. 12: "A formula has its main field of usefulness in the appraisal of minor investment projects. . . . Major projects tend to be less amenable to formula solutions."

Taylor [6] cites nine non-MAPI formula situations, six of which are specified by Terborgh in *Business Investment Policy.*

1. Future capital additions during the lifetime of the proposed equipment.

2. Present capital additions to the existing equipment, because it extends the life period of the equipment beyond the 1-year test for which the formula is designed.

3. Existing equipment that for any reason has a more than 1-year economic life.

4. Predictable changes in the real cost of the project resulting in favorable or unfavorable future prices (not inflationary or deflationary changes).

5. Equipment not of the "deterioration and obsolescence" type, such as the one-horse shay class or the military aircraft class (termed by MAPI as "predictable total obsolescence").

6. The situation termed "predictable partial obsolescence," which occurs when a proposed machine of the deterioration and obsolescence type is expected to be replaced suddenly by one that is known to be under development (i.e., combined deterioration-obsolescence and military aircraft type).

The following are non-MAPI formula situations not specifically referred to in Terborgh's book:

7. The direct comparison of new pieces of equipment.

8. The comparison of income-expansion alternatives.

9. Equipment having discrete functional degradation, namely, discrete economic life periods.

e. The Capital Budgeting Problem Revisited

We defined capital budgeting as the allocation of capital to investment projects. In the previous paragraphs we became acquainted with a number of techniques and approaches to evaluate projects as to their desirability. In such cases we considered only one project at a time even though we compared several alternative investments to perform the same task or project.

In practice, many projects will compete for funds and the responsible manager will have to decide which ones to approve and which not to accept. One common way to approach this problem is to rank all projects which satisfy the minimum requirements, such as minimum rate of return or positive present worth, in the order of their desirability. Available funds are allocated by approving projects with the highest degree of desirability first and then projects that are less desirable until the funds are exhausted. There are, however, some facts which complicate the issue and which might even make the application of this selection approach impossible:

1. Indivisibilities of projects might cause a suboptimal allocation of funds to projects. Let us assume that we have ranked our projects according to their ratio of present value to investment cost and that we want to find the allocation of a fixed total which maximizes the total present value of all investment projects approved. It is possible that a single large project has a high ratio of present value to cost but that it consumes almost all the capital available, leaving enough for only a low-ranked project or perhaps none at all. Investment in a number of smaller projects might together yield a higher net present value through fuller exploitation of the total budget.

2. The potential investment projects might not be independent of each other. They might represent alternatives; i.e., the approval of one specific project excludes the acceptance of one or more others. They might be related to one another in that the approval of one project necessitates the approval of another project. The other project might not even be among the projects which satisfy the minimum requirements.

3. In some cases the projects will require investments not in one but in several time periods. Since specific budget constraints must be met in each of these periods as well as in the current one, the solution which satisfies the budget constraints of the present

period might allow only suboptimal solutions in the future periods.

4. In none of the above-mentioned approaches have we considered total systems implications. Particularly in the case of investments for expansion, the methods described might point to a machine which we are not using fully even under the present circumstances. In any case, even if the suggested machine type is fully used at present, none of the methods can tell us which investment will increase our profit most, taking account of all other production constraints.

To take account of these complexities, more powerful techniques for overall system optimization have to be used. One of them is linear programming, the use of which we shall study in Sec. C.

C. Use of Mathematical Programming for Capital Budgeting

I. THE LORIE-SAVAGE PROBLEM AND OTHER PROBLEMS IN CAPITAL BUDGETING

In 1955, J. H. Lorie and L. J. Savage, in their article "Three Problems in Rationing Capital" [7], first pointed to some of the problems of capital budgeting and suggested possible approaches which might be employed to obtain acceptable solutions. Their major concern was that of allocating a fixed capital budget to potential investment projects such that the sum of the present values of the accepted projects is at a maximum without violating the capital constraints. The cost of capital is assumed to be known and independent of the investment decisions.

To solve this problem, which we shall call the Lorie-Savage problem, the following approach was suggested.

a. Single-Period Case

If all investments for all projects have to be made in one single period (1 year) or if there are budgeting constraints in only one time period, Lorie and Savage suggest ranking all projects by their ratio of present value to cost and then selecting projects from the top of the list until the budget is exhausted.

This procedure, which we previously discussed, will, in fact, lead to an optimum if

1. All projects, particularly the marginal ones, are divisible.

2. There are no dependencies between the projects.
3. All investments of future periods, such as major repairs and additional investments, can be neglected with respect to capital constraints.

b. Multiperiod Case

For the multiperiod case, i.e., when the investment projects require outlays in more than one period in which capital constraints have to be met, Lorie and Savage suggest a slightly modified approach. They do not provide a computationally efficient procedure; in fact, their technique breaks down under certain conditions. The logic of their approach is very interesting, however, and gives much insight into the problem area. In addition, we shall be able to interpret the linear programming approach much better after becoming familiar with the Lorie-Savage model. We shall use the following notation:

P_j = net present value of project j
C_{ij} = present value of capital outlays required in period i for project j
C_j = present value of capital available in period i
W_{ij} = ratio of present value of project j to its capital outlays in period i.

Let us consider the first year only and rank all projects according to their present-value-to-cost ratio:

$$W_{1j} = \frac{P_j}{C_{1j}}. \tag{5-9}$$

We now allocate capital to projects, starting at the top of the list, until our resources for the first time period, C_1, are exhausted or the remainder is too small to accept another project. Let us assume that the last accepted project is project k. Then

$$\sum_{j=1}^{k} C_{1j} \leq C_1; \tag{5-10}$$

i.e., the sum of the capital outlays of the accepted projects for period 1 is smaller or equal to the capital budget of period 1. W_{1k}, the ratio of the last of the accepted projects, is the *cutoff ratio* for period 1. We shall denote this ratio by W_1. If we now compute the quantities

$$Q_j = P_j - W_1 C_{1j},$$

then these will be positive or zero for all accepted projects and negative for all rejected projects. Thus, if we only accept projects with nonnegative Q_js, W_1 works like a Lagrangian multiplier and we can ensure nonviolation of our capital constraint by choosing an appropriate W_1. In fact, each W_1 in the range of

$$\frac{P_{k+1}}{C_{1,k+1}} < W_1 < \frac{P_k}{C_{1,k}} \qquad (5\text{-}11)$$

will act as an separator between acceptable and nonacceptable projects. We could therefore choose an arbitrary W_1, see whether

$$C_1 - \sum_{j=1}^{k} C_{1j}$$

is positive or negative, and then adjust W_1. This trial-and-error method can now be extended to the multiperiod case. Our problem would then become the following: Find a sequence of evaluators $W_j, j = 1, 2, \ldots, T$, such that the quantities

$$Q_j = P_j - \sum_{i=1}^{T} W_j C_{ij} \qquad (5\text{-}12)$$

are nonnegative for projects to be accepted and negative for nonacceptable projects.

Let us illustrate the process by the following two-period example, borrowed from the above-mentioned article by Lorie and Savage.

Example 5-11

See Table 5-6. The present values of the budget ceilings are assumed to be \$50 and \$20, respectively, in the two periods. We now have to find values for W_1 and W_2 such that, if we accept all projects (from the top of the list) for which

$$Q_j = P_j - W_1 C_{1j} - W_2 C_{2j}$$

Table 5-6 Capital Budgeting Problem

Investment	Outlay Period 1 ($)	Outlay Period 2 ($)	Present Value of Investment ($)
A	12	3	14
B	54	7	17
C	6	6	17
D	6	2	15
E	30	35	40
F	6	6	12
G	48	4	14
H	36	3	10
I	18	3	12

is nonnegative and reject all others, the sum of the net values of the accepted projects is maximized and the capital constraints are not violated. Using $W_1 = 1$ and $W_2 = 3$ would lead to the acceptance of project D only; i.e., we would still be far below our budget ceilings. $W_1 = .1$ and $W_2 = .5$, however, would make all projects acceptable; i.e., we would violate our capital constraints. Using $W_1 = .33$ and $W_2 = 1$, projects A, C, D, F, and I become acceptable. This leads to total capital outlays of \$48 and \$20 respectively in the two time periods; the best solution we could hope for with indivisible projects.

It should by now be obvious that the determination of the optimal set of Ws in the multiperiod case can be a very difficult task if it has to be done by trial and error. We shall show, however, how one can obtain similar evaluations by the use of linear programming.

So far we have considered independent investment projects. The Lorie-Savage approach can, however, be modified to include certain classes of interdependent projects also. Let us use Weingartner's classification of projects [8]:

> Independent projects. When the worth of individual investment proposals is not profoundly affected by the acceptance of others.
>
> Mutually exclusive projects. When acceptance of one proposal of a certain group renders all others in that group clearly unacceptable, or even unthinkable.
>
> Contingent projects. When acceptance of one proposal is dependent on acceptance of one or more other proposals.
>
> Compound projects. When contingent projects are combined with the projects on which they depend, the independent projects and the compound projects may be treated as mutually exclusive alternatives.

To select an optimal set of investment projects from a group containing independent and mutually exclusive projects, the Lorie-Savage method has to be modified as follows: Regard each independent project as the sole member of a set of mutually exclusive projects. Choose trial values for W_i and select tentatively from within each set of mutually exclusive projects that one for which Q_j is largest and nonnegative. Check, by adding the required outlays for the selected projects, if the budget constraints are satisfied. If the budget constraints are violated, the W value referring to this period is increased. If not, all funds of this period are used as the respective W value is decreased. This procedure is repeated until a satisfactory set of projects is obtained.

Summarizing, we can say that Lorie and Savage have suggested a very interesting approach to solve certain problems in capital budgeting. Their approach, however, does not offer a computationally efficient procedure, particularly for the multiperiod case and when indivisibilities are present.

II. APPLICATION OF LINEAR AND INTEGER PROGRAMMING TO CAPITAL BUDGETING: LINEAR PROGRAMMING

We can formulate the Lorie-Savage problem as a linear programming problem. The only difference from our problems in Sec. B is that we can accept *at most one* of each of the proposed investment projects. Using the number of projects of each kind accepted as our variables, we would therefore have to restrict our variables X_i to be between zero (rejected) and 1 (fully accepted). Thus our LP problem becomes

$$\text{maximize} \quad Z = \sum_{i=1}^{n} P_i X_i$$

$$\text{subject to} \quad \sum_{i=1}^{n} C_{ij} X_i \leq C_j, \quad j = 1, 2, \ldots, T \tag{5-13}$$

$$0 \leq X_i \leq 1,$$

where T is the number of relevant time periods.

In contrast to the Lorie-Savage procedure, linear programming examines sets of projects, rather than single projects, until it arrives at an optimal set which maximizes the objective function subject to the constraints.

Applying the LP formulation to Example 5-11, we obtain the linear programming problem [9] shown in Fig. 5-7.

Table 5-7, where the S_is are the slack variables of the primal problem and the w_js and v_js are the dual variables corresponding to the first two and last nine primal constraints, respectively, shows the solution to this problem and the corresponding $Z_j - C_j$ values of the optimal primal solution, which gives, as we know, the solution to the dual problem.

Table 5-7 Noninteger Solution to Example 5-11[a]

Project	X	S	W	V
A	1.0	0	0	6.7727
B	0	1.0	3.4090	0
C	1.0	0	0	5.000
D	1.0	0	0	10.4545
E	0	1.0	29.3181	0
F	0.9697	0.0303	0	0
G	0.0455	0.9545	0	0
H	0	1.0	0.500	0
I	1.0	0	0	3.9545

[a] $S_1 = 0$, $S_2 = 0$, $W_1 = .1363$, $W_2 = 1.8636$, and $Z_{\text{opt}} = 70.2727$.

Maximize $Z = 14x_1 + 17x_2 + 17x_3 + 15x_4 + 40x_5 + 12x_6 + 14x_7 + 10x_8 + 12x_9$

subject to $\begin{array}{l} 12x_1 + 54x_2 + 6x_3 + 6x_4 + 30x_5 + 6x_6 + 48x_7 + 36x_8 + 19x_9 \leqslant 50 \\ 3x_1 + 7x_2 + 6x_3 + 2x_4 + 35x_5 + 6x_6 + 4x_7 + 3x_8 + 3x_9 \leqslant 20 \end{array} \Bigg\} \alpha$

$$\left.\begin{array}{rl} x_1 & \leqslant 1 \\ x_2 & \leqslant 1 \\ x_3 & \leqslant 1 \\ x_4 & \leqslant 1 \\ x_5 & \leqslant 1 \\ x_6 & \leqslant 1 \\ x_7 & \leqslant 1 \\ x_8 & \leqslant 1 \\ x_9 & \leqslant 1 \end{array}\right\} \beta$$

$$X_i \geqslant 0$$

Figure 5-7. LP formulation.

Table 5-8   Integer Solution to Example 5-11[a]

Project	X	S	W	V
A	1.0	0	0	3.8571
B	0	1.0	0	0
C	1.0	0	0	9.7083
D	1.0	0	0	8.2698
E	0	1.0	27.837	0
F	1.0	0	0	0
G	0	1.0	0	0
H	0	1.0	0	0
I	1.0	0	0	0.1761

[a] $S_1 = 2.00$, $S_2 = 0$, $W_1 = 0$, $W_2 = 1.8174$, and $Z_{\text{opt}} = 70.00$.

For convenience, S_j represents the slack variables and the X_is are the variables representing investment projects. We observe that the total present value is $70.2727, which is slightly higher than the Lorie-Savage solution. This is due to the acceptance of fractional projects, a topic we shall return to later.

The solution of this problem took 6.1 seconds on an IBM 7094 computer. We had to pay for this efficient solution, however, by achieving only a non-integer solution. Fractions of projects F and G have been included in the solution. It can be shown that at most as many fractional projects can be included in the optimal solution as the number of time periods considered.

There is one further advantage of the noninteger solution, apart from the higher efficiency with which it can be obtained. In contrast to the integer solution, the dual solution gives valuable information and insight into the structure of our primal solution.

For analytical reasons, let us distinguish two kinds of dual variables: dual variables which correspond to the *structural primal constraints* or budget constraints, i.e., the primal constraints per time period, and dual variables which correspond to the upper-bound constraints per project. We shall denote the former by W_j, $j = 1, 2, \ldots, T$, and the latter by V_i, $i = 1, \ldots, n$.

We can then write our dual problem as

$$\text{minimize } g = \sum_j W_j C_j + \sum_i V_i \cdot 1$$
$$\text{subject to } \sum_j W_j C_{ij} + V_i \geq P_i \qquad (5\text{-}14)$$
$$W_j, V_i \geq 0.$$

We may now recognize the meaning of our optimal dual variables $W_{j,\text{opt}}$: They are the shadow prices of our budget constraints in periods j, or the present value which we can gain by adding an additional dollar to the budget in period j. That implies that $W_{j,\text{opt}}$ has to be zero if the capital budget in period j is not binding, i.e., if we can accept all projects without reaching our budget ceiling. If the budget is "very restrictive," we would expect W to be very high. This is very similar to the evaluation W_j used by Lorie and Savage, and, in fact, as Weingartner shows, the Lorie-Savage evaluations can be interpreted as optimal values of the dual variables corresponding to the budget constraints.

We used all $Z_j - C_j \geq 0$ as an optimality criterion, which meant that the $(Z_j - C_j)$s for all variables *not* in the final solution had to be nonnegative. Thus in the final tableau of our problem the $(Z_j - P_j)$s of the rejected projects have to be nonnegative.

The optimal primal solution has to be equal to the optimal dual solution, i.e., $Z_{j,\text{opt}} = \sum_j W_{j,\text{opt}} C_{i,j} + \sum_i V_{i,\text{opt}}$ and so $Z_j - C_j$ for this tableau becomes

$$(Z_{j,\text{opt}} - C_j) = \sum_j W_j C_{i,j} + \sum_i V_{i,\text{opt}} - P_i \geq 0.$$

Remember that the C_js are the P_is in our present problem.

Let us first look at rejected projects: Here $X_{i,\text{opt}} = 0$, $S_{i,\text{opt}} = 1$, and

$V_{i,\text{opt}} = 0$. Hence

$$\sum_j W_{j,\text{opt}} C_{i,j} - P_j > 0$$

or

$$\sum_j W_{j,\text{opt}} C_{i,j} > P_j.$$

Verbally, the present values of the rejected projects are smaller than the sum of their discounted outlays in all time periods. The $W_{j,\text{opt}}$ functions thereby as the discounting rate and can be interpreted as the capital cost or the opportunity cost of capital.

If only a fraction of a certain project is accepted, then $0 < X_{i,\text{opt}} < 1$, $0 < S_{i,\text{opt}} < 1$, and $V_{i,\text{opt}} = 0$, and we obtain

$$(Z_j - C_j) = \sum_{j,\text{opt}} C_{i,j} - P_i = 0$$

or

$$\sum_j W_{j,\text{opt}} C_{i,j} = P_i.$$

These projects are marginal in the sense that their present values are *equal* to the sum of their discounted outlays in all time periods; i.e., their acceptance would neither increase nor decrease the value of our present solution.

Recalling the Lorie-Savage approach, we observe that the $(Q_j = P_i - W_j C_{ij})$s, which have to be nonnegative for accepted projects, are very similar to the $(Z_j - C_j)$s; they merely divide *marginal projects* into both the acceptable and the nonacceptable projects and therefore do not obtain unique optimal values for W_j. We saw before that W_j could vary within a certain range and still be functional.

Mutually exclusive and contingent projects can easily be handled within the linear programming formulation. For *mutually exclusive* projects we would just have to add one additional constraint of the form

$$\sum_i X_i \leq 1$$

for each set of mutually exclusive projects. The subscript i would have to run over all indices of the mutually exclusive projects of this set.

Contingent projects can be handled similarly. We form compound projects which include the contingent projects and then proceed as above for mutually exclusive projects.

We have not yet solved the problem of indivisibilities of potential projects. Theoretically this does not pose a severe problem. There exist a number of integer programming algorithms which guarantee a mixed-integer solution (a solution in which some variables have to be integers) in a finite number of steps. One of these was devised for this particular problem by Laughhunn [10].

The two major disadvantages of most of these algorithms are

1. They have not yet been shown to be computationally efficient.
2. The primal-dual relationships mentioned above no longer hold; i.e., we cannot read the dual prices off the final integer tableau.

Table 5-8 shows the final integer solution of the problem of Example 5-11, obtained from Gonnory's mixed-integer algorithm. The solution took 10.1 seconds on the same IBM 7094 computer that was used to find the noninteger solution. We see that the solution is identical to the Lorie-Savage solution and we are tempted to believe that the additional information compared to the noninteger solution does not justify the additional computational effort.

There is, however, one approach which in the past few years has shown promising results in solving integer programming problems. This method, which we shall study in more detail in Chap. 6, is called *branch and bound*. We shall illustrate the basic approach in Example 5-12.

Example 5-12 [11]

We want to allocate \$37,000 to five different projects. The necessary investments and the possible annual profits are as follows:

Project	Investment (\$)	Annual profit (\$)
1	17,000	11,000
2	16,000	14,000
3	21,000	16,000
4	8,000	8,000
5	12,000	7,000

The optimal allocation can be found by solving the following problem:

$$\text{maximize } Z = 11x_1 + 14x_2 + 16x_3 + 8x_4 + 7x_5$$
$$\text{subject to} \quad 17x_1 + 16x_2 + 21x_3 + 8x_4 + 12x_5 \leq 37 \quad (5\text{-}15)$$
$$0 \leq X_i \leq 1, \text{ integer.}$$

This is an integer programming problem with five variables. We shall try to solve this problem by solving simpler subproblems, hoping that the solution to the subproblems is also the solution to the original problem. By fixing the value of one of the variables we can split Eq. (5-15) into two subproblems with only four variables each. Equation (5-16) can, for instance, be split into Eqs. (5-17) and (5-17a) by fixing the value of x.

$x_1 = 0$ yields

$$\text{maximize } Z = 14x_2 + 16x_3 + 8x_4 + 7x_5$$
$$\text{subject to} \quad 16x_2 + 21x_3 + 8x_4 + 12x_5 \leq 37. \tag{5-16}$$

$x_1 = 1$ yields

$$\text{maximize } Z = 11 + 14x_2 + 16x_3 + 8x_4 + 7x_5$$
$$\text{subject to} \quad 16x_2 + 21x_3 + 8x_4 + 12x_5 \leq 20. \tag{5-16a}$$

Both problems could now be split again into two subproblems by fixing the value of x_2: For Eq. (5-15), $x_2 = 0$ yields

$$\text{maximize } Z = 11 + 16x_3 + 8x_4 + 7x_5$$
$$\text{subject to} \quad 21x_3 + 8x_4 + 12x_5 \leq 20. \tag{5-17}$$

$x_2 = 1$ yields

$$\text{maximize } Z = 25 + 16x_3 + 8x_4 + 7x_5$$
$$\text{subject to} \quad 21x_3 + 8x_4 + 12x_5 \leq 4. \tag{5-17a}$$

A complete decomposition of Eq. (5-15) into 2^5 subproblems can be illustrated by the decision tree shown in Fig. 5-8.

Each path from the root of the tree to one of the end points represents a solution to Eq. (5-15).

A decomposition of Eq. (5-17a) shows, however, that the constraint will be violated for $x_3 = 1$ and obviously for all further variables set equal to 1. It is therefore not necessary to pursue this line of decomposition because all solutions on this path will be infeasible.

We shall try to reduce the computational effort further by assigning to each of the subproblems (nodes of the tree) a number which indicates the *chance* that the optimal solution will be found by further following that path. In our example such an indicator could be the potential profit that can be reached on that path. This indicator, which we shall call a *bound*, is 56 for Eq. (5-15), 45 for Eq. (5-16), and 31 for Eq. (5-17).

Starting with Eq. (5-15), we shall now follow the following procedure:

1. Decompose the problem with the highest bound.
2. Terminate a branch whenever the constraint is violated.

This approach results in the reduced tree shown in Fig. 5-9. The numbers at the nodes indicate the bounds and the remaining capital to be allocated.

As can be seen from this reduced tree, only 3 problems (nodes 17, 19, and

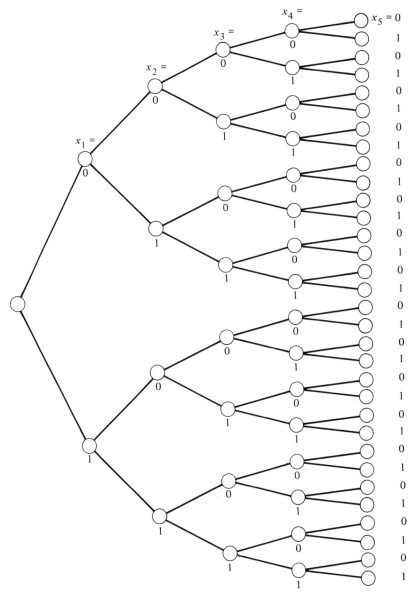

Figure 5-8. Complete decision tree.

25), or 3 complete paths, had to be evaluated to find the optimal solution rather than 32 paths as shown in the original design tree.

The optimal solution (node 17) is $x_1 = 0$, $x_2 = 1$, $x_3 = 1$, $x_4 = 0$, $x_5 = 0$. The optimal annual profit is $30,000.

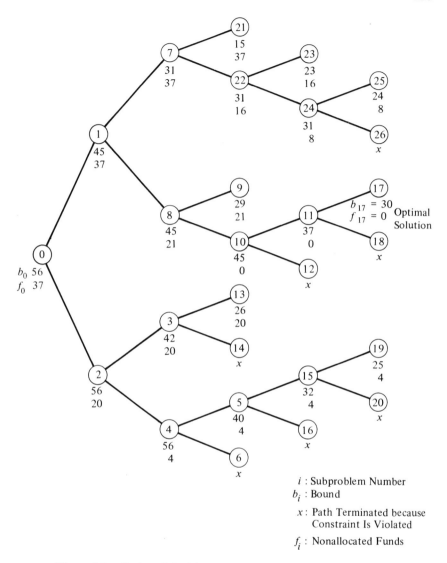

Figure 5-9. Reduced decision tree.

In examining the capital budgeting problem up to this point we have assumed that the data required for the calculation of present value and cost were easily available and independent of decisions on other projects. This is certainly not always true. We shall examine an example to show the interdependency when each of three types of machines are part of the same process. Therefore the decision on how to invest in additional equipment must be looked at for the process rather than treating the three types individually.

Example 5-13. Expansion Problem

Company A produces three products, A, B, and C, each of which has to be processed in three departments: the cutting department, the milling department, and the grinding department. These departments have monthly capacities of 5000, 9000, and 4000 machine-hours, respectively.

Let us assume that Company A is operating at the optimal product mix (see Chap. 6) found by solving the following linear programming problem:

$$\text{maximize profit} = 10x_1 + 15x_2 + 5x_3$$

$$\text{subject to} \quad 2x_1 + x_2 \qquad\qquad \leq 5000$$

$$3x_1 + 3x_2 + x_3 \leq 9000$$

$$x_1 + 2x_2 + 2x_3 \leq 4000$$

$$x_j \geq 0,$$

where the x_js are the levels of the three products produced and the coefficients in the constraints are the number of machine-hours required to produce one unit of the product in each department.

After three iterations we shall arrive at the following final optimal simplex tableau:

C_j	X_1	X_2	X_3	X_4	X_5	X_6	b
10	1	0	$-\frac{2}{3}$	$\frac{2}{3}$	0	$-\frac{1}{3}$	2000
0	0	0	-1	-1	1	-1	0
15	0	1		$-\frac{1}{3}$	0	$\frac{2}{3}$	1000
$Z_j - C_j$	0	0	8.33	1.66	0	6.66	

The management of Company A now decides to spend $85,000 for expansion investments. The following investment alternatives are available:

Cutting machines for $20,000 a piece.
Milling machines for $15,000 a piece.
Grinding machines for $18,000 a piece.

All machines have a monthly capacity of 300 machine-hours. "Conventional" investment evaluation methods point to the purchase of milling machines as being most profitable.

From our above tableau, however, we see that

1. The slack variable corresponding to the milling machines (second

constraint) is in the final solution, indicating that our milling capacity is not fully used.

2. The shadow prices of our resources, which can be found in the $Z_j - C_j$ row of the corresponding slack variables, are 1.66, 0, and 6.66, respectively. This indicates that we could increase our optimal total profit by $1.66 for each additional cutting hour and by $6.66 for each additional grinding hour.

Since the capacities of all machines are equal, it seems appropriate to buy a grinding machine. It should, however, be kept in mind that the shadow prices are valid only for the final optimal tableau under present conditions.

If we expand our grinding capacity, we change our original requirement vector b and thereby our optimal solution vector. Let us call the additional grinding capacity ΔX_6 (since it means an expansion of the slack line of grinding machine capacity). Then our new requirement vector would be

$$b' = \begin{pmatrix} 5000 \\ 9000 \\ 4000 + \Delta X_6 \end{pmatrix}$$

and our new solution vector would be

$$b'' = B^{-1} b',$$

where B^{-1} is the inverse of the current basis.

$$b'' = \begin{pmatrix} \frac{2}{3} & 0 & -\frac{1}{3} \\ -1 & 1 & -1 \\ -\frac{1}{3} & 0 & \frac{2}{3} \end{pmatrix} \begin{pmatrix} 5000 \\ 9000 \\ 4000 + \Delta X_6 \end{pmatrix}$$

$$b'' = \begin{pmatrix} 2000 - \frac{1}{3}\Delta X_6 \\ 0 - \Delta X_6 \\ 1000 + \frac{2}{3}\Delta X_6 \end{pmatrix}.$$

This solution will be optimal and feasible until one of its components becomes negative. We can easily check that this will happen for any $\Delta X_6 > 6000$. That means that we can buy additional $6000/300 = 20$ grinding machines before our shadow prices would change. The available capital allows us to buy $85,000/18,000 = 4$ grinding machines, which would give us an additional profit, assuming an optimal product mix, of $1200 \times 6.66 = \$8000$ per month.

If we consider an expansion in our cutting machine capacity, we shall find that we could expand the available capacity by 3000 cutting hours before the present optimal solution becomes infeasible. That would mean 10 cutting machines. Available capital would allow the purchase of $85,000/15,000 = 5$ cutting machines, which would lead to an additional profit of $5 \times 300 \times 1.66 = \$2490$ per month.

It should be observed that the above profit figures were obtained taking into account all implications underlying linear programming models. This means, on the one hand, that we took into account effects which a change in one type of capacity would have on all other types of capacities. On the other hand, we had to assume that costs and profits increase or decrease linearly with changes in production levels. This might be an assumption which is not adequate in some practical situations.

III. SIMULTANEOUS DETERMINATION OF OPTIMAL INVESTMENT AND PRODUCTION PROGRAMS

As shown by the previous example, a close interrelationship exists between production and investment. The link between these two is the capacity, which is created by investment and used by production.

Until now, we have, however, treated production programs and investment programs separately as if they would not influence each other. Let us now try to determine the optimal production and investment program. We shall illustrate one possible formulation of the problem by the following example, which differs from the previous example in a change in profit per item with new equipment and limits on total sales.

Example 5-14 [12]

A firm assembles two products, p_1 and p_2. Presently two bottlenecks, capacity I with 3000 machine hours and capacity II with 10,000 machine-hours, restrict the production. The required capacities are

product 1: 2 machine hours of capacity I
4 machine hours of capacity II
product 2: 3 machine hours of capacity I
3 machine hours of capacity II.

We can sell 1500 units of each of the products.

The question is now whether the firm should buy new equipment to substitute for capacity of type I. The capacity would be unchanged, 3000 hours, but it would only take 1 and 2 hours, respectively, to finish one unit of product 1 or 2. Due to the shorter operation times, the profit per unit sold would increase from $10 to $11 for product 1 and $9 to $11 for product 2. The fixed cost for the new equipment is $5000 per year in contrast to $1300 for the old equipment.

We shall use the following symbols for production activities:

$$p_{11} = \text{units of product 1 made by old equipment}$$
$$p_{12} = \text{units of product 1 made by new equipment}$$
$$p_{21} = \text{units of product 2 made by old equipment}$$
$$p_{22} = \text{units of product 2 made by new equipment}$$

Also, we shall use

$$I_1 = 0, 1 \text{ variable for the old capacity I equipment}$$
$$I_2 = 0, 1 \text{ variable for the new capacity I equipment.}$$

Our problem is then

maximize $z = 10p_{11} + 9p_{21} + 11p_{12} + 11p_{22} - 1300I_1 - 5000I_2$

such that
$$2p_{11} + 3p_{21} \qquad\qquad\qquad - 3000I_1 \leq 0$$
$$4p_{11} + 3p_{21} - 4p_{12} + 3p_{22} \qquad\qquad \leq 10{,}000$$
$$p_{12} + 2p_{22} \qquad - 3000I_2 \leq 0$$
$$I_1 + I_2 = 1$$
$$p_{11} \qquad\qquad p_{12} \qquad\qquad\qquad \leq 1{,}500$$
$$p_{21} \quad + p_{22} \qquad\qquad \leq 1{,}500$$

$I_i, p_{ij} \geq 0$, I_i integer.

After four iterations with the simplex method, we arrive at the tableau shown in Table 5-9 (s_is are slack variables):

The optimal solution is

$$p_{12} = \quad 1500$$
$$p_{22} = \quad 750$$
$$z = 19{,}750$$
$$I_2 = \quad 1 \qquad \text{(i.e., invest in new equipment).}$$

The optimal solution without considering the new investment was $p_{11} = 1500$, $z = 13{,}700$.

SUMMARY

In Sec. A.I. we stated that for an investment decision to be optimal three conditions have to be satisfied:

1. For each alternative, all costs, cost savings, additional income streams, and other consequences have to be considered.

Table 5-9

c_i	P_B	p_{11}	p_{21}	p_{12}	p_{22}	I_1	I_2	s_1	s_2	s_3	s_4	s_5	s_6	b
g	p_{21}	$\frac{2}{3}$	1			-1000		$-\frac{1}{3}$			$-4,500$	$-\frac{5}{2}$		0
0	s_2	$-\frac{1}{2}$				-5000		-1	1	$-\frac{3}{2}$	$1,500$	$-\frac{1}{2}$		1,750
11	p_{22}	$-\frac{1}{2}$			1	1500				$-\frac{1}{2}$	1			750
-5000	I_2					1	1							1
11	p_{12}	1		1				$-\frac{1}{3}$		$-\frac{1}{2}$	$-1,500$	1		1,500
0	s_6	$-\frac{1}{4}$				-500						$\frac{1}{2}$	1	750
$z_j - c_j$		$\frac{3}{2}$	0	0	0	3800	0	3	$\frac{11}{2}$	$\frac{11}{2}$	11,500	$\frac{11}{2}$	0	19,750

2. The evaluation criteria and techniques or models have to be economically sound.

3. All relevant alternatives have to be considered.

In Secs. A–C we only considered consequences within the financial sector of the firm directly due to the single investment alternative. We disregarded consequences of the single investment project on other potential projects and we neglected consequences of the investment on other areas of the firm, such as production capacity, product mix, and sales.

This obviously violated our first condition of considering *all* consequences. Using "traditional" decision rules, such as described in Secs. A–C, it is generally impossible to include secondary consequences and effects of investment decisions on other sectors of the firm. Rather, we have to use more powerful tools of simultaneous optimization such as linear programming.

In Sec. D we showed how the production area can be included in our considerations. Without major difficulties it is also possible to include other areas when using mathematical programming methods.

REFERENCES

1. M. B. Solomon, "Uncertainty and Its Effect on Capital Investment Analysis," *Management Science* (1966), B-334–339.

2. D. B. Hertz, "Risk Analysis in Capital Investment," *Harvard Business Review* (Jan.–Feb. 1964), 95–106.

3. G. A. Taylor, *Managerial and Engineering Economy*, Van Nostrand Reinhold, New York, 1964, p. 118.

4. G. A. Taylor, *ibid.*, pp. 364–369.

5. George Terborgh, *Business Investment Policy*, Machinery and Allied Products Institute, Washington, D.C., 1958.

6. G. A. Taylor, *op. cit.*, pp. 373–375.

7. J. H. Lorie and L. J. Savage, "Three Problems in Rationing Capital," *Journal of Business*, 28, No. 4 (Oct. 1955), 229–239.

8. H. W. Weingartner, *Mathematical Programming and the Analysis of Capital Budgeting Problems*, Prentice-Hall, Englewood Cliffs, N.J., 1963, p. 11.

9. H. W. Weingartner, *op. cit.*, p. 18.

10. D. J. Laughhunn, "Quadratic Binary Programming with Application to Capital-Budgeting Problems," *Operations Research*, 18, No. 3 (May–June 1970), 454.

11. F. Weinberg, *Einführung in die Methode Branch and Bound*, Springer, Berlin, 1968.

12. P. SWOBODA, "Die Simultane Planung von Rationalisierungs-und Erweiterungsinvestitionen und von Produktionsprogrammen," *Zeitschrift für Betriebswirtschaft*, 35 (1965), 148–163.

PROBLEMS

1. Compare the annual costs of machines A and B for 10-year service using a minimum attractive rate of return of 10% before income taxes. See Table P-1.

Table P-1

	Machine A ($)	Machine B ($)
First cost	2400	5000
Estimated salvage value	500	None
Annual operating cost	650	350
Annual repair cost	200	120

2. A manufacturing plant has to purchase a special lathe. A secondhand machine which will be satisfactory will cost $6000; a new machine will cost $13,000. Annual disbursements for labor are estimated as $8100 with the secondhand lathe and $7050 for the new lathe. Annual maintenance costs are estimated as $400 and $300, respectively. The annual increase of maintenance costs is estimated to be $150 for the secondhand lathe and $100 for the new one. Annual property taxes and insurance will be 3% of the investment for each machine. The expected period of service is 12 years. At the end of this period the secondhand machine will have no salvage value, while the new machine will have a salvage value of $3800. Tabulate the differences in cash flows of these two machines. Compare the two investment alternatives assuming a 11% rate of return before income tax.

3. A company is considering the installation of their own power plant for generating electricity for production operations. The installation of a steam-powered plant will cost $420,000 and will consume $12,000 in fuel annually. It would have an estimated life of 25 years and annual maintenance costs of $4000. A gas-powered installation would cost $370,000 but would have an annual fuel consumption of $15,000. The estimated life is 10 years and annual maintenance costs are $5000. Taxes and insurance costs amount to 3% for the steam-powered plant and 4% of first cost annually for the gas-powered plant. All other costs are about the same for both installations. It is anticipated that the plants will be needed for at least 25 years. Capital is worth not less than 12% to the company. Compute the annual cost, present worth, and internal rate of return of both installations. Which installation should be carried out?

4. A bank considers installing an automatic protection system in one of its branches. The average amount of money held in the safe, which could be

stolen, is $500,000. Each available system has an expected life of 20 years and no value at the end of this period. The systems provide protection against holdups to different degrees. The data in Table P-4 on costs and probabilities of successful holdups are available. Invested capital should be earning at least 10%. Which system should be chosen, if any, by comparing total expected annual costs.

Table P-4

System	Probability of Successful Holdup	Installation Costs ($)
None	.01	0
A	.005	100,000
B	.003	120,000
C	.001	250,000

5. a. A new machine costs $100,000. The old machine is sold for $20,000. The new machine will save $20,000 in the first year in labor costs. Deterioration for both the old and new machines would be about $1,000 per year. Obsolescence has been estimated at 3% of new price per year for this type of equipment over the last half-century. The company uses sum-of-the-year's-digits depreciation and the standard MAPI projection. Salvage value probably will not be any different than what is now obtained for the old machine. Neglecting taxes, what is the MAPI urgency rating?

   b. Is this an optimal model for replacement of capital equipment? Why or why not (short answer)?

   c. In what ways is the MAPI method more explicit than return on investment (short answer)?

   d. What dangers are there in use of the MAPI method? Be specific.

6. A company is considering the purchase of a special type of equipment used in their operations. Two alternative models of that equipment are available: Equipment A costs $20,000 and causes annual costs of $5,000. Equipment B costs $36,000 and causes annual costs of $1,000. None of the machines will have an appreciable salvage value. The minimum return on this type of equipment should be 10%. Since the length of time this type of equipment will be needed is highly uncertain, it is desired to perform a sensitivity analysis. Determine the rates of return for useful lives of 4, 8, and 12 years and comment on the results.

7. The Rome Foundry has just received a 2-year contract to manufacture 6000 items of a casting per month for the Ready Robert rocket. Since this rocket style will be obsolete by the end of the contract, no additional orders are expected. Some old casting equipment which has no foreseeable use in the future is being stored by Rome at an estimated cost of $200 a year because no one wanted to spend money to have it hauled away. This equipment can be rebuilt to produce the rocket casting at a cost of $6000. It will require $600 per month

of direct labor and maintenance to produce the 6666 parts needed to get 6000 acceptable parts. Defective parts are melted back down. At the end of the 2 years the machine can be sold for the cost of hauling it away. A new centrifugal casting machine can be bought for $30,000 and will produce 500 parts per day at a cost of $30 a day for direct labor and maintenance. The machine is expected to produce about 2% defectives. During the first year no other use for the machine exists, but during the second, idle time can be subcontracted at a total charge of $65 per day. The company works 22 days per month. At the end of the 2 years the machine can be sold for $15,000. At present most of Rome's work is in highly speculative lines. Management, therefore, feels that only projects which are expected to yield 25% or more per year are worth undertaking. The government contract was taken because it was a sure thing and would help stabilize the business. Which alternative should be followed in producing the castings?

8. Three cost reduction opportunities are available in a certain plant and each requires an extra investment of $10,000. The first has annual savings of $3400, the second $3007, and the third $2888. The salvage values are all estimated to be zero.

    a. Which of these will be selected by a test of payout periods if the period may not exceed 3 years?

    b. Which of these will be selected by a rate of return analysis if the economic lives are first project, 3 years; second, 6 years; and third, 9 years? The minimum required rate of return is 15%.

See Table P-8.

Table P-8

	Years		
	3	6	9
Single-payment compound factor	1.0303	1.0615	1.0937
Capital recovery factor	.3400	.1725	.1167

9. John urgently needs $1000. A bank offers him two different loans: Either John has to repay $1210 at the end of 2 years (alternative A) or he has to repay $1000 at the end of the first year and an additional $122.10 at the end of the second year (alternative B). Which alternative is the better deal for the bank. Compute present worth and rate of return for the alternatives and discuss the results.

10. Compute the rates of return for the project shown in Table P-10. Discuss the result. What are the reasons for the astonishing results?

11. A company produces four products, A, B, C, and D, which have to be processed in three departments: the cutting department, the milling department, and the grinding department. The products need the machine times shown in Table P-11(a). Profits per piece for the products are $12, $11, $5, and $4,

Table P-10

Year	Cash Flow ($)
0	−1,000
1	+7,000
2	−10,000

respectively. The present departments have the monthly capacities shown in Table P-11(b).

Table P-11(a)

Product	Hours per Piece			
	A	B	C	D
Cutting	2	1	3	1
Grinding	0	2	3	1
Milling	4	2	1	0

Table P-11(b)

Department	Capacity (hr/month)
Cutting	6000
Grinding	5000
Milling	7000

a. $110,000 is available for the expansion of the present capacities. A new cutting machine costs $12,000, a new grinding machine costs $18,000, and a new milling machine costs $15,000. The capacities of all machines, considering maintenance and breakdowns, are 334 hours per month. Which machines should be bought so as to maximize total profits?

b. New types of grinding and milling machines have been designed. The new grinding machines reduce the processing time of the products to 1 hour per piece for product B, 2 hours per piece for product C, and .5 hour per piece for product D. The new milling machines would reduce the times to 3, 1, and .5 hours per piece for products A, B, and C, respectively. The company believes that the purchase of one extra machine of each type which would cost $22,000 and $17,000, respectively. The expected useful life is 5 years. Depreciation of a presently used milling machine is $3500 per year and $3000 for a grinding machine. Should the two machines or either of them be bought?

chapter 6

Aggregate Production Planning

A. The Problem of Aggregate Production

I. INTRODUCTION AND DEFINITION

The preceding chapters have discussed the prerequisites for production: the size, location, and the design of the plant. The chapters following this will discuss the detailed operation of the production process. Aggregate production planning is the link between these long-run and short-run problems of the firm. As such it is one of the most difficult, most varied, and most important functions of production management.

Aggregate production planning can be defined as the intermediate-range matching of variable inputs to the fixed inputs of the production process with the objective of meeting demand at least cost. Obviously, the time frame is essential in this definition. In general the time frame is about 1 year. For various firms it ranges from perhaps a monthly to a 5-year horizon. Within this time period the production facilities can be considered fixed, although small increments may be made in connection with the capital budgeting process. The amounts and types of raw materials, manpower, inventories, and the product mix are variable to a large degree within this time frame.

We can distinguish the aggregate planning function from that of design and of control. Design decisions have the widest range of flexibility because very few limitations exist, since the plant is still being planned. On the other hand, control decisions focus on such details as the particular colors and sizes and the particular item inventory and production levels since the other variables cannot be changed in the short run. Aggregate planning focuses on total production, inventory, and manpower.

It is the necessity of making intermediate-range commitments for raw material inventories, sales and advertising campaigns, labor negotiations, storage and transportation contracts, and new equipment orders that makes aggregate production planning essential for most firms. It is usually difficult and costly to change these commitments.

There are some firms for whom aggregate planning is easy. The demands of their customers are known and constant. Their suppliers deliver immediately when requested. Their production process is in complete control and no new technology is ever introduced. These firms can move directly to scheduling, bypassing the aggregate planning function, but not many firms match this description.

There are many firms that do avoid much of the aggregate planning process. They merely wait until the problems show up at scheduling time. They are the firms that cannot meet delivery promises, much less take on additional orders. They are always short of some essential raw materials or parts and have excesses of others. Some departments are always on overtime while others sit idle. Layoffs are frequent and turnover is high. Their machinery is old and inappropriate to their product mix. Unfortunately these look like scheduling problems, but increased short-term efficiency is not the answer for these firms. Adequate planning is the answer.

II. THE IMPORTANCE OF AGGREGATE PLANNING

We shall discuss one example in order to get a better understanding of some particular problems which arise in aggregate planning. In later sections we shall discuss some general models for solving these problems.

The example firm is actually a division of a large manufacturer of control devices. It manufactures and assembles metal valve devices. There are about 2600 different assemblies which are final products. The number of subassemblies is about 6000 and the number of parts about 15,000. Some products are shipped directly to customers and others to divisions of the same company. About 600 people are engaged in the manufacture of the parts from metal stock and the assembly of the parts. More than half of these people are engaged in the design, control, and operation of the process rather than in the actual manufacture. The complete process from placement of an order to delivery takes about 3–6 months, although management would like to reduce this considerably and believes it possible. A diagram of the steps in the production sequence is shown in Fig. 6-1. Demand is seasonal. The products

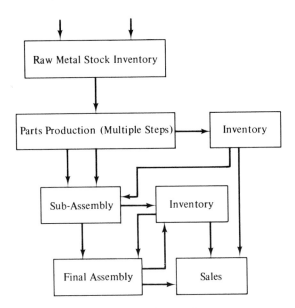

Figure 6-1.   Example production flow.

are essentially customized items made to customer specifications from standard components. The firm has had considerable difficulty meeting delivery dates.

The particular problems the firm faces in aggregate planning are

1. Raw material procurement takes a long time. Therefore raw material orders must be placed before the orders for valves are received.

2. The parts are made in economic lot sizes† because of high setup costs. This would be a scheduling problem except that demand is not constant for a long period. Instead, most items are popular only for a time which is not a large multiple of the time to produce and consume a lot. Therefore the demand estimates must be made based on sales forecasts updated in the same time frame as aggregate planning.

3. The assembly lines have to be run for a fairly long time on one item or assembly is expensive. An economic lot size system is used, but the assembly lines are few in number and common to many different subassemblies that each have fluctuating demands.

---

†If the reader is not familiar with the concept of economic lots or economic order quantities, the first part of Chap. 7 should be read.

Therefore scheduling of assembly cannot be done at the last minute on a short-term basis.

4. If parts inventories are not available, the assembly lines have to cease operation. As noted above, parts are common to many subassemblies. Because parts runs are long and infrequent, assembly runs are also long and infrequent. If several long assembly runs in succession call for the same part, then the part will probably become in short supply.

5. The plant runs three shifts for 6 days per week, so that there is not much extra capacity available if the workload becomes heavy.

This firm obviously has some very difficult problems. Their current planning technique is essentially only a yearly budget, a very common situation. Since much of the work is of a job-shop nature, it is harder to estimate departmental workloads from total sales than it would be for a purely assembly process. The yearly budget is based on a forecast of sales by item, which is more detailed than most companies prepare. The yearly sales are converted to departmental activity by matching the sales forecast against a computerized listing of parts and labor hours required for each item and totaling. The departmental activities are based on labor hour estimates which assume job times and lot sizes. This conversion to departmental activity is the reason for the detailed sales forecast. From the forecasted departmental activities or workloads, yearly operating and capital expenditures budgets are prepared, which are used for cost control and cost estimating. The operating budget is a rough manpower planning device. Raw material purchases are also based on the yearly sales estimate.

Thus far we see that the firm has prepared aggregate production plans for capital expenditures, manpower, raw materials, and sales planning. Unfortunately the planning is stopped at this point. The yearly sales estimate is not used for planning parts or assembly inventories. The difficulties the company faces are primarily the result of the interaction of the production of parts and the assembly operations. The production of parts and assemblies are controlled strictly on a lot-size and reorder point scheduling rule for each item independently, as shown in Fig. 6-2. Each part, subassembly, and assembly has a lot size based on forecasted annual demand. Production of a lot is scheduled as orders come in and reduce the inventory of either a part or assembly below the reorder point for a lot. This treatment ignores the interaction of the parts and assembly operations. Consequently large orders for assemblies may deplete the inventories of any particular part which happens to be used in several consecutive assemblies. This causes a rush order for the part and/or shutdown of the assembly lines. As a result, the actual lot sizes are decreased in an effort to get some parts out quickly. Additional setups are then needed, and so the total job time is increased above that estimated

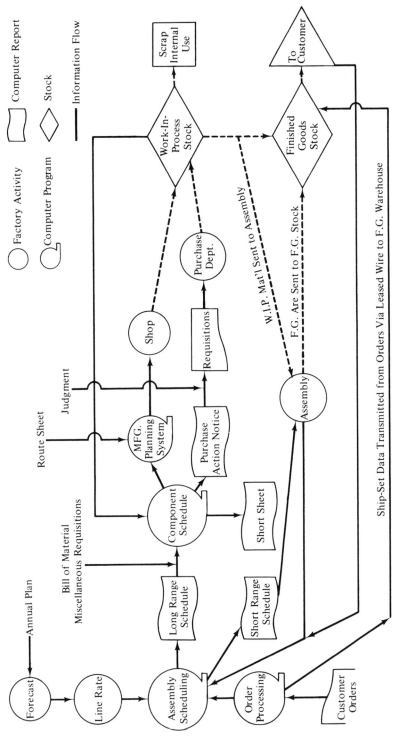

Legend:
- ⬭ Factory Activity
- ⬭ Computer Program
- ▭ Computer Report
- ◇ Stock
- ─ Information Flow

Forecast → Line Rate → Assembly Scheduling

Annual Plan

Long Range Schedule

Bill of Material
Miscellaneous Requisitions

Component Schedule

Route Sheet   Judgment

MFG. Planning System

Purchase Action Notice

Short Sheet

Short Range Schedule

Order Processing

Customer Orders

Shop

Purchase Dept.

Requisitions

Assembly

Work-In-Process Stock

Scrap Internal Use

Finished Goods Stock

To Customer

W.I.P. Mat'l Sent to Assembly

F.G. Are Sent to F.G. Stock

Ship-Set Data Transmitted from Orders Via Leased Wire to F.G. Warehouse

Figure 6-2. Example production control system.

and budgeted on the basis of standard lot sizes. Soon the entire system is far behind. Seasonal variations make the problem even worse, since these are not planned for in the system at all, but are present.

A partial answer to this problem has been aggregate planning of the assembly lines. Product groups, not individual assemblies, should be scheduled for assembly in a sequence as based on the beginning inventory and yearly sales forecast. Parts production can still be in lots, but the runs should be sequenced to make available the items necessary for the assembly plan, since many parts are common across the product group.

III. THE INTERRELATIONSHIP OF AGGREGATE PRODUCTION PLANNING AND OTHER DECISIONS

Aggregate production planning cannot be effective if it is separated from the other decisions of the firm. That was one problem of the firm in the example above.

Aggregate production planning is the major interface of production management and the marketing and financial management functions of the firm. The coordination with the marketing function must determine an intermediate-term production plan which meets fluctuations in demand or there will be constant battles between marketing and production managers regarding urgent orders to be met, inadequate leadtime and capacity, etc.

Similarly, it is essential to plan raw material inventories and seasonal inventories as well as work in process with the knowledge of the firm's financial planners. Otherwise sudden layoffs or shortages may result when cash is not available. More important than merely avoiding the problems is that these three groups have the ability to plan profitable operations through the many trade-offs that exist between the functions. For example, the marketing department can help avoid seasonal production problems by selling in advance. Alternatively, financial managers may be able to give discounts for early orders. If each function merely tries to do its own job best, the firm may have large sales orders, high production, and tight financial control and still go bankrupt from broken delivery promises, obsolescent inventories, bad labor relations because of fluctuations, and high setup costs because of inventory shortages. If these three parts of the firm can cooperate in an aggregate plan for the firm, profitable results are much more likely.

Unfortunately, in many firms the aggregate planning is performed separately by the marketing and finance departments. Often the only production planning is short-term. Consequently not all the necessary links between the groups are made. Then everyone's time is devoted to explaining why profit was not as high as that indicated by the financial plan instead of seeing that there is an effective way of interrelating the actual decisions.

Figure 6-3 illustrates the relationships of aggregate planning and other decisions within the firm. The figure is essentially that shown in William Holstein's article "Production Planning and Control Integrated" [1]. The aggregate planning function depends on the long-term capacity planning function for forecasts of future demand and for long-term capacity plans. On the basis of actual orders and inventory status, it issues production and inventory plans to the short-term scheduling and inventory control functions. It works in parallel with capital budgeting for marginal capacity decisions. It receives reports on current status through the scheduling function as discrepancies between schedules and actual work occur.

It is obvious that aggregate production planning must be closely coordinated with the other functions of the firm depicted in Fig. 6-3. Information flows between functions are not adequate in themselves. Decisions in each function must be made with an overall view, as will be further discussed in Chap. 10 and in the next few paragraphs.

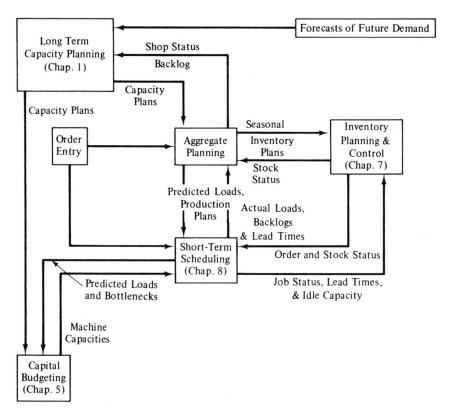

Figure 6-3.   Relationship of aggregate planning to other production decisions.

There seem to be several ways to accomplish the integration of the necessary information and coordination.

1. Centralize the information flows so that at least one group is in constant touch with all the relevant data. This usually requires a highly automated system because the information is very detailed.

2. Create a special operating group to serve as coordinators for aggregate production planning but without operational responsibility. This staff group must perform all staff functions shown in Fig. 6-3 and still keep in close touch with operations.

3. Spend a very large amount of time in meetings between the various groups so that everyone understands the interrelationships as actual issues arise.

4. Hire an extremely able plant manager who can make sure that the process is synchronized.

5. Develop a simulation model that is used for scheduling on a day-to-day basis but can be run off-line to explore the effects of projected inventory build-up and plant changes and otherwise test aggregate plans. Because the model is used daily for scheduling, the information must be current and correct. Its use as a by-product in planning will then be inexpensive. This type of model removes many of the guesses by the planners which are otherwise necessary. The planner usually spends most of his time finding out what is wrong in Fig. 6-3 and has to guess how to correct it. The model allows the staff and operations personnel to speak the same language and operate from the same data base in coming up with plans to correct the difficulties. We shall discuss these models later in this chapter.

IV. AGGREGATE PRODUCTION PLANNING FOR REPETITIVE AND NONREPETITIVE PRODUCTION PROCESSES

To a large extent the example in Sec. A.II was one in which the same items are produced repetitively. There are some production processes such as construction which are designed for producing only one or a few items, each of which is a major new project. The aggregate production planning problem is still the same, that of the timely matching of fixed and variable resources. In the matching for nonrepetitive processes, certain questions become more important or less important than with repetitive production.

The question that becomes more important is that of the sequence in which the parts of the project are undertaken. Because of the complexity of the project, there are many different sequences in which the operations can be performed. This would not ordinarily be true in the repetitive aggregate planning situation, unless the entire production plan for the firm is considered to be one project. In that case the repetitive and nonrepetitive problems become equivalent, which is one justification for their common treatment in this chapter.

The question which becomes less important is that of inventory. Since only a few items are being produced, inventory is fairly easy to control. In the following two sections we shall address the nonrepetitive and then the repetitive processes.

B. Planning Large Projects

I. CONVENTIONAL METHODS

Many large projects have been undertaken throughout the centuries. It is tempting to say that they were not as technologically complex as modern projects but this may be a relative matter. More likely they were just performed with less success or efficiency than desirable. The usual techniques for dealing with complexity included

1. Informal coordination, either through the genius of some one individual such as Michelangelo, or
2. Through considerable investment in cultural training, such as the Egyptian priesthood, or
3. By simply employing many coordinators who spent their time seeing that everyone had what they needed, as in the World War II efforts in the United States.

Another approach was to borrow techniques from planning for repetitive production. The Gantt chart, a repetitive production scheduling technique, can show what is being done in each of the activities of a large project. It can even show when each activity has to be done. A Gantt chart is basically a representation of activity along a time axis, as shown in Fig. 6-4, which is a progress chart for the assembly of fuses. Brackets indicate the planned start and stop dates of production. The current date is October 11 and the assembly of fuses is on schedule since the cumulative production bar reaches the check mark. Fuse body manufacture is behind. The various operations are planned so that initial assemblies can be made on October 8. Parts and subassemblies must be started and some amount finished by the date of final assembly. The numerals indicate specific operations in the activity which must be complete in order to provide the initial flow of finished product.

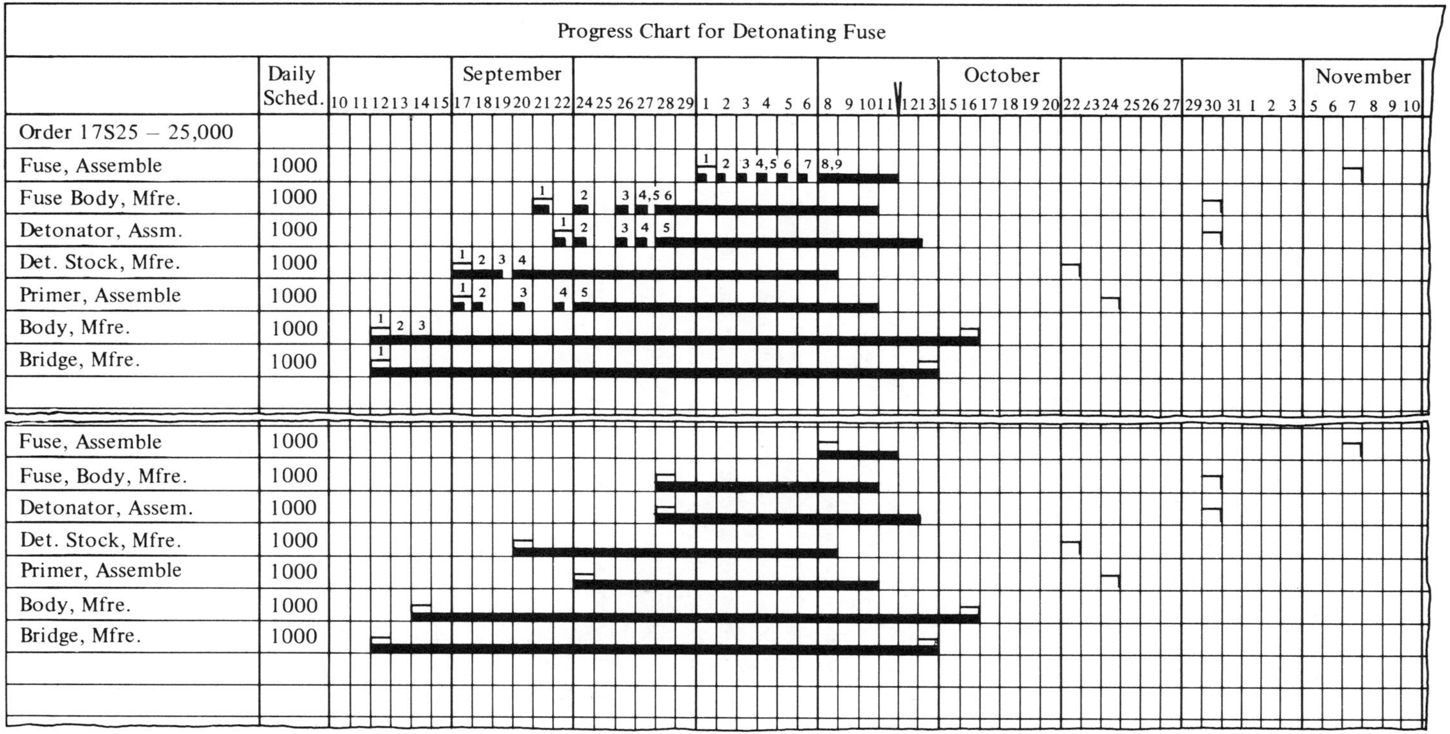

245

Progress Chart for Detonating Fuse

Figure 6-4. Early Gantt chart.

Source: David B. Porter, "The Gantt Chart as Applied to Production Scheduling and Control," NLRQ, 15, No. 2 (June 1968), 312. Courtesy of Naval Logistics Research Quarterly.

The advantages of a Gantt chart are quite obvious:

1. It can be used as a planning tool and as a control device as well.
2. The progress of work is recorded on a time scale. Therefore the Gantt chart is instructive even for the nonspecialist. He can quite easily read from it the present status of completion of the different operations and compare it with the planned status.

The severe disadvantages are probably not quite so visible:

1. The structure of the project (i.e., the sequence of the planned operations) and the time planning have to be performed simultaneously. If either the sequence of the operations or the time of one or more of the operations changes, the entire chart may have to be redrawn.
2. There is no way of optimizing the sequence of operations in a Gantt chart since it does not give any information about other possible sequences.
3. It does not give any information about the impacts of delays of a single operation on the completion time of the entire project.
4. If the number of operations to be planned is high, it is hard or even impossible to maintain an overview in a Gantt chart.
5. A Gantt chart is not directly convertible to computerization.

Because of the above-mentioned points, a Gantt chart seems to be more appropriately used *after* the use of the critical path methods (CPMs), which will be introduced in the next section. The use of a Gantt chart as a final aid is shown in Fig. 6-26.

II. NETWORK PLANNING

The need for improved planning and control methods became particularly obvious in the early 1950s when the U.S. government experienced severe delays in the completion of important defense contracts, such as the development of missiles and the like. This led to the development of so-called network planning methods. The three most important methods of network planning became public in 1957–1958:

1. PERT (Program Evaluation and Review Technique) was developed by the U.S. Navy and was first used in connection with the construction of the Polaris missile system.
2. CPM (Critical Path Method) was developed by E. I. Du Pont and Remington-Rand. It was first applied to maintenance scheduling in the chemical industry.

3. MPM (Metra Potential Method) was developed by the "Sema," a European consulting group. It was first applied to construction of atomic power plants.

In the meantime numerous other network planning methods have been worked out. They are all similar to the three major techniques mentioned above.

a. The Arrow Diagram of CPM

CPM planning begins with an element by element analysis of the project. Every element, which we call operation, activity, or work element, of the entire project has to be uniquely defined and the sequence of elements determined. The definition of the element determines the level of detail, i.e., whether turning the nut or installing the door will be the smallest activity examined. The level of detail of the analysis depends largely on the purpose of the plan and on the planner's ability to identify individual activities.

To provide a visual representation of the project, activities are depicted by arrows or by circles, depending on which method is used. We first turn to the arrow notation used in CPM. Here the arrows represent activities (operations or periods of time) and the nodes joining the arrows represent events (points in time). Consider the following project with 10 operations: Operations B, C, and D cannot be started before activity A is completed. Operations E and F can be started upon completion of B and C. Operation G can start after completion of D. Operation H can be started after completion of D, E, and F. Activity I can be started only after F and D have been completed and activity J can start upon the completion of operations G, H, and I.

The project can be described by the precedence matrix of Fig. 6-5. The marks in the columns below the operations indicate the immediate predecessors of the respective operations. For instance, operation H has the immediate predecessors D, C, and F, and operation A has no predecessors. The project network representing our 10-activity project is shown in Fig. 6-6. Arrows representing activities are labeled by capital letters. Nodes representing the respective starting or finishing events are labeled by numbers. The lengths of the arrows do not correspond to the durations of the operations, which have not yet been specified. Only the relative position of the arrows has any significance.

There are some important details of the graphical representation:

1. Between nodes 2 and 3 we find a so-called *dummy activity* indicated by a broken-line activity arrow. It is necessary so that activities can be distinguished by their starting and finishing events, i.e., by two node numbers. Activities B and C have a common starting event and a common finishing event. They could, there-

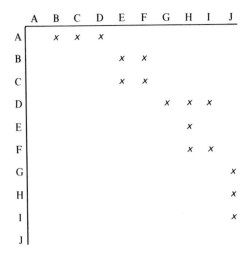

	A	B	C	D	E	F	G	H	I	J
A		x	x	x						
B					x	x				
C					x	x				
D							x		x	
E								x		
F								x	x	
G										x
H										x
I										x
J										

Figure 6-5. Immediate precedence matrix.

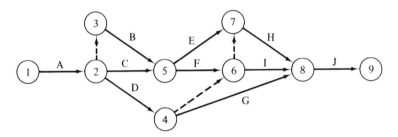

Figure 6-6. Example of CPM network structure.

fore, not be distinguished by node numbers. By introduction of the dummy, which has zero duration, the common starting event is split in two. Now B and C can be uniquely identified by node numbers.

2. If activities H and I were joined with E and F the same way as E and F are joined with B and C by event 5, then the graphical representation would indicate that both E and F were predecessors of both H and I. However, this is not true; I has only the predecessors D and F. This situation can be depicted correctly by introducing the two dummy activities. Dummy activities are used to make activities with common starting and finishing events distinguishable and to maintain correct precedence relationships between activities not connected by actual work elements.

b. Critical Path and Critical Operations in a CPM Network

After the structure of the project has been described, the timing analysis can be started. Figure 6-7 shows our project network in which durations have been assigned to the different operations.

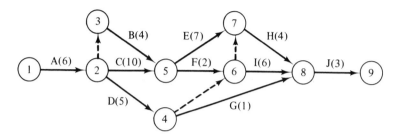

Figure 6-7. Example of CPM network durations.

The computations of the time analysis are performed in three phases:

1. Compute an earliest and latest time for each event.
2. On the basis of these two event times, compute four activity times for each activity.
3. Determine buffer times, critical operations, and critical paths.

We shall discuss each step in the following paragraphs.

The earliest time (ET) of an event is the time at which this event can first take place. It is subject to the condition that *all* activities leading from the beginning of the project to the event have been performed. The earliest time of event i is therefore the longest path from the start of the project to event i.

The longest path can be computed by adding the durations of all operations along the paths leading to event i. If two or more paths merge at an event, we have to choose the latest ET. Figure 6-8 depicts above each node the ETs of our project with 10 operations. The ET of the last event, event 9 of our project, equals the minimum total project time.

To find the latest time (LT) of an event, we determine the longest path from the end of the project to the event. The LT is found by subtracting from the minimum total project time the durations of the operations along the longest path from the end of the project to the event. At events where several paths merge, we now have to choose the smallest LT possible. Figure 6-9 shows our network with all ETs and LTs in the event circles with ET above LT.

From the ETs and LTs we now compute four times for each operation

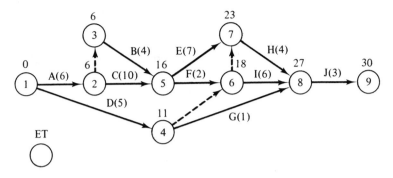

Figure 6-8. CPM network with earliest times of events.

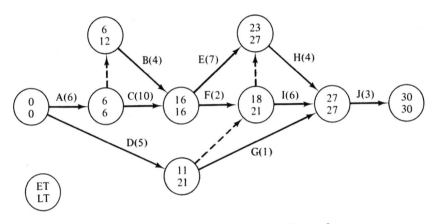

Figure 6-9. Network with earliest and latest times of events.

according to the following rules, where index i indicates the starting event, index j indicates the finishing event, and d_{ij} is the duration of operation ij:

$$\text{earliest starting time of} \\ \text{operation between events } i \text{ and } j = \text{EST}_{ij} = \text{ET}_i$$

$$\text{earliest finishing time} = \text{EFT}_{ij} = \text{ET}_i + d_{ij}$$

$$\text{latest starting time} = \text{LST}_{ij} = \text{LT}_j - d_{ij}$$

$$\text{latest finishing time} = \text{LFT}_{ij} = \text{LT}_j.$$

Finishing times are also often called completion times.

The longest path (or paths) of a CPM network is called the critical path and all the operations along a critical path are *critical operations*. The length of the critical path corresponds to the minimum total project time. A delay of any of the critical operations results in the same delay of the completion of the project. Noncritical operations have some leeway or *float* in their start and completion times. Two types of float are normally considered: total float and free float. Total float (TF) is defined as the leeway available for the operation if all operations preceding the one in question are finished as early as possible and all succeeding activities are started as late as possible. It can be computed as

$$\begin{aligned} TF_{ij} &= LT_j - ET_i - d_{ij} \\ TF_{ij} &= ET_j - EFT_{ij}. \end{aligned} \tag{6-1}$$

Free float (FF) is the leeway available for the activity if all other activities in the network are started as early as possible:

$$\begin{aligned} FF_{ij} &= ET_j - ET_i - d_{ij} \\ FF_{ij} &= ET_j - EFT_{ij}. \end{aligned} \tag{6-2}$$

Critical operations are easily identified by computing the total float for each operation because the total float for critical operations is zero. In our example the following operations have a total float of zero: A, C, E, H, I, and J. The critical path in our project network is therefore 1–2–5–7–8–9.

c. The Circle Diagram of the Metra Potential Method

In the MPM technique the activities are represented by the nodes of the network and the arrows indicate precedence relationships only. Our project with 10 activities described in Figs. 6-5 and 6-6 is shown in *circle notation* in Fig. 6-10. The arrows are drawn where Xs appeared in Fig. 6-5, the imme-

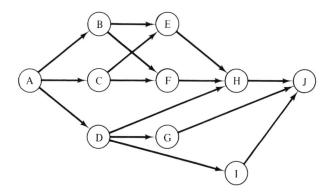

Figure 6-10.   Network in circle notation.

diate precedence matrix. In contrast to the CPM, we do not need any dummies to correctly depict precedence relationships or to differentiate two or more operations. There exist only two "dummies" in MPM which are used if the beginning and the end of the project are not determined by one operation each but by several. In this case a dummy *project start* and another dummy *project end* are introduced.

d. The Time Analysis in MPM

MPM is a more sophisticated method than CPM. The coverage of situations which can be represented by MPM tools is more comprehensive than in CPM. Because MPM uses the circle notation, operations only need one index for their identification. In contrast to CPM, which provides only one type of sequential relationship of operations, MPM allows for four kinds. We use the following definitions: $t(i)$ is the starting time of operation i, $t(0)$ is the starting time of the project, and $b(i)$ and $c(i, j)$ are time intervals between starting times of operations as defined below; operation i precedes operation j. The four possible types of interrelationships can now be defined by inequalities:

Relationship I. Operation i has to start *at least* $b(i)$ units after the start of the project:

$$t(i) \geq t(0) + b(i) \quad \text{or} \quad t(i) - t(0) \geq b(i). \tag{6-3}$$

For a graphic represention, see Fig. 6-11.

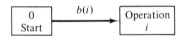

Figure 6-11.

Relationship II. Operation i has to start *at most* $b'(i)$ units after the beginning of the project:

$$t(i) \leq t(0) + b'(i) \quad \text{or} \quad t(0) - t(i) \geq -b'(i). \tag{6-4}$$

For a graphic representation, see Fig. 6-12.

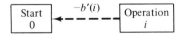

Figure 6-12.

Relationship III. Operation j has to start *at least* $c(ij)$ units later than operation i:

$$t(j) \geq t(i) + c(ij) \quad \text{or} \quad t(j) - t(i) \geq c(ij). \qquad (6\text{-}5)$$

For a graphic representation, see Fig. 6-13.

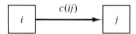

Figure 6-13.

Relationship IV. Operation j has to start *at most* $c'(ij)$ units after operation i:

$$t(j) \leq t(i) + c'(ij) \quad \text{or} \quad t(i) - t(j) \geq -c'(ij). \qquad (6\text{-}6)$$

For a graphic representation, see Fig. 6-14.

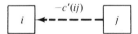

Figure 6-14.

Summarizing at this point,

1. MPM uses only *start-start* relationships; i.e., $b(i)$, $c(ij)$, $b'(i)$, and $c'(ij)$ denote the time intervals between the starting times of consecutive operations.
2. There are two *minimum conditions* (types I and III) and two *maximum conditions* (types II and IV).
3. The intervals $c(ij)$ and $b(i)$ which define the interval between the starting times are not necessarily equal to the job durations; i.e., they can be set arbitrarily.

Point 3 may need some elaboration. Due to the fact that the time interval between the starting times does not have to equal to the duration of the operation, different situations can be represented just by choosing $c(ij)$ and $b(i)$ appropriately. We use the type III relationship as an example:

1. If $d(i) = c(ij)$, then operation j may start immediately after operation i has terminated.

2. If $d(i) < c(ij)$, there will be a gap between the termination of operation i and the start of operation j.

3. If $d(i) > c(ij)$, operations i and j may overlap.

The ability to handle these situations brings the MPM method closer to reality, where setup times and overlaps are sometimes important. For example, an activity may be painting each of 10 parts. As soon as half of the parts are finished the next operation, baking, can be started.

Since condition III is a minimum condition, all operations j can be delayed (pushed to the right) without violating the condition. The situation is shown graphically in Fig 6-15. Combinations of different sequencing conditions are possible. For instance, see Fig. 6-16, which shows that operation j has to start as soon as operation i has terminated. Or note Fig. 6-17, which shows that operations i and j have to start at the same time, or Fig. 6-18, which shows that operations i and j have to be terminated at the same time.

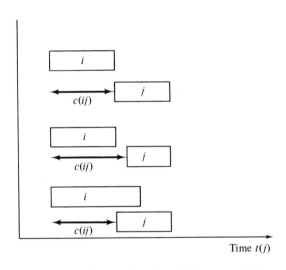

Figure 6-15. Gantt chart for minimum conditions.

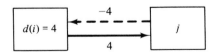

Figure 6-16.

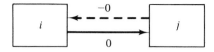

Figure 6-17.

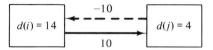

Figure 6-18.

e. Critical Path in MPM

The determination of critical operations and of the critical path consists of five phases:

1. Determination of the earliest start times of the activities on the basis of all $b(i)$ and $c(ij)$ in a manner similar to CPM.
2. Investigation of whether the type II and IV conditions are met and correction of the earliest start times if the maximum conditions are violated.
3. Determination of the latest starting times on the basis of $b(i)$ and $c(ij)$ as in CPM.
4. Determination of whether the maximum conditions are violated and correction of latest start times if violations exist.
5. Determination of the critical operations or operations with no slack time. Slack time is the difference between latest and earliest start times (LST − EST) of the respective operations.

The phases described above are illustrated in the following example. Figure 6-19 shows an eight-operation project in which earliest start times have been computed.

We now check the maximum conditions, of which three are assumed and are represented by the dotted arrows:

$t(c) - t(b) \geq -2$ c has to start at least 2 units after the beginning of b; this condition is met

$t(f) - t(e) \geq -4$ this condition is also satisfied

$t(e) - t(d) \geq -7$ operation e has to start not later than 7 units after the beginning of d; this condition is not met and the

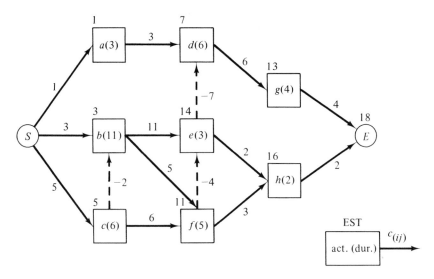

Figure 6-19. MPM network with earliest start times.

earliest start time of d has to be increased from 4 to 7; this again has an effect on the earliest start of g, which has to be increased from 10 to 13.

After the same calculations have been performed for the backward determination of the latest starting times, we arrive at the network shown in Fig. 6-20. The critical path is S–b–e–h–E, as indicated by the zero difference between EST and LST. Operation c is critical because of the maximum condition imposed on operations b and c.

MPM and CPM treat the durations of the activities as deterministic. PERT (program evaluation and review technique) takes into account that these activity durations are stochastic. By using three time estimates for each element rather than one, PERT estimates the probability distribution of total project time on the critical path. PERT has been described in the several references [2, 3]. Although it is clear that element times are probabalistic in aggregate planning decisions, uncertainty is usually assumed to be controlled in scheduling. The general idea of examining the possible variance is useful, however.

III. THE PROBLEM OF CAPACITY CONSTRAINTS

a. Introduction

The schedules obtained by using the above-mentioned methods may turn out to be infeasible in practice in cases where resources are limited, i.e., where

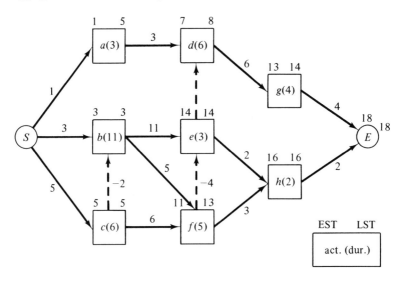

Figure 6-20. MPM network with earliest start times and latest start times.

only a certain number of machines or men are available to perform the different tasks. Rather than scheduling the operations without consideration of resources available as above, we might schedule them so that the total requirement for each resource does not exceed the amount available at any time. We call this *resource scheduling.* Alternatively, we might start as above but want to smooth the requirements for certain resources in different time intervals. We call this *resource leveling.*

Let us first look at the resource-scheduling problem, which can be formulated as an integer programming problem. Because of the computational limitation of the integer programming approach, a number of heuristic approaches have been developed. These do not necessarily optimize but they are computationally more feasible. We shall first look at one which is based on CPM networks.

Assume that we have drawn the CPM network and that we know the earliest start time (EST), latest finish time (LST), and total float (TF) values for each operation. We also assume that we know the exact amount of the resource available at any time. In this case only one man is available. Figure 6-21 is an example of a simple network. To avoid dummy activities, we have drawn the network using circle notation. After operation 1 has been finished, we could start on operations 2 and 3. We cannot start both of them since that would exceed the available resources. Thus we have to select one operation to start first. One possible criterion for this selection is the *urgency* of the job,

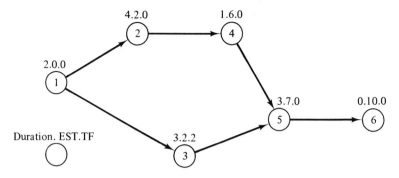

Figure 6-21.   MPM network for capacity constraints.

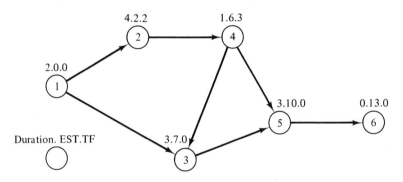

Figure 6-22.   Capacity contrained network.

indicated by its total float. Since the total float of job 2 (zero) is smaller than the total float of job 3, we shall start on job 2.

After job 2 has been finished, jobs 3 or 4 could be started. Comparing their total floats, we find that the total float of job 4 is smaller than that of job 3. Note that the total float of job 3 may be reduced from its original value but that it is still positive. Therefore we start job 4, and job 3 still has to wait. Upon finishing job 4, we compare jobs 3 and 5. Again the total float of job 5 is smaller than that of job 3. However, one of the immediate predecessors of job 5—namely, job 3—has not yet been completed. Therefore we have to complete job 3 before we start job 5.

Our sequence of decisions which required performing job 4 before job 3 amounts to drawing an additional arrow from node 4 to node 3, as in Fig. 6-22. This arrow or precedence constraint would not have been necessary in normal unconstrained networks. As the next step we can now finish job 5 and then job 6. Note that our project completion time has increased to 13 units. This method can easily be extended to larger networks and a larger number of resources. It can be and has been programmed for computers and has proved to be rather efficient and easy to use. If we keep track of the resource utilization by using a Gantt bar chart, we can summarize and formalize the procedure by the flow diagram of Fig. 6-23.

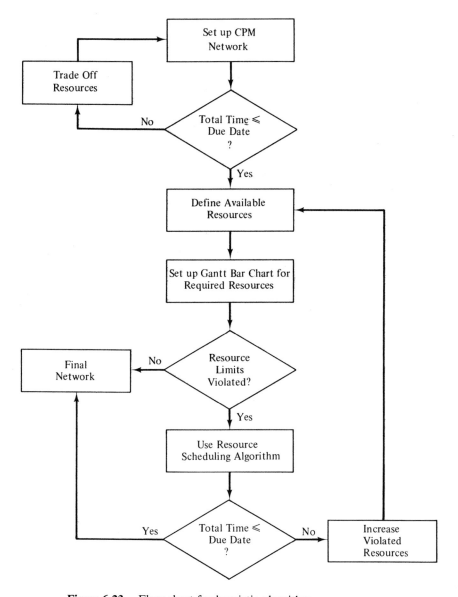

Figure 6-23.   Flow chart for heuristic algorithm.

b. Heuristic Methods

Most of the available computer programs use the following approach: Schedule all *nonrestricted* activities, those with no resource constraints, until there is none left that can be scheduled without scheduling at least one restricted activity first. If several restricted activities could now be scheduled, use *priority rules* to decide the sequence of the restricted activities. Then proceed with nonrestricted activities until restricted activities have to be scheduled again. Possible priority rules are

1. Select the activity with the smallest total float.
2. Select the activity with the smallest duration.
3. Select the activity with the smallest EST.
4. Select the activity with the smallest LST.
5. Select the activity for which the sum of float and duration is smallest.
6. Select externally specified priorities based on management policy, union work rules, or esthetics.

The impact of resource constraints on the sequence of operations and the total project time is illustrated by the example which we shall develop in the next few pages.

Double arrows in the arrow diagram (Fig. 6-24) indicate that these activities require 1 unit of the scarce capacity, exactly 1 unit of which is available. See Table 6-1.

Resolving these problems means determining sequences in which the six activities competing for the available unit of capacity are scheduled. There

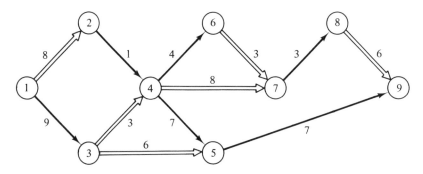

Figure 6-24.   Example project.

Source: H. Müller-Merbach, "Ein Verfahren zur Planung des optimalen Betriebsmitteleinsatzes bei der Terminierung von Grossprojekten," AWF-Mitteilungen, No. 2, 1967, 5–9.

Table 6-1   Constrained Network Calculation

1, Activity No.	2, i	3, j	4, Dura- tion	5, Resource Require- ment	6, EST	7, EFT	8, LST	9, LFT	10, Float	11, 29-LFT
1	1	2	8	1	0	8	3	11	3	18
2	1	3	9	—	0	9	0	9	0	20
3	2	4	1	—	8	9	11	12	3	17
4	3	4	3	1	9	12	9	12	0	17
5	3	5	6	1	9	15	16	22	7	7
6	4	5	7	—	12	19	15	22	3	7
7	4	6	4	—	12	16	13	17	1	12
8	4	7	8	1	12	20	12	20	0	9
9	5	9	7	—	19	26	22	29	3	0
10	6	7	3	1	16	19	17	20	1	9
11	7	8	3	—	20	23	20	23	0	6
12	8	9	6	1	23	29	23	29	0	0

are $6! = 720$ possible sequences of six elements. Twenty-four possible sequences remain feasible after excluding all sequences which are not feasible because of existing precedence relations, i.e., activities 3 and 4 must never come before activity 1.

Table 6-2 lists the feasible sequences and the resulting total project times, which vary between 36 and 58 time units.

Using priority rule 3, based on EST, we arrived at the schedule shown in Table 6-3 for our example project. As can be seen from Table 6-3, we arrived at a total project time of 38, which is not quite optimal according to Table 6-2, which shows a minimum time of 35.

c. Linear Programming Methods

Let us now turn to the linear programming formulation. The use of linear of linear programming is, of course, only possible if the linearity conditions are satisfied. In this case element times are additive, i.e., linear. Since the formulation of the scheduling problem with linear programming requires some integer constraints, we have to use integer programming techniques to find an optimal solution to the problem.

Consider a hypothetical project in which 12 jobs have to be performed, all requiring the use of three limited resources. Figure 6-25 shows the standard CPM network without consideration of resource limitations.

For purposes of illustration it is assumed that there will be a maximum amount of resources A, B, and C available. The maximum amount available

Table 6-2   Possible Sequences of Constrained Operations

Activity No.	Sequence	Total Project Time
1	1-4- 5- 8-10-12	35
2	1-4- 5-10- 8-12	42
3	1-4- 8- 5-10-12	38
4	1-4- 8-10- 5-12	36
5	1-4- 8-10-12- 5	45
6	1-4-10- 5- 8-12	42
7	1-4-10- 8- 5-12	50
8	1-4-10- 8-12- 5	49
9	1-5- 4- 8-10-12	38
10	1-5- 4-10- 8-12	42
11	4-1- 5- 8-10-12	47
12	4-1- 5-10- 8-12	51
13	4-1- 8- 5-10-12	47
14	4-1- 8-10- 5-12	45
15	4-1- 8-10-12- 5	54
16	4-1-10- 5- 8-12	51
17	4-1-10- 8- 5-12	49
18	4-1-10- 8-12- 5	58
19	4-5- 1- 8-10-12	47
20	4-5- 1-10- 8-12	51
21	5-1- 4- 8-10-12	46
22	5-1- 4-10- 8-12	50
23	5-4- 1- 8-10-12	47
24	5-4- 1-10- 8-12	51

Table 6-3   Feasible Schedule of Example Project

1, Activity No.	2, i	3, j	4, Duration	5, Resource	6, EST	7, EFT
1	1	2	8	1	0	3
2	1	3	9	—	0	9
3	2	4	1	—	8	9
4	3	4	3	1	9	12
5	3	5	6	1	12	18
6	4	5	7	—	12	19
7	4	6	4	—	12	16
8	4	7	8	1	18	26
9	5	9	7	—	19	26
10	6	7	3	1	26	29
11	7	8	3	—	29	32
12	8	9	6	1	32	38

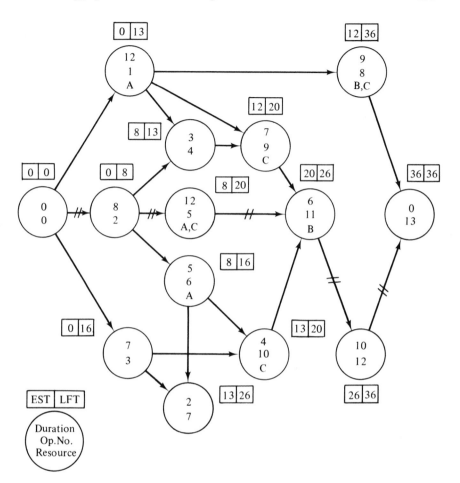

Figure 6-25.   Example project.

of each resource is

Resource	Amount
A	2 units
B	1 unit
C	2 units

As shown in Fig. 6-25, operations 1, 5, 6, 8, 9, 10, and 11 require the use of one or more of these resources. Only operations 5 and 8 require more than 1 unit of one resource. To help illustrate the network's resource requirements, Fig. 6-26 shows the initial Gantt bar chart and required resource levels for the project. Although we could relax the assumption of a predetermined sequence for the operations, we shall maintain this assumption to make comparison with our last model easier. Let us now restate our problem.

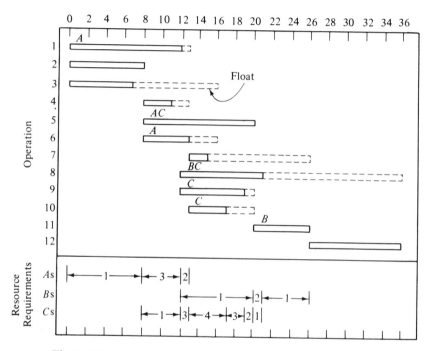

Figure 6-26. Gantt chart without resource considerations.

We want to minimize the project time under the constraints that

    1. The resource requirements never exceed our available resources.
    2. The operations are performed in the predetermined order.

We shall look at one resource at a time and formulate the constraints for all operations requiring use of that resource.

Resource A. Operations 1, 5, and 6, which require resource A, generate the following constraints based only on technological requirements:

$$t_1 \geq t_0 + y_0$$
$$t_5 \geq t_2 + y_2 \qquad (6\text{-}7)$$
$$t_6 \geq t_2 + y_2,$$

where t_i = earliest start time of operation i
y_i = duration (working time) of operation i.

These constraints merely say that an operation can start once the operation on which it is dependent is completed. A feasible solution satisfying the resource A requirements occurs when two or less of operations 1, 5, and 6 are in progress at any time because each operation requires 1 unit of resource A but resource A is limited to 2 units during any time period. To accommodate resource A's conditions, we have to make sure that one of the three operations begins *after* the two other have been terminated. If operation 6 were to begin after operations 1 and 5 have been terminated, either of the following two inequalities would have to hold:

$$t_6 \geq t_1 + y_1$$
$$t_6 \geq t_5 + y_5. \qquad (6\text{-}8)$$

If operation 5 were to start last, either

$$t_5 \geq t_1 + y_1 \quad \text{or} \quad t_5 \geq t_6 + y_6 \qquad (6\text{-}9)$$

would have to hold. If operation 1 were to be the last, either of the following two constraints would have to hold:

$$t_1 \geq t_5 + y_5 \quad \text{or} \quad t_1 \geq t_6 + y_6. \qquad (6\text{-}10)$$

In each case we want only *one* of the six constraints to be enforced. If we would include all six constraints in our linear program, one constraint would be unnecessary and the rest would be inconsistent with the constraint we want to be enforced. The dilemma is solved by introducing zero-one variables and modifying our original six restrictions by adding an integer variable in the second term:

$$t_6 + T(1 - X_{1,6}) \geq t_1 + y_1$$
$$t_6 + T(1 - X_{5,6}) \geq t_5 + y_5$$
$$t_5 + T(1 - X_{1,5}) \geq t_1 + y_1$$
$$t_5 + T(1 - X_{6,5}) \geq t_6 + y_6 \qquad (6\text{-}11)$$
$$t_1 + T(1 - X_{5,1}) \geq t_5 + y_5$$
$$t_1 + T(1 - X_{6,1}) \geq t_6 + y_6,$$

where T = any large number exceeding the expected project duration
$X_{i,j}$ = integer 0 or 1, where i is the initial operation and j the following operation; a 1 indicates that operation j follows operation i; a zero indicates that i and j occur simultaneously.

Furthermore, it is necessary to add the following constraint:

$$X_{1,5} + X_{1,6} + X_{5,1} + X_{5,6} + X_{6,1} + X_{6,5} = 1, \qquad (6\text{--}12)$$

which is called the selector or indicator constraint for resource A. Thus, using the selector constraint, one of the restraints becomes effective and the other five become redundant. For example, let $X_{5,1} = 1$. The remaining $X_{i,j}$ terms are zero; therefore the constraints reduce to

$$
\begin{aligned}
t_1 &\geq t_5 + y_5 \\
t_1 &\geq t_6 + y_6 - T \\
t_5 &\geq t_1 + y_1 - T \\
t_5 &\geq t_6 + y_6 - T \\
t_6 &\geq t_1 + y_1 - T \\
t_6 &\geq t_5 + y_5 - T.
\end{aligned}
\qquad (6\text{-}13)
$$

For a value of T sufficiently large the last five relationships are clearly redundant. The first relationship is effective and restricts operation 1 from starting until operation 5 is finished.

We use the same approach for resources B and C.

Resource B. Operations 8 and 11 require 1 unit of resource B of which only 1 unit is available. The technological restraints for these operations are

$$
\begin{aligned}
t_8 &\geq t_1 + y_1 \\
t_{11} &\geq t_9 + y_9 \\
t_{11} &\geq t_5 + y_5 \\
t_{11} &\geq t_{10} + y_{10}.
\end{aligned}
\qquad (6\text{-}14)
$$

These restraints must be augmented by resource restraints along with a selector constraint:

$$
\begin{aligned}
t_8 + T(1 - y_{11,8}) - t_{11} + y_{11} \\
t_{11} + T(1 - y_{8,11}) - t_8 + y_8 \\
Y_{8,11} + Y_{11,8} = 1,
\end{aligned}
\qquad (6\text{-}15)
$$

where $Y_{i,j}$ = integer 0 or 1 is the selector variable for resource B.

Resource C. From Fig. 6-25 it is seen that operations 5, 8, 9, and 10 each require 1 unit of resource C. The technological relationships for these operations are

$$
\begin{aligned}
t_5 &\geq t_2 + y_2 & t_9 &\geq t_4 + y_4 \\
t_8 &\geq t_1 + y_1 & t_{10} &\geq t_6 + y_6 \\
t_9 &\geq t_1 + y_1 & t_{10} &\geq t_3 + y_3.
\end{aligned}
\qquad (6\text{-}16)
$$

Two units of C are available; thus the ordering must be for two operations to follow the other two. A total of 12 constraints are required for resource requirements. Stating these restrictions in a form suitable for solution yields

$$T(1 - Z_{5,9}) + t_9 \geq t_5 + y_5$$
$$T(1 - Z_{5,10}) + t_{10} \geq t_5 + y_5$$
$$T(1 - Z_{5,8}) + t_8 \geq t_5 + y_5$$
$$T(1 - Z_{8,5}) + t_5 \geq t_8 + y_8$$
$$T(1 - Z_{8,9}) + t_9 \geq t_8 + y_8$$
$$T(1 - Z_{8,10}) + t_{10} \geq t_8 + y_8 \qquad (6\text{-}17)$$
$$T(1 - Z_{9,5}) + t_5 \geq t_9 + y_9$$
$$T(1 - Z_{9,8}) + t_8 \geq t_9 + y_9$$
$$T(1 - Z_{9,10}) + t_{10} \geq t_9 + y_9$$
$$T(1 - Z_{10,5}) + t_5 \geq t_{10} + y_{10}$$
$$T(1 - Z_{10,8}) + t_8 \geq t_{10} + y_{10}$$
$$T(1 - Z_{10,9}) + t_9 \geq t_{10} + y_{10},$$

where $Z_{i,j}$ = integer 0 or 1 is the selector variable for resource C.

To select a solution where 2 of the restraints are effective and the remaining 10 are redundant requires 5 additional selector constraints:

$$Z_{5,9} + Z_{5,10} + Z_{5,8} + Z_{8,5} + Z_{9,5} + Z_{10,5} = 1$$
$$Z_{8,5} + Z_{8,9} + Z_{8,10} + Z_{5,8} + Z_{9,8} + Z_{10,8} = 1$$
$$Z_{9,5} + Z_{9,8} + Z_{9,10} + Z_{5,9} + Z_{8,9} + Z_{10,9} = 1 \qquad (6\text{-}18)$$
$$Z_{10,5} + Z_{10,8} + Z_{9,10} + Z_{5,10} + Z_{8,10} + Z_{10,9} = 1$$
$$Z_{5,6} + Z_{5,10} + Z_{5,8} + Z_{8,5} + Z_{8,9} + Z_{8,10}$$
$$+ Z_{9,5} + Z_{9,8} + Z_{9,10} + Z_{10,5} + Z_{10,8} + Z_{10,9} = 2.$$

The last selector constraint allows only two of the $Z_{i,j}$ to be selected. Therefore two operations will follow the other two so that the resource will not exceed its availability limit of 2 units. The technological constraints, resource restraints, and selector constraints ensure the existence of a meaningful solution based on the scheduling of operations utilizing the same resource. However, in this problem operations 5 and 8 use two resources and have been considered separately in two different resource operation sets. If further restrictions were not introduced, the influence of such *joining* operations using more than one resource would result in inconsistent answers.

For example, if $X_{5,1} = 1$ and $Z_{8,5} = 1$, it would mean a self-contradictory solution, since activity 1 is a predecessor of 8 and the two variables indicate that activity 1 follows 5 and activity 5 follows 8. See Fig. 6-27. As shown there the following and preceding operations would form an infeasible loop. This undesirable combination could be removed from consideration by adding

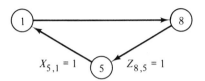

Figure 6-27.

the constraint

$$X_{5,1} + Z_{8,5} \leq 1,$$

where $X_{i,j}$ and $Z_{i,j}$ are integers 0 or 1.

An examination of this problem for such cycles reveals that six improper solution combinations exist. Necessary additional restrictions to prohibit such occurrences are

$$X_{5,1} + Z_{8,5} \leq 1$$
$$Z_{8,9} + Y_{11,8} \leq 1$$
$$Y_{11,8} + Z_{8,10} \leq 1$$
$$Z_{10,5} + X_{5,6} \leq 1 \qquad (6\text{-}19)$$
$$Z_{9,5} + X_{5,1} \leq 1$$
$$Y_{11,8} + Z_{8,5} \leq 1,$$

where $X_{i,j}$, $Y_{i,j}$, and $Z_{i,j}$ are integers 0 or 1.

Adding the remaining technological constraints and formulating the objective function of minimizing the total project duration results in the final, total formulation of the model, as shown in the matrix in Fig. 6-28. The objective function is easily stated as minimizing the time when the last operation, which has a duration time of zero, starts; i.e., minimize t_{13}.

A total of 57 constraints and 33 variables are required to set up this problem. This 57 by 33 matrix is shown in Fig. 6-28.

The optimal solution to this problem is

$$Z = 39$$

$$t_1 = t_2 = t_3 = 0, \qquad t_4 = t_5 = 8, \qquad t_6 = 12, \qquad t_7 = 17, \qquad t_8 = 29,$$
$$t_9 = 12, \qquad t_{10} = 12, \qquad t_{11} = 23, \qquad t_{12} = 29, \qquad t_{13} = 39$$

Figure 6-28. L_p tableau.

Row block annotations at right: rows 1–17 = *Technological Restrictions*; rows 18–25 = *A*; rows 26–29 = *B*; rows 30–51 = *C*.

Objective row: **Minimize** with 1 in column Z_{13}.

	Z_1	Z_2	Z_3	Z_4	Z_5	Z_6	Z_7	Z_8	Z_9	Z_{10}	Z_{11}	Z_{12}	Z_{13}	$X_{1,5}$	$X_{1,6}$	$X_{5,1}$	$X_{6,1}$	$X_{6,5}$	$Y_{8,4}$	$Y_{4,8}$	$U_{5,6}$	$U_{5,8}$	$U_{5,10}$	$U_{6,5}$	$U_{6,9}$	$U_{6,10}$	$U_{9,5}$	$U_{9,8}$	$U_{9,10}$	$U_{10,5}$	$U_{10,8}$	$U_{10,9}$	R.H.S.
Minimize													1																				
1												-1	1																				≥ 10
2							-1				1																						≥ 9
3										-1	1																						≥ 6
4					-1						1																						≥ 2
5								-1	1																								≥ 7
6						-1			1																								≥ 12
7									-1	1																							≥ 4
8							-1	1																									≥ 8
9		-1						1																									≥ 7
10	-1							1																									≥ 12
11				-1				1																									≥ 3
12	-1						1																										≥ 12
13				-1	1																												≥ 5
14			-1		1																												≥ 7
15	-1			1																													≥ 8
16	-1		1																														≥ 8
17	-1	1																															≥ 8
18	-1		1											-62																			≥ -50
19	-1			1											-62																		≥ -50
20	1		-1													-62																	≥ -50
21			-1	1													-62																≥ -50
22				-1														-55															≥ -50
23			1	-1														-55															≥ -50
24														1	1	1	1	1															≥ 1
25														-1	-1	-1	-1	-1															≥ -1
26							-1			1									59														≥ -50
27							1			-1										-56													≥ -50
28																			1	1													≥ 1
29																			-1	-1													≥ -1
30							-1			1											-62												≥ -50
31							-1			1												-62											≥ -50
32							-1				1												-62										≥ -50
33								1		-1														-59									≥ -50
34								-1	1																-59								≥ -50
35								-1		1																-59							≥ -50
36						1			-1																		-57						≥ -50
37								1	-1																			-57					≥ -50
38									-1	1																			-57				≥ -50
39						1					-1																			-54			≥ -50
40								1			-1																				-54		≥ -50
41									1		-1																					-54	≥ -50
42																					1	1	1	1			1			1			≥ 1
43																					-1	-1	-1	-1			-1			-1			≥ -1
44																					1			1	1	1		1			1		≥ 1
45																					-1			-1	-1	-1		-1			-1		≥ -1
46																						1			1		1	1	1			1	≥ 1
47																						-1			-1		-1	-1	-1			-1	≥ -1
48																							1			1			1	1	1	1	≥ 1
49																							-1			-1			-1	-1	-1	-1	≥ -1
50																					1	1	1	1	1	1	1	1	1	1	1	1	≥ 2
51																					-1	-1	-1	-1	-1	-1	-1	-1	-1	-1	-1	-1	≥ -2
52																		-1				-1											≥ -1
53																			-1					-1									≥ -1
54																			-1								-1						≥ -1

$$X_{1,6} = 1 \text{ (op. 1 is followed by op. 6)}$$
$$Z_{5,8} = 1 \text{ (op. 5 is followed by op. 8)}$$
$$Z_{9,10} = 1 \text{ (op. 9 is followed by op. 10)}$$
$$Y_{11,8} = 1 \text{ (op. 11 is followed by op. 8)}.$$

Figure 6-29 shows the optimal utilization of available resources. This

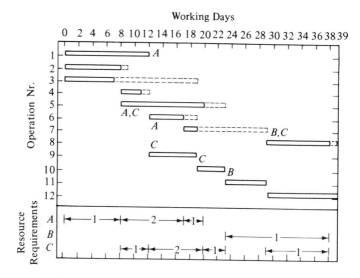

Figure 6-29. Feasible Gantt chart.

hypothetical example possessed many simplifications:

1. Only 12 operations.
2. Only 7 operations require resources.
3. Only 2 operations require more than 1 unit of one resource type.
4. Only three types of resources were considered as limited.

It is very doubtful that in reality we shall ever find a situation that can be simplified to this extent. Formulating more complex problems is entirely feasible; however, the solution for more complex projects is not always found with the existing computerized integer programming routines. The solution to the above problem took 5.31 minutes on an IBM 7094 computer.

It should be obvious that many real problems will be of enormous size if many products are included. Although there are efficient computer programs available to solve large-sized linear programming problems on most of the large computers, integer programs are much less efficient and reliable. The reader is advised to investigate other methods of approach such as dynamic programming or branch and bound methods, which we shall discuss next.

d. Branch and Bound Methods

For the purpose of illustration, let us use the 12-operation project shown in Fig. 6-30, which is Fig. 6-24 changed to circle notation and is the problem solved by the heuristic method.

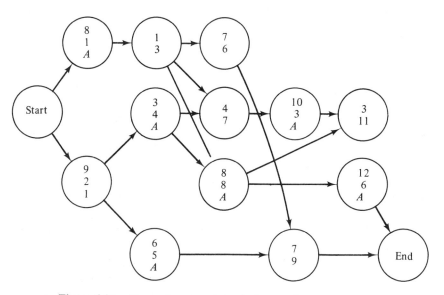

Figure 6-30.   Example network in circle notation.

Source: H. Müller-Merback, "Ein Verfahren zur Planung des optimalen Betriebsmitteleinsatzes bei der Terminierung von Grossprojekten," AWF-Mitteilungen, No. 2, 1967, 5–9.

As before, operations 1, 2, 4, 5, 8, 10, and 12 need 1 unit of resource A each. The capacity of resource A is exactly 1. If we analyze the project neglecting the capacity constraints, we arrive at a total project time of 29 time units. This is a lower bound (unachievable) for the achievable process time taking account of scarce resources. If we use the heuristic method described above, we arrive at a project time of 38 time units, as can be seen from Table 6-4. We have noted that the total project time depends on the sequence in which the operations requiring capacity are performed.

Table 6-4   Project with Resource Constraints

Operation No.	Duration	Required Capacity	EST	EFT
1	8	1	0	8
2	9	—	0	9
3	1	—	8	9
4	3	1	9	12
5	6	1	12	18
6	7	—	12	19
7	4	—	12	19
8	8	1	18	26
9	7	—	19	26
10	3	1	26	29
11	3	—	29	32
12	6	1	32	38

In our project exactly 24 sequences of the constrained operations are possible. Our problem is to find the sequence which leads to the shortest total project time. The problem can be represented by a decision tree with 24 paths, as shown in Fig. 6-31. The tree is drawn to show every possible sequence of the operations 1, 4, 5, 8, 10, and 12 which require the scarce resource.

The goal of branch and bound methods is to solve problems represented by decision trees without enumerating and evaluating all existing paths. Any of these problems can be solved by complete enumeration but that takes too long. The reduction in effort is achieved by constructing the branches of the decision tree by stepwise addition of operations and checking at each step whether the branches can be terminated because they lead to infeasible or nonoptimal solutions. The reference standard for this checking procedure is a bound or limiting value on solutions, which will be considered further. In our case two lower bounds on the time for the project are readily avaiable:

1. The project time neglecting the capacity constraints.
2. The sum of all times requiring limited capacity divided by the capacity available. This represents the schedule in which the capacity is always fully used.

We shall use these two bounds and the heuristic solution with a total project time of 38 units. We can proceed to compute the EFTs of all *free operations* (operations which do not require scarce resources) until the first constrained operation has to be put into the sequence of operations. Then we check the bounds for all constrained operations which could be placed into the next position by computing the EFTs of the different constrained operations and calculating the resulting bound or minimal project time in

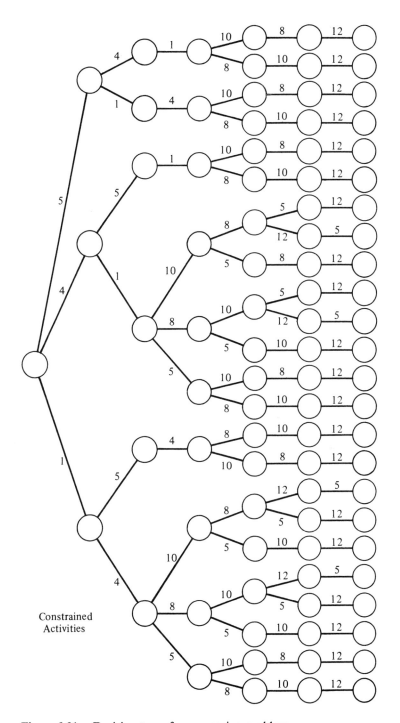

Figure 6-31. Decision tree of a sequencing problem.

two ways:

1. The sum of the EFT of the operation already in the branch and the total time of the remaining project, not considering capacity constraints.
2. The sum of the EFT of the operation already in the branch and the total remaining required times on capacity-limited resources, divided by the units of the resource available. If several resources are constrained, each must be checked and the maximum selected.

Both these values are compared to the best total project time known, which is 38 units at the beginning. The branch of the decision tree is terminated if the value is higher, since only longer project times could result. A new branch is selected by returning to the decision tree. As soon as a better complete sequence has been determined, i.e., as soon as we complete a branch of the decision tree which results in a shorter total project time than the one already known, we replace our old total project bound by this better solution.

Table 6-5   Branch and Bound Solution

Step No.	Sequence	EFT of Last Constrained Operation + Minimal Remaining Project Time	EFT of Last Constrained Operation + Remaining Capacity Requirements
1	1-4-5-8-10-12 (heuristic sol.)	38	38
2	1-	29	34
3	1-4-	29	35
4	1-4-5	35	35
5	1-4-5-10-	38[a]	35
6	1-4-8	33	35
7	1-4-8-5	38[a]	35
8	1-4-8-10-	36	35
9	1-4-8-10-5-	36	35
10	1-4-8-10-5-12	36	36[b]
11	1-4-8-10-12	45[a]	38[a]
12	1-4-10-	36[a]	39[a]
13	1-5-	35	35
14	1-5-4-	35	35
15	1-5-4-8-	38[a]	35
16	1-5-4-10-	42[a]	39[a]
17	4-	41[a]	43[a]
18	5-	38[a]	43[a]

[a]Bounds are violated.
[b]Optimal solution.

The solution steps for our project are depicted in Table 6-5. The corresponding part of the decision tree is shown in Figs. 6-31 and 6-32. For illustrative purposes let us do the computations of the two bounds of step 5 (38 and 25, respectively) in detail:

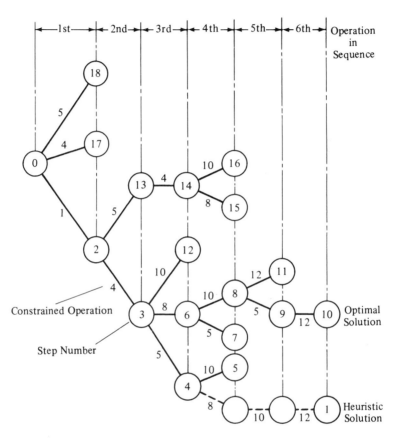

Figure 6-32.   Finding the optimal sequence by branch and bound.

Bound 1:

$$EFT_{10} = EFT_4 + d_5 + d_{10} = 12 + 6 + 3 = 21$$
$$\text{min. remaining proj. time} = d_8 + d_{11} + d_{12} = 17$$
$$21 + 17 = 38.$$

Bound 2:

$$EFT_4 + d_8 + d_{11} + d_{12} = 21 + 8 + 6 = 35.$$

(Each of the operations 8, 11, and 12 requires exactly 1 unit of resource.)

In our example the computational effort is relatively high (18 partial evaluations for 24 possible complete sequences). In other examples the effort is less and sometimes is less than 1 % of the effort compared to complete enumeration techniques [4].

IV. PROJECTS WITH CONTROLLABLE OPERATION LENGTH

a. Introduction

Until now we have assumed that operation times are fixed, not controllable. Even in PERT when the operation times were considered as stochastic variables, their means are assumed not to be under our control. This is not always true; to a certain extent the durations of the activities can be shortened by assigning more of the work force to them, by working overtime, or by intensifying the work effort.

In Fig. 6-33, T_1 is the project length which would, for instance, satisfy

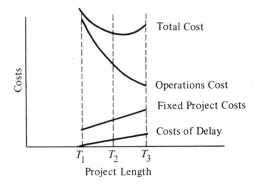

Figure 6-33.   Costs as a function of project length.

our customers completely with no penalty. T_3 might be the project time which we arrived at by means of normal CPM computations and T_2 is the project time with the minimal cost.

In trying to determine the project duration with the minimal cost, one normally assumes the time-cost function of operation cost shown in Fig. 6-34 and Table 6-6.

In most cases a decrease of the duration requires an increase in cost. This gives rise to the following problem. The total project time is no longer uniquely determined by the number and the kind of operations which have to be performed. It can be varied to a certain extent. Since these variations have

Operation Cost of an Activity

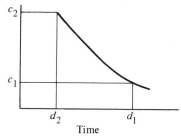

Figure 6-34. Cost as a function of operation time.

cost consequences, it is possible and meaningful to determine total project times which minimize the cost.

The costs which have to be taken into account are essentially

1. *The operation costs,* which consist mainly of variable costs such as wages, raw materials, and repairs. This cost may decrease as the project is extended if better use of personnel and less waste of materials are possible.

2. *Fixed project costs,* which are normally constant per time unit so that the total amount rises as the total project time increases.

3. *Costs of delay,* which are costs, such as lost profit, lost rent, and penalties for not fulfilling delivery contracts, which arise as soon as the total project time surpasses a certain limit.

The overall tendency of these costs as a function of project length is shown in Fig. 6-33 for a general case.

Costs will increase as the time required to finish one operation decreases. The cost curve will be convex and will end at a certain *crash duration* d_2 at which a further decrease of required time becomes impossible. For computational purposes the convex cost curve is approximated by a linear function.

If C_{1ij} is the cost of operation ij finished in the normal time and C_{2ij} is the cost of the same operation performed in the shorter duration d_{2ij}, then

$$\frac{C_{2ij} - C_{1ij}}{d_{1ij} - d_{2ij}} = \text{ASCC}_{ij}, \qquad (6\text{-}20)$$

the average slope of the cost curve or the average cost of shortening the required time by 1 unit. This is also the negative slope of the linear approximation to the cost function.

Table 6-6   Network with Controllable Operation Times

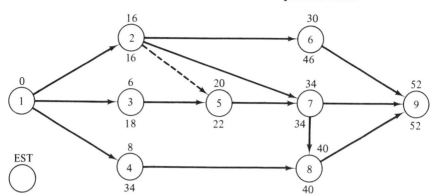

Operation				Costs at		
		Normal	Crash	Normal	Crash	
i	*j*	*Duration*	*Duration*	*Duration*	*Duration*	*ASCC*
(1)	*(2)*	*(3)*	*(4)*	*(5)*	*(6)*	*(7)*
1	2	16	8	6200	9400	400
1	3	6	5	2200	2400	200
1	4	8	6	1800	2600	400
2	5	0	0	0	0	0
2	6	24	16	6000	6800	100
2	7	18	12	2800	4300	250
3	5	4	4	1000	1000	0
4	8	6	5	900	1400	500
5	7	3	1	1160	1560	200
5	8	18	16	5000	5600	200
6	9	6	5	2400	3000	600
7	8	6	6	1800	1800	0
7	9	14	8	3000	5100	350
8	9	12	6	4200	7200	500

b. The Crash Heuristic

There are two possible approaches to reducing the total project time by
decreasing the times required to perform each operation:

  1. Decrease the duration of the critical path operation starting with
     the one with the lowest ASCC until either it reaches the crash
     duration or until other operations become critical. Proceed by

choosing the critical operation with the next lowest ASCC until the desired project time is reached.

2. Decrease all operation durations to their crash durations. Then allow stepwise increase of the durations of the critical operations with the highest ASCC until the desired project time has been reached.

The first approach is illustrated by the following example (Table 6-6).†
Fig. 6-35(a)–(f) illustrates the stepwise decrease of total project time. Table 6-7 shows which operations were involved at each step and the additional cost from decreasing the total project time. The critical path at the start is 1, 2, 7, 8, and 9.

Unfortunately, this heuristic may not produce optimal results. An optimal method is available for solving this problem. It is a multiple-step network flow algorithm devised by Ford and Fulkerson to find the least-cost time reduction on the critical path for any project length [5].

Let us assume that the project cost and cost due to delay shown in columns 5 and 6 of Table 6-8 have been determined for our project. This table is consistent with the steps of Table 6-7 but adds delay costs and fixed costs. From Table 6-8 it becomes obvious that the minimal project time of 32 time units determined by the heuristic is not the project time leading to the least total cost. The total project time with the least cost is 35 time units.

It should be obvious by now that the determination of optimal networks and the consideration of resource constraints always require the elementary time analysis of the respective networks using CPM, MPM, or PERT. Which of the methods should be used for the first step depends on the specific requirements of the project to be controlled. This can be decided only after a thorough investigation of the particular situation.

V. SYSTEMS CONSIDERATIONS IN NETWORK PLANNING

The sections above have developed several algorithms for dealing with the networks which represent production projects. In this section we shall present a discussion of the use of these techniques in project management. Included are discussions of the information system required for not only the planning but also the control phase of the network, the allocation of float, the leveling of resources, the costing of activities in planning and control, and financial planning and control considerations. The last topic may require some justification. The production manager is often bewildered when told he cannot just go out and do the job to be done because of financial limitations.

---

†H. J. Zimmermann, *Netzplantechnik*, Walter DeGruyter & Co., Berlin, 1971, pp. 66–70. Courtesy of Walter DeGruyter & Co.

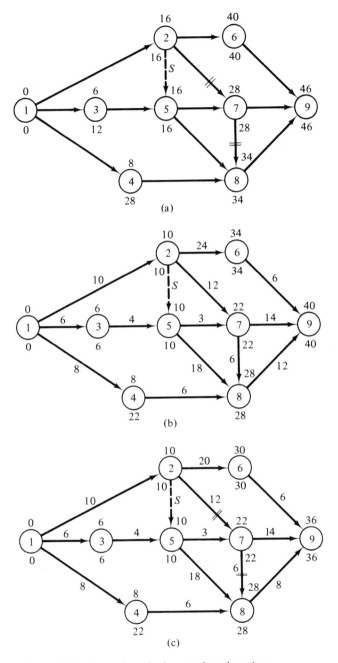

Figure 6-35. Steps in reducing total project time.

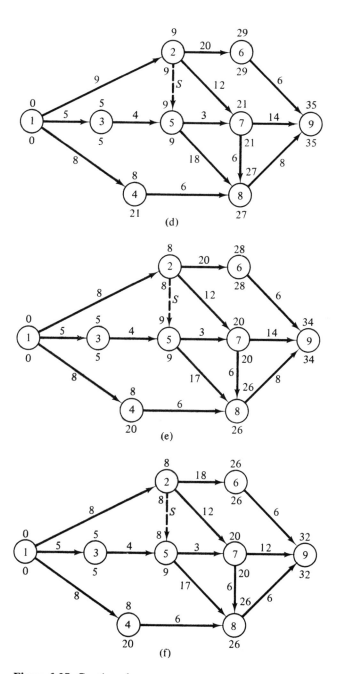

Figure 6-35. Continued

**Table 6-7   Stages of Heuristic Algorithm:
Normal Project Time of 52 Units**

Decrease Time on Operation	Time Units Reduced	Additions to Critical Path	ASCC	Crash
1 (2-7)	6	(2-5-8) (2-6-9)	250	(2-7)
2 (1-2)	6	(1-3-5)	400	
3 (8-9) (2-6)	4	(7-9)	500 100	
4 (1-2) (1-3)	1	—	400 200	(1-3)
5 (1-2) (5-8)	1	—	400 200	(1-2)

6 (8-9)
   (7-9)
   (2-6)
	2	—	500
			350
			100
				(8-9)

Table 6-8   Total Cost as a Function of Project Time

Plan No. (1)	Project Time (2)	Cost at Normal Duration (3)	Costs of Acceleration (4)	Costs of Delay (5)	Fixed Project Costs (6)	Total Costs (7)
0	52	38,460	0	11,050	3500	53,210
1	46	38,460	1500	8,860	3080	52,100
2	40	38,460	3900	6,380	2660	51,600
3	36	38,460	6300	3,560	2380	50,900
4	35	38,460	6900	1,630	2310	49,500
5	34	38,460	7500	1,550	2240	50,050
6	32	38,460	9400	0	2100	50,160

This can occur in project management and we shall attempt to show how this factor can be built into the project manager's model.

a. Information for Network Planning and Control

Network planning methods are specifically designed for large projects. It is not surprising that a detailed planning technique for large projects would have quite large information and data-processing requirements. In fact, organization of the information has been one of the major benefits of network techniques. On the other hand, many firms involved in large detailed projects have found that substantial problems can occur unless special data-handling procedures are adopted. These procedures are designed to make the handling of network planning data both routine and inexpensive. Otherwise the costs of the control system may overshadow the possible savings. On the other hand, not every firm will have to adopt procedures such as those described below in order to make use of network planning. Substantial benefits may accrue from unsophisticated systems in the following cases:

1. The basic concepts of a critical path can be useful in scheduling without detailed use of CPM or MPM. For example, the Gantt chart can be made more accurate if the scheduler keeps in mind that the total task length is determined by the longest path(s).
2. Simple network plans for overall coordination of a project without detailed activity analysis are often seen in the offices of higher management. These may have some utility. They are essentially an overall Gantt chart.

One lesson from the experience of major U.S. construction companies is the fact that the data and possibly diagrams should be processed by computer, particularly if updating is frequent. Many complete computer packages are available from computer manufacturers, consulting firms, and other companies who have designed their own packages. A brief description of several systems is shown in Table 6-9.

A second lesson is that the preparation of standardized data for computer processing can itself consume a large fraction of possible savings unless standardized methods are devised. Flow sheets and prepunched activity cards can be prepared for many simple standard operations so that the engineer merely checks off certain options and indicates significant parameters. If diagrams are standardized and data procedures and checks are established, it may not even be necessary to resort to computers if trained clerical help is available. This is the case in many European applications.

Third, a standard methodology for breaking down large projects into a number of smaller diagrams must be developed so that everyone knows how his activities fit into the total project. On large-scale aerospace projects, for example, many subcontracting companies must coordinate their activities into one plan. A master CPM diagram is a useful technique if the updating can be accomplished centrally, but this is difficult because of widely varying computerized network planning programs which may be in use by the subcontractors. The techniques for breaking down the network start with simple physical breakdown of the master diagram with coordinates established for relating the parts. At the other extreme are complex routines for condensing detailed networks into simpler networks. The routine represents all the nodes at the interfaces between portions of the diagram for each contractor but summarizes the activities within each portion into only a few activities [6].

Table 6-9 Network Computer Programs[a]

Name and Source	Objectives	Orientation	Method	Multiple Project Capability	Minimal Configuration	Output	Node Capacity	
							Minimal Computer Configuration	Maximal Computer Configuration
GRASP, IBM	Time & capacity planning & reporting	Activity	CPM	No	IBM 360/30	Lists, network diagram	5000	—
PMS, IBM	Time, cost, & capacity planning & reporting	Activity	CPM	Yes	IBM 360/30	Lists, network diagram	—	200,000
PERT TIME/COST, CDC	Time, cost, & capacity planning	Activity or event	PERT	?	CDC 3100	Lists, network diagram	3000	6,000
CPM, Honeywell	Time planning & reporting	Activity	CPM	No	H 110	Lists, network diagram	200	3,800
SINETIK, Siemens	Time, cost, capacity, & financial planning	Activity or event	CPM, MPM, or PERT	Yes	Siemens 4004/35	Lists, tables, network diagram	1000	20,000

[a]From H. J. Zimmermann, *Netzplantechnik*, Walter De Gruyter, Berlin, 1971, p. 128. Courtesy of Walter De Gruyter & Co.

Up to this point CPM methods have been treated strictly as planning techniques. One of the problems with information in CPM is the need to update the networks for the next step in management, control. Because CPM planning is so detailed, control uses the same technique as planning, with frequent review. Control depends on updating the planning network.

As soon as the project has begun, the actual durations become relevant and the network may need to be changed. Although there may be thousands of activities in the network, only hundreds will need to have their durations changed. Many of these will be noncritical and therefore will affect only a small portion of the network, but some will be important enough to require recalculation of the critical path. Therefore the procedures for the original calculation should provide for easy recalculation.

A reporting system is needed to get the information concerning actual durations into the project planning and control system. A first step in setting up the reporting system is to draw time contours on the network, i.e., connect by dotted lines the activities with equal start times or prepare a time-axis display of the events such as in a Gantt chart. This will enable the manager to determine when important events should be happening so that a reporting schedule can be set up.

For reporting purposes it is often worthwhile to break long operations up into weekly or monthly suboperations. Otherwise the weekly or monthly reports will not show that there are any problems with the operations until it is too late to rectify them. A form such as Table 6-10 should be required periodically to make sure that both the project manager and the individual responsible for a long operation are aware of its criticality and how to stay or get back on schedule and are planning ahead to future suboperations.

Periodic reporting of the status of the project is an important part of the network system. In principle the critical path(s) provides a means of translating the principle of management by exception into a specific reporting procedure. Progress on critical paths should be most closely monitored since other activities are not as crucial. Examination of the float of paths and activities gives a crude priority for management attention, as explained below.

b. Allocation of Float

You will recall that two floats were defined in Sec. B.II.b, total float and free float. Total float is the amount of leeway an activity has if every preceding activity is started as early as possible and every following activity is started as late as possible with all durations as planned. It is zero on any critical path. It is therefore actually the float of an entire path. Each activity on the path has the same total float and must share the total float, as will be discussed below. Free float of an activity is the leeway between the earliest starting time and the earliest finishing time—in other words, how much leeway there

Table 6-10 CPM Control Report

Date: Nov. 7, 1971
Project: Tropospheric Scatter System
Operation: 123   Supervisor: Mr. Mahlke

Suboperation (1)[a]	Scheduled Starting Date (2)	Scheduled Finishing Date (3)	Float (4)	Status, Started, % Finished (5)	Expected Finishing Date[b] (6)	Resources Required (7)	Resource Scheduled, Yes, No, or Additional Problems Described (8)
1231							
1232							
1233							
1234							
1235							
1237							

[a]*Note:* Computer or central headquarters prepares columns 1, 2, 3, 4, and 7.
[b]If later than scheduled, provide proposed action to correct if free float is exceeded.

is without affecting the right of *following* activities to start early. On a critical path, free float is zero. The sum of free float on a path is the total float.

The reporting of total float should emphasize that float must be shared by all activities on the path. If reports are broken down by workshops or departments so that only a portion of the path is shown, each department may attempt to use the same total float. If the total float of any one activity is used, the whole path becomes critical. For example, suppose that department 1 notes that total float on an activity is 3 weeks; therefore it decides to start it 3 weeks later than its earliest start time. No harm has yet been done, although the path has become critical. Meanwhile department 2 has looked at the activity following the activity in department 1 and has also noted the 3 weeks of float. Since the department is currently working on a different activity with zero float, the foreman tells the chief mechanic to delay his vacation until the next month when they will be working on an activity with float. The foreman figures that this may increase the duration of the second activity by half a week but that it does not matter because of the float. Now the project completion will be delayed unless additional steps are taken.

One means of avoiding this problem is to allocate the total float of the path to the activities so that departmental or activity managers have a guide for how much of the float they can use. General Electric, for example, has a routine which allocates to each activity a portion of the total float. The allocation routine examines three factors: (1) the placement of the activity in the diagram, with early activities given more leeway or float; (2) the duration of the activity, with longer durations given more float; and (3) an index of the amount of control of the duration which can be exercised by management. Even with this effort, coordination between departments is necessary because not everyone stays within his allocation.

c. Leveling of Resources

In Sec. B.III, algorithms for assigning constrained resources to activities were described. In practice the optimal scheduling of networks with resource constraints is still rudimentary because solution routines for large networks are still inefficient. In previous paragraphs we described some integer programming formulations for solving this problem. Some experimental integer programs specifically designed for this problem have been programmed using the branch and bound technique. For an example, see the thesis by Patton [7]. However, these routines have not yet found general use. Therefore most examination of the scheduling of resources follows a more indirect approach. Some programs do have the ability to display the amounts of resources required by the CPM network. Others have the ability to stay within assigned resource limitations in any time period while generating the CPM network. A plot of resource requirements versus time can be derived from the network diagram if each activity is coded for the resources required. Limits can also be placed on the resources available. When these limits are reached, the start of activities is delayed by the routine and the starting times are moved forward. An example is described below.

The example is from a construction project where the basic resources are categories of labor. Two useful references in construction networks are [8, 9]. Figure 6-36 shows the resource, total construction labor, as a function

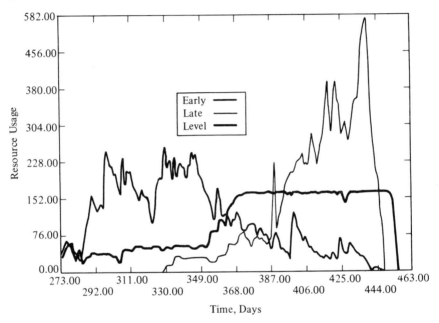

Figure 6-36.   Resource schedule.

of time:

1. The double line with the early peak shows the resource schedule if all jobs start at their earliest starting time.
2. The single line with the latest peak shows the resource schedule if all jobs start at their latest starting time.
3. The triple line shows the resource schedule if all jobs start at their latest starting time except that the total labor resource is constrained and activities are moved back toward their earliest starting time as far as necessary to stay within the resource limit.

The difference between curves 1, 2, and 3 demonstrate that the network plan alone does not provide enough information for scheduling.

A further refinement of the schedule is accomplished by taking the timing of the activities given by the leveled schedule shown by line 3 and breaking down total labor by the skill groupings to get a rough schedule for each type of labor in each time period. Then the network is run again with the size of each skill limited to a fraction of the peak requirement for that skill. A total schedule is obtained. This schedule has resource utilization which is more level than that of Figure 6-36. It gives a usable schedule for each skill but in this case requires nearly 25% more than the minimal time at the construction site.

In Sec. B.IV we discussed a technique for optimizing the network when activities could be shortened at additional cost. Unfortunately, realistic cost curves for these algorithms are difficult to develop. In practice a good deal of the objective is met merely by having management look at the critical activities. They can either shift resources from noncritical activities or purchase additional resources to reduce the duration of critical activities. A float report by activity is useful for this purpose, such as Table 6-10.

d. Costing

There have been several attempts at reporting costs along with the network planning and control [10]. Many CPM computer routines have this capability. In large projects this is a desirable objective because of the difficulty of assessing cost performance before the end of the project. The difficulty arises in tying the actual work done to the planned costs up to that date. The work schedule often changes from that originally estimated. Consequently it is difficult to determine whether cost performance is satisfactory unless each activity and its cost are identified as completed or not completed.

The network diagram can be used for this purpose. An example of a PERT/COST report is shown in Fig. 6-37. Unfortunately it is often difficult to tie the activities in the network plan to the cost accounting definitions of activities. Problems in implementation of PERT/COST have led to its virtual abandonment by the U.S. Department of Defense. The variety of network planning models and the detailed requirements for their implementation have come under criticism. President Nixon's Blue Ribbon Defense Panel [11] reported as follows:

> *Imposed on Program Management is a proliferation of reporting requirements for a wide variety of cost, schedule and technical data to satisfy the the management and reporting systems specified by all higher headquarters, which preoccupy the manager's time to the exclusion of substantive management. . . . So many management control systems now exist that the process of review and analysis, to determine what should be the revisions and consolidations and/or cancellations of the thousands of existing management control systems documents, consumes an inordinate amount of time.*

PERT TIME AND COST STATUS REPORT

Project _____
Contract No. _____
Month Ending _____

	Identification			Time Status					Cost Status			
	Begin Event No.	End Event No.	Activity Account No.	Expected Elapsed Time (t_e)	Scheduled Elapsed Time (t_s)	Scheduled Completion Date (T_S)	Latest Allowable Completion Date (T_L)	Activity Slack ($T_L - T_S$)	Contract Estimate ($)	Actual Costs ($)	Latest Revised Estimate ($)	Overrun/(Underrun) ($)
BASIC												
By Activities	165	168	71829-01	5.0	5.0	9/8/61	8/25/61	-2.0	20,000	25,000	30,000	10,000
	168	182	71829-02	10.0	10.0	11/17/61	11/3/61	-2.0	35,000	18,000	30,000	(5,000)
	165	182	71829-03	8.0	8.0	9/15/61	11/3/61	7.0	15,000	6,000	25,000	10,000
(Direct Costs only)									70,000*	49,000*	85,000*	15,000*
FIRST SUMMARY												
By Individual Hardware Items	165	182	71829	15.0	15.0	11/17/61	11/3/61	-2.0	70,000	49,000	85,000	15,000
									◆105,000	◆74,000	◆128,000	◆23,000
(Total Costs)									175,000*	123,000*	213,000*	38,000*
SECOND SUMMARY												
By Major Hardware Categories	051	325	718	30.0	30.0	1/26/62	1/12/62	-2.0	500,000	300,000	600,000	100,000
(Total Costs)												

Notes:
◆ = Indirect Costs
* = Totals

Figure 6-37. PERT time and cost status report.

Thus we have perhaps come the full cycle from undercontrol to over-control. As with any input, there is an optimum level of control. When new systems and opportunities such as computerization become available, it is difficult for management to select the proper level and type of control without expensive experimentation.

e. Financial Planning and Control

Although associating both estimated and actual costs with an operation can be difficult, there are additional benefits when financial control during the project is necessary. For example, in the the construction industry where cost networks are more common than in other industries, payments may be tied to both completion and expenditure of funds, or a fixed payment schedule may have been specified. In either case the construction company may have to delay starting some operations if their expenditures are running too far ahead of payments. Also, the rate of actual expenditures versus planned expenditures provides a good means of determining whether the original estimates of time and resource requirements were accurate. If the rate of expenditures is higher than planned and the network is only on schedule or behind, then there are definitely difficulties arising in the fulfillment of the original estimates.

When payments to the construction company are scheduled at completion of certain events, some interesting trade-offs occur. The construction company wants to reach the events which will bring payments as soon as possible, but this may mean starting the activities which lead up to the payment event earlier. Unfortunately, these activities usually require payments by the construction company for labor and the like. Therefore the advancement of the payment dates and the delay of performance of costly activities may conflict and make a trade-off necessary. Consider the simple network in Fig. 6-38 with one cost at node 2 and two payments at nodes 3 and 4.

This looks like a quite reasonable contract for the construction company, which makes $1000 net, and for the buyer, who gives partial payment at node 4 but holds the last payment until the last node. The critical path is of length 11 through node 3. Certainly the final payment should encourage the construction company to finish on time in the shortest length of 11.

The earliest starting times for the nodes are (0, 2, 8, 11). However, the construction company might delay activity 2 in order to delay the payment of the $5000. If they delay it 1 day, the path through node 2 becomes critical. Interestingly enough, if they delay it 2 days, their discounted cash flow will be even higher, even though the project and their final payment will be delayed 1 day.

To see this problem from the construction company's viewpoint, we assume that money has a time value and that flows out should be delayed and money

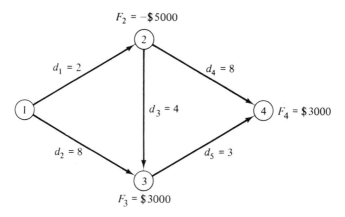

Figure 6-38.

flows in should be advanced. We could discount all cash flows back to the beginning of the project and choose a schedule that will maximize the present value of the flows. It is much simpler, however, to avoid the interest calculations and simply treat money as a resource which can be spent or collected from various days and to minimize the dollar-days used, or

$$\min \sum_{i=1}^{4} F_i T_i = -5000 T_2 + 3000 T_3 + 3000 T_4$$

in our example network. Russell [12] uses the present value but approximates it with one term which turns out to do the same thing. The usual CPM constraints must be obeyed:

$$T_2 - T_1 \geq 2 \quad \text{or} \quad T_2 \geq 2 \qquad \text{if } T_1 = 0 \text{ for convenience}$$
$$T_3 - T_1 \geq 8 \quad \text{or} \quad T_3 \geq 8$$
$$T_3 - T_2 \geq 4$$
$$T_4 - T_2 \geq 8$$
$$T_4 - T_3 > 3,$$

where the right-hand side is the duration, d_j. Although this could be handled by LP, a very simple flow maximization can be performed instead. We write the dual of the problem above:

$$\max \sum_{j=1}^{5} f_i d_j,$$

where f_i is the dual variable which we shall treat as a flow in an arc of the network. The constraints are (we shall explain the equality in a moment)

$$f_1 - f_3 - f_4 = -5000$$
$$f_2 + f_3 - f_5 = 3000$$
$$f_4 + f_5 = 3000.$$

We can get an additional constraint by addition,

$$f_1 + f_2 = 1000,$$

or by figuring the net and attaching it to the source. Returning to the net-work, note that the constraints are exactly the balances on directed flows into the nodes; for example, at node 2, flow from activity 1 minus flows from activities 3 and 4 $= -5000$, F_2. See Fig. 6-39. The solution to the dual is

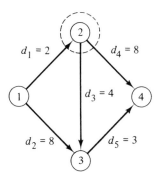

Figure 6-39.

to pick the flows that obey the flow balance equations and which maximize the sum of the product of flow and duration:

$$\max \sum_{j=1}^{5} f_j d_j.$$

This is easy in the simple networks. Since 5000 must come out of node 2 and we want to send as much as possible on the higher duration, we look first at sending the 5000 out on arc 4. However, only 3000 can come in to node 4 by the third constraint, and so we send 2000 down arc 3. Node 2 is balanced. Looking at node 3, nothing can go out since node 4 is already receiving its 3000. By the second constraint node 3 must also receive 3000 and so it must get 1000 from node 1, which also balances node 1 by the last constraint and checks with the zero flow in arc 2 which was assumed in the balance of node 2.

The equality constraints in the dual are explained by the fact that at optimality only flows can occur in arcs with zero float. Therefore we can derive the critical path from our flows. Thus node 3 must be reached at 8, node 2 at 4, and node 4 at 12. Note that this is one day longer than the critical path.

A quick check of the optimality shows that, indeed, this is the best decision for the construction company:

Start Times	Dollar-Days
(0, 2, 8, 11)	$-10{,}000 + 24{,}000 + 37{,}000 = 47{,}000$
(0, 3, 8, 11)	$-15{,}000 + 24{,}000 + 33{,}000 = 42{,}000$
(0, 4, 8, 12)	$-20{,}000 + 24{,}000 + 36{,}000 = 40{,}000$
(0, 5, 9, 13)	$-25{,}000 + 27{,}000 + 39{,}000 = 41{,}000$

The 2-day delay is optimal because an additional day of delay will also delay the payment at node 3.

Russell presents an algorithm which will solve for the schedules with optimal discounted cash flow. It is a modification of the out-of-kilter algorithm and will also perform the minimization above for fairly large networks.

C. Repetitive Aggregate Production Planning Models

I. INTRODUCTION

As we discussed in Sec. A, aggregate production planning concerns the choice of amounts of each product, manpower skill, raw materials, and inventories as well as the timing of these production decisions. Useful tools include sales forecasts, capital and operating budgets, and schedules as well as experience. None of the mathematical models we shall present can do the entire aggregate planning job, but they can be quite helpful in organizing the myriad of data and in providing a problem-solving or optimization approach.

Some of these models were among the first management science efforts, probably because of the importance of the problem and its suitability for mathematical programming. In Sec. C.II we shall discuss a series of models based on production and work-force smoothing equations. In Sec. C.III some heuristic models will be presented. In Sec. C.IV we shall briefly explore a group of linear programming and dynamic programming aggregate scheduling models.

II. PRODUCTION SMOOTHING MODELS

a. Introduction

Often the major issue in aggregate production planning is the trade-off between inventories and manpower fluctuations. Rather than lay off and rehire personnel when sales are low, we can smooth the production level by producing for inventory during slack seasons. There is a whole series of smoothing models based on the realization that production and the work force should be changed slowly. These smoothing relationships are like those of exponential smoothing, a forecasting technique discussed in Appendix B. In general the relationships are

$$P_t = aW_{t-1} + (1 - a)P^*$$
$$W_t = bW_{t-1} + (1 - b)W^*, \tag{6-21}$$

where P_t is the aggregate production level at time t and W_t is the total work force at time t. The constants a and b are called smoothing constants and are between 0 and 1. P^* and W^* are "idealized" levels of the work force or production, which are related in most models to inventory levels and to forecasted sales. For example, the "ideal" inventory in these models is often taken as one half the sum of the economic order quantities for each item. This is a major assumption since in practice inventories result not only from this type of consideration but also from obsolescence of items and stock-out buffers. Also, there are the seasonal inventories which can be explicitly considered in the model. However, this is probably not a bad planning assumption where setup costs are high, as in a paint factory, because the other inventories will be small and independent of the production smoothing decisions. The "ideal" production force is just the force required at normal pay rates to produce the amount specified by the production schedule. It is estimated by standard time methods as described in Chapter 4.

The models devised differ amazingly in the means by which the smoothing constants a and b are chosen. This wide selection of models is of value to the production manager because aggregate planning situations vary widely. A tabular summary and comparison of the four models discussed below, as well as a linear programming formulation which will be discussed later, is contained in Table 6-11.

Table 6-11 Methods of Production Smoothing

Author, Model, & Reference	Cost Structure	Parameter Estimation	Forecast Requirements	Result	Computability	Optimization Technique
1. Holt et al., linear decision rule [13]	Quadratic approx. for layoff & hiring, overtime & regular payroll, inventory & shortages	Historical curve fitting or estimates	Monthly shipments over yearly horizon	Linear decision rule for P_t, W_t as function of W_{t-1}, I_t.	Difficult for first time; easily applied rules	Matrix inversion of differentiated cost
2. Hanssmann and Hess, linear program [14]	Linear approx. to layoffs & hiring, overtime & regular, inventory shortages	Same as above except piecewise linear approx.	Monthly shipments over 6-month horizon (multiperiods increase computational difficulty)	Optimal values of P_t, W_t	Must be run each time period	Linear programming
3. Jones, parametric production planning [15]	Quadratic or linear as above or arbitrary	Same as above	As desired	Smoothing rule for P_t, W_t as function of W_{t-1}, I_t	Difficult first time	Parameter search for good parameter values
4. Bowman, management coefficients [16]	Not required	Management's past decisions on P, W	As desired	Smoothing rule for P_t, W_t as above	Relatively easy	Regression for smoothing equations
5. Taubert, search decision rule [17]	Arbitrary	Historical curve fitting or estimates	As desired	Optimal values for P_t, W_t	Difficult to easy, depending on cost structure	Gradient search

b. Models for Solving the Smoothing Problem

1. The Holt-Modigliani model—the linear decision rule (LDR). The first of these models was the application of classic economic optimization of the type described in Chap. 2 to the aggregate production and work-force levels of a paint factory. This work is a standard reference in management science and is a masterpiece of applied research. Its success has been in spawning the whole set of additional models that we shall list below rather than in the number of direct applications of the technique.

The following costs are considered in the model:

1. The regular payroll costs per time period as a function of the size of the work force. These costs are a straight line from the origin at a slope equal to the average worker's monthly rate, C.
2. Hiring and layoff cost as a function of the change of the work force. These costs increase as the work force goes up or down. A quadratic function is used as an approximation $C_2(W_t - W_{t-1})^2$, as shown in Fig. 6-40.

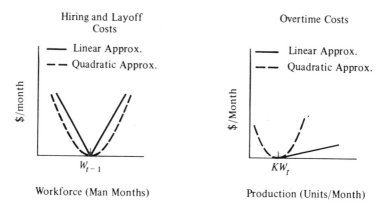

Figure 6-40.

3. Overtime cost. Regular time productivity per worker is K, and so if P is greater than KW, the regular time production, overtime must be paid to get extra production. It can be approximated as

$$C_3(P - KW_t)^2 - C_5 P - C_6 W_t,$$

where C_5 and C_6 are constants which help fit a quadratic function, as shown in Fig. 6-40.

4. Inventory, back-order, and setup costs. Assuming that the usual setup, back-order, and inventory-carrying cost models for the economic lot size are applied to each item, there will be a total inventory which will be optimal for a group of unrelated items. The cost of departing from this "ideal" inventory, I^*, can be approximated by

$$C_7(I^* - C_8 - C_9 S)^2,$$

where S is the shipment rate per time period. The costs are shown in Fig. 6-41.

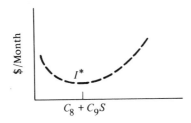

Figure 6-41.   Inventory costs.

The total cost is simply the sum of the four costs over the decision horizon. The constants C_1 through C_9 are estimated in the study from accounting and engineering data. The optimal P and W are found by differentiation with respect to the decision variables W and P, although here for convenience P was taken as a function of S and I, and I was made the decision variable. The resulting set of equations was solved along with an inventory balance constraint,

$$I_{t-1} + P_t - S_t = I_t, \tag{6-22}$$

for each t in the decision horizon. Linear decision rules of the following form were found for the paint company:

$$
\begin{aligned}
P_t &= \sum_i F_i S_i + .9W_{t-1} + 153 - .4I_{t-1} \\
W_t &= .7W_{t-1} + 2 - .01I_{t-1} + \sum_i F_i S_i,
\end{aligned}
\tag{6-23}
$$

where $F_i S_i$ is a weighted forecast of future shipments.

It can be seen that these rules are of the general smoothing form given in Eqs. (6-21). That is, the decision variables at t are a function of their values at $t - 1$ and of inventory and sales. The constants on work force and inventory are between 0 and 1 and are, therefore, smoothing constants. In this model, sales were forecasted for each period in the decision horizon. The optimal forecast weights, F_i, were derived in solving the linear equation system. Yance [18] has rigorously shown the equivalence of this model to the smoothing models. We shall compare this model with the others after presenting each model. As a test the model was compared to the paint company's actual results, but the comparison is clouded by the Korean War and by the fact that the model has parameters obtained from information gathered over the entire period. This information could not have been available to the decision maker. Such a comparison is a common fault in evaluation of these models.

2. Jones' parametric production planning method (PPP). Jones suggests that the basic smoothing equations be taken as

$$W_t = AW_{t-1} + (1 - A)W_d, \qquad (6\text{-}24)$$

where W_d, the desired work force as defined below, is based on a forecast of sales and a standard least-cost work force for each sales level. In particular Jones assumed that

$$W_d = \sum_{t=1}^{E} b_t K(F_t) + b_{t-1}K(I^* - I_t), \qquad (6\text{-}25)$$

where B like A is a fractional smoothing constant, used raised to a power in

$$b_t = \frac{B^t}{\sum_{t=1}^{E} B^t}. \qquad (6\text{-}26)$$

Therefore b_t is a weighting function on the forecast of sales of the ith period. E is the planning horizon, $K(F_t)$ is the work force with least variable cost for production of the quantity in parentheses, I^* is the ideal inventory, and F_t is a forecast of sales for the t period.

The production rule is of the form

$$P_t = (1 - C)K^{-1}(W_t) + \sum_t d_t F_t + d_{t+1}(I^* - I_t), \qquad (6\text{-}27)$$

where $K^{-1}(W_t)$ is the least unit-cost production by W_t workers, and W_t is a number already set by the first rule. C is a constant to be determined. $d_t = D^t/\sum_{t=1}^{E} D^t$ is the forecast weighting for the ith period, and D is a forecast weighting factor, a constant to be determined.

These rules, Eqs. (6-25) and (6-27), for W and P are obviously rules of the general smoothing form. The difference in Jones' method is the method of deriving the smoothing constants A, B, C, and D. Whereas Holt et al. derived optimal coefficients for a particular quadratic cost function, Jones generalized to a search for values for the constants that will optimize any specified cost function. This can be done by simply assuming a quadratic cost structure such as in the LDR study; computing costs for various combinations of the parameters A, B, C, and D; and finally selecting the lowest-cost set of parameter values. This is the method of direct search. It can also be done with any arbitrary cost function or even historical data or simulation results.

Jones compared the parametric production planning model with the LDR model. Table 6-12 shows the costs for combinations of A, B, C, and D parameters and demonstrates the method of direct search. First the quadratic cost structure of the LDR model was assumed. The parametric planning equations for W_t and P_t above were used to determine decisions for the entire time horizon of the LDR model. The decision values were plugged into the quadratic cost equation to obtain a total cost. This was done with each of the 625 possible combinations of A, B, C, and D with each variable set to each of the values .00, .25, .50, .75, and 1.00. The least-cost set of parameters has a cost of $2.056 million and values of .25 for A, 1.0 for B, and .50 for D.

This type of search is inexact and relatively wasteful compared to the more sophisticated search procedures such as golden section or Fibonacci search, which might be applied; see Wilde and Breightler [19]. However, the answer is within $933 of the LDR cost, or a difference of less than 1 %. It is interesting to note in Table 6-12 that some quite different values of the parameters lead to almost identical costs.

The complete equations for the paint factory model obtained by Jones differ from the LDR equations only in the constants and the forecast weighting. The derivation of the form of Jones' model is computationally easier than the LDR model and is more general. It should, therefore, be preferable, particularly since the ideas could be extended to additional decision variables. The LDR model has been proved to be optimal for the quadratic cost structure under nondeterministic forecasts [13]. Such a comparison has not been established for Jones' model.

3. Bowman's management coefficients model. Bowman argued that what is important in planning is the application of a set of consistent rules. He suggested a smoothing model structure because he believed that managers' actual behavior is "more erratic than biased." In his method, historical production decisions for work force and production based on historical sales and inventory levels were used to fit a linear regression with the form of the smoothing rule as the linear function. For example, one management coefficients model [20] has the following smoothing equations:

$$P_t = a + bW_{t-1} - cI_{t-1} + dF_{t+1}$$
$$W_t = a' + b'W_{t-1} + d'F_{t+1}. \tag{6-28}$$

Table 6-12 PPP on Paint Factory—Four-Dimensional Universe Cost Values
(All Figures in Millions of Dollars)[a]

$$A_1 = B_1 = C_1 = D_1 = .00$$
$$A_2 = B_2 = C_2 = D_2 = .25$$
$$A_3 = B_3 = C_3 = D_3 = .50$$
$$A_4 = B_4 = C_4 = D_4 = .75$$
$$A_5 = B_5 = C_5 = D_5 = 1.00$$

		A_1					A_2					A_3					A_4					A_5				
		B_1	B_2	B_3	B_4	B_5	B_1	B_2	B_3	B_4	B_5	B_1	B_2	B_3	B_4	B_5	B_1	B_2	B_3	B_4	B_5	B_1	B_2	B_3	B_4	B_5
D_1 C_1		14.001	14.001	14.001	14.001	14.001	2.835	2.474	2.254	2.192	2.579	2.824	2.408	2.168	2.128	2.740	3.388	2.485	2.165	2.138	2.826	5.037	2.729	2.188	2.150	2.879
C_2		2.551	2.551	2.551	2.551	2.551	2.375	2.236	2.137	2.092	2.151	2.697	2.350	2.159	2.086	2.190	3.372	2.526	2.196	2.098	2.219	5.037	2.866	2.253	2.111	2.243
C_3		2.242	2.242	2.242	2.242	2.242	2.260	2.176	2.115	2.083	2.112	2.632	2.334	2.168	2.094	2.138	3.377	2.582	2.241	2.114	2.185	5.037	3.026	2.344	2.136	2.180
C_4		2.235	2.235	2.235	2.235	2.235	2.240	2.177	2.132	2.109	2.137	2.611	2.346	2.196	2.126	2.163	3.400	2.658	2.304	2.157	2.185	5.037	3.212	2.466	2.194	2.206
C_5		2.291	2.291	2.291	2.291	2.291	2.267	2.215	2.178	2.163	2.196	2.268	2.389	2.248	2.183	2.224	3.411	2.758	2.391	2.225	2.248	5.037	3.429	2.626	2.283	2.271
D_2 C_1		14.001	14.001	14.001	14.001	14.001	2.835	2.474	2.254	2.192	2.579	2.824	2.408	2.168	2.128	2.740	3.388	2.485	2.165	2.138	2.826	5.037	2.729	2.188	2.150	2.879
C_2		2.754	2.754	2.754	2.754	2.754	2.392	2.241	2.137	2.093	2.169	2.662	2.328	2.145	2.084	2.126	3.238	2.464	2.170	2.095	2.250	4.467	2.729	2.209	2.106	2.276
C_3		2.251	2.251	2.251	2.251	2.251	2.247	2.159	2.098	2.067	2.098	2.584	2.280	2.134	2.074	2.126	3.106	2.447	2.178	2.088	2.148	4.308	2.729	2.234	2.102	2.169
C_4		2.187	2.187	2.187	2.187	2.187	2.193	2.132	2.089	2.066	2.090	2.469	2.250	2.131	2.078	2.117	2.991	2.434	2.189	2.098	2.138	4.012	2.729	2.264	2.117	2.158
C_5		2.195	2.195	2.195	2.195	2.195	2.177	2.128	2.094	2.077	2.104	2.414	2.234	2.134	2.091	2.132	2.889	2.425	2.204	2.116	2.155	3.754	2.729	2.248	2.142	2.177
D_3 C_1		14.001	14.001	14.001	14.001	14.001	2.835	2.474	2.254	2.192	2.579	2.824	2.408	2.168	2.128	2.740	3.388	2.485	2.165	2.138	2.826	5.037	2.729	2.188	2.150	2.879
C_2		3.222	3.222	3.222	3.222	3.222	2.445	2.263	2.148	2.107	2.217	2.680	2.331	2.141	2.094	2.280	3.204	2.442	2.158	2.104	2.320	4.485	2.671	2.188	2.115	2.350
C_3		2.329	2.329	2.329	2.329	2.329	2.284	2.174	2.102	2.072	2.116	2.568	2.276	2.124	2.076	2.150	3.649	2.405	2.152	2.087	2.174	4.056	2.620	2.188	2.097	2.196
C_4		2.180	2.180	2.180	2.180	2.180	2.218	2.138	2.085	2.059	2.083	2.485	2.241	2.113	2.067	2.109	2.923	2.376	2.147	2.079	2.130	3.726	2.578	2.188	2.090	2.150
C_5		2.161	2.161	2.161	2.161	2.161	2.199	2.130	2.081	2.056	2.076	2.434	2.220	2.106	2.063	2.102	2.827	2.353	2.143	2.077	2.123	3.479	2.544	2.188	2.090	2.144
D_4 C_1		14.001	14.001	14.001	14.001	14.001	2.835	2.474	2.254	2.192	2.579	2.824	2.408	2.168	2.128	2.740	3.388	2.485	2.165	2.138	2.826	5.037	2.729	2.188	2.150	2.879
C_2		4.525	4.525	4.525	4.525	4.525	2.579	2.334	2.190	2.151	2.346	2.777	2.381	2.162	2.129	2.438	3.264	2.473	2.172	2.139	2.490	4.474	2.682	2.197	2.150	2.526
C_3		2.696	2.696	2.696	2.696	2.696	2.452	2.274	2.165	2.135	2.235	2.758	2.374	2.170	2.132	2.288	3.200	2.484	2.189	2.141	2.345	4.118	2.668	2.216	2.150	2.345
C_4		2.296	2.296	2.296	2.296	2.296	2.428	2.273	2.172	2.133	2.174	2.779	2.401	2.195	2.135	2.206	3.217	2.531	2.222	2.142	2.227	3.949	2.704	2.251	2.150	2.247
C_5		2.212	2.212	2.212	2.212	2.212	2.508	2.330	2.207	2.139	2.140	2.909	2.490	2.243	2.140	2.160	3.376	2.646	2.277	2.144	2.177	4.016	2.823	2.309	2.150	2.195
D_5 C_1		14.001	14.001	14.001	14.001	14.001	2.835	2.474	2.254	2.192	2.579	2.824	2.408	2.168	2.128	2.740	3.388	2.485	2.165	2.138	2.826	5.037	2.729	2.188	2.150	2.879
C_2		6.870	6.870	6.870	6.870	6.870	2.781	2.463	2.280	2.248	2.640	2.931	2.472	2.213	2.199	2.768	3.364	2.540	2.213	2.206	2.835	4.538	2.735	2.234	2.217	2.879
C_3		4.043	4.043	4.043	4.043	4.043	2.845	2.565	2.389	2.366	2.707	3.121	2.617	2.334	2.327	2.797	3.507	2.697	2.337	2.329	2.845	4.374	2.858	2.355	2.337	2.879
C_4		3.086	3.086	3.086	3.086	3.086	3.250	2.888	2.641	2.575	2.777	3.621	2.998	2.626	2.549	2.826	4.036	3.111	2.638	2.548	2.855	4.723	3.262	2.657	2.553	2.879
C_5		2.894	2.894	2.894	2.894	2.894	4.859	3.951	3.310	2.947	2.851	5.761	4.373	3.443	2.955	2.855	6.424	4.630	3.512	2.961	2.865	7.144	4.847	5.558	2.957	2.879

[a] From Curtis R. Jones, "Parametric Production Planning," *Management Science*, 13, No. 11 (July 1967), 862. Courtesy of The Institute of Management Science.

These linear relationships have coefficients a, b, c, and d fitted by a multi-variate regression. The observed production or work-force decisions were the dependent variables. The independent variables were the historical values of earlier work force and inventory and a forecast of sales.

Bowman also explored the use of the management coefficients model on the paint factory. If the quadratic cost structure is assumed to be correct, the management coefficients model gives costs of 129% of the LDR costs. However, the actual decisions had a cost of 138% of the LDR costs. The management coefficients model may, of course, lead to lower costs than the LDR model with the actual, unknown cost structure.

One of the main criticisms of Bowman's model is that it is not self-adjusting. If the managers rely on the model for decisions, it will be impossible to obtain independent data for adjusting the coefficients when new conditions arise. The model would have to be discontinued whenever significant changes occurred until management's behavior stabilized again.

4. Taubert's search decision rule (SDR). Taubert has taken the next logical step in creating a flexible production and work-force planning rule. He suggests that if a cost or net profit structure can be written as a function of a reasonably limited number of decision variables, then any of several optimization techniques can be used. In particular he suggests a "pattern search" method of Hooker and Jeeves, which is a rather crude, but in this particular case an apparently effective, search technique which starts with a feasible solution and evaluates "steps" (increases or decreases) in each one of the n decision variables. If one of these changes results in a higher value of the objective function, a longer step is made in that "direction" of n space. A flow diagram of the procedure appears in Fig. 6-42.

Gradient search techniques or the technique used by Jones or branch and bound procedures are also available to optimize the objective function instead of using pattern search. The SDR model is not limited to any particular form of cost function or particular set of decision variables such as W_t and P_t, and it is therefore merely a return to the economic optimization of Chap. 2. As an example Taubert takes the LDR paint factory and aggregate planning variables P_t and W_t. The results are extremely close to the LDR model with perfect forecasts. SDR does not provide forecast weights as do the LDR and PPP models. This feature could be added to the model but at some computational expense. Computation time for SDR was very short for the paint factory data, however.

In Sec. C.IV, a linear programming model for smoothing will be examined. The advantage of linear programming models is that additional products or constraints can be included. However, the problem then rapidly becomes a detailed scheduling problem which requires considerable computation for each set of decisions. The first three methods each determine a simple smoothing rule which can be used over a long horizon without recomputation of

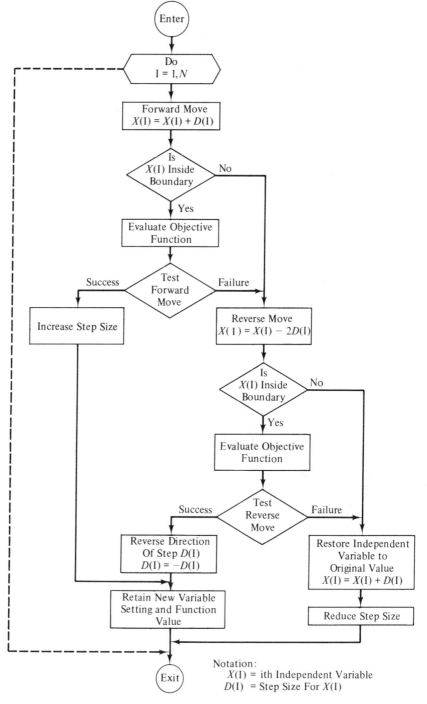

Figure 6-42. Flow chart for search algorithm.

Source: William H. Taubert, "A Search Decision Rule for the Aggregate Scheduling Problem," Management Science, *14, No. 6 (Feb. 1968), B-349. Courtesy of The Institute of Management Science.*

coefficients. Both the SDR and linear programming models require computation each period.

III. HEURISTIC AND SIMULATION AGGREGATE PLANNING MODELS

a. Introduction

The primary criticism of the smoothing models for aggregate production planning is that they are aggregated beyond a useful level. That is, the production rate is simply not that easily related to the total sales. The sales mix and even the seasonal fluctuation of sales may significantly affect production rates. It is probably this reason which has prevented the widespread implementation of the models of Sec. C.II.

One answer would be to disaggregate the model. A firm could forecast sales by relevant product groups and then find production and work-force levels by the methods above for each group. For an approach to disaggregation, see [21]. However, this approach would ignore the interrelationships of the various products. After all, the products are generally made in the same plant by the same people. Separate decisions for each product might produce scheduling conflicts for facilities or personnel. Of course, constraints could be added to the problem to reflect the interrelationships. Indeed, this is the approach of the last group of aggregate planning techniques, linear programming, as discussed in Sec. C.IV, but the advantage of the aggregate models has been their relative lack of constraints, which simplifies solution. This is the chief difference between aggregate planning models and scheduling. Therefore, before we move a bit farther in the direction of scheduling with the linear programming models, we shall examine a different approach, the heuristic.

The basic idea of this approach is to analyze the structure of the major decisions which determine how sales are transformed into production schedules in the plant. If we can quantitatively represent this structure with fair precision by a few simple rules, we may be able to get a good representation of the future response of the plant to a particular set of sales. This representation may be adequate for planning purposes.

b. Heuristics for Aggregate Production Planning

1. Introduction. The term *heuristic* appeared earlier in this chapter and others. A heuristic method is one which obtains a "good" solution but one that is not guaranteed to be optimal in the mathematical sense. Optimality is relatively less important for techniques which deal with problems which have ill-defined criteria or are of an exceedingly large scale or have very poor

data. Since these conditions are often met in aggregate production planning, it is worthwhile exploring heuristics in some detail. They can be described by the following steps:

1. Identification of the major decisions, bottlenecks, and problems.
2. Specification of the major variables in the decision process: run time, product characteristic, material usage, etc.
3. Observation of the rules of thumb by which the decisionmaker transforms the observed variables into a decision such as a production schedule or an order-handling sequence.
4. Determination of the parameters in the rule by matching of decisions with observed input variables or by regression.

This process is a simplification of the modeling steps in Chap. 1. The results will never be able to entirely duplicate the performance of the human decision maker because of his wide range of adaptability. There will be subclassifications of the variables or unusual values of the variables which will arise too infrequently to be represented in the heuristic model. However, the objective here is not to replace the production scheduler but to get a reasonable representation of his later aggregate schedule for early aggregate planning purposes.

2. Examples of heuristic studies of aggregate production planning. (a) A job-shop problem. Hurst and McNamara [22] studied the wool textile production process shown in Fig. 6-43. In this plant a weekly schedule is made up for the nine carding machines from a sequence of the back orders on hand and actual machine conditions, but it is desirable to have a longer-range idea of the schedule in order to purchase raw materials. A heuristic to model the scheduling process was developed and tested.

First the scheduling of the carding operation was determined to be the controlling operation. In the carding schedule, the important variables are the characteristics of the orders on hand and of the machines which will finish current jobs. In particular, the due date, the process time, the material blend, and the thread count currently of each job are important. The thread count setup on the machine and the blend being fed to the carding machines were the major machine characteristics. The due date and process time were converted to one variable, slack time. Slack time is the due date minus a constant minus the carding process time minus the processing time for later processes.

A linear functional relationship of the variables seemed to be indicated by the schedules observed and so the following linear relationship was chosen:

$$y_i = b_1 x_{i1} + b_2 x_{i2} + \sum_{k=1}^{4} \sum_{j=1}^{4} a_{jk} Z_{ijk}, \qquad (6\text{-}29)$$

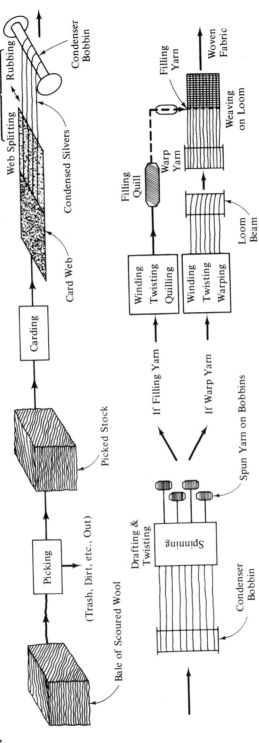

Figure 6-43.

*Source: E. Gerald Hurst and A. B. McNamara, "Heuristic Scheduling in a Woolen Mill,"
Management Science, 14, No. 4 (Dec. 1967), B-184. Courtesy of The Institute of Management Science.*

Wool Textile Production — Flow Chart

where

x_{i1} = change in thread count for decision i

x_{i2} = slack time for decision i

Z_{ijk} = 1 if blend j is on the machine and blend k is on the job list at decision i

Z_{ijk} = 0 otherwise

y_i = priority index for decision on which job to process next, a 0 or 1 variable as below.

The b_i and a_{jk} coefficients were obtained by regression of the linear relation on 25,000 observations of decisions whether or not to schedule a job on a particular carding machine with the dependent variable set to 0 for no and 1 for yes. The table of priority indices, Table 6-13, resulted. A decision to schedule a job on a carding machine that becomes open is made with this matrix. A maximax decision rule is used to make the weekly schedule, as described below.

1. For the first machine which becomes available, look down the column for a maximum priority.

2. Look across that row for a machine with an even higher priority on that job. If there is one, schedule that job on that machine. If not, schedule the job on the first machine.

3. Eliminate the assigned job, put the assigned machine on the schedule, and repeat steps 1 and 2.

The results of the model versus the actual plan are shown in Table 6-13.

(b) An assembly line example. A second quite different example is the heuristic developed for planning the products and number of shifts to employ in a multiline bottling plant by Gordon [23]. Gordon developed specific models for each of three different approaches to aggregate planning: a linear decision rule, two management coefficients rules, and a simple heuristic program for determining the number of line shifts, which was the relevant manpower variable. The rule for number of line shifts which Gordon found the company to be using was to stablize the number of line shifts over the horizon while maintaining inventory between limits which were adjusted to minimize the number of line-shift changes. The flow chart for the program is shown in Fig. 6-44.

The cost results of each of the models over one year of operation of the bottling plant were as shown in Table 6-14. Each of the models and the actual performance show roughly the same total costs, but each has quite different distributions of types of cost. Payroll costs predominate in each method.

Table 6-13 Priority Indices[a]

Job No.	Machine Number				
	1	*2*	*3*	*4*	*4 (Recomputed)*
1	12.38	10.69	2.63	11.00	10.89
2	11.21	9.52	4.01	9.83	9.43
3	2.15	.46	28.15	.77	.63
4	13.67	14.56	3.95	14.87	Eliminated
5	12.25	13.11	2.49	13.42	12.21
6	12.28	10.59	2.52	10.90	9.10
7	8.11	6.42	.77	6.74	5.33
8	11.97	10.28	2.21	11.59	11.01
9	4.64	2.95	3.17	3.25	2.79
10	1.53	.16	27.52	.15	.10

The Comparative Schedules

Card Number	Model's Predicted Schedule (By Job Numbers)	Planner's Actual Schedule (By Job Numbers)	Comments
		First Week	
1	34	34	Same job—same card
2	27	41	Predicted job *not* scheduled by production planner
3	4	4	Same job—same card
4	28	28	Same job—same card
5	15	15	Same job—same card
6	9	9	Same job—same card
7	48	48	Same job—same card
8	1	1	Same job—same card
9	19	11	Predicted job *not* scheduled by production planner
		Second Week	
1	56	56	Same job—same card
2	44	39	Predicted job *not* scheduled by production planner
3	58	58	Same job—same card
4	26	36	Predicted job *not* scheduled by production planner
5	24	24	Same job—same card
6	25	25	Same job—same card
7	33	33	Same job—same card
8	47	47	Same job—same card
9	51	20	Predicted job *not* scheduled by production planner

[a]From E. Gerald Hurst and A. B. McNamara, "Heuristic Scheduling in a Woolen Mill," *Management Science*, 14, No. 4 (Dec. 1967), B-195. Courtesy of The Institute of Management Science.

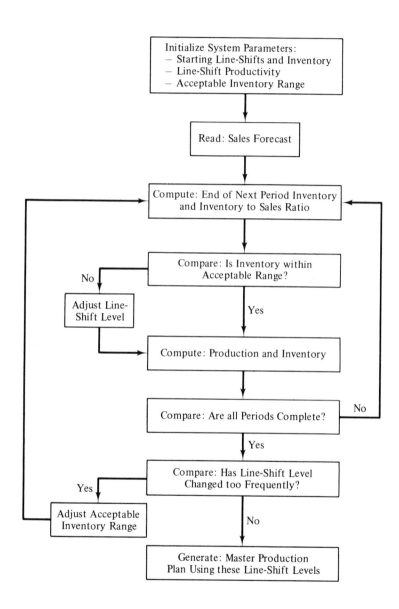

Figure 6-44.   Flow chart of planning procedure.

*Source: J. R. M. Gordon, "A Multi-Model Analysis of an Aggregate Scheduling Deci-
sion." Unpublished Ph.D. dissertation, Sloan School of Management, M.I.T., 1966.*

Table 6-14   Comparative Cost Evaluation of
Simulated Aggregate Schedules[a]

Model	Payroll	Overtime	Inventory	Work-Force Change	Inventory[b] Adjustment	Total
Expressed as a Percentage of LDR Costs						
LDR	100.0	100.0	100.0	100.0	100.0	100.0
Actual	117.0	41.0	82.6	189.2	48.1	110.8
#1 Management	110.6	6.9	123.9	84.9	107.8	107.0
#2 Coefficient	117.4	12.5	80.9	77.8	24.4	107.1
Heuristic	117.6	1.0	108.5	158.4	59.3	111.2
Expressed as Percentage Composition of Total Cost for Each Model						
LDR	84.7	3.7	5.9	1.9	3.8	100.0
Actual	89.4	1.4	4.4	3.2	1.6	100.0
#1 Management	87.6	.3	6.9	1.4	3.8	100.0
#2 Coefficient	92.9	.4	4.5	1.3	.9	100.0
Heuristic	89.6	.1	5.7	2.6	2.0	100.0

[a]The total cost base for these calculations is approximately $700,000.

[b]Because the level of inventory at the end of the test period differed from plan to plan and from the beginning inventory, an asset adjustment due to embedded value must be made (Gordon [23]).

The heuristic program would be the simplest quantitative model for a manager to develop. Its results appear to be reasonably close to those of alternative methods. We cannot conclude that the LDR costs are the "best" because the quadratic cost structure was arbitrarily assumed. Since the aggregate plan is almost always changed later in the scheduling stage, absolute precision is not as necessary as understanding of the method by management. This is a major advantage of heuristics.

Other heuristic aggregate planning models can be found in Dutton [24, 25]. Most firm's aggregate planning methods are heuristic in nature.

c. Simulation Models for Aggregate Production Planning

1. Introduction. There is a rather fine line between the preceding heuristic models and the use of simulation models for aggregate production planning. There are two main differences between these techniques.

1. The heuristic models result in fairly simple rules for planning. They do not require a computer once they are derived. The simulation models are used only when simple procedures are not applicable.

2. The heuristic models can best be used when there is one common unit of sales or production and/or one major controlling stage or process of production. If large numbers of orders for a variety of products are to be handled in many semi-independent stages of production, simulation will be of more value for aggregate planning than heuristics. A large data base is a characteristic of computer simulation models.

2. An example of an aggregate planning simulation model. An example of a simulation model used for aggregate planning is the 90-day scheduling model for movements to and from the West Coast and Hawaii developed by Matson Research Corporation [26]. Twelve freighters and 12 cargo classes are specified since cargo and freighter type must be matched. The company publishes a 90-day schedule of sailings from Hawaii and the three major West Coast areas, the Northwest, San Francisco, and Los Angeles. A short-term schedule is released 1 to 2 weeks in advance. It reflects last-minute adjustments and specifies the particular days the ships will be in particular ports within the San Francisco area, for example.

The aggregate planning problem for this firm can be thought of as a multiperiod, multicommodity transportation problem with queuing at the origins and destinations and requiring integer solutions. This would be difficult to optimize directly and so a simulation approach is warranted. For example, the model is more complicated than merely a queuing situation because a series of economic decisions must be made. The ships can be sent to additional West Coast areas before Hawaii. They can be dropped from the schedule if not enough cargo is available. The flow chart of the model shown in Fig. 6-45 indicates these decisions as well as the cargo and ship movements. The criterion for these decisions is net profit contribution for each sailing, based on cargo revenue and operating cost data. Minimum frequencies of service are also built into the scheduling rules. Because of the prevalence of westbound cargo, the crucial step is scheduling the westbound movements, denoted as WB in Fig. 6-45.

Manipulation of the decision rules for dropping ships from the schedule and changes in operating rules can result in different ship schedules and different profit contributions. The simulation measures the profit given the decisions and input data.

The basic input data for the simulation are

1. Ninety-day forecasts of cargo.
2. The status of ships and cargo at the beginning of the simulation.
3. Economic data on rates and costs.
4. The description of the physical characteristics of the system, ship capacities, handling facilities, and distances.

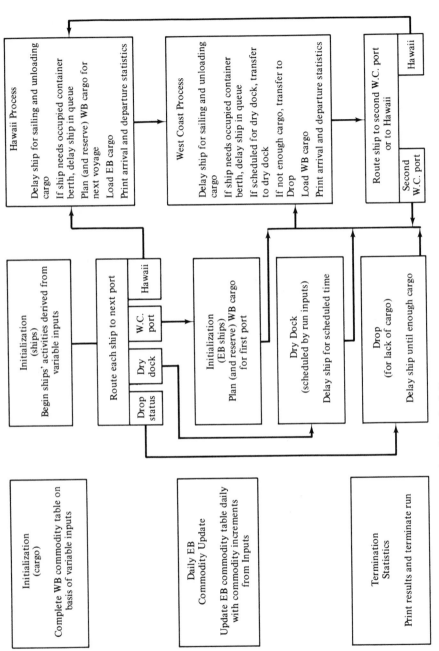

Figure 6-45. General flow chart for ship scheduling.

Source: C. A. Olson, E. E. Sorenson, and W. J. Sullivan, "Medium-Range Scheduling for a Freighter Fleet," Operations Research, 17, No. 4 (July–Aug. 1969), 576. Courtesy of the Operations Research Society of America.

The physical system and the status data are reasonably simple compared to a job-shop production system. Since there are only a dozen ships, changes in the physical system are infrequent. The only information difficult to obtain is the cargo forecast. However, this was already a major responsibility of the company's freight agents. Besides, the information is all needed for the short-term scheduling, although not in computer format, with the exception of the more distant cargo forecasts. For these reasons it is practical to make use of the computer model only for aggregate or medium-range scheduling, without using it for detailed scheduling.

3. Simulation scheduling models for aggregate planning. Although simulation models are useful for aggregate planning, they would rarely be built for use only in aggregate planning. One reason is that the data base can be kept up to date only by constant use. Another reason is that the cost of building and maintaining the model and data base is usually too high for a problem that is strictly planning. The result of these two considerations is that simulation models will be available for aggregate production planning only if they are also used for scheduling. Certainly a good scheduling model can be used along with forecasted orders to produce an aggregate plan. It may be rather costly to do so because the data requirements will be more detailed than for the usual aggregate planning model, but it is possible—and almost certainly desirable—if the scheduling model is available.

As we have noted, usually the model is available because of its primary use for scheduling, most likely in production processes where simulation is most useful for scheduling. We have already looked briefly at the structure of an information system for a job-shop in Chap. 4 (Figs. 4-9 and 4-10). We remarked then that the structure could be used to prepare a simulation for scheduling. A typical example is the job-shop simulation model described by Steinhoff et al. [27]. Let us look again at Figs. 4-9 and 4-10 and note how a simulation of this system could be used an an aggregate planning device as well as a scheduler. Figure 4-9 describes the physical system in computer format. Figure 4-10 shows the decision procedure for handling each order and how the queues of orders are held. These figures show the system as an information system or control system. All the simulation does is repeatedly process orders through the information and decision flow chart of Fig. 4-10.

The change from a control system to a simulation model requires an ability to switch the monitoring of the progress of jobs through the shop from actual observation to simulated estimates of the completion of each operation. Then changes in the decision rules can be examined, such as the first-in, first-out priority rule directly below the dotted line in Fig. 4-10. The basic change from a controller-scheduler to an aggregate planning device is the time frame. Since current orders cover only a small time period, a forecast of future orders is necessary. These relationships are shown in Fig. 6-46.

The forecast of orders is run against the existing system and decision rules

Production Process Controller

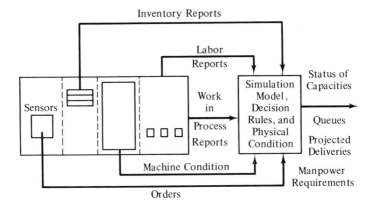

Simulation Scheduler

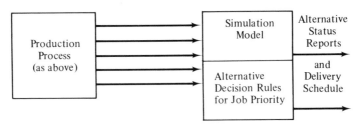

Aggregate Production Planner

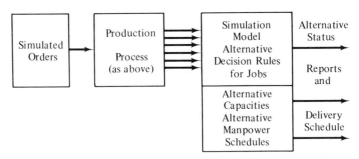

Figure 6-46. Simulation model as information control system, simulation scheduler, and aggregate production planning model.

to identify problems in handling the orders such as bottlenecks or parts shortages. Decision rules can be changed in an attempt to eliminate the problem. Finally, changes in the simulated system such as increased capacity or manpower can be made in order to find their effects, thus accomplishing aggregate planning functions.

IV. LINEAR AND DYNAMIC PROGRAMMING MODELS FOR AGGREGATE PRODUCTION PLANNING

a. Introduction

The use of mathematical programming models in production scheduling has grown to become a major area. It would be theoretically possible to build mathematical programming models for the entire firm down to the scheduling level [28, 29]. Many entire refineries are operated according to linear programming models and these are being extended back to crude oil production and transportation and forward into delivery and inventory decisions in the marketing system, as will be noted in Chap. 10.

For such a process, aggregate planning could make use of the scheduling model to examine longer-run detailed decisions such as capacity or workforce expansion, just as detailed simulation scheduling models were suggested for aggregate planning in the previous section. However, the refinery is in a limited sense a bottleneck or one major facility. Most processes have not been as fully scheduled by linear programming methods. In particular we shall examine some problems and approaches to job-shop type systems. These approaches are based on dynamic and linear programming and finally the meshing of these techniques through the decomposition method of linear programming. First, a linear programming approach to a simple smoothing aggregate planning problem and the make-or-buy question are examined. Next a simple dynamic programming scheduling problem which has scheduling uses in its own right will be examined. Then this dynamic program is embedded in a linear programming formulation for aggregate production planning of the regular and overtime work force.

b. A Linear Programming Model for Production Smoothing

We shall first develop an LP model for the scheduling of a single product only. It is easy to expand the range of the model to several products afterward. This problem is essentially the same as the smoothing problem examined with other techniques in Sec. II.c.

Let us use the following notation:

d_j = demand in the jth period (week, month)

P_j = production in the jth period

s_j = stock at the end of the jth period

c_1 = unit cost of decreasing production capacity from one period to the other, i.e., firing

c_2 = unit cost of increasing production capacity from one period to the other, i.e., hiring

c_3 = cost of carrying one unit in stock from one period to the next.

We shall assume that inventory cost and unit production cost remain unchanged over the entire planning period. Our inventory at the end of the first planning period will be equal to the production in this period plus the inventory carried into this period from the period prior to it minus the sales of this period, or

$$s_1 = P_1 + s_0 - d_1. \tag{6-30}$$

Rearranging the terms, we can write

$$P_1 + s_0 - s_1 = d_1.$$

Also, in general,

$$P_j + s_{j-1} - s_j = d_j. \tag{6-31}$$

The change in production from one period to the next is

$$P_j - P_{j-1} = z_j. \tag{6-32}$$

The z_j could be positive or negative, depending on the direction of the change. Since we want all variables in linear programming to be nonnegative, we shall denote a negative change with n_j and a positive change (increase in production) with z_j. If we restrict z_j and n_j to be nonnegative, we can write

$$P_j - P_{j-1} = z_j - n_j. \tag{6-33}$$

We can now formulate our problem as

$$\text{minimize TC} = c_1 \sum_{j=1}^{n} n_j + c_2 \sum_{j=1}^{n} z_j + c_3 \sum_{j=1}^{n} s_j \tag{6-34}$$

$$\text{subject to } P_j + s_{j-1} - s_j = d_j$$

$$P_j - P_{j-1} - z_j + n_j = 0 \tag{6-35}$$

$$P_j, s_j, z_j, n_j \geq 0.$$

In this model s_0 and s_n, the stock at hand at the beginning of the first period and at the end of the nth period have to be determined before we start the computations. Before pointing to some possible variations of the model, let us look at a small numerical example.

A company wishes a monthly schedule for a 5-month period for their main product. The following data are known:

$$d_1 = 12,000 \qquad P_0 = 14,000$$
$$d_2 = 18,000 \qquad s_0 = 4000$$
$$d_3 = 32,000 \qquad s_5 = 4500$$
$$d_4 = 17,000 \qquad c_1 = \$.01$$
$$d_5 = 18,000 \qquad c_2 = \$.02$$
$$\qquad\qquad\qquad\quad c_3 = \$.05.$$

The problem can now be written as

$$\text{minimize TC} = .01(n_1 + n_2 + n_3 + n_4 + n_5)$$
$$+ .02(z_1 + z_2 + z_3 + z_4 + z_5) \qquad (6\text{-}36)$$
$$+ .05(s_1 + s_2 + s_3 + s_4)$$

$$
\begin{array}{ll}
P_1 - s_1 & = 8000 \\
s_1 + P_2 - s_2 & = 18,000 \\
s_2 + P_3 - s_3 & = 32,000 \\
s_3 + P_4 - s_4 & = 17,000 \\
s_4 + P_5 & = 22,500 \\
P_1 \quad -z_1 + n_1 & = 0 \\
-P_1 \quad + P_2 \quad -z_2 + n_2 & = 0 \\
\quad -P_2 \quad + P_3 \quad -z_3 + n_3 & = 0 \\
\quad\quad -P_3 \quad + P_4 \quad -z_4 + n_4 & = 0 \\
\quad\quad\quad -P_4 \quad + P_5 \quad -z_5 + n_5 & = 0 \\
& p_j, s_j, z_j, n_j \geq 0.
\end{array}
$$

The solution to this problem is

$$P_1 = 14,000 \qquad s_1 = 6000$$
$$P_2 = 22,000 \qquad s_2 = 10,000$$
$$P_3 = 22,000 \qquad s_3 = 0$$
$$P_4 = 19,750 \qquad s_4 = 2750.$$
$$P_5 = 19,750$$

The minimal total costs are $\text{TC} = 1600$.

The model can easily be expanded to many products or to include the use of regular time, overtime, and subcontracting. In the case of subcontracting we would have to take into account the unit production cost. Also, we could treat different versions of the same product as different products. For instance, the parts of the product obtained from overtime, regular time, and subcontractors could be treated as different products.

c. The Make-or-Buy Decision Model

The make-or-buy decision, i.e., the decision whether to manufacture an item with the firm's own productive resources or to purchase it from another firm, is an important and common decision in industry. By purchasing, the firm can uncouple the production program from the sales program and it can smooth production when demand is fluctuating.

Make-or-buy decisions are commonly made using the incremental cost rule (ICR) which states that the firm should manufacture an item if the incremental cost of manufacture is less than the purchase price. We shall show that this rule is optimal only under very limited conditions. It does not take into account multiproduct situations, nor does it consider system implications such as effects on capacity utilization or overtime levels. We shall first develop an extension of the previous model to the make-or-buy decision and then modify it for comparison to the ICR.

The limitations on the methodology for the make-or-buy decisions can be eliminated by expanding the model described in the last paragraph to include the make-or-buy decision. We have to supplement the symbols used in the model above as follows:

s_{ij} = stock of item i in period j

q_{ij} = amount of item i bought in period j

p_{ij} = amount of item i manufactured in period j

d_{ij} = demand for item i in period j

c_{1k} = unit cost of decreasing the amount of resource k

c_{2k} = unit cost of increasing the amount of resource k

c_{3i} = unit variable cost of product i

c_{5i} = unit purchase price of product i

c_{6i} = cost of carrying one unit of product i in stock from one period to the next

l_{ik} = required units of resource k per unit of product i

b_k = available amount of resource k per period.

By arguments similar to those of the last model the following relationships hold:

$$P_{ij} + s_{i(j-1)} - s_{ij} + q_{ij} = d_{ij}. \tag{6-37}$$

The change in production in terms of changes in the variable scarce resources is

$$(P_{ij} - P_{i(j-1)})l_{ik} - z_{ijk} - n_{ijk} = 0. \tag{6-38}$$

Our capacity constraints are

$$P_{ij}l_{ik} \leq b_k. \tag{6-39}$$

Since we want to minimize total cost, our problem is

$$\begin{aligned} \text{minimize TC} = \sum_{ijk} c_{1k}z_{ijk} + \sum_{ijk} c_{2k}n_{ijk} + \sum_{ij} c_{3i}P_{ij} \\ + \sum_{ij} c_{5i}q_{ij} + \sum_{ij} c_{6i}s_{ij} \end{aligned} \tag{6-40}$$

such that

$$\begin{aligned} P_{ij} + s_{i(j-1)} - s_{ij} + q_{ij} = d_{ij} \\ (P_{ij} - P_{0(j-1)})c_{ik} - z_{ijk} + n_{ijk} = 0 \\ \sum_i P_{ij}l_{ik} \leq b_k \end{aligned} \tag{6-41}$$

$$z_{ijk}, n_{ijk}, P_{ij}, q_{ij}, s_{ij} \geq 0.$$

The model above [Eqs. (6-40) and (6-41)] is very general and includes smoothing considerations as well as multiple items. In comparing linear programming models with the ICR it seems appropriate to separate the two effects. We shall therefore limit our comparison model to a single-period model, i.e., a model in which no smoothing occurs. This limitation is appropriate because the ICR does not consider multiple periods. In addition, we shall consider labor as the only scarce factor.

Under these circumstances the notation would have to be slightly changed as indicated; the other notation is the same as before:

w_{ik} = labor absorption of one unit of product i in work center k

P_i = amount produced of product i

q_i = amount purchased of product i

d_i = demand for product i

b_k = maximal number of workers assignable to work center k

w_k = number of workers assigned to work center k

o_k = overtime (in hours) performed in work center k

α = regular number of hours per worker

c_{3i} = unit variable cost of product i excluding labor

c_{7k} = hourly wage rate of regular time in work center k

c_{8k} = hourly wage rate of overtime in work center k.

The model now reads as follows:

$$\text{minimize } Z = \sum_i (c_{3i}P_i + c_{5i}q_i) + \sum_k (w_k \alpha c_{7k} + c_{8k}o_k) \quad (6\text{-}42)$$

$$\text{Subject to } P_i + q_i \geqq d_i$$

$$\sum_i w_{ik}P_i - \alpha w_k - o_k \leqq 0, \qquad w_k \leqq b_k$$

$$P_i, q_i, w_k, o_k \geqq 0.$$

The dual problem to Eq. (6-43), with β_i, ∂_k, and δ_k the dual variables corresponding to the first, second, and third primal constraints, is

$$\text{maximize } Z' = \sum_i d_i\beta_i + \sum_k b_k\delta_k \quad (6\text{-}43)$$

$$\text{subject to } \beta_t - \sum_k w_{ik}\partial_k \leqq c_{3i}$$

$$\beta_i \leqq c_{5i}$$

$$\alpha \partial_k - \delta_k \leqq c_{7k} \quad (6\text{-}44)$$

$$\partial_k \leqq c_{8k}$$

$$\beta_i, \partial_k, \delta_k \geqq 0.$$

Using the notation above, the ICR can be stated as

if $c_{5i} \geqq c_{3i} + \sum_k w_{ik}c_{7k}$, set $p_i = d_i$, $q_i = 0$

if $c_{5i} \geqq c_{3i} + \sum_k w_{ik}c_{7k}$, set $p_i = 0$, $q_i = d_i$ \quad (6-45)

if $c_{5i} = c_{3i} + \sum_k w_{ik}c_{7k}$, set p_i and q_i such that $p_i + q_i = d_i$.

Using dual relationships, we shall now find optimal cost relationships which can be compared to the ICR. Let us assume that the optimal solution to (6-43) indicates that product i is to be manufactured and not purchased. From the theorem of complementary slackness we can state that

$$P_i(\beta_i - c_{3i} - \sum_k w_{ik}\partial_k) = 0, \quad (6\text{-}46)$$

and since $P_i > 0$ by assumption,

$$\beta_i = c_{3i} + \sum_k w_{ik}\partial_k. \quad (6\text{-}47)$$

In other words, the dual prices corresponding to the first primal constraints
have to be equal to actual cost, considering multiitem constraints on capacity.
It is easy to show that the following relationship has to hold for (6-47) to
be optimal,

$$c_{5i} > c_{3i} + \sum_{k} w_{ik}\, \partial_{k}, \qquad (6\text{-}48)$$

because according to the theorem of complementary slackness for $q_i = 0$,

$$q_i(c_{5i} - \beta_i) = 0. \qquad (6\text{-}49)$$

Also, since $\beta_i < c_{5i}$, in conjunction with (6-47)

$$c_{5i} > c_{3i} + \sum_{k} w_{ik}\, \partial_{k}. \qquad (6\text{-}50)$$

It can also be shown that (6-48) is not only a necessary but also a sufficient
condition for optimality of the decision $p_i = d_i$ and $q_i = 0$. Similarly, it can
be proved that the optimality condition for $p_i = 0$ and $q_i = d_i$ is

$$c_{5i} < c_{3i} + \sum_{k} w_{ik}\, \partial_{k}. \qquad (6\text{-}51)$$

The necessary and sufficient condition for $p_i > 0$, $q_i > 0$ is

$$c_{5i} = c_{3i} + \sum_{k} w_{ik}\, \partial_{k}. \qquad (6\text{-}52)$$

In this case the size of p_i, however, can be determined only by solving programming problem (6-43).

Comparing the three ICR equations [Eqs. (6-45)] with the optimality conditions arrived at by linear programming [Eqs. (6-48), (6-51), and (6-52)],
we observed that the two sets have the same structure. They differ only with
respect to the prices used. While ICR uses the purchase prices and variable
costs of single products, the LP conditions use the dual prices, as expected.
This implies that the ICR does not have to be optimal and can lead to severe
nonoptimalities whenever the real prices differ from dual prices. The prices
will differ whenever one or more of the labor constraints are *binding*, i.e.,
if there is not enough labor available to manufacture in regular time all
the products which should be manufactured rather than bought according
to the ICR. In these cases the ICR will understate the manufacturing cost.

At this point we would recommend using the LP conditions rather than
the ICR for make-or-buy decisions. However, it would be difficult to do so
because the dual prices can only be established ex post, i.e., after solving the
LP problem. Burton and Laughhunn [30] therefore establish bounds on the
basis of LP considerations which can be used in advance of solving the LP
problem. They are more informative than the ICR and they can also be used

to decrease the number of variables and constraints of the LP problem to be solved subsequently:

$$m_{iL} = c_{3i} + \sum_k w_{ik} c_{7k}. \tag{6-53}$$

If $c_{si} \leq m_{iL}$, then it will always be optimal to purchase product i rather than buy it. The highest possible manufacturing cost, on the other hand, will occur when product i has to be manufactured by using overtime in all work centers. These costs can be used as an upper bound on manufacturing cost. They are

$$m_{iL} = c_{3i} + \sum_k w_{ik} c_{8k}. \tag{6-54}$$

Whenever $c_{si} \geq m_{iu}$, it will be optimal to manufacture rather than purchase product i. That leaves the zone of

$$m_{iL} \leq c_{si} \leq m_{iu} \tag{6-55}$$

as the *zone of ignorance*, i.e., the interval in which an optimal solution can be made only after solving the above-mentioned LP problem. The following numerical example shows the nonoptimality of the ICR.

Consider the three-product, three-work-center problem shown in Table 6-15. Application of the ICR to the three products yields

$$IC_1 = 258.75 \leq c_{51} = 300.00$$
$$IC_2 = 267.50 \leq c_{52} = 275.00$$
$$IC_3 = 141.24 \leq c_{53} = 175.00,$$

which results in a production schedule of

$$p_1 = 2400$$
$$p_2 = 1200$$
$$p_3 = 400$$
$$q_1 = q_2 = q_3 = 0.$$

Table 6-16 shows the corresponding results using lower and upper bounds and linear programming, respectively. As can be seen from Table 6-16, the ICR solution was not optimal and incurred a penalty of approximately 2.5% by purchasing when it was not optimal. The use of upper and lower bounds leads to the optimal result.

Similar calculations can be carried out to estimate the error of the ICR by not taking into consideration smoothing effects of the make-or-buy decision.

Table 6-15   Example Make-or-Buy Problem

Parameter	Worker Center		
	$k = 1$	$k = 2$	$k = 3$
α	40	40	40
c_{7n}	200	250	300
c_{8k}	7.5	9.38	11.25
b_k	650	170	800

Parameter	Product		
	$i = 1$	$i = 2$	$i = 3$
d_i	2400	1200	400
c_{3i}	100	200	50
c_{5i}	300	275	175
w_{1i}	10	8	6
w_{2i}	3	2	5
w_{3i}	12	2	4

Table 6-16   Solutions for the Example Problem

Variable	ICR	Bounding	LP
p_1	2,400	2,400	2,400
p_2	1,200	0	0
p_3	400	400	400
q_1	0	0	0
q_2	0	1,200	1,200
q_3	0	0	0
Total cost	$1,041,534	$1,016,000	$1,016,000

d. The Dynamic Programming Lot-Size Scheduling Model

The usual economic order quantity problem specifies a setup or order cost as well as carrying costs. In such a case an inventory problem results even when the demand for an item is deterministic but not constant.

We begin with a simple example. Suppose that the delivery schedule for boilers over the next 4 months is three in January, two in February, three in March, and one in April. No one buys boilers in the summer and we expect to redesign before next fall. Because of automation, the production time is short but a $500 setup cost is involved each time we prepare to produce a batch of boilers. If we have any inventory on hand at the end of a month, our accountants assess a $200 inventory charge for each boiler. The question is how many boilers to produce each month if there is no initial inventory and we must meet demand.

We adopt the following notation:

$$I_t = \text{inventory at time } t$$
$$h_t = \text{inventory carrying cost at time } t$$
$$A_t = \text{order cost or setup cost}$$
$$q_t = \text{amount produced, nonnegative}$$
$$r_t = \text{known demand at } t$$
$$N = \text{length of the horizon}$$
$$Z(q_t) = 0 \text{ if } q_t = 0 \text{ and } 1 \text{ if } q_t = 0.$$

Then total cost to be minimized is

$$\text{TC} = \sum_{t=1}^{N} h_t I_t + A_t Z(q_t) + h_0 I_0 \qquad (6\text{-}56)$$
$$\text{subject to } I_t = I_{t-1} + q_t - r_t. \qquad (6\text{-}57)$$

We cannot apply our usual calculus methods because of the discontinuous cost structure. Instead, we apply the dynamic programming approach of examining a series of problems. For any given initial inventory, I_0, we want the function $f(I_0)$ which minimizes the expression above disregarding the last term for initial inventory cost, or

$$f(I_0) = \min_t \sum_t [h_t I_t + A_t Z(q_t)] \qquad \text{or holding cost plus setup cost} \qquad (6\text{-}58)$$
$$\text{subject to } I_t = I_{t-1} + q_t - r_t. \qquad (6\text{-}59)$$

Consider the Nth period,

$$f_N(I_{N-1}) = \min A_N Z(q_N), \qquad (6\text{-}60)$$

since there need be no further holding cost.

Obviously we produce only if we do not have enough inventory on hand to meet the demand constraint. Now we examine the preceding time period or stage:

$$f_{N-1}(I_{N-2}) = \min [A_N Z(q_{N-1}) + A_N Z(q_N) + h_{N-1} T_{N-1}]. \qquad (6\text{-}61)$$

With the information gained from the Nth period [Eq. (6-60)] this can be written, using the constraint for substitution of I_{N-1} twice, as

$$f_{N-1}(I_{N-2}) = \min [A_{N-1} Z(q_{N-1}) + h_{N-1}(I_{N-2} + q_{N-1} - r_{N-1})$$
$$+ f_N(I_{N-2} + q_{N-1} - r_{N-1})]. \tag{6-62}$$

In general we can write

$$f_t(I_{t-1}) = \min [A_t Z_t + h_t I_t + f_{t-1}(I_t)]. \tag{6-63}$$

With these relationships we can work backward, stage by stage, to the optimal set of decisions at each time period for any I_0, as will be shown in the example.

In the problem above there were four periods and demand in the last period was 1. For simplicity we note that it would never pay to carry more than one unit into the fourth period and so $I_3 = 0$ or 1. From the expression above for the last period,

$$f_N(I_{N-1}) = \min A_N Z(q_N)$$
$$\text{if } I_3 = 0, \quad f_4(0) = 500, \text{ because we must produce one} \tag{6-64}$$
$$\text{if } I_3 = 1, \quad f_4(1) = 0.$$

Next we use the expression for $f_{N-1}(I_{N-2})$ and various possibilities for I_3:

$$\text{if } I_2 = 0, \quad f_3 = \min [500 + 200(0 + q_3 - 3) + f_4(0 + q_3 - 3)]. \tag{6-65}$$

We know that q_3 must be at least 3 to meet demand, but it could also be 4. The decision on q_{N-1} also sets I_3 so that we can use the results for $f_4(I_3)$ above in performing the minimization:

$$f_3(0) = 500 + 200(0) + f_4(0) = 1000 \qquad \text{if } q_3 = 3$$

or

$$500 + 200(1) + f_4(1) = 700 \qquad \text{if } q_3 = 4 \tag{6-66}$$

Obviously, $f_3(0) = 700$ and $q_3 = 4$ if $I_2 = 0$.

We can work through each other possible value of I_2, computing $f_3(I_2)$ and making use of $f_4(I_3)$ in each case. Then we proceed to the $f_2(I_1)$ stage and finally to the $f_1(I_0)$ stage. Then for any I_0 we can follow the optimal decisions at each stage or time period. Table 6-17 gives the results in terms of cost and optimal production quantity for each time period.

It enables the decision maker to select the optimal production schedule for each time period even if at some later period one of the forecasts of sales is proved to be incorrect.

In performing the calculations for Table 6-17, certain rules become obvious,

Table 6-17   Dynamic Programming Schedule

Inventory	$f_1(I_0)$ Production Cost	Qty	$f_2(I_1)$ Production Cost	Qty	$f_3(I_2)$ Production Cost	Qty	$f_4(I_3)$ Production Cost	Qty
0	1600	5	1200	2	700	4	500	1
1	1600	4	1000	5	700	3	0	2
2	1600	3	700	0	700	2	—	—
3	1200	0	900	0	500	0	—	—
4	1200	0	1100	0	200	0	—	—
5	1100	0	1100	0	—	—	—	—
6	1500	0	1000	0	—	—	—	—
7	1500	0	—	—	—	—	—	—
8	2100	0	—	—	—	—	—	—
9	2200	0	—	—	—	—	—	—

such as

1. Never produce in a period and carry inventory into the same period (except for the first period).
2. Produce amounts equal to the sum of demands over some number of periods into the future (except for perhaps the first period).

If the beginning inventory is known, the problem is more easily solved by a forward algorithm—in other words, by starting with I_0 and working toward the final inventory of zero.

These problems can be generalized to include average inventory costs, constraints on maximum production, and backlogging of orders, and other costs such as costs of changing production level may be added. Changes to the algorithm are also necessary, however. For detailed description of these extensions, see Wagner [31] and Zangwill [32]. An application of the model at several installations of the Northrop Corporation is discussed in a recent article by Schussel and Price [33]. In this particular use, dates for factory requirements are known and various vendors submit bids with amounts offered if delivery is taken in certain sized lots or at certain times. The total cost functions may not be strictly concave. Several interesting methods for overcoming this problem are discussed.

When demand is not known deterministically, the problem becomes an inventory problem, such as discussed in Chap. 7.

e. Lot-Size Scheduling by the Decomposition Technique

The technique for lot-size production scheduling, discussed in the preceding paragraphs, is quite adequate for a single product but cannot easily be extended to several products. We shall now discuss a method for the aggregate planning of lot sizes for many products, all of which use the same facilities but which are not necessarily done in the same sequence. This problem was first formulated as a linear programming problem by Manne [34]. It entails aggregate planning for a job-shop that is manpower-limited. Essentially the problem is how many splits should be made in production lots to meet a given schedule and minimize overtime costs. In a later work [35] the method was extended to include regular time and layoff and hiring costs. It is aggregate planning because sequence conflicts and machine capacities are not considered, as would be necessary in a detailed scheduling model.

The number and timing of setups again play an important role and must now be specified for each product, i. The alternative timings of setups are referred to as a sequence such as $(1, 0, 0, 0,)$, where in this example the nine boilers required in our earlier dynamic programming problem are all produced in the first of the four periods.

The labor coefficients in the model are a matrix B_{ijt} of the amount of labor required to produce product i in period t using sequence j. A setup and unit labor requirement can be included in each element b_{ijt}. Demands are now a vector R_{it} for the required deliveries of each item in each time period. Let y_t be overtime labor and w_t the regular time of the work force. We are solving for X_{ij}, the fraction of the total requirement for the ith part to be supplied by the jth sequence of setups. We want all X_{ij} to be 0 or 1, since a sequence is either used or not used. The problem can be stated as follows:

$$\text{minimize} \sum_t y_t$$

$$\text{subject to} \sum_{j=1}^{J} X_{ij} = 1 \text{ (demands are met by the sequence)}$$

$$\sum_{i=1}^{I} \sum_{j=1}^{J} B_{ijt} X_{ij} - y_t = w_t, \qquad t = 1, \ldots, T \tag{6-67}$$

$$x_{ij} \text{ nonnegative.}$$

The only trouble with this formulation is the large number of sequences that may be possible, $I \times 2^{T-1}$.

The creation of this many vectors and the inclusion of them all in the LP problem would make it very difficult to compute. Instead, various authors have suggested a decomposition approach. The sequences are treated as a block in the decomposition. We can see the usefulness of this procedure by examining the matrix that results from the equations above:

$$
\begin{aligned}
X_{11} + \quad X_{12} + \quad X_{13} + \qquad \cdots \qquad\qquad\qquad &= 1 \\
X_{21} + \quad X_{22} \cdots &= 1 \\
b_{111} X_{11} + b_{121} X_{12} + b_{131} X_{13} \cdots b_{211} X_{21} + b_{221} X_{22} \cdots &= b_1 \\
b_{112} X_{11} + b_{122} X_{12} + b_{132} X_{13} \cdots b_{212} X_{21} + b_{222} X_{22} \cdots &= b_2.
\end{aligned}
\tag{6-68}
$$

This problem falls into the class of easily decomposable problems of the form

$$
\begin{bmatrix}
A_1 & A_2 & A_3 \\
B_1 & 0 & 0 \\
0 & B_2 & 0 \\
0 & 0 & B_3
\end{bmatrix}
[X] = [B].
\tag{6-69}
$$

Since there are large areas or partitions of these problems that are empty, it is useful to attack the partitions of the problem individually. Any solution to the entire problem must be a linear combination of solutions to the partitioned problem. In our particular problem we can examine the entire upper portion of constraints as a partition, $\sum_j x_{ij} = 1$. The solution to this is a closed set and so any solution is a linear combination of the vertices of the convex hull of the set. We shall denote one of the H vertices as ϕ_h, a vector of I dimension. These vertices are merely the intersections of the simultaneous equations $\sum_j X_{ij} = 1$. Then $X_{ij} = \sum_h \lambda_h \phi_h$, the linear combination of vertices, where $\sum_n \lambda_h = 1$.

We can rewrite the problem, substituting for the X_{ij}s, as

$$
\text{minimize} \sum_t y_t
$$

$$
\text{subject to} \sum_i, \sum_j, \sum_h b_{ij} - \lambda_h \phi_h - y_t = b_t
\tag{6-70}
$$

$$
\sum \lambda_h = 1, \qquad \lambda_h \geq 0,
$$

where the λ_h now are the variables.

This linear program has fewer rows but a number of variables equal to the number of vertices.

Suppose that we are performing a revised simplex solution of this problem. The reader may wish to refer to Appendix D for a short explanation of the revised simplex. We have a basis and are about to search for a new column of elements $b_{ijt}\phi_h$ to bring into the solution. The top row of the revised simplex tableau contains the shadow prices, π. We evaluate the proposed column vectors for the basis by multiplying the shadow price row times the column. We shall pick the column that maximizes this term-by-term product:

$$
\max_h \left(\sum_t \pi_t b_{ijt} \phi_h \right)
$$

$$
\text{subject to} \sum_j X_{ij} = 1.
\tag{6-71}
$$

We recall that b_{ijt} is made up of a setup labor component and a regular labor component. We note that the problem of generating "good" vectors to bring into the linear programming solution is just the same as the dynamic programming scheduling problem if we treat each item separately. We set $x_{ij} = 1$ for product i if j is the minimal cost sequence using the π_t from the first row of the revised simplex as the unit labor cost and $X_{ij} = 0$ otherwise. The π_t represent the value of overtime in the current solution in each time period. Having performed the maximization, we compile these values into a new vertex, ϕ_h. The vertex is multiplied by the appropriate b_{ijt} to become the new column in the revised simplex tableau.

Another difficulty arises in this problem. Some of the solutions may not be integer, although partial solutions are difficult to interpret. However, most problems will contain only a minor number of fractional solutions. For further explanation, see Dzielinski and Gomory [36]. An application to tire production planning is given by Gorenstein [37]. An approach which reduces the size of the problem is given in [38].

The same general technique of decomposition and generation of optimal vectors at an iteration in the linear program has been applied to many other combinational problems, such as cutting stock problem, by Gilmore and Gomory [39]. Balinski has examined a whole set of problems using this technique [40]. Glassey [41] has shown that the technique can be extended to problems where sequence of operations must be considered, although still without machine constraints in any time period.

SUMMARY

The aggregate planning function is the key to successful production management. Here the personnel and material resources of the firm are first scheduled into the sequence of activities which will reach the economic goals. A major subdivision is made between repetitive versus one-time projects. A series of network models is available for the single large project. These techniques are widely used. For repetitive production aggregate planning is much more varied and a great variety of optimization and heuristic models were explored. The make-or-buy problem is also discussed.

REFERENCES

1. WILLIAM HOLSTEIN, "Production Planning and Control Integrated," *Harvard Business Review* (May–June 1968), 9.

2. ROBERT W. MILLER, *Schedule, Cost and Profit Control with PERT*, McGraw-Hill, New York, 1963.

3. J. J. MODER and C. R. PHILLIPS, *Project Management with CPM and PERT*, Van Nostrand Reinhold, New York, 1964.

4. Hans-Jurgen Zimmermann, *Netzplantechnic*, Walter DeGruyter, Berlin, 1971, p. 63.

5. L. R. Ford and D. R. Fulkerson, *Flows in Networks*, Princeton University Press, Princeton, N.J., 1962, p. 151.

6. Robert W. Blanning and A. G. Rao, "A Note on Decomposition of Project Networks," *Management Science*, 12, No. 1 (Sept. 1965), 145.

7. George T. Patton, *Optimal Scheduling or Resource Constrained Projects*, Unpublished thesis, Stanford University, Stanford, Calif., Aug. 1968.

8. James A. Antill and R. W. Woodhead, *Critical Path Methods in Construction Practice*, Wiley-Interscience, New York, 1970.

9. Eric Jenett, "Experience with and Evaluation of Critical Path Methods," *Chemical Engineering* (Feb. 10, 1961), 96.

10. Army Management Engineering Training Agency, *PERT/COST*, AMETA, Rock Island, Ill., n.d.

11. Blue Ribbon Defense Panel, "Report to the President and the Secretary of Defense in the Department of Defense," GPO, Washington, D.C., 1970, p. 82.

12. A. H. Russell, "Cash Flows in Networks," *Management Science*, 16, No. 5 (Jan. 1970), 357.

13. Charles C. Holt, F. Modigliani, J. Muth, and H. Simon, *Planning Production Inventories and Work Force*, Prentice-Hall, Englewood Cliffs, N.J., 1960, p. 127.

14. Fred Hanssmann and S. W. Hess, "A Linear Programming Approach to Production and Employment Scheduling," *Management Technology* (Jan. 1960), 46.

15. Curtis H. Jones, "Parametric Production Planning, *Management Science*, 13, No. 11 (July 1967), 843.

16. Edward H. Bowman, "Consistency and Optimality in Managerial Decision-Making," *Magagement Science*, 9, No. 2 (Jan. 1963), 310.

17. William H. Taubert, "A Search Decision Rule for the Aggregate Scheduling Problem," *Management Science*, 14, No. 6 (Feb. 1968), B-343.

18. J. V. Yance, "Marshallian Elements in the Carnegie Tech Rules." Unpublished mimeograph paper, M.I.T., Cambridge, Mass.

19. Douglas J. Wilde and C. S. Beightler, *Foundations of Optimization*, Prentice-Hall, Englewood Cliffs, N.J., 1967.

20. Howard Kunreuther, "Extensions of Bowman's Theory on Managerial Decision-Making," *Management Science*, 15, No. 8 (April 1969), B-415.

21. KLAUS ZOLLER, "Optimal Disaggregation of Aggregate Production Plans," *Management Science*, 17, No. 8 (April 1971), B-533.

22. E. GERALD HURST and A. B. McNAMARA, "Heuristic Scheduling in a Woolen Mill," *Management Science*, 14, No. 4 (Dec. 1967), B-182.

23. J. R. M. GORDON, "A Multi-Model Analysis of an Aggregate Scheduling Decision," Unpublished Ph.D. dissertation, M.I.T., Sloan School of Management, Cambridge, Mass., 1966.

24. JOHN M. DUTTON, "Simulation of an Actual Production Scheduling and Work Flow Control System," *International Journal of Production Research* (Dec. 1962), 21.

25. JOHN M. DUTTON, "How Charlie Schedules Run Time," *Research Toward the Development of Management Thought* (Dec. 1966), 48.

26. C. A. OLSON, E. E. SORENSON, and W. J. SULLIVAN, "Medium-Range Scheduling for a Freighter Fleet," *Operations Research*, 17, No. 4 (July–Aug. 1969), 565.

27. HARRY W. STEINHOFF, M. H. BULDIN, and J. L. COLLEY, "Load Forecasting, Priority Sequencing and Simulation in a Job Shop Control System," in *Readings in Production and Operations Management* (E. S. Buffa, ed.), Wiley, New York, 1966, p. 166.

28. GARY L. BERGSTROM and BARNARD E. SMITH, "Multi-item Production Planning: An Extension of the HMMS Rules," *Management Science*, 16, No. 10 (June 1967), 614.

29. K. O. KORTANEK, D. SODARO, and A. L. SOYSTER, "Multi-Product Production Scheduling Via Extreme-Point Properties of Linear Programming," *NLRQ*, 15, No. 2 (June 1968), 287.

30. R. M. BURTON and D. J. LAUGHHUNN, "A Make-Buy Decision in a Production Planning Contest," *Journal of Business Administration*, 1, No. 2 (Winter 1969–1970), 53.

31. HARVEY M. WAGNER, *Principles of Operations Research*, Prentice-Hall, Englewood Cliffs, N.J., 1969, p. 291.

32. WILLARD I. ZANGWILL, "A Deterministic Multi-product, Multi-facility Production and Inventory Model," *Operations Research*, 14, No. 3 (May–June 1966), 486.

33. GEORGE SCHUSSEL and STEVE PRICE, "A Case History in Optimum Inventory Scheduling," *Operations Research*, 18, No. 1 (Jan.–Feb. 1970), 1.

34. ALAN S. MANNE, "Programming of Economic Lot Sizes," *Management Science*, 4, No. 2 (Jan. 1958), reprinted in *Mathematical Studies in Management Science* (A. F. Veinott, ed.), Macmillan, New York, 1965.

35. BERNARD P. DZIELINSKI, C. T. BAKER, and A. S. MANNE, "Simulation Tests of Lot-Size Programming," *Management Science*, 9, No. 2 (Oct. 1963), 229.

36. BERNARD P. DZIELINSKI and R. E. GOMORY, "Optimal Programming of Lot Sizes, Inventory and Labor Allocations," *Management Science*, 11, No. 9 (July 1965), 874.

37. SAMUEL GORENSTEIN, "Planning Tire Production," *Management Science*, 17, No. 2 (Oct. 1970), B-72.

38. L. S. LASDON and R. C. TERJUNG, "An Efficient Algorithm for Multi-item Scheduling," *Operations Research*, 19, No. 4 (July–Aug. 1971), 946.

39. P. C. GILMORE and R. E. GOMORY, "A Linear Programming Approach to the Cutting Stock Problem," *JORSA*, 9, No. 6 (Nov.–Dec. 1961), 849.

40. M. L. BALINSKI, "On Some Decomposition Approaches to Linear Programming," Unpublished mathematical paper, Princeton, N.J.

41. C. R. GLASSEY, "Dynamic Linear Programs for Production Scheduling," *Operations Research*, 19, No. 1 (Jan.–Feb. 1971), 45.

42. T. M. WHITIN, *Optimal Plant under Conditions of Uncertainty*, Netherlands School of Economics Report 2701, Rotterdam, March 20, 1967.

PROBLEMS

1. a. Indicate the critical path on the network in Fig. P-1.

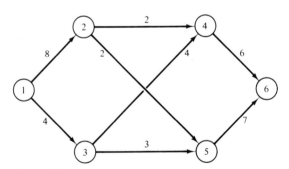

Figure P-1.

b. Write this problem in a primal longest route linear programming unit flow form using X_{ij} as the flow from node i to node j and with proper flow conservation constraints.

c. Write this problem in a dual form. Of what use are dual variables in network problems?

2. Demand for the product of a shop is as follows:

Week	1	2	3	4
Demand:	3	2	3	2

The holding cost for any items left at end of the week is $1 per unit. Demand must be satisfied. Production can be 0, 3, or 4 units per week. The initial inventory is 0. Production is instantaneous. The production cost is $10 in any week in which there is production greater than zero. Inventory is limited to less than 6. Use a dynamic programming approach to solve the problem for minimum production and holding costs.

3. Activities in the project shown in Fig. P-3 and Table P-3 involve two resources which must be present during the activity in the amounts shown.

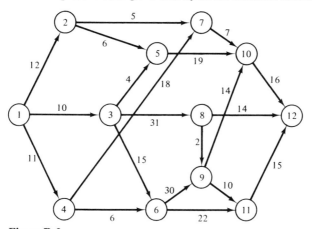

Figure P-3.

Table P-3

Activity	Duration	Resources I	Resources II	Activity	Duration	Resources I	Resources II
(1, 2)	12	3	—	(5, 10)	19	17	—
(1, 3)	10	2	—	(6, 9)	30	6	13
(1, 4)	11	—	4	(6, 11)	22	10	—
(2, 5)	6	—	—	(7, 10)	7	—	—
(2, 7)	5	2.1	—	(8, 9)	2	—	1
(3, 5)	4	—	1.3	(8, 12)	14	6	6
(3, 6)	15	2	2	(9, 10)	14	—	7
(3, 8)	31	3	14	(9, 11)	10	2	2
(4, 6)	6	1	—	(10, 12)	16	8	1
(4, 7)	18	5	5	(11, 12)	15	5	5

    a. Find the critical path.
    b. If every activity starts at its earliest start time, how many units of each resource are needed?
    c. Suppose that only 20 units of resource 2 are available. Which activities should be given priority?
    d. If only 14 units of resource 2 are available, what is the time to completion?
4. Figure P-4(a) is a node network for a nine-task project. Table P-4 gives the limits on the feasible linear combinations of units of labor and time for each of the tasks. Labor must be integer.

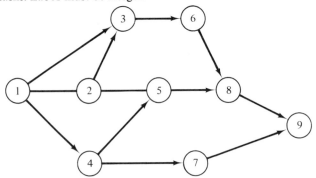

Figure P-4(a).

Table P-4   Feasible $A_j T_j$ Combinations

Task	Labor, A_j	Time, Z_j	Labor, A_j	Time Z_j
1	12	2	3	8
2	12	2	4	6
3	12	3	4	9
4	12	2	2	12
5	12	3	3	12
6	12	1	3	4
7	12	1	4	3
8	12	3	4	9
9	12	3	3	12

    a. Write the 12 constraints representing the sequence of tasks on the network.
    b. Write the 36 constraints which represent these combinations of resources and time. For task 1 they are $Z_1 \geq 2$, $A_1 \geq 3$, $A_1 \geq 3Z_1 \geq 18$, $4A_1 + 3Z_1 \geq 36$.
    c. If there are only 10 men available, write the 12 pairwise constraints which reflect this constraint and the network sequencing.
    d. As an objective function, suppose that we want to minimize the completion time once started, $X_9 - X_1$. A lower bound can be calculated at 24 days.

It is possible that the limits on manpower allowed on the tasks and the sequence constraints would not allow the 24-day completion. A student "solved" the linear integer programming problem and obtained the solution shown in Fig. P-4(b). Can you do better by hand?

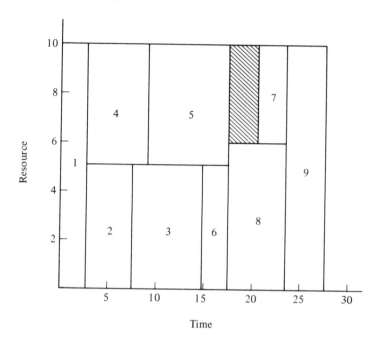

Resources vs. Time

Figure P-4(b).

5. Suppose that the cost of producing an item is a function only of the square of the change in production level, in particular, production cost $= 80(P_t - P_{t-1})^2$. Inventory cost is a function of the square of the difference between the ending inventory I_t and a desired level of inventory of 12, in particular, inventory cost $= 20(I_t - 12)^2$. Sales for the next 4 months are forecasted at 30, 15, 45, and 20. Solve by the Holt-Modigliani-Muth model if $I_0 = 10$ and $P_0 = 15$.

6. A greeting card manufacturer wishes to diversify his line. His designers have been experimenting with a new plastic material. It is available in thin sheets and lends itself to some unusual effects. The designers have come up with two alternative card designs, both of which appear to be totally acceptable. Because special equipment is required to print and cut this new material, the production manager wants to carefully consider the advantages of either card or the possibility of making both of them. The following data have been made available to him.

	Card A	Card B
Time to print card on one special machine	2.4 min	2.4 min
Time to cut and fold card on one special machine	4.8 min	1.6 min
Material required	80 in.^{2}	240 in.^{2}
Estimated profit per card	$.70	$.80

The company works a 40-hour week and has 833 square feet of the material on hand and cannot obtain more in the near future. Assume no cutting waste and the requirement that the job be completed within 1 week. What product mix should the production manager plan to use?

7. A telephone manufacturer reported a problem of selecting the monthly production of phones which was solved by linear programming as follows. The yearly cost function to be minimized was the sum of the average inventory during the month, $(I_i + I_{i+1})/2$, times a holding cost C_1, plus C_2 times the increase, U_i, in production rate for any month requiring an increase, plus C_3 times any decrease, V_i.
   a. Write the objective function.
   b. A safety stock, S, was specified to meet variations in forecasted monthly D_i. Write the inventory balance constraint as a function of production rate X_i.
   c. The production rate in month i is $X_i = (X_{i-1} + U_i - V_i)$, where $U_i V_i = 0$. Rewrite the inventory balance constraints. The manufacturer reported $60,000 annual savings in inventory by the use of this model.

8. Suppose that three plants are available to supply a certain warehouse which requires D_1, D_2, and D_3 thousand units in the next 3 weeks. Variable production costs at the plants are C_1, C_2, and C_3 per thousand units. Transportation costs to the warehouse are T_1, T_2, and T_3 per thousand units. Storage costs at the central warehouse are S per period per thousand units. Capacities of the plants are K_1, K_2, and K_3 per thousand units per period where D is large with respect to any of K_1, K_2, or K_3. Set up a planning algorithm.

9. An order for 20 pieces of length 2, 10 pieces of length 3, and 20 pieces of length 4 is to be cut from stock lengths 5, 6, and 9 with costs of 6, 7, and 10, respectively.
   a. Set up a revised simplex tableau for this problem.
   b. Why would anyone want to solve the following problem?

   $$\max C_B B^{-1} P_j > C_j$$
   $$\text{subject to } 9 \geq 2a_1 + 3a_2 + 4a_3.$$

   c. Give an ad hoc solution to problem b.
   d. Perform a revised simplex iteration using the solution vector of problem c.
   e. Why is the dynamic program routine used, and how do you know when to use it?
   f. Outline the solution to the dynamic programming routine.

10. Whitin [42] has suggested the following problem to illustrate the difficulty of planning when uncertainty is introduced. Two "plants" could be built, one with

a constant marginal cost of \$1.80 per unit or one with costs of \$2.60, \$1.50, and \$2.60 for 1, 2, and 3 units. Demand is distributed $P(D)$ $\frac{1}{4}, \frac{1}{2}, \frac{1}{4}$ for 1, 2, and 3 units, respectively. Price is \$9 and so the payoffs are as shown in Fig. P-10(a)

(i, x)	Outgoing Inventory 0	1	2	q_i Expected Single-Period Payoff
0, 3	21.6 [1/4]	12.6 [1/2]	3.6 [1/4]	12.6
1, 2	23.4 [1/4]	14.4 [1/2]	5.4 [1/4]	14.4
2, 1	25.2 [1/4]	16.2 [1/2]	7.2 [1/4]	16.2

Figure P-10(a). Constant cost plant.

(i, x)	Outgoing Inventory 0	1	2	3	4	q_i Expected Single-Period Payoff
0, 3	19.2 [1/4]	10.2 [1/2]	1.2 [1/4]			10.2
1, 2	24 [1/4]	15 [1/2]	6 [1/4]			15
2, 2		24 [1/4]	15 [1/2]	6 [1/4]		15
3, 2			24 [1/4]	15 [1/2]	6 [1/4]	15
4, 0		27 [1/4]	18 [1/4]	9 [1/4]		18

Figure P-10(b). U-shaped cost plant.

and (b). The left-hand border of each figure, (i, x), represents the inventory and production policy. For example, (1, 2) represents the policy "if initial inventory is one unit, produce 2 units." The row bordering the top indicates the levels of outgoing inventory. The numbers in the boxes in the lower right-hand corner cell contain the probabilities for each possible level of outgoing inventory. As seen in Chaps. 6 and 7, optimal production and inventory decisons are related. Here we see that the plant capacity is also related. We first must solve for the

optimal production and inventory by the technique of Chap. 7. A discount rate
of $B = \frac{1}{1} + r$ is assumed.

a. Obtain the discounted value of profit $V(i, x)$ to the horizon assuming stationarity of the demand distribution for the constant cost plant. Recall from Chap. 7 that $V(0, 3) = q_0 - B[\frac{1}{4}V(0, 3) - \frac{1}{2}V(1, 2) - \frac{1}{4}V(2, 1)]$, etc.

b. The values for the U-shaped plant are $V(0, 3) = 140.32$, $V(1, 2) = 145.12$, $V(2, 2) = 147.75$, $V(3, 2) = 149.39$, and $V(4, 0) = 150.75$. If you have calculated correctly, the conclusion is that the highest-profit choice is the constant cost plant, unless there is some initial inventory available free from some other source.

Part III

CONTROL
OF THE
PRODUCTION PROCESS

Chapters 7, 8, and 9 set forth short-run questions on inventories, scheduling, and maintenance, such as

1. When and how much of materials and products should be placed in noncyclical inventories?
2. When and where should products be produced, on a very short-range and detailed basis?
3. What maintenance should be performed and how should the maintenance force be scheduled?

Control takes up where planning leaves off. Models for answering these questions are detailed. It is the translation of the plan into the detailed accomplishments. Personnel, materials, and facilities are matched in a schedule which includes the interruptions from maintenance.

Chapter 7 contains a number of models for optimizing inventories and a discussion of systems for applying the models including computerization.

Chapter 8 separately treats the scheduling of product-oriented systems or assembly lines. For process-oriented systems, a number of assignment techniques are specified for optimally matching resources and jobs.

Chapter 9 first sets forth the general problem of maintenance policies. Then models for frequency and type of maintenance are specified. Finally the size and scheduling of maintenance crews are addressed.

chapter 7

Inventory Control

A. Contents and Importance of Inventory Control

I. IMPORTANCE

It is neither physically possible nor economically sound to have goods delivered to a system precisely when demands for them occur or to produce goods at precisely the same time and rate that they are asked for by customers. In addition, the different stages of a production system are normally not perfectly balanced with respect to their capacities. Without the use of inventories to uncouple different production facilities, interruptions in the production process would occur, as discussed in Chap. 4.

We can distinguish three fundamental types of inventories according to their main purposes:

1. Inventories of raw materials and purchased parts, which are inputs to the production system.

2. Unfinished goods and *work-in-process* inventories, which are buffer inventories between the different stages of our production process.

3. Finished goods inventories, which contain the outputs of the production process, i.e., products ready for sale.

The problems of the first and the last kind of inventory are very similar. The problems of the second kind of inventory are more difficult, because different stages of the production process have to be considered simultaneously. Models dealing with the second kind of inventory are therefore generally more complex than the models dealing with the first and last types.

II. GENERAL INVENTORY PROBLEMS

In controlling the inventory of any item, two fundamental questions have to be answered:

1. When should the inventory be replenished?
2. How much should be added to inventory?

These two questions must be answered for a variety of inventory systems with consideration of a variety of costs. We shall arrive at different operating rules for these different types of systems and costs. We shall try to find optimal decision rules under different assumptions. These rules result in the minimum cost that can be achieved by operating an inventory system under these assumptions. In the final section of this chapter we shall briefly discuss the applications of the results of inventory theory to the practice of controlling inventories.

III. THE HISTORY OF INVENTORY THEORY

The first attempts to employ analytical techniques in studying inventory problems were found at the beginning of the twentieth century. In 1915 F.W. Harris derived what is often called the "simple lot-sized formula." The same formula was developed by R. H. Wilson in 1918. The first full-length book dealing with inventory problems was written by F. E. Raymond in 1931, while he was at M.I.T. It does not contain any explicit theory or derivations but explains how various extensions of the simple lot-size model can be used in practice. After World War II, detailed attention was focused on inventory problems, particularly in the emerging management sciences and in operations research. Since that time a variety of different inventory models have been formulated and analyzed. One of the first papers which provided a mathematical treatment of the simple type of inventory model was the article by Arrow et al. [1], which appeared in 1951 in *Econometrica*. Since then, inventory theory has become one of the most heavily studied areas of management science.

B. Basic Inventory Models

I. DETERMINATION OF OPTIMAL ORDER QUANTITIES AND CYCLES

a. The Economic Order Quantity

1. The relevant costs and their characteristics. Three kinds of costs are significant in an inventory system:

1. The cost of carrying inventories.
2. The cost of incurring shortages.
3. The cost of replenishing inventories.

We shall refer to these costs as carrying cost, shortage cost, and replenishment cost, respectively, and we shall call the sum of these three kinds of costs the total cost.

The first kind of cost, the cost of carrying inventories, contains costs that are quantity- and time-dependent and costs that are value- and time-dependent. In particular, the quantity- and time-dependent costs included in the carrying cost are the cost of storage space, light, heat, maintenance, rent, etc.; the cost of holding inventory (pilferage, deterioration, spoilage); and the cost of handling, reshuffling, and packaging inventories. The value-dependent costs are capital cost, cost of insurance, cost of obsolescence, etc.

Replenishment costs are costs which depend on the amount being ordered or manufactured, such as commissions, transportation, insurance, customs, taxes, materials, wages, etc. Other elements of replenishment depend only on the number of orders placed, such as review and control cost, purchasing cost, cost of internal transportation, cost of incoming inspection, etc.

The cost of incurring shortages is the cost of overtime payments due to stock outs, of special administrative or control efforts due to stock outs, and of loss of goodwill, loss of sales, etc.

An optimization of inventory systems is possible because the costs mentioned above behave differently as inventory variables change. These variables are the amount of inventories carried, the number of orders, the time period, or the order quantity. We shall consider the cost of carrying inventories first.

Figure 7-1 shows the inventory carrying cost as a function of the order size or the size of the inventory carried. It is assumed that the cost is linearly dependent on the average inventory, which in turn depends linearly on the order size (see Fig. 7-4).

Figure 7-2 shows the replenishment cost, that is, the cost of ordering or setup per time period as a function of the order size. It is obvious that this

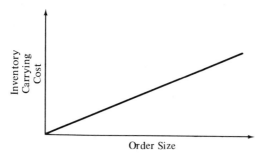

Figure 7-1. Order size and inventory carrying cost.

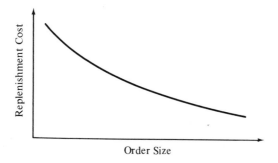

Figure 7-2. Order size and replenishment cost.

cost falls as the order size increases, because the number of orders per time period will decrease.

Our problem is to find the order quantity for which the sum of the replenishment cost and the inventory carrying cost is at a minimum.

Figure 7-3 shows carrying cost, replenishment cost, and total cost as a function of the order quantity. The optimal or economic order size would obviously be q_0.

2. The mathematical model. For the following conditions we want to find the economic order quantity (EOQ) for which the total costs are at a minimum:

1. The demand is deterministic and occurs at a constant rate over the entire interval.

2. Replenishments are made whenever inventory reaches its zero level. The replenishment rate is infinite, i.e., replenishment occurs instantaneously. Therefore no stock-outs are allowed and so stock-out costs do not have to be considered.

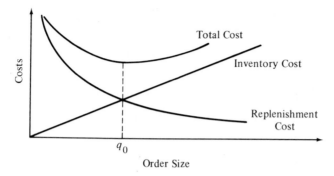

Figure 7-3. Order size and total cost.

3. The replenishment size or order quantity is constant.
4. The unit carrying cost is constant.
5. The replenishment cost consists of a fixed part or order cost and a variable part or unit cost.

Figure 7-4 illustrates the size of inventory as a function of time in the system described above.

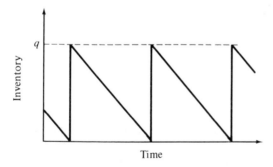

Figure 7-4. Inventory pattern for constant order size and instantaneous replenishment.

The following symbols will be used:

q = order quantity

c_F = fixed replenishment cost per order

c_v = variable replenishment cost per unit of product

c_r = replenishment cost per order

c_c = unit carrying cost per time unit and unit of product

d = demand rate = demand per time unit

p = unit price of product

C_R = total replenishment cost per time unit

C_C = total inventory carrying cost per time unit

TC = total cost per time unit

t = cycle time.

The total costs that have to be minimized are then

$$\text{TC}(q) = C_R + C_C, \tag{7-1}$$

where $C_R = (c_F + qc_v)$
$C_C = (q/2)c_c.$

It is obvious from Fig. 7-4 that the average amount of inventory in our model is $q/2$. Our total cost function is therefore

$$\text{TC}(q) = \frac{q}{2}c_c + (c_F + qc_v)\frac{d}{q}. \tag{7-2}$$

This cost equation was shown graphically in Fig. 7-3. By differentiating the cost equation with respect to q, writing c_r for the replenishment cost per order, and setting the first derivative equal to zero, we arrive at an economic order quantity of

$$q_o = \sqrt{\frac{2dc_r}{c_c}}. \tag{7-3}$$

3. Limitations of the model. Although we arrived at an "optimal" order quantity for our model, the significance and the "optimality" of that order size are very much limited by the assumptions that were made and by some premises that were implied without being stated explicitly.

The main limitations of the model, some of which will be relaxed in some of our later models, are

1. Only one product is being considered.
2. The demand of the entire period is known and constant and the replenishment rate is infinite, and so no stock outs have been considered.
3. The price of the product is independent of the size of demand.

4. No additional constraints from other parts of our system such as production or finance have been taken into account.

We shall make changes in each of these assumptions, but at the price of more complicated models.

b. Optimal Order Cycles and Frequencies

Having found the economic order size, it is not difficult to determine the economic reorder cycle or the economic order frequency. Of course, the same limitations are valid as for the economic order size.

The economic number of orders per time period, r_o, is

$$r_o = \frac{d}{q_o} \quad \text{or} \quad r_o = \sqrt{\frac{dc_c}{2c_r}}. \tag{7-4}$$

The economic ordering cycle is then

$$t_o = \frac{1}{r_o}$$
$$t_o = \sqrt{\frac{2c_r}{dc_c}}. \tag{7-5}$$

c. The Economic Order Quantity When Discounts Are Granted

We shall now relax one of the premises of our basic model: the assumption that prices are constant. Very often quantity discounts are granted when the order size passes a certain limit. That means a decrease in purchase price, which, of course, influences the size of the economic order quantity.

Looking at our basic cost equation, we see that a change in the purchase price affects only the inventory carrying cost and not the replenishment cost.

Let us assume that the price will change above a certain order quantity q_r and that we are charged the price P_1 for orders smaller than q_r and the price P_2 for orders above q_r. The new situation is illustrated in Fig. 7-5, which shows two different inventory carrying cost curves and two different total cost curves. Cost I refers to buying at P_1 and cost II refers to buying at P_2. The economic order quantity will now be either $q_{1\ min}$, $q_{2\ min}$, or q_r, where $q_{1\ min}$ is q_o computed for P_1 and $q_{2\ min}$ is q_o for P_2.

Situation 1: If $q_{1\ min} < q_r < q_{2\ min}$ the economic order quantity will be $q_{2\ min}$ since the total cost is at a minimum for that order size. See Fig. 7-5.

Situation 2: If $q_r < q_{1\ min}$, $q_{2\ min}$ and $TC_1 > TC_2$ at q_r, then the economic order quantity will presumably be $q_{2\ min}$ since we get the quantity discount choosing the least-cost order quantity $q_{2\ min}$. See Fig. 7-6.

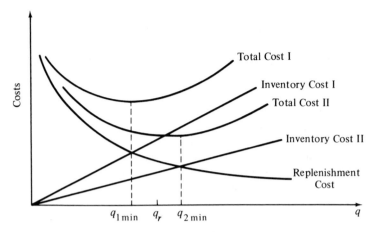

Figure 7-5. Quantity discounts: Situation 1.

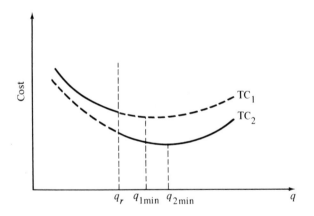

Figure 7-6. Quantity discounts: Situation 2.

Situation 3: In this case we have $q_r > q_{1\,min}$, $q_{2\,min}$, and $TC_1 > TC_2$ at q_r. Since, however, the total cost for q_r is lower than the total cost for $q_{1\,min}$, the economic order quantity will be q_r. See Fig. 7-7.

To determine the economic order quantity in the case of quantity discounts, we therefore have to compute the total cost for three different order quantities: the economic order quantity for price 1, the economic order quantity for price 2, and for the order quantity q_r at which the price break occurs. Since prices change, the expenses for purchasing the total quantity have to be included in the total cost. The following example is an illustration.

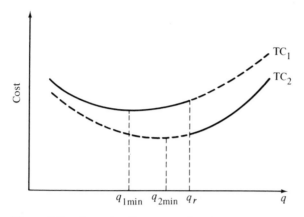

Figure 7-7. Quantity discounts: Situation 3.

Example 7-1

An automobile manufacturer needs 20,000 transmissions per year. The price for the transmission is $200 and the replenishment costs per order are $400. The inventory carrying costs are 20% per year. Above a certain order size q_r, the price will be $195. We want to compute the economic order quantities for price breaks at 500 pieces, 1000 pieces, and 10,000 pieces to show the different relationships of q_r and $q_{1\,min}$ and $q_{2\,min}$. The relevant data are

$$T = 1 \text{ year}$$
$$D = 20,000 \text{ units}$$
$$P_1 = \$200$$
$$P_2 = \$195$$
$$c_r = \$400$$
$$c_c = .20.$$

Case 1 $(q_r = 500)$: The economic order quantities for the prices $P = \$195$ and $P = \$200$ are

$$q_{1\,min} = q_{01} = \sqrt{\frac{2 \times 400 \times 20,000}{.20 \times 1 \times 200}} = 632$$

$$q_{2\,min} = q_{02} = \sqrt{\frac{2 \times 400 \times 20,000}{.20 \times 1 \times 195}} = 641.$$

Total cost now includes the purchase cost of the items:

$$TC = C_R + C_c + \frac{P_i D}{T}.$$

The total costs per year for prices P_1 and P_2, respectively, are then

$$TC_1 = \$4,012,563.20$$
$$TC_2 = \$3,912,564.20.$$

Since $q_r < q_{01}, q_{02}$, the economic order quantity will be either q_{01} or q_{02}. Since the total cost for q_{02} is lower than the total cost for q_{01}, the economic order quantity will be $q_{02} = 641$ pieces.

Case 2 $(q_r = 1000)$: In this case $q_r > q_{01}, q_{02}$. Therefore we have to compare the total cost for q_{01} and q_{02} with the total cost that occurs at the order size q_r. Using p_2 for the calculation of a total cost for q_r, the results are

$$
\begin{array}{lll}
P_1 = 200 & q_{01} = 632 & TC_1 = \$4,012,563.20 \\
P_2 = 195 & q_{02} = 641 & TC_2 = \$3,912,564.20 \\
P_r = 195 & q_r = 1000 & TC_r = \$3,908,100.00.
\end{array}
$$

The lowest total cost is the cost for the order quantity $q_r = 1000$, which in this case is therefore our economic order quantity.

Case 3 $(q_r = 10,000)$. Here again q_{02} is smaller than the order quantity at which the price break occurs. The economic order quantity is therefore found by comparing total cost at q_{01} and q_r. In this case,

$$
\begin{array}{lll}
P_1 = 200 & q_{01} = 632 & TC_1 = \$4,012,563.20 \\
P_2 = 195 & q_r = 10.000 & TC_r = \$3,901,800.00.
\end{array}
$$

The economic order quantity is therefore $q_r = 10,000$.

In cases in which more than one price break occurs, the economic order quantity is found by the computations described above applied to each price break.

d. The Influence of Stock Outs

1. *The lost-sales case.* In the basic model it was assumed that there is always inventory on hand when demand occurs. Let us now consider the case in which we might deliberately be out of inventory when demand occurs. We shall further assume that whenever demand occurs at the time when there is no inventory available the potential sales are lost. This situation is illustrated in Fig. 7-8.

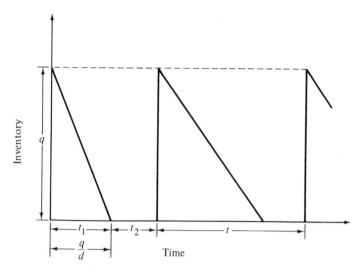

Figure 7-8. Lost sales case.

To analyze this situation mathematically, we shall start again from our total cost function, which has to be supplemented by the term for possible stock-out costs. Let us assume that for each unit of demand that we cannot satisfy, a stock-out cost of c_S will occur. In addition, we shall split the time of the order cycle into two parts, the time interval t_1 in which we can satisfy demand and the time interval t_2 in which there is no stock available. The total cost function is then

$$\text{TC} = C_C + C_R + C_S$$

$$\text{TC} = \frac{q^2}{2(q + dt_2)} c_c + \frac{d}{q + dt_2} c_r + \frac{d^2 t_2}{q + dt_2} c_S. \tag{7-6}$$

This is the total cost equation (7-2) adjusted by q/d and supplemented by the cost of stock outs.

We want to determine the optimal values of q and t_2. Differentiating the total cost function with respect to t_2 and setting the first derivative equal to zero yields

$$\frac{\partial \text{TC}}{\partial t_2} = 0 = -\frac{1}{[q + dt_2]^2}\left[d^2 c_r + \frac{q^2 d}{2} c_c + d^3 t_2 c_S\right] + \frac{d^2 c_s}{q + dt_2}$$

$$dc_s = \frac{dc_r}{q} + \frac{q}{2} c_c \tag{7-7}$$

$$q_0 = d\frac{c_s}{c_c} \pm \sqrt{\left(\frac{dc_s}{c_c}\right)^2 - \frac{2dc_r}{c_c}}.$$

This quadratic equation has real solutions only if the expression under the square root is nonnegative, i.e., if

$$(dc_s)^2 \geq 2dc_r c_c.$$

Let us examine briefly the consequences of different values of q on t_2. Differentiating the total cost function with respect to q and setting the result equal to zero yields

$$\frac{\partial TC}{\partial q} = 0 = -\frac{1}{[q + dt_2]^2}\left[dc_r + \frac{q^2}{2}c_c + d^2t_2c_s\right] + \frac{qc_c}{q + dt_2}$$

$$dc_r = \frac{q_o^2}{2}c_c - d^2t_2c_s + q_odt_2c_c.$$

Substituting q_o yields

$$dt_2 = -\frac{dc_s}{c_r} \pm \sqrt{\left(\frac{dc_s}{c_c}\right)^2 - \frac{2dc_r}{c_c}} \tag{7-8}$$

for $0 < t_2 < \infty$ and $0 < q < \infty$.

Since there are only real values for q if

$$(dc_s)^2 \geq 2dc_r c_c,$$

the roots for t_2 can only be smaller than zero because in this case

$$\frac{dc_s}{c_r} > \sqrt{\left(\frac{dc_s}{c_c}\right)^2 - \frac{2dc_r}{c_c}}. \tag{7-8a}$$

For $(dc_s)^2 = 2dc_r c_c$ all values of t_2 are optimal. The obvious conclusion is that it is always cheaper to run the system without any stock outs than to allow stock outs to occur [2].

2. The back-ordering case. Let us now assume that our customers are more patient than in the last model, i.e., that they are prepared to wait if their demand cannot be satisfied at once. The demands occurring during the time the system is out of stock are back-ordered until the new replenishment arrives. The back-ordered demand is then satisfied before any of the new stock is used to meet other demands. This situation is illustrated in Fig. 7-9. If the back ordering would not cost anything, it would, of course, be optimal never to have any inventory on hand. If, on the other hand, back orders are extremely expensive, stock outs should never occur. In the intermediate range, allowing back orders might be optimal.

Let us, for the time being, assume that the back-order cost function is of the type

$$B = c_b + c_b't.$$

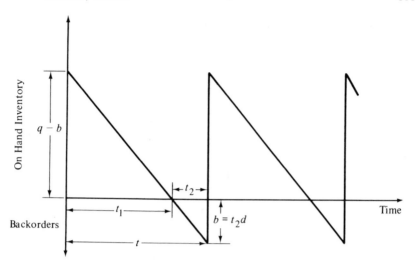

Figure 7-9. Back-ordering case.

Each back-ordered demand causes a fixed cost c_b and variable cost c_b' which is proportional to the time the demand has to remain back-ordered. Let b be the accumulated amount of back-ordered demand when the new shipment arrives. Our total cost function is then

$$\text{TC} = C_C + C_R + C_B = \frac{(q-b)^2}{2q}c_c + \frac{d}{q}c_r + \left[\frac{db}{q}c_b + \frac{b^2}{2q}c_b'\right]. \quad (7\text{-}9)$$

Total costs are obviously a function of q and b. To find the optimal values of q and b, the condition

$$\frac{\partial \text{TC}}{\partial q} = \frac{\partial \text{TC}}{\partial b} = 0$$

must hold. It can be written as

$$\frac{\partial \text{TC}}{\partial q} = -\frac{1}{2q^2}[p(q-b)^2 c_c + 2dc_r + dbc_b + b^2 c_b'] = 0$$

or

$$q_0^2 = \frac{2d}{c_c}\left[c_r + bc_b + \frac{b^2}{d}c_b'\right] + b^2. \quad (7\text{-}10)$$

Differentiating partially with respect to d yields

$$\frac{\partial \text{TC}}{\partial b} = -\frac{1}{q}[(q-b)c_c - dc_b - bc_b'] = 0$$

$$b_0 = \frac{q}{c_b' + c_c} - dc_b.$$

Substituting this expression into our expression for q_o^2,

$$q_o^2 = \frac{2d}{c_c}\left[c_r + \frac{bc_bc_c}{qc_c + c_b'} - \frac{dc_b^2}{c_c + c_b'}\right]$$
$$+ \left[\frac{c_b' + c_c}{c_c}\frac{qc_c - dc_b^2}{c_c + c_b'}\right]$$

$$q_o = \sqrt{\frac{c_b' + c_c}{c_b'}}\sqrt{\frac{d}{c_c}\left(2c_r - \frac{c_b}{c_c + c_b'}\right)}. \qquad (7\text{-}11)$$

Obviously we have to require that c_b' is not equal to zero, because otherwise we could not divide by this figure.

This result can be simplified for the case in which no fixed back-order costs are charged. For $c_b = 0$ our optimal q becomes

$$q_o = \sqrt{\frac{c_b' + c_c}{c_b'}}\sqrt{\frac{2dc_r}{c_c}}. \qquad (7\text{-}12)$$

If we call the economic order quantity in the case where neither back ordering nor lost sales are allowed EOQ, then the optimal order quantity in the back-ordering case with no fixed back-order charges becomes

$$q_{ob} = \sqrt{1 - \frac{c_c}{c_b'}}\,\text{EOQ}. \qquad (7\text{-}13)$$

e. The Economic Lot Size

In our basic model we assumed that the replenishment occurred instantaneously, which is sometimes a valid assumption for the purchasing area if you have very cooperative suppliers. We therefore called the optimal amount to be ordered the economic order quantity. Also it was assumed that deliveries normally occur at a certain point in time and not at a rate over a period.

If, however, we are considering inventories within the production area of a manufacturing firm in which the production takes place in lots, the assumption of instantaneous replenishment or of an infinite production rate will in many cases no longer be true. Let us therefore study our basic deterministic model with no stock outs and under the assumption that we have a finite production rate or replenishment rate r. This situation is illustrated in Fig. 7-10, where the slope of the line DB is the rate of demand d, the slope of the line AC is the replenishment rate r, and the slope of the line AF, which is the difference between the replenishment and the demand rate, is the rate at which inventory is accumulated during the production time. The average inventory is now no longer $q/2$. Time t_1 is the time that is needed for the production of one lot. If t is equal to q/r and the distance EF denotes the inventory q' that

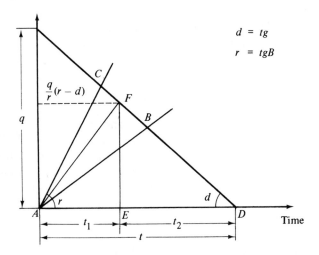

Figure 7-10.   Inventory pattern for continuous replenishment.

has been accumulated during the time t_1, then

$$q' = t_1(r - d)$$
$$= \frac{q}{r}(r - d).$$

The average inventory is therefore

$$I_a = \frac{q}{2}\left(1 - \frac{d}{r}\right).$$

The total cost function has to include inventory carrying cost and replenishment cost and is therefore

$$\mathrm{TC} = C_C + C_R$$
$$= \frac{q}{2}\left(1 - \frac{d}{r}\right)c_c + \frac{d}{q}c_r. \tag{7-14}$$

Finding the optimality conditions by differentiation leads to

$$\frac{\partial \mathrm{TC}}{\partial q} = 0 = \frac{1 - (d/r)}{2}c_c - \frac{d}{q^2}c_r$$
$$q_0 = \sqrt{\frac{2dc_R}{c_c[1 - (d/r)]}}. \tag{7-15}$$

To indicate that q_o is the optimal size of the order for the case of a finite replenishment rate which occurs mainly in the production area of manufacturing firms, we shall call it *economic lot size* in contrast to the economic order quantity which we derived in our first model.

II. ELEMENTARY INVENTORY CONTROL SYSTEMS

In deriving the economic order quantity and the economic lot size, it was assumed that the demand rate was constant for the time interval considered. In practice this assumption will seldom be true. Therefore inventory control systems have been developed which allow for variations of the demand rate and still assure a proper control of inventory levels. We shall study two of these basic models for the case of instantaneous replenishment with lead time. It is not difficult, however, to introduce a finite replenishment rate into these models. Two basic types of inventory control systems can be distinguished which are equivalent with respect to optimality under deterministic conditions or with constant rates of demand: the perpetual model (q model) and the periodic inventory control model (p model).

a. Perpetual Inventory Control Systems

In discussing stock outs in the deterministic case, it was already established that stock outs should never be allowed if sales are lost and that they should occur only to a certain degree if unsatisfied demand can be backlogged. To control stock outs, the basic p model as well as the basic q model provides a certain stock in addition to the normal *working inventory*. This is the so-called safety stock or buffer stock. The function of this buffer stock is to control the amount of stock outs due to unforeseen demand increases or delivery delays. In later sections we shall discuss how the size of the optimal buffer stock can be determined.

In the perpetual inventory control system the order quantity q, which will normally be the economic order quantity, is fixed. Whenever a certain *reorder level* is reached, a new order of size q is placed. The order level (or reorder point) is determined in such a way that our working inventory should reach the zero level when the new replenishment arrives. The reorder level, s, is therefore

$$s = s_s + zd, \qquad (7\text{-}16)$$

where s_s denotes the amount of buffer stock and z the lead time between ordering and replenishment. Figure 7-11 illustrates this situation. The maximum inventory that we can have in stock is

$$S = s_s + q.$$

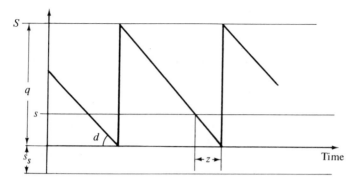

Figure 7-11. Inventory pattern for perpetual inventory control systems.

b. Periodic Inventory Control Systems

In the periodic inventory control system, orders for replenishment are placed at fixed time intervals. The amount ordered is determined such that the total inventory is always replenished up to a certain level S. This maximum inventory level is identical to the maximum inventory level S in the perpetual inventory control system. In contrast to the perpetual control system, however, the periodic control system keeps the ordering intervals constant and varies the size of the replenishment. Figure 7-12 illustrates inventory situations in a periodic inventory control system in which there are zero lead times for replenishment. Extensions of these two basic inventory models will be treated in Sec. C of this chapter.

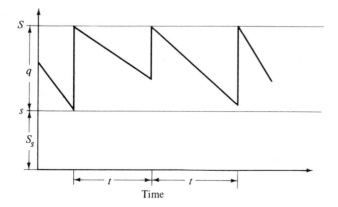

Figure 7-12. Inventory pattern for periodic inventory control systems.

III. SENSITIVITY OF INVENTORY POLICIES

To use any of the derived decision rules for the optimal order quantity, optimal order size, or optimal reorder cycle, one needs to know the numerical values of the parameters contained in the formulas. In our case these parameters are essentially the size of the order cost, the inventory carrying cost, and sometimes the stock-out cost. To provide such parameters, statistical estimation techniques can be used when a sample of observations is obtainable, or if data are not available, management can use accumulated experience to set the appropriate parameters. In either case the estimates are likely to be in error. If the results from inventory decisions (i.e., the size of the total cost) are sensitive to estimation errors of the parameters, then the value of using such models is limited by the need to provide accurate parameter inputs into the models. It is therefore important to know how sensitive the derived decision rules are with respect to errors of the relevant parameters. Let us therefore consider the problem of sensitivity in more detail for the perpetual inventory control model.

For this model we found a total cost of

$$TC(q) = \frac{q}{2}c_c + \frac{d}{q}c_r$$

and an economic order quantity

$$q_o = \sqrt{\frac{2dc_r}{c_c}}, \tag{7-17}$$

not considering the cost of stock outs. Let

$$c_r' = \text{estimated reorder cost}$$
$$c_c' = \text{estimated inventory carrying cost}$$
$$a = \text{percentage error in estimating } c_r'$$
$$f = \text{percentage error in estimating } c_c'.$$

Use of the estimated parameters to compute the EOQ results in

$$q_o' = \sqrt{\frac{2dc_r'}{c_c'}},$$

and since $c_r = c_r'(1 + a)$ and $c_c = c_c'(1 + f)$,

$$q_o' = q_o\sqrt{\frac{1+a}{1+f}} = q_o k.$$

Substituting q' into our total cost function results in the total minimum cost due to estimated parameters:

$$TC(q') = \frac{q'}{2}c'_c + \frac{d}{q'}c'_r$$

$$E = \frac{TC(q')}{TC(q)} = \frac{1 + k^2}{2k}$$

or

$$E = \frac{1}{2} \frac{2 + a + f}{\sqrt{(1 + a)(1 + f)}}. \tag{7-20}$$

Now the measure of sensitivity E is in a form suitable for interpretation. It is obvious that E depends only on a and f.

Since errors in estimating the parameters will certainly not improve our total cost situation, E will always be greater than q. How much does E rise above q? The following examples give some indications of the sensitivity of TC with respect to errors in parameter estimation.

Case 1: $f = +100\%$; $a = +100\%$:

$$E = \frac{1}{2}\left(\frac{2 + 1 + 1}{2}\right) = 1.$$

This result is rather surprising as it says that if you overestimate or underestimate the parameters by the same percentage amount, then you incur no penalty in making a decision.

Using the decision rule for our EOQ, we can see this to be true since it depends on the *relative* cost and not on the absolute amounts. If both these costs are estimated with the same percentage errors, then we make the optimal decision.

Case 2: $f = +100\%$; $a = -50\%$:

$$E = \frac{1}{2}\left(\frac{2 + 1 - .5}{2 \times .5}\right) = 1.25.$$

A 100% overestimate of c_c and a 50% underestimate of c_r results in cost rising 25% above the optimum cost.

Case 3: $f = +100\%$; $a = +50\%$:

$$E = \frac{1}{2}\left(\frac{3.5}{\sqrt{3}}\right) = 1.01.$$

Comparing case 2 with case 3, it can be seen that for any given degree of error in *one* parameter the value of E is lower if the other parameter contains an error in the same direction.

Table 7-1 shows the values of E for different ratios of c_c'/c_c and c_r'/c_r. As can be seen from Table 7-1, the sensitivity of total cost with respect to errors in parameter estimates is very small if the errors are in the same direction. The total costs are more sensitive to errors which are in different directions.

Table 7-1   Sensitivity of q Systems

d'/d	1.2	1.0	1.2	.8	1.0	1.2
c_c'/c_c	1.2	1.0	.8	1.2	1.2	1.2
c_r'/c_r	1.2	1.0	1.2	1.2	1.0	.8
q'/q_o	1.1	1.5	1.35	.9	1.0	.9
E	1.005	1.083	1.042	1.006	1.005	1.06

C. Advanced Inventory Models

I. MULTIITEM MODELS

The models considered so far were deterministic in demand and considered only the inventory of one product. In the following pages these models will be extended in two directions: We shall consider some of the difficulties caused by multiproduct inventories and we shall relax the assumption of deterministic demand.

a. Additional Constraints

One possible limitation might arise because of limited availability of storage space or capital resources that can be invested in inventory. Let us assume that the company needs two different products, which have to be ordered at the same time. The available storage capacity is L and the storage space needed per unit of product i is l_i. Then the following condition must be satisfied:

$$L - \sum_{i=1}^{2} q_i l_i \geq 0. \tag{7-21}$$

Again we want to determine the economic order quantity—this time, however, under the condition that the available storage space must not be exceeded. Thus our problem is

$$\text{minimize TC} = \text{TC}_1 + \text{TC}_2$$

$$\text{such that } L = \sum_{i=1}^{2} q_i l_i \geq 0.$$

Assuming that the constraint has to hold as an equality, we can use the method of the Lagrangian multipler to solve the programming problem. Substituting the total cost of products 1 and 2 into our total cost function, we can write the Lagrangian function as

$$\min TC'(q, q_2, \lambda) = \sum_{i=1}^{n} \frac{q_i}{2} c_{c_i} + \frac{d_i}{q_i} c_{r_i} + \left(L - \sum_{i=1}^{2} q_i l_i\right).$$

Since the last term is zero, it does not affect TC. Again we find the optimality conditions by partially differentiating the Lagrangian function with respect to q_1, q_2, and λ:

$$\frac{\partial TC'}{\partial q_i} = 0 = c_{c_1} - \frac{1}{q_1^2} d_1 c_{r_1} - \lambda l_i$$

$$\frac{\partial TC'}{\partial q_2} = 0 = c_{c_2} - \frac{1}{q_2^2} d_2 c_{r_1} - \lambda l_2$$

$$\frac{\partial TC'}{\partial \lambda} = 0 = L - (q_1 l_1 + q_2 l_2).$$

Our economic order quantities for products 1 and 2, respectively, are then

$$q_{io} = \sqrt{\frac{2 d_i c_{r_i}}{c_{c_i} - \lambda l_i}}. \tag{7-22}$$

We did not compute λ explicitly, which we could have done rather easily in this case. The value of λ is the gain from another unit of capacity L. However, we can find the optimal value of λ by trial and error in many cases in which it is difficult to determine it analytically.

Example 7-2 [3]

A company produces three different products and does not want to invest more than \$14,000 in inventory. An inventory carrying charge $c_c = .2$ has been established.

Table 7-2 shows demand, price, and reorder cost for the three products.

Table 7-2   Inventory Control with Capital Constraints

	Product		
	1	*2*	*3*
Demand, d_i	1000	500	2000
Price, p_i	\$20	\$100	\$50
Reorder cost, c_{r_i}	\$50	\$75	\$100

Computing the economic order quantities separately results in

$$q_{01} = 158$$
$$q_{02} = 61$$
$$q_{03} = 200.$$

The total maximum inventory would then amount to

$$T = \sum_{i=1}^{3} q_{oi} = 158 \times 20 + 61 \times 100 + 200 \times 50 = 19{,}260.$$

This obviously exceeds our available capital resources. Using the Lagrangian technique, we arrive at

$$q_{01} = 144$$
$$q_{02} = 44 \qquad \lambda_0 = .091$$
$$q_{03} = 145.$$

Our total invested capital is now

$$\text{TI} = 144 \times 20 + 44 \times 100 + 145 \times 50 = 13{,}930,$$

which is within the limits set by the additional capital restrictions, allowing for rounding.

b. Batch Production

If several items are manufactured on a single facility, the production will normally be carried out in batches or in lots. The production of one lot takes a certain time and we assume that the different products can only be manufactured successively (and not simultaneously). The question arises whether the demand for the different products can always be satisfied if the production for the item is carried out using the normal economic lot size. In many cases we shall find that even if we use an optimal sequence of the products to be manufactured, one or the other of the items will be out of stock before one lot of each of the products has been manufactured. Our problem is then to find those lot sizes that minimize total cost subject to the condition that demand for the different products has to be satisfied at least to a certain predetermined degree.

Figure 7-13 illustrates the batch production of two products in which the normal economic lot sizes also satisfy the existing demand requirements. Times t_1 and t_2 are the production times necessary to manufacture one lot of product 1 or 2, respectively, while t_4 and t_5 are the time intervals in which the existing demand can be satisfied by one lot of the respective products. Since $t_4 < t_2$, the time interval available between two necessary production periods

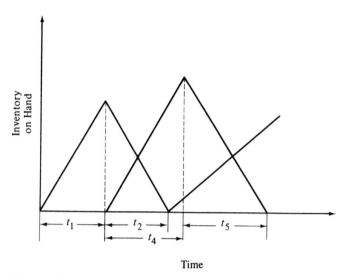

Figure 7-13.   Multiproduct inventories.

for product 1 is long enough to finish one lot of product 2, as can be seen from Fig. 7-13. If $t_4 > t_2$, there would be stock outs of product 1 in the time period $t_4 - t_2$.

Eilon [4] has suggested a method to decrease the optimal lot sizes of the different products until the demand or capacity requirements are met. He assumes that the total cost function is rather flat. He decreases lot sizes successively until all products can properly be manufactured within one cycle. The solution is considered optimal as soon as the total cost of that solution does not deviate more than 5% from the optimal total cost for the nonrestricted case.

Another approach is that of finding the optimal cycle time or the optimal number of cycles per year by optimizing the total cost function that contains the cost of all items that have to be considered. Figure 7-14 shows one production cycle for one product. The inventory of the different products will vary only with respect to the values of r_i, d_i, and q_i. The total costs are the reorder cost and inventory carrying cost for all products. Thus

$$TC = \sum_i C_{Ci} + C_{Ri} = \sum_i \frac{q_i}{2r_i}(r_i - d_i)c_{ci} + \sum_i nc_{ri},$$

where n is the number of cycles per period. Since $q_i = d_i/n$,

$$TC = \sum_i \frac{d_i}{2r_i n}(r_i - d_i)c_{ci} + \sum_i nc_{ri}.$$

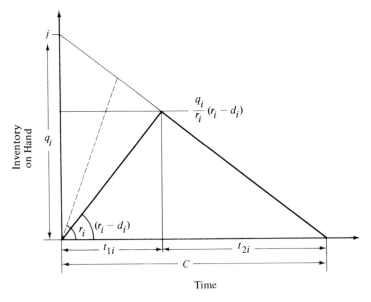

Figure 7-14.   Optimal cycle times.

The optimality conditions for n are then

$$\frac{\partial TC}{\partial n} = 0 = -\frac{1}{n^2} \sum_i \frac{d_i}{2r_i}(r_i - d_i)c_{c_i} + \sum c_{r_i}$$

or

$$n_0 = \sqrt{\frac{\sum d_i(r_i - d_i)c_{c_i}}{2 \sum r_i c_{r_i}}}. \tag{7-23}$$

The optimal number of cycles n_o has to be an integer. If the computed n_o is not integer, we have to check the nearest integers in order to find their number of cycles with the lowest total cost.

Note that the following conditions have to hold for n_o to be optimal:

1. We are assuming one-stage production processes.
2. Within each cycle each product has to be produced once, a somewhat restrictive assumption.
3. Setup costs for the different products are considered to be constant and independent of the sequence in which the products are manufactured.
4. Each product uses $(d_i/r_i)C$ of the available capacity. Therefore

the following condition must hold:

$$\sum_i \frac{d_i}{r_i} \le 1.$$

Otherwise one cycle would not be long enough to produce all products at least once.

5. Initial inventory conditions consist of an optimal mix of products.

II. STOCHASTIC INVENTORY MODELS

We now want to relax the assumption that the parameters—especially the demand rate—are deterministic. We shall consider essentially the same models that were considered in Sec. B, but this time with stochastic demand rates.

If the demand is stochastic, rather than minimizing total cost we now wish to minimize the expected total cost. If the demand distribution is discrete, we find the total expected cost by summing the different total costs for each situation weighted by their probabilities. If the distribution of the demand is continuous, the total costs are also distributed continuously and we wish to minimize the mean value of the total cost function or the integral of the distribution times the costs. There are essentially four possible decision variables, two of which can be relevant for each of the different inventory systems:

$t = $ length of one reorder cycle, review cycle, or scheduling cycle

$q = $ order quantity or lot size

$s = $ reorder level, i.e., inventory level at which a new replenishment order has to be issued or at which a new replenishment arrives

$S = $ maximum inventory level up to which the inventory is restocked.

In the inventory models discussed below we shall either fix one of the parameters and then find the optimal value of the other parameter, or we shall try to find optimal values for two of the parameters. The inventory systems will be labeled according to the parameters and decision variables which determine the behavior of the system: They are the (t, S), the (s, q), and the (s, S) systems.

a. (t, S)-type Systems

1. Systems with zero lead time. In this system the review or ordering period is fixed and the optimal order level S_0 has to be determined. Since there is no lead time, reordering and replenishment take place at the same time and the

replenishment is assumed to occur instantaneously. Let us assume that the demand occurs with a uniform pattern; i.e., the demand rate is constant during any one cycle. Figure 7-15 describes this system. Since at the end of any order cycle we order up to the inventory level S, the order size is equal to the demand during the previous cycle.

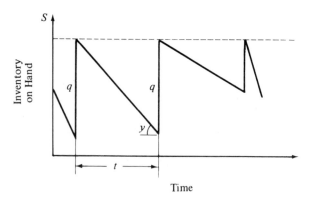

Figure 7-15.   Inventory pattern of (t, S) systems.

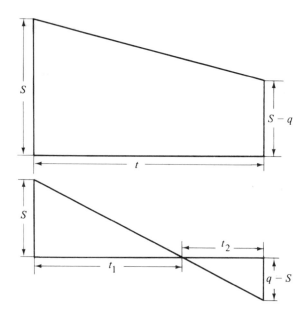

Figure 7-16.   Possible inventory patterns depending on the sizes of S and q.

Let us assume a continuous probability density $f(q)$ for the demand d during t equal to the replenishment q. In computing the optimal maximal inventory level S_0, we shall take into consideration stock-out cost and inventory carrying cost, since order cost is a constant for fixed t. Depending on the relative values of S and q, two situations will arise. They are described in Fig. 7-16. For a given demand, $d = q$, the average inventory, $I(q)$, will be

$$I(q) = \begin{cases} \dfrac{S + (S - q)}{2} & \text{if } S \geq q \\[2ex] \dfrac{S^2}{2q} & \text{if } S \leq q. \end{cases}$$

The average shortage is

$$I_s(q) = \begin{cases} 0 & \text{if } S \geq q \\[2ex] \dfrac{(q - S)^2}{2q} & \text{if } S \leq q. \end{cases}$$

Total expected costs of operating this system are then

$$\text{TC} = \int If(q)\,dq c_c + \int I_s f(q)\,dq c_s$$

$$+ \left[\int_0^S \frac{S + (S - q)}{2} f(q)\,dq c_c + \int_S^\infty \frac{S^2}{2q} f(q)\,dq \right] c_c$$

$$+ c_s \int_S^\infty \frac{(q - S)^2}{2q} f(q)\,dq. \tag{7-24}$$

Differentiating the total cost function with respect to S and setting the result equal to zero will yield the optimality condition for S:

$$\frac{\partial \text{TC}}{\partial S} = 0 = \left[\int_0^S f(q)\,dq + \frac{S}{2} f(S) + \int_S^\infty \frac{S}{q} f(q)\,dq - \frac{S}{2} f(S) \right] c_c$$

$$+ c_s \int_S^\infty \frac{(S - q)}{q} f(q)\,dq$$

$$0 = (c_c + c_s) \left[\int_0^S f(q)\,dq + \int_S^\infty \frac{S}{q} f(q)\,dq \right] - c_s$$

$$\int_0^{S_0} f(q)\,dq + \int_{S_0}^\infty \frac{S_0}{q} f(q)\,dq = \frac{c_s}{c_c + c_s}. \tag{7-25}$$

This can intuitively be interpreted as picking S to equate the expected amount of stock-out times c_s to the expected amount of inventories to be carried times c_c. This optimality condition does not permit the explicit computation of S_0, the optimal value of S. For certain probability functions, for example, the exponential [5], $f(q)$, it is possible to obtain numerical values for S_0.

If the demand fluctuates considerably, possibly following a seasonal pattern, the assumption of a constant demand rate is no longer justified and we have to modify our (t, S) model slightly. An extreme case of a fluctuating demand can be described as follows.

At the beginning of our reviewing period we have to order up to a certain maximum level S, thus determining our initial inventory. At the end of a known time interval t_1, a demand y, the amount of which is a stochastic variable with the density function $f(y)$, occurs instantaneously and reduces our initial inventory level S. If y is larger than S, a stock-out cost will occur for the remaining period t_2. If y is smaller than S, we shall have to keep in store the remaining inventory for the period t_2. We want to find the optimal level S_0 which minimizes expected total cost. This situation can be described by Fig. 7-17. The total average inventory I is then

$$I(S, y) = \begin{cases} t_1 S + t_2(S - y) & \text{if } S \geq y \\ t_1 S & \text{if } S \leq y, \end{cases}$$

and the total average stock out is

$$I_S(S, y) = \begin{cases} 0 & \text{if } S \geq y \\ t_2(y - S) & \text{if } S \leq y. \end{cases}$$

Total expected costs are then

$$TC = c_c \left[\int_0^S t_1 S + t_2(S - y)f(y)\, dy + \int_S^\infty t_1 S f(y)\, dy \right]$$
$$+ c_s \int_S^\infty t_2(y - S)f(y)\, dy.$$

Substituting $t_2 = t - t_1$ and rearranging,

$$TC = c_c \int_0^S St - y(t - t_1)f(y)\, dy + \int_S^\infty c_c St_1$$
$$+ c_s[(y - S)(t - t_1)]f(y)\, dy. \qquad (7\text{-}26)$$

We find the minimum conditions for S by differentiating the cost function with respect to S and setting the first derivative equal to zero:

$$\frac{\partial TC}{\partial S} = 0 = \int_0^S c_c t f(y)\, dy + \int_S^\infty [c_c t_1 - c_s(t - t_1)]f(y)\, dy.$$

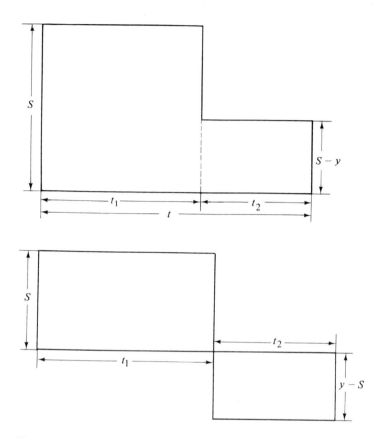

Figure 7-17. Inventory pattern if demand is instantaneous.

Substituting

$$F(S) = \int_0^S f(y)\, dy$$

and

$$\int_0^\infty f(y)\, dy = 1$$

yields

$$0 = F(S)(t - t_1)(c_c + c_s) - c_c t_1 - c_s (t - t_1)$$

$$F(S_0) = \frac{t_1}{t - t_1} - \left[\frac{c_s}{c_c + c_s} \frac{t}{t - t_1} \right]. \tag{7-27}$$

The inventory level S is optimal if S is chosen such that the probability that the demand y is smaller or equal to S is equal to the right-hand side of Eq. (7-27). S_0 therefore depends on the ratio of t_1/t and the ratio of the inventory carrying cost to the stock-out cost.

If in addition to instantaneous replenishment and instantaneous withdrawal of inventories, the time of ordering and the time of withdrawal are the same, the model can be simplified. Figure 7-18 describes this situation. There

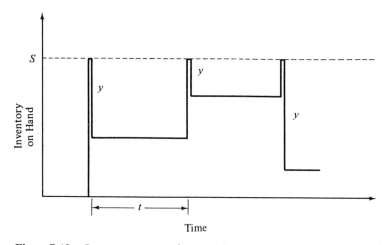

Figure 7-18. Inventory pattern for special cases of instantaneous demand.

is no longer the carrying cost of the full inventory between the time of ordering and the time of withdrawal and so our total cost function reduces to

$$\text{TC}(S) = c_c \int_0^S (S - y)f(y)\,dy + c_s \int_S^\infty (y - S)f(y)\,dy.$$

The optimality condition is then [6]

$$F(S_0) = \frac{c_s}{c_s + c_c}. \tag{7-28}$$

We see that the optimal order level no longer depends on the time ratios but only on the ratio of carrying cost to stock-out cost. The optimal cost will be lower than in the case in which ordering occurred at the beginning of the period and withdrawal at a later point. Therefore one should try to estimate the time of withdrawal as well as possible and thus approximate the second model.

Example 7-3: A Variation of the Newsboy Problem

As a numerical example for extreme cyclic fluctuation of demand, let us consider an ice-cream stand. Every Friday night a big truck from the ice-cream manufacturing company passes by, giving the proprietor of the ice-cream stand an opportunity to replenish his stock of ice cream. Saturday morning the horse races near that stand begin and the ice-cream stand sells the ice cream. If not all ice cream is sold, it has to be stored in a commercial freezer until the next weekend. If the demand is higher than the available ice cream at the stand, the proprietor loses the potential profit of the ice cream that he could have sold if he had had enough.

Let us assume that the proprietor of the ice-cream stand knows that the demand is normally distributed with a mean of $\bar{y} = 400$ units and a standard deviation of $\sigma = 80$ and that he loses \$3 per carton of ice cream that he does not sell. The storage of a carton of ice cream for 1 week costs 40 cents. The proprietor now wants to know up to which level he should restock his inventory every Friday night.

His total cost will be minimized if

$$F(S_o) = \frac{c_s}{c_s + c_c} = \frac{3}{.4 + 3} = .8824.$$

Using a table of the cumulative standardized normal distribution, we find that this corresponds to a standard deviation of 1.187. Using the transformation equation $S_0 = \bar{y} + S_z$, we find the optimal ordering level to be

$$S_0 = 400 + 1.187 \times (80) = 494.96 \text{ cartons.}$$

2. Systems with finite lead time. Until now we have assumed that there is no time lag between ordering and replenishment. If there is a constant lead time between these two actions, this will not affect the results so far derived for the (t, S) model *so long as the lead time is shorter than one reviewing period.* It will only affect the time period for which stock-out protection has to be calculated. However, if the lead time exceeds one reviewing cycle, the model must be changed.

In many cases demand will not occur continuously but rather instantaneously or be described by discrete variables, with $P(q)$ the probability distribution of the demand. Then the integral signs in the above equations have to be replaced by summation signs and the density functions $f(q)$ by the probabilities $P(q)$. In our treatment of inventory systems we shall restrict ourselves, however, to continuous probability distributions.

b. (s, q)-Type Systems

Here the inventory level is watched continually. Whenever the inventory level reaches a certain reorder level s, a new order of the size q is issued. This order arrives in inventory after an additional lead time of t_1. Decision variables are therefore q and s. This situation is illustrated in Fig. 7-19.

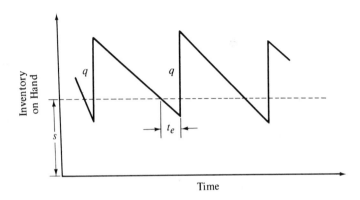

Figure 7-19.   Inventory pattern of (s, q) systems.

For the determination of the optimal reorder level s_0 and the optimal order quantity q_0, we shall follow the same path as in our preceding models. We shall find the optimality conditions by differentiating the total cost function and setting the first derivative equal to zero.

We shall take into consideration reorder cost, stock-out cost, and inventory carrying cost. For the stock-out cost we shall assume that back ordering is possible and that a back order causes a cost of c_b per unit for the time the order has to be back-ordered.

The total cost function is again the sum of total inventory carrying cost, total back-order cost, and total reordering cost. We shall examine these costs in turn.

Reorder cost: Let d again be the demand per time unit and q the order quantity; then the cost of ordering per unit of time is

$$C_r = \frac{d}{q} c_r.$$

Inventory carrying cost: If we assume a constant lead time of t_1 and if x is the demand during that lead time with $f(x)$ the density function of this demand, our inventory at the end of the period I_b is

$$I_b = \int_0^\infty (s - x)f(x)\, dx.$$

In the case of constant lead times this is equal to the size of our safety or buffer stock.

Suppose, however, that the lead time is a random variable with the density function $g(t_1)$; then the average inventory is

$$I_b = \int_0^\infty \int_0^\infty (s - x)f(x)g(t_1)\, dx\, dt_1$$

$$= \int_0^\infty (s - x)h(x)\, dx,$$

where $h(x)$ is the convolution of $f(x)$ and $g(t_1)$, or

$$h(x) = \int_0^\infty f(x)g(t_1)\, d(t_1).$$

If we define

$$\bar{x} = \int_0^\infty xh(x)\, dx,$$

the mean demand during a variable lead time, then the buffer stock I_b is

$$I_b = \int_0^\infty (s - x)h(x)\, dx = s - \bar{x},$$

and total inventory carrying cost C_c is

$$C_c = c_c p\left(\frac{q}{2} + s - \bar{x}\right).$$

Cost of back orders. The number of back orders per cycle is

$$b(x, s) = \begin{cases} 0 & \text{if } s \geq x \\ x - s & \text{if } s < x. \end{cases}$$

Since x is a random variable, we find that the expected number of back orders per period is

$$\bar{b}(x, s) = \int_s^\infty (x - s)h(x)\, dx$$

$$= \int_s^\infty xh(x)\, dx - \int_s^\infty sh(x)\, dx.$$

Since

$$\int_{s}^{\infty} sh(x)\, dx = sH(s),$$

we define $H(s)$ as the complementary cumulative distribution of $h(x)$, or as 1 minus the sum of $h(x)$ and simplify:

$$\bar{b}(x, s) = -sH(s) + \int_{s}^{\infty} xh(x)\, dx.$$

The average back-order cost under the assumption that only fixed back-order costs are charged per back order is therefore

$$C_B = \frac{d}{q} c_b \left(\int_{s}^{\infty} xh(x)\, dx - sH(s) \right).$$

We can now define our total cost function as

$$\text{TC} = c_r \frac{d}{q} + c_c \left(\frac{q}{2} + s - \bar{x} \right) + c_b \frac{d}{q} \left(\int_{s}^{\infty} xh(x)\, dx - sH(s) \right). \qquad (7\text{-}29)$$

For values of q_0 and s_0 between zero and s_0 our optimality conditions are

$$\frac{\partial \text{TC}}{\partial q} = 0 = \frac{c_c}{2} - \frac{1}{q^2}[dc_r + dc_b \bar{b}]$$

$$\frac{\partial \text{TC}}{\partial s} = 0 = c_c - c_b \frac{d}{q} H(s)$$

or

$$q = \sqrt{\frac{2(dc_r + dc_b \bar{b})}{c_c}}$$

$$= \sqrt{\frac{2dc_r}{c_c}} + \sqrt{\frac{2dc_b}{c_c} \int_{s}^{\infty} xh(x)\, dx - sH(s)} \qquad (7\text{-}30)$$

$$H(s) = \frac{qc_c}{c_b d} \qquad (7\text{-}31)$$

A numerical example illustrating the solution of these two simultaneous equations is given in Hadley and Whitin [7], pp. 169ff. There we also find a very interesting discussion of the relationships between s and q. The solution starts with approximating q by the standard EOQ.

c. (s, S)-Type Policies

This section is concerned with inventory systems in which the inventory on hand is reviewed periodically and an order is placed if the inventory has reached a certain minimum level. The order placed will then replenish the inventory up to a certain maximum level. Again we shall assume, for the sake of simplicity, that there are no lead times.

Up to this point in our analysis we have quietly assumed that the systems considered are stationary and thus that the distribution function of demand or lead time does not change over time. We also have not taken into account the time value of money. These two assumptions made it possible to analyze a single period and apply the results to the dynamic system.

If one of these assumptions is not true, this approach can no longer be used. Future periods have to be taken into account when determining optimal values for the decision variables of any single period.

An approach which is widely used in treating systems in which the parameters change over time, which we shall call dynamic systems, is dynamic programming. As should be remembered from earlier chapters, dynamic programming uses a recursive approach to find optimal policies starting with the last or first period. It is therefore necessary to find optimal values for the decision variables for single periods of the inventory systems. Therefore we shall first illustrate the determination of optimal values of an (s, S)-type system for a single period. The results may then be used as a basis for dynamic analysis.

1. Single-period model. (a) No setup cost. Let us assume that the demand during the period under consideration can be described by the random variable y with the density function $f(y)$. The inventory at the beginning of the period is S. The unit production cost is c and no recorder costs are charged. The inventory carrying costs per period, c_c, are to be charged at the end of the period. We want to determine the starting inventory S which minimizes total cost.

In the deterministic case, the starting inventory should be set equal to the demand y during the period, resulting in a zero stock level at the end of the period. In this case no inventory carrying cost and no stock-out cost would occur.

If, however, demand is stochasticly distributed, a zero stock level at the end of the period cannot be guaranted. The optimality conditions for S will be derived in the usual way by setting the first derivative of the total cost function equal to zero. A special case of this type of model was already analyzed in the framework of stationary (t, S) models in Example 7-3. The expected value of total production and inventory carrying cost is given by

$$E[C_c] = \int_0^S c_c(S - y)f(y)\,dy + cy.$$

The expected value of total cost for stock outs is

$$E[C_S] = \int_S^\infty c_s(y - S)f(y)\,dy,$$

resulting in an expected value of total cost of

$$E[\text{TC}] = C(S) = \int_0^S c_c(S - y)f(y)\,dy + cy + \int_S^\infty c_s(y - S)f(y)\,dy.$$

$$(7\text{-}32)$$

Assuming that this cost function is convex, we find the optimality conditions for S to be

$$\frac{\partial C(S)}{\partial S} = 0 = c_c \int_0^S f(y)\,dy - c_s \int_S^\infty f(y)\,dy + c.$$

Denoting the cumulative distribution by $F(S)$,

$$F(S) = \int_0^S f(y)\,dy.$$

Since

$$\int_0^\infty f(y)\,dy = 1,$$

the optimality conditions can be written as

$$c_c F(S) - c_s[1 - F(S)] + c = 0$$

or

$$F(S) = \frac{c_s - c}{c_c - c_s}.$$

$$(7\text{-}33)$$

The expected value of total cost is thus minimized if the inventory level S at the beginning of the period is such that $F(S)$ equals the expression on the right-hand side of Eq. (7-33).

If our actual inventory at the beginning of the period is v, an optimal replenishment policy is the following:

$$\text{if } v < S, \quad \text{order up to } S \qquad [\text{order } (S - v)]$$
$$\text{if } v \geq S, \quad \text{do not order.}$$

Figure 7-20 shows the expected value of total cost $C(v)$ as a function of the initial inventory v and demonstrates that our optimality conditions for $S = v_0$ are valid only for total expected cost functions which are convex functions.

(b) Single-period model with setup cost. If a setup cost or reorder cost c_R is included, our total cost function can be written as

$$E[\text{TC}] = \begin{cases} C_R + c(S - v) + H(S) & \text{for } S > v \\ H(S) & \text{for } S = v, \end{cases}$$

$$(7\text{-}34)$$

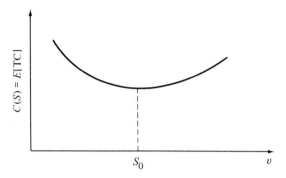

Figure 7-20.

with $H(S) = $ combined carrying and stock-out cost:

$$H(S) = c_c \int_0^S (S - y)f(y)\, dy + c_s \int_S^\infty (y - S)f(y)\, dy.$$

S was defined as the initial inventory which minimized $cy + H(s)$; i.e., any other v will result in higher expected total cost.

If $S < v$, we might consider placing an order by examining the following cost inequality:

$$C_R + c(S - v) + H(S) > H(s).$$

The left-hand side of our inequality shows the cost if an order is placed. The right-hand side shows the cost if no ordering occurs. If is obvious that no order should be placed if $v > S$, because this would result in higher cost than necessary.

Let us now define s as the smallest value of v for which

$$cs + H(s) = C_r + cS + H(S).$$

For this v the additional cost of placing an order, i.e., replenishing our stock up to S, just balances the cost disadvantage of having a nonoptimal starting inventory.

If $s < v < S$, the following relationship holds:

$$C_R + cS + H(S) \geq cv + H(v)$$
$$C_R + c(S - v) + H(S) > H(v) \qquad \text{for } S > v.$$

It is evident that not ordering is less expensive than ordering.

If, finally, $v < s$, then

$$C_R + cS + H(s) < cv + H(v);$$

i.e., it pays to place an order.

We can now summarize the optimal ordering policy as follows: Given the value of S from

$$F(S) = \frac{c_s - c}{c_c + c_s}$$

and the value of s as the smallest v which satisfies the condition

$$cs + H(s) = C_R + cS + H(S)$$

and assuming a convex cost function, an optimal ordering policy is

$$
\begin{aligned}
&\text{order up to } S &&\text{if } v < s \\
&\text{do not order} &&\text{if } S > v > s.
\end{aligned}
\tag{7-35}
$$

2. Multiperiod (s, S) models. The decision rule derived for the one-period model is in general not optimal for multiperiod cases. For multiple periods, rather than review only at certain periods as in the P system or wait until a reorder level is reached as in the Q system, we must look at the decision to order an amount during each and every period to ensure optimality. Because this is a very general approach, we shall limit the discussion of possible costs to an only fairly general class of models: those where the loss function for holding and shortage costs is strictly convex (for example, linear holding costs and nonzero density functions).

Over a finite horizon the last period can be treated as a single-period decision and a dynamic programming approach can be used to work backward period by period, to a set of optimal decisions. If is necessary to use the scrap value from the single-period model, since the inventory is carried over into the next period. In general the complete period-by-period dynamic programming approach must be used, but some rules have been derived for the case of a convex loss function. If there is no order cost, the optimal policy says merely to order up to a level S if inventory is less then S. If the scrap cost of the last period is equal to C and the last period's penalty is a back-order cost of C, the level S can be obtained from

$$\frac{\partial C(S)}{\partial S} + C(1 - \alpha) = 0, \tag{7-36}$$

where α is the discount rate.

As a simple example of a dynamic programming approach, suppose that demand D for an item in one period has the following stationary distribution:

D	0	1	2
$P(D)$	$\frac{2}{3}$	0	$\frac{1}{3}$

The multiperiod problem can be treated as a Markov process and the policy iteration method of Howard [8] can be applied to test an arbitrary policy for optimality or improve it if it is not optimal. Assume an arbitrary policy such as "order one unit (the maximum in this simple problem) when initial inventory is zero." Inventory at the end of the period is down to zero or 1. Costs are $3 per unit ordered, $1 per unit held over, and $6 per unit short. The cost matrix for the arbitrary policy and the transition probability matrix are as follows:

Transition Probability Matrix (p_{ij})

Next Period's Initial Inventory

		0	1	2
State of initial inventory	0	$\frac{1}{3}$	$\frac{2}{3}$	0
	1	$\frac{1}{3}$	$\frac{2}{3}$	0
	2	$\frac{1}{3}$	0	$\frac{2}{3}$

Cost Matrix (c_{ij})

Next Period

		0	0	2
Initial period	0	4	4	∞
	1	2	1	∞
	2	0	∞	2

stage rewards: $r_0 = 4, \quad r_1 = \frac{4}{3}, \quad r_2 = \frac{4}{3},$

where ∞ costs mean that the transition cannot occur.

Define the one-stage reward,

$$r_1 = \sum_i p_{ij} c_{ij},$$

for each state i. Then the recursive equation

$$R_i = r_i + \sum_{r=0}^{2} p_{ij} r_j \qquad (7\text{-}37)$$

gives the discounted expected cost starting any state i under the assumed policy. We obtain the R_is from the simultaneous equations, for which we shall assume a discount rate of .9:

$$R_0 = 4 + .9(1/3v_0 + 2/3v_1) = 8$$
$$R_1 = 4/3 + .9(1/3v_0 + 2/3v_1) = \tfrac{28}{3}$$
$$R_2 = 4/3 + .9(1/3v_0 + 2/2v_2) = \tfrac{28}{3}.$$

To test for optimality, the alternative policy for each initial state is tested with the present costs to see if cost can be lowered. The transition probability and cost matrices for the alternative policy—order 1 only when initial inventory is 1 or 2—are needed:

Transition Probability Matrix

Next Period's Initial Inventory

		0	1	2
Initial inventory	0	$\tfrac{1}{3}$	$\tfrac{2}{3}$	0
	1	$\tfrac{1}{3}$	0	$\tfrac{2}{3}$
	2	$\tfrac{1}{3}$	0	$\tfrac{2}{3}$

Cost Matrix

Next Period's Initial Inventory

		0	1	2
Initial inventory	0	$\tfrac{1}{3} \cdot 6 + 3$	4	∞
	1	3	∞	5
	2	0	∞	2

stage rewards: $r_0 = \tfrac{13}{3}, \quad r_1 = \tfrac{13}{3}, \quad r_2 = \tfrac{4}{3}.$

Then the R_is are compared, and if the arbitrary policy has minimal cost for each R_i, it is optimal. If at least one R_i is not the least, change the policy in the case and reiterate the process. Here the "arbitrary" policy is optimal, as shown below:

$$R_i = r_i + \alpha \sum_{j=0}^{2} p_{ij} r_j \qquad (\text{note}: \quad R_1 = R_2 = \tfrac{28}{3}!)$$

initial inventory $= 0$
$$\begin{cases} \text{policy 1:} & R_0 = 4 + .9(\tfrac{8}{3} + \tfrac{20}{9}) \approx 8.4 \qquad \text{(best)} \\ \text{policy 2:} & R_0 = \tfrac{13}{3} + .9(\tfrac{8}{3} + \tfrac{20}{9}) \approx 8.7 \end{cases}$$

$= 1$
$$\begin{cases} \text{policy 1:} & R_1 = \tfrac{4}{3} + .9(\tfrac{8}{3} + \tfrac{20}{9}) \approx 5.9 \qquad \text{(best)} \\ \text{policy 2:} & R_1 = \tfrac{13}{3} + .9(\tfrac{8}{3} + \tfrac{20}{9}) \approx 8.7 \end{cases}$$

$= 2$
$$\begin{cases} \text{policy 1:} & R_2 = \tfrac{4}{3} + .9(\tfrac{8}{3} + \tfrac{20}{9}) \approx 5.9 \\ \text{policy 2:} & R_2 = \tfrac{4}{3} + .9(\tfrac{8}{3} + \tfrac{20}{9}) \approx 5.9. \end{cases} \qquad \text{(tie)}$$

This example assumes a particular structure to make the dynamic programming approach easier. The first policy is optimal. The same problem can be solved by linear programming [9].

Problems with more general structures lead to far more complicated recursive equations and are solvable only under certain restricted circumstances.

d. Comparison of (s, q), (t, S), and (s, S) Policies

So far three different inventory policies have been discussed as examples for possible stochastic inventory models. Each of these policies was optimal in a certain sense and it seems natural to ask which of these policies leads to the best results in terms of total cost.

This question can be answered only for certain classes of inventory systems. It can, for instance, be shown that in certain cases the (s, S) policy is always better or at least equal to an (s, q) policy and that an (s, q) policy is always better or equal to a (t, S) policy. This does not hold in general however. If one wants to determine the optimal policy under certain conditions, one will have to define the different policies, determine the optimal values for their decision variables, calculate the resulting optimal cost, and then find out which of the "optimal" policies leads to minimal total cost. Naddor [5] shows that the (t, S) policy, a special case of the (s, q) policy, is inferior to an (s, q) policy. We shall now follow Naddor's argument and show that the (s, S) policy leads to better results than the use of an (s, q) policy.

Let the optimal reorder point in an (s, q) system be s_o, and the optimal lot size q_o. The expected total variable cost of the (s, q) policy using s_o^q and q_o is designated by C_o^q. For an (s, S) policy using the same system, the optimal quantities are s_o^S, S_o, and C_o^S. For any arbitrary s and q or s and S, the expected total costs are C^q and C^S, respectively.

For reasons of simplicity let us consider the discrete case. If in an inventory system an (s, q) policy is used, the inventory at the beginning of any reorder cycle I_q may lie anywhere between $s + 1$ and $s + q$. In the same system using an (s, S) policy, the beginning inventory I_s will always be S. Thus while the starting inventory varies for an (s, q) policy, it is fixed at S for an (s, S) policy.

$C^S(s, S)$ is the expected total cost using an (s, S) policy, i.e., starting with inventory S and replenishing when s is reached. Starting with inventory I_q and replenishing when the reorder point s is reached will lead to the expected total cost of $C^S(s, I_q)$. The latter policy, however, is an (s, q) policy for which the total expected cost can be written as

$$C^q(s, q) = \sum_{I=s+1}^{s+q} w_I C^S(s, I), \tag{7-38}$$

where the w_Is are weighting factors, which correspond to the frequency of the reordering periods starting with the different values of I. Since the w_Is are frequencies, it is obvious that

$$1 \leq w_I \leq 0, \qquad \sum_{I=s+1}^{s+q} w_I = 1.$$

Since only one value of I_q can be equal to S_o, even policies using the optimal reorder level will be suboptimal compared to the optimal (s, S) policy:

$$C_o^q = \sum_{I=S_o^q+1}^{s+q_o} w_I C^S(S_o^q, I) \geq \sum_{I=S_o^q+1}^{S_o^q+q_o} w_I C_o^S = C_o^S, \qquad C_o^q \geq C_o^S. \tag{7-39}$$

The above considerations lead to the conclusion that the following relationship holds:

$$C_o^t \geq C_o^q \geq C_o^S \tag{7-40}$$

where the C_o^t are the expected optimal costs of a (t, S) system.

It should, however, be emphasized again that these considerations cannot be generalized to all inventory systems and that in some cases it might be very hard to determine an optimal policy.

D. Inventory Control in Practice

I. INTRODUCTION

The optimal rules for inventory control that have been derived in the first sections are usually simplified in practice. An "optimal" operational inventory control system must handle several additional considerations: the large volume of transactions, the high cost of the information systems, the necessity to forecast demand, the policies of vendors of multiple items, and the integration with the production system or distribution system. We shall address these problems in the order given above.

II. RULES FOR ORDERING

a. Rules of Thumb

For many years inventory control was based on rules of thumb such as "hold from 3 to 6 months of demand in inventory." These rules are inadequate because they do not explicitly take into account the value of inventory or the cost of ordering or back ordering. If the decision maker balanced the ordering cost against the cost of having excess or inadequate inventory, this rule could be equivalent to the (s, q) policy.

Most companies have now moved to more formalized systems. Most existing systems are adaptations of the periodic or perpetual inventory systems discussed in Sec. B with economic order size considerations and allowance for a buffer stock against uncertainty, as discussed in Sec. C. Therefore they are also slight adaptations of the (t, S) and (s, q) policies previously described.

Although we presented the optimal models in previous sections, most computerized inventory systems and most manually operated systems follow the slightly simplified models which we shall develop in the next sections. These models are generally reduced to a table or other simple statement of rules for order size and buffer stocks.

b. Perpetual Systems

In Sec. C.II it was noted that the (s, q) system is essentially a perpetual inventory system as described in Sec. B.II with the addition of a provision of a buffer stock for protection against shortages or back orders. With the assumptions that the time during which demand cannot be met is negligible when measuring inventory holding costs and that lead time is constant, total costs including back ordering are

$$\text{TC} = \frac{d}{q}c_r + c_c\left(\frac{q}{2} + s - \bar{x}\right) + \frac{c_b d}{q}\int_s^\infty (x - s)f(x)\,dx, \qquad (7\text{-}41)$$

where the first term is the order cost and the second term is the inventory holding cost. Here $s - \bar{x}$ is the difference between the reorder point, s, and the average demand during the lead time period, $\bar{x}$, or the average level of the buffer stock that is used to protect against stock outs. The third term is the expected cost of back ordering, where c_b is a back-order cost per unit and x is demand during the lead time. The integral is the expected number of units back-ordered, since demand during lead time is assumed to be distributed continuously. Equating the derivative with respect to s to zero gives

$$P(x > s) = \frac{qc_c}{c_b d},$$ (7-42)

which is exactly Eq. (7-30) except that the equation has the convolution of lead time and demand instead of the cumulative distribution of demand. The derivative with respect to q gives

$$q = \frac{2d(c_r - c_b \cdot \text{expected number of back orders})^{1/2}}{c_c},$$ (7-43)

which is the same as Eq. (7-31) except for the convolution.

Here the expected number of back orders is

$$\int_s^\infty (x - s) f(x)\, dx.$$

Equation (7-42) is simply a restatement of the condition for stocking with the (s, q) model, since qc_c/d is simply the cost of holding an item unsold from one ordering period to the next. If we move c_b to the other side of the equation, this optimality condition merely says "Choose s to balance the cost of a back order with the cost of the holding time until the next order." Equation (7-43) is simply the formula for q from the model under certainty except that the order cost has been increased by the cost of the average number of back orders.

It is not possible to solve Eq. (7-42) and (7-43) sequentially or simultaneously because of the presence of q in the s equation and the presence of expected back-order costs, which are a function of s, in the equation for q. However, in most applications the cost of the expected back orders is small. Therefore one method of solving for the optimal q and s is to calculate q based on the standard EOQ formula without the expected back-order costs, then to compute s based upon this q, and finally to find the expected back-order cost and see if it is negligible compared to the order cost.

The result in the case where sales are lost rather than back-ordered if inventory is not available to meet demands is only slightly different from that obtained above. However, because the expected size of the inventory after arrival of any order is larger for the lost sales case, since no back orders are immediately sent out, there is a higher inventory carrying cost. Consequently, the optimal reorder point is higher:

$$P(x > s) = \frac{qc_c}{c_s d + qc_c}.$$ (7-44)

Equation (7-43) is unchanged with lost sales except for the use of expected number of stock outs instead of back orders. Usually the additional term in the denominator is negligible, as noted in the procedure for solution given above.

As an example we take the following data for a q system with a lead time of 1 week:

> $d = 100$ items per week or 5200 per year, the mean demand distributed normally with a standard deviation of 10 items per week
>
> $c_r = \$50$ order cost
>
> $c_c = \$10$-per-year inventory carrying charge
>
> $c_b = \$100$ back-order cost

approx. $q = \left(\dfrac{2dc_r}{c_c}\right)^{1/2} = 228$

$P(x > s) = \dfrac{qc_c}{dc_b} = \dfrac{228 \cdot 10}{520,000} = .00438$, or 2.65 standard deviations from the mean of the standardized normal distribution.

See Appendix G for the normal distribution table or see Fig. 7-22. The buffer stock which will have a probability of .00438 of being inadequate is 2.65 standard deviations or 2.65×10 in this problem or 26.5 units. We shall discuss a simple graphical method for this calculation at the end of the next section. The reorder point is equal to the buffer plus the average demand during lead time:

$$s = 2.65 \times 10 + 100 = 126 \text{ units.}$$

As a check of the negligibility of the expected cost of stock outs in the economic order quantity, we can compute the number of stock outs. This check is usually neglected and the standard EOQ formula is assumed to be a valid approximation. For demonstration of the check, we use the example above:

$$\text{check } q \overset{?}{=} \frac{1}{c_c}\left[dc_r - c_b \int_s^\infty (x - s)f(x)\,dx\right]^{1/2}$$

$$\int_s^\infty (x - s)f(x)\,dx = \int_{2.65}^\infty (x - s)f(x)\,dx \quad \text{in std. deviations from the mean}$$

$$= \int_{2.65}^\infty xf(x)\,dx - s\int_{2.65}^\infty f(x)\,d(x)$$

$$= f(2.65)\dagger - 2.65 \times .00438$$
$$= .012 - .0105$$
$$= .0015$$
$$q = \left(\frac{2 \times 5200 \times 50 - 100 \times .0015}{10}\right)^{1/2} = 228.$$

c. Periodic Review Systems

With a periodic review information system, at each time period t an order is placed to bring the amount on hand plus that on order up to S. Periodic review or P models can be handled by techniques very similar to those used for Q models. We introduced the P system with a buffer stock in Sec. D.II.b. Now we shall show how to calculate the buffer stock.

Equation (7-45) gives the total cost of operating the periodic review system with constant lead time:

$$\text{TC} = \frac{c_r}{t} + c_c\left(S - \frac{dt}{2} - \bar{x}\right) + \frac{c_b}{t}\int_S^\infty (y - S)f(y)\,dy, \qquad (7\text{-}45)$$

where y is the demand during a lead time plus an inventory review period. The second term is holding cost, again ignoring the effect of the stock out on holding cost. Taking the derivative of the total cost with respect to S, the reorder level gives

$$P(y > S) = \frac{c_c t}{c_s}. \qquad (7\text{-}46)$$

This is the counterpart of Eq. (7-42) except that q has been replaced with t, the review period. Solving for optimal t is more difficult in practice; however, t is usually set by other considerations. Total cost can be determined by the total cost equation [Eq. (7-45)] for values of t, each using the optimal S from Eq. (7-46) and determining a minimum cost value of t.

In the lost-sales case,

$$P(y > S) = \frac{pc_c t}{c_s - pc_c t} \qquad (7\text{-}47)$$

is found to hold. This is again similar to Eq. (7-43) for the Q model.

An important difference between the Q and P models is that the buffer stock for the Q model must meet demands during the lead time. In the P

$\dagger \int_a^\infty yg(y)\,dy = g(a)$. In this case $f(x)$ is the height of the normal distribution curve at 2.65.

model it must meet demand during the entire period between orders plus a lead time. For example, if the earlier problem involved a P system with orders placed every 2 weeks, using Eq. (7-46) we would set

$$P(x > S) = \frac{10 \times 2}{100 \times 52} = .00385,$$

but in the P system we must examine demand over a 3-week period, the 2 weeks between orders plus 1 week of lead time. In that period demand has a mean of 300 but a standard deviation of

$$(3)^{1/2} \times 10 = 17,$$

and so S is $2.6 \times 17 + 300$ or 344 instead of 126 for the Q system, greatly increasing the inventory required.

In our example the term for the cost of the expected number of stock outs was very small. We therefore did not have to revise the economic order size. This will usually be true and often the check is neglected.

d. Service Level Versus Back-order Cost

In practice it is difficult to estimate the back-order cost. It is often more convenient to specify an upper limit on the probability of having a stock out occur during a lead time for the Q system or during a lead time plus review period for the P system. The probability of not having a stock out is called the service level. Service level can be defined either in terms of the probability of stock out not occurring or as the percentage of total items ordered which are filled. We shall use the probability of no stock out as our service level. The probability of a stockout is the probability that demand exceeds the reorder point during the lead time in a Q system, denoted $P(x > s)$. For a P system it is the probability that the demand exceeds the stocking level S in a review period plus lead time, $P(y > S)$. In our previous example we could have set the probability of a stock out at .004 instead of specifying the stock-out cost of \$100. The service level would then be 99.6%. Management sometimes feels better establishing a policy on service level rather than explicitly stating a stock-out cost, although one can be derived from the other and the costs by the appropriate relationship, such as $P(x > s) = qc_c/c_s d$ for the Q system. In our example the \$100 stock-out cost and 99.6% service level are consistent. Reinterpreting existing service levels as stock-out costs can often persuade management that a particular service level policy is or is not appropriate.

A final note is that the service level of 99.6% for a Q system does *not* mean that only 99.6% of *all* orders are filled, in our definition of service level. Since the lead time is usually short compared to the time between orders, the probability of a stock out over a long period is much less than during a lead time. Therefore far fewer than .4% of orders are not filled.

Figure 7-21 shows the relationship of service level to inventory level.

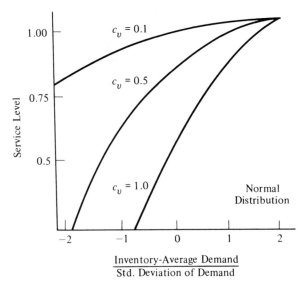

Figure 7-21.   Service level as a function of inventory for three values of coefficient of variation.

Source: J. Buchan and E. Koenigsberg, Scientific Inventory Management, *Prentice-Hall, Inc., Englewood Cliffs, N.J., 1963, p. 348. Courtesy of Prentice-Hall, Inc.*

Note the non-linearity. A tool to aid management in the setting of a stock-out cost or a service level is the exchange curve. An exchange curve is simply a graph of two measures of effectiveness or costs which result from the policy such as dollar value of safety stock inventory and stock outs. This type of presentation may help management make the difficult trade-off between customer service and investment by showing clearly how sensitive one variable is to the decision on the other.

e. Nomogram for Calculation of Buffer Stock

Figure 7-22 is a nomogram which gives a short-cut calculation method for the buffer stock for both the P and Q systems. The calculation starts at the point on the left marked with an asterisk. Project a line through the point from the required service level line to the axis to obtain the number of standard deviations. Then project a line from that spot, the number of standard deviations, to the standard deviation of demand during a lead time for the Q

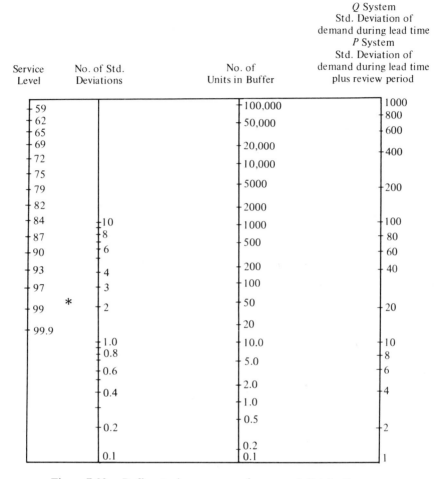

Service Level	No. of Std. Deviations	No. of Units in Buffer	*Q* System Std. Deviation of demand during lead time *P* System Std. Deviation of demand during lead time plus review period
59		100,000	1000
62		50,000	800
65			600
69		20,000	400
72		10,000	
75			
79		5000	200
82		2000	
84	10	1000	100
87	8	500	80
90	6		60
93	4	200	40
97	3	100	
99	2	50	20
		20	
99.9	1.0	10.0	10
	0.8	5.0	8
	0.6		6
	0.4	2.0	4
		1.0	
	0.2	0.5	2
	0.1	0.2 0.1	1

Figure 7-22. Buffer stock nomogram for normal distribution.

system or lead time plus a review period for the *P* system on the last axis and read the number of units in the buffer stock in the middle. The standard deviation must be for the lead time for the *Q* system and for lead time plus review time for the *P* system. The average demand must be added to buffer stock to obtain the reorder point or reorder level.

We shall now discuss the application of these rules in large systems.

III. INFORMATION-PROCESSING REQUIREMENTS AND COST

Much of the problem in application of inventory theory is in the collection and processing of the data needed for the calculations indicated.

For this reason most large companies have resorted to computerized inventory control for their largest inventories. However, these systems can be quite costly. Even if computers are not used, the systems must be reduced to simple standardized routines. The cost of running the information system has not been included in the total cost equations formulated in this chapter. Since different inventory systems require different amount of information, it is important to consider this cost. In most cases this will be determined by calculating the costs of alternative systems such as P and Q systems and adding the relevant costs of information systems. We shall discuss this question in detail later.

There are integrated computer packages available from the manufacturers which edit data, forecast, set reorder points, set order quantities, examine discounts, etc. Many large companies find it worthwhile to develop their own systems, however. In the following paragraphs we shall deal with some of these problems.

a. The ABC Classification

The data-processing requirements can often be reduced by categorization of inventory items. ABC classifying simply means dividing all the items of the inventory into subcategories for different treatment. Sometimes the relevant categories are the quantity demanded of the item, sometimes they are the dollar volume, and sometimes they are the number of customers or even location. The classifications can be combined into cross classifications in any fashion if the result is a category which deserves special treatement. In most cases, it will be found that only a small proportion of the items in inventory are important enough in number or value of transactions to require formalized inventory control, as in Fig. 7-23. The ABC classification identifies them. The

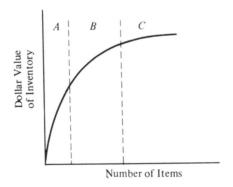

Figure 7-23.   ABC classification.

attention of the inventory manager can then be focused on the most important items. Different inventory control systems can be used for different
items. The low volume and/or low cost or C items may not be put under the
computerized control of a Q system, for example. A simple two-bin system
with the second bin as the buffer stock may be sufficient for these items. For
the intermediate group of items the buffers can be large and the review period
quite long.

b. Costs of the System

The inventory manager may be able to choose between installing P and Q
systems. We shall consider the costs of carrying inventory, costs of ordering,
and costs of operating the system while holding the same service level for both
systems and setting the review period equal to the time to consume an EOQ:

$$t = \frac{d}{q}.$$

1. Cost of ordering. Since t is equal to d/q, the same number of orders are
placed by each system for any one item. However, ordering costs may be
influenced by savings from grouping orders for several items on one order
form or from discounts or transportation savings. If orders for several items
can be determined at roughly the same time, these savings might be realized.
These ordering savings would occur more often for the P system, since the
orders for different items could be combined at the review period. Usually
these group discounts require special handling in our models, which we shall
examine later under the heading of joint replenishment.

2. Costs of carrying inventory. If t does not equal d/q, the average inventory less buffer stock would be quite different for the two systems, and so we
shall maintain that assumption. The buffer stock must be larger for the regular
P system because the buffer stock protects against stock out during the entire
time between orders plus a lead time rather that just *the* lead time. Often,
however, it is possible to "review" the inventory when it gets to zero; that is,
you know when your inventory is zero even in the P system because you
realize when you have none available to fill the order. In this case a two-bin
version of the Q system may be practical. A buffer stock adequate for the
lead time is maintained separately from the other stock. When the buffer
stock is opened, an order is placed. This special or modified P system is also
called a base stock system and requires the same buffer stock as the Q system.

3. Information system costs. A perpetual inventory system or Q system
requires that every order be processed by the inventory control system as it
arrives so that a perpetual inventory balance is available. The cost of such an
information-processing capability was not included in our total cost models.
Keeping a perpetual inventory for a Q system can be very expensive if you

must install new equipment. In other cases it may have very little additional cost because the withdrawal of an item from inventory is already processed in the computer for other reasons. A Q system may or may not have higher information costs than a P system, depending on the information system.

4. Other costs. One of the main reasons for inventory is the uncoupling of sales and production. If the production control and inventory systems were completely separate, the choice of P or Q inventory system would not matter. But most production planning is tightly linked to inventory levels and many production systems are based almost directly on EOQ calculations, as noted in Chap. 6. There is some advantage to the regular P system in uncoupling of the production system from inventory since production plans can be made at the review period and no surges in demand will disturb the production plan.

The advantage of the P system in uncoupling production from inventory may not show up in total cost savings of the system. If demand fluctuates, the Q system may provide more immediate warning so that total costs can be minimized even if the production schedule has to be disturbed. The modified P system or base stock system, which includes a review when inventory reaches zero, would have the same advantage in the case of fluctuating demand.

In summary, the following quotation is appropriate [10]:

> *Although the periodic system is more costly with respect to inventory carrying cost, the perpetual system tends to cause higher clerical processing costs due to the higher processing costs for each transaction. Thus, the reorder point system (Q system) will be more appropriate if*
>
> 1. *The number of transactions is low compared to annual usage.*
> 2. *The processing costs of transactions are very low compared with ordering costs.*
> 3. *Unit price of the item is very high.*
> 4. *The required service level or degree of protection against stock outs is high.*
> 5. *Sales fluctuations are very high and difficult to predict.*
> 6. *Inventory carrying costs are high.*
>
> *The reverse holds true for the periodic ordering system.*

IV. FORECASTING

The forecasting of demand for 10,000 items, which is not an unusual number, is a major problem in itself. Two approaches frequently occur. Some companies have fairly reliable yearly sales plans. The sales estimates are usually made by category of model rather than by parts needed or even by particular models because of the inherent difficulties of forecasting. It may therefore be necessary to further break down the estimate of the sales categories.

An "explosion" or breakdown of the sales into production parts can be made by a computerized or manual scanning of the bill of materials, which tells what subassemblies or parts go directly into each assembly. The totals by part can then be used for the period's demand in the inventory calculations. We examined this type of yearly forecast in Chap. 6. See problem 4-5.

Often the sales estimates are not sufficiently accurate. A projection based on usage to date can be obtained for each part by the method of exponential smoothing, as discussed in Appendix B or in Brown [11]. Seasonality and trend of demand can be taken into account through this method. Manual projection of demand for newly designed parts and careful editing for the elimination of obsolete parts or products is necessary or serious mistakes will be made.

The forecasts made with computer routines generally use a measure of variation called the mean absolute deviation (MAD) rather than the standard deviation. This approximation is simply the sum of the absolute value of the deviations divided by the number of deviations. It is used rather than the square root of the sum of the squares of the deviations divided by the number of deviations. For the normal distribution,

$$\text{MAD} = .8 \times \text{standard deviation.} \qquad (7\text{-}48)$$

An additional forecasting problem is that of translating annual demand forecasts into estimates of the demand distribution during a lead time, which is necessary for setting the buffer inventory level in the Q system or lead time plus the review period for the P system. This can be done mathematically by convolution if the form of the demand distributions is known, as noted in Sec. C.II. For some simple distributions, such as the normal, Poisson, and exponential distributions, both the mean and variances are additive. Often the lead time is also a probablistic variable and the demand during lead time is then doubly stochastic. If the demand and lead-time distributions are normal, a simple estimate of demand variance can be obtained as

$$\sigma^2 = \bar{t}\sigma_{DD}^2 + \bar{u}^2\sigma_L^2, \qquad (7\text{-}49)$$

where $\bar{t}$ = average length of lead time
       σ_{DD}^2 = variance of daily demand
       $\bar{u}$ = average daily demand (or other period)
       σ_L^2 = variance of lead time.

In most other cases convolution or simulation is required to obtain the distribution of demand during lead time, as was done in Sec. C.II.a.2.

The effect of variation in lead time can be quite drastic. For example, suppose that demand has an average of 10 units per day and a standard deviation of only .2 while the lead time averages 5 days and has a standard deviation of only .3 days. The standard deviation of demand during a lead time assuming normality and using Eq. (7-49) is

$$(5 \times .04 + 100 \times .09)^{1/2} = 3.$$

The safety stock will have to be almost seven times as high as when lead time is a constant 5 days since the standard deviation during a lead time is only approximately .45, $(5^{1/2} \times .2)$.

V. MULTIITEM VENDORS

For inventories of items which are each purchased individually, most computer inventory control programs available are straightforward applications of the rules derived in Sec. D.II with demands forecasted by exponential smoothing. Figure 7-24 is taken from the IBM 360 text and shows the rela-

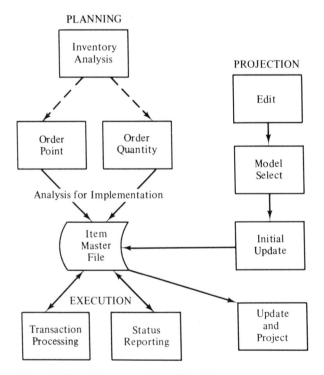

Figure 7-24. General relationship of inventory programs.

Source: Reprinted by permission from "S/360 Wholesale IMPACT Program Library Version 2 Application Description," GH20-0173-2. Courtesy of IBM.

tionship between the parts of the program. We shall discuss each component of the diagram.

The inventory analysis section at the top of the diagram performs an ABC classification. The order point routine calculates average demand plus buffer stock during a lead time for the Q model or buffer stock for a lead time plus time between orders for the P model. The order quantity routine calculates an EOQ for the Q model. For the P system the sum of the buffer stock plus average demand during lead time plus the time between orders is calculated. For the Q system, the master item file keeps track of the amount of inventory of each item and the status reporter prints out an EOQ instruction when the reorder point is reached. For the P system the withdrawals are batched and processed at the review time. The difference between S and inventory plus any undelivered replenishments is output by the status reporter.

For both models the individual order data are edited and passed to a routine which selects an exponential smoothing forecasting model with either a trend, seasonal, or constant pattern. The routine then produces a projected demand for use in the EOQ and buffer stock calculations.

For items that are related because they are purchased from the same vendor, or use the same transportation, or are made in the firm's own plant or own facility, the system must be more complicated because of the need to take into account the savings from writing only one order, purchase discounts for the total of an order, and transportation rate breaks or joint setup costs. These are referred to as joint order problems.

Joint order strategies are available in most computerized inventory systems. The user specifies which items are ordered from each vendor. Whenever any of the items in inventory reaches the reorder point, all items from that vendor are purchased. The user may specify that the order must meet some amount to qualify for a discount or transportation savings. The system will order enough of each item from that vender to bring all items up to the same inventory position in terms of days of demand on hand. If there are many items, this policy can result in carrying what amounts to very large buffer stocks because some item is bound to reach a reorder point almost daily, triggering an order of all items from the vendor. A calculation of whether the order can be delayed at lower total cost is a good procedure and can be provided by some computer systems.

Figure 7-25 shows the IBM Impact system, which includes either a fixed interval, P system or variable interval, Q system with joint order routines. The allocation program looks at the current inventory of each item and the projected demand. When an item reaches its reorder (service) point, the allocation routine orders enough of each item to

1. Meet the minimal size for discount.
2. Bring the supply of each item up to the same number of days of demand as for every other item.

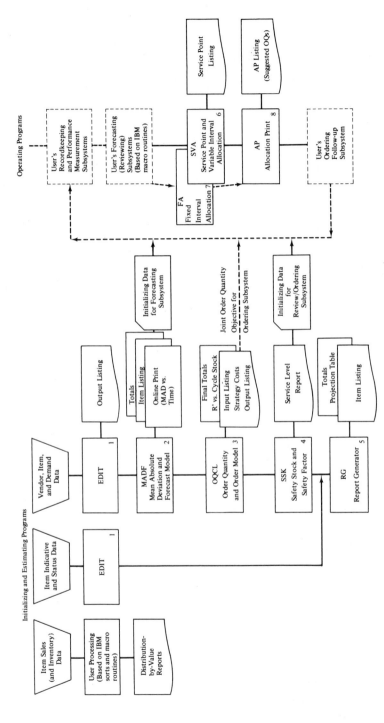

Figure 7-25. General systems chart—System/360 wholesale impact program library.

Source: Reprinted by permission from "S/360 Inventory Control Application Description," GH20-0471-1. Courtesy of IBM.

3. Check whether the increase in inventory holding costs would be higher than the savings from joint ordering. If so, it orders only the item whose service point is reached.

VI. INTEGRATION OF INVENTORY AND PRODUCTION

An example of the integration of production and inventory planning is the use of a computerized inventory system for a producer of over 2000 vegetable oil products, the Foods Division of Anderson, Clayton, & Co. of Dallas, Texas.

The system controls all orders nationwide for the products, maintains inventory records at over 100 warehouses, prints invoices and shipment directives with bills of lading, and issues a production schedule for all four plants. Orders and inventories are updated by leased wire so that the computer can depend on the accuracy of the inventories when directing shipments to meet orders.

The production scheduling is based on economic order quantities with joint order strategy. Any products which have a similar oil content and packaging and are produced at the same plant are listed as coming from one "vendor." Because the production facility is a simple single-stage processor, the problem is actually the standard many-product-with-one-facility problem for batch production. The inventory system can handle production scheduling because the solution technique is the same for both the multiproduct one-facility production problem and the multiitem, single-vendor problem. The solution is to obtain supplies of each item which will satisfy demand for the same length of time.

For each item in a production run or "vendor" grouping, the program compares the balance on hand against its reorder point to determine whether any order for the group should be placed. If so, then the program determines production quantities to bring the supply of each item in the group up to a supply which should last the same time for each item. The length of time of the supply is based on an EOQ calculation for the entire group. Figure 7-26 gives a detailed account of the steps in the functioning of the system. The system has certain disadvantages, primarily the fact that centralized decision making takes time, at least overnight, even with leased line communication. In this industry very rapid service is desired which makes the cost worthwhile. Also, production schedules must be examined on a local basis and adjusted when other production groups are required within a short time or when changeover costs between production groups indicate that sequencing should be changed. These changes may disturb the centrally produced schedule.

IMPACT PROCESSING —

After the daily inventory recordkeeping functions are performed (that is, after customer orders, shipments, production, and production orders are processed), the IMPACT processing can begin. A number of IMPACT and Foods Division programs are used to review the inventory position of the approximately 2000 finished products at the four plants to determine suggested production quantities for items needing replenishment.

Review

Using finder cards containing order points, "peek" points, and other ordering criteria for each product, the review run punches out order cards for non-

IMPACT items (items not controlled by IMPACT because usage figures are not yet available or because demand is low or erratic), for independent items (items that can be ordered or produced independently of other items), and for joint replenishment items (items produced along with other items of similar specifications).

Ordering

Using the joint replenishment order cards as input, a series of IMPACT runs is performed to determine production requirements. All items for a given production run are considered together. (The IMPACT programs are ordinarily set up to determine joint replenishment quantities for "vendors". To convert "vendors" to "production runs", items

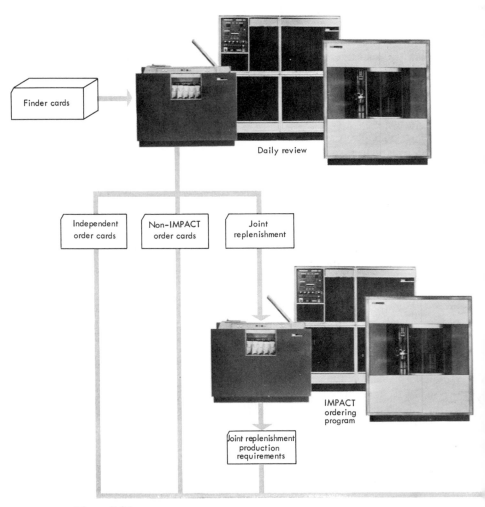

Figure 7-26.

Source: Reprinted by permission from "Centralized Order Entry, Billing, Inventory, and Production Requirements Planning Using IBM IMPACT," IBM Application Brief, K 20–0075–0, pp. 4–7. Courtesy of Foods Division of Anderson, Clayton & Co. and IBM.

which have the same oil specifications, and which use the same packaging line, and which are produced at the same plant are coded in such a manner as to be treated as coming from one "vendor".)

The IMPACT allocation runs first analyze joint replenishment groups where one or more of the items have fallen below minimum level, in order to decide which groups can wait to be produced and which should be produced now. Next the programs determine how much of each product in the group should be produced to result in an economic production run for that group of items and punches order cards with this information. These order cards are then combined with the order cards for non-IMPACT and independent items and are used to print the daily report of production requirements.

The next day, this report is used as the basic input in establishing the production and packing schedules at the various plants. The coordinator responsible for a given plant, knowing the capabilities of that plant, how far ahead it is scheduled, what can be produced on one shift, etc., arrives at a production schedule by considering these factors along with the production requirements shown on the report. A daily printout of the entire finished goods inventory is also provided for the coordinator's information.

The final production orders are then transmitted to the plants and sent to the data processing department, where the item numbers and quantities of the items to be produced are punched in cards. The cards are then processed on the 1401 to update the finished goods inventory records.

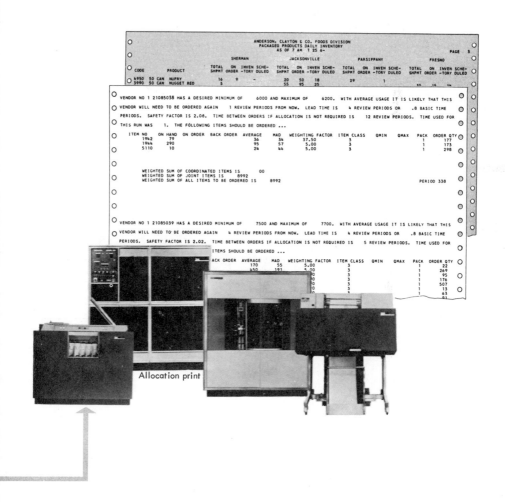

Allocation print

Figure 7-26. Continued

399

VII. MULTIECHELON INVENTORY SYSTEMS

An inventory system may consist of many steps between the manufacturer and the consumer. There may be a warehouse at the plant and a regional distribution warehouse. There may also be inventories at local sales offices. A typical system is shown in Fig. 7-27. Managing this multiechelon inventory system is very difficult. Recently we attempted to purchase a large quantity of "the" pipe mixture in a chain tobacconist shop in Monterey, California. They had only a small amount on hand. Their next step was to contact the Los Angeles distributor who was out of stock and was forced to order from New York. By that time, as it happened, the purchaser would be in New York himself.

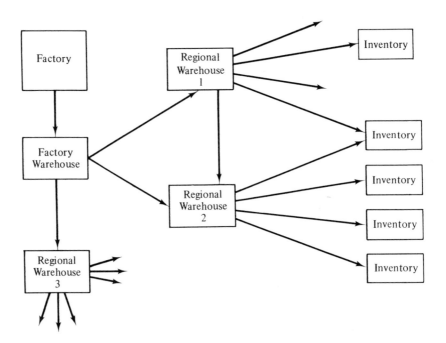

Figure 7-27. Multiechelon inventory system.

Obviously at least two alternatives are available which were apparently not anticipated by the chain:

1. Transfers of stock from one branch to another was possible geographically but not allowed by administrative procedures.
2. The distributor could have served as a central stocking point with enough inventory to virtually avoid ever running out. By not

providing this service, the distributor will soon induce each branch to hold its own buffer inventories. With perishable commodities this is probably not an optimal policy.

Unfortunately the determination of optimal policies in multiechelon systems is still in its infancy.

The optimality criterion for this problem is similar to the others, the minimization of stock out and holding costs of inventory plus, in this case, a transportation cost. In the long run or in the design phase we have returned to the distribution center decision of Chap. 2. We shall consider here only the short-range problem, how to control the stocks at the various levels, and generally not concern ourselves with transportation costs, which must be paid in any event. If the customer will not order unless the item is on hand at the branch, the problem becomes somewhat simpler. We can treat each branch as an independent inventory and compute order quantities and reorder levels. The significant step comes in the treatment at the next stage up the line, the regional distributor.

It is unlikely that the regional distributor will have so many branches that he can treat demand as a stationary distribution. If the reorder quantities from several branches arrive at the same time, the distributor may run out of stock, in which case he will place a large order at the manufacturing warehouse. This type of behavior is fairly obviously unstable, as the number of inventory points at each level becomes fewer and orders become larger. That is, large orders at irregular intervals will occur, producing stock outs.

Instead, the regional distributor and manufacturer should be notified of the branch sales so that they can produce and stock to *sales* rather than to the large, infrequent orders placed by the regional distributors.

A few general principles for multiechelon systems seem to have emerged:

1. Keep buffer stocks centrally.
2. Watch for transportation savings.
3. Stock branches in proportion to their demands.
4. Keep track of demand or sales data centrally and produce to meet sales, not inventory orders.

Figure 7-28 shows such a system, which requires considerable investment in high-speed communication system.

There has been a certain amount of development of the theory of multiechelon systems. To date optimal policies have been derived only for relatively simple systems. In general a dynamic programming approach is necessary. These techniques can be justified only for very expensive items, but there is a significant class of such items, called repairables, which include jet engines. Several models have been developed and some implementation has occurred [12, 13].

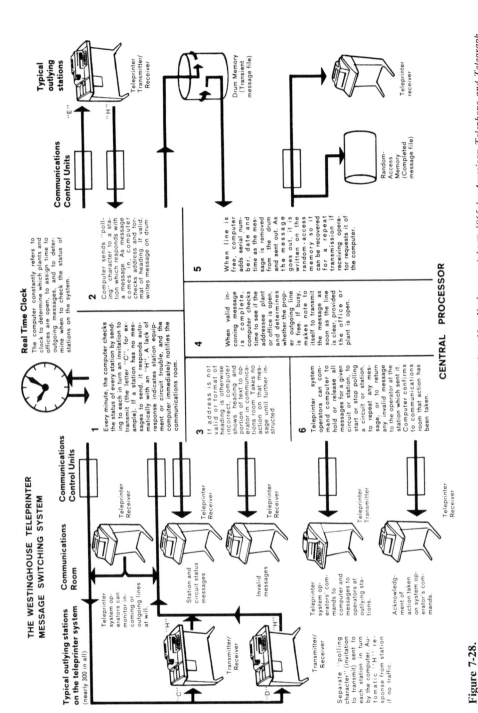

Figure 7-28.
Source: E. C. Gentle, Jr., Data Communications in Business—An Introduction, New York, copyright © 1965 by American Telephone and Telegraph Company, pp. 34–35. Courtesy of American Telephone and Telegraph Company.

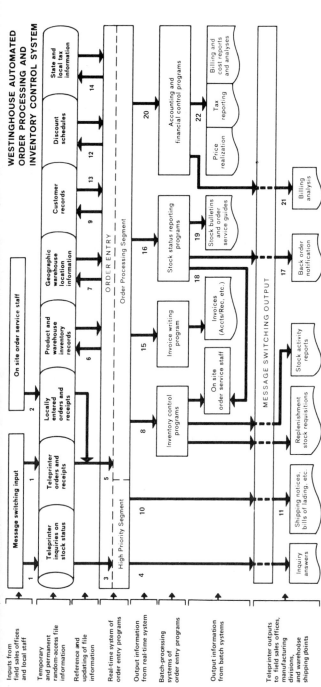

WESTINGHOUSE AUTOMATED ORDER PROCESSING AND INVENTORY CONTROL SYSTEM

Message switching program receives and directs incoming messages:

1 recognizes stock-states inquiries, customer orders, and stock receipt reports, and writes them on random-access section from which order entry program receives all job assignments. **2** On-site order entry program may receive messages via channels other than teleprinter. In such cases, they may enter information directly to the order entry program, by-passing the teleprinter switching input.

Stock-status inquiries receive priority: order-entry program **3** checks warehouse inventory for availability of ordered items; any designated warehouse, or alternate warehouses, if necessary; and **4** replies in standard form through message switching output whose program also gives priority to stock-status messages.

Customer orders are processed as received. **5** They contain coded customer billing and shipping address, product identification, and preferred warehouse. **6** Order-entry program searches preferred warehouse inventory. **7** For items

not available at preferred warehouse, program uses geographic warehouse file to find items at warehouses progressively closer to factory, and finally at factory itself.

8 As items are assigned to an order, inventory totals are reduced accordingly. Inventory control program constantly monitors inventory records. When reorder point is reached, program includes the item in daily inventory-control batch run which sends teleprinter stock-replenishment information to factories, calculated for economical production quantities.

Order-entry program performs shipment paperwork: **9** extracts customer special requirements and shipping address from random-access file and **10** sends shipping notices to selected warehouses via teleprinter switching output program. **11** Teleprinter at warehouses print the actual labels, bills of lading and all paperwork necessary to make shipment.

Order-entry program extracts from random-access file **6** pricing information, **12** discount schedules for each item, **13** customer billing address and discount classification;

and **14** state and local tax data, completing information for printing invoice **15** and stores on tape for periodic invoice-printing runs (several per day) and accounts-receivable input information.

If an item is out of stock: **16** the sales office and the customer are notified through daily back-order run, which also generates teleprinter notification **17** of back-ordered items; **18** order service staff at Tele-Computer Center is notified via printed reports, run several times daily. **19** Stock-status reporting program also generates weekly stock bulletins on active items; monthly stock statistics for manufacturing division planning; and a periodic order service guide to the entire product file.

At end of each day, **20** order-entry program initiates daily accounting and financial control program. **21** Information for billing analyses is automatically collected for each manufacturing division. **22** price realization reports, tax reports and billing-versus-cost reports and analyses are printed.

Figure 7-28. Continued

Inputs from
field sales offices
and local staff

Temporary
and permanent
random-access file
information

Reference and
updating of file
information

Real-time system of
order entry programs

Output information
from real-time system

Batch-processing
systems of
order entry programs

Output information
from batch systems

Teleprinter outputs
to field sales offices,
manufacturing
divisions,
and warehouse
shipping points

403

404 Control of the Production Process

SUMMARY

This chapter has set forth a series of models ranging from extremely simple decision rules to some complex computational methods. Fortunately in many production situations the majority of items in inventory can be handled by simple techniques such as the two-bin system. When inventory decisions cannot be easily separated from production decisions or when the item is expensive, inventory control becomes a very difficult task and must be considered as a part of the aggregate planning system. The cost and timeliness of information processing become very important factors in the control systems built to handle these problems. Unfortunately it is not yet possible to give optimal procedures for design of such a system. We hope that the examples given here and in Chap. 6 will enable the production manager to begin the search for such a system both forearmed and forewarned.

REFERENCES

1. K. J. ARROW, T. HARRIS, and J. MARSHAK, "Optimal Inventory Policy," *Econometrica*, 19, No. 3 (July 1951), 250–272.

2. G. HADLEY and T. M. WHITIN, *Analysis of Inventory Systems*, Prentice-Hall, Englewood Cliffs, N.J., 1963, p. 48.

3. G. HADLEY and T. M. WHITIN, *ibid.*, p. 59.

4. S. EILON, *Elements of Production Planning and Control*, Macmillan, New York, 1962.

5. ELIEZER NADDOR, *Inventory Systems*, Wiley, New York, 1966, p. 306.

6. E. NADDOR, *ibid.*, p. 155.

7. G. HADLEY and T. M. WHITIN, *op. cit.*, pp. 169ff.

8. RONALD HOWARD, *Dynamic Programming and Markov Chains*, M.I.T. Press, Cambridge, Mass., 1960.

9. ALAN S. MANNE, "Linear Programming and Sequential Decisions," *Management Science*, 6, No. 3 (April 1960), 259.

10. H. J. ZIMMERMANN, "Periodic vs. Perpetual Inventory Control Systems," *Production and Inventory Management* (Oct. 1966), 79.

11. ROBERT G. BROWN, *Smoothing Forecasting and Prediction of Discrete Time Series*, Prentice-Hall, Englewood Cliffs, N.J., 1962.

12. HOWARD H. HAMILTON, *Solution of a Multi-echelon Inventory Model with Possible Item Repair*, Unpublished thesis available from Defense Documentation Center, Cameron Station, Va., Sept. 1971.

13. GEORGE HADLEY and T. M. WHITIN, "An Inventory-Transportation Model with *N* Locations," in *Multi-stage Inventory Models and Techniques* (H. E. Scart, D. M. Gilford, and M. W. Shelly, eds.) Stanford University Press, Stanford, Calif., 1963, p. 116.

14. ROBERT G. BROWN, *Decision Rules for Inventory Management*, Holt, Rinehart & Winston, New York, 1967.

15. EARL E. BOMBERGER, "A Dynamic Programming Approach to the Lot-Size Scheduling Problem," *Management Science*, 12, No. 11 (July 1966), 778.

16. MARTIN F. STANKARD, JR., and S. K. GUPTA, "A Note on Bomberger's Approach to Lot Size Scheduling: Heuristic Proposed," *Management Science*, 15, No. 7 (March 1969), 449.

17. THOMAS J. HODGSON, "Addendum to Stankard's and Gupta's Note on Lot Size Scheduling," *Management Science*, 16, No. 7 (March 1970), 514.

18. J. G. MADIGAN, "Scheduling a Multi-Product Single Machine System for an Infinite Planning Period," *Management Science*, 14, No. 11 (July 1968), 713.

19. KENNETH R. BAKER, "On Madigan's Approach to the Deterministic Multi-Product Production and Inventory Problem," *Management Science*, 16, No. 9 (May 1970), 636.

20. SALAH E. ELMAGHRABY, "The Machine Sequencing Problem—Review and Extension", *NLRQ*, 15, No. 2 (June 1968), 205.

21. SALAH E. ELMAGHRABY, A. K. MALLIK, and H. L. W. NUTTLE, "The Scheduling of Lots on a Single Facility," *AIIE Trans.*, 2, No. 3 (Sept. 1970), 203.

22. SAMUEL EILON, "Multi-product Scheduling in a Chemical Plant," *Management Science*, 16, No. 2 (Feb. 1969), B-267.

23. DAVID R. DENZLER, "A Comparison of Three Multi-product, Multi-facility Batch Scheduling Heuristics," Paper #271, Herman C. Krannert Graduate School of Industrial Administration, Purdue University, Lafayette, Ind., Feb. 1970.

PROBLEMS

1. The distribution of demand per day is as follows:

Demand (units), D	1	2	3
Probability of demand, $P(D)$	.4	.3	.3

The distribution of lead time is as follows:

Lead time (days), L	1	2
Probability of lead time, $P(L)$	.5	.5

  a. What is the distribution of demand during a lead time?

  b. If the inventory manager wants to have a 90% chance of meeting demand during a lead time, how many items should be in stock when he orders a replenishment?

2. An inventory is presently reviewed every month. Weekly demand for the item is normally distributed with a mean of 20 units and a standard deviation of 3. Lead time is 1 week. The order cost is $1. The inventory carrying charge is 10%. The unit cost is $12. The shortage cost is $100.

  a. What should the reorder level, S, be?

  b. If the cost of reviewing inventory is $2.40, is a 1-month review period a good period?

  c. If the cost of keeping records for a perpetual inventory system for this item is $50 per year, would it pay to install a Q system? (*Hint*: Compare buffer stock costs.)

3. If an inventory consists of two items with unit costs C_1 and C_2 and constant demand rates R_1 and R_2 and average inventory is limited to $I\$(000)$,

  a. Show that the optimal order quantity is

$$Q_1 = \frac{2I(R_1/C_1)^{1/2}}{(C_2R_2)^{1/2} + (C_1R_1)^{1/2}}.$$

  b. Generalize the solution above.

  c. Is it surprising that ordering and holding costs drop out of the problem?

  d. What is assumed about initial inventory?

  e. Suppose that the constraint on inventory was one of physical space. Would you be able to simply take the 2 out of the formula above?

4. Demand for the product is known to be $r_1 = 3$, $r_2 = 2$, $r_3 = 3$, $r_4 = 1$ in four periods. There is a setup charge or order charge of $A = \$.50$ in any period in which production is greater than zero. The production cost is $1 each. The inventory holding cost is 20 cents per unit per time period for ending inventory of each period. The initial inventory is zero.

  a. What is the optimal production plan? Show work. Begin by listing possible order plans.

  b. Why do we not use a $Q = \sqrt{2DS/IC}$ model here (short answer)?

  c. What if there are constraints on inventory or production amounts?

  d. Why don't you use an LP model?

  e. If you were forced to use an LP model, what could you do?

  f. Why isn't this approach (a) used in most inventory scheduling problems? (*Hint:* What kind of constraints cannot be added and still have reasonable computations?)

5. In Sec. B.III.c the determination of when to change EOQs to take advantage of discounts was discussed. In [14], Brown determines that the largest order Q which should be placed to take advantage of a discount of $d\%$ if the usual order is Q_0 is

$$Q_1 = \frac{2ds}{2r} - (1 - d)Q_0.$$

Brown uses a discounted cost model to prove this. Since the EOQ is an infinite horizon model, the same result can be obtained more simply.

a. Show that this is true by equating costs and savings of taking the discount.

b. Apply the result to the automotive example, Example 7-1.

c. Could the discount ever make the new EOQ rise above the minimum amount required for the discount if the previous EOQ was below the minimum amount required?

6. The setting of an inventory carrying charge may seem to be a strictly factual parameter, but it is usually quite difficult. Therefore it is wise to perform a sensitivity analysis on the effect of varying this parameter. For example, Brown [14] presents the data for a P system shown in Table P-6.

Table P-6 Annual Replenishment Orders and Total Stock Investment for Several Carrying Charge Values

Carrying Charge, r	Number of Orders per Year	Average Investment in Total Stocks	
		90% Service ($)	95% Service ($)
.14	38,429	1,353,874	1,654,060
.16	40,570	1,355,031	1,653,881
.18	42,529	1,356,375	1,654,045
.20	44,327	1,357,703	1,654,340
.22	45,995	1,359,049	1,654,754
.24	47,547	1,360,325	1,655,204
.26	48,989	1,361,419	1,655,591
.28	50,351	1,362,487	1,656,014
.30	51,639	1,363,503	1,656,443

Source: Robert G. Brown, *Decision Rules for Inventory Management*, Holt, Rinehart & Winston, Inc., New York, 1967, Table II, p. 191. Reprinted by permission of Holt, Rinehart & Winston.

a. What happens to investment as the carrying charge increases? Is this normal?

b. What carrying charge would you recommend?

c. Brown mentions that the following practical adaptations have been made in the system from which these data were obtained:

(1) Minimum order is one item and 1 week's supply.

(2) No negative safety stocks are allowed.

(3) Some multiple-item vendors are included.
(4) Service is defined as percentage of orders filled without shortage over a year.

Would these help explain the above trend?

d. Brown asserts that the trend above is caused by the fact that "the value of the working stock is more than offset by the decrease in the safety stock required." Evaluate.

7. The choice of a stock-out cost or definition of a service level criterion is a non-trivial resource allocation problem, which can be stated as follows. Given a parametric amount of investment in inventory by the firm, how should the investment be allocated among the numerous items of inventory? In this chapter we assumed that there was a dollar value which the firm could attach to

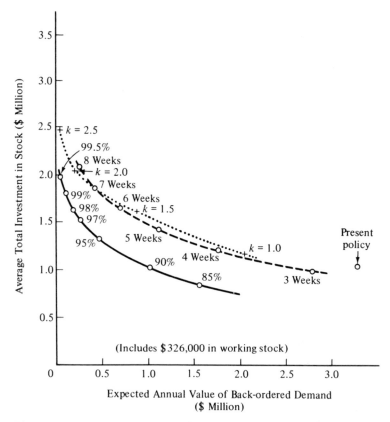

Figure P-7.

Source: Robert G. Brown, Decision Rules for Inventory Management, *Holt, Rinehart & Winston, Inc., New York, 1967, p. 190. Reprinted by permission of Holt, Rinehart & Winston, Inc.*

the occurrence of any stock out, independent of the size of stock out, during a lead time or reorder period. Needless to say, this is difficult. Instead service levels are often set. Even the proper definition of a service level is difficult to determine, much less at what level it should be set. Brown [14] presents the exchange curve in Fig. P-7 for spare parts inventories in a case study. The dotted line is for a number-of-weeks-supply rule of thumb. The dashed line is for an equal probability of stock-out occurrence for each item. The solid line is for equal dollar value of expected stock outs.

a. Is there any relationship between the relative positions of the exchange curves and the precise measures shown on the axes?

b. Is there any relationship between annual value, i.e., the sum of the manufacturing cost of the items back-ordered, and the usual stock-out cost?

c. In a decentralized economic system, what "costs" should be passed between firms—in particular with regard to inventories of spare parts; i.e., who should bear the costs of interruption of service for lack of spare parts?

d. Later in the case described by Brown [14] an estimate of a cost to expedite the processing of the order for items on which stock outs occur is used as a stock-out cost. Will the items for which stock outs occur under this system be the same as the class of items which have stock outs under the equal dollar value of the stock-out policy?

8. Devise an approximate P or periodic inventory system for an item with the following characteristics. Daily demand is Poisson-distributed but can be "approximated" by a normal distribution with a mean of 10 and a standard deviation of 2. A year has 250 days. Lead time has the following distribution:

Number of days	0	1	2	3	4
Frequency	0	0	.6	.4	0

The sales price of the item is \$1.80. The purchase cost is \$1.00. The inventory carrying charges are 20%. The shortage cost is \$1.60 per item-day. The order cost is \$2.00. Remember that the variance of demand during any varying period is equal to the sum of the variance of daily demand times the average number of days in the period plus the square of the daily demand times the variance of the length of the period.

a. How often should inventory be reviewed?

b. How is the order size established at each review period?

c. What important assumptions have been made concerning the inventory and concerning the relationship between decision variables? How would you check the assumption of the relationship between the decision variables?

d. Relate the probability you obtained in devising the system to the service level or chance of not being able to fulfill an order.

e. How might you have used the transform or convolutions to advantage in this problem?

f. What is the strong point of the use of Markov chains for examining possible inventory policies?

g. Carefully describe the inventory problem in terms of the queuing model.
9. We return to the problem discussed in Sec. C.I.b. Suppose that n products are to be produced on one machine. Setup times and production rates are known (see Table P-9). Demand is known and constant.

Table P-9

Part No.	Setup Cost, s ($)	Piece Cost, c ($/unit)	Prod. Rate, p (unit/day)	Demand, r (unit/day)	Setup Time, t (hr)
1	15	.0065	30000	100	1
2	20	.1175	8000	100	1
3	30	.1275	9500	200	2
4	10	.1000	7500	400	1
5	110	2.7850	2000	20	4
6	50	.2675	6000	20	2
7	310	1.5000	2400	6	8
8	130	5.9000	1300	85	4
9	200	.9000	2000	85	6
10	5	.0400	15000	100	1

a. Compute the economic lot size and cost for each product.
b. Check whether there is enough capacity to set up and produce the n products on the one machine over some long period so that setup time is included.
c. Now, however, the question of inteference arises. The ELS assumed that the new batch arrived just as the old ran out. This may not be possible to arrange. Try it.
d. One approach is to make all lots produce an amount which will last the same time or have the same cycle. Then there would be no interference as long as demand is constant. Each product would run out as the cycle called for it to begin production. What would you do if demand had a small variance?
e. The equal production should, of course, be found in an optimal manner given the *equality*. This was done in this chapter. Use the appropriate result to find the "cycle time" and lot sizes for each product.
f. What assumption is made about initial stocks in this problem?
10. (related to Problem 9).
a. Bomberger [15] suggested that although a single cycle would solve the interference problem, it did force some products to be set up much more often than would be required by ELS. Observe whether this occurs in the example.
b. Bomberger [15] noted that even if some products were set up only at some multiple of the cycle time there would be no interference. He suggested a dynamic programming solution for determining the multiples. In the data above, try a 40-day cycle for all products except product 7, which has a 120-day cycle. How much is saved?
11. (continuation of Problem 10). Stankard and Gupta [16] observed that Bomberger's idea could be extended even further by simply grouping the products by

frequency of production according to the standard ELS. Create M groups, where the first group is produced K times per unit, where K is determined from a simple calculation balancing holding and setup costs for all products. The other groups are produced every $M - 1$ repetitions of the first group.

a. For Bomberger's problem, compute the costs for group 1, products 2, 4, 6, 8, and 10; group 2, product 9; and group 3, products 1, 3, 5, and 7, which give a schedule as follows: 2, 4, 6, 8, 10, 9, 2, 4, 6, 8, 10, 1, 3, 5, 7, 2, 4, 6, 8, 10, 9, 2, 4, . . . , with a K of 4. The cost is actually less than Bomberg's solution and no dynamic programming is needed. This method has been generalized by Hodgson [17]. Other heuristics have been suggested in [18, 19].

b. What initial inventories are assumed in this model?

12. (continuation of Problem 11). The models above have not described the relationship of initial inventories to the scheduling of the lot sizes. In many cases this would be a crucial question. Typically, managers have to reduce lot sizes in order to produce an item which is short. Sometimes a small safety stock would eliminate the problem, but when should that be produced? Elmaghraby [20] suggests that a more desirable approach is to start with known inventories and schedule production over a finite horizon to meet the known demand rates. This is basically the approach used in the dynamic programming aggregate planning problem over a finite horizon with known (varying) demands in Chap. 6 but allowing for the fact that several items are produced in the same capacity. This problem could conceivably be attacked directly with a multiple-state variable dynamic program for n products, but the computation would be difficult. Instead, Elmaghraby makes the assumption that each product will be produced only *once* in the finite horizon and formulates a branch and bound sequencing problem. This is a sequencing problem which reduces to scheduling one lot of each product for the known demand out to the horizon less the beginning inventory. It is assumed that the horizon contains enough machine time to set up and produce the one lot of the demand to the horizon. A back-order cost must be included because the assumption of one lot may force some late deliveries. The nonconstrained case serves as a lower bound. A branch and bound algorithm has been designed to solve the problem [21].

13. Eilon [22] and Dentzler have studied the following problem:

> The plant manufactures five products, each product being subject to a normal demand distribution with a known mean. The plant has four machines (1, 2, 3 and 4), each can produce only one product at a time, but not all are capable of producing all the products. The rate of production is indicated by R_{ijk}, which is the number of machine-hours required to produce 10^3 lbs of product i on machine k. Table 1 gives values of R_{ik} and also shows which machines cannot be used to produce certain products. Each machine has production capacity of 168 hours per week.
>
> Changing-over from one product to another on a given machine requires a setup time, as shown in Table 2; this setup time s mainly depends on which product is being replaced and to a lesser extent on the machine. Table 3 gives the sales price G for each product; Table 4 shows the

running cost C per machine-hour. An investigation of the setup costs in this plant suggested that they may be taken as sC (where s and C are given in Tables 2 and 4). The cost of raw materials is c = 10 per lb for all the products.

Planning is carried out by weekly schedules and production in any one week is available to satisfy demand in that week. If demand exceeds the

Table 1   Production Rates (hr/1000 lb), R_{ik}

			Product, i		
Machine, k	1	2	3	4	5
1	6.28	4.21	4.95	—	—
2	3.02	—	—	3.31	—
3	—	4.95	—	—	3.29
4	6.02	5.05	4.95	6.28	4.90

Table 2   Setup Times (hr)

				From		
Machine	Product	1	2	3	4	5
	To					
1	1	0	3	24	—	—
	2	4	0	24	—	—
	3	6	5	0	—	—
2	1	0	—	—	3	—
	4	3	—	—	0	—
3	2	—	0	—	—	2
	5	—	3	—	—	0
4	1	0	4	25	3	5
	2	3	0	24	4	5
	3	5	6	0	5	4
	4	5	3	26	0	3
	5	3	5	25	4	0

Table 3   Sales Price/lb

Product 1	Price, G_i
1	23
2	27
3	26
4	21
5	25

Table 4   Running Costs

Machine	Cost/hr, C_k	Capacity (hr/wk)
1	500	168
2	450	168
3	400	168
4	550	168

available stock outstanding orders are recorded as "unsatisfied demand."
Example of demand is given in the table below.

Three Cases of Mean Demand *D* (in thousands)

Case	Coefficient of Variation *v*	Product 1	2	3	4	5
A1	.3	25.0	44.0	6.0	22.5	28.0
A2	.5					
B1	.3	31.0	55.0	7.0	28.0	35.0
B2	.5					
C1	.3	37.0	66.0	8.0	33.5	42.0
C2	.5					

We shall see in the following chapter that this problem has many aspects of scheduling problems, i.e., setup depends on previous profit as well as inventory, and so it serves as a good bridge to the scheduling chapter. Eilon suggests that one method for dealing with this problem is the *n*-product, one-machine cyclical formula developed in Problem 9.

a. How should the four-machine problem be reduced to a one-machine problem? Assume that capacity is at least equal to demand and is known.

b. Find a cyclical schedule for the chemical plant.

c. How is initial inventory taken care of in this problem?
   Eilon also suggests a linear programming approach to this problem on a 1- or 2-week basis so that initial inventory can be included. He assumes that demand is known for at least 1 week.

d. What are the formulas for quantity produced, cost of materials, revenue and production, *ignoring setup time* and stock-holding costs.

e. What is the profit function for part a?

f. What are the constraints, ignoring setup time?

14. Dentzler formulates a fixed charge problem which includes an approximation for the setup costs:

$$\text{minimize } z = \sum_{i=1}^{n} \sum_{j=1}^{m} \sum_{k=1}^{l} C_{ij} X_{ijk} + K_{ij} \delta_{ijk} + I_i Y_{ik}^{+} + B_i Y_{ik}^{-},$$

where C_{ij} = variable production cost associated with product *i* and machine *j*
       K_{ij} = fixed batch setup charge associated with product *i* and machine *j*
       I_i = inventory holding cost associated with product *i*
       B_i = backlogging cost associated with product *i*
       X_{ijk} = number of units of product *i* made on machine *j* in period *k*
       Y_{ik}^{+} = number of units of product *i* in inventory at the end of period *k*
       Y_{ik}^{-} = number of units of product *i* backlogged at the end of period *k*
       $\delta_{ijk} = \begin{cases} 0 & \text{if } X_{ijk} = 0 \\ 1 & \text{if } X_{ijk} > 0, \end{cases}$

subject to production capacity constraints,

$$\sum_{i=1}^{n} a_{ij} X_{ijk} \leq b_{jk} \qquad \text{for } i = 1, 2, \ldots, n \text{ and } k = 1, 2, \ldots, l,$$

and demand requirement constraints,

$$Y_{i,k-1}^{+} - Y_{i,k-1}^{-} + \sum_{j=1}^{m} X_{ijk} - Y_{ik}^{+} + Y_{ik}^{-} = d_{ik}.$$

a. Why is an approximation to setup costs necessary?
b. Dentzler uses a "fixed charge simplex method" to solve the above problem [23], which selects the new vector to enter the basis in a way slightly different from the usual simplex. Suggest a method.

chapter 8

Short-Term Scheduling and Line Balancing

A. Introduction

Schedule control or scheduling is the area in our production control system in which the preplanned activities such as aggregate production schedules and aggregate inventory levels are projected on a detailed time scale. The detailed allocation of jobs and materials to human and physical resources, man and machines, takes place in scheduling.

Schedules are based on the aggregate planning or the master schedules of Chap. 6, the established optimal lot sizes of Chap. 7, and the knowledge of available resources. The scheduler tries to find detailed schedules which are optimal with respect to meeting due dates, high machine utilization, low unit cost, and possible other goals. These approximate goals are necessary because it is hard to define long-run profit in the short-run situation where it often appears that all costs are fixed. Results of the scheduling activities are fed back to the other planning and control areas to improve their decision making. For example, a continually tight schedule on a machine is a signal to capital budgeting that additional capacity is needed.

To differentiate between different schedules and to select the best one, we have to have some measures of effectiveness, as in other areas where we want to "optimize," with which we can compare the different solutions. In general we want to minimize either the length of operation time such as total processing time, completion time for certain products, average finishing time, total project times, etc., or we want to maximize machine utilization, i.e., minimize idle times, or we want to minimize certain costs such as the unit cost of production, total cost, etc. The underlying notion for all these objectives is that of profit maximization. Examining the different measures of effectiveness more closely we shall find that some of them are not applicable for certain problems and that, what is worse, many of them are contradictory. Here we face "the dilemma of scheduling," which is particularly evident in job-shop production:

1. On the one hand, we want to decrease the average in-process time of our work orders, thus decreasing in-process inventory and increasing the likelihood of meeting due dates.
2. Also, we want to increase the degree of utilization of equipment, thus increasing the return on our investment in physical facilities.

To achieve our first goal, we would be led to select the schedule with the smallest in-process time for a certain product or the smallest average in-process time for all our products. Denoting p_{jm} as the processing time of product j on machine m, t_{jm} as the transportation time of product j to machine m, w_{jm} as the waiting time of product j for machine m, and s_{jm} as the setup time for the processing of product j on machine m, we would pick the schedule that *minimizes* the total in-process time:

$$\min T = \sum_{m=1}^{M} p_{jm} + \sum_{m=1}^{M} t_{jm} + \sum_{m=1}^{M} s_{jm} + \sum_{m=1}^{M} w_{jm}, \qquad j = 1, 2, \ldots, N.$$

$$(8\text{-}1)$$

This objective focuses on the jobs to be done and implies moving them rapidly through the production process.

To achieve our second goal, we would want to pick the schedule that maximizes the utilization of existing capacity, U, or

$$\max U = \frac{\sum_{j=1}^{N} \sum_{m=1}^{M} p_{jm} + s_{jm}}{\sum_{j=1}^{N} \sum_{m=1}^{M} p_{jm} + s_{jm} + i_{jm}}, \qquad (8\text{-}2)$$

where s_{jm} is determined by the set of operations to be performed, and i_{jm} is the idle time on machine m before processing product j. This objective focuses on the machines and implies arrangement of jobs to suit the machines.

It is easily seen that a schedule which is optimal with respect to T does not have to be optimal with respect to U. It should, however, be noted that the contradiction of these goals exists only for rather short planning horizons or if information concerning future orders is very uncertain. In the long run, the minimum cost goal, including capital cost and inventory cost, includes most of the other *subobjectives* of minimum in-process inventory or maximum utilization of machine capacity.

From the two major objectives above a number of secondary measures of effectiveness can be derived which take into account some aspects of the overall problem or focus on important factors which influence the total result:

1. Minimize the time the facilities are occupied, or

$$\min B = \sum_{m,j} p_{jm} + \sum_{m,j} s_{jm} + \sum_{m,j} w_{jm}. \qquad (8\text{-}3)$$

2. Minimize total idle time:

$$\min I = \sum_{m,j} i_{jm}. \qquad (8\text{-}4)$$

3. Minimize total waiting time of products:

$$\min W = \sum_{m,j} w_{jm}. \qquad (8\text{-}5)$$

4. Minimize the total lateness, i.e., the times that it takes to finish products after they were due for delivery:

$$\min PT = \sum_{j=1}^{N} (F_j - T_j), \qquad (8\text{-}6)$$

where T_j = due date for product j
F_j = completion date of product j.

In some cases we might want to weight the lateness with different weights corresponding to different penalties which we have to pay for lateness of different products or corresponding to different degrees of importance of finishing the different products on time.

In the following pages several different criteria will be used. It should, however, be kept in mind that we are only *sub*optimizing if we use any of the single measures of effectiveness as a criterion other than total cost and that we would need an objective function incorporating several of the above-mentioned measures to achieve an overall optimum. It should further be kept in mind that this chapter is concerned with *production* scheduling and line balancing only. We would have to include other areas of our planning and control system if we wanted to achieve a solution which is optimal with respect to our entire system.

In the preceding pages we have assumed that the physical layout, i.e., location and size of our production facilities, has already been determined, as discussed in Chaps. 2, 3, and 4. This is generally true in the case of functionally oriented facilities. However, if our facilities are arranged in a product-oriented form, i.e., if we have manufacturing or assembly lines, then an additional problem arises. Let us take a close look at an assembly line.

A number of tasks or operations have to be performed in order to finish our product. The durations of these operations are known and they are independent of the durations of other operations. The operations have been analyzed by time and motion study, as described in Chap. 4. Some of the operations may be performed at almost any point of the production line, while others have to be performed in a specific sequence. This implies that we have to determine an "optimal" sequence of the operations subject to the existing technological precedence relationships and the production rate desired. A product is completed when it leaves the last operation. We assume that the assembly line is to be set up for the assembly of one product only.

Generally the product will move through the assembly line with a constant pace. This pace is determined by the cycle time, the time between units completed. The cycle time in turn depends on the production rate. If we denote the production rate by r and the cycle time by c, then $c = 1/r$. For example, if we require the production of $r = 10$ cars per hour, then the cycle time $c = \frac{60}{10} = 6$ minutes; i.e., every 6 minutes one car has to leave the assembly line. In general the operations that have to be performed in the framework of an production line are grouped in *stations*. The work content at each station is the sum of the durations of the operations at that station. If all the stations have the same *work content*, then there will be no idle time in any of the stations. We call such an assembly line perfectly balanced. Since production rates do occasionally change, a flexible balance is desirable. It is not possible to perfectly balance an assembly line for all cycle times. Assembly lines which are perfectly balanced for one cycle time may show idle times for other cycle times.

The problem of determining the groupings of operations for production lines is usually called *line balancing*. It can be formulated† as follows. Find the minimum number of stations for a given set of operations and a given cycle time so that

1. The work contents of each station are not larger than the cycle time.
2. All precedence relationships of operations in the line are satisfied.

Another formulation would be the following: For a given number of stations, minimize the cycle time so that conditions 1 and 2 above are satisfied. Both formulations imply the minimization of idle time due to an unbalanced line.

The balancing of subsystems in a functional layout, as we discussed in Chap. 4, is done on a rather permanent basis. Assembly lines have to be newly balanced for each new cycle time or for each new product assembled on that line. This makes line balancing very similar to scheduling in that both attempt

---

†In two ways, depending on the given circumstances.

to fit a given amount of work into a fixed time with minimum idleness. In fact, line balancing and scheduling are very closely interrelated. We shall therefore discuss line balancing in greater detail in this chapter after some of the problems of scheduling have been analyzed.

Let us now turn to the major fields of production scheduling. As already mentioned, the production schedule tells us which department or machine should be doing what, and when. The main problems which have to be solved in scheduling are

1. Coordinating our production levels in different time periods and departments with demand, i.e., *smoothing* production over time.
2. Assigning jobs to specific machines from among those alternative machines on which they can be performed at specific costs.
3. Determining the order in which operations and jobs should be performed on different machines if alternative orderings and routings are possible. This problem is commonly known as *sequencing*.

We shall now examine these areas in more detail.

B. Production Smoothing

In Chap. 6 we studied the use of critical path methods for the planning and controlling of projects. CPM methods, however, are not used only for controlling single projects. They are also the basis of most of the production control programs offered by software houses and producers of EDP equipment for any type of production.

A forerunner of the CPM methods discussed in Chap. 6, the line of balance method, is particularly suited for the control of repetitive, job-shop-type production. Although it contains most of the elements of modern CPM methods, it is simpler to use than these methods. It was devised by G. F. Fouch in 1942 and expanded and reinstated by the U.S. Department of the Navy in February 1958.

The use of the LOB technique requires two types of information: first, the knowledge of the delivery requirements or demands, and, second, the standard production times of the different stages of production. LOB proceeds as follows:

1. On the basis of the known demand, a cumulative production chart is drawn. This chart is used to compare total planned production with total actual production. It provides aggregate information, which is, however, not sufficient to initiate specific corrective measures if the actual does not match the planned.

2. A second stage is necessary to get the required detailed information. By knowing the technological structure of the production process and the total production time per lot in each of the departments, the scheduler computes the volume of work which should have passed through each department or stage at any particular time if the delivery requirements are to be maintained. This is the line of balance, indicating balanced production by all departments.

The use of the LOB technique will be illustrated with the following example.

Example 8-1

See Tables 8-1, 8-2, and 8-3. From Tables 8-2 and 8-3 we can draw the aggregate control chart in Fig. 8-1, which indicates a backlog of 7 by week 7. Let us assume the structure of production shown in Fig. 8-2, where we divide the work into elements performed at different departments or work stations indicated by the numbered nodes. By the fourth week a total volume of 25 units is required at control point 13 (the last work station). To accomplish this and to continue to support the planned program, the volume of work

Table 8-1   Weekly Requirements

Week No.	Number of Items Required	Week No.	Number of Items Required
0	0	6	6
1	5	7	2
2	4	8	8
3	6	9	6
4	10	10	6
5	5	11	5

Table 8-2   Cumulative Requirements

Week No.	Cumulative Requirements	Week No.	Cumulative Requirements
0	0	6	36
1	5	7	38
2	9	8	46
3	15	9	52
4	25	10	58
5	30	11	63

Table 8-3   Actual Production

Week No.	Actual Prod.	Week No.	Actual Prod.
0	0	6	3
1	4	7	
2	4	8	
3	4	9	
4	8	10	
5	6	11	

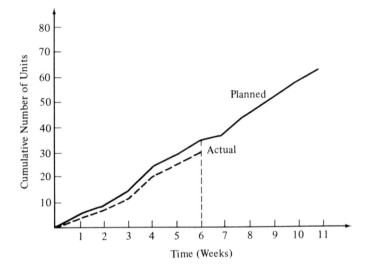

Figure 8-1.   Cumulative production.

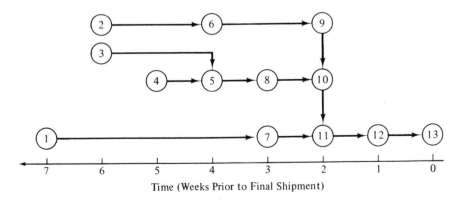

Figure 8-2.   Plan of operation.

which should have passed through point 12 should be equivalent to the volume of finished output at week 4 + 1, since 1 week is the time interval between points 12 and 13. Similarly, the required volumes of work for the other points can be computed by adding the requirements for each of the weeks from final shipment, as shown in Table 8-4.

Table 8-4   Required Volume of Work by Week 4

Control Point	Required Volume	Control Point	Required Volume
1	63	8	38
2	58	9	36
3	58	10	36
4	52	11	36
5	46	12	30
6	46	13	25
7	38		

The LOB chart for week 4 (Fig. 8-3) can be constructed from Table 10-4. The shaded areas in the LOB chart indicate cumulative actual production of the various departments or control points by week 4. Departments with

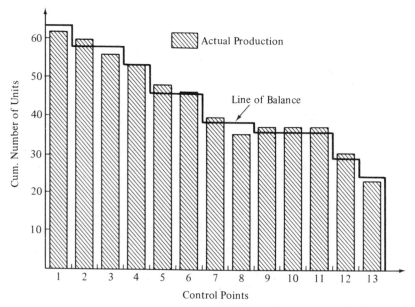

Figure 8-3.   Production requirements at the end of the fourth week.

underperformance can easily be seen and corrective actions can be started in a more effective way than would have been possible on the basis of an aggregate control chart.

C. The Assignment Problem

I. GENERAL PROBLEM FORMULATION

In addition to the control of the "when" and "how much" of production we have to make some decisions concerning the "how." Our problem is now to assign the predetermined tasks or production jobs to the available machines. In many cases this choice will be technologically determined by technical features of available machines. Thus drilling jobs can be performed only on drilling machines, grinding jobs on grinding machines, etc. In a number of cases, however, there might be numerous machines which are capable of performing certain jobs, particularly in the case of multipurpose facilities. If these machines are not identical, the efficiency with which they can perform a certain job will differ. Our task is to find the optimal way of assigning the required jobs to the available machines. The term *optimal* with respect to the job assignment has a slightly different meaning than it had in the smoothing problem because the quantities to be produced in the specific time period are fixed. They cannot be changed. We can only try to use the available capacity as efficiently as possible to produce the required quantity. Let us therefore search for the least-cost assignment of jobs to machines subject to the capacity constraints by type of available machine.

Suppose that we decide that within a certain time period the quantities p_1, p_2, p_3, . . . , p_n of the products 1, 2, 3, . . . , n should be produced. Let us assume that we have m machine types with the capacities $b_1, b_2, b_3, \ldots, b_m$ in machine-hours. All are capable of performing the necessary jobs, although some have different efficiencies or rates of production for the various jobs. Denote the time which machine 1 needs to produce 1 unit of product 1 as $t_{1,1}$ and 1 unit of product 2 by $t_{2,1}$, etc. In general the time which machine j needs to finish 1 unit of product i is $t_{i,j}$. The quantity of product i produced on machine j is $p_{i,j}$.

According to our problem definition, the quantities of product 1 produced on the different machines 1, 2, . . . , m have to add up to the total requirement of product 1, i.e., p_1. Thus

$$p_1 = p_{1,1} + p_{1,2} + \cdots + p_{1,m} = \sum_{j=1}^{m} p_{1j}.$$

The same condition must hold for all products:

$$p_j = \sum_{j=1}^{m} p_{i,j}, \qquad i = 1, 2, \ldots, n. \tag{8-7}$$

Since by definition we cannot expand our machine capacities, the time that machine 1 spends for the production of different products must not exceed its capacity b_1. If machine 1 needs $r_{1,1}$ minutes to produce 1 unit of product 1, it will use $p_{1,1}r_{1,1}$ to produce $p_{1,1}$ units of product 1, and it will use $p_{i,1}r_{i,1}$ minutes to produce $p_{i,1}$ units of product i. The sum of these times must not exceed b_1, or

$$b_1 \geq p_{1,1}r_{1,1} + p_{2,1}r_{2,1} + \cdots + p_{n,1}r_{n,1} = \sum_{i=1}^{n} p_{i,1}r_{i,1}.$$

Since the same conditions hold for the other machines, we arrive at our next set of constraints:

$$b_j \geq \sum_{i=1}^{n} p_{i,j}r_{i,j}, \qquad j = 1, 2, \ldots, m. \qquad (8\text{-}8)$$

Let us now turn to our objective function. If the cost of producing 1 unit of product i on machine j is $c_{i,j}$ and if we want to minimize our total production cost, then our objective function becomes

$$\text{minimize TC} = \sum_{j=1}^{m} \sum_{i=1}^{n} c_{i,j}p_{i,j}, \qquad j = 1, 2, \ldots, m. \qquad (8\text{-}9)$$

Thus we have to solve the problem

$$\text{minimize TC} = \sum_{j=1}^{m} \sum_{i=1}^{n} c_{i,j}p_{i,j}$$

$$\text{subject to } \sum_{i=1}^{n} p_{i,j}r_{i,j} \leq b_j, \qquad j = 1, 2, \ldots, m$$

$$\sum_{j=1}^{n} p_{i,j} = p_i, \qquad i = 1, 2, \ldots, n \qquad (8\text{-}10)$$

$$p_{i,j} \geq 0$$

This is a standard linear programming problem which can be solved by using any of the well-known LP algorithms. If the production costs are dependent only on the running time of the respective machine and not on the kind of product which is produced, then the objective function can be simplified to read

$$\text{minimize TC} = c_j \sum_{j=1}^{m} \sum_{i=1}^{n} p_{i,j}, \qquad (8\text{-}11)$$

where c_j is the unit production cost on machine j.

Another kind of assignment problem is the assignment of personnel to jobs. This problem may be more difficult to solve than the job to machine assignment since the performance of a man in a specific job is not as easily predictable as the productivity of a machine performing a certain operation. Therefore personnel assignment problems are sometimes stochastic problems which have to be solved by methods other than the machine assignment. An interesting approach to the solution of this problem is presented by W. R. King, "A Stochastic Personnel Assignment Model in Operations Research," *Operations Research, 13* (1965), 67-81.

II. OVERTIME AND SUBCONTRACTING AS ALTERNATIVE MODES OF PRODUCTION

In Chap. 6 we assumed certain available machine capacities. These capacities are certainly subject to fluctuations due to breakdowns of machines on the one hand and the possibility of the use of overtime and subcontracting on the other. If we want to take account of the fact that we can use overtime to a certain extent and also subcontracting when assigning jobs to facilities, we have to change slightly the model above. We can treat the quantities of one product manufactured by regular time, overtime, and subcontracting, respectively, as quantities of different products. We also have to consider available regular time, overtime, and subcontracting for the same type of machine as distinguishable capacities. That means that we have to split each of our constraints [Eq. (8-8)] into three constraints and that we have to add two more variables for each product.

Assuming linear production cost functions with unit costs c_{ij} and neglecting fixed production cost, our cost functions might have the shape shown in Fig. 8-4. The underlying assumption is that overtime is more expensive than

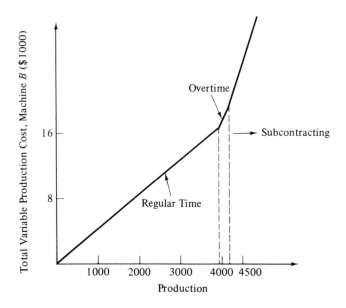

Figure 8-4. Total production cost of machine B.

regular time and that subcontracting is more expensive than overtime. Our linear programming model then becomes

$$\min TC = \sum_{j=1}^{m} \sum_{i=1}^{n} (c_{i,j,1}p_{i,j,1} + c_{i,j,2}p_{i,j,2} + c_{i,j,3}p_{i,j,3})$$

$$\text{subject to } \left. \begin{array}{l} \sum_{i=1}^{n} p_{i,j,1}r_{i,j,1} \leq b_{j,1} \\[1em] \sum_{i=1}^{n} p_{i,j,2}r_{i,j,2} \leq b_{j,2} \\[1em] \sum_{i=1}^{n} p_{i,j,3}r_{i,j,3} \leq b_{j,3} \end{array} \right\} \quad j = 1, 2, \ldots, m$$

$$\sum_{i=1}^{n} p_{i,j,1} + p_{i,j,2} + p_{i,j,3} = p_i, \quad i = 1, 2, \ldots, n$$

$$p_{i,j} \geq 0,$$

(8-12)

where the third subscript of the ps, rs, and cs and the second subscript of the bs denote regular time, overtime, or subcontracting, respectively. Let us demonstrate this by a simple example which can easily be expanded.

Example 8-2

A company produces three products. For the first quarter of the year 2000 units of product I, 5000 units of product II, and 6000 units of product III are scheduled. Two different kinds of facilities or machines are available each of which can produce each product. The variable cost of machine A is $2.00 and of machine B $4.00 per hour of regular working time. Overtime is 50% more expensive. Subcontracting is possible only for machine C and each subcontracted hour costs $7.00. The capacity of each machine is 4000 hours. They can be expanded by 500 hours each by using overtime. The various efficiencies of machines A and C when producing products I, II, or III, respectively, are as shown in the following table. They are the same whether regular time, overtime, or subcontracting is used.

Hours Needed for 1 Unit of Product

	Product I	Product II	Product III
Machine A	1.7	1	1
Machine B	.8	1.1	.8

The company wants to know which product should be produced on which machine and how much overtime and subcontracting should be used to minimize the total variable production cost.

To facilitate the formulation of the objective function, let us compute the unit production cost per product for the different ways of production (see Table 8-5).

Table 8-5   Unit Production Cost

	Machine A	Machine B
Product I		
Regular time	3.4	3.20
Overtime	5.75	4.80
Subcontr.	—	5.60
Product II		
Regular time	2	4.40
Overtime	3	6.60
Subcontr.	—	7.70
Product III		
Regular time	2	3.20
Overtime	3	4.80
Subcontr.	—	5.60

Total production costs are

Product I $3.4p_{1,A,1} + 5.75p_{1,A,2} + 3.20p_{1,B,1} + 4.8p_{1,B,2} + 5.60p_{1,B,3}$

Product II $2p_{2,A,1} + 3p_{2,A,2} + 4.40p_{2,B,1} + 6.60p_{2,B,2} + 7.70p_{2,B,3}$

Product III $2p_{3,A,1} + 3p_{3,A,2} + 3.2p_{3,B,1} + 4.8p_{3,B,2} + 5.6p_{3,B,3}.$

Numbering our variables consecutively, we arrive at our objective function as

$$\text{minimize } z = 3.4p_1 + 5.75p_2 + 3.2p_3 + 4.8p_4 + 5.6p_5 + 2p_6$$
$$+ 3p_7 + 4.4p_8 + 6.6p_9 + 7.7p_{10} + 2p_{11}$$
$$+ 2p_{12} + 3.2p_{13} + 4.8p_{14} + 5.6p_{15}$$

subject to the following constraints:

$1.7p_1$		$+p_6$	$+p_{11}$	≤ 4000
	$.8p_3$	$+1.1p_8$	$+8p_{13}$	≤ 4000
$1.7p_2$		$+p_7$	$+p_{12}$	≤ 500
	$.8p_4$	$+1.1p_9$	$+8p_{14}$	≤ 500
$p_1+p_2+p_3+p_4+p_5$				$= 2000$
		$p_6+p_7+p_8+p_9+p_{10}$		$= 5000$
			$p_{11}+p_{12}+p_{13}+p_{14}+p_{15}$	$= 6000$
				$p_i \geq 0.$

The solution to this problem is

Product I:	subcontract 2000 units for machine B
Product II:	produce 4000 units on machine A, regular time
	produce 125 units on machine A, overtime
	subcontract 875 units on machine B
Product III:	produce 375 units on machine B, overtime
	produce 5000 units on machine B, regular time
	subcontract 625 units on machine B.

The total cost for this solution is $46,437.50.

III. SPECIALIZED ALGORITHMS FOR SCHEDULING: USE OF THE TRANSPORTATION ALGORITHM

It is obvious that the size of our problem will increase tremendously as the number of machines or products increases. Therefore we look for a simpler or more efficient way of solving our problem than the standard simplex method of linear programming.

Often assignment problems have the form where the sum of the requirements is equal to the sum of the total available capacities. An even simpler form is where the assignments cannot be split between several machines, or it can be transformed into this form by adding dummy variables or dummy constraints. This special case of linear programming can then be solved by the transportation model.

Let us illustrate this by solving another example of the assignment problem where only one lot of each product is to be made using the *Hungarian method*.

Example 8-3

We want to assign the production of four products to four out of five product lines. The product lines have to be set up for the product they are going to produce. We do not want to change the assigned job during the planning interval because the setup cost is very high. The production costs for 1000 units of each of the products on each product line have been determined in advance. They are shown in Table 8-6. Our objective is to minimize total variable production cost. Since our problem does not yet conform to the required form for the transportation or assignment model, we add one dummy product in the form of a row of zeros, thus arriving at Table 8-7. Now our problem has the required format and we can start searching for an optimal assignment.

The first step in the Hungarian method is to reduce the cost matrix by subtracting the minimum cost element in each row from all elements of this row. Reducing Table 8-7, we arrive at Table 8-8. This step can be interpreted

Table 8-6   Production Cost for 1000 Units (Thousands of $)

	Product Line				
	A	*B*	*C*	*D*	*E*
Product I	12	10	15	22	18
Product II	10	18	25	15	16
Product III	11	10	3	8	5
Product IV	6	14	8	13	13

Table 8-7   Augmented Cost Matrix

	Product Line				
	A	*B*	*C*	*D*	*E*
Product I	12	10	15	22	18
Product II	10	18	25	15	16
Product III	11	10	3	8	5
Product IV	6	14	8	13	13
Dummy	0	0	0	0	0

Table 8-8   First Reduced Cost Matrix

	Product Line				
	A	*B*	*C*	*D*	*E*
Product I	2	0	5	12	8
Product II	0	8	15	5	6
Product III	8	7	0	5	2
Product IV	0	8	2	7	7
Dummy	0	0	0	0	0

as the search for a set of opportunity costs: If we can assign all our jobs to the product lines by which they can be produced most cheaply, we do not incur any opportunity cost. If there are, however, conflicts, e.g., if two or more products have the same preferred production line, we have to assign at least one of the products to a product line which is not the "most preferred." In this case we incur opportunity costs which amount to the difference between our lowest assignment and the actual assignment. These are the costs shown in Table 8-8.

We see that there is conflict between products II and IV on product line A. The only zeros for the first and the fourth row are both in column 1. That means we could not achieve an optimal assignment in the first step. Additional computations are necessary and the following iterative scheme may be used, which will yield an optimal assignment in a finite number of steps:

1. Draw the minimum number of horzontal and/or vertical lines that will pass through all zeros in the reduced matrix.
2. Select the smallest of the elements not covered by a line. Add this element to all elements that occur at the intersection of two lines and substract it from all elements that do not have a line through them.
3. Check for an optimal set of assignments and repeat steps 1–3 if an optimal assignment is not yet reached.

Application of step 1 to Table 8-8 results in Table 8-9. Step 2 transforms Table 8-9 into Table 8-10. We can see that we still have not found our optimal assignment. We repeat steps 1 and 2, which yields Tables 8-11 and 8-12.

An optimal assignment can now be made: Assign product I to product line B, product II to product line A, product III to product line E, product IV to product line C, and do not use product line D, the dummy assignment. The total costs for this assignment are

$$TC = \$10,000 + \$10,000 + \$5,000 + \$3,000 = \$28,000.$$

Table 8-9   Step 1: Minimum Number of Lines

	Product Line				
	A	B	C	D	E
Product I	2	0	5	12	8
Product II	0	8	15	5	6
Product III	8	7	0	5	2
Product IV	0	8	2	7	7
Dummy	0	0	0	0	0

Table 8-10   Step 2: Modified Reduced Tableau

	Product Line				
	A	B	C	D	E
Product I	2	0	5	10	6
Product II	0	8	15	3	4
Product III	8	7	0	3	0
Product IV	0	8	2	5	7
Dummy	2	2	2	0	0

Table 8-11   Step 1: Minimum Number of Lines

	Product Line				
	A	B	C	D	E
Product I	~~2~~	~~0~~	~~5~~	~~10~~	~~6~~
Product II	~~0~~	8	15	3	4
Product III	~~8~~	~~7~~	~~0~~	~~3~~	~~0~~
Product IV	~~0~~	8	2	5	7
Dummy	~~2~~	2	2	~~0~~	~~0~~

Table 8-12   Step 2: Final Modified Reduced Tableau

	Product Line				
	A	B	C	D	E
Product I	4	0	5	10	6
Product II	0	6	13	1	2
Product III	10	7	0	3	0
Product IV	0	6	0	3	5
Dummy	4	2	4	0	0

It should be noted that the same approach can be used for certain investment or replacement decisions: If we want to find out whether we should replace one of our production lines by another or not, we can add the proposed product line and a dummy product to our tableau. The assignment of our dummy product will then indicate which product line should be discontinued or not be started.

D. Product Sequencing

I. INTRODUCTION

Throughout the last sections we have assumed that the sequence in which jobs are performed or in which products are produced by a set of available machines was either technologically completely predetermined, which we assumed when using CPM, or that the sequence of the jobs was irrelevant for our problem of finding optimal schedules. Unfortunately that is not always true.

Suppose that we have to produce a number of products, each of which requires several operations to be performed on one or more machines. The sequence in which the operations are performed is of no importance as long as all operations for all products are performed in the same sequence and the times required for the different operations are equal. As long as we make sure that there is no idle time between the operations, we shall achieve the shortest possible in-process production time.

There are difficulties, however, when the operation sequences of the different products are different from each other if they can be varied at least within limits or if the operation times are different. We shall illustrate the point with an example.

Example 8-4

We want to produce three products, each of which requires three operations. The sequence in which the operations are performed is arbitrary. There are three machines available, each of which can process one product at a time. The character of the products requires that one operation has to be finished before we start the next, i.e., no overlapping.

Figure 8-5 shows the possible sequences for the case that the required processing times are all equal. We can easily see that the total production times for all six alternatives are equal. Let us look at the same case with different processing times. Table 8-13 gives the processing times for our products I, II, and III on machines A, B, and C. Figure 8-6 shows the different possible sequences of operations and their total process time.

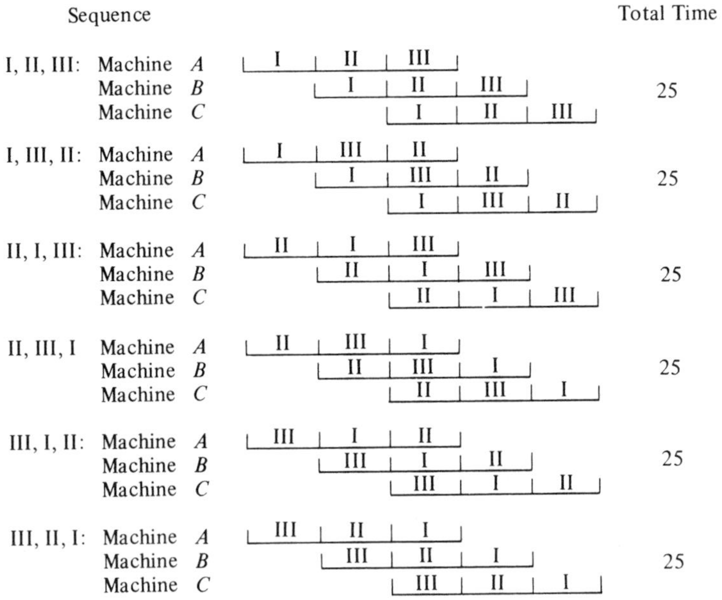

Sequence							Total Time
I, II, III:	Machine A	I	II	III			
	Machine B		I	II	III		25
	Machine C			I	II	III	
I, III, II:	Machine A	I	III	II			
	Machine B		I	III	II		25
	Machine C			I	III	II	
II, I, III:	Machine A	II	I	III			
	Machine B		II	I	III		25
	Machine C			II	I	III	
II, III, I:	Machine A	II	III	I			
	Machine B		II	III	I		25
	Machine C			II	III	I	
III, I, II:	Machine A	III	I	II			
	Machine B		III	I	II		25
	Machine C			III	I	II	
III, II, I:	Machine A	III	II	I			
	Machine B		III	II	I		25
	Machine C			III	II	I	

Figure 8-5. Processing three products on three machines.

Table 8-13 Processing Times (Hours)

	Machine A	Machine B	Machine C	Total
Product I	2	7	3	12
Product II	3	3	4	10
Product III	3	3	5	11
Total	8	13	12	

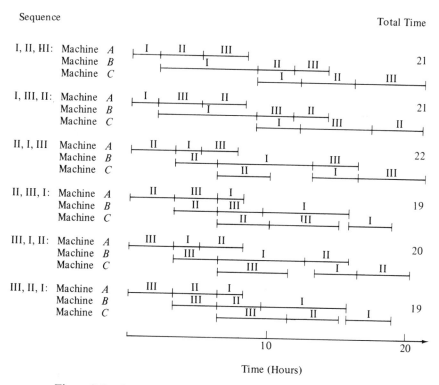

Figure 8-6. Processing three products on three machines.

We see that the time required to finish all products varies between 19 and 22 hours depending on the sequence used. The shortest total time of 19 hours is, furthermore, not reached by choosing the shortest operation first (sequences I, II, III and I, III, II) but is reached in sequences 4 and 6, where we start with product II or III, respectively. Hence it would seem fallacious to assume, as is very often done, that minimum total processing time is achieved by setting priorities either in favor of the longest or the shortest job. We shall, however, see that the assignment of high priorities to the short jobs has certain advantages.

We could obviously decrease our total process time considerably by buying another machine and processing two or more products simultaneously, for instance, at the beginning. That would decrease the overall utilization of our equipment and therefore the return on our investment. One of our other objectives was to maximize return. How, then, can we find optimal or near-optimal solutions to our sequencing problem? We shall look at two major approaches: the direct approach of examining the sequences and the indirect approach of assigning priorities to jobs.

II. DIRECT APPROACHES TO SEQUENCING

a. Enumeration

The most straightforward approach for finding the optimal sequence is to list all possible sequences, eliminate those which are infeasible because of technological reasons, and then select the one with the smallest total process time if we are mainly interested in finding the sequence with the shortest total process time. The number of possible sequences for n jobs is n factorial $= n!$ $= n(n - 1)(n - 2) \cdots 0$. It grows very rapidly with the number of operations. For $n = 5$ the number of alternatives is 120, and for $n = 7$ it is 5040. For any moderate-sized real problem it is difficult to find some means of evaluating all possible schedules within a reasonable time and for reasonable cost. Even high-speed computers are, for the time being, not able to do that.

In Figure 8-6 notice that one reason for long total process times is the idle time of machines which have to wait because one of the other machines has not yet finished a preceding operation. For instance, the total process time of alternative 3 would decrease by 2 hours if idle time was eliminated. The reason for idle machine time is that product I has not finished its operation on machine B when the second operation of product I is ready to be performed on machine C. We can change the sequence in order to eliminate or reduce time. In changing the sequence of jobs we would have to ensure that operation 1 on machine B is longer or equal to operation 2 on machine A, that operation 1 on machine C is longer or equal to operation 2 on machine B, which in turn has to be longer or equal to operation 3 on machine A, etc.

In general the following relationships would have to hold in order to eliminate idle time (we change machine notation from A, B, C to 1, 2, 3 for convenience):

$$t_{1,2} \geq t_{2,1}$$

$$t_{1,3} \geq t_{22} \geq t_{31}$$

$$\vdots$$

(8–13)

$$t_{1j} \geq t_{2,j} \geq \cdots \geq t_{i-1,2} \geq t_{i,1}, \quad \text{for } i \text{ and } j = 1, 2, \ldots, m.$$

There are a number of similar rules which can be employed to decrease the number of schedules which have to be evaluated. In general, however, the number is still too large to be handled computationally.

Giffler et al. [1], for instance, developed an algorithm based on the Gantt chart. They examine only "active" feasible schedules. Active schedules have the following properties:

1. No machine is idle for a length of time sufficient to process a product which is also idle.
2. When a product has been assigned to a machine, processing is begun at the earliest time that both machine and product are idle.

Giffler et al. investigated the problem of scheduling six items over n machines. Table 8-14 lists the number of "active" schedules found and the computation

Table 8-14   Active Schedules

No. of Machines, n	Number of Active Schedules	Computer Time (min)
1	36	.00
2	290	.09
3	914	.48
4	7,546	4.82
5	84,802	70.18

time required on an IBM 704 computer. The results seem to indicate that enumeration of active schedules as a method of scheduling complex operations is impractical with such facilities.

b. Linear Programming for Sequencing

In Chap. 6 we used the linear programming approach to solve the problem of allocating and assigning limited resources to a number of activities which had to be performed in a predetermined sequence, i.e., CPM. You might wonder whether that approach cannot be used to solve the problem of sequencing a number of jobs on a limited number of machine resources. The answer is yes because the problems are very similar. The main difference is that we have one additional set of variables, the sequence of the jobs. Rather than allowing only one sequence of operations, as we did in Sec. B, we shall now include different possible alternatives and leave it to the program to determine the respective 0 and 1 values for our *selector variables*. If we have to allow for a great number of technologically possible sequences, this will, of course, increase the number of variables considerably. This fact limits the applicability of the linear integer programming approach to rather small problems, at least until more efficient integer programming algorithms have been developed. Decomposition approaches similar to the one in Chap. 6 have also been tried for this problem.

c. Branch and Bound for Sequencing

A new approach which seems to point in the right direction is the so-called branch and bound techniques, which have been used in two ways: first, to make integer programming algorithms more efficient and better suited for solving sequencing problems, and, second, to solve sequencing problems directly. The basic idea of branch and bound is that under certain conditions multivariable decision problems can be decomposed into many single-variable subproblems. For the decomposed problem a decision tree can be drawn. In the decision tree each path from beginning to any of the end points represents one complete solution to the original problem. A completely decomposed problem will in many cases be represented by a huge decision tree which is by far too large to be treated by conventional methods of optimization, such as enumeration. Branch and bound techniques—although essentially enumeration methods—try to minimize the computational effort by cutting off as many branches of the tree as possible. This is done by computing bounds for the different branches and terminating the branching activity whenever the bound has been violated. The general branch and bound procedure can be described as follows:

1. Definition of the set of all solutions and determination of a first lower bound.
2. Selection of a subset of solutions which has not yet been decomposed, for instance, the subset with the lowest cost at that point.
3. Decomposition of this subset into at least two new subsets and calculation of their bounds.
4. If one of the subsets contains a complete solution the bound of which is lower than the bounds of all subsets not yet decomposed, this solution is optimal. If this is not the case, proceed with step 2.

We shall illustrate the fundamentals of branch and bound by solving the following sequencing problem.

Example 8-5: Sequencing Five Jobs on Four Machines [2]

Five jobs, A–E, have to be performed by four machines, 1–4. The sequence of jobs has to be the same for all machines. Table 8-15 gives the lengths of

Table 8-15 Operation Times, T_i, on Machine i

Machine, i	Job					
	A	B	C	D	E	Total $\sum T_i$
1	5	2	9	4	1	21
2	5	1	5	3	7	21
3	5	3	2	6	4	20
4	3	7	2	8	1	21

the operations on the different machines. We want to find the job sequence which results in the shortest total process time. This is the sequence which has the earliest completion time of the last operation. From the viewpoint of any machine variations in the total process time for different sequences are caused by

1. Idle time of the machine before the beginning of its first operation (IT_i).
2. The sum of the operation times of the last job on the remaining machines (OT_i).
3. Idle time between operations due to sequence constraints.

Let us assume that we start with the sequence B-E-D-A-C. The total processing time of that sequence is found to be 33 days by laying out a Gantt chart such as Fig. 8-7. We shall now try to improve the sequence by branch and bound, first bounding and then branching. For our sequence B-E-D-A-C, the

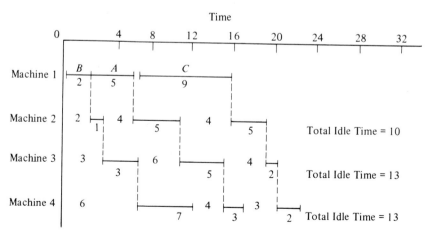

Figure 8-7. Gantt chart for sequence B-A-C.

IT_is and OT_is for the different machines can easily be determined. The sum of IT_i, OT_i, and of all operation times T_i of machine i is a lower bound for the total process time TT. That is, any sequence with B first and C last is at least this long.

Machine	$\sum T_i$	IT_i	OT_i	$\sum T_i + IT_i + OT_i$
1	21	—	9	30
2	21	2	4	27
3	20	3	2	25
4	21	6	—	27

The maximum lowest bound is 30. Obviously the machine with maximum time determines the bound on the total process time. The known sequence is therefore not necessarliy optimal since its length of 33 is more than the bound.

We now begin branching by constructing possible permutations of the jobs. We stop whenever the known lowest bound for a machine (best known total time $[33 - \sum (T_i + OT_i)]$) is reached by the sum of all idle times:

Machine	Bound $33 - (\sum T_i + OT_i)$
1	3
2	8
3	11
4	12

Sequence No.	Sequence	Idle Times of Machines 1	2	3	4
1	A	—	5	10	15[a]
2	B	—	2	3	6
3	B-A	—	6	9	10
4	B-A-C	—	10[a]	13[a]	13[a]
5	B-A-D	—	6	9	13[a]
6	B-A-E	—	6	11[a]	13[a]
7	B-C	—	10[a]	13[a]	11
8	B-D	—	5	6	8
9	B-D-A	—	7	7	8
10	B-D-A-C	—	11[a]	11[a]	9
11	B-D-A-E	—	7	9	9
12	B-D-A-E-C	—	7	10	11

[a]Violation of stage 1 bound.

For illustration we compute the idle times for sequence 4 (B-A-C) using the Gantt chart of Fig. 8-7. The sequence B-D-A-E-C needs 32 days. Therefore it is a new lower bound for the total time.

Stage 2   New Lower Bound $= 32 - (\sum T_i + OT_i) = $ 2, 7, 10, 11

Sequence No.	Sequence		Idle Times		
13	B-D-C	—	11^a	11^a	8
14	B-D-E	—	5	7	8
15	B-D-E-A	—	5	8	10
16	B-D-E-A-C	—	5	8	10

[a]Violation of stage 2 bound.

New sequence: B-D-E-A-C with total time $= 31$ days.

Stage 3   New Bounds: 1, 6, 9, 10

Sequence No.	Sequence		Idle Times		
17	B-D-E-C	—	5	8	8
18	B-D-E-C-A	—	5	11^a	13^a
19	B-E	—	2	7	7
20	B-E-A	—	2	8	12^a
21	B-E-C	—	4	10^a	11^a
22	B-E-D	—	2	7	12^a
23	C	—	9^a	14^a	16^a
24	D	—	4	7	13^a
25	E	—	1	8	12^a

[a]Violation of stage 3 bound.

The sequence B-D-E-A-C turns out to be optimal with a total time of 31 days. To arrive at that result we had to evaluate 25 of 120 ($n!$) possible sequences.

In all the approaches mentioned above we assumed that the processing times are exact and are known in advance. We neglect any unforeseen delays in processing caused by breakdowns, absenteeism, materials shortage, etc. Furthermore, we look at the scheduling problem form the standpoint of a "superscheduler," e.g., *one* central department which establishes schedules for the entire plant. This can normally be the case only for master schedules which do not go into the details of machine assignment, machine loading, and *microsequencing*. In other words, only aggregate planning can be done centrally in most plants. Even if the centrally established master schedules would assign all jobs to machines at exact times, problems would arise in the actual functioning of the plant. There is a certain time lag between the establishment of the schedule and the execution of the different operations. Within this time conditions may change or more information may be available, and corrections to the original schedule must be made. This final step of the production scheduling process is called *dispatching* and it is one of the main functions of foremen, supervisors, etc.

Here we must answer the question, What should be done next? The answers to this question represent the machine schedule actually performed, which may or may not differ from the original schedule. If we look at a machine as a service channel, then the jobs waiting in front of that machine form a waiting line or queue. In this connection dispatching can be considered to operate according to a priority system: Each job or class of jobs has assigned to it a certain index, called *priority*. When a machine becomes vacant because one job is finished, the operator chooses from the jobs waiting to be performed on that machine the one with the highest priority. There are different ways of assigning these priorities to the different jobs. The mechanism used to assign priorities affects certain characteristic values of the queuing system such as waiting time of jobs, idle time of machines, etc. The approach presented in the following pages uses these priorities as a tool to control the flow of jobs in the production system.

III. SEQUENCING BY PRIORITY ASSIGNMENTS (DISPATCHING)

There is a large number of ways to assign priorities to jobs. These priorities can take into consideration characteristics of the entire production system or major parts of it, such as utilization of the overall capacity at the time of the dispatching decision, the structure of the overall capacity such as bottlenecks and the like, and the presence of other jobs. On the other hand, they can be limited to characteristics of a single machine or of the jobs to which they are assigned. The former rules are called *global priority rules*, and the latter *local priority rules*.

Even for local rules it is intuitively obvious that different methods of assigning priorities will affect the relative progress of many scheduled jobs. It has also been shown that the choice of the priority assignment procedure can affect aggregate measures of shop performance such as average inventory. The application of priority rules is not costly because simple priority rules can be applied by any foreman or machine operator. It is therefore quite valuable to study them. In fact, even if an operator does not use priority rules consciously, he is applying some kind of priority rule unconsciously; otherwise he could not make a choice between two jobs which are waiting to be done.

The major loading or priority rules are

1. Choose a job at random (random rule).

2. FOFO (first off, first on), SIO (shortest imminent operation) or SOR (shortest operation rule): A strictly decreasing sequence of priorities is assigned to jobs as they require more time on the machine. The job with the highest priority is selected for assignment.

3. LRT (longest remaining time): Here the priority is directly related to the amount of remaining time for the job on following machines. Maximum priority is given to the job for which the sum of the processing time for all remaining operations is a maximum.

4. SRT: With the shortest remaining time (SRT) rule, priority is inversely related to the total remaining processing time. Maximum priority is given the job for which the sum of the processing times for all remaining operations is a minimum.

5. MRO: Priority is directly related to the number of remaining operations. Maximum priority is given to the job with the most remaining operations (MRO).

6. FRO: Priority is inversely related to the number of remaining operations. Maximum priority is given to the job with the fewest remaining operations (FRO).

7. LO: Maximum priority is given to the job with the longest operation (LO) on the machine in question.

8. FCFS: Maximum priority is given to the job that arrives first. The jobs are on a first-come, first-served (FCFS) priority basis.

9. Due date: The priority value is inversely related to the due date of the job. The job with the earliest due date has the highest priority.

10. Slack time: Priority is inversely related to the remaining slack time. Maximum priority is given to the job for which the time remaining to due date less the remaining processing time is a minimum.

11. Value: Priority is directly related to the (dollar) value of the job. The priority is taken to be equal to the value of the job.

12. Class value: Priority depends on the (dollar) value of the job. Jobs are divided into two classes—a high-value class and a low-value class. All high-value jobs are assigned greater priorities than all low-value jobs. Within the class, priority is assigned in arrival order (FOFO or SIO rule).

The effects of using one or another of these loading rules in complex queuing systems are largely unknown. For some rules and for rather simple systems better insight has been gained. Let us first look at a single-channel system in which the SOR is applied.

Consider n jobs which have to be sequenced on one machine. Each of these jobs may have very different properties in terms of urgency, value, size, etc. If

p_{ij} = value for the ith job of the jth property
t_i = processing time of the ith job,
T_i = time at which the ith job is completed (corresponding to total processing time in our last example);

then, applying the SOR, the jobs are performed (sequenced) such that

$$s_1 \leq s_2 \leq s_3 \leq \cdots \leq s_n.$$

It can be shown that in this case we shall

1. Minimize the total completion time: $\sum_{i=1}^{n} T_i$.
2. Minimize the average completion time: $\sum_{i=1}^{n} T_i/n$.
3. Minimize the average number of jobs in process: $\sum_i T_i/\max_i T_i$.
4. Minimize the average waiting time: $\sum_{i=1}^{n} (T_i - s_i)/n$.
5. Minimize the *average lateness*: $\sum_{i=1}^{n} (T_i - d_i)/n$, where d_i is the due date of job i.

The same will be true for $\sum_{i=1}^{n} p_{ij}T_i$ rather than $\sum_{i=1}^{n} T_i$ if the jobs are sequenced such that

$$\frac{t_1}{p_{ij}} \leq \frac{t_2}{p_{2j}} \leq \cdots \leq \frac{t_n}{p_{nj}}.$$

These results can be generalized to more complex systems only under very limiting assumptions.

Unfortunately we shall hardly find such "simple" situations in reality. Therefore the most efficient way, and very often the only feasible way, to study more complex systems with respect to the effects of different loading rules is the simulation of these systems. This is true at least for the near future, e.g., until complex queuing systems have been more thoroughly explored analytically. For the SOR and the LOR very interesting results have been found by Conway and Maxwell [3]. These results give us valuable insight into some aspects of the use of priority rules and we shall look at them briefly.

Conway and Maxwell simulated a system with the number of jobs equal to 2, 4, and 6 times the number of machines. The number of jobs was held constant at each point of time and two extreme types of systems, a job-shop model and a pure flow shop, were studied. The sample size was 2000 jobs in each case. The following loading rules were considered:

1. Random rule (R): Jobs are selected for assignment at random from among those waiting. This rule was selected to represent the class of local rules that do not consider processing time, FCFS, rank by value, select at random, etc., which are assumed to be equivalent with respect to mean system measures.

2. SOR (S): Jobs are selected for assignment that will take the least amount of processing time. Ties are solved by FCFS. It is assumed that the processing time for each operation is known.

3. SOR under imperfect information (S, X): Same as SOR except that the processing times are not precisely known a priori. X is an index of the ability to predict the processing times. For a processing time S the errors of estimate were approximately normally distributed with mean zero and standard deviation x_s. (Any negative estimates that resulted were taken to be zero.) Note that $S, 0 = S$, and $S, \infty = R$.

4. Two-class SOR ($2S$, B): Jobs are considered to be either short or long, preference being given to short jobs. A job is short if its processing time (which is precisely known a priori) is less than B.

5. Truncated SOR ($2S$, C): Same as SOR except that an upper bound, C, is placed on the time that a job can spend in any one queue. When a job has waited for C time units, it takes precedence in assignment regardless of its processing time. Note that TS, $0 = FCFS$ and TS, $\infty = S$.

6. Alternating SOR and FCFS rule (ST, P): The SOR and FCFS rule are used alternatively for periods of fixed length. The cycle is 400 time units in each case (40 times the mean processing time) and P indicates the proportion of the cycle during which the SOR is used. Note that SF, $1 = S$ and SF, $0 = FCFS$.

7. Subsequent operation rule (A, K) (not a strictly local rule): The dispatcher looks ahead to see where the job would go after leaving the machine in question. Preference is given to jobs that will go to a "critical" queue, a critical queue being one with less than K time units of work waiting. Among jobs that will go on to critical queues, selection is by the SOR.

Figure 8-8 shows the results concerning idle time in percent for different loading rules and for different shop sizes for the job shop. Table 8-16 finally compares the mean flow times and their variances of the FCFS rule, the random rule, and the SOR.

Two main properties of the SOR—compared to other rules—can clearly be read from Table 8-16:

1. The mean flow time is minimized.

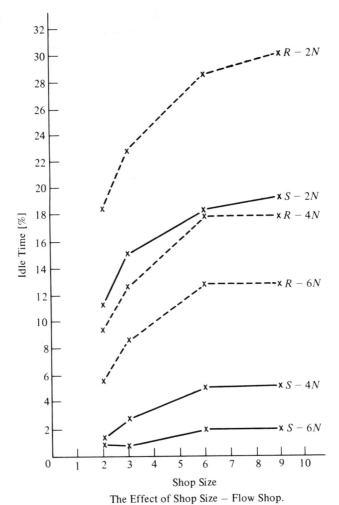

The Effect of Shop Size – Flow Shop.

Figure 8-8. Idle time for different loading rules.

Table 8-16   Characteristics of Scheduling Rules

Rule	Mean of Distribution of Flow Time	Mean of Distribution of Flow Time/Operation	Variance of Distribution of Flow Time	Variance of Distribution of Flow Time/Operation
FCFS	344.7	72.0	61.785	16.933
R	344.4	72.3	93.074	46.221
S	283.1	59.5	388.672	356.801

2. The variance of the flow times is maximized.

These are results which intuitively we would have expected with the SOR. Jobs with long operation times have to wait until all short-operation jobs are cleared out. In fact, when there are enough short-operation jobs the long-operation jobs will never be done.

One way to reconcile the advantages of the SOR with its disadvantages would be to

1. Alternate the SOR with a low variance rule to periodically clear the shop of jobs with long operations.
2. Truncate the SOR by imposing a limit on the delay that individual jobs can have at one station.

Both ways have been suggested and tested by Conway and Maxwell. In their studies the second way seemed to yield more favorable results. More research will have to be done, however, before definite and applicable rules can be stated.

In many practical cases the testing of alternative loading rules by simulating the relevant condition will point to priority rules which yield the best results with respect to certain desirable results.

E. Line Balancing

I. INTRODUCTION

As pointed out at the beginning of this chapter, line balancing is closely related to scheduling. In fact, line balancing can be considered as a very special sequencing problem. For the purpose of discussing this problem in more detail, let us use the following definitions:

Work element: a rationally indivisible element of work which has to be performed by *one* operator, i.e., perform a single task, return a tool, etc.

Work station: a location at which certain operations or work elements are performed. Assembly line stations can be manned by one or more operators. In certain cases one operator may man more than one work station.

Station work content: the total amount of work measured in units of time to be performed at a single work station.

Total work content: the aggregate amount of work of the total production line that is needed to assemble or produce one item.

Cycle time: the amount of time elapsed between successive units (products) as they move down the line; i.e., the cycle time is the time that elapses between completion of units leaving the line.

Balance delay: the total amount of idle time due to imperfect division of the total work content between the work stations—the imbalance of the line.

a. Problem Definition

We are now ready to formulate the problem of line balancing in mathematical terms. If we write d for the balance delay, t_i for the duration of the ith work element, N for the number of work stations, C for the cycle time, and J for the total sum of work elements, the balance delay in general is

$$d = NC - \sum_{i=1}^{J} t_i, \qquad N \text{ integer.} \qquad (8\text{-}14)$$

b. Objective Function

We want to minimize the balance delay, d. This objective reduces to minimizing the product NC, assuming that the sequence of the operations does not influence their duration. Therefore possible goals are either

1. Minimize the number of work stations for a given cycle time, or
2. For a given number of work stations, minimize the cycle time.

Which of the goals is chosen depends on the problem situation. If the capacity or number of stations is rather inflexible because of fixed size of machines or fixed layout, optimizing means finding the minimum cycle time, given the existing work stations. If, however, the output of the production line has to be constant, the corresponding cycle time has to be held constant and the minimum number of stations should be determined. Obviously the line has to be rebalanced whenever the cycle time is changed.

c. Balancing Restrictions

The objective function has to be minimized subject to the following restrictions:

1. The cycle time has to be larger than the duration of the largest work element:
$$t_{i\,\text{max}} \leq C.$$

2. The work content of any single station (in units of time) has to be smaller than the cycle time:
$$\sum_{i=1}^{J} t_i X_{ij} \leq C, \qquad j = 1, 2, \ldots, N, \qquad (8\text{-}15)$$

and

$$X_{ij} = \begin{cases} 1 & \text{if work element } i \text{ is assigned to work station } j \\ 0 & \text{if work element } i \text{ is not assigned to work station } j. \end{cases}$$

3. Each work element is to be assigned only once:

$$\sum_{j=1}^{N} X_{ij} = 1, \qquad i = 1, 2, \ldots, J. \tag{8-16}$$

4. Technological restrictions referring to the sequence of the operations can be formulated as a precedence matrix or precedence graph and must not be violated. The same holds for other technological restrictions imposed by fixed facilities on the line or by specific required positions of operators or work stations.

II. LINE-BALANCING METHODS

a. General Remarks

The problem of line balancing has been approached from several directions. Figure 8-9 surveys well-known methods that have been suggested. They are classified as to their authors and the basic techniques. Using Jackson's example [4], we shall demonstrate some of the characteristic approaches.

Example 8-6

Table 8-17 shows the basic data of our Figures 8-10 and 8-11, which show respectively the precedence matrix and precedence graph. In the precedence matrix an entry of 1 indicates that operation i directly precedes operation j and no entry that operation i does not directly precede operation j. In the precedence graph the precedence relationships are indicated by arrows and the numbers above the circles indicate the duration of the operations (circles).

The balance delay, d, can be plotted as a function of the cycle time, C. Figure 8-12 shows the relative balance delay as a function of C or N, respectively, for our numerical example:

$$d' = 100 \frac{d}{NC} \%. \tag{8-17}$$

It is obvious that a perfect balance ($d = 0$) can be reached only for $C = 23$, which means that $N = 2$. In calculating the balance delay for Fig. 8-12, precedence restrictions and other technological restrictions were neglected. Thus the absolute minimum of the balance delay is at a cycle time of 23. It can be considered a boundry value which can be achieved only if we are completely free to chose the cycle time. Generally, additional restrictions will

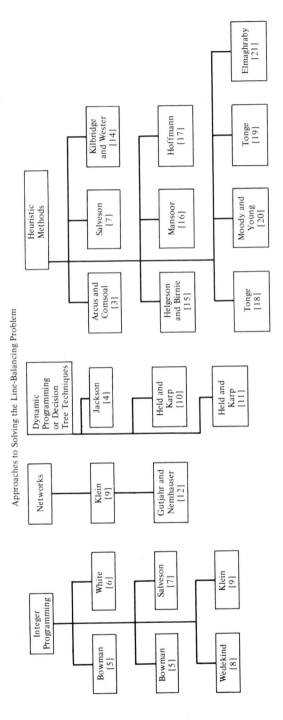

Figure 8-9. Methods and models of line balancing.

Table 8-17   A Numerical Example

Work Element	Duration	Direct Predecessors
1	6	—
2	2	1
3	5	1
4	7	1
5	1	1
6	2	2
7	3	3, 4, 5
8	6	6
9	5	7
10	5	8
11	4	9, 10

i \\ S	1	2	3	4	5	6	7	8	9	10	11
1		1	1	1	1						
2						1					
3							1				
4							1				
5							1				
6								1			
7									1		
8										1	
9											1
10											1
11											

Figure 8-10.   Precedence matrix for numerical example.

limit the range of possible cycle times and thereby shift the minimum achievable balance delay to a value higher than zero.

Let us assume that in our example the required cycle time is $C = 10$. In this case the required number of the stations has to satisfy the following

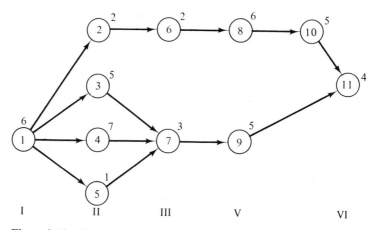

Figure 8-11. Precedence graph for numerical example.

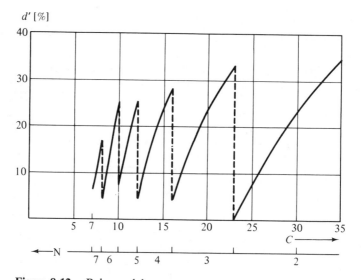

Figure 8-12. Balance delay.

conditions:

$$N_{\min} = \min\left\{ n \geq \frac{\sum\limits_{i=1}^{J} t_i}{C} \right\} \tag{8-18}$$

$N_{\min}$ has to be integer.

For $C = 10$ these conditions are met by $N_{\min} = 5$. If there are no additional constraints, the relative balance delay according to Fig. 8-12 is

$$d_{\min} = 1 - \frac{\sum_{i=1}^{J} t_i}{N_{\min}C} = 8\%.$$

Using different techniques we shall now study to what degree this theoretical balance delay can be achieved considering additional technological or precedence restrictions.

b. The Linear Programming Model

As an example of the existing linear programming formulations of a line-balancing problem, we want to discuss Bowman's model and apply it to our 11-element numerical example.

Example 8-7

We want to find the minimum number of work stations for the cycle time $C = 10$. Since we do not know whether the theoretically minimal number of work stations, $N_{\min} = 5$, is sufficient considering the existing constraints, the model is formulated for a larger number of working stations. In our example we chose seven work stations (A–G). Writing A_1 for the duration of work element 1 if assigned to station A, A_2 for the duration of work element 2 if assigned to station A, etc., we get the following constraints:

1. Capacity constraints:

$$A_1 + A_2 + A_3 + \cdots + A_{11} \le 10$$
$$B_1 + B_2 + B_3 + \cdots + B_{11} \le 10$$
$$\vdots \qquad \vdots \qquad \vdots \qquad\qquad \vdots \qquad \vdots \qquad\qquad (8\text{-}19)$$
$$G_1 + G_2 + G_3 + \cdots + G_{11} \le 10.$$

2. Constraints to assign each work element only once:

$$A_1 + B_1 + C_1 + \cdots + G_1 = 6$$
$$A_2 + B_2 + C_2 + \cdots + G_2 = 2$$
$$\vdots \qquad \vdots \qquad \vdots \qquad\qquad \vdots \qquad \vdots \qquad\qquad (8\text{-}20)$$
$$A_{11} + B_{11} + C_{11} + \cdots + G_{11} = 4.$$

3. Indivisibility constraints for the work elements:

$$\tfrac{1}{6}A_1 + A_1' = 1, \tfrac{1}{6}B_1 + B_1' = 1, \ldots, \tfrac{1}{6}G_1 + G_1' = 1$$
$$\tfrac{1}{2}A_2 + A_2' = 1, \tfrac{1}{2}B_2 + B_2' = 1, \ldots, \tfrac{1}{2}G_2 + G_2' = 1$$
$$\vdots \qquad \vdots \qquad \vdots \qquad \vdots \qquad \vdots \qquad \qquad (8\text{-}21)$$
$$\tfrac{1}{4}A_{11} + A_{11}' = 1, \tfrac{1}{4}B_{11} + B_{11}' = 1, \ldots, \tfrac{1}{4}G_{11} + G_{11}' = 1.$$

There are 77 constraints in which the variables $A_1', \ldots, G_{11}'$ can be 0 or 1.

4. Precedence constraints:

$$\tfrac{1}{2}A_2 \le \tfrac{1}{6}A_1$$
$$\tfrac{1}{2}B_2 \le \tfrac{1}{6}A_1 + \tfrac{1}{6}B_1$$
$$\tfrac{1}{2}C_2 \le \tfrac{1}{6}A_1 + \tfrac{1}{6}B_1 + \tfrac{1}{6}C_1$$
$$\vdots \qquad \vdots \qquad \vdots \qquad \vdots \qquad (8\text{-}22)$$
$$\tfrac{1}{4}G_{11} \le \tfrac{1}{5}A_{10} + \tfrac{1}{5}B_{10} + \tfrac{1}{5}C_{10} + \tfrac{1}{5}D_{10} + \tfrac{1}{5}E_{10} + \tfrac{1}{5}F_{10} + \tfrac{1}{5}G_{10}.$$

There are 91 precedence constraints in our example.

For our example there are 186 constraints with 154 integer variables. The objective function for the problem is

$$\min Z = 1F_{11} + 5G_{11}. \qquad (8\text{-}23)$$

The objective function contains only the work stations that have been added to the minimal number of work stations, in our example work stations F and G. These work stations are weighted with increasing cost factors to ensure that the work elements without direct successors (in our case, work element 11)—and therefore all other work elements—are assigned to the least number of work stations.

For the example the following optimal solution could be obtained:

station A: work elements 1,2,6
station B: work elements 5,8
station C: work elements 3,10
station D: work elements 4,7
station E: work elements 9,11.

The optimal number of stations is therefore 5 and the minimal relative balance delay is 8%. In this case the theoretical minimum has been reached.

c. Network Model

Another interpretation of the line-balancing problem is the search for the shortest path in a directed finite network. We have mentioned that the minimization of the balance delay, given a certain cycle time, is identical to the minimization of the number of work stations. If we construct a network in which the edges correspond to the work stations and the vertices correspond to the feasible sequences, then the optimal solution to the line-balancing problem corresponds to the path through the network which has the least number of edges.

Example 8-8

For the purpose of illustration, we shall apply the approach of Gutjahr and Nemhauser [12] to our numerical example. We start with assignments A_i, $i = 0, 1, \ldots, r$, which are sets that contain a feasible sequence of operations; that is, each can be accomplished without predecessors not in the set. A_r is the set that contains all work elements and A_0 is the empty set that contains no work elements. We now assign to each such set a number which is equal to the sum of the durations of the work elements contained in that set or which equals total work content:

$$t(A_0) = 0$$
$$t(A_i) = \sum_{x \in A_i} t_x, \qquad i = 1, \ldots, r \qquad (8\text{-}24)$$
$$t(A_r) = \sum t_x, \qquad x = 1, \ldots, r.$$

We now construct a network linking the A_i and we assign the feasible sequence A_i to the vertex i. We next draw an edge (i, j) from vertex i to vertex j if and only if the set A_i is contained in the set A_j and if

$$t(A_j) - t(A_i) \leq C, \qquad (8\text{-}25)$$

i.e., if the additional assignment is within the cycle time. The expression for the length of the edge is defined as

$$l(i, j) = C - [t(A_j) - t(A_i)] \geq 0 \qquad (8\text{-}26)$$

and corresponds to the idle time of station (i, j).

Since no edge leads to vertex 0 and no edge leads from vertex r, the network is a finite directed network from vertex 0 to vertex r. Each path from vertex 0 to vertex r corresponds to an assignment of the work elements to the work stations. The length of this path corresponds to the total balance delay of the work stations. For the case of N edges the balance delay is

$$d = NC - t(A_r). \qquad (8\text{-}27)$$

Since $t(A_r)$ is a constant, the optimal solution to our problem will be a path with the minimal number of edges (stations).

For the purpose of completeness we want to outline one method that can be used to find feasible sequences $(A_0, A_1, \ldots, A_r)$: We define as the *immediate successor* of sequence A an element that is a direct successor of at least one element of A and that has no predecessor not contained in A. Starting from the empty set A_0 (stage 0), an element without predecessor is selected. A list of all immediate successors is made and all combinations of the original element and the immediate successors are formed. This process is repeated until all elements are in the set.

Table 8-18 shows the result of applying this method to the numerical example. Table 8-18, which was constructed by using a shortest route tech-

Table 8-18   Determination of the Shortest Path

Minimal Number of Edges to Vertices	Vertex No.	Edges to Vertex
0	0	1, 2, 5, 8, 17
1	1	3, 4, 6, 7, 10, 11, 13, 14, 18, 20, 22, 28
	2	19, 23, 31
	5	
	8	
	17	
2	3	9, 12, 15, 16, 29
	4	21, 24, 25, 30
	6	33
	7	26, 34
	10	
	11	
	13	
	14	27
	18	
	19	
	20	
	22	
	23	
	28	41, 42, 44
	31	46
3	9	32, 35
	12	36, 37
	15	
	16	39
	21	38

Table 8-18   (Cont.)

Minimal Number of Edges to Vertices	Vertex No.	Edges to Vertex
	24	
	25	
	26	
	27	
	29	
	30	43, 45
	33	
	34	47, 48
	41	
	42	
	44	
	46	49
4	32	40
	35	
	36	
	37	
	38	50
	39	
	43	
	45	
	47	
	48	
	49	51
5	$51 = r$	

nique, shows that vertex 51, which corresponds to the feasible sequence A_{51}, was reached for the first time from vertex 49 by a path including five edges (see Fig. 8-13). These five edges represent the five stations to which the 11 work elements are assigned as follows:

$$\text{Station 1:} \quad A_2 = \{1, 2\}$$
$$\text{Station 2:} \quad A_{31} - A_2 = \{5, 6, 8\}$$
$$\text{Station 3:} \quad A_{46} - A_{31} = \{3, 10\}$$
$$\text{Station 4:} \quad A_{49} - A_{46} = \{4, 7\}$$
$$\text{Station 5:} \quad A_{51} - A_{49} = \{9, 11\}.$$

Retracing the path from vertex 51 to vertex 0, we find that the shortest path contains the vertices 0, 2, 31, 46, 49, and 51, which leads to the above-mentioned optimal result. Again the number of work stations is five and the relative balance delay is 8%, even though the assignment is slightly different from the one found by linear programming.

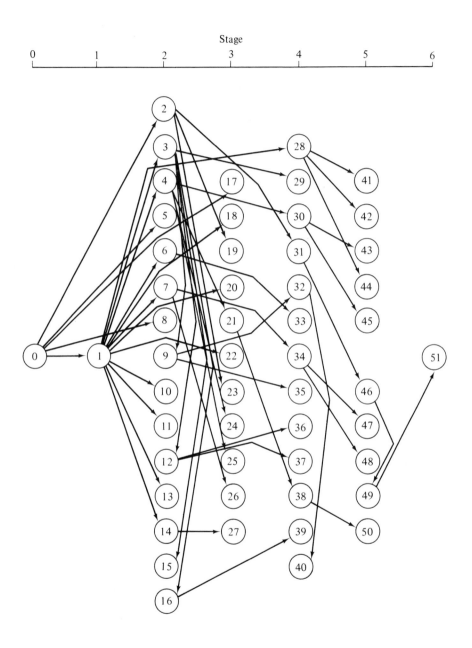

Figure 8-13.   Network.

d. Dynamic Programming Model

Another method to find an exact optimal solution is the dynamic programming approach. As an example we shall apply the method of Held and Karp [11] to the numerical example to determine the minimum number of work stations required. Only feasible sequences A_i are considered. We measure for each feasible sequence the work accomplished by $(k - 1)C + l_k$, where k is the number of used work stations, C is the cycle time, and l_k is the work content of the last work station.

A stagewise minimization of time required can be accomplished by the following recursive algorithm which refers to feasible sequences only:

1. We start with any feasible sequence which contains only one element. Then $T(A_1) = t_1$.
2. We go to the next stage where the measure $T(A_j)$ is computed by adding to $T(A_j)$ the duration t_1 of the added task I_1 if thereby the capacity of a work station is not violated. If it is violated, we must add a new station with the time of t_1 and the idle station time in the old station.

Mathematically,

$$T(A_j) = \min_{J_1 \in A_j} \sum [T(A_j) - \{I_1\} + \Delta(T(A_j - \{I_1\}), t_1)] \tag{8-28}$$

$$A_j - \{J_1\} \text{ feasible}$$

where the sign Δ means the following: If the integer part of

$$\left\{ \frac{T(A_j - \{I_1\}) + t_1}{C} \right\} \tag{8-29}$$

is equal to the integer part of

$$\frac{T(A_j - \{I_1\})}{C} \tag{8-30}$$

or if the expression in braces is integer itself (in other words, the added task fits into the station), then

$$\Delta(T(A_j - I_1), t_1) = t_1, \tag{8-31}$$

of the added work time is the task length. If this is not true, then a new station is added and

$$\Delta(T(A_j - \{I_1\}), t_1) = C\left[\frac{T(A_j - \{I_1\} + t_1}{C}\right] + t_1 - T(A_j - \{I_1\}). \tag{8-32}$$

Example 8-9

Applying the algorithm to the numerical example, we start with the feasible sequences shown in Table 8-19. The computations then start with

$$T(\{1\}) = t_1 = 6$$

$$T(\{1, 2\}) = T(\{1\}) + (T\{1\}, t_2) = 6 + \Delta(6, 2) = 8$$

$$T(\{1, 3\}) = T(\{1\}) + (T\{1\}, t_3) = 6 + \Delta(6, 5) = 15$$

$$T(\{1, 4\}) = T(\{1\}) + (T\{1\}, t_4) = 6 + \Delta(6, 7) = 17$$

$$T(\{1, 5\}) = T(\{1\}) + (T\{1\}, t_5) = 6 + \Delta(6, 1) = 7$$

$$T(\{1, 2, 3\}) = \min \begin{bmatrix} T(\{1, 2\}) + \Delta(T(\{1, 2\}), t_3) \\ T(\{1, 3\}) + \Delta(T(\{1, 3\}), t_2) \end{bmatrix}$$

$$= \min \begin{bmatrix} 8 + \Delta(8, 5) = 15 \\ 15 + \Delta(15, 22) = 17 \end{bmatrix}$$

$$T(\{1, 2, 3\}) = 15.$$

Table 8-19 Generation of Feasible Sequence

Stage	Number	Work Elements	Duration	Immediate Successors
		Assignment		
0	0	Empty set	0	1
1	1	1	6	2 3 4 5 6
2	2	1, 2	8	6
	3	1, 3	11	
	4	1, 4	13	
	5	1, 5	7	
	6	1, 2, 3	13	6
	7	1, 2, 4	15	6
	8	1, 2, 5	9	6
	9	1, 3, 4	18	
	10	1, 3, 5	12	
	11	1, 4, 5	14	
	12	1, 2, 3, 4	20	6
	13	1, 2, 3, 5	14	6
	14	1, 2, 4, 5	16	6
	15	1, 3, 4, 5	19	7
	16	1, 2, 3, 4, 5	21	6 7
3	17	1, 2, 6	10	8
	18	1, 2, 3, 6	15	8
	19	1, 2, 4, 6	17	8
	20	1, 2, 5, 6	11	8
	21	1, 2, 3, 4, 6	22	8

Table 8-19   (Cont.)

Stage	Number	Work Elements	Duration	Immediate Successors
	22	1, 2, 3, 5, 6	16	8
	23	1, 2, 4, 5, 6	18	8
	24	1, 3, 4, 5, 7	22	9
	25	1, 2, 3, 4, 5, 6	23	8
	26	1, 2, 3, 4, 5, 7	24	9
	27	1, 2, 3, 4, 5, 6, 7	26	8 9
4	28	1, 2, 6, 8	16	10
	29	1, 2, 3, 6, 8	21	10
	30	1, 2, 4, 6, 8	23	10
	31	1, 2, 5, 6, 8	17	10
	32	1, 2, 3, 4, 6, 8	28	10
	33	1, 2, 3, 5, 6, 8	22	10
	34	1, 2, 4, 5, 6, 8	24	10
	35	1, 3, 4, 5, 7, 9	27	—
	36	1, 2, 3, 4, 5, 6, 8	29	10
	37	1, 2, 3, 4, 5, 7, 9	29	—
	38	1, 2, 3, 4, 5, 6, 7, 8	32	10
	39	1, 2, 3, 4, 5, 6, 7, 9	31	—
	40	1, 2, 3, 4, 5, 6, 7, 8, 9	37	10
5	41	1, 2, 6, 8, 10	21	—
	42	1, 2, 3, 6, 8, 10	26	—
	43	1, 2, 4, 6, 8, 10	28	—
	44	1, 2, 5, 6, 8, 10	22	—
	45	1, 2, 3, 4, 6, 8, 10	33	—
	46	1, 2, 3, 5, 6, 8, 10	27	—
	47	1, 2, 4, 5, 6, 8, 10	29	—
	48	1, 2, 3, 4, 5, 6, 8, 10	34	—
	49	1, 2, 3, 4, 5, 6, 7, 8, 10	37	—
	50	1, 2, 3, 4, 5, 6, 7, 8, 9, 10	42	11
6	51 = r	1, 2, 3, 4, 5, 6, 7, 8, 9, 10, 11	46	

These computations are repeated until all elements are assigned. Starting from $T(A_r)$, we then find the optimal sequence after further iterations to be

$$1, \quad 2, \quad 5, \quad 6, \quad 8, \quad 3, \quad 10, \quad 4, \quad 7, \quad 9, \quad 11,$$

with a $T(A_r)$ of 49. This is the same sequence that we found by the network model.

e. Two Heuristic Models

The methods described above guarantee the optimal solution of the line-balancing problem. Since the computational efforts are usually very high, some authors have developed heuristic models. These are algorithms leading to rather good solutions with much less effort. These solutions *can* be optimal but the heuristic methods do not *guarantee* optimal solutions.

Example 8-10

We shall apply the methods suggested by Kilbridge und Webster [14] and by Elmaghraby [21] to the numerical example. The point of departure for the first method is the precedence graph shown in Fig. 8-11. In this precedence graph the work elements are then exchanged in a way such that the precedence relationships are not violated and such that a good balance of the work stations (columns of the graph) is achieved. First, the work elements are arranged in a table according to the columns of the precedence graph (see Table 8-20). The remarks in column B, for instance, 3 with (7, 9), indicate

Table 8-20   Table of the Precedence Graph

(A) Column of P Graph	(B) Work Elements	(C) Remarks	(D) Duration	(E) Total Duration	(F) Cumulative Duration
I	1		6	6	6
II	2		2		
	3 (with 7, 9)	→ III	5		
	4 (with 7, 9)	→ III	7		
	5 (with 7, 9)	→ III	1	15	21
III	6		2		
	7 (with 9)	→ IV	3	5	26
IV	8		6		
	9	→ V	5	11	37
V	10		5	5	42
VI	11		4	4	46

that work element 3 can be shifted together with work elements 7 and 9. The arrows in column C indicate to which station the respective work elements can be shifted. Work element 1 has to stay in work station I. Work elements of station II which can be assigned to work station I are numbers 2 and 5 in row II. The additional assignment of any other work element would exceed the cycle time of 10. That leaves in work station II the work elements 3 and 4 with the total duration of 12. Since the cycle time is only 10, we assign work element 4 to work station II, shift work element 3 to work station III, and also shift work element 6 to work station II.

Work element 3 together with the elements 7 and 9 was shifted down to stations IV and V, respectively. Now the remaining work elements are assigned as follows:

1. Work elements 3 and 7 to work station III.
2. Work element 8 to work station IV.
3. Work elements 9 and 10 to work station V.
4. Work element 11 to work station VI.

The final assignment for work elements is shown in Table 8-21.

Table 8-21   Final Assignment of Work Elements to Work Stations

(A) Column of P Graph	(B) Work Elements	(C) Remarks	(D) Duration	(E) Total Duration	(F) Cumulative Duration
I	1		6		
II	2		2		
	5		1	9	9
	4		7		
III	6		2	9	18
	3		5		
IV	7		3	88	26
	8		6	6	32
V	9		5		
	10		5	10	42
VI	11		4	4	46

Elmaghraby [21] suggests the following heuristic algorithm: From the precedence matrix M of Fig. 8-10, construct a matrix M' which has an entry 1 in position ij if task i occurs prior to task j. Calculate *positional weights* w_i, which are the sum of the durations of each specific task and all tasks which must follow. The vector $w = (w_1, w_2, \ldots, w_r)$ of the positional weights can easily be obtained from

$$w = (I_r + M')\{t_1, t_2, \ldots, t_r\}, \qquad (8\text{-}33)$$

where I_r is an identity matrix of rank r. Now sort the weights w_i in decreasing order $w_{(1)} \geq w_{(2)} \geq \cdots \geq w_{(r)}$ and assign tasks to stations in the following fashion:

1. Assign the task corresponding to $w_{(1)}$ to the first station.
2. Calculate $1 = C - t_{(1)}$.
3. Assign the task corresponding to $w_{(2)}$ to station 1 if
   a. The immediate predecessor of this task was assigned to station 1.

b. $t_{(2)} \leq 1$.

Otherwise go to $w_{(3)} \cdots w_{(r)}$ and repeat the test.

4. After the task corresponding to $w_{(r)}$ has been analyzed, repeat steps 1–4 for station 2. Continue until all tasks have been assigned.

Example 8-11

For the numerical example we get the following results: From the precedence matrix M we derive the matrix M' shown in Fig. 8-14. Assuming again

i \ j	1	2	3	4	5	6	7	8	9	10	11
1	1	1	1	1	1	1	1	1	1	1	1
2		1				1		1		1	1
3			1				1		1		1
4				1			1		1		1
5					1		1		1		1
6						1		1		1	1
7							1		1		1
8								1		1	1
9									1		1
10										1	1
11											1

Figure 8-14. Matrix M' for numerical example. Vector $w = (I_n + M')$ $\{t_1, t_2, \ldots, t_{11}\}$ is $w = (46, 19, 17, 19, 13, 17, 12, 15, 9, 9, 4)$, and in decreasing order, $w = (46, 19, 19, 17, 17, 15, 13, 12, 9, 9, 4)$.

that $C = 10$ and executing steps 1–4 until all tasks are assigned, we arrive at the result shown in Table 8-22. Comparing the result with that previously obtained with the network model, it becomes obvious that the optimal result was not reached. The computational effort, however, was smaller.

Table 8-22 Assignment of Tasks to Stations

Station, j	Task, i	Positional Weight, w_i	Immediate Predecessor	Duration, t_i	$\sum s_j t_i$	$\begin{array}{c}1 = 10 \\ -\sum s_j t_i\end{array}$
1	1	46	—	6	6	4
	2	19	1	2	8	2
	6	17	2	2	10	0
2	4	19	1	7	7	3
	5	13	1	1	8	2
3	3	17	1	5	5	5
	7	12	3, 4, 5	3	8	2
4	8	15	6	6	6	4
5	9	9	7	5	5	5
	10	9	8	5	10	0
6	11	4	9, 10	4	4	6

SUMMARY

In this chapter we have discussed the control element of the production scheduling process. First the problem of criteria for short-term control problems was discussed since there is a conflict between a high level of machine utilization and a quick response to meet deliveries. The goal is to maximize long-run profit. This may require several different subgoals in the short run. Next the distinction between job shops and assembly line or functional production systems was recalled from Chap. 4, since scheduling is different for each type. In Sec. B several techniques for completing the aggregate production plans on time with least-cost resources were presented—the line of balance and the assignment method of linear programming.

In Sec. D the job-shop sequencing problem was presented. The question is which jobs should receive priority in a situation when some must wait. Simulation results for various rules of thumb are discussed. The optimizing approach was formulated but rejected for large problems because of the computational difficulties.

In the final section we returned to the functional or assembly line production process to look at the detailed man-machine scheduling or line-balancing problem. Several heuristic methods were presented in order to demonstrate the problem. Again linear programming models were formulated but computation is a difficulty. A network model and a dynamic programming method were also presented since calculation is somewhat reduced with these techniques.

REFERENCES

1. B. GIFFLER, G. L. THOMPSON, and V. VAN NESS, "Numerical Experience with Linear and Monte Carlo Algorithms for Solving Scheduling Problems," in *Industrial Scheduling* (J. F. Muth and G. L. Thompson, eds.), Prentice-Hall, Englewood Cliffs, N.J., 1963, pp. 21–38.

2. H. MÜLLER-MERBACH, "Ein Verfahren zur Lösung von Reihenfolgeproblemen der industriellen Fertigung," in *Zeitschrift für Wirtschaftliche Fertigung*, 61 (1966), 147–152.

3. R. W. CONWAY and W. L. MAXWELL, "Network Scheduling by the Shortest Operations Discipline, in Muth and Thompson [1], *op. cit.*, pp. 277–307.

4. J. R. JACKSON, "A Computing Procedure for a Line Balancing Problem," *Management Science*, 2 (1956), 261–271.

5. E. H. BOWMAN, "Assembly Line Balancing by Linear Programming," *Operations Research*, 8, No. 3 (1960), 385–389.

6. W. W. WHITE, "Comments on a Paper by Bowman," *Operations Research*, 9 (1961), 274–276.

7. M. E. SALVESON, "The Assembly Line Balancing Problem," *The Journal of Industrial Engineering*, 6, No. 3 (1955), 18–25.

8. H. WEDEKIND, "Linearer Programmansatz für das Fließbandproblem," *Ablauf- und Planungsforschung*, 4 (1963), 245–261.

9. M. KLEIN, "On Assembly Line Balancing," *Operations Research*, 11, No. 2 (1963), 274–281.

10. M. HELD and R. M. KARP, "A Dynamic Programming Approach to Sequencing Problems," *Journal of the Society for Industrials and Applied Mathematicss*, 10, No. 10 (1962), 196–210.

11. M. HELD, R. M. KARP, and RICHARD SHARESHIAN, "Assembly Line Balancing—Dynamic Programming with Precedence Constraints," *Operations Research*, 11, No. 3 (1963), 442–459.

12. A. G. GUTJAHR and G. L. NEMHAUSER, "An Algorithm for the Line Balancing Problem," *Management Science*, 11, No. 2 (1964), 308–315.

13. A. L. ARCUS, "Comsoal: A Computer Method of Sequencing Operations for Assembly Lines," in *Readings in Production and Operations Management* (E. S. Buffa, ed.), Wiley, New York, 1966, pp. 336-360.

14. M. D. KILBRIDGE and L. WESTER, "A Heuristic Method of Assembly Line Balancing," in *Readings in Production and Operations Management* (E. S. Buffa, ed.), Wiley, New York, 1966, pp. 291–307.

15. W. R. HELGESON and D. P. BIRNIE, "Assembly Line Balancing Using the

Ranked Positional Weight Technique," *The Journal of Industrial Engineering*, 12, No. 6 (1961), 394–398.

16. E. M. MANSOOR, "Assembly Line Balancing Improvement of the Ranked Positional Weight Technique," *The Journal of Industrial Engineering*, 15, No. 2 (1964), 73–77.

17. T. R. HOFFMANN, "Assembly Line Balancing with a Precedence Matrix," *Management Science*, 9, No. 4 (1963), 551–562.

18. F. M. TONGE, *A Heuristic Program for Assembly Line Balancing*, Prentice-Hall, Englewood Cliffs, N.J., 1961.

19. F. M. TONGE, "Assembly Line Balancing Using Probabilistic Combinations of Heuristics," *Management Science*, 11, No. 7 (1965), 727–735.

20. G. L. MOODY and H. H. YOUNG, "A Heuristic Method of Assembly Line Balancing for Assumptions of Constant or Variable Work Element Times," *The Journal of Industrial Engineering*, 16, No. 1 (1965), 23–29.

21. S. E. ELMAGHRABY, *The Design of Production Systems*, Reinhold, New York, 1966, pp. 278–279.

PROBLEMS

1. A railroad company has to meet daily cyclic loads. The varying demand is met either by attaching additional cars to trains up to a certain technological limit L or by setting up additional trains as soon as it is economical. Establish decision rules for varying the length of the first train and/or for setting up additional trains for the cases of increasing, constant, and decreasing marginal costs. Given data: fixed costs, F_j (occur only while train is running); marginal costs, m_{ij}; average costs, a_{ij}; startup posts per train, S_j; and shut-down costs per train, N_i.

2. A company has six turret lathes and as many jobs to be run on them. Each job will take approximately 1 day regardless of the lathes on which they are run. The lathes vary as to manufacturer, date of manufacture, speeds and feeds available, hourly overhead cost, and so forth, so that costs are not the same for a given job from lathe to lathe. From standard data, labor rates, and overhead rates, the cost matrix in Table P-2 is constructed, the elements being the cost of each order if it is produced on the lathe in question. The object of the problem, of course, is to minimize total costs. Determine the optimal assignments.

3. The network in Fig. P-3 gives the precedence relationships for the tasks in assembly of an engine. The tasks and times are given in the following table. The cycle time is set at 10 minutes. Use the network technique to find the optimal number and assignment of stations.

Node and task no.	1	2	3	4	5	6	7	8	9	10	11
Time for task	6	2	5	7	1	2	3	6	5	5	4

Table P-2   Turret Lathe

Job	A	B	C	D	E	F
1	27.62	31.27	32.09	28.47	34.29	31.24
2	25.74	28.62	27.49	26.31	30.91	24.79
3	32.67	32.48	33.91	30.47	34.72	34.62
4	23.47	23.92	28.62	27.61	25.47	28.62
5	33.08	39.62	37.41	38.62	31.42	39.72
6	32.97	28.62	29.47	31.26	33.49	34.72

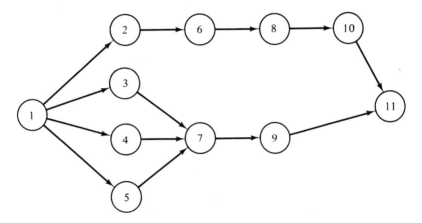

Figure P-3.

4. a. The following tasks are to be performed on an assembly line with three stations. Group the tasks into feasible groups for the three stations with no line
balance delay.

Tasks	Must be Preceded by	Time (min)
a	—	2
b	—	1
c	a	4
d	b	3
e	a	5
f	c, d	2
g	e, f	3
h	c, d	4
i	c, d	2
j	i	2
k	g, h, j, l	1
l	—	1
		30

b. What would the production rate be from this line? Suppose that you wanted five units per hour instead; what different actions could be taken?

5. a. Sequence the following jobs on two machines if all jobs are done first on machine A and then on machine B. The objective is to finish all operations as soon as possible.

	Job				
	1	*2*	*3*	*4*	*5*
Time on A, A_i	3	6	8	3	4
Time on B, B_i	4	5	7	6	2
Start lag, a_i	2	3	3	1	2
Stop lag, b_i	1	2	5	2	3

b. What would you do if the jobs didn't have to go on machine A first but could be scheduled for B and then A?

c. Sequence the following jobs on three machines. Explain why this is possible, in relation to the problem above.

	Job					
	1	*2*	*3*	*4*	*5*	*6*
Time on A	6	9	5	11	10	3
Time on B	2	3	0	2	2	3
Time on C	12	7	7	4	4	8

6. Company A produces three types of detergents in two plants. The daily production rates (in tons) are the following:

	Detergent		
	A	*B*	*C*
Plant I	100	130	90
Plant II	90	110	110

The capacities of the two plants are 20 days per month. By working overtime the capacities can be increased by 10% in plant I and by 15% in plant II. The variable costs per ton of detergent are as given in the following table:

	Detergent		
	A($)	B($)	C($)
Plant I	100	110	80
Plant II	120	100	90

When working overtime, these costs increase by 40%. The demand for the first quarter of the year is estimated as follows:

Detergent	Demand in		
	Jan.	Feb.	March
A	3000	2500	2800
B	1500	1700	1800
C	2000	1500	1600

Limited storage space is available: 1000 tons can be stored in plant I and 1200 tons in plant II. Storage costs for 1 month are $2 per ton. Determine the production schedule which maximizes profit assuming that the prices are constant.

7. Four products have to be assigned to three product lines. The rates of production in units per day are known to be as follows:

Product Line	Products				Maximum Line Capacity (days)
	1	2	3	4	
1	150	80	400	400	20
2	250	80	700	400	20
3	180	70	700	600	18
Total requirements (units)	2000	2500	2800	6000	

The cost of using the lines is $600, $500, and $400, respectively. Determine the optimal assignment.

8. The sales forecasts for a product are as follows:

Period	Units	Period	Units
1	1100	6	800
2	1000	7	900
3	900	8	1200
4	700	9	1000
5	800	10	1000

The production capacity is 900 units per period (regular time) and 250 units per period (overtime). Subcontracting can be relied on up to a capacity of 400 units per period. Costs are overtime, $30 per unit more than regular time; subcontracting, $25 per unit more than regular time; and storage, $8 per unit per period.

a. Suggest an optimal production schedule for the 10 periods if the initial inventory is 250 units.

b. Find the total cost of this program.

c. Draw the stock level variations during the 10 periods.

chapter 9

Maintenance

A. Introduction

I. THE MAINTENANCE SYSTEM

At this point in the book we have examined most of the production subsystems. The proper functioning of these elements will ensure a smooth operation of the total production system. We have decided on the quantitative and qualitative aggregate capacity, the location of our facilities both within the economy and within our plant, and the kind and quantity of product to manufacture. We have also considered when and on what machine we produce which item and how much inventory we shall have to carry to support our production and to satisfy demand. In all our considerations we assumed that the productive facilities—once they were bought and installed—remained in good condition. This, however, will not be true if they are not properly maintained. The physical facilities of our productive capacity are susceptible to failure or deterioration due to age and the effects of their use. Failure or excessive deterioration of the equipment might result in losses of production and in the enforced idleness of allied equipment or personnel within the same system. We should point out that we concentrate on the nonhuman portion of the system because of the lack of models for the "maintenance" of the human portion.

Losses due to failure can be reduced to a minimum by maintaining facilities in good working condition. Such preventive maintenance, however, involves significant costs in itself. It is one of the major goals of the maintenance system to minimize the total of maintenance cost and cost of losses from breakdowns. Before trying to determine the maintenance levels which are optimal in this sense, we shall briefly discuss the nature of maintenance operations, the organization and contents of the total maintenance system, and the various decisions that are made in designing and operating the maintenance system. Since production systems differ, so does maintenance of the systems. Before we can determine optimal maintenance decisions we have to determine the systems characteristics because these characteristics limit the strategies available.

Four fundamental questions have to be answered:

1. What is to be maintained?
2. What kind of maintenance will be applied?
3. Who is to perform the maintenance?
4. By which means, ongoing or shutdown, should the maintenance be performed?

a. Items To Be Maintained

The objects or systems to be maintained are the portions of our productive facilities which are subject to failure or deterioration such as machines, weapon systems, roads, gardens, etc. From a systems point of view we could distinguish between

1. Entire systems to be maintained.
2. Single machines or facilities to be maintained.
3. Parts of machines or facilities to be maintained, for instance, the moving parts of a machine only.

The following distinctions are also relevant for the purpose of decision making in the maintenance area.

1. Integrated versus separated systems. The degree to which a facility is integrated into the production flow determines to a large extent the maintenance effort which is justified. If it is integrated, it must be kept operable in order to avoid severe disturbances of the entire production system. A lathe which is part of a flowshop will, for instance, require a higher degree of maintenance than a lathe which is part of a job shop if the total cost of maintenance and breakdowns is to be minimized.

2. Observable versus nonobservable deterioration. To a certain extent the types of possible maintenance strategies are determined by the deterioration

characteristics of the element to be maintained. By observing moving parts of a machine (e.g., bearings or tires of a car), we can determine the degree of deterioration. We can measure the wear and tear of the part or the facility. This type of equipment has two very important features. First, we can determine the degree of deterioration by simple inspection or measurement, and on the basis of these inspections we can estimate rather well the future states of operability. Second, up to a certain time we are free to decide whether or not we want to perform any maintenance operation or replacement. The equipment does not break down suddenly and without warning but rather slowly becomes inefficient in operation.

On the other hand, objects such as light bulbs do not signal their failure in advance. They operate properly until they break down completely. Inspection would not help to detect the occurrence of failure. In contrast to the first type, the second type of deterioration often forces a decision for replacement. After the light bulb has failed, the operation has ceased completely and it can be started again only after repair or replacement of the detective parts.

3. Continuous operation versus interrupted operation versus continuous preparedness. The two extreme cases, continuous operation and continued preparedness or standby, pose the most difficult problems for maintenance. In the first case the operation has to be interrupted to perform maintenance operations, which might interrupt the entire production flow, for instance, furnaces, atomic power reactors, and assembly lines operated on a 24-hour basis. In the second case we have to perform experiments which might destroy the facility to test the operability, for instance, emergency generators or ammunition. Maintenance operations are much easier to schedule without interfering with the production flow if the facilities operate with interruptions during which maintenance operations can be performed.

4. Maintainable while operating versus not maintainable while operating. It is obvious that some of the problems of scheduling maintenance operations disappear if the systems can be maintained while operating. No interruption of the production flow is necessary and even facilities integrated into the production flow can be maintained without adverse effects on the remaining operating systems.

b. Classifications of Maintenance

Maintenance operations are technically as complex as production operations. They can involve drilling, cutting, welding, or greasing, depending on the facilities which have to be maintained. When we talk of different kinds of maintenance in this text, however, we mean different types of maintenance classified from the managerial point of view as follows:

1. *Inspection*, the first and sometimes the only step of maintenance, which may include

a. Visual inspection only.

b. Measurement of certain physical indicators while the facility is operating or continuous observation of control instruments such as instruments in the cockpit of a plane.

c. Careful periodic analysis of weak spots of the facility.

2. *Normal maintenance* such as greasing, oiling, and readjusting operations, which normally will be carried out together with inspection operations.

3. *Emergency maintenance*, which often is called *repair*. These are maintenance operations which are performed after the facility has broken down or after it has deteriorated to a degree which renders proper production operations impossible or unadvisable; i.e., the quality of the output might have dropped to a level at which it can hardly be sold.

4. *Preventive maintenance*. Precautionary maintenance operations to prevent breakdown are advisable in cases in which inspection indicates an impending breakdown of the facility or in which the lifetime of the facility can be determined probabilistically. The latter case holds when the lifetime distribution of the facility has a rather small variance and in cases in which a breakdown of the facility has severe adverse effects on other facilities of the production system. These preventive measures are carried out according to predetermined maintenance plans or schedules. One of the most important tasks of maintenance management is to design optimal schedules for this kind of maintenance.

The goal of each type of maintenance is to keep the equipment in effective working condition. It can be achieved in two ways, which have important differences:

1. By reworking or readjusting the defective part of machine. This is often called *repairing*.

2. By *replacing* the defective parts or the entire facility with new parts or entities. If defective parts are replaced by new and even more effective parts, an increase of efficiency of the entire system can often be achieved. Maintenance then turns into improvement, because the equipment is better than the old when it was new.

Which of the alternatives—repair or replacement—is chosen is mainly an economic question which has to be answered within the framework of maintenance management. It is obvious that there exist close ties to investment decisions, as discussed in Chap. 2 and 5.

c. Maintenance: Personnel and Organization

Maintenance operations can be performed by either

1. The service personnel of the production facilities, or
2. Special maintenance or service crews within the firm, or
3. External maintenance personnel.

While the first will generally be possible if the maintenance operations are easy to perform the second or third is sometimes called for if maintenance operations are more complicated and demand special training, experience, or skill.

Having the service crew on one's own payroll means that in general we shall be served more promptly because we can control and schedule the maintenance crew. It also means increased fixed costs for tools and fixtures. There may be smoothing problems with respect to the work load of the service crew if the services of the maintenance crew are demanded cyclically or sporadically.

In either case, decisions made within our maintenance system will strongly depend on decisions made in other subsystems such as facility design, aggregate capacity, and aggregate planning decisions. In turn, maintenance decisions will also have considerable impact on the areas of production scheduling. Figure 9-1 depicts the major problems of the maintenance system and their interrelationships to each other and to other functional areas.

II. ECONOMIC CONSIDERATIONS

Whether we talk about optimal replacement policies, the optimal level of preventive maintenance, the optimal size of the service crew, or the optimal size of maintenance, repair, and operating supplies (MRO) of inventories, the term *optimal* always refers to the least-cost alternative. The maintenance function is a special case of the production function, and so we seek optimal combinations of inputs, optimal capacities, optimal schedules, etc.

The "optimal" level of preventive maintenance is an example. Figure 9-2 shows the relationship between the amount of preventive maintenance performed, the cost of maintenance, and the cost of failures. The curves are total cost curves. A marginal cost analysis would, however, lead to the same results.

The manager will try to determine the level of preventive maintenance which minimizes total cost. If maintenance falls below this level, the cost of failures will increase more than is saved in maintenance. If the maintenance effort rises above this level, the additional maintenance cost is not justified by the resulting (smaller) decrease in cost of failures. It is obvious that the

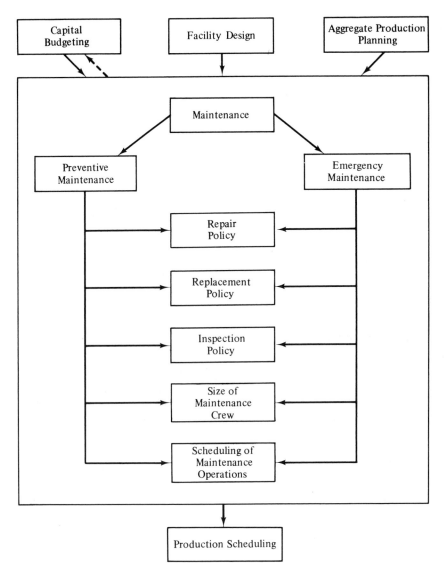

Figure 9-1. Maintenance system.

curves of Fig. 9-2 are generally not known to the decision maker—otherwise decision making would be easy. In the following paragraphs we shall discuss methods to solve some of the major problems of maintenance management optimally or at least to establish some heuristic rules as an aid to decision making in the maintenance system.

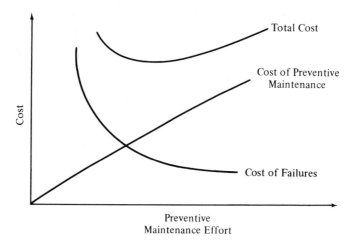

Figure 9-2. Cost of maintenance.

B. Information Requirements

I. INFORMATION REQUIREMENTS

For the design of optimal maintenance strategies, information concerning the system to be maintained is needed. It is often extremely difficult or even impossible to obtain all or even a major part of the needed information within an acceptable time and without incurring excessive cost. In these cases approximation to reality or assumptions about real relationships have to substitute for complete information.

Before looking at some of the necessary information in more detail, let us structure the total information requirements.

The following information refers primarily to the total system to be maintained:

1. List of all facilities to be maintained.
2. Degree of integration of a facility into a production system.
3. Distribution function of short-term availability of maintenance material, personnel, and spare parts.
4. Cost of breakdowns.

The following information primarily concerns single facilities:

1. Description of functions, design, and raw material of the facility.
2. Age or time of usage.

3. State of deterioration of facility.
4. Methods for determination of states of deterioration.
5. Search procedures to localize failures and malfunctions.
6. List of past failures and major maintenance operations applied to the facility.
7. Deterioration characteristics: distribution function of breakdown or length of useful life of facility or the mathematical or statistical description of deterioration characteristics of facilities.
8. Durations of possible maintenance operations.
9. Costs of possible maintenance operations and breakdowns.

In the short run, the main concern of maintenance management is to determine optimal maintenance strategies based on the information mentioned above and assuming a given size of the service crew. In particular, the following have to be extablished: maintenance operations, maintenance periods or frequencies, and priorities for cases in which several breakdowns occur at the same time. In the long run the size of the service crew can and ought to be optimized as an additional degree of freedom. Optimization refers to the kind and number of personnel and equipment and the quantities and kinds of maintenance materials. This, in turn, has to be fed back to the short-run optimization using the information mentioned above, which obviously is effected by decisions concerning the service crew.

Information requirements for deterioration and maintenance duration warrant special attention because of their importance to maintenance models.

II. DETERIORATION AND MAINTENANCE CHARACTERISTICS

a. Breakdown Distributions and Durations of Maintenance Operations

Distributions of breakdown times can be expressed as probability distribution functions or as density functions, such as shown in Fig. 9-3.

Let us use the following notation:

t = useful life of a facility

T_e = expected value of t

$F(t)$ = fraction of facilities not yet broken down by time t or the probability that a facility will not break down before time t

$d(t)$ = density function of breakdowns

$P(t)$ = probability that no breakdown occurs within the randomly chosen interval t

$F(t), P(t)$ = abbreviations for $F_0(t)$ and $P_0(t)$ as compared to $F_k(t)$ and $P_k(t)$, which refers to K breakdowns.

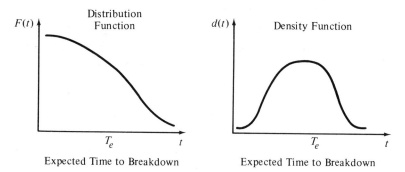

Figure 9-3.   Breakdown time distribution.

The following important relationships hold as a result of these definitions:

$$\int_0^\infty d(t)\, dt = 1 \tag{9-1}$$

$$d(t) = -\frac{dF(t)}{dt} \tag{9-2}$$

$$F(t) = 1 - \int_0^t d(t)\, dt = \int_t^\infty d(t)\, dt \tag{9-3}$$

$$T_e = \int_0^\infty t\, d(t)\, dt = \int_0^\infty F(t)\, dt = \frac{1}{\lambda} \tag{9-4}$$

$$P(t) = \lambda \int_t^\infty F(t)\, dt, \tag{9-5}$$

where λ is the average occurrence rate of breakdowns and μ is the average service rate.

Often the representation of the probabilities of breakdown by a discrete probability distribution is considered sufficient. In some cases it is possible to describe the breadkown time distributions adequately by continuous functions such as the Poisson, Erlang, Hyperexponential, or Normal distributions. Figure 9-4 shows these three distribution functions as applied to service time distributions [1]. Figure 9-4(a) depicts the exponential distribution. Many practical cases can be approximated by this distribution, particularly if the system to be maintained consists of many moving parts. Figure 9-4(b) shows Erlang distribution functions, which can often be used as good approximations if the system has only a few moving parts or if we consider a single part to be maintained. Due to the small variance of the breakdown time distribution, preventive maintenance is often advisable to avoid breakdowns. Distribution such as in Fig. 9-4(c) indicates the contrary situation, hyperexponential distributions with a higher variance than the Poisson distribution. Here very short and very long times between breakdown times are more frequent. This distribution function is often observed for machines which need several exact adjustments. If they are adjusted properly, they run for quite a while. If the adjustments are not performed carefully, a new adjustment is necessary very soon.

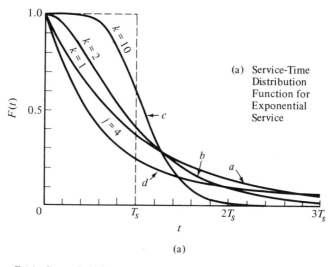

(a) Service-Time Distribution Function for Exponential Service

(a)

$F_0(t)$, the probability that the service operation takes longer than time t. Curve a ($k = 1$) is for exponential service. The dashed curve is for constant service time. Time $t = T_s = 1/\mu$ is the average service time.

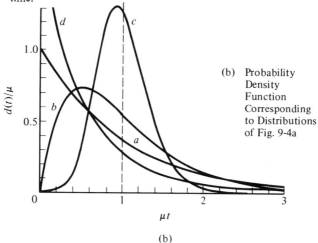

(b) Probability Density Function Corresponding to Distributions of Fig. 9-4a

(b)

Figure 9-4. Examples of service time distribution functions.

Source: Philip M. Morse, Queues, Inventories and Maintenance, *John Wiley & Sons, Inc., New York, 1958, pp. 8, 11. Courtesy of John Wiley & Sons, Inc.*

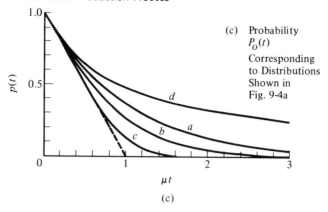

(c)   Probability $P_0(t)$

Corresponding to Distributions Shown in Fig. 9-4a

(c)

Probability density $d(t)/\mu$ of completion of service at time t and probability $p_0(t)$ that no service completion occurs in interval of length t chosen at random, for service characteristics corresponding to those shown in Fig. 9-4(a). Dashed curve is limiting case of constant service time.

Figure 9-4. Continued

Poisson processes are of great importance when applying queuing theory to maintenance problems. These are random processes in which (1) the events (breakdowns) are stochastically independent of each other and of time. This means the probability that an event occurring during time period $t + \Delta t$ does not depend on what happens before or after $t + \Delta t$. (2) The above-mentioned probabilities are a function of Δt only, i.e., of the length of the time interval considered. (3) The probability that more than one event occurs during Δt approaches zero for small Δt.

Such a process can be described by

$$d(t) = \lambda e^{-\lambda t} \tag{9-6}$$

$$F(t) = P(t) = e^{-\lambda t} \tag{9-7}$$

$$F_k(t) = P_k(t) = \frac{1}{k!}(\lambda t)^k e^{-\lambda t}.$$

In Fig. 9-5 λt or t/T_L is the expected value of the number of breakdowns in an arbitrarily choseni nterval of length t. Calling this expected value Z, we can easily derive the well-known Poisson formula

$$\frac{1}{k}Z^k e^{-z}$$

from our expression for $F_k(t)$. This is then the probability that k events have occurred; i.e., it is discrete with respect to k.

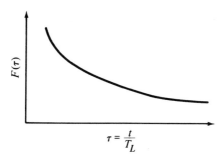

$$\tau = \frac{t}{T_L}$$

Figure 9-5. Probability $F(\tau)$ that τ time units after the occurrence of an event, no other event has occurred.

For any given λ, the $F_k(t)$s therefore represent a family of exponential distributions. For each t there is one distribution function. Also, the durations of maintenance operations, or the time intervals between the ends of maintenance operations, can be represented by the above type of distribution function. We shall discuss these functions for the cases discussed below.

Distribution functions with smaller or larger variances can be obtained using the exponential distribution function and simulation. As an example we choose the Erlang distribution and as a vehicle for its derivation we assume a one-phase *arrival timing channel*. In this channel each of the subsequent phases is described by the same exponential distribution function $le^{-l\lambda t}$ Figure 9-6 depicts such a channel schematically. It operates as follows:

1. Pick one element from the queue.
2. Process this element in phase 1 and pass it on to phase 2 and so on to L.
3. After it has passed phase L, we proceed with the next element according to step 1.

The distribution of the output of this series of channels can be described by [2]

$$a(t) = l\lambda(l\lambda t)^{l-1}\frac{e^{-l\lambda t}}{(l-1)!}; \qquad T_a = \frac{1}{\lambda}$$

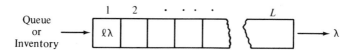

Figure 9-6. Arrival timing channel.

$$A_0(t) = e^{-l\lambda t} \sum_{n=0}^{l-1} \frac{(l\lambda t)^n}{n!} = E_{l-1}(l\lambda t)$$

$$U_0(t) = e^{-l\lambda t} \sum_{n=0}^{l-1} \left(1 - \frac{n}{l}\right)\frac{(l\lambda t)^n}{n!} = D_{l-1}(l\lambda t)$$

$$A_n(t) = e^{-l\lambda t} \sum_{s=0}^{l-1} \frac{(l\lambda t)^{s+nl}}{(s+nl)!}; \qquad \Delta t_a = \frac{1}{\lambda\sqrt{l}}$$

$$U_n(t) = e^{-l\lambda t} \sum_{s=0}^{l-1} \left[\left(1 - \frac{s}{l}\right)\frac{(l\lambda t)^{nl-s}}{(nl-s)!} + \left(1 - \frac{s+1}{l}\right)\frac{(l\lambda t)^{nl+s+1}}{(nl+s+1)!}\right],$$

where $a(t)$ = probability density of arrivals
$A_0(t)$ = arrival time distribution
$A_n(t)$ = probability that n more arrivals will occur within a time t after the last arrival
$U_n(t)$ = probability of n arrivals in interval t, randomly chosen
$U_0(t)$ = arrival time distribution, for randomly chosen t.

Figure 9-7 depicts the distributions of the output of the above-described system. Table 9-1 shows the values of the Erlang density function. By arranging several stages or phases of one "simulator" in series, we arrived at an Erlang-distributed output, the variance of which was smaller than the variance of the exponential distributions. If we want to arrive at an hyperexponentially distributed output (with increased variance), we could use a similar devise in which the "phases" are arranged in parallel. Figure 9-8 and Table 9-2 [3] show the distribution functions and the values of the density function, respectively, at which we would arrive.

b. Processes of Deterioration

It is difficult to ascertain breakdown distributions. It is generally even more difficult to describe the process of deterioration analytically or statistically. Sometimes the process can be described by homogeneous Markov chains. We shall illustrate this approach by the following example.

Example 9-1

Let us assume that a specific deterioration process can be described by a homogeneous Markov chain and that possible states are perfect = 1, just operable = 2, and defective (breakdown) = 3. We now choose a time interval such that no more than one change of state can occur. It will be assumed possible, however, to carry on maintenance operations or replacements

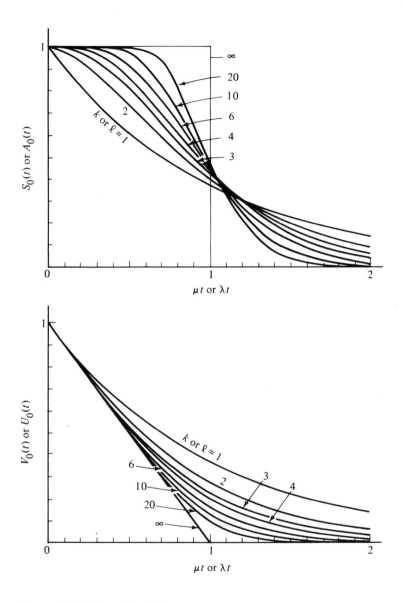

Figure 9-7. Erlang distributions. Probability that the next arrival or the next service completion will occur *after* time interval t. For S_0 or A_0, the interval starts just after the last arrival or service completion. For V_0 or U_0, time in the interval t is started at random. Case k or $l = 1$ is the simple exponential case.

Table 9-1   Erlang Density Function:[a]
Values of $ke_{k-1}(kx) = [k(kx)^{k-1}e^{-kx}/(k-1)!]$

x	$k = 1$	2	3	4	6
0	1.0000	0.0000	0.0000	0.0000	0.0000
.1	.9048	.3275	.1000	.0286	.0021
.2	.8187	.5363	.2964	.1534	.0375
.3	.7408	.6586	.4940	.3470	.1562
.4	.6703	.7189	.6506	.5513	.3612
.5	.6065	.7358	.7531	.7218	.6049
.6	.5488	.7229	.8034	.8361	.8261
.7	.4966	.6905	.8101	.8899	.9799
.8	.4493	.6461	.7838	.8905	1.0485
.9	.4066	.5951	.7349	.8499	1.0369
1.0	.3679	.5414	.6721	.7815	.9638
1.1	.3329	.4875	.6025	.6972	.8518
1.2	.3012	.4354	.5312	.6067	.7222
1.3	.2725	.3862	.4618	.5171	.5914
1.4	.2466	.3405	.3968	.4329	.4702
1.5	.2231	.2987	.3374	.3569	.3644
1.6	.2019	.2609	.2844	.2904	.2761
1.7	.1827	.2269	.2379	.2335	.2052
1.8	.1653	.1967	.1976	.1858	.1499
1.9	.1496	.1700	.1631	.1464	.1078
2.0	.1353	.1465	.1339	.1145	.0764

x	$k = 8$	10	12	16	20
.1	0.0001	0.0000	0.0000	0.0000	0.0000
.2	.0086	.0019	.0004	.0000	.0000
.3	.0660	.0270	.0108	.0017	.0002
.4	.2223	.1323	.0771	.0252	.0079
.5	.4763	.3627	.2704	.1444	.0746
.6	.7669	.6884	.6050	.4492	.3227
.7	1.0137	1.0140	.9932	.9158	.8170
.8	1.1600	1.2408	1.2995	1.3703	1.3980
.9	1.1886	1.3176	1.4299	1.6189	1.7734
1.0	1.1169	1.2511	1.3724	1.5875	1.7767
1.1	.9778	1.0853	1.1794	1.3388	1.4706
1.2	.8079	.8736	.9251	.9970	1.0396
1.3	.6357	.6605	.6720	.6687	.6438
1.4	.4798	.4734	.4574	.4103	.3562
1.5	.3495	.3241	.2943	.2332	.1788
1.6	.2467	.2131	.1803	.1240	.0825
1.7	.1694	.1353	.1058	.0621	.0353
1.8	.1136	.0833	.0597	.0296	.0142
1.9	.0745	.0498	.0326	.0134	.0054
2.0	.0480	.0291	.0173	.0059	.0019

[a]From Philip M. Morse, *Queues, Inventories and Maintenance*, John Wiley & Sons, Inc., New York, 1958, p. 187. Courtesy of John Wiley & Sons, Inc.

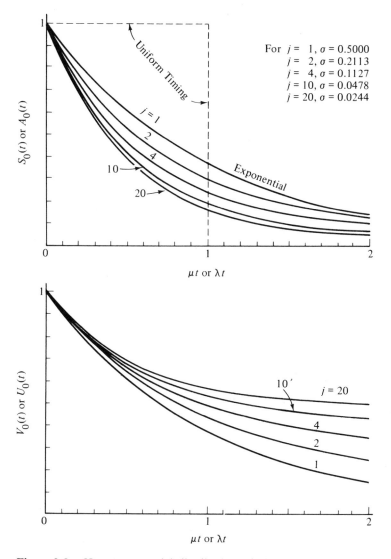

Figure 9-8. Hyperexponential distributions. Values of σ are chosen so that the variability Δt is equal to $\sqrt{j/\mu}$ or $\sqrt{j/\lambda}$ and thus ranges from $(1/\mu)(\sigma = \frac{1}{2})$, the exponential or Poisson case, to infinity ($\sigma = 0$). These are to be compared to the set of Erlang distributions shown in Fig. 9-7, which have variabilities less than $(1/\mu)$. Between the two sets, most operational situations can be simulated.

Source: Philip M. Morse, Queues, Inventories and Maintenance, *John Wiley & Sons, Inc., New York, 1958, p. 54. Courtesy of John Wiley & Sons, Inc.*

Table 9-2   Distribution Functions for Hyper-Exponential Channels
Hyper-exponential Distribution Functions $V_0(t) = \frac{1}{2}e^{-2\sigma x} + \frac{1}{2}e^{-2(1-\sigma)x}$
$S_0 = -(dV_0/dx)$ and $(s/\mu) = -(dS_0/dx)$, where $x = \mu t$.[a]

x		j → 1	2	4	10	20
x	σ	0.5000	0.2113	0.1127	0.0477	0.0244
0	(s/μ)	1.0000	1.3333	1.6000	1.8182	1.9048
	(s/μ)	.8187	.9894	1.1284	1.2436	1.2897
0.2	S_0	.8187	.7695	.7298	.6974	.6845
	V_0	.8187	.8242	.8286	.8322	.8336
	(s/μ)	.6703	.7373	.7974	.8510	.8734
0.4	S_0	.6703	.5981	.5393	.4904	.4709
	V_0	.6703	.6883	.7027	.7147	.7195
	(s/μ)	.5488	.5521	.5651	.5827	.5915
0.6	S_0	.5488	.4701	.4044	.3487	.3262
	V_0	.5488	.5821	.6092	.6316	.6406
	(s/μ)	.4493	.4159	.4019	.3994	.4007
0.8	S_0	.4493	.3740	.3087	.2517	.2282
	V_0	.4493	.4981	.5384	.5722	.5858
	(s/μ)	.3679	.3154	.2873	.2742	.2716
1.0	S_0	.3679	.3013	.2404	.1852	.1619
	V_0	.3679	.4309	.4839	.5289	.5473
	(s/μ)	.3012	.2411	.2066	.1885	.1843
1.2	S_0	.3012	.2460	.1915	.1394	.1169
	V_0	.3012	.3765	.4410	.4967	.5197
	(s/μ)	.2466	.1861	.1498	.1300	.1250
1.4	S_0	.2466	.2036	.1562	.1079	.0863
	V_0	.2466	.3317	.4064	.4722	.4996
	(s/μ)	.2019	.1451	.1098	.0900	.0851
1.6	S_0	.2019	.1706	.1305	.0862	.0656
	V_0	.2019	.2943	.3779	.4530	.4845
	(s/μ)	.1653	.1145	.0815	.0627	.0578
1.8	S_0	.1653	.1449	.1115	.0711	.0514
	V_0	.1653	.2629	.3538	.4373	.4729
	(s/μ)	.1353	.0914	.0614	.0440	.0395
2.0	S_0	.1353	.1244	.0973	.0606	.0418
	V_0	.1353	.2361	.3329	.4242	.4636

[a]From Philip M. Morse, *Queues, Inventories and Maintenance*, John Wiley & Sons, Inc., New York, 1958, p. 192. Courtesy of John Wiley & Sons, Inc.

$((P_{da}))$:

Initial State d ＼ Next State a	1	2	3
1	P_{11}	P_{12}	P_{13}
2	0	P_{22}	P_{23}
3	1	0	0

during operation. By determining the probabilities for transitions from one state to another, we arrive at the following matrix of transition probabilities

The probability $P_d^{(n)}$ of being in state d during the nth interval of operation is then

$$P_d^{(n)} = P^{(0)}((P_{da}))^n,$$

where $P^{(0)}$ is the initial-state vector.

An inspection is carried out every Nth interval and a part is replaced whenever the inspection shows it to be in state 2. The probability for the occurrence of replacement is $P_2^{(n)}$. The probability for a breakdown in the period 1 to N is

$$\sum_{n=1}^{N} P_3^{(n)}. \tag{9-9}$$

c. Time and Cost of Maintenance Operations

We are primarily interested in knowing the average duration of preventive maintenance operations, T_m, and of repairs, T_s; the average idle time due to breakdown, T_i; and the cycle time of the maintenance cycle and the breakdown cycle. The maintenance cycle is the sum $T_m + T_p$, where T_p is the operating time between preventive operations. The breakdown cycle is $T_b + T_s$, where T_b is the mean value of operating times before breakdown, which depends on the breakdown distribution and on T_p. See Fig. 9-9.

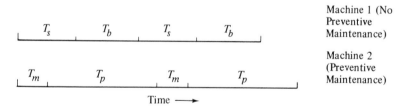

Figure 9-9. Diagram of breakdown and maintenance cycles.

Given the above-mentioned times and cycles, we shall determine distribution functions or at least characteristic parameters which allow an approximate determination of distributions. The difficulties are essentially the same ones we faced dealing with breakdown time distributions. We should point out, however, that maintenance times and cycles can generally be controlled to a higher degree than breakdown times. In many cases they are the decision variables when designing optimal maintenance strategies.

We mentioned that cost plays the essential role in optimizing maintenance strategies. We can influence cost of maintenance and cost of breakdowns and repairs by the level and the frequency of preventive maintenance. Depending on the model we are using, costs will be distinguished according to

1. The kind of event, such as cost of preventive maintenance, cost of repair, cost of breakdown, etc.
2. Variable and fixed cost elements. Here we have to distinguish between variability with respect to single maintenance actions and with respect to the entire maintenance system.

Suppose, for instance, that a machine breaks down and has to be repaired by a mechanic sent by the company which manufactured it. To the company owning the machine, the travel expense of this mechanic is a fixed cost in contrast to the additional cost caused by repair time and material if he performs preventive maintenance on additional machines. Wages and depreciation on the company's own maintenance equipment, however, are essentially fixed costs. In this case variable costs are the material and spare parts used for repair and maintenance.

III. SOME TYPES OF MAINTENANCE STRATEGIES

We shall follow I. J. McCall in his classification of maintenance strategies into strategies which can be applied if the breakdown distribution is known and those few cases in which this distribution is not known. For the former strategies the data base is rather limited and minimax-type policies will have to be applied. They do not require much information but they yield the least satisfactory results. If at least the mean and variance of the breakdown time distributions are known but not the distributions themselves, we can use bounding techniques. Bounds on the distributions can be established within which certain maintenance operations are advisable.

In *adaptive* strategies, new information concerning the deterioration characteristics is collected as time goes on and the maintenance strategies are improved. A similar approach is used when applying *sequential* strategies. They are particularly suitable if the useful life of the system to be maintained is short compared to maintenance cycles and if the breakdown distribution or cost parameters change over time. This may occur because of changes of prices of raw material or spare parts or of labor. Cost parameters can also change because of restructuring of the maintenance department or improved performance of maintenance operations. Sequential strategies are particularly suitable wherever improvement of technology plays an important role.

If the breakdown characteristics are sufficiently known, *periodic* strategies can be applied. These strategies are sets of optimal maintenance intervals and maintenance operations determined once and for all. The maintenance system then becomes a stationary system or process which is changed only by exogenous actions or changes in breakdown time distributions. Periodic strategies can be worked out and put into practice much easier than most of the other types of strategies. Figure 9-10 depicts four different types of strategies. The following symbols are used:

X = preventive maintenance operation
(X) = repair (emergency maintenance)
$\uparrow$ = breakdown.

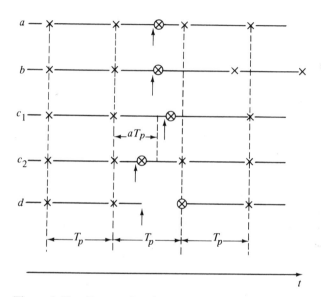

Figure 9-10. Types of maintenance strategies: a, periodic strategy; b, strategy with constant maintenance interval; c, parts which failed shortly before maintenance operation are slipped in next period; and d, idle time until next scheduled maintenance operation is scheduled.

Figure 9-11 shows the results of choosing different values of T_p for strategy b. Repair costs are assumed higher than the cost of preventive maintenance.

The total cost of maintenance per unit of time during the maintenance cycle has a damped oscillation approaching the size of the cost of repair.

In the neighborhood of point 1, preventive maintenance operations occur just in time to prevent most of the breakdowns. Around point 2, however, preventive maintenance is not performed early enough to avoid failure. The

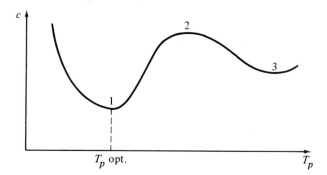

Figure 9-11. Cost of maintenance as a function of the maintenance cycle. The notation is C, cost of maintenance; $c = t =$ per minute of time; $C =$ total cost of maintenance $=$ number of repairs, x cost per repair $+$ number of prevented maintenance actions $\times$ cost per action.

low cost of maintenance at point 3 can be explained by the fact that parts which have been replaced after breakdown near point 1 are maintained just in time to prevent the next unpredicted breakdown.

Until now our criterion for classifying maintenance strategies was the amount of information concerning the distribution of breakdown times. Another way of classifying strategies is that of considering the time pattern of utilization of the system which is to be maintained. If a system has to operate continuously, decreases in effectiveness or breakdown can generally be observed quickly and without excessive extra effort. If, however, the system performs only infrequently or even just stands by ready to operate in an emergency, then the system has to be inspected frequently or even tested with trial runs to detect failures.

In practice, often the specific maintenance operations called for depend on the state of deterioration of the equipment. Frequently there are three states considered: operable, still operable but requiring service, and not operable.

As already mentioned, the theory of Markov chains or simulation might be helpful in designing optimal strategies. This is particularly true for the design of any complicated policies or for the determination of optimal *opportunistic strategies*, which consider several items as one maintainable entity. The problem then poses more involved combinational aspects.

As an example, let us mention neon streetlights with two bulbs each. The switches have a useful life of several thousand switching operations. If one of the bulbs fails after approximately the estimated useful life, the second bulb will also be replaced in order to avoid the costs which are caused by each repair. If the failure occurs after a short time, however, a substantial useful life can still be expected for the other bulb, and only the defective bulb will be replaced.

IV. DETERMINATION OF MAINTENANCE FREQUENCIES

a. Optimal Maintenance Frequency for Given Size of Service Crew and a Single Machine

The strategy to be analyzed includes preventive maintenance as well as repairs. Preventive maintenance needs, on the average, T_m time units and is performed with a cycle time of T_p if no breakdown occurs during this time period. Obviously two different maintenance cycles exist:

1. The "usual" cycle has the length $T_p + T_m$ with a relative frequency of $F_0(T_p)$. The average fraction of time during which the facility operates is then $T_p/(T_p + T_m)$ during the usual cycle.
2. The "unusual" cycle of the length $T_b + T_s$ which has the relative frequency of $1 - F_0(T_p)$.

For the unusual cycle the expected time before breakdown is

$$T_b = \frac{1}{1 - F_0(T_p)} \int_0^{T_p} t\, d(t)\, dt$$

$$= \frac{1}{1 - F_0(T_p)}\left[\int_0^{T_p} F_0(t)\, dt - \left| t F_0(t) \right|_0^{T_p} \right]$$

$$= \frac{1}{1 - F_0(T_p)}[T_i - T_i P_0(T_p) - T_p F_0(T_p)], \tag{9-10}$$

where

$$P_0(t) = \frac{1}{T_i} \int_t^\infty F_0(X)\, dX \tag{9-11}$$

$$T_i = \int_0^\infty F_0(X)\, dX. \tag{9-12}$$

Assuming that preventive maintenance puts the facility into the same state as repair operations, the resulting cycle time is

$$F_0(T_p)[T_p + T_m] + [1 - F_0(T_p)](T_b - T_s). \tag{9-13}$$

If we set $\alpha = T_m/T_i$, $\beta = T_s/T_i$, and $u_p = T_p/T_i$, then the fractions of time the machine is working, F_w, and the fractions of preventive maintenance time, F_m, and repair time, F_s, respectively, are

$$F_w = \left[1 + \alpha \frac{F_0(u_p)}{1 - P_0(u_p)} + \beta \frac{1 - F_0(u_p)}{1 - P_0(u_p)} \right]^{-1} \tag{9-14}$$

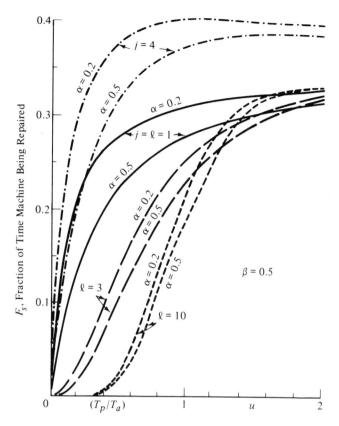

Figure 9-12. Fraction of time machine is undergoing repair after break-down. Fraction of time F, the machine is undergoing repair after break-down, corresponding to the curves of Fig. 9-13 for F_w and F_m.

Source: Philip M. Morse, Queues, Inventories and Maintenance, John Wiley & Sons, Inc., New York, 1958, p. 164. Courtesy of John Wiley & Sons, Inc.

$$F_m = F_w \alpha \frac{F_0(u_p)}{1 - P_0(u_p)} \qquad (9\text{-}15)$$

$$F_s = F_w \beta \frac{1 - F_0(u_p)}{1 - P_0(u_p)}. \qquad (9\text{-}16)$$

These functions are depicted in Figs. 9-12, 9-13, and 9-14 for different $F(u_p)$s [4]. The curves show the Erlang distributions with $k = 3$ and 10, respectively; the exponential distributions with $k = 1$; and the hyperexponential distribution with $j = 4$. For each distribution of breakdown time a

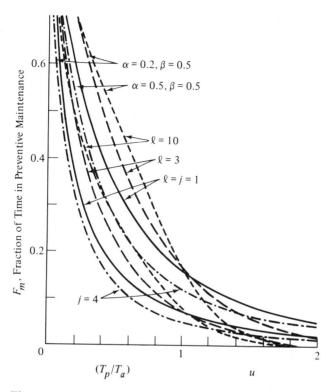

Figure 9-13. Fraction of time machine is in preventive maintenance.

Source: Philip M. Morse, Queues, Inventories and Maintenance, *John Wiley & Sons, Inc., New York, 1958, p. 163. Courtesy of John Wiley & Sons, Inc.*

curve with $\alpha = .2$ and $\beta = .5$ and one with $\alpha = .5$ and $\beta = .5$ is shown. α and β were chosen rather large in order to show their effects more clearly. Figure 9-14 shows clearly that an increase of the fractional time the machine is working can be achieved by using preventive maintenance if

1. The maintenance period is chosen advantageously.
2. The distribution of breakdown times has a rather small variance, i.e., if the breakdowns can be predicted accurately.
3. $\alpha < \beta$, which implies that $T_m < T_s$.

In practice α and β are often very small compared to u or to 1. If that is true, the above formula can be simplified to read

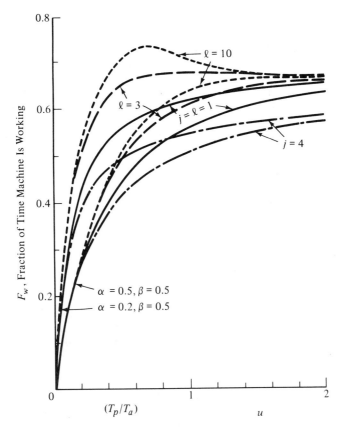

Figure 9-14. Fraction of time machine is working. Fraction of time F_w the machine is working as a function of $u = (T_p/T_i)$, the ratio between preventive maintenance period and machine breakdown time, where $\beta = (T_p/T_i)$ and $\alpha = (T_m/T_i)$, for different kinds of machine breakdown distributions. Solid curves for $j = l = 1$ are for exponential breakdown distributions, dashed lines and dotted lines for Erlang distributions $l = 3$ and $l = 10$, and dot-dash curves are for hyperexponential distribution $j = 4$.

Source: Philip M. Morse, Queues, Inventories and Maintenance, *John Wiley & Sons, Inc., New York, 1958, p. 161. Courtesy of John Wiley & Sons, Inc.*

$$F_w \simeq 1 - \alpha \frac{F_0(u_p)}{1 - P_0(u_p)} - \beta \frac{1 - F_0(u_p)}{1 - P_0(u_p)} \qquad (9\text{-}17)$$

$$F_m \simeq \alpha \frac{F_0(u_p)}{1 - P_0(u_p)} \qquad (9\text{-}18)$$

$$F_s \simeq \beta \frac{1 - F_0(u_p)}{1 - P_0(u_p)}. \qquad (9\text{-}19)$$

In certain situations F_w may be used to choose a good T_p since $u_p = T_p/T_i$. This is justified whenever the costs of idle time are considerably larger than all other costs of maintenance. Define G as the output of the machine in dollars per unit or productive time, C_m as the hourly cost of maintenance, and C_s as the hourly cost of repair. If direct maintenance costs are of great importance in contrast to the fixed cost of personnel, then the net income per hour from this machine is

$$I = G - \alpha(G + C_m)\frac{F_0(u_p)}{1 - P_0(u_p)} - \beta(G + C_s)\frac{1 - F_0(u_p)}{1 - P_0(u_p)}. \qquad (9\text{-}20)$$

The first derivative of this function with respect to u_p becomes zero for

$$\frac{T_m(G + C_m)}{T_s(G + C_s)} = \frac{(d(t)T_p)(1 - P_0(u)) - F_0(u_p)(1 - F_0(u_p))}{d(t)T_p(1 - P_0) + F_0(u_p)^2}. \qquad (9\text{-}21)$$

Figure 9-15 [5] depicts the right-hand side of this equation as a function of

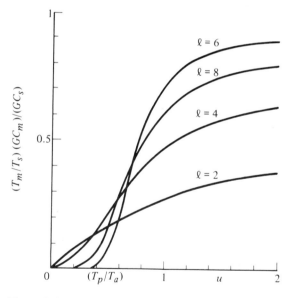

Figure 9-15. Curves for determining optimal T_p.

Source: Philip M. Morse, Queues, Inventories and Maintenance, John Wiley & Sons, Inc., New York, 1958, p. 166. Courtesy of John Wiley & Sons, Inc.

T_p for different Erlang distributions. Since the right-hand side and the Erlang distributions are known, the optimal T_p can be determined.

b. Optimal Replacement Policies

If the depreciation pattern of a facility can be described by

$$A(t) = A_0 e^{-\lambda t}, \tag{9-22}$$

where A_0 = initial investment
   λ = depreciation constant, representing obsolescence and inferiority
   of the process.

If the accumulated cost of maintenance follows approximately the function

$$C(t) = C_0(e^{\mu t} - 1), \tag{9-23}$$

the cost of the facility per unit of time t amounts to

$$c(t) = \frac{1}{t}[A_0(1 - e^{-\lambda t}) + C_0(e^{\mu t} - 1)]. \tag{9-24}$$

We observe that costs are derived as a function of time t. We can find the optimal t or the useful life from this expression.

Costs are at a minimum for $dc(t)/dt = 0$ or for

$$\frac{1 - e^{-\lambda t}(1 + \lambda t)}{1 - e^{-\mu t}(1 - \mu t)} = \frac{C_0}{A_0}. \tag{9-25}$$

It is not easy to solve this equation for t. Therefore diagrams and tables have been developed to aid in determining the optimal time of replacement, which is the end of useful life of the facility to be replaced.

Example 9-2

Let us assume a situation which can be characterized by the following parameters:

$$A_0 = \$35 \qquad C_0 = \$1470$$
$$\lambda = .029 \qquad \mu = .058.$$

We find that $A_0/C_0 = .24$ and that $\lambda/\mu = .5$.

We now use the nomogram shown in Fig. 9-16. Draw a line from the origin to .5 on the λ/μ axis. The intersection of this line with the A_0/C_0 curve for 24 determines the coordinates on the λt and μt axes. In our case $\lambda t = .86$ and $\mu t = 1.7$. Hence

$$t_{opt} = \frac{\mu t}{\mu} = \frac{1.7}{.058} \simeq 2.9 \text{ years.} \tag{9-26}$$

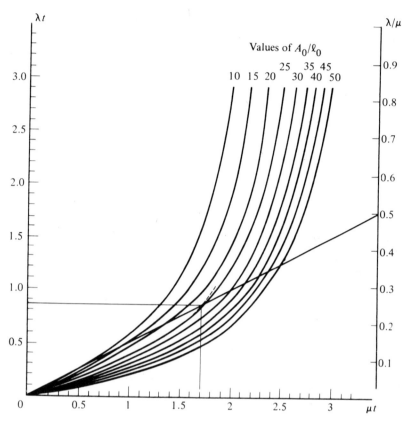

Figure 9-16. Nomogram for the determination of optimal replacement times.

Source: A. Kaufmann, Methods and Models of Operations Research, *Prentice-Hall, Inc., Englewood Cliffs, N. J., 1963, p. 435. Courtesy of Prentice-Hall, Inc.*

We would, of course, find the same value using the λt value. This model has very wide applicability for replacement of equipment. It can be used to determine economic life in conjunction with the models of Chap. 5; of course, the determination of λ and μ may be difficult.

c. Optimal Replacement or Overhaul Policy by Dynamic Programming

In contrast to the last model in which cost was the basis, we could include revenue of the machine in our considerations. We shall use the following symbols:

$R_t^A(s)$ = present value of revenue minus cost for all the years $t \cdots T$, for
policy A and for machine of age s

$r_t(s)$ = yearly revenue in year t for machine of age s

$u_t(s)$ = yearly maintenance cost in year t for machine of age s

$c_t(s)$ = cost of overhaul; an overhaul places the machine in the same
state as a new machine

$t = 1, 2, \ldots, T$ years

T = planning horizon

s = age of the machine (in years)

a = discounting factor.

We want to consider the following two alternative decision possibilities:

$$x_t = \begin{Bmatrix} A: \text{ overhaul} \\ B: \text{ no overhaul} \end{Bmatrix}.$$

The optimal strategy is now determined by searching all possible strategies
for the strategy that results in the highest value of revenue minus cost over the
planning horizon. The optimal strategy is determined recursively beginning in
year $t = T$. If at the beginning of year t, the decision was made to overhaul
the machine ($x = A$), then revenue minus cost of year t plus the discounted
revenue minus cost of all future years until T is

$$R_t^A(s) = r_t(0) - u_t(0) - c_t(s) + aR_{t+1}(1). \tag{9-27}$$

If it was decided not to overhaul, we arrive at

$$R_t^B(s) = r_t(s) - u_t(s) + aR_{t+1}(s + 1). \tag{9-28}$$

The optimal alternative for any one year t to be chosen can be found by

$$R_t^0 = \max_{A,B} [R_t^A(s), R_t^B(s)]. \tag{9-29}$$

Example 9-3

We assume that we start with a machine which is 3 years old. The planning
horizon is $T = 10$, and $r_t(s)$, $u_t(s)$, and $c_t(s)$ are shown in Table 9-3. We shall
consider $a = 1$ first, no discounting. For three t-s combinations we show the
computations in detail:

$$R_{10}^0(1) = \max \begin{cases} A: & 155 - 5 - 225 + 0 = -75 \\ B: & 140 - 10 + 0 = 130 \end{cases} = 130.$$

Table 9-3 Yearly Revenue, Maintenance Cost, and Cost of Overhaul

s \ t	1	2	3	4	5	6	7	8	9	10	
0	90	100	110	115	120	125	135	140	150	155	$r_t(s)$
	20	15	15	15	10	10	10	5	5	5	$u_t(s)$
	200	200	200	210	210	210	210	220	220	220	$c_t(s)$
1		85	90	105	110	115	120	125	135	140	r
		20	20	15	15	10	10	10	10	10	u
		220	220	220	215	215	220	220	230	225	c
2			80	80	100	100	115	110	110	125	r
			25	20	20	20	15	10	10	10	u
			240	240	240	220	220	230	230	240	c
3	60			75	75	95	90	110	105	105	r
	55			25	25	20	20	15	15	15	u
	250			250	250	250	225	225	240	240	c
4		60			70	70	90	80	105	100	r
		55			30	25	25	25	20	15	u
		260			255	255	255	230	230	250	c
5			50			70	65	80	70	100	r
			55			30	30	25	25	20	u
			270			260	260	260	235	235	c
6				50			70	65	70	60	r
				60			35	30	30	30	u
				280			265	265	265	240	c
7					50			60	65	60	r
					60			40	35	30	u
					280			270	270	270	c
8						40			60	65	r
						60			45	35	u
						290			270	270	c
9							40			60	r
							60			50	u
							290			270	c
10								40			r
								65			u
								300			c
11									30		r
									65		u
									300		c
12										30	r
										70	u
										310	c

The optimal decision $x_{10}^0(1) = B$,

$$R_{10}^0(2) = \max \begin{cases} A: & 155 - 5 - 240 + 0 = -90 \\ B: & 125 - 10 + 0 = 115 \end{cases} = 115,$$

and $x_{10}^0(2) = B$,

$$R_9^0(1) = \max \begin{cases} A: & 150 - 5 - 230 + 130 = 45 \\ B: & 135 - 10 + 115 = 240 \end{cases} = 240$$

$$x_9^0(1) = B.$$

The complete set of all R_t^0s and x_t^0s for $a = 1.0, s, \ldots, 12$ and $t = 1, \ldots, 10$, is listed in Table 9-4. Table 9-5 lists the results for a discounting factor of

Table 9-4 Optimal Policies and Their Results:
$R_t^0(s), x_t^0(s), a = 1, T = 10$

s \ t	10	9	8	7	6	5	4	3	2	1
1	130B	240B	310B	385B	465B	390B	435B	455B	490B	t
2	115B	195B	275B	360B	295B	345B	385B	425B		
3	95B	175B	260B	215B	265B	325B	370B			310A
4	85B	165B	145A	190B	245A	320A			285B	
5	80B	75B	125B	175A	240A			280B		
6	30B	70B	110A	170A			285B			
7	36B	60B	105A			295A				
8	30B	25B			210A					
9	10B			145A						
10			75A							
11		-25A								
12	-40B									

$a = .86$ (15%) and Fig. 9-17 depicts the optimal policies for $a = 1$ and $a = .86$. Figure 9-18 shows a flow chart, summarizing the dynamic programming algorithm for this problem.

The close relationship to the models in Chaps. 2 and 5 should be noted. Decisions of the type described above cannot be made without taking into account other investment decisions and decisions affecting total operating capacity.

It should also be noted that the information requirements are quite high. We would have to know the cost and deterioration characteristics of all machines at different times to use the model effectively; see Table 9-3.

Table 9-5 $R_t^0(s)$ and $x_t^0(s)$ for $a = .86$ (15%)

s \ t	10	9	8	7	6	5	4	3	2	1
1	130B	224B	283B	347B	415B	349B	387B	401B	431B	
2	115B	182B	251B	324B	265B	312B	340B	372B		
3	95B	163B	237B	195B	238B	261B	325B			250B
4	85B	154B	120B	173B	191A	255A			246B	
5	80B	71B	115B	132A	187B			240B		
6	30B	66B	87B	127A			245B			
7	30B	56B	71A			230A				
8	30B	24B			156A					
9	10B			102A						
10			41A							
11		−43A								
12	−40B									

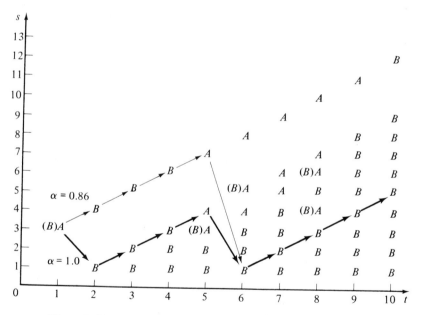

Figure 9-17. Optimal policies for one machine.

V. THE SIZE OF THE MAINTENANCE CREW

In the previous section we treated short-run problems where the crew size was fixed. Now we shall treat the long-run problem of setting crew size.

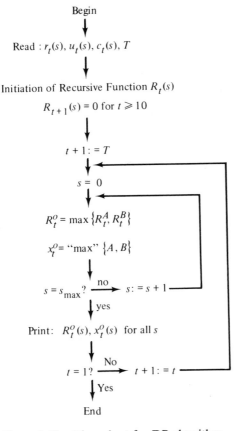

Begin

$\downarrow$

Read : $r_t(s)$, $u_t(s)$, $c_t(s)$, T

$\downarrow$

Initiation of Recursive Function $R_t(s)$

$R_{t+1}(s) = 0$ for $t \geqslant 10$

$\downarrow$

$t + 1: = T$

$\downarrow$

$s = 0$

$\downarrow$

$R_t^O = \max \{R_t^A, R_t^B\}$

$x_t^O = $ "max" $\{A, B\}$

$\downarrow$

$s = s_{max}$? $\xrightarrow{\text{no}}$ $s: = s + 1$

$\downarrow$ yes

Print : $R_t^O(s)$, $x_t^O(s)$ for all s

$\downarrow$

$t = 1$? $\xrightarrow{\text{No}}$ $t + 1: = t$

$\downarrow$ Yes

End

Figure 9-18.   Flow chart for DP algorithm.

a. Single-Machine Case

The distribution of breakdowns of a machine is assumed to be $F(t)$ with a mean of $T_a = 1/\lambda$. We shall further assume that the cost of the maintenance department is proportional to the rate $\mu = 1/T_s$ with which the repair can be carried out on the average after the facility has broken down. Cost also depends on C_s, which is a machine-dependent constant. The monthly cost of the service department is thus C_s/T_s. The value of monthly output of the machine is again G. The average fraction of time the machine is working per month is $T_a/(T_a + T_s)$. We can now determine the optimal size of the service crew in terms of T_s by differentiating the *output function* of the service department and setting the first derivative to equal zero:

$$\frac{d}{dT_s}\left[\frac{GT_a}{T_a - T_s} - \frac{C_s}{T_s}\right] = 0 = -\frac{GT_a}{(T_a + T_s)^2} + \frac{C_s}{T_s^2} \qquad (9\text{-}30)$$

or

$$T_{s\,\mathrm{opt}} = \frac{T_a}{\sqrt{GT_a/C_s} - 1}. \tag{9-31}$$

b. Multimachine Case

Let us illustrate a possible approach to solving this problem by again using an example.

Example 9-4

A manufacturer of machines has in his workshop 50 identical machines which have to be maintained by a service crew. How many mechanics should be on the payroll of the service department in order to optimally maintain the workshop? No preventive maintenance is intended. In addition to the symbols we have been using, let us introduce the following notation:

T_i = average idle time of a machine between breakdown and repair
T_0 = average time the machine is operating between termination of service and the next breakdown
n = number of machines maintained by one mechanic
c_i = cost of idle time of machine per time unit
c_s = cost per unit of service time (excluding labor)
c_L = cost of operator per time unit
c = total cost of machine operation per unit of time
c_u = cost of output per time unit per machine
m = machine running time per unit.

Since the machines are identical, we can assume that breakdowns are random events and that no interrelationships exist between breakdowns. If there were good correlations to some of the parameters or if the breakdown times were distributed with a small variance so we could estimate the occurrence of breakdowns, then the size of the service crew could be determined much more easily.

As is common practice, machines are repaired according to a FCFS priority rule. For the time being let us assume that repair times are constant and equal, i.e., the coefficient of variation, which is defined to be standard deviation/mean, equals zero.

Our goal is to determine the size of the service crew such that the sum of total wages and total cost of idle time is minimized. The ratio of

$$\frac{\lambda}{\mu} = \frac{\text{mean number of breakdowns per unit of time}}{\text{mean service rate}}$$

can physically be taken to be the fraction of time the machine is being serviced divided by the fraction of time it is operating. If we call $\lambda/\mu = k$, then

$$k = \frac{[T_s/(T_s + T_i)] + T_0}{[T_0/(T_s + T_i)] + T_0} = \frac{T_s}{T_0}. \tag{9-32}$$

The mathematical justification for this equivalence is available in Palm and Fetter [7]. It should be stressed again that T_s includes only service time and not the time a machine waits for service.

Total cost per time unit per machine when n machines are serviced by one operation is

$$c = T_0 c_0 + T_s c_s + T_i c_i + \frac{c_L}{n}. \tag{9-33}$$

Since $c_u = c/m$,

$$c_u = c_0 + k c_s + \frac{T_i c_i + c_L/n}{m T_0}. \tag{9-34}$$

An optimal assignment will depend on the ratios of costs as well as on the service constant k. For certain ranges of k and c_i/c_L, Palm calculated the optimum assignment n, and Mangelsdorf portrayed the results as depicted in Figs. 9-19 and 9-20 for constant and exponentially distributed service times [8].

Example 9-5

Let us assume for our example now that the total time considered is 10,250 hours and that a repair time of 719 hours was observed. c_i is \$1077 and c_L is \$2.80. It is $k = 719/10{,}250 = .07$ and $c_i/c_L = 177/2.80 = .64$. If we now determine the value of n which corresponds to $k = .07$ and $c_i/c_L = .64$ in Fig. 9-15, we find that $n = 10$. Hence for 50 machines we would need $\frac{50}{10} = 5$ service men. Using the curves of the above figures, we can also determine the sensitivity of our results with respect to the total repair time or the type of distribution function assumed for service times. For an increase of repair time of 100%, we would find $k = 1440/10{,}250 = .14$, leading to $n = 7$ rather than 5 as before.

If the service times were distributed exponentially, we would find by using Fig. 9-19 than $n = 10$ and $n = 6$, respectively. We observe that the results do not deviate much from the results found for constant service times. This indicates that other distribution functions—lying between exponential and constant service time distributions—can be approximated fairly well using Fig. 9-19 or 9-20.

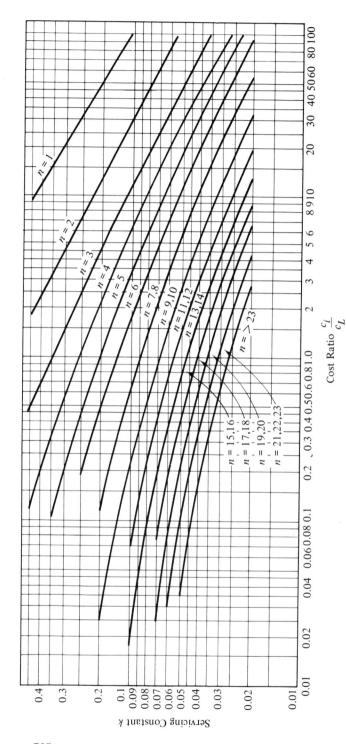

Figure 9-19. Optimal assignment for constant service time.

Source: I. M. Mangelsdorf, "Waiting Line Theory Applied to Manufacturing Problems," Analysis of Industrial Operations (E. H. Bowman and R. B. Fetter, eds.), Richard D. Irwin, Inc., Homewood, Ill., 1959, p. 263. Courtesy of Richard D. Irwin, Inc.

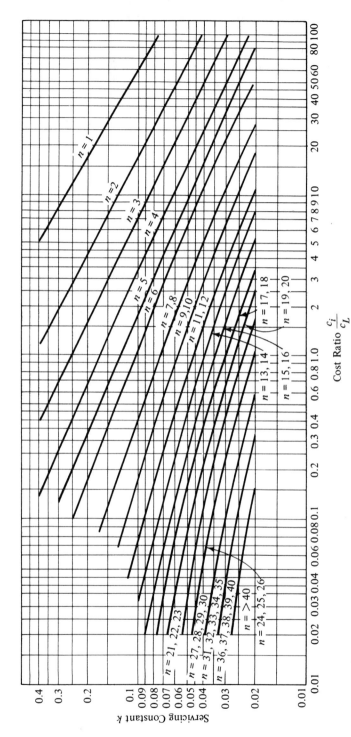

Figure 9-20. Optimal assignment for exponentially distributed service times.

Source: I. M. Mangelsdorf, "Waiting Line Theory Applied to Manufacturing Problems," Analysis of Industrial Operations (E. H. Bowman and R. B. Fetter, eds.), Richard D. Irwin, Inc., Homewood, Ill., 1959, p. 264. Courtesy of Richard D. Irwin, Inc.

VI. SIMULTANEOUS DETERMINATION OF SIZE
OF SERVICE CREW AND MAINTENANCE FREQUENCY

a. Single-Machine Case

If in contrast to the case treated in Sec. B.V.a, fixed cost, C_F, of the maintenance department is included in the considerations, then the profit per hour, P, is [9]

$$P(T_s, m, u_p) = G - \alpha\left(G + \frac{c_m}{T_a}\right)\frac{F_0}{1 - P_0} - \beta\left(G + \frac{c_s}{T_a}\right)$$

$$\times \frac{1 - F_0}{1 - P_0} - \frac{C_F}{T_s}. \tag{9-35}$$

Differentiating this expression partially with respect to T_s and u_p and setting the partial derivatives equal to zero, we arrive at the following optimality conditions for T_s and u_p, respectively:

$$T_s = \left[\frac{c_s T_a(1 - P_0)}{G(1 + \{[F_0(T_m - T_s)]/T_s\}}\right]^{1/2}$$

$$\frac{T_m G + c_m}{T_s G + c_s} = \frac{d(u_p)/\lambda(1 - P_0) - F_0(1 - F_0)}{(d(u_p)/\lambda)(1 - P_0) + F_0^2}. \tag{9-36}$$

It would be very unwieldy to attempt a simultaneous solution of these two equations. Vergin [9] suggests the following iterative procedure:

1. Estimate the left-hand side of Eq. (9-36). Calculate the value of u from this same equation, the right-hand side of which is tabulated for several Erlang distributions in Fig. 9-14.
2. Using this u_p, solve Eq. (9-35) for T_s.
3. Using this T_s, solve Eq. (9-36) for u.
4. Repeat steps 2 and 3 until T_s and u remain constant.

The resulting T_s and u are optimal. The recursive process will generally not require more than two or three iterations.

Example 9-6

$$G = \$100$$
$$T_a = 100 \text{ hours}$$
$$T_m = .5T_s$$
$$c_m = \$40$$

$$c_s = \$2$$
$$c_F = \$40$$
$$l = 8.$$

If we estimate the right-hand side of Eq. (9-36) to be approximately .5, we find u to be .8 (from Fig. 9-15). Substituting this into Eq. (9-35), T_s turns out to be 6.74 hours.

Substituting $T_s = 6.74$ into Eq. (9-36), the right-hand side becomes .461, and from Fig. 9-15 we find that $u = .78$. This again leads to $T_s = 6.74$.

The optimal policy is therefore to undertake preventive maintenance every 78 hours and have a service crew which is able to maintain the machine in the average time of 6.74 hours.

b. Integrated Production Systems

Most real production systems which have to be maintained involve more than one machine and very often a large number of different machines. In these cases, considering each machine individually would lead to nonoptimal results. It would also be very inefficient to expand single-machine models directly to multimachine systems. It seems more appropriate to design integrated production-maintenance systems which are operationally feasible. They will not always guarantee optimal results, but they can improve the operation of systems by supplying heuristic rules.

Bovaird [10], for instance, suggested the following approach as an operational model for the optimization of maintenance in an integrated production system. Figure 9-21 sketches the interrelationships he takes into consideration. He determines

1. The time between periodic maintenance operations.
2. The number of maintenance men.
3. The time periods in which each item is inspected.

The following information is needed:

1. Deterioration and failure probabilities for each item.
2. Average required man-hours for preventive inspection and for preventive maintenance.
3. Average time required for emergency diagnosis and repair.
4. Setup cost for periodic maintenance.
5. Cost of maintenance men.
6. Cost of down time.

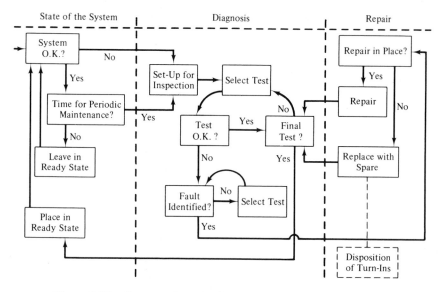

Figure 9-21. Integrated production system.

Source: R. L. Bovaird, "Characteristics of Optimal Maintenance Policies," Management Science, *Providence, R. I., 7, 1961, 239. Courtesy of* Management Science.

Assuming situations which can be approximated by a change of state of the system, Bovaird achieves optimization by using the following equation to find the value of k_i which minimizes c_i:

$$c_i = \frac{1}{k_i T} c_{1i} + \frac{P_i}{k_i T} c_{2i} + \frac{E_i}{k_i T} c_{3i}. \tag{9-37}$$

The annual cost attributable to the items of the system are thus given by

$$\sum_i C_i.$$

The cost coefficients C_0 and C_m together with the minimum values of $\sum_i C_i$ are then used in the following equation to find the values of T and M which give the least annual cost from maintenance of the system of items:

$$C = \frac{1}{T} C_0 + M C_m + \sum_i C_i. \tag{9-38}$$

The symbols used have the following meanings:

C_{1i} = annual cost of maintenance of the ith item

k_iT = number of years between the periodic maintenance operations of item i

P_i = probability of preventive maintenance after N_i time intervals between preventive inspections of the ith item

E_i = probability for the breakdown of item i within one maintenance period

C_{1i} = marginal cost of a preventive inspection of item i

C_{2i} = marginal cost of a preventive repair of item i

C_{3i} = cost of resulting emergency diagnoses and repair attributable to a failure of item i

C_0 = periodic setup cost

C_m = manpower costs

M = number of maintenance men in the service crew.

Bovaird illustrates his model by means of a simple hypothetical example with 100 identical subsystems. He uses the following basic data:

W_1 = average man-hours for 1 preventive inspection = .2 man-hours

W_2 = average man-hours for 1 preventive maintenance operation = 1 man-hours

D = 4.0 hours = average downtime for diagnosis and repair

C_0 = $5000

C_m = $10,000 per man-year

G = opportunity cost per hour interruption of the system operation = $500 per hour = cost of down time.

Figure 9-22 shows the failure characteristics and maintenance cost characteristics of his hypothetical system.

For a four-men maintenance crew and $T = \frac{1}{6}$ (bimonthly inspection) the following costs result:

preventive inspection:	$ 25 × 6	=	150
preventive repairs (from Fig. 9-22):	$ 130 × 1.7	=	220
breakdowns [from Fig. 9-22 (a)]:	$2000 × .5	=	1000
			$1370
for 100 items:			$137,000
periodic setup costs:	$ 5,000 × 6	=	30,000
manpower costs:	$10,000 × 4	=	40,000
	total		$207,000.

Similarly, the cost of other T-M combinations can be calculated. Table 9-6 depicts the resulting total costs in thousands of dollars. The optimal T-M

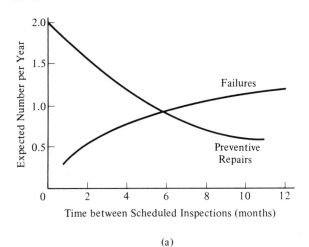

Time between Scheduled Inspections (months)

(a)

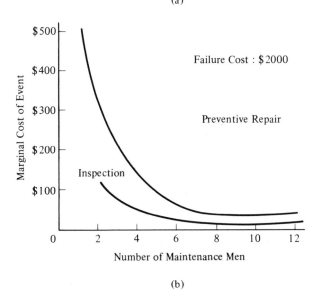

Number of Maintenance Men

(b)

Figure 9-22.   Failure characteristics and cost of maintenance.

combination is found to be a service crew of four men and a periodic maintenance interval of $2\frac{1}{2}$ months, which results in total costs of $202,000.

c. Linear Programming for Smoothing the Work Load of the Service Crew

In maintenance departments, as in other departments, it is desirable to
smooth the work load over time by scheduling preventive maintenance opera-

512 Control of the Production Process

Table 9-6   Total Annual Maintenance Costs

		Number of Maintenance Men				
		1	*2*	*4*	*8*	*12*
	1	286	248	222	236	265
Time	2	267	218	207	226	260
between periodic	4	252	219	217	246	283
inspections	8	246	232	241	275	313
	12	247	241	253	289	328

tions. LP .models can be used to minimize the deviations of the periodic maintenance work load from a certain standard. In presenting one of these models [11], we shall use the following notation:

$w = 1, 2, \ldots, W =$ week in the total scheduling period

$p = 1, 2, \ldots, P =$ number of the maintenance project

$\{S_p\} =$ set of possible starting weeks with $1 \leq S_p \leq W$

$X_{p,s} = 1$, if project p starts in week s; 0, otherwise

$t_p =$ duration of project p; within that duration, the project weeks are indexed as $t_p = 1, 2, \ldots, T_p$

$M_{p,t} =$ manpower required for project p in prjecot week if $1 \leq t \leq T_p$; 0, otherwise

$\Delta M_{p,t} = M_{p,t} - M_{p,t+1} =$ change in required manpower for project p and weeks t and $t - 1$

$\Delta M_W = \sum_{p=1}^{P} \sum_{s \in S_p} \Delta M_{p,w-s+1} X_{p,s} =$ total change in required manpower between calendar week w and $w + 1$.

The linear programming model has the following form:

$$\min \qquad \sum_{w=1}^{W-1} |\Delta M_W|$$

$$\text{such that} \qquad \sum_{s \in S_p} X_{p,s} = 1$$

$$\sum_{p=1}^{P} \sum_{s \in S_p} \Delta M_{p,w-s+1} X_{p,s} = \Delta M_w \qquad (9\text{-}39)$$

$$\Delta M_{p,t} - M_{p,t} + M_{p,t+1} = 0$$

$$M_{pit}, M_w \geq 0$$

A feasible schedule requires that each X_{ps} be either 0 or 1 and that the M_{pt}s are integers. This implies that normal linear programming techniques could not be used but that integer programming algorithms would have to be used. These integer programming algorithms, however, are not yet efficient enough to handle very large programming problems. Therefore use may be made of some rounding prodedures. Two possible approaches for our problem would, for instance, be

1. Immediate rounding (IR): For each project p choose that week as a starting week for which the X_{ps} is closest to 1.
2. Repeated rounding (RR): Solve the standard linear programming problem and determine the largest X_{ps}. Add an equality constraint that assures that this $X_{ps} = 1$. Solve the new linear programming problem and look for the largest X_{ps}. Assure that this $X_{ps} = 1$. Repeat this procedure until all starting dates have been determined.

Obviously the computational effort is largest when integer programming routines are used and it is smallest when immediate rounding procedures are employed. It will be somewhere in between for repeated rounding methods. Experience shows, however, that the results do not necessarily improve with effort. Which of the three approaches works best depends very much on the special structure.

Example 9-7

The data used by Wagner et al. [11] are shown in Table 9-7. The three sets of constraints are shown in Tables 9-8, 9-9, and 9-10. The objective function in our model is

$$\text{minimize } Z = \sum_{w=1}^{9} \Delta M_w. \tag{9-40}$$

Table 9-7   Basic Data

Project, p	Manpower Requirements, $M_{p,t}$					Total	Starting Dates, S_p
	$t = 1$	$t = 2$	$t = 3$	$t = 4$	$t = 5$		
1	10	10				20	3, 4, 5
2	5	20	5			30	6, 7, 8
3	5	10	15			30	1, 2, 3
4	10	10	20	20		60	6, 7
5	10	20	10			40	1, 2, 3, 4
6	25	10	10	25	10	80	5, 6
7	5	5	5	25		40	1, 2, 3
8	10	5	5	10		30	4, 5, 6, 7
						330	

Table 9-8 Project Equations

Project	X_{13}	X_{14}	X_{15}	X_{26}	X_{27}	X_{28}	X_{31}	X_{32}	X_{33}	X_{46}	X_{47}	X_{51}	X_{52}	X_{53}	X_{54}	X_{65}	X_{66}	X_{71}	X_{72}	X_{73}	X_{84}	X_{85}	X_{86}	X_{87}	
1	1	1	1																						= 1
2				1	1	1																			= 1
3							1	1	1																= 1
4										1	1														= 1
5												1	1	1	1										= 1
6																1	1								= 1
7																		1	1	1					= 1
8																					1	1	1	1	= 1

Table 9-9 Total Manpower Required Per Week (M_w)

Week	X_{13}	X_{14}	X_{15}	X_{26}	X_{27}	X_{28}	X_{31}	X_{32}	X_{33}	X_{46}	X_{47}	X_{51}	X_{52}	X_{53}	X_{54}	X_{65}	X_{66}	X_{71}	X_{72}	X_{73}	X_{84}	X_{85}	X_{86}	X_{87}	
1							5					10						5							= M_1
2							10	5				20	10					5	5						= M_2
3	10						15	10	5			10	20	10				5	5	5					= M_3
4	10	10						15	10				10	20	10			25	5	5					= M_4
5		10	10						15					10	20	25			25	5					= M_5
6			10	5						10					10	10	25			25					= M_6
7				20	5					10	10					25	10				10				= M_7
8				5	20	5				20	10					10	25				5	10			= M_8
9					5	20				20	20						10				5	5	10		= M_9
10						5					20										10	5	5	10	= M_{10}

Explanatory note: Project 1, requiring 10 men in the first week and 10 men in the second week, can begin in week 3, 4, or 5.

Table 9-10 Total Change in Required Manpower Per Week (M_w)

Week	X_{13}	X_{14}	X_{15}	X_{26}	X_{27}	X_{28}	X_{31}	X_{32}	X_{33}	X_{46}	X_{47}	X_{51}	X_{52}	X_{53}	X_{54}	X_{65}	X_{66}	X_{71}	X_{72}	X_{73}	X_{84}	X_{85}	X_{86}	X_{87}	
1–2							−5	−5											−5						$= \Delta M_1$
2–3	−10						−5	−5	−5											−5					$= \Delta M_2$
3–4		−10					+15	−5	−5			−10	−10	−10				−20			−10				$= \Delta M_3$
4–5			−10					+15	+15			+10	+10	−10	−10			−25	−20		+5	−10			$= \Delta M_4$
5–6				−5								+10	+10	+10	−10	−25			+25	−20	−5	+5	−10		$= \Delta M_5$
6–7					−15						−10	+10	+10	+10	+10	+15	−25			+25	−5	+5	+5	−10	$= \Delta M_6$
7–8					+15	−5				−10	−10					−15	+15				+10	−5	−5	+5	$= \Delta M_7$
8–9					+5	−15				−10	−10					+15	−15					+10	−5	−5	$= \Delta M_8$
9–10						+15				+20						+10	+15						+10	−5	$= \Delta M_9$

Explanatory note: If project 1 begins in week 3, 10 men will be required in both weeks 3 and 4. The *change* in manpower in going from week 2 to week 3 will be $(0 - 10) = -10$; in going from week 3 to week 4, $(10 - 10) = 0$; and in going from week 4 to 5, $(10 - 0) = +10$.

The results of the computations using linear programming (LP), approach 1 (IR), approach 2 (RR), and integer programming (IP) are shown in Table 9-11.

The best but infeasible solution is arrived at by using LP. It is inferior to the IP solution if simply rounded to achieve integer values.

Table 9-11   Programming Solutions

	LP	IR	RR	IP
X_{13}	.218			
X_{14}				1
X_{15}	.782	1	1	
X_{26}	.621	1	1	1
X_{27}	.274			
X_{28}	.105			
X_{31}	1.000	1	1	
X_{32}				1
X_{46}				
X_{47}	1.000	1	1	1
X_{51}	.729	1	1	1
X_{52}				
X_{53}				
X_{54}	.271			
X_{65}	.645	1	1	1
X_{66}	.355			
X_{71}	.979	1	1	
X_{72}				
X_{73}	.024			1
X_{84}				1
X_{85}				
X_{86}			1	
X_{87}	1.000	1		
M_1		20	20	10
M_2		35	35	25
M_3		30	30	25
M_4		25	25	30
M_5		35	35	40
M_6		25	35	40
M_7		50	45	50
M_8		45	45	45
M_9		35	40	35
M_{10}		30	20	30
Objective function Z	32,324	90	70	60

C. Simulation and Maintenance

I. SIZE OF MAINTENANCE CREW AND PRIORITIES

Realistic maintenance systems are in most cases highly probabilistic and determined by many more factors than could be considered in the models treated so far. To find optimal strategies for these systems, one often has to resort to simulation models.

Input data to these models include
1. Deterministic data such as costs of material, labor costs, breakdown costs, effects of maintenance operations on the operability of machines.
2. Parameters such as maintenance intervals, kind and level of maintenance operations, and size of service crew; priorities for assigning jobs to maintenance personnel; and ratio of maintenance performed by own service crew to maintenance subcontracted.
3. Stochastic data such as breakdown distributions, maintenance distributions, distribution of maintenance costs. By varying the parameters, we try to find the optimal set of parameters with respect to some of the following criteria:
a. Total costs of maintenance.
b. Total down time.
c. Total costs of maintenance, production, and down time.
d. Fraction of down time compared to total time.
e. Average queue length of machines waiting for maintenance.
f. Average utilization of maintenance resources.

A rough sketch of these relationships is shown in Fig. 9-23.

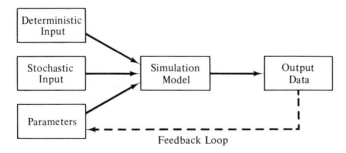

Figure 9-23.   Simulation data.

To obtain adequate results by systematically varying the parameters, either long time periods have to be simulated or a short time period has to be simulated repeatedly, possibly using different sets of random numbers.

In an example, let us assume that we want to find the optimal size of the service crew (parameter 1) and the optimal priority rules (parameter 2). We could be looking for the set of parameters which minimizes the sum of the costs of down time and the labor costs of the service crew. The structure of the basic simulation model is shown in Fig. 9-24. P indicates parameter; S, stochastic input data; D, deterministic input data; and R, results of the simulation model.

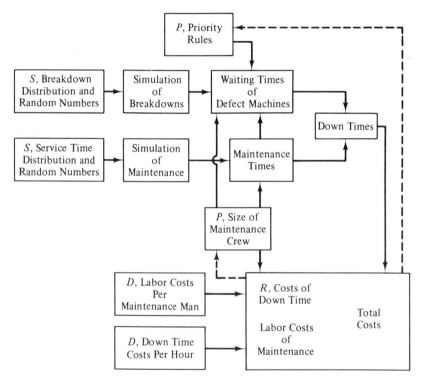

Figure 9-24. Simulation model for the determination of optimal maintenance crew size and optimal priorities.

II. OPTIMAL MAINTENANCE STRATEGIES

In the last paragraph we did not discuss any of the details of the simulation analysis. We shall now illustrate in more detail the design of an optimal maintenance strategy.

Example 9-8

In a workshop there are a number of machines working at a high degree of utilization. Each of these machines has a gearbox containing four gears. A maintenance strategy for these gearboxes has to be developed which minimizes costs. The following strategies are possible:

    I. In the case of a broken tooth, replace all four gears.
    II. In the case of a broken tooth, replace the two gears which mesh.
    III. Replace all four gears after each tooth break—at least, however, after x hours, where the optimal x has to be determined.

The following data have been found:

	Down Time (hr)	Repair Time (hr)
Preventive replacement of 4 gears	4	4
Replacement of 2 gears after breakdown	5	4
Replacement of 4 gears after breakdown	6	5

1 maintenance hour costs:	$6
1 down-time hour costs:	$40
Gears 1 and 2 (together) cost new:	$70
Gears 3 and 4 (together) cost new:	$150
Additional cost if tooth breaks:	$80

Considering the costs above, each replacement incurs the following costs:

Strategy I: $570.
Strategy II: If gear 1 or 2 breaks, $370.
               If gear 3 or 4 breaks, $450.
Strategy III: Preventive replacement, $400.
               Replacement after breakdown, $570.

Figure 9-25 shows the survival distribution functions of gears 1 and 2 and of gears 3 and 4, which were determined emperically.

Random sequences of survival times were generated by using a table of random numbers which were distributed between 0 and 100. The survival times were then read from the respective distribution functions as shown in Fig. 9-26. Ten thousand hours of operation time were simulated, the results of which are shown in Table 9-12.

Evaluating the results of the simulation, we arrive at the cost figures shown in Table 9-13.

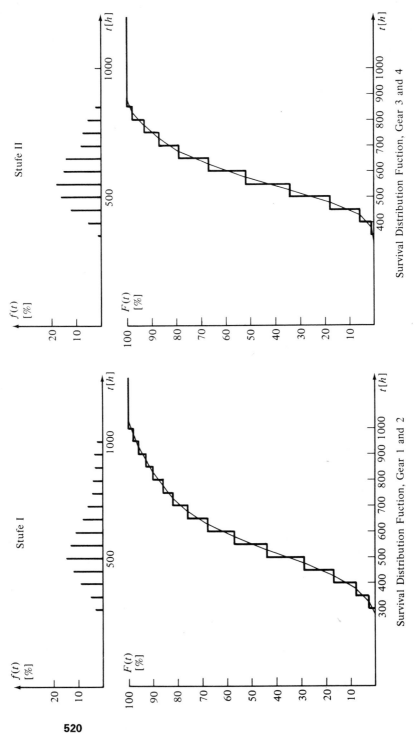

Figure 9-25.

Table 9-12 Simulation of Breakdowns and Replacements for a Period of 10,000 Hours

	Strategy I				Strategy II							Strategy III						
	Random Numbers					Random Numbers						Random Numbers				Replacing All Gears		
	Gears 1 & 2		Gears 3 & 4		Time of Replacing All 4 Gears	Gears 1 & 2		Gears 3 & 4		Repl. 1 & 2	Repl. 3 & 4	Gears 1 & 2		Gears 3 & 4				
	Pr.	R.N.	R.N.	Pr.		Pr.	R.N.	R.N.	Pr.			Pr.	R.N.	R.N.	Pr.	x = 500	x = 450	x = 400
1	40	510	760	91	510	37	500	500	26	500	500	95	900	600	59	500	450	400
2	80	710	550	42	1060	79	700	610	64	1200	1100	12	400	550	41	B900	B850	B800
3	53	560	610	64	1620	62	600	760	91	1800	1870	41	520	800	95	1400	1300	1200
4	97	950	580	55	2200	61	530	720	87	2390	2590	63	610	480	19	B1880	1750	1600
5	71	650	620	66	2820	54	560	600	49	2950	3130	85	760	780	93	2380	2200	2000
6	25	460	570	50	3280	40	510	460	15	3460	3650	75	670	450	11	B2830	B2650	2400
7	69	630	530	34	3810	63	600	620	66	4060	4270	05	350	690	81	B3180	B3000	B2750
8	30	820	510	28	4320	55	670	440	10	4630	4710	04	330	600	60	B3510	B3330	B3080
9	28	470	430	07	4750	83	740	520	32	5370	5230	38	510	550	42	4010	3780	3480
10	9	380	670	64	5130	94	830	370	01	6260	5600	46	530	470	16	B4480	4230	3880
11	62	600	670	77	5730	38	370	750	90	7230	6350	44	530	710	84	4980	4680	4280
12	15	420	400	03	6130	18	430	370	01	7660	6720	85	760	450	13	B5430	5130	4680
13	16	420	730	88	6550	31	840	750	90	8500	7470	10	390	760	91	B5820	B5520	B5070
14	09	380	450	11	6930	42	520	500	26	9020	7970	85	760	440	10	B6270	B5960	5470
15	35	500	530	37	7430	64	610	720	87	9630	8630	08	380	470	18	B6650	B6340	B5850
16	72	650	580	54	8010	55	570	470	16		9160	86	780	690	82	7150	6790	6250
17	57	570	770	92	8580			440	10		9600	89	810	470	17	B7620	7240	6650
18	93	870	810	96	9390			810	81			75	670	480	13	B8070	7690	7050
19	31	480	820	97	9870							21	440	570	49	B8510	B8130	7450
20	27	470	570	48								80	710	830	98	9010	8580	7850
21												39	510	460	16	B9470	9030	8250
22												04	330	600	58	9800	B8360	8650
23												58	580	610	62		9810	B8980
24												76	680	470	17			9380
25												86	770	570	50			9780

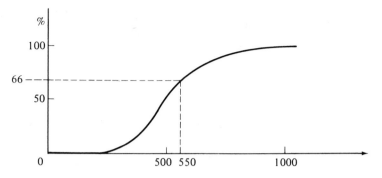

Figure 9-26. Generation of survival times.

Table 9-13   Comparison of Costs

Strategy I
    20 replacements @ $570 = $11,400
Strategy II
    1 replacement   @ $570 = $570
    15 replacements @ $370 = $5,550
    17 replacements @ $450 = $7,650
    Total $13,770
Strategy III
    $x = 500$ hours
    14 replacements @ $570 = $7,980
    9 replacements @ $400 = $3,600
    Total $11,580
    $x = 450$ hours
    9 replacements @ $570 = $5,130
    15 replacements @ $400 = $6,000
    Total $11,130
    $x = 400$ hours
    $5\frac{1}{2}$ replacements @ $570 = $3,140
    $20\frac{1}{2}$ replacements @ $400 = $8,200
    Total $11,340

As can be seen from Table 9-13, strategies I and III lead to almost the same cost, while strategy II incurs higher costs. Strategy III is the least-cost strategy for $x = 450$. We should take into account, however, that for this strategy we have to keep track of the running time of all gearboxes in order to replace them at least every 450 hours. If this control is expensive, strategy I might be preferable to strategy III.

SUMMARY

In this chapter we have presented a series of models to give the reader a feeling for the problems in even conceptually maintaining control of the physical state of the production process through maintenance. As explained in Sec. A, almost all facilities are subject to deterioration and failure. Unfortunately, these processes vary widely and therefore maintenance policies and planning are complex. The stochastic nature of the problem is stronger here than in any other chapter.

For this reason, in Sec. B the analytical models for determining the maintenance frequency and crew size make considerable use of distributions which are new to this book, such as the Erlang distribution, which can represent much failure data.

In Sec. C some of the assumptions required in Sec. B were relaxed by the use of simulation to solve the same problems. These models require large amounts of data and special structuring for the individual situation. Therefore it is wise to try out the analytical models first in case that is all that is required.

REFERENCES

1. P. M. MORSE, *Queues, Inventories and Maintenance*, Wiley, New York, 1958, pp. 8 and 11.

2. P. M. MORSE, *op. cit*, p. 42.

3. P. M. MORSE, *op. cit.*, p. 43.

4. P. M. MORSE, *op. cit.*, pp. 161, 163, 164.

5. P. M. MORSE, *op. cit.*, p. 166.

6. A. KAUFMANN, *Methods and Models of Operations Research*, Prentice-Hall, Englewood Cliffs, N.J., 1963, p. 435.

7. R. B. FETTER, "The Assignment of Operations Research To Service Automatic Machines," *Journal of Industrial Engineering* (Sept.–Oct. 1955), 22–30; D. C. PALM, ibid., *Journal of Industrial Engineering*, (Jan.–Feb. 1958), 28–42.

8. I. M. MANGELSDORF, "Waiting Line Theory Applied to Manufacturing Problems," in *Analysis of Industrial Operations*, (E. H. BOWMAN and R. B. FETTER, eds.), Irwin, Homewood, Ill., 19, 59, 252.

9. R. C. VERGIN, "Scheduling Maintenance and Determining Crew Size for

Stochastically Failing Equipment," *Management Science*, 13 (1967), B52–65.

10. R. L. BOVAIRD, "Characteristics of Optimal Maintenance Policies," *Management Science*, 7 (1961), 238–253.

11. H. M. WAGNER, R. J. GIGLIO, and R. G. GLASER, "Preventive Maintenance Scheduling by Mathematical Programming," *Management Science*, 10 (1964), 316–334.

PROBLEMS

1. Determine the optimal replacement interval t_{opt} using Eq. (9.24) and the nomogram of Fig. 9-16 for the following data: $A_0 = 40, $c_0 = 1800, $\lambda = .031$, and $\mu = .049$. Compare your result with the result of Example 9-2 and comment on the sensitivity of t_{opt}.

2. a. Determine the optimal replacement policy for the problem given in Example 9-3, taking into account a discounting rate (interest rate) of 25%.
   b. Use an interest rate of 35% and compare the optimal policies for 0, 15, 25, and 35%.

   How does the interest rate influence your optimal policy?

3. The workshop of Company XYZ consists of 100 machines of approximately the same type. Complaints have been coming in about very high down times in this workshop. The company has a maintenance crew of nine repair men and is considering an increase of this number. A statistical investigation yields the following data for the last month:

Total time	12,750 hours
Average idle time of a machine between breakdown and repair	2 hours
Average time the machine is operating between termination of repair and the next breakdown	113.3 hours
Average repair time per machine	8.2 hours
Cost of idle time per machine hour	$1.96
Cost of 1 hour of service time (including labor)	$2.80.

Machines are repaired on a FCFS basis. It is assumed that the breakdowns are Poisson-distributed. Determine the optimal size of the service crew assuming exponentially distributed repair times (Fig. 9-20). What would you recommend to the management of Company XYZ. Would your advice be different if the maintenance times were constant?

4. A car manufacturer considers taking up preventive maintenance for the final assembly line. The maintenance manager wants to know what size of service crew this would require and how many times a week preventive maintenance would have to be performed (a week = 80 hours). The following data are known:

Value of monthly output, G	$2,000,000
Average breakdown time, T_a (per week)	3 hours
Average time of preventive maintenance, T_m	$.5T_s$
Cost per hour of service time, c_s	$3.50
Fixed costs of the maintenance department, c_F	$500
Cost per hour of maintenance, c_m	$30.

Determine the optimal size of the service crew and the optimal maintenance interval by using Eqs. (9-35) and (9-36).

chapter 10

Summary

A. Review of the Objectives and the First Nine Chapters

In Chap. 1 we set forth our objectives in presenting quantitative models for production management problems:

1. To serve as a conceptual basis for a detailed understanding of the factors involved in production management decisions.
2. To indicate the extent to which problems in the production management area can be solved by modeling techniques.

We also stated that our approach to the first objective would be twofold: first, to outline a framework for each of the major functional problems and, second, to build up the modeling skill of the reader.

The first step is somewhat the easier. We began by establishing our emphasis on an economic approach in Chap. 2. In these times we feel some need to explain this emphasis. Many current production management problems seem largely noneconomic: pollution, labor management, motivation for quality, production for minority groups, and even the presence of drugs in the factory. We wish there were quantitative models to solve these problems, but there are not. We hope that the additions to the nation's resources produced by economic design and operation of the production system can help to solve these problems. In addition, we believe that an understanding of the economics of the production processes is necessary to design new processes which avoid the production problems of pollution, workers' monotony, and uniformity of output.

In each of the chapters we defined the structure of the major decisions in economic terms, such as

1. In capacity planning, the choice of output where marginal revenue equals marginal cost of production.
2. In location, the choice of number and location of sites with maximum profit.
3. In plant design, the arrangement of equipment and facilities to minimize operating cost.
4. In capital budgeting, the choice of alternative equipment or processes to maximize return on investment.
5. In aggregate planning for operation of the firm, the matching of men and equipment to tasks to complete projects at minimum cost within time constraints. Also, the choice of employment and seasonal inventory policies to minimize cost.
6. In inventories, the choice of the amount and frequency of orders to minimize investment and operating costs of the inventory system including those from customer reaction.
7. In scheduling, the choice of when and where to make each product to minimize variable production costs within the constraints of the existing production system.
8. In maintenance, the choice of size and service level of the maintenance force to minimize its cost plus the costs which result from breakdowns.

These decisions and these objectives as outlined will continue to be major decisions for production management for a long time to come. The general framework will be applicable even when improved models become available. The decisions may become more integrated, as we shall discuss later in this chapter.

We next proceeded to the second step of building a model or set of models, i.e., identifying the most economic solutions to the problem. As pointed out in Chap. 1, the final decision in a solution will usually include factors in addition to the more easily quantified economics of the model.

The models presented in each chapter are basically illustrative. Few of them were shown in sufficient detail to represent an actual decision. We hope that with the feeling for model structure acquired from this text, and perhaps with additional background in techniques or with the aid of professional model builders, many production managers can see their way to the preparation of more detailed models reflecting their particular problems.

The models presented include a wide variety of model types:

1. In the chapter on capacity planning, the models are adaptations of engineering realtionships and cost factors into economic production functions or cost functions.
2. In the chapter on location, the revenue models are basically demographic and the cost models are economic linear activity models.
3. In the chapter on plant design, there are iconic models and also some which are similar to the cost models for location.
4. In the chapter on capital budgeting, the longest-run models are simply the economic models of capital theory. The budget-constrained models are activity models.
5. In the chapter on aggregate planning, the variety is especially wide, from rules of thumb and sequencing calculations to smoothing rules and many varieties of activity analysis.
6. In the chapter on inventory, the models are essentially the marginal economic analysis under uncertainty or risk.
7. In the chapter on scheduling, the models are linear economic activity models and simple priority rules.
8. In the chapter on maintenance, there are probabilistic models of the costs of various policies.

In addition, a variety of techniques for solution of the models has been displayed. The techniques range from the classic optimization techniques of continuous functions, i.e., calculus, through linear programming to branch and bound methods and simulation:

1. In capacity planning, solution techniques are classic continuous optimization techniques such as calculus.
2. In location, the revenue techniques tend to be simulation or classic techniques because of nonlinearities. The cost models are mostly variations of linear programming.
3. In plant design, some graphical techniques and some linear programming models were presented.
4. In capital budgeting, simple explicit formülas and linear and quadratic programming are useful.
5. In aggregate planning, a wide range from computer adaptations of graphical techniques to heuristics, linear programming, and dynamic programming was presented.

6. In inventory systems, the statistical treatment of the problem was foremost, with confidence statements derived and classical calculus optimization of the probability models.

7. In scheduling, because of the constraints, mathematical programming was the major tool.

8. In maintenance, classical optimization of the probability models was supplemented with simulation.

In summary, we believe the exposure to this collection of structured problems, models, and techniques has demonstrated the potential of quantitative models for production management. What is most sorely needed is the implementation of these models according to the philosophy expressed in Chap. 1, as follows:

1. Adequate understanding of the problem is essential. Understanding requires communication with physical reality and with the persons involved.

2. Accuracy and timeliness of data and sound engineering are essential to a system which solves rather than complicates the problem.

3. Final selection between solutions require judgment on many factors, particularly behavioral factors, which are not quantifiable.

4. Implementation of a solution is strongly affected by how the problem was solved and cannot rest solely on the virtues of the solution. Procedures for passing from present conditions to the solution are required. Thus it is not only the solution which the manager must examine but the feasibility of reaching the solution within the system, which must be changed through time. Unfortunately, many analyses are strictly comparisons of static equilibrium positions and neglect the time path of changes between static solutions.

B. Integration of Production Management Decisions

I. THE PROBLEM

In each of the chapters of this book we considered a particular production decision and modeled that decision. These decisions are not independent; they are, in fact, highly interdependent. We resolved the interdependencies by implicitly assuming a certain time sequence of problems. We started with the first decisions as if there were no existing production system. Capacity, location, and plant design were all treated as design decisions for a new system. Then we considered the decisions which would be made after the system was ready to operate but which are middle range in time: aggregate planning and capital budgeting. Finally, we treated those problems which recur daily: inventory, scheduling, and maintenance. In progressing through this time sequence, we often referred to the other chapters and noted some interdependencies, but the time sequence minimized the interdependencies. In existing systems, the feedbacks are much more evident. Sometimes the feedbacks could be more accurately described as conflicts, as per the following scenario:

> *"Maintenance" wants to keep to their preventive maintenance down-time schedule even though "scheduling" says they need the machine running because "inventory" made a mistake (bad inventory control system). Throughout the dispute "maintenance" will emphasize that management should have okayed the replacement for that equipment long ago but that they were too busy pouring money into that new plant in the South.*

In Chap. 6, on aggregate planning, we did emphasize the interrelationships of several of the production decision areas. Refer back to Fig. 6-3 for the summary diagram. In a sense aggregate planning is a controlling or decision-making device for the entire production system, but it is only a planning control; that is, its time frame is too long for daily decisions. Despite good planning, control decisions are required to straighten out the problems which arise in any plan because of uncertainties. That, of course, is the job of scheduling, but scheduling cannot do the job alone, as witness the short scenario above. Scheduling will often be dependent on other areas to help it resolve short-run problems: maintenance, capital budgeting, and inventory. The system needs a short-run integrating device.

We have briefly discussed such a system already. In the chapter on design we presented the problem of design of the information and control system for the production system. At that time we had not presented all the decision areas, however. If we can refer back to Figs. 4-9 and 4-10, we see the information data base and decision information required for a functionally oriented shop. In Fig. 6-3 we showed in less detail the requirements for information for all the firm's decisions. A computerized system as well as noncomputerized alternatives were shown in Chap. 6. Without this information it will be very difficult for production management to solve short-run problems. The models in each area must be designed to provide data for use in other areas. Moreover, the models must be structured so that information from other decisions can be considered, in order to avoid the suboptimization problem, each area making its own decisions with its own models without consideration of the effect on other areas.

The following case study and suggestions for solution are presented to illustrate the interrelations of the production decisions and the models used for solution.

II. AN EXAMPLE OF INTEGRATION OF PRODUCTION DECISIONS

As an example of the application of quantitative models across a variety of production decisions and some of the necessary linkages between the decisions, we shall describe and analyze a small psuedofirm, Pop-Rite, Inc. We are indebted to Professors Robert Ferguson and Curtis Jones for the use of this example [1].

Pop-Rite, Inc. is a well-known California soft drink bottling firm. Mr. Fizzle, Pop-Rite's president, is particularly concerned about finished goods inventory positions, the use of overtime, and second-shift employment. For a variety of reasons, we have agreed to devote our initial efforts to the area of production planning.

Problem environment: A preliminary investigation of operations at Pop-Rite, Inc. has produced the following information:

1. *Marketing:* Pop-Rite's product line consists of five brands of soft drinks. The sales price and the cost of material vary from brand to brand (Table 10-1). Historical demand data indicate both a marked seasonality and a slight growth pattern for all five brands of the product (Table 10-2). Cyclamates and all other health scare ingredients were removed from Pop-Rite's soft drinks prior to 1967. Mr. Fizzle is not planning any major changes in his firm's product line or marketing policy.

2. *Production:* All five brands of soft drinks are produced on a single bottling line. A rather complicated and time-consuming conversion is required when shifting from the production of one brand to another; the setup time varies by brand. Production output averages 150 cases per hour regardless of brand. First-shift production can be varied between a minimum of 140 hours per month and a maximum of 200 hours per month. The regular labor rate of $225 per hour applies from 140 to (and including) 160 hours per month. The overtime labor rate of $300 per hour applies beyond 160 to (and including) 200 hours per month. A second shift of production with the same cost and output characteristics as the first shift can be employed in whole month increments. A $3000 start-up cost and a $2000 shutdown cost are incurred when initiating and terminating second-shift operations.

3. *Inventory:* Mr. Fizzle has indicated that monthly inventory carrying costs should be applied in accordance with Table 10-1.

Table 10-1 Pop-Rite, Inc.

Brand	Sales Price ($)	Material Cost ($)	Setup Time (hr)[a]	Monthly Inventory Carrying Cost, 2% ($)	Year-end Inventory Positions (cases)	Lost Sales Cost ($)	Allocation Factor
1	16.05	4.10	2.0	.32	1250	2.00	.05
2	14.00	3.60	4.0	.28	2545	1.75	.10
3	11.85	2.75	4.0	.24	2203	1.50	.15
4	10.10	2.60	8.0	.20	8941	1.25	.30
5	7.95	2.05	2.0	.16	6558	1.00	.40

[a] Production line conversions require the effort of an entire shift's labor force.

Table 10-2 Pop-Rite, Inc. Sales

1967 Sales for Months 1–12 and Year

	1	2	3	4	5	6	7	8	9	10	11	12	Year
Brand 1	1139	1097	1160	1,189	1,246	1,290	1,344	1,410	1,359	1,298	1,240	1205	14,977
Brand 2	2350	1883	1501	1,967	2,335	2,651	2,878	3,046	3,086	2,992	2,818	2592	30,099
Brand 3	2098	2515	3111	3,455	3,806	4,285	5,108	4,865	4,280	3,573	2,935	2567	42,598
Brand 4	7583	6629	7156	9,111	10,607	11,331	11,540	12,103	12,182	11,266	10,628	8629	118,765
Brand 5	6231	7427	8915	10,419	11,854	13,535	14,710	13,514	12,261	10,889	9,640	8578	127,973

1968 Sales for Months 1–12 and Year

	1	2	3	4	5	6	7	8	9	10	11	12	Year
Brand 1	1145	1101	1148	1,195	1,243	1,306	1,362	1,408	1,359	1,287	1,248	1193	14,995
Brand 2	2290	1937	1520	1,945	2,300	2,651	2,884	3,034	3,061	3,100	2,885	2562	30,139
Brand 3	2065	2548	3017	3,581	4,284	4,878	5,444	5,114	4,202	3,613	3,076	2697	44,519
Brand 4	8414	6714	7751	9,601	10,851	11,173	11,550	12,072	11,907	10,824	9,914	9792	120,563
Brand 5	6361	7841	9464	10,636	12,593	14,040	16,084	14,620	13,099	11,481	10,315	8767	135,301

Inventory positions as of December 31, 1968, are also indicated in Table 10-1. Pop-Rite's inventory storage area is sufficiently large so as to be considered unlimited.

We begin by examining the aggregate planning problem for this firm. First we identify the basic variable costs. We could state them as follows:

total variable costs = inventory carrying costs + shortage costs
+ shift change cost + overtime cost.

The company has a significant employment smoothing problem because of the highly seasonal nature of demand. Regular-time production is 24,000 cases per month but demand fluctuates from 20,000 to 37,000 per month, as shown in Table 10-2. First we obtain a rough idea of the costs of alternatives to this problem. Overtime for 50 persons on the line costs $.25 per case. Only an additional 6000 cases can be produced in overtime. A second shift can be employed but the start-up and shutdown costs come to $5000, or about $.24 per case, if only the minimum 21,000 cases are produced from running the line 1 month. At the maximum regular-time capacity of 30,000 cases, the cost is $.16. Another alternative is storage, but the storage cost is 2% per month, or about .20 on the weighted average case. Since the seasonal problem would require long storage if employment were kept level, the costs of storage as the major method of smoothing would be considerably more than the cost of overtime or adding a second shift. Shortage costs (lost profits) are $1–$2 per case, and so ignoring shortages is not the answer. Overtime cannot provide the only answer either. If we arrange for only one start-up and shutdown of the second shift and run both lines at minimal level for, say, the first three heavy months, we can bring the incremental production costs to about $.08 per case plus some storage costs in the following heavy months.

A more complete and rigorous answer to this problem can be formulated by a linear programming method adapted for the fixed charge of the setup costs. We reject the short-term smoothing methods because of the importance of the setup cost. Monthly decisions might lead to several setups. Table 10-3 contains the setup of the problem as a transportation method of linear programming. Production comes from initial inventory, regular or overtime, first or second shift in each month. Costs include overtime premium, extra shift costs, and storage. The extra shift cost must be separately computed for 1, 2, and 3 months of continuous running and for each possible starting month. Each separate tableau, such as Table 10-3, would have to be solved. A rolling schedule of perhaps 12–18 months in advance could be calculated each month.

To finish the aggregate planning as above, we must have an estimate of the build-up to total inventory desired in addition to meeting the forecasted

Table 10-3 Pop-Rite Aggregate Planning Model

Source				Months												Total
Month	Shift	Regular Time	Overtime	1	2	3	4	5	6	7	8	9	10	11	12	
1	1	1		0	.20	.40	.60	.80	1.00	1.00	1.40	1.60	1.80	2.00	2.20	21
1	1		1	.25	.45	.65	.85	1.05	1.25	1.45	1.65	1.85	2.05	2.15	2.25	9
1	2	1		.24	.44	.64	.84	1.04	1.24	1.44	1.64	1.84	2.04	2.24	2.44	21
1	2		1	.49	.69	.89	1.09	1.29	1.49	1.69	1.89	2.09	2.29	2.49	2.69	9
2	1	1		—	—											21
2	1		1	—	—											9
2	2	1		—	—											21
2	2		1	—	—											9
3	1	1		—	—	—										
3	1		1	—	—	—										
3	2	1		—	—	—										
3	2		1	—	—	—										
4	1	1		—	—	—	—						—			
4	1		1	—	—	—	—						—			
4	2	1		—	—	—	—						—			
4	2		1	—	—	—	—						—			
5	1	1		—	—	—	—	0	.20	.40	.60	.80	—			
5	1		1	—	—	—	—	.25	.45	.65	.85	1.05	—			
5	2	1		—	—	—	—	.24ᵃ	.44	.64	.84	1.04	—			
5	2		1	—	—	—	—									
6	1	1														
etc.																
Demands				21.15	20.7	—	—									

ᵃ If second shift in two adjoining months, .12, .32, .52; if used in three adjoining months, .08, .28, .48; if used in four adjoining months, .06, .26, .46.

demand of twice this year's sales less last years sales. The present inventory may not be adequate. There are two problems in setting this inventory: the single production facility and the necessity of providing protection against possible errors in the forecast.

Because the brands are all made on the same machine and a setup cost is incurred each time brands are changed, we must produce in a cycle of batches which takes into account setup and carrying costs. This problem was discussed in Chap. 7 where the formula below was developed for the number of cycles:

$$n^o = \left(\frac{\sum d_i(r_i - d_i)C_{ci}}{2 \sum_i r_i C_{ri}} \right)^{1/2},$$

where d_i = demand rate
r_i = production rate
C_{ci} = carrying cost
C_{ri} = setup cost.

See Table 10-4. Here we take demand at the average monthly rate for the year. The seasonality will actually require larger inventories and so the number of cycles is understated. We might take 1 cycle per month as a convenient approximation.

Table 10-4   Cycle Calculation

Brand	d_i (000)	$r_i - d_i$ (000)	$d_i(r_i - d_i)$ (000, 000)	$r_i = 24,000$
1	1.25	22.750	28.4	$\sum c_{ri} = 3000$
2	2.5	21.500	54.0	$n = \left(\frac{88.2}{144} \right)^{1/2}$
3	3.7	20.300	75.0	
4	10	14.000	140.0	$n^o = .77$ cycles/month
5	11.2	12.800	144.0	1.3 months/cycle
			441.4	

Because of the cycle, it is necessary to have an average of one half of the cycle's inventory on hand at all times. In addition, we would need buffer stock inventory to safeguard against errors in estimation of demand. Because of the production cycle, this is essentially a periodic review model. In Chap. 7 we presented the following formula for buffer stock:

$$P(x > S) = \frac{C_c t}{C_s},$$

where t = cycle time or review time
C_c = carrying cost

$C_s = $ shortage cost

$S = $ stock for a lead time plus a review period.

In our case, then,

$$P(x > S) = \frac{\$.32 \times 1.0}{2.00} \qquad \text{for Brand 1}$$

$$= .16.$$

We can assume that lead time is short.

We now need an estimate of the distribution of demand for the cycle time. If we examine the demand data for brand 1, we see no growth in sales. Also for this particular brand there is very little seasonality. We can then take the 24 observations and calculate a mean average derivation (MAD) of 78 and multiply by 1.25 to estimate the sample standard deviation as 98. If we make a heroic assumption of normality of the distribution of demand during the month, we can now find in the standardized normal table that $P(x > S)$ $= .16$ is 1 standard derivation or 98 units away from the mean. We then need a buffer stock of 98, or about 100 items. One month's cycle stock is 1250 for brand 1. Our inital inventory, also 1250, is large enough to allow us to start the cycle with any brand and have almost enough stock to cover the buffer stock since we shall begin the production of brand 1 in less than a month.

We should now calculate the safety or buffer stock for each other brand and examine the adequacy of initial stocks. Some of the other brands have growth and seasonality which must be taken into account. The safety stock of the seasonal items should be higher in the summer than during the off-season. Any adjustments for additional or lower buffer and cycle inventories must be made in the demands in the aggregate planning tableaus.

Detailed scheduling: We now reveal that there remain considerable detailed decisions in the Pop-Rite operating system. The information presented should be supplemented as follows:

1. *Product line:* The historical demand by flavor within brand is displayed in Table 10-5.
2. *Bottling line conversions:* Setup times are composed of a brand changeover plus a flavor adjustment (Table 10-6). There is no technological requirement to produce all flavors following a brand changeover.
3. *Raw materials:* Each case of finished goods requires 1 gallon of syrup ingredients, 5 gallons of sparkling water, 4 cardboard cartons, 24 disposable bottles, 24 labels, and 24 bottle caps. The sparkling water is essentially a free good: unlimited supply, zero cost, and no lead time. The costs and lead times of other raw materials is indicated in Table 10-7. In every instance, the item

Table 10-5 1967 Demand for Months 1-12

	1	2	3	4	5	6	7	8	9	10	11	12
Brand 1	1139	1097	1160	1,189	1,246	1,290	1,344	1,410	1,359	1,298	1,240	1205
Flavor A	733	724	848	955	999	959	1,077	959	1,121	1,025	834	832
Flavor B	406	373	312	234	247	331	267	451	238	273	406	373
Brand 2	2350	1883	1501	1,967	2,335	2,651	2,878	3,046	3,086	2,992	2,818	2592
Flavor A	591	803	816	854	1,252	1,054	993	1,130	1,314	1,606	1,203	1025
Flavor B	1287	479	280	679	496	1,118	523	1,176	734	546	686	573
Flavor C	320	340	237	296	386	319	1,146	441	726	499	612	614
Flavor D	152	261	168	137	201	160	216	299	312	340	317	379
Brand 3	2098	2515	3111	3,455	3,806	4,285	5,108	4,865	4,280	3,573	2,935	2567
Flavor A	620	708	1336	1,654	985	1,350	1,145	1,082	1,336	834	997	859
Flavor B	366	683	801	704	937	1,242	987	1,692	801	679	709	399
Flavor C	757	519	442	652	859	642	1,209	788	1,237	442	584	409
Flavor D	286	465	377	334	764	709	1,123	836	683	960	449	631
Flavor E	69	140	155	112	261	342	645	467	224	659	196	270
Brand 4	7583	6629	7156	9,111	10,607	11,331	11,540	12,103	12,182	11,266	10,628	8629
Flavor A	2499	1240	1830	1,485	2,908	3,229	3,646	4,794	5,287	3,361	2,815	2025
Flavor B	582	2008	825	2,761	1,452	2,550	1,562	1,019	1,583	2,884	1,563	1302
Flavor C	2058	1584	2426	1,933	997	1,411	2,004	1,822	1,040	1,235	2,832	1110
Flavor D	526	435	580	544	679	641	585	1,068	819	593	865	696
Flavor E	548	386	436	485	782	877	584	1,325	699	1,199	624	460
Flavor F	384	508	460	523	972	1,322	928	823	1,003	591	650	735
Flavor G	580	199	217	560	2,061	917	1,669	395	336	422	543	1202
Flavor H	406	268	380	819	757	385	563	857	1,413	980	735	1099
Brand 5	6231	7427	8915	10,419	11,854	13,535	14,710	13,514	12,261	10,889	9,640	8578
Flavor A	2929	3286	3503	5,621	6,915	8,149	5,642	8,577	4,400	6,008	5,448	4121
Flavor B	2039	3080	4133	3,236	2,863	3,348	5,673	2,996	3,728	2,424	2,146	2201
Flavor C	1263	1062	1279	1,562	2,075	2,038	3,396	1,941	4,133	2,457	2,046	2256

Table 10-6   **Bottling Line Conversions**^a

Brand	Changeover (hr)	Flavor Change (hr)	Total Conversion Time[b] (hr)
1	1.0	.5	2.0
2	2.0	.5	4.0
3	2.5	.3	4.0
4	2.4	.7	8.0
5	1.25	.25	2.0

[a]*Note:* The bottling line was set up for brand 3, flavor E, at the close of December 31, 1968.
[b]If all flavor changes are made and all flavors are produced.

Table 10-7   **Raw Materials Purchasing Data**^a

Material	Brand	Item Cost ($)	Order Cost ($)	Lead Time (days)
Syrup ingredients	1	2.55	100.00	6
	2	2.10		
	3	1.40		
	4	1.30		
	5	.85		
Cartons	1, 2[b]	.20	500.00	10
	3, 4, 5[b]	.15		
Bottles	1, 2, 3[b]	.45	800.00	5
	4, 5[b]	.40		
Labels and caps	1	.25	175.00	12
	2	.20		
	3	.15		
	4	.15		
	5	.15		

[a]*Note:* There was no material on order as of December 31, 1968.
[b]Indicates raw material item which is common to two or more brands.

cost refers to the quantity of raw material required to produce one case of soft drink. Annual raw material inventory carrying costs are calculated at 25% of line item costs. The 1968 year-end raw material inventory positions, in case equivalents, are listed in Table 10-8. The last column in Table 10-8 lists 1968 year-end finished goods positions.

4. *Syrup distillation process:* At the bottling line stations, the syrup and sparkling water are injected into the bottles, and the bottles are capped, labeled, and cartoned, yielding the finished product which we have come to know so well. The syrup itself, however,

Table 10-8   Inventory on Hand December 31, 1968[a]

	Syrup Ingredients	Cartons	Bottles	Labels and Caps	Finished Goods
Brand 1					
Flavor A	1,825			2,275	842
Flavor B	950			1,300	408
Brand 2		5,850[b]			
Flavor A	2,425			4,025	1,203
Flavor B	950			850	411
Flavor C	875			650	422
Flavor D	675			725	519
Brand 3			9,450[b]		
Flavor A	2,725			2,400	621
Flavor B	1,375			1,675	543
Flavor C	1,300			1,825	517
Flavor D	1,425			1,450	318
Flavor E	725			1,075	204
Brand 4					
Flavor A	3,825			4,225	2,236
Flavor B	2,925			4,050	1,924
Flavor C	2,650			2,550	1,572
Flavor D	1,000			1,700	1,313
Flavor E	1,075			1,750	654
Flavor F	1,650			2,075	636
Flavor G	875			675	255
Flavor H	750			725	351
Brand 5		38,925[b]	38,500[b]		
Flavor A	8,950			8,275	3,312
Flavor B	5,725			7,125	2,165
Flavor C	4,825			6,650	1,081
Total	49,500	44,775	47,950	58,050	21,497

[a]*Note:* All numbers are in case or case equivalents.
[b]Total inventory for group.

is the product of a process which is shrouded in considerable mystery. Mr. Sauer, Pop-Rite's brewmaster, is intent upon preserving the secrets which ensure the unique taste of each brand and flavor of soft drink. He is, however, anxious to receive assistance in controlling this manufacturing process, and he has for this reason furnished certain information:

a. The syrup is produced by a distilling process in one of three stills whose characteristics are described in Table 10-9.

b. The syrup is distilled in batches by flavor and brand. The size of the batch may be less than the still size; however, the time

Table 10-9   Syrup Distillation[a]

Still	Maximum Batch (gal)	Time Required (hr)	Fixed Cost ($)
A	400	4	50
B	200	4	30
C	100	2	20

[a]*Note:* There was 600 gallons of syrup for brand 1, flavor A, on hand at the close of December 31, 1968.

> required and the fixed cost do not vary. One gallon of syrup yields one case of soft drink.
>
> c. Because of the rapid deterioration of the distilled syrup, inventory is limited to 1000 gallons of syrup.

The first question concerns the effect of the flavors within each brand. Since the setup cost has already been included in the aggregate, the cycle time is not affected. We do have an additional safety stock problem since each flavor must have its own safety stock rather than a pool for the brand. Because of the nonlinear behavior of variance, the total safety stock will increase but the methodology is the same as for brands.

The next question is that of raw material inventories. Again carrying costs are high. The use of the linear programming aggregate plan will allow us to tie raw material orders directly to planned production rates with only a buffer stock for variations. An EOQ system should not be used here because inventories can be tied directly to usage.

The final question is the scheduling of the production of flavors. Again the aggregate plan can be used to tell when to produce the flavors so that they are available for the bottling of the brand.

This procedure will not be adequate if the flavors do not follow the brand sales pattern. This is true for some flavors; see, for example, flavor G of brand 4 in 1967. In this case there are two possible problems. The first is that there is actually much more variance in demand for the individual flavors than for the brand. On the other hand, it is quite likely that the apparent variance is created by the system. We have probably produced that flavor in the month with high demand and therefore sold it, unconsciously creating the surge or even consciously creating the high demand by advertising or otherwise pushing a particular flavor. If this is the reason for the extreme variance, we should deal with the problem by planning rather than statistical techniques.

If the extreme fluctuations are a valid measure of demand and we cannot "switch" customers to another flavor, there are at least two possible solutions. One is to carry much larger buffer stock inventories than we previously determined, with each buffer stock figured for one flavor. The other is to make the production system able to respond to the fluctuations directly by producing the flavor when needed. Even the highest monthly demands for a flavor can be met in a few days' worth of production. This would require adequate syrup stocks, however. Since each brand is made monthly, the peak flavor can probably be detected early enough and produced heavily in the regular cycle for that brand. Also, we see that the detailed data place a much lower penalty on breaking up the sequence of the cycle to make one flavor than was previously stated for the brand.

The final problem is that of the production and stocking of syrups. According to Table 10-9, the upper limit on production of syrup is 200 gallons per hour versus 150 gallons per hour consumed by the process. The limitation of 1000 gallons of syrup in inventory essentially requires the production of the syrup within 6 hours of final bottling of the drink, not including time the process is not running. Therefore virtually no inventories can be maintained. Since the production time per batch is short, there should be no problem in adapting the syrup production to the bottling schedule as long as the stills do not break down. Breakdowns would require second- or third-shift production. In fact, most breakdowns would be very costly because the production line would have to stop in a very short time, and so maintenance is important.

If we leave the area of planning inventory and scheduling, we can see how important the analysis of these areas is to the others, such as capital budgeting. It is easy to imagine someone selling Mr. Fizzle a new production line because its increased capacity will solve his problems. From what we have seen, this is a very expensive approach and will almost certainly be unsuccessful. Similarly, more syrup distillation facilities are not required. The major improvement needed in the system is not equipment but a method of making the best use of it.

C. Interrelationships with Marketing

The production decisions discussed in the chapters of this book have usually involved only the production system, which we defined in Chap. 1 as the "nonmarketing" subsystem of the firm. There have been several important exceptions to this emphasis, where we have included part of the marketing system:

1. In capacity planning (Chap. 2), it is essential to have information of how the prices of products and inputs will vary (or not vary) with the level at which the production system is operated.

2. In location decisions (Chap. 3), the revenue factor has been as important as cost, although the emergence of national markets has somewhat eclipsed this factor for some products. International

marketing decisions, however, will probably throw the emphasis over to revenue again. For location decision models we need information on how sales will vary with transportation charges.

3. In plant design, we need estimates of both the total production level which can be sold at the planned prices and of the mix of products that we expect to sell, down to model type, color, and other characteristics which will require special treatment. Otherwise the design will not be suitable for actual production.

4. In the chapter on capital budgeting, we examined problems such as expansion and change in product mix which are often encountered in practice. These desisions require estimates of total sales levels by product as well as price information. The information can be given as ranges, such as minimum amounts required to satisfy steady customers, or as an upper limit at which price will have to be lowered.

5. Repetitive aggregate planning decisions often center on smoothing of seasonal sales. Obviously, to perform this function well, the degree of seasonality must be predictable. Price discounts are often used to help smooth production.

6. In Chap. 7 we saw that inventory decisions concerning products hinge on estimates of how customers will react to shortages or back orders. The best source for this information is the marketing function, not "off the top of the production manager's head."

7. Some of the major constraints in most scheduling problems examined in Chap. 8 are the delivery promises made by the marketing function.

We can see from this quick review that marketing information is vital to good production decisions. The production manager must be sure that the marketing function in his firm can supply this information. Unfortunately, this responsibility is often not clear because of the organizational structure of many firms, which separates marketing and production. In Chap. 6 we discussed the role that the aggregate planning production system must play in coordinating the marketing and production systems in the medium range. The coordination is equally important in the short run and long run. Good location and capacity decisions cannot be made by ignoring either cost or revenue. Scheduling and inventory problems are often caused by lack of coordination between the production and marketing functions. For example, delivery promises are made that are technologically impossible. Inventories are often not coordinated with sales efforts. Market information that changes the parameters required for the production decisions, as outlined above, often fails to reach the production manager until too late. On the other hand, a cooperative production manager could often save or create sales for the marketing function by seeing that certain orders or custom models receive top priority in production or inventory systems.

Unfortunately, the development of models and systems that can solve the joint problems of marketing and production has not been well developed to date. One attempt is the *industrial dynamics* approach, which we shall demonstate in the following section. Another approach is centered on the *logistics* approach to the management of the firm. This approach calls for the centralization of all the decisions on flow of materials through the firm. It would thus incorporate the aggregate planning and inventory and scheduling production decisions along with the order-processing, purchasing, and physical distribution functions which are tied to the marketing subsystem. Often this centralized decision making is performed by a computer-based organization which has access to the required information. This fundamentally sound approach has not been a panacea because

1. It is often found that these decision makers are too far removed from either the market or the product functions. That is, they do not receive information on sales plans, machine breakdowns, etc.
2. The capability of computerized systems with regard to hardware and, particularly, software has too often not been adequate to handle the information flows in timely fashion.
3. The decision models for the complete systems have not yet been developed. That is, a distribution, scheduling, and inventory model for multiple plants down to the individual machine, worker, and piece of raw material and every product simply has not been formulated. This is the reason that the production manager remains an important part of the production function.

D. Large-Scale Models for Integrated Production Management

In Sec. B we discussed tying the models for various production decision areas together into a management information and decision system. An alternative to this approach is to develop a single large-scale model for the entire production system which can generate solutions for all or most of the decision areas. We shall now discuss two of these approaches.

Although these two approaches may span the range of available techniques and models, they by no means completely cover the variety of approaches possible. For instance, the accounting system of any firm can be thought of as a management information system and even a decision system if a few obviously implied rules are explicitly implemented, e.g., "Don't produce products which lose money." But the accounting system has usually failed to be sufficient and we are forced to turn to alternatives or perhaps extensions of it. We hope, however, that in the longer run it will become more useful than it currently is.

The first approach we shall examine is the use of linear programming models of refineries as an integrated information and decision system for several production decisions. The second approach is a simulation approach, industrial dynamics.

I. LINEAR PROGRAMMING AS AN INTEGRATED PRODUCTION DECISION MODEL

In Chaps. 6 and 8 we examined linear programming models for aggregate planning and for scheduling. In addition, we have used linear programming models of processes in Chap. 2 on location analysis for incremental additions to the distribtuion system. We also used them in Chap. 5 when examining incremental additions to equipment. It is conceivable that these models could be brought together to produce an integrated model which would allow many different production decisions to be made with the same model. This procedure would have the advantages that all the decisions would be based on the same set of assumptions and on the same data base. Often it is difficult to coordinate decisions simply because of differences in these.

In the preceding chapters, the models which come closest to this degree of integration are the aggregate planning linear programming models—particularly the decomposition model of Dzielinski and Gomory on the job shop, since it includes capacity and manpower constraints as well as the complete scheduling technology. This model could be used for capital budgeting and aggregate planning as well as scheduling. In fact, it could conceivably be useful in long-run capacity planning and in location decisions if appropriate data were available for the processes under these greatly different conditions. It is very doubtful that any two job shops would be created that much alike, however. We shall take a simpler production process, a refinery, as an example.

A field in which linear programming has reached perhaps its most comprehensive use is the operation of refineries. Refineries are flow processes and therefore are fairly simple. They have only one major input, crude oil, in addition to manpower. Through the use of standardized "recipes" for operation, the nonlinearities in the system can be overcome. The field has highly trained technical personnel with extensive predictive models of technical relationships. The economics of the industry are complex. For all these reasons linear programming has become well developed in the opera-

tion of refineries. These refineries in terms of investment are some of the
largest productive processes in the world.

Besides functioning as an operational model for scheduling the separation
and blending of the various fractions of oil, the refinery LP models can be
used to answer other decisions in aggregate planning, capital budgeting,
inventory control, and even maintenance policies. Since the refineries are
almost always only a portion of integrated world wide networks of oil production, transportation, and marketing and because the refinery equipment
is somewhat internationally standardized, the models can even be used for
location and capacity planning.

We quote from a survey of the field by G. W. Sears of Shell Oil Co. Ltd.
that appeared in *Progress in Operations Research*:†

> *On the other hand, very real side benefits have been obtained from the
> operation of these models partly from gaining a better understanding of the
> nature of the interactions between the various plants but more particularly
> from the sharper and more copious information which is thrown up as a
> byproduct of the final solution. For example, the marginal costs associated
> with plant capacity limitations are automatically generated, and these not
> only indicate where "debottlenecking" may be desirable, but also go a long
> way towards giving an integrated estimate of the savings which would be
> consequent on such debottlenecking. In the same way, the marginal costs of
> finished products are generated, and a parametric routine will show how
> these are related to product demand and thus provide valuable information
> for the negotiation of contracts for additional business. Running the model
> with and without a "good-will" sale will give a genuine evaluation of the cost
> of that sale, etc. . . .*
>
> *Logically, therefore, the next step for an integrated company was to take
> a closer look at its allocation of overall crude oil availability to the refineries
> under its control. This entailed the aggregation of individual models into a
> multirefinery model covering a geographically coherent marketing region
> such as "East of the Rockies," "whole of the U.K.," "Common Market," etc.
> Essentially this requires that additional flexibility should be built in by allow-
> ing for interchange of product components between refineries and for alterna-
> tive sources of supply for the main installations serving local markets; the
> integrated model is linked together by these additional facilities, by the
> transportation elements which go with them, and by the overall constraints
> on crude oil availability.*
>
> *Several such models are known to have been constructed and are in regular
> and evolving use in the examination of medium and long-term programs.*

The following simplified example of linear programming is taken from a
paper by Munjal, which also discusses nonlinear models in refinery planning
[3].

---

†From *Progress in Operations Research*, Volume II, edited by D. B. Hertz and R. T.
Eddison. Copyright © 1964 by John Wiley & Sons, Inc. Reprinted by permission.

The distillation capacity of the main refinery column is 1600 barrels per day (B/D), about one-hundredth the size of an actual refinery. The main distillation unit has only two streams, an overhead distillation unit and a bottom distillation unit, with capacities of 600 and 400 B/D, respectively, as shown in Fig. 10-1, where it is seen that only up to 1000 B/D of finished

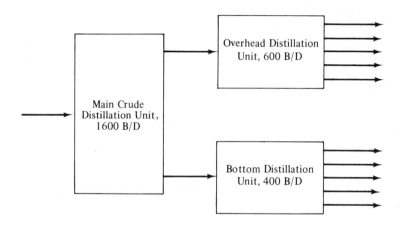

Capacity of Overhead Distillation Unit = 600 B/D
Capacity of Bottom Distillation Unit = 400 B/D
Capacity of Main Crude Distillation Unit = 1600 B/D

Figure 10-1.   Simplified flow diagram of refinery's major distillation units.

products can be produced unless we increase the current capacities of the overhead or bottom distillation units. The company has two crudes, x_1 and x_2, available for this refinery. Two other crudes, x_3 and x_4, are obtained from an independent supplier. Crudes have different physical and chemical properties and yield different quantities of the finished products per barrel. Based on these properties, the marketing department has determined different netbacks (revenue minus cost) for each one of the crudes. The percentage yield for the overhead and bottom capacities for various crudes along with their netback is given in Table 10-10.

Based on Table 10-10, we can then write the following set of equations, where x_6 and x_7 are slack variables for overhead and bottom capacity, x_1–x_4 are scaled by a factor of 10, and the redundant constraint on overall capacity is neglected:

$$8x_1' + 9x_2' + 7x_3' + 2x_4' + x_5 = 600$$
$$2x_1' + x_2' + 3x_3' + 8x_4' + x_6 = 400$$
$$6x_1' + 20x_2' + 18x_3' + 8x_4' = z \text{ (max)}.$$

Table 10-10 Composition and Price Data for Various Crude Oils

Crude	% Overhead Yield	% Bottom Yield	Netback, $/bbl
x_1	80	20	.60
x_2	90	10	2.00
x_3	70	30	1.80
x_4	20	80	.80
x_7	75	25	1.89

The final tableau for this problem is

Basic Variables	Admissible Variables (Including Slacks)							Constants
	x'_1	x'_2	x'_3	x'_4	x_5	x_6	$-z$	
x'_3	$\frac{6}{5}$	$\frac{7}{5}$	1	0	$\frac{4}{25}$	$-\frac{1}{25}$	0	80
x'_4	$-\frac{1}{5}$	$-\frac{2}{5}$	0	1	$-\frac{3}{50}$	$\frac{7}{50}$	0	20
$-z$	-14	-2	0	0	$-\frac{12}{5}$	$-\frac{2}{5}$	1	-1600

In ordinary operation the model would be used to select the amount of each crude—here, 800 B/D of x_3 and 200 B/D of x_4, with a profit of $1600. We have assumed no constraints on demand. If there were minimum amounts of some products required, we would have to model the blending process, which we shall avoid for simplicity.

As an example of the use of the model in capital budgeting decisions, we might have three methods for increasing capacity. If a new type of column heater is purchased, it will increase the overhead distillation capacity by 10% at a cost of $23 B/D, which includes the investment and the increased fuel. Additional capacity up to 20% of the rated capacity can be obtained by maintenance such as cleaning the boilers on overhead and bottom units at a cost of $1.50 per B/D of capacity. Additional capacity above this increase can be obtained by redesign such as welding fins on boilers at a cost of $3.00 per B/D of capacity. Let

y_1 = increase in overhead capacity by new heaters

y_2 = increase in overhead capacity by cleaning of boilers

y_3 = increase in bottom capacity by cleaning boilers

y_4 = increase in overhead capacity by welding fins to boilers

y_5 = increase in bottom capacity by welding fins to boilers:

$$8x'_1 + 9x'_2 + 7x'_3 + 2x'_4 - y_1 - y_2 - y_4 + x_5 = 600 \text{ B/D}$$
$$2x'_1 + x'_2 + 3x'_3 + 8x'_4 - y_3 - y_5 + x_6 \qquad = 400 \text{ B/D}$$
$$y_1 + y_2 + y_3 + y_4 + y_5 + x_7 \qquad\qquad = 600 \text{ B/D}$$
$$y_1 + x_8 \qquad\qquad\qquad\qquad\qquad = 60 \text{ B/D}$$
$$y_2 + x_9 \qquad\qquad\qquad\qquad\qquad = 120 \text{ B/D}$$
$$y_3 + x_{10} \qquad\qquad\qquad\qquad\qquad = 80 \text{ B/D.}$$

Objective function:

$$6x'_1 + 20x'_2 + 18x'_3 + 8x'_4 - \tfrac{23}{60}y_1 - 1.5y_2$$
$$- 1.5y_3 - 3y_4 - 3y_5 = z \text{ (max)}.$$

The optimum solution is shown as follows:

This solution, which uses both methods of increasing overhead capacity, could have been foreseen by the shadow prices on the overhead and bottom constraint in the final tableau of the original problem. The shadow piece is six times as high on overhead capacity, $\tfrac{12}{5}$ versus $\tfrac{2}{5}$.

For longer-range problems, such as location, transportation, and total capacity planning, larger models such as referred to by Sears are required.

II. INDUSTRIAL DYNAMICS AS AN INTEGRATED PRODUCTION MODEL

Industrial dynamics is the name given by its originator, Jay W. Forrester of M.I.T., to a type of model which is based on feedback loops, as shown in Fig. 10-2. A system to be modeled is described as an interacting set of feedback loops. Commodity flows (material, orders, personnel, money, equipment) and information flows are modeled. All variables are described as rates or levels or auxiliary variables. Levels are integrations of rates, and differences between levels supply the potential which produces rates of flow. Auxiliaries are used to calculate desired rates.

A simple feedback loop is shown in Fig. 10-2. Levels are calculated at present time K and rates for past or future periods at JK or KL, as shown in Fig. 10-3. The length of time, JK or KL, is set by the model builder at DT. The level of inventory at time K in the simple feedback loop of Fig. 10-2 can be written as

$$\text{INV }(K) = \text{INV }(J) - DT \cdot \text{FLO }(JK).$$

The rate controller or decision rule might be

$$\text{FLO }(KL) = \text{constant} - \text{INV }(K).$$

Matrix of Admissible Variables (Including Slacks)

Basic Variables	x_1'	x_2'	x_3'	x_4'	y_1	y_2	y_3	y_4	y_5	x_5	x_6	x_7	x_8	x_9	x_{10}	$-z$	Constants
x_3'	$\frac{6}{5}$	$\frac{7}{5}$	1				$-\frac{1}{25}$	$-\frac{4}{25}$	$\frac{1}{25}$	$\frac{4}{25}$	$-\frac{1}{25}$		$\frac{4}{25}$	$\frac{4}{25}$			$\frac{544}{5}$
x_4'	$-\frac{1}{5}$	$-\frac{2}{5}$		1			$-\frac{7}{50}$	$\frac{3}{50}$	$-\frac{7}{50}$	$-\frac{3}{50}$	$\frac{7}{50}$		$-\frac{3}{50}$	$-\frac{3}{50}$			$\frac{46}{5}$
x_7							1	1	1			1	-1	-1			420
y_1					1								1				60
y_2						1								1			120
x_{10}							1								1		80
$-z$	-14	-2					$-\frac{11}{10}$	$-\frac{3}{5}$	$-\frac{13}{5}$	$-\frac{12}{5}$	$-\frac{2}{5}$		$-\frac{121}{60}$	$-\frac{9}{10}$		1	-1829

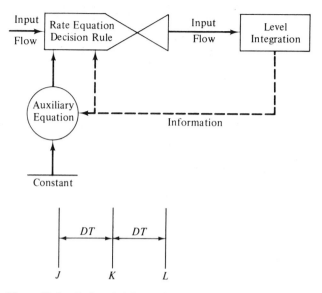

Figure 10-2.   Industrial dynamics feedback loop and time period diagram.

These level and rate equations have been standardized, along with a variety of useful functions in compilers called DYNAMO [4] and DYNFOR [5]. Table 10-11 gives the standard functions available. DYNFOR also accepts FORTRAN statements. These compilers greatly simplify the building and interpretation of industrial dynamics models.

An example of an inventory model using DYNFOR is shown in Fig. 10-3. Customers place orders (ORDR) in the unfilled order bin (UORD). Information on orders is sent to the shipping department (SHPS), which ships out of inventory (XINV) if the item is in stock and notifies the customer if the order must be back-ordered. Information on orders and inventory level flows to the purchase order department (PORDS), where orders are placed with suppliers whose shipping departments (SHPR) send the goods to the inventory. Figure 10-4 gives the DYNFOR program for the problem complete with initial values. Figure 10-5 is a graph of the output.

One difficulty with industrial dynamics models has been that they have usually been designed as descriptive rather than optimizing models. In the example inventory problem it would be necessary to try out various inventory rate rules by changing NWIDS, the amount of inventory desired, and test which was the best value. With the FORTRAN compatibility of DYNFOR, we can write optimizing subroutines for the rate equations to furnish auxiliary variables for optimized decisions.

In the past the most successful industrial dynamics models have been those which dealt with large-scale problems not easily formulated in optimi-

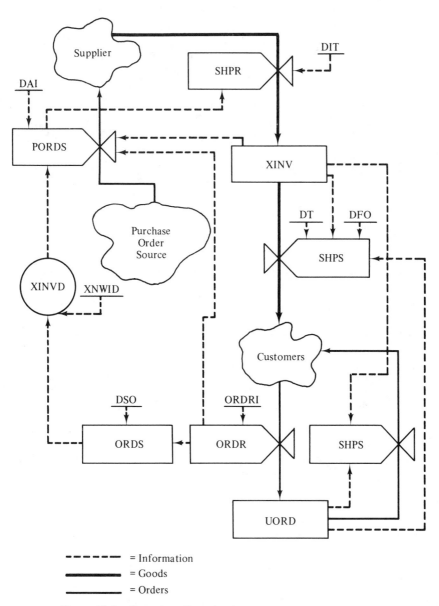

Figure 10-3. Inventory flow chart.

Source: R. L. Nolan, DYNFOR: A General Business and Economic Systems Simulator, *TR #5, Graduate School of Business Administration, University of Washington, Seattle, 1970, p. 19. Courtesy of the Graduate School of Business Administration, University of Washington.*

Table 10-11 General Form for Algebraic Functions and Equivalent DYNFOR Form[a]

DYNAMO/DYNFOR Equation Number	General Form	DYNFOR Form
Levels		
FN1	V(K)=V(J)+DT*(P+Q)	V(K)=FN1(V(J),P,Q)
FN52	V(K)=V(J)+DT*(P+Q+R+S)	V(K)=FN52(V(J),P,Q,R,S)
FN2	V(K)=V(J)+DT*(P+Q+R+S+T+U)	V(K)=FN2(V(J),P,Q,R,S,T,U)
FN3	V(K)=V(J)+DT*(1/Y)*(P+Q)	V(K)=FN3(V(J),Y,P,Q)
FN4	V(K)=V(J)+DT*(1/Y)*(P+Q+R+S+T+U)	V(K)=FN4(V(J),Y,P,Q,R,S,T,U)
FN5	V(K)=V(J)+DT*(1/Y)*(P+Q)+(1/Z)*(R+S)	V(K)=FN5(V(J),Y,P,Q,R,S,Z)
Sums and products		
FN6	V=P	V=FN6(P)
FN7	V=P+Q	V=FN7(P,Q)
FN8	V=P+Q+R	V=FN8(P,Q,R)
FN9	V=P+Q+R+S	V=FN9(P,Q,R,S)
FN10	V=P+Q+R+S+T+U	V=FN10(P,Q,R,S,T,U)
FN11	V=P+Q+R+S+T+U+W+X	V=FN11(P,Q,R,S,T,U,W,X)
FN12	V=P*Q	V=FN12(P,Q)
FN13	V=P*Q*R	V=FN13(P,Q,R)
FN14	V=P+Q*R	V=FN14(P,Q,R)
FN15	V=P*Q+R*S	V=FN15(P,Q,R,S)
FN16	V=P*Q+R*S+T*U+W*X	V=FN16(P,Q,R,S,T,U,W,X)
FN17	V=P*Q*R+S*T*U+W*X*Y	V=FN17(P,Q,R,S,T,U,W,X,Y)
FN18	V=P*(Q+R)	V=FN18(P,Q,R)
FN19	V=P*(Q+R+S+T)	V=FN19(P,Q,R,S,T)
Ratios		
FN20	V=P/Q	V=FN20(P,Q)
FN44	V=P*Q/R	V=FN44(P,Q,R)
FN42	V=P/Q*R	V=FN42(P,Q,R)
FN46	V=(P*Q*R)/(S*T*U)	V=FN46(P,Q,R,S,T,U)
FN21	V=(P+Q)/Y	V=FN21(Y,P,Q)
FN24	V=(P+Q+R+S+T+U)/Y	V=FN24(Y,P,Q,R,S,T,U)
FN22	V=(P*Q+R*S)/Y	V=FN22(Y,P,Q,R,S)
FN23	V=(P+Q)/Y+(R+S)/Z	V=FN23(Y,P,Q,Z,R,S)
FN27	V=P/Q+R	V=FN27(P,Q,R)

FN40	$V=P+(R+S)/Q$	$V=FN40(P,Q,R,S)$
FN25	$V=P+(R+S+T+U+W+X)/Q$	$V=FN25(P,Q,R,S,T,U,W,X)$
FN48	$V=P/Q+R$	$V=FN48(P,Q,R)$
FN50	$V=P*Q/R+S$	$V=FN50(P,Q,R,S)$
FN26	$V=(P+Q+R)/(S+T+U)$	$V=FN26(P,Q,R,S,T,U)$

Special functions

Exponentiation	$V=P*e^Q$	$V=FN28(P,Q)$
Natural logarithm	$V=P*\log(Q)$	$V=FN29(P,Q)$
Square root	$V=P*\sqrt{Q}$	$V=FN30(P,Q)$
Trigonometric sine	$V=P* \sin (2*\pi*Q/R)$	$V=FN31(P,Q,R)$
Trigonemetric cosine	$V=P* \cos (2*\pi*Q/R)$	$V=FN32(P,Q,R)$
Uniform random numbers	$V=$ (random number uniformly distributed between $-P/2.$ and $+P/2.$)	$V=NOISE(P)$
Normally distributed random number	$V=P*$ (random number normally distributed with mean Q and standard deviation R)	$V=NORMRN(P,Q,R)$
Third-order delay	$V=$ (third-order exponentially delayed output from input P, with delay constant C)	$V=DELAY3(P,C)$
Pulse function	$V=$ (pulse output of height P and width DT when TIME $=Q$, and at succeeding intervals of length R, between pulses $V=0.$)	$V=PULSE(P,Q,R)$
Step function	$V=$ (0., until TIME exceeds Q when it becomes P)	$V=STEP(P,Q)$
Ramp function	$V=$ (0., until TIME exceeds Q when it becomes $\sum_{i=Q}^{TIME} DT*P_i$)	$V=RAMP(P,Q)$
Sampling function	$V=$ (P at intervals on length Q, and 0. between samples)	$V=SAMPLE(P,Q)$
Maximum function	$V=$ (the greater of P or Q)	$V=XMAX(P,Q)$
Minimum function	$V=$ (the smaller of P or Q)	$V=XMIN(P,Q)$
Clip function	$V=$ (P, if R is greater than or equal to S; otherwise Q)	$V=CLIP(P,Q)$
Switch function	$V=$ (P, if $R=0.$; otherwise Q)	$V=SWITCH(P,Q)$
Summing function	$V=$ (sum of all P from TIME $=$ 0. to current time period; summation stops when TIME $=$ X)	$V=SUM1(X,P)$
	$V=$ (sum of all P*Q to current period, until TIME $=$ X)	$V=SUM2(X,P,Q)$
	$V=$ (sum of all P*Q*R to current period, until TIME $=$ X)	$V=SUM3(X,P,Q,R)$

[a]From R. L. Nolan, *DYNFOR: A General Business and Economic Systems Simulator*, TR #5, Graduate School of Business Administration, University of Washington, Seattle, 1970, p. 9. Courtesy of the Graduate School of Business Administration, University of Washington.

```
C
C
C                    GENERAL INVENTORY MODEL
C
C
C    SPECIFICATION SECTION
C
         IMPLICIT REAL (I,J,K,L,M,N)
         INTEGER J,K,L,JK,KL
         DIMENSION  INV(502), INVD(502),UORD(502),ORDS(502),SHPS(502),
        XPORDS(502),SHPR(502),ORDR(502)
C    SPECIFY VALUES FOR DT, LENGTH, PRTPER, PLTPER
         CALL SPECS (.1,50.,1.,,3)
C    SET UP SUBSCRIPTS AND DT AS VARIABLE NAMES, RECEIVING INITIAL VALUES BACK.
C    FROM THE DYNFOR SIMULATED COMPILER
         CALL SETUP (J,K,L,JK,KL,DT)
C    SPECIFY OUTPUT HEADINGS
         REAL*8 NAMES(8)/ 'INV', 'INVD','UORD','ORDR','SHPS','PORDS',
        X'SHPR','ORDS'/
C    TRANSMIT LITERAL HEADINGS TO  COMPILER  AND SPECIFY HOW MANY THERE ARE
         CALL HEDING (NAMES,8)
C
C    CONSTANT SECTION
C
C    ORDER RATE INITIALLY (UNITS PER WEEK)
         ORDRI=1000.
C    DELAY IN SMOOTHING ORDERS (WEEKS)
         DSO=4.
C    DELAY IN TRANSIT (WEEKS)
         DIT=2.
C    DELAY IN FILLING ORDERS (WEEKS)
         NWID=3.
C    DELAY IN FILLING ORDERS (WEEKS)
         DFO=1.
C    DESIRED ADJUSTMENT IN INVENTORY
         DAI=4.
C    MEAN ORDER RATE (UNITS PER WEEK)
         MOR=0.
C    STANDARD DEVIATION
         SD=100.
C    LOWER AND UPPER LIMITS OF ONE AXIS
         A=2500.
         B=5000.
C    LOWER AND UPPER LIMITS OF SECOND AXIS
         C=750.
         D=2100.
C
C    INITIALIZATION SECTION

C
         INVD(J)=ORDRI*NWID
         INV(J)=INVD(J)
         ORDR(JK)=ORDRI
         UORD(J)=DFO*ORDR(JK)
         ORDS(J)=ORDRI
         PORDS(J)=ORDRI
         SHPR(J)=ORDRI
         SHPS(J)=ORDRI
C
C    MODEL EQUATIONS
C
C BEGIN LOOPING AND RECEIVE INCREMENTED SUBSCRIPT VALUES FOR EACH  TIME PERIOD
1        CALL DYNGO (J,K,L,JK,KL)
C
```

Figure 10-4.

Source: R. L. Nolan, DYNFOR: A General Business and Economic Systems Simu-lator, TR #5, Graduate School of Business Administration, University of Washington, Seattle, 1970, pp. 30–31. Courtesy of the Graduate School of Business Administration, University of Washington.

```
C              LEVELS
C
C  ACTUAL INVENTORY IS A FUNCTION OF PREVIOUS ACTUAL INVENTORY AND THE RATE OF
C  CHANGE BETWEEN THE PREVIOUS AND CURRENT PERIOD (SHIPMENTS RECEIVED-SHIPMENTS
C  SENT)
       INV(K)=FN1(INV(J),SHPR(JK),-SHPS(JK))
C  UNFILLED ORDERS ARE CALCULATED IN A SIMILAR MANNER
       UORD(K)=FN1(UORD(J),ORDR(JK),-SHPS(JK))
C  ORDERS SMOOTHED IS A SMOOTHED AVERAGE OF THE WEEKLY ORDER RATE OVER
C  THE LAST DSO WEEKS
       ORDS(K)=FN3(ORDS(J),DSO,ORDR(JK),-ORDS(J))
C
C              AUXILIARY
C
C  DESIRED INVENTORY IS A FUNCTION OF AVERAGE ORDERS RECEIVED
       INVD(K)=FN12(NWID,ORDS(K))
C
C              RATES
C
C  SHIPMENTS SENT IS THE SMALLER OF SHIPMENTS NEEDED TO FILL PROCESSED
C  ORDERS AND THE AMOUNT OF INVENTORY ON HAND
       SHPS(KL)=XMIN(UORD(K)/DFO, INV(K)/DT)
C  PURCHASE ORDERS SENT IS DETERMINED BY ORDERS RECEIVED IN THE PREVIOUS
C  PERIOD AND THE AMOUNT OF INVENTORY ADJUSTMENT NEEDED (DESIRED--ACTUAL)
       PORDS(KL)=FN40(ORDR(JK),DAI,INVD(K),-INV(K))
C  SHIPMENTS RECEIVED IS A DELAYED FUNCTION OF PURCHASE ORDERS SENT
       SHPR(KL)=DELAY3(PORDS(JK),DIT)
C  ORDERS RECEIVED IS THE INPUT WHICH DRIVES THE MODEL.  AN INITIAL,
C  CONSTANT ORDER RATE IS ASSUMED TO CHECK FOR A STEADY STATE.  THEN A
C  NORMALLY DISTRIBUTED ORDER RATE WITH MEAN XMOR AND STANDARD DEVIATION
C  SD IS INTRODUCED AT TIME=4.  AT TIME=20., A STEP INCREASE OF 500
C  UNITS PER WEEK IS INTRODUCED.
       ORDR(KL)=FN8(ORDRI,STEP(XNORM(1.,MOR,SD),4.),STEP(500.,20.))
C
C              OUTPUT
C  PRT8 PRINTS OUT ALL VALUES FOR THE 8 VARIABLES GIVEN
       CALL PRT8 ( INV(K), INVD(K),UORD(K),ORDR(KL),SHPS(KL),PORDS(KL),
      X SHPR(KL),ORDS(KL))
C  THE SAME VARIABLES ARE PLOTTED BY GIVING THE QUANTITY NAMES (NO TIME
C  SUBSCRIPT) FOLLOWED BY THE LOWER AND UPPER LIMITS IN THE RANGE OF EACH
C  VARIABLE, EITHER A AND B OR C AND D
       CALL PLT8 ( INV,A,B, INVD,A,B,UORD,C,D,ORDR,C,D,SHPS,C,D,PORDS,C,D
      X SHPR,C,D,ORDS,C,D)
C  END OF LOOP
C
       CALL DYNEND (&1)
       END
```

Figure 10-4. Continued

zation terms, such as multilevel inventory systems, industry structure, capacity growth, etc. A recent set of four articles in *Management Science* shed more heat than light on the usefulness of industrial dynamics [6, 7, 8, 9]. Unfortunately, those who wait to try the approach until enough evidence of successful applications is available may find they are far behind the field.

III. SIMULATION AND OPTIMIZATION MODELS FOR INTEGRATED PRODUCTION SYSTEMS

In Sec. D.I and D.II we examined linear programming and a special simulation approach, industrial dynamics, for integrated production systems. Unfortunately, we cannot endorse either of these approaches as a general

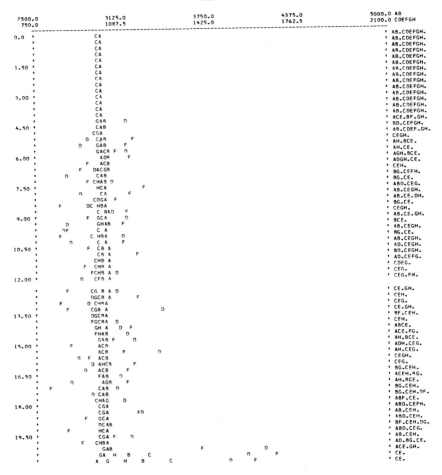

Figure 10-5.

Source: R. L. Nolan, DYNFOR: A General Business and Economic Systems Simulator, *TR #5, Graduate School of Business Administration, University of Washington, Seattle, 1970, pp. 26–27. Courtesy of the Graduate School of Business Administration, University of Washington.*

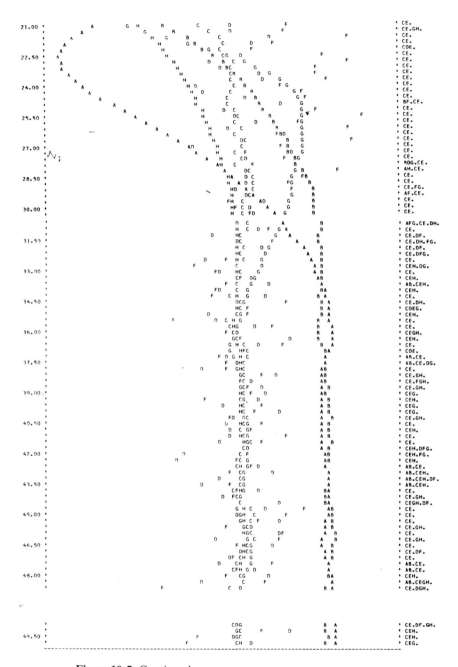

Figure 10-5. Continued

panacea to all integrated systems. Some systems simply cannot be meaning-fully linearized within present ranges of compatibility. Sears [10] pointed out this problem in refineries as follows:

> *In principle there would, of course, be no difficulty in building bigger and better (linear) models to include all the refineries operated by a single corporate entity, or to study the whole of the industry's operations in (say) the United States. But to do so in the same amount of detail as that required for a two- to three-refinery model would be completely impractical; the major oil companies operating worldwide, for example, are individually concerned with between twenty and fifty existing or projected refineries, and there are approximately three hundred refineries in the United States alone.*
>
> *Models for corporate planning purposes must necessarily, therefore, be "broader brush" than those used for refinery programming. Inevitably this entails the deliberate suppression of flexibility, consideration of only the major products, aggregation of individual crude oils into crude oil types, etc. Condensation of the model in this way without seriously impairing its relevance and utility requires a great deal of experience both of the company's operations and of the significance of the results of exploratory runs during the evolution of the model. It should be remarked also that whereas individual refinery models have for the most part been developed within the manufacturing part of the organization, the corresponding corporate models have frequently been prepared by an independent group within the central planning function. It is hardly surprising that this has engendered cross-criticism of the respective approaches.*

Simulation of large systems soon reaches the point where the number of variables makes it very difficult to provide answers to problems without immense quantities of computer time. Most large-scale systems have failed for some of the following reasons:

1. The complexity of the simulation model and of the required programming effort is exceedingly difficult to manage. Errors and costs grow beyond reasonable levels.

2. The analyst may fail to ask whether the simulation will be able to answer the relevant questions even if it can be completed. Very seldom is an experimental design established before the model. Experimental scientists have long realized that design of the model should be preceded by the design of the experiment. The treatment of the many variables in simulation models should be specified before simulation to be sure that the question can be answered.

3. Adequate experimental designs for complex simulation models require large numbers of hours of expensive computer time. This is true because an experimental design for optimization requires varying many parameters and observing enough results for statis-

tical analysis. The number of combinations of parameter values that must be tested to find optimality can become intractable even with truncated experimental designs.

An alternative for analysis is to first explore the problem with an optimization approach, such as linear programming, at an aggregate level. Experience with the aggregate model can help define what questions can best be answered by simulation, as well as what questions can be answered only by optimization after additional detailed information is obtained by simulation. The rationale for this strategy is that most questions that the analyst is trying to solve are at least partial optimizations, but it is difficult to answer anything more than feasibility questions with simulation unless an adequate experimental design is conceived and carried out. Formulation of problems for an optimization technique focuses the analyst's attention on solving the problem rather than merely on modeling it.

This approach uses both simulation and optimization methodologies in a complementary manner rather than performing an analysis with an extremely large model of either the simulation or optimization type. The optimization model gives final policy guidance on questions of resources or schedules, while the simulation model furnishes operational data such as productivities and tests the schedules in a more detailed environment. For a description of this relationship, see Fig. 10-6. Figure 10-7, which is described in later pages, is an example of this relationship for three particular models.

Example 10-1: Recursive Use of Optimization and Simulations in a Large-Scale Transportation Problem

An example of this procedure for analysis has been the modeling for the

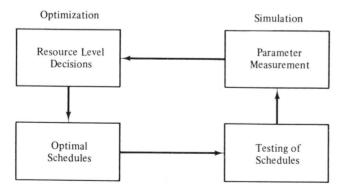

Figure 10-6. Complementary relationship of optimization and simulation models.

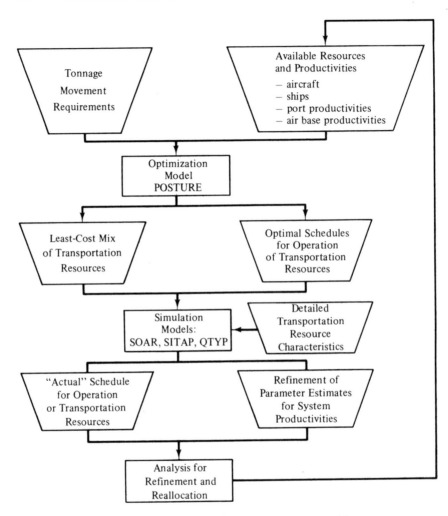

Figure 10-7.   Approach to military transportation problem.

strategic mobility or transportation problem described in considerable detail at the end of Chap. 1. In this case a linear programming model, POSTURE, is used in a recursive fashion with several simulation models, SITAP, SOAR, and QTYP. We shall briefly describe each model and their interrelationships [11].

POSTURE is a linear programming matrix generator for relating the various airlift, sealift, and prepositioning alternatives to movement requirements. The matrix is solved with a linear programming algorithm. POSTURE has the following features:

1. It generates time-phased requirements (5-day periods) for troops, tons of equipment, and supplies by theater.

2. It generates constraints for readiness of U.S. forces and availability of supplies at worldwide locations.

3. It generates a large number of mobility resource alternatives: airlift (C-5A, C-141, CRAF), sealift [merchant marine ships, national defense reserve fleet (NDRF) ships, MSTS-controlled ships, forward floating depot (FFD)], and prepositioned equipment and supplies expressed in tons per time period delivered on each route.

4. It generates constraints on cargo throughput processing at nodes depending on node resources deployed or specified limits.

5. It generates movement requirements for mobility support resources at seaports, aerial ports, and in-theater routes.

The POSTURE matrix can be solved for the optimal numbers and types of aircraft and ships and levels and location of prepositioning given the number of troops and tons to be moved and the costs and availabilities of alternative ways to move tons per time period. The linear programming solution also produces an optimal schedule for allocation of resources such as aircraft to a given set of delivery requirements in several theaters. However, POSTURE aggregates a number of system variables such as individual seaports in a theater. This makes it difficult to determine the effects of queuing at nodes and indirect routes between sources and destinations. POSTURE also has the usual linear programming of difficulties with discrete entities and has omniscient information requirements. Fractions of ships can become large and important. The information requirement becomes crucial because in reality the complete schedule of deployment is often not known in advance, but the model must be given the information and can optimize with it while actual schedule makers would be denied this opportunity.

Two simulation models, SOAR and SITAP, were developed to be used in conjunction with POSTURE to generate system parameters and to more operationally test the "optimality" of the POSTURE movement schedule in ways not possible with POSTURE. For example, the reduction of productivity of ships because of queues in ports can be estimated with the simulation models and the revised productivities can be placed in the optimization model. The revised optimal schedule is then tested by simulation to see if comparable queuing occurs.

SOAR is a model of the strategic airlift system designed to simulate deployments of up to 90 days and to estimate

1. Airlift productivity by aircraft type.

2. Airlift utilization rates (flying hours per day).

3. Air base throughput capacities in aircraft departures per day.

Through repeated applications of SOAR, marginal productivities or airlifts as a function of the node resource levels are measured. The information obtained from SOAR is used to revise POSTURE resource productivities and constraints.

SITAP is a model of the military transportation system designed for detailed analysis of nodes. SITAP has the following features:

1. Movement requirements can be generated by a predetermined schedule or by an inventory reorder policy.
2. Cargo attributes include vehicle type (capacities and limitations) and cargo-handling rates at nodes.
3. Cargo-handling systems at nodes can operate serially or in parallel.
4. Simple rules approximating scheduling behavior are used for routing vehicles.

SITAP provides information concerning the detailed operation of nodes during a deployment. It is used to determine the productivity of node resources and whether the right types and numbers have been deployed. In addition, SITAP is used to operationally test the optimal POSTURE movement schedule in a more realistic representation of discrete vehicles, queuing, and convoying.

Figure 10-7 is a summary flow chart showing the recursive use of POSTURE and SOAR/SITAP to determine the least-cost set of resources required to meet deployment objectives. First, POSTURE provides the optimal schedule for operating the resources. Then POSTURE results are used to provide input to the simulation models. The first recursion used SOAR. SOAR accepted the set of resources from POSTURE and generated airlift system parameters that contributed to aircraft productivity. The aircraft productivity function was determined by analyzing environmental constraints such as weather, congestion, and resource constraints at air bases such as fueling, maintenance, and flight crews. The resulting productivity parameters for the aircraft were used to revise POSTURE data. Again, a least-cost set of resources was determined along with an optimal schedule. The airlift resources were then input to SOAR to operationally test the POSTURE "optimal" schedule. Operationally testing the schedule led to further constraints for POSTURE and revised productivities.

This recursive analysis is also shown using POSTURE and SITAP. SITAP is used to expand the analysis to include mobility support resources at nodes. Productivities and constraints from SITAP are input to POSTURE. Then SITAP is used to test capabilities assumed in POSTURE with additional details, such as convoying.

In summary, the analysis evolves by including more and more components in the transportation system. An optimization framework is used to determine "optimal" movement schedules. A simulation framework is used to generate system parameters and operationally test "optimal" schedules, which, in turn, generate more realistic constraints. The process is recursive suboptimization evolving toward greater overall system optimization. It is not necessary for one model containing all the detail of the system to be asked the most involved questions with massive experimental designs.

Currently, computer speed and capacity limit the three models described above to a batch mode of solution with fairly long turnaround because of their size. A large step toward an on-line management information and decision system for this problem was taken by the preparation of a fourth model, called QTYP. QTYP is operated on line from a terminal and can answer many deployment capability questions in seconds or minutes.

QTYP uses the same level of aggregation and data base as POSTURE, the linear programming optimization model. It therefore represents the detailed simulation models SOAR and SITAP as they are reflected in POSTURE, but its method of solution is a straightforward calculation by a priority rule with the human decision maker establishing only which route or set of routes will be used to fulfill each theater's demands. Having observed many optimal schedules generated by POSTURE and using common sense, the decision maker and QTYP can often perform quite well compared to POSTURE. Thus we have the convenience of a quick response model without losing much quality in the solution. POSTURE is used to check the better QTYP results when time permits.

QTYP solutions can also be used to screen out bad combinations of variables and therefore reduce the size of experimental designs for the other models.

Example 10-2: A Programming and Simulation Model for Aggregate Production Planning

Another model using some of the iterative nature of the model described above for integrated production planning and transportation has been described by Chambers et al. of Corning Glass [12]. The model minimizes the total cost, shown in Table 10-12, of inventory holding and shortages, hiring and layoffs, start-up and shutdown, as well as production and transportation costs at four plants for a range of 10 products.

A mathematical programming model, as shown in Table 10-13, is used to generate a large number of close to "optimal" production plans, which are then sent to a detailed simulation model with the detailed cost structure shown in Fig. 10-8. The lower-cost plans are sent to a transportation linear programming model to have a shipping plan generated. Then the various solutions and costs are presented to management, who may select one or suggest revi-

Table 10-12   Mathematical Model of the Objective Function

I_{hij} = beginning inventory of size h in plant j in period i

X_{hijk} = demand of size h by customer k allocated to plant j in period i

X^*_{hijk} = amount of size h that is *shipped* in period i from plant j to customer k

U_{hijk} = shipping equalization cost function for size h from plant j to customer k in period i

L_{ij} = number of lines required to produce $\sum P_{hij}$ units in plant j in period i

L_{hij} = number of lines required to produce P_{hij} units of size h in plant j in period i

$c_{1hj}(I_{h(i+1)j})$ = inventory-carrying *cost function* for size h per period assignable to plant j in period i

$c_{2h(\text{amount short})}$ = shortage *cost function* for size h per period

$c_{3,g,i,j}(\Delta L_{ij})$ = hiring *cost function* in plant j of skills g in period i

$c_{4,g,i,j}(\nabla L_{ij})$ = laying-off *cost function* in plant j of skills g in period i

P_{hij} = number of units of size h to produce in plant j in period i

$M(P_{hij})$ = manufacturing *cost function* for various production levels of product size h for plant j in period i

$S_1(\Delta L_{ij})$ = 0, when $\Delta L_{ij} = L_{ij} - L_{(i-1)j} \leq 0$; positive value, when $L_{ij} - L_{(i-1)j} > 0$

$S_2(\nabla L_{ij})$ = 0, when $\nabla L_{ij} = L_{(i-1)j} - L_{ij} \leq 0$; positive value, when $L_{(i-1)j} - L_{ij} > 0$

$S_1(\Delta L_{ij})$ = cost involved in starting a line in plant j in period i; this does not include the hiring cost

$S_2(\nabla L_{ij})$ = cost involved in shutting down a line in plant j in period i, excluding the layoff cost

Where period $i = 1, \ldots, 13$, periods in the planning horizon
plant $j = 1, \ldots, 4$
sizes $h = 1, 2, 3, 4, 5, 6, \ldots, 10$
customer $k = 1, \ldots, 8$

$$
\begin{aligned}
\text{Total cost} = \sum_i \{ &\sum_{h,j,k} c_{1hj}(P_{hij} + I_{hij} - X_{hijk}) && \text{inventory carrying cost} \\
+ &\sum_{h,j,k} c_{2,h}(X_{hijk} - P_{hij} - I_{hij}) && \text{shortage cost} \\
+ &\sum_{g,j} c_{3,g,i,j}(L_{ij} - L_{(i-1)j}) && \text{hiring cost} \\
+ &\sum_{g,j} c_{4,g,i,j}(L_{(i-1)j} - L_{ij}) && \text{layoff cost} \\
+ &\sum_{h,j} M(P_{hij}) && \text{manufacturing cost} \\
+ &\sum_j S_1(L_{ij} - L_{(i-1)j}) && \text{start-up cost} \\
+ &\sum_j S_2(L_{(i-1)j} - L_{ij}) && \text{shutdown cost} \\
+ &\sum_{h,j,k} U_{h,i,j,k} X^*_{h,i,j,k} \} && \text{transportation cost}
\end{aligned}
$$

Table 10-13 Constraints of the Model

Subject to

$$\sum_{hk} [P_{hij} - X_{hijk} + I_{hij}] \leq W_{ij}$$

where W_{ij} = storage capacity of the warehouse in plant j in period i

$$\sum_{h} P_{hij} \leq D_{ij}, \qquad D_{ij} \leq 0$$

where D_{ij} is the maximum capacity of plant j in period i

$$P_{hij} \leq D_{hij}, \qquad D_{hij} \geq 0$$

where D_{hij} is the maximum capacity of plant j to make size h in period i

$$\sum_{h} P_{hij} \geq D_{ij}^*$$

where D_{ij}^* is the minimum level of capacity specified by management at which plant j must operate in period i

$$X_{hijk}^* = \begin{cases} X_{hijk} & \text{if } P_{hij} + I_{hij} \geq X_{hijk} \\ P_{hij} + I_{hij} & \text{if } P_{hij} + I_{hij} < X_{hijk} \end{cases}$$

$$
\begin{aligned}
L_{ij}(\sum_{h} P_{hij}) = 0 \quad & \text{when } \sum_{h} P_{hij} = 0 \\
= 1 \quad & \text{when } 0 < \sum_{h} P_{hij} \leq \sum_{h} P_{hij}^1 \\
= 2 \quad & \text{when } \sum_{h} P_{hij}^1 < \sum_{h} P_{hij} \leq \sum_{h} P_{hij}^2 \\
= 3 \quad & \text{when } \sum_{h} P_{hij}^2 < \sum_{h} P_{hij} \leq \sum_{h} P_{hij}^3 \\
= 4 \quad & \text{when } \sum_{h} P_{hij}^3 < \sum_{h} P_{hij} \leq \sum_{h} P_{hij}^4 \\
= 5 \quad & \text{when } \sum_{h} P_{hij}^4 < \sum_{h} P_{hij} \leq \sum_{h} P_{hij}^5
\end{aligned}
$$

Because of learning curves and the different mix of sizes, $\sum_{h} P_{hij}$ is not a fixed number. It is fixed for a given period and a given configuration.

$$W_{ij}, P_{hij}, X_{hijk}, I_{hij} \geq 0$$

---

sions to be further analyzed. The steps in the procedure are shown in Fig. 10-9.

A FINAL NOTE

In summary we wish to make the following last attempts to guide the reader in his quest for better production management decisions:

1. Information must be reliable and available if analyses for decisions are to be made with a quantitative model. We refer again to Fig. 4-10 and the need to plan for an adequate information system.

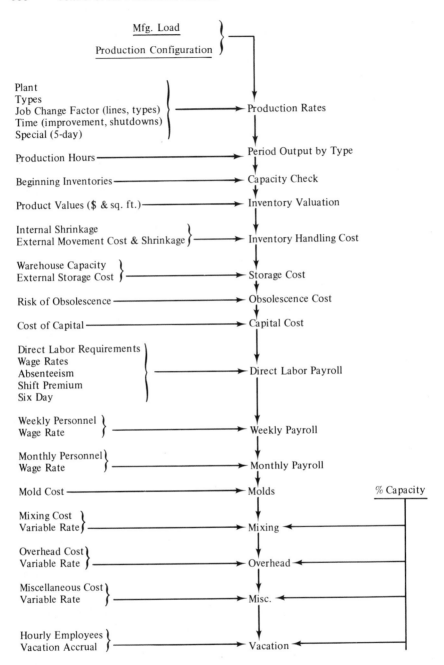

Figure 10-8.   Production allocation model.

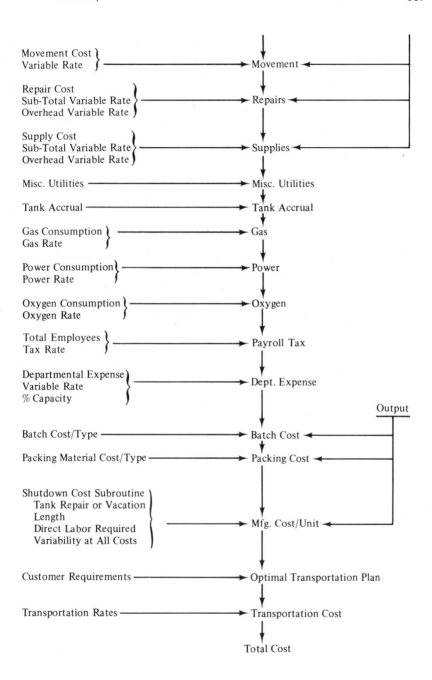

Figure 10-8. Continued

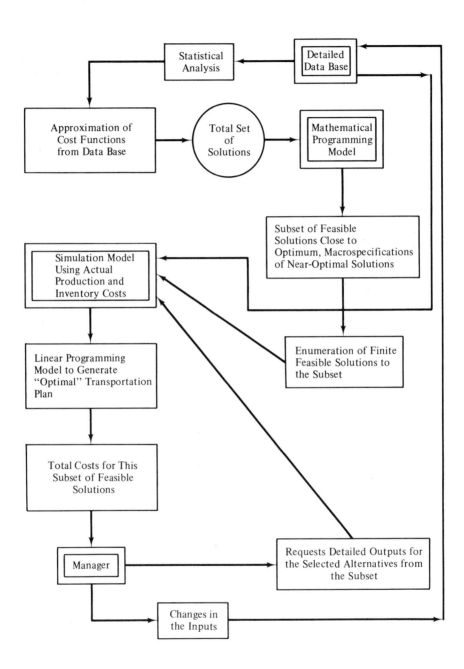

Figure 10-9.   Flow chart of calculation procedure for deriving solutions.

2. Quantitative models can be designed for almost any production process at almost any phase of design, planning, and control. Specialists are available to help in this process, but the manager must be able to evaluate their work. Merely because a model can be built does not mean it will contribute enough to pay for itself. This investment analysis should always be performed.

3. Production decisions are interrelated. We refer again to the Fig. 6-3 and the models of this chapter. Beware of subotimization.

4. The final decisions must be tempered with talented prediction of the behavioral effect on the organization and the individuals within it.

We wish you good luck.

REFERENCES

1. CURTIS H. JONES and ROBERT L. FERGUSON, "An Innovative Approach to Management Information Systems Education," International Conference of TIMS, London, July 1970.

2. G. W. SEARS, "Petroleum," in *Progress in Operations Research*, Vol. II (David B. Hertz and R. T. Eddison, eds.), Wiley, New York, 1964, pp. 269–270.

3. PREM K. MUNJAL, "Use of Mathematical Programming in Sensitivity Analysis of Allocation of Various Crude Oils in Refineries," Joint ORSA-TIMS Meeting, San Francisco, May 1, 1968.

4. JAY W. FORRESTER, *Industrial Dynamics*, M.I.T. Press, Cambridge, Mass., 1961.

5. RICHARD L. NOLAN, *DYNFOR: A General Business and Economic Systems Simulator*, TR #5, Graduate School of Business Administration, University of Washington, Seattle, 1970.

6. H. IGOR ANSOFF and DENNIS P. SLEVIN, "An Appreciation of Industrial Dynamics," *Management Science*, 14, No. 7 (March 1968), 383.

7. JAY W. FORRESTER, "Industrial Dynamics—After the First Decade," *Management Science*, 14, No. 7 (March 1968), 398.

8. H. IGOR ANSOFF and DENNIS P. SLEVIN, "Comment on Professor Forrester's 'Industrial Dynamics—After the First Decade,'" *Management Science*, 14, No. 9 (May 1968), 600.

9. JAY W. FORRESTER, "Industrial Dynamics—A Reply to Ansoff and Slevin," *Management Science*, 14, No. 9 (May 1968), 601.

10. G. W. SEARS, *op. cit.*, p. 271.

11. RICHARD L. NOLAN and MICHAEL G. SOVEREIGN, "A Recursive Approach to Analysis with Optimization and Simulation with an Application to Transportation Systems," *Management Science*, 18, No. 12 (August 1972), B626.

12. J. C. CHAMBERS, SATINDER K. MULLICK, and BRUCE C. GILBERT, "Strategic Short-Term Planning Models," TIMS Meeting, Mexico City, Aug. 22, 1967.

PROBLEMS

1. Finish the analysis for Pop-Rite, Inc.
   a. Set up the complete aggregate planning model.
   b. Calculate buffer stocks.
   c. Describe the scheduling of flavor mixes in detail.
   d. What other steps are necessary?
2. Apply the information system requirements of Chaps. 4 and 6 to the specification of a real-time simulation control device for the Corning Glass model.
3. The strategic mobility model can be handled by a simple scheduling algorithm of the job-shop type. Formulate decision rules for this schedule.

Part IV

APPENDICES

appendix A

Review of Microeconomics

A. Introduction

The following material will serve as a review of basic microeconomic concepts used in Chap. 2. It is assumed that the student has had a course in the principles of microeconomics and is familiar with simple calculus techniques. A book such as J. M. Henderson and R. E. Quandt, *Microeconomic Theory, A Mathematical Approach*, McGraw Hill, Inc., 1958, is more than adequate as a reference for this material.

For illustration, a one-output, two-input production function $q = f(x_1, x_2)$ is assumed, where q is the quantity of output which results from input quantities x_1 and x_2 of inputs 1 and 2, respectively.

B. Productivities

The average productivity of a factor, x_1, is defined as $AP_1 = q/x_1 = AP_1$, where the amount of factor x_2 is fixed or $q = f(x_1, x_2^0)$, where the superscript indicates that the factor is held constant. In words, AP is the output per unit of an input holding other inputs constant. In economics, a *marginal* measure is also of great usefulness. The marginal productivity with respect to the factor x_1 is

$$\mathrm{MP}_{x1} = \frac{\partial f(x_1, x_2^0)}{\partial x_1} = \frac{\partial q}{\partial x_1} = \mathrm{MP}_1.$$

MP is the change in output per unit of an input, holding other inputs constant.

The economist postulates a law of diminishing marginal productivity which says that beyond a certain level of input of x_1 the MP of x_1 decreases. Graphically, q can be plotted as a function of x_1 with x_2 fixed. In Fig. A-1, $\partial q/\partial x_1$

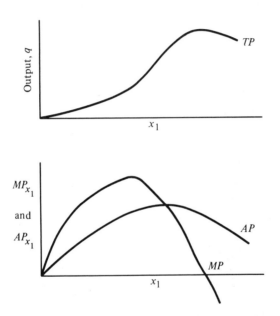

Figure A-1.   Total, average, and marginal productivity.

$=$ MP$_1$ is the slope of the curve and AP is the slope of the tangent to the curve from the origin. Prove to yourself that the MP and AP curves should cross at the level of x_1, which gives the highest total productivity. The particular curves hold only for one particular level of fixed x_2. For example, for the production function $q = 24x_1x_2 - 10x_1^2 - 8x_2^2$ with different levels of x_2 the total productivity curve is as shown in Fig. A-2 for two levels of x_2^0. This is a two-dimensional representation of a three-dimensional production surface with the two inputs and output as the three dimensions.

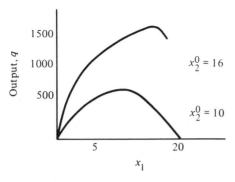

Figure A-2.   Total productivity as a function of the constant input.

C. Complements and Substitutes

If the amount of q always increases when x_2^0 is increased, as shown in Fig. A-2, or $\partial \mathrm{MP}_1/\partial x_2 \geq 0$, then x_1 and x_2 are said to be complementary inputs. The factors are substitutes whenever both MPs with respect to the factors are positive: $\mathrm{MP}_1, \mathrm{MP}_2 > 0$. Factors are often complementary substitutes; thus complementarity and substitution are *not* mutually exclusive terms as in demand theory. To further extend the idea of substitution, economists define the rate of technical substitution (RTS), as

$$\mathrm{RTS} = -\frac{dx_2}{dx_1},$$

where q is held constant. This corresponds to the negative of the slope of the isoquant shown in Fig. 2-1. On an isoquant the change in output is zero by definition. The expression for the total differential is

$$dq = \frac{\partial q}{\partial x_1}dx_1 + \frac{\partial q}{\partial x_2}dx_2,$$

The implicit function rule can be applied:

$$0 = \frac{\partial q}{\partial x_1}dx_1 + \frac{\partial q}{\partial x_2}dx_2$$

or

$$-\frac{dx_1}{dx_2} = \frac{\partial q/dx_2}{\partial q/\partial x_1} = \frac{\mathrm{MP}_2}{\mathrm{MP}_1} = \mathrm{RTS}.$$

The RTS is numerically just the ratio of MPs at the particular level of x_1 and x_2.

D. Elasticity

To further develop the relationship between the factors of production and output, the concept of elasticity must be introduced. Elasticity is often used in demand analysis where price elasticity is defined as the relative or percentage change in quantity sold divided by the relative or percentage change in price. Price elasticity estimates are useful in predicting the change in total revenue when prices are changed. When price elasticity is numerically greater than 1 (elastic), total revenue will increase when price is increased. Total revenue will decrease when price is decreased if the elasticity is numerically less than 1 (inelastic). Similarly, define the *marginal elasticity of a factor i* as

$$E_i = \frac{\% \text{ change in total product}}{\% \text{ change in input}}.$$

Then

$$E_i = \frac{\Delta q/q}{\Delta x_i/x_i} = \frac{\Delta q}{\Delta x_i} \frac{x_i}{q}.$$

If the limit is taken as Δ approaches 0,

$$E_i = \frac{\partial q}{\partial x_i} \frac{x_i}{q} = \frac{\text{MP}_i}{\text{AP}_i}.$$

Both MP_i and AP_i change with x_i. As long as $E_i > 1$, or in other words MP is greater than AP, then the production process is showing increasing average returns to factor x_i.

Stop for the moment and compute the above measures for one of the production functions given above. If $q = 24x_ix_2 - 10x_1^2 - 8x_2^2$, $\text{MP}_1 = \partial q/\partial x_1 = 24x_2 - 20x_1$ and the MP is decreasing over any positive x_1. (It is customary to consider only positive levels of factors and product.) $\partial \text{MP}_1/\partial x_2 = 24(\partial \text{MP}_2/\partial x_1)$, and so the factors x_1 and x_2 are always complements. $\text{MP}_2 = \partial q/\partial x_2 = 24x_1 - 16x_2$. The MPs are never both positive, and so the factors are not substitutes. The average productivity of factor x_1 is

$$\text{AP}_1 = \frac{q}{x_1} = 24x_2 - 10x_1 - 8\frac{x_2^2}{x_1}$$

and

$$\text{AP}_2 = \frac{q}{x_2} = 24x_1 - 10\frac{x_1^2}{x_2} - 8x_2.$$

The AP also decreases as the variable factor increases. The elasticity of factor x_1 holding x_2 constant is

$$E_1 = \frac{MP_1}{AP_1} = \frac{(24x_2 - 20x_1)x_1}{24x_1x_2 - 10x_1^2 - 8x_2^2}$$

$$E_2 = \frac{MP_2}{AP_2} = \frac{(24x_1 - 16x_2)x_2}{24x_1x_2 - 10x_1^2 - 8x_2^2}.$$

E. Scale Coefficient

We shall define this relationship as the elasticity of production or scale coefficient.

$$E = \frac{\% \text{ change in total output}}{\% \text{ change in all factors}},$$

where all factor proportions are held constant.

There are increasing returns to scale if $E > 1$, constant returns to scale if $E = 1$, and decreasing returns to scale if $E > 1$.

There is a simple link between marginal elasticities of the factors E_i and the elasticity of production E. The total differential change in q is

$$dq = \frac{\partial q}{\partial x_1}dx_1 + \frac{\partial q}{\partial x_2}dx_2 = \sum \frac{\partial q}{\partial x_i}dx_i \qquad \text{for all } i \text{ factors.}$$

Multiply the denominator and numerator by x_i and factor the constant dx_i/x_i:

$$dq = \sum \frac{\partial q}{\partial x_i} \frac{x_i}{x_i} dx_i = \frac{dx_i}{x_i} \sum \frac{\partial q}{\partial x_i} x_i.$$

Then rearrange and divide by q:

$$\frac{dq}{dx_i} \frac{x_i}{q} = \frac{\sum (\partial q/\partial x_i)x_i}{q} = \sum \frac{MP}{AP} = \sum E_i.$$

However,

$$\frac{dq}{dx_i} \frac{x_i}{q} = \frac{dq/q}{dx_i/x_i} = \frac{\text{relative change in } q}{\text{relative change in } x_i} = E.$$

For the example production function above,

$$E = \sum E_i = \sum \frac{MP_i}{AP_i} = \frac{24x_2x_1 - 20x_1^2}{24x_1x_2 - 10x_1^2 - 8x_2^2} + \frac{24x_1x_2 - 16x_2^2}{24x_1x_2 - 10x_1^2 - 8x_2^2}$$
$$= 2.$$

For this function, increasing the factors proportionally by 1%,

$$q(500, 600) = 1,820,000; \qquad q(505, 606) = 1,856,582$$
$$\Delta q = 36,582, \qquad \text{approximately 2\% increase in output.}$$

In general, E will be a function of x_1 and x_2 rather than a constant. For example, compute E for the simple additive production function $q = a_0 + a_1 x_1 + a_2 x_2$.

F. Homogeneous Production Functions

The class of production functions with constant elasticity of productivity, E, such as our example above, has been of considerable interest to economists. These production functions are called homogeneous of degree E because if all inputs are multiplied by a scale factor t, output is multiplied by t^E, or

$$f(tx_1, tx_2) = t^E f(x_1, x_2)$$

defines a homogeneous function of degree E. Our example is homogeneous of degree 2, as verified by the computation above.

For $E = 1$, the so-called linear homogeneous function, the behavior of MPs is unusual. We take the derivative of the equation above for $E = 1$ with respect to x_1 to find the MP of the linear homogeneous function,

$$\frac{\partial f(tx_1, tx_2)}{\partial x_1} = t \frac{\partial f(x_1, x_2)}{\partial x_1}.$$

By the function of a function rule,

$$t \frac{\partial f(tx_1, tx_2)}{\partial x_1} = t \frac{\partial f(x_1, x_2)}{\partial x_1},$$

or

$$\frac{\partial f(tx_1, tx_2)}{\partial x_1} = \frac{\partial f(x_1, x_2)}{\partial x_1},$$

which says that the MP_{x_1}s do not change with a proportional change of all factor inputs. Since for linear homogeneous functions both E_i and MPs are constant with proportional changes in inputs, it is obvious that APs are constant for proportional changes in inputs since $E_i = MP/AP$. This will help to establish an important connection later on in limitational production function theory.

In the case of a linearly homogeneous production function, $q = x_1 MP_1 + x_2 MP_2$, or output is the sum of the input level times the MP for each input, since MPs are constant for proportional factor increases from zero up to any level of input (or prove by Euler's theorem). This equation can be generalized to any nonhomogeneous production function at a particular point as $q = \sum x_i MP_i$, which follows from the derivation of the scale coefficient.

With one more definition this section can be brought to a close. It will be necessary to examine lines in the factor diagram where MPs of pairs of factors are held in a constant ratio. Any such line is termed an isocline. One set of such lines is known from the discussion of linear homogeneous production functions. All homogeneous production functions have isoclines which are straight lines through the origin because the MPs stay constant for proportional factor increases. See Fig. A-3.

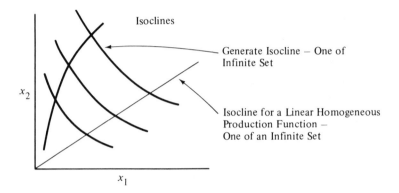

Figure A-3.

G. Proof of the Tangency of Isoquant and Isocost at Optimum

Graphically, the factor diagram shows solution given as Fig. A-4. The isoquant for q^0 is tangent to an isocost line C, which is established by its

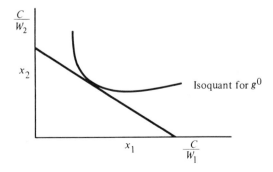

Figure A-4.

intercept $x_1 = c/W_2$, $x_2 = C/W_2$. This is the lowest isocost line which touches q^0. Since the q^0 curve and the isocost line are tangent at the optimum, their slopes are the same. The slope of the isocost is

$$-\frac{x_2 \text{ intercept}}{x_1 \text{ intercept}} = \frac{CW_2}{CW_1} = \frac{W_1}{W_2}.$$

The slope of the isoquant is, by the implicit function rule,

$$0 = \frac{\partial f(x_1, x_2)}{\partial x_1} dx_1 + \frac{\partial f(x_1, x_2)}{\partial x_2} dx_2$$

$$\frac{dx_2}{dx_1} = -\frac{[\partial f(x_1, x_2)]/\partial x_1}{[\partial f(x_1, x_2)]/\partial x_2} = \frac{MP_{x1}}{MP_{x2}}.$$

Again, then, $W_1/W_2 = MP_{x1}/MP_{x2}$ is the shadow or opportunity cost of the restriction $= \partial C/\partial q$, or the amount that C could be reduced if q^0 is reduced by 1 unit. This corresponds to the marginal cost of the last unit.

appendix B

Moving Averages and Exponential Smoothing for Forecasting

In practice the short- to medium-range forecasting problem for individual items is best attacked with the exponential smoothing technique. The moving average is similar but has considerably less desirable computational requirements. The least-squares technique is better suited to long-range forecasting and is computationally inferior for repeated short-term use.

Averaging and smoothing can be used under the basic assumption that sales or other processes are either (1) constant or changing only by occasional discrete jumps with random noise effects disguising the constant level, (2) changing with a linear trend (can be growing negatively) again with noise, or (3) either 1 or 2 with a seasonal or cyclical pattern. The best procedure in the last case is to seasonally adjust the data before attempting to forecast.

The moving average forecast is simply an average of the sales over the last N periods. Each new period's data replace the oldest data in the calculation. The number of periods included in the average governs the forecast's response to changes in the process. A large number of periods is desirable to average out random effects. On the other hand, an average over a large number of periods, N, means that any change in the process cannot be fully realized in the forecast until at least N periods have passed.

Since the average of a random sample is an unbiased estimator of the population mean, the moving average is a "good" forecast mechanism for the case of a constant process with only random noise.

The computation of moving averages requires the storage of all data observed for the last N periods. If storage becomes a problem, each observation can be approximated by the average or forecast at any time. We define the moving average for N periods as

$$M_t = \frac{1}{N} \sum_{i=t}^{t-N+1} x_i = \frac{1}{N}(x_t + x_{t-1} + x_{t-2} + x_{t-N+1}),$$

where only the first and last terms change as new data are received. Observe that we can rewrite this as

$$M_t = M_{t-1} + \frac{x_t - x_{t-N}}{N},$$

and if x_{t-N} is then approximated by M_{t-1},

$$M_t = M_{t-1} + \frac{x_t - M_{t-1}}{N}.$$

For example,

$$x_1 = 3, \quad x_2 = 4, \quad x_3 = 5$$
$$M_t = \tfrac{1}{3}(12) = 4 \qquad \text{for a 3-month moving average.}$$

Now suppose that another piece of data becomes available, $x_5 = 6$:

$$\text{approximate } M_t = 4 + \frac{6-4}{3} = 4 + \frac{2}{3}.$$

The unapproximated moving average would have been

$$M_t = \frac{4+5+6}{3} = 5.$$

The approximate M_t can be written as

$$\frac{1}{N} x_t + \left(1 - \frac{1}{N}\right) M_{t-1}.$$

This leads to the definition of exponential smoothing, a forecasting procedure which is a weighted average of the last observation and the previous forecast, or $S_t = \alpha x_t + (1 - \alpha)S_{t-1}$, where the weights add to 1. The major difference is that no observations are dropped out of the computation. By repeatedly replacing the forecast at time t with the previous forecast, we obtain

$$S_t = \alpha \sum_{k=0}^{t-1} (1 - \alpha)^k x_{t-k} + (1 - \alpha)^t x_0,$$

or S_t is a linear combination of all past observations. The oldest observations have little influence on the forecast because of the high exponential power of the fraction by which they are weighted. The average age of the data, $\bar{k}$, is the sum of all ages times each one's weighting factor, $\beta^k = (1 - \alpha)^k$:

$$\bar{k} = 0\alpha\beta^0 + 1\alpha\beta^1 + \cdots + k\alpha\beta^k + \cdots$$

$$= \alpha \sum k\beta^k = \alpha\frac{\beta}{(1 - \beta)^2} = \frac{\beta}{\alpha},$$

since $\alpha = 1 - \beta$, which will be useful below.

The expected value of S_t is simply the average of the process, and so it is also a "good" forecast in the unbiased sense. The effect of changes in the process can be rapidly reflected in the exponential smoothing method by choosing a high weight (α) for the last observation. A high weighting for the previous forecast (β) promotes stability.

The choice of a value for the smoothing constant α is very difficult, being largely a matter of judgment of past and present changes in the process and observation or simulation. For discussion of such techniques, see Brown [1] or Chow [2].

Example B-1: Constant Process with Noise

Initial estimate $= 10$, $\alpha = .1$, and $S_t = \alpha X_t + \beta S_{t-1}$:

	$t = 0$	$t = 1$	2	3	4
Observation, X_t	—	11	10	11	15
Forecast, S_t	10	10.1	10.09	10.181	10.6629

So far only the process with a constant or occasionally changing parameter has been considered. If a linear trend $x_t = a + bt$ is suspected, the data should be "double-smoothed" by an exponential smoothing (or moving average) of the result from the first smoothing. If the data have a linear trend, as shown in Fig. B-1, the smoothed data will lag behind the observations. The first smoothing will lag by $(\beta/\alpha)b$, because of the age of the data. The second smoothing will again lag by $(\beta/\alpha)b$. From these two smoothing estimates, the coefficient b, using Fig. B-1, can be estimated as follows:

$$\hat{x}_t = S_t + (S_t - S_tS_t) = 2S_t - S_tS_t,$$

where S_tS_t means double-smoothed. Now substituting and solving,

$$\frac{\beta}{\alpha}b = 2S_t - S_tS_t$$

$$\hat{b}_t = \frac{\alpha}{\beta}(S_t - S_tS_t).$$

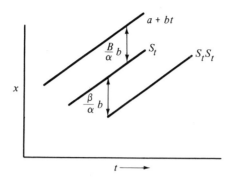

Figure B-1.   Linear trend and single and double smoothing.

Measuring t from the present $a_t = x_t$,

$$a_t = 2S_t - S_tS_t.$$

Example B-2: Linear Trend and Noise

Initial estimate $= 10$, $a = 2S_t - S_tS_t$, $b = (\alpha/\beta)(S_t - S_tS_t)$, and the forecast for T periods ahead $= a_t + b_tT$:

	0	*1*	*2*	*3*	*4*	*5*
X_t	—	11	12	13	13	16
S_t	1	2	3	4	4.9	6.01
S_tS_t	−8	−7	−6	−5	−4.01	−3.008
a	10	11	12	13	13.81	15.028
b	1	1	1	1	.99	1.002
Forecast for $t + 1$	11	12	13	14	14.8	16.03

The only trick in double smoothing is coming up with the initial values for S_t and S_tS_t. Here we assume an initial guess that the process is something like $a + bt$ with $a = 10$ and $b = 1$. Then by solving the following equations for S_t and S_tS_t,

$$a = 2S_t - S_tS_t$$

$$b = \frac{\alpha}{\beta}(S_t - S_tS_t),$$

we obtain the solutions

$$S_t = a - \frac{\beta}{\alpha}b = 1$$

$$S_tS_t = a - 2\frac{\beta}{\alpha}b = -8.$$

Thus double smoothing provides a method for estimating a linear trend without having to store all previous observations, as is required for least-squares estimation of the coefficients. The coefficient estimates obtained by double smoothing also minimize the squared deviations of the observations from the predicted line, as in least squares. The method is also flexible in that the weighting factor can be adjusted.

For data that are likely to contain seasonal fluctuations there are two basic approaches:

1. Use a model which includes periodic fluctuations such as a higher-degree polynomial or a trigonometric function.
2. Adjust the data for seasonal fluctuations before introducing the data into the model and readjust the deseasonalized forecasts for seasonal variation.

Exponential smoothing can be readily extended to triple smoothing for quadratic polynomials: $x_t = a + bt + ct^2$. The use of trigonometric functions requires considerable computation.

A method which eliminates seasonal fluctuations in the data is the use of a 12-month moving average. Another method for seasonally adjusting the data is the method of ratio seasonals. A seasonal ratio F_t is established for each period and the revised forecast RS_t is

$$RS_t = \alpha \frac{S_t}{F_{t-1}} + (1 - \alpha)S_{t-1}.$$

The seasonal factor F_{t-1} can be continually updated by new observations.

appendix C

Duality in
Constrained Optimization

A. Introduction

The solution to constrained optimization problems contains valuable information concerning the effect of the constraint(s) on the achievable value of the objective function. We shall discuss the solution techniques of Lagrangian multipliers, linear programming, nonlinear programming, and the Kuhn-Tucker conditions. For each subject we shall emphasize the interpretation of the effect of the constraints.

B. Lagrangian Techniques

As noted in Chap. 2, if we are given a problem

$$\text{optimize } z = f(x_i), \qquad x = 1, \ldots, m$$
$$\text{subject to } F_j(x_i) = 0, \qquad j = 1, \ldots, n, n \leq m,$$

we can rewrite this as an unconstrained problem in $n + m$ variables where there is one new variable called a Lagrange multiplier for each constraint. We write the Lagrangian function as

$$\text{optimize } L(x_i, \lambda_j) = f(x_i) - \lambda_1 F_1(x_i) - \lambda_2 F_2(x_i) - \cdots - \lambda_m F_m(x_i).$$

Optimizing this function in the usual manner results in an optimal solution to the original problem, as proved below.

Proof for the one-constraint, two-variable case:

$$\max z = f(x_1, x_2)$$
$$\text{subject to } F(x_1, x_2) = 0.$$

Since we must maintain the equality, we must remain on the hyperplane of the constraint; the total differential of the constraint must be equal to zero:

$$dF = \frac{\partial F}{\partial x_1} dx_1 + \frac{\partial F}{\partial x_2} dx_2 = 0$$

or

$$\frac{dF}{dx_1} = \frac{\partial F}{\partial x_1} + \frac{\partial F}{\partial x_2} \frac{dx_2}{dx_1} = 0.$$

We have seen before in Appendix A that we can rearrange this to give the rate of technical substitution if F is a production function:

$$\frac{dx_2}{dx_1} = -\frac{\partial F/\partial x_1}{\partial F/\partial x_2}.$$

At the optimum for z there can be no change in z from a differential change in x_1 or x_2:

$$dz = \frac{\partial f}{\partial x_1} dx_1 + \frac{\partial f}{\partial x_2} dx_2 = 0$$

or

$$\frac{dz}{dx_1} = \frac{\partial f}{\partial x_1} + \frac{\partial f}{\partial x_2} \frac{dx_2}{dx_1} = 0.$$

Substituting for dx_2/dx_1 from above,

$$\frac{\partial f}{\partial x_1} - \frac{\partial f}{\partial x_2} \frac{\partial F/\partial x_1}{\partial F/\partial x_2} = 0,$$

or we can obtain the following equality of ratios, which we shall call λ:

$$\frac{\partial f/\partial x_1}{\partial F/\partial x_1} = \frac{\partial f/\partial x_2}{\partial F/\partial x_2} = \lambda.$$

A final rearrangement would give the optimality conditions:

$$\frac{\partial f}{\partial x_1} - \lambda \frac{\partial F}{\partial x_1} = 0, \qquad \frac{\partial f}{\partial x_2} - \lambda \frac{\partial F}{\partial x_2} = 0,$$

recalling that we have substituted from $F(x_1 x_2) = 0$. Now we note that the following expression has the same optimality conditions:

$$L(x_1, x_2, \lambda) = f(x_1, x_2) - \lambda F(x_1, x_2)$$

$$\frac{\partial L}{\partial x_1} = \frac{\partial f}{\partial x_1} - \lambda \frac{\partial F}{\partial x_1} = 0$$

$$\frac{\partial L}{\partial x_2} = \frac{\partial f}{\partial x_2} - \frac{\partial F}{\partial x_2} = 0$$

and

$$\frac{\partial L}{\partial \lambda} = F(x_1, x_2) = 0.$$

Therefore the Lagrangian technique is equivalent to optimizing with equality constraints.

As shown in the proof above, the constraint F_j is the partial derivative of the Lagrangian function L with respect to the new variable λ_j. At the optimum, the Lagrangian function and the objective-function have the same value. The value of λ_j at the optimum can thus be intrepeted as the change in the objective function with a marginal change in b_j, the constant term of the constraint. In short, we can call λ_j the *cost* or *marginal cost* variable for the jth constraint; we shall also call λ_j a *dual* variable for the jth constraint, as shown in the next section.

As an example of the Lagrangian technique, consider the profit function

$$P(x, y) = x + 4y + xy - x^2 - y^2 + 10,$$

where $x =$ investment (\$000)
$y =$ labor cost (\$000)
$P =$ profit (\$0000).

With no constraints, the optimal values for x and y can be obtained from the simultaneous solution of the first derivatives equated to zero:

$$\frac{\partial P}{\partial x} = 1 + y - 2x = 0$$

$$\frac{\partial P}{\partial x} = 4 + x - 2y = 0.$$

Therefore $x^* = 2$, $y^* = 3$, and $p = 17$, and second-order conditions tell us that this is a maximum. Suppose, however, that there are limits to the finances available. One half of the investement and all the labor cost must come from funds available, s, or

$$\frac{x}{2} + y = s.$$

To solve, set up the Lagrangian $L_p = x + 4y + xy - x^2 - y^2 + 10 -$

$\lambda[(x/2) + y - s]$:

$$\frac{\partial L_P}{\partial x} = 1 + y - 2x - \frac{\lambda}{2} = 0$$

$$\frac{\partial L_P}{\partial y} = 4 + x - 2y - \lambda = 0$$

$$\frac{\partial L_P}{\partial \lambda} = \frac{x}{2} + y - s = 0.$$

These three simultaneous equations can be solved easily by substituting $y = s - (x/2)$ from the third equation back into the first two equations and solving:

$$x = \tfrac{4}{7}s - \tfrac{2}{7}, \quad y = \tfrac{5}{7}s + \tfrac{1}{7}, \quad \lambda = -\tfrac{6}{7}s + \tfrac{24}{7}.$$

This parametric solution depends on the amount of funds available, s. Suppose that $s = 4$; then $\lambda = 0$ and the Lagrangian becomes identical to the profit function, and so

$$x^* = 2, \quad y^* = 3.$$

Graphically, we are on the line $s = (x/2) + y = 4$; see Fig. C-1. If s is less than 4, say 3, then

$$x = \tfrac{12}{7} - \tfrac{2}{7} = \tfrac{10}{7}$$
$$y = \tfrac{15}{7} + \tfrac{1}{7} = \tfrac{16}{7}$$
$$P = 16\tfrac{4}{7}$$
$$\lambda = \tfrac{6}{7},$$

where λ is the marginal cost of a change in the constraint.

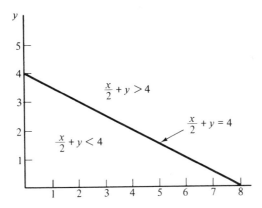

Figure C-1.

If s is greater than 4, say 5, we find that the sign of λ has changed to negative, which is a clue that we should not spend the entire amount of funds available:

$$\lambda = -\tfrac{6}{7}$$
$$x = \tfrac{18}{7}$$
$$y = \tfrac{26}{7}$$
$$P = 16\tfrac{4}{7}.$$

We can see that the constraint should be $(x/2) + y \leq s$ since we are free not to invest the entire amount. This leads us to inequality-constrained problems solved with linear programming and the Kuhn-Tucker conditions.

C. The Dual Problem of Linear Programming

Suppose that we have the following linear programming problem, which we call the primal:

$$\max z = \sum_j c_j x_j, \qquad j = 1, \ldots, m$$
$$\text{subject to } \sum_j a_{ij} x_j \leq b_i, \qquad i = 1, \ldots, n, \ n \leq m.$$

The dual theorem of linear programming asserts that we can write another program called the dual,

$$\min z' = \sum_i b_i y_i, \qquad i = 1, \ldots, n$$
$$\text{subject to } \sum_i a_{ji} y_i \geq c_j, \qquad j = 1, \ldots, m,$$

and that at optimality

$$\min z' = \max z.$$

Moreover, y_i is the dual variable for the ith constraint of the primal and can be interpreted as the cost of the ith constraint. Finally, the roles of the two problems can be reversed; i.e., the x_j are dual variables for the constraints of the minimization problem.

As an example of duality and a quick review of linear programming by the simplex method, take the following problem:

$$\text{maximize profit } z = 6x_1 + 9x_2$$
$$\text{subject to } 2x_1 + 6x_2 \leq 30$$
$$4x_1 + 3x_2 \leq 36$$
$$x_1, x_2 \geq 0,$$

3. Final primal tableau:

c_i					
9	0	1	$\frac{2}{9}$	$-\frac{1}{9}$	$\frac{8}{3}$
6	1	0	$-\frac{1}{6}$	$\frac{1}{3}$	7
$z_j - c_j$	0	0	1	1	66

4. First dual tableau:

c_i	30	36					
	u_1	u_2	u_3	u_4	b_i	θ	
0	2	4	1	0	6	3	(infeasible)
0	6*	3	0	1	9	$\frac{3}{2}$	
$z_j - c_j$	-30	-36	0	0	0		

5. Second dual tableau:

	0	0	3*	1	$-\frac{1}{3}$	3	1
	30	1	$\frac{1}{2}$	0	$\frac{1}{8}$	$\frac{25}{8}$	$\frac{45}{4}$
$z_j - c_j$		0	-21	0	$\frac{15}{4}$	$\frac{375}{2}$	

6. Final dual tableau:

36	0	1	$\frac{1}{3}$	$-\frac{1}{9}$	1
30	1	0	$-\frac{1}{8}$	$\frac{2}{9}$	1
$z_j - c_j$	0	0	7	$\frac{22}{3}$	66

st we note that the solution to the dual problem appears in the $z_j - c_j$ ɪplex multiplier row of the primal problem under the slack variables. ual variables y_1, y_2, and y_3 can be intrepreted as the value of another f resource 1 or 2 since the simplex multiplier is just the change in the ive function from one more unit of the activity, where in this case the y is the *slack* activity, which is an additional unit of the constrained ce. Also, the dual solution contains the primal solution since 7 and $2\frac{2}{3}$ he simplex multiplier row are the solution to the primal. ear programming problems can be approached from either the dual or

Duality in Constrained Optimization

painters and carpenters, who require certain quar
resources, for example, 30 square yards and \$36 per
combination of inputs which will allow us to make a
their services within our two constraints. The problem

$$\text{minimize } z' = 30u_1 + 36u_2$$
$$\text{subject to } 2u_1 + 4u_2 \geq 6$$
$$6u_1 + 3u_2 \geq 9.$$

Here the dual variables u_1 and u_2 can be intrepreted
constrained resources which will just exhaust the profit
optimal inputs as rates.

To solve the primal, you will recall that the simplex
following steps:

1. Introduce slack variables x_3, x_4.
2. Compute $z_j - c_j = \sum_i c_i a_{ij} - c_j, j = 1, \ldots$
   technology matrix coefficient and c_j is the p
3. Select column c with minimum $z_j - c_j$, neg
4. Select row r with minimum $\theta = b_i/a_{ic}$, posit
5. Divide row r by a_{rc}.
6. Add multiples of the new row r to other rov
   other rows of column c.
7. Repeat steps 2–6 until all $z_j - c_j \geq 0$.

Primal solution:

1. First primal tableau:

c_i	6	9				
	x_1	x_2	x_3	x_4	b_i	θ
0	2	6*	1	0	30	5
0	4	3	0	1	36	12
$z_j - c_j$	−6	−9	0	0	0	

2. Second primal tableau:

9	$\frac{1}{3}$	1	$\frac{1}{6}$	0	5	15
0	3*	0	$-\frac{1}{2}$	1	21	7
$z_j - c_j$	−3	0	$\frac{3}{2}$	0	45	

the primal. In Chap. 2 we presented the problem of minimizing cost subject to an output constraint. We also presented maximization of output subject to a cost constraint. If the right-hand side of the cost constraint is equal to the minimum cost from the first problem, the maximum output will be the same as the right-hand side of the output constraint in the second problem.

D. The Lagrangian and the Saddle Point of Nonlinear Programming

A generalization of duality applies to nonlinear programming. We define that a pair of vectors X^*, U^* with nonnegative components is a *saddle point* of a function $G(X, U)$ if

$$G(X, U^*) \leq G(X^*, U^*) \leq G(X^*, U)$$

for all pairs of $X \geq 0$, $U \geq 0$.

As an example, the optimal solution vector to a linear program and the vector of dual variables are the saddle point of the Lagrangian of the linear program. If we take a linear program

$$\max z = \sum_j c_j x_j, \qquad j = 1, \ldots, m$$

$$\text{subject to } \sum_j a_{ij} x_j \leq b_i, \qquad i = 1, \ldots, n,$$

and introduce a slack vector to remove the inequality in both the primal and dual X or U, i.e., a variable x_k or U_k

$$\text{primal: } \max z = \sum_j c_j x_j + x_k$$

$$\text{subject to } \sum_j a_{ij} x_j + x_k \leq b_i, \qquad i = 1, \ldots, n,$$

or

$$\text{dual: } \min z' = \sum_i b_i u_i$$

$$\text{subject to } \sum_i a_{ij} u_i - u_k \geq c_j,$$

we can write the Lagrangian functions

$$L_z = \sum_{j=1}^{k} c_j x_j - \sum_i \lambda_i \left(\sum_{i=1}^{k} a_{ij} x_j - b_i \right)$$

$$L_{z'} = \sum_{i=1}^{k} b_i u_i - \sum_j \lambda_j \left(\sum_{i=1}^{k} a_{ij} u_j - c_j \right).$$

It can be seen that $L_z = -L_{z'}$ since $\lambda_i = U^*$ and $\lambda_j = X^*$, after which the terms all match.

The saddle point obtains its name from the geometric representation. If a saddle point exists for a function $F(X, U)$, then there is a hyperplane which is tangent to the surface of the function at the point $G(X^*, U^*)$ and lies above $F(X, U)$ as U varies or $G(X, U^*)$ is concave in X and $G(X^*, U)$ is convex in U. This concavity and convexity is an additional condition on the saddle point theorem. Graphically, the saddle point lies at the center of a saddle where the horse's back is one surface and the horn and back of the saddle trace the other.

As an example of a saddle point, take our linear programming problem. If we write the Lagrangian of the primal as

$$L_z = 6x_1 + 9x_2 + U_1(2x_1 + 6x_2 - 30) + U_2(3x_1 + 3x_2 - 36),$$

the optimal X^* vector is $(7, \frac{2}{3})$ and the optimal U^* vector is $(1, 1)$. We take any other feasible X vector, say $(6, 3)$, and U vector, $(2, \frac{1}{2})$. If we test the saddle point,

$$L_z(X, U^*) \le L_z(X^*, U^*) \le L_z(X^*, U)$$
$$50 + (0) + (-3) \le 66 \le 66 + 0 + 0$$

or

$$47 \le 66 \le 66.$$

The X and U must be feasible because they both must belong to the function which contains the linear constraints.

The general non-linear programming problem

$$\max z = f(x_i), \qquad i = 1, \ldots, m$$
$$\text{subject to } F_j(x_i) \le 0, \quad x_i \ge 0, \qquad j = 1, \ldots, n, \; m \le n,$$

is just the original problem addressed in Sec. B except that the equality has been replaced by an inequality. Necessary and sufficient conditions for X^* to be a maximum are that we form a Lagrangian function L_z which is a function of X and U, the primal and dual (or Lagrangian λ) variables, and that X^*, U^* are the saddle point of L_z. This requires that we optimize L_z, or

$$\frac{\delta L_z}{\delta x_i} = \frac{\delta f}{\delta x_i} - \sum_j U_j \frac{\delta F_j}{\delta x_i} \le 0 \qquad \text{for all } i, \text{ and if } < \text{ holds, } x_i = 0$$

$$\frac{\delta L_z}{\delta U_j} = F_j(x_i) \le 0 \qquad\qquad \text{for all } j, \text{ and if } < \text{ holds, } U_j = 0.$$

We call these the Kuhn-Tucker necessary conditions. We shall develop these conditions more slowly in the following pages. Then we shall apply the Kuhn-Tucker conditions to our linear programming problem as an example.

E. An Exposition of the Kuhn-Tucker Necessary Conditions for Inequality-Constrained Optimization

The general unconstrained first-order conditions for optimization involve equating derivatives of the objective function to zero. For equality-constrained optimization, additional terms are added to the optimization function to obtain the Lagrangian function, which includes the equality constraints in implicit form. The first-order conditions merely equate partial derivatives to zero again. Inequality constraints, i.e., $(x \leq k)$, cannot be expressed as implicit equations without introducing additional slack variables. The Kuhn-Tucker conditions merely add inequality conditions to the equating of the partial derivates to zero in order to take care of the inequalities in the constraints. *Example*: $\pi = -(x - 2)^2$, where π is profit and x is output, nonnegative. First-order condition (see Fig. C-2):

$$\frac{d\pi}{dx} = f'(x) = 0$$

$$-2(x - 2) = 0$$

$$-2x = -4$$

$$x = 2$$

and we have no boundary problem.

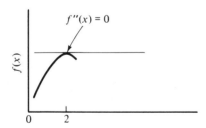

Figure C-2.

Suppose that we change the profit function to $\pi = -(x + 2)^2 + 4$ and x is not to be negative. See Fig. C-3. Then $f'(x) = -2x - 4 = 0$ or $x = -2$, which does not have meaning as an output, and so we would want to produce at the zero level. Therefore the condition for profit maximization really is

$$f'(x) \leq 0, \quad \text{if } < \text{ is true } [f'(x) \text{ negative}], \text{ then } x = 0.$$

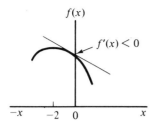

Figure C-3.

However, this condition is not complete. Suppose that a restriction other than nonnegativity is introduced, say $x \leq 1$ for the problem

$$\max \pi = -(x - 2)^2 + 4$$

$$\text{subject to } x \leq 1.$$

The optimality condition above gives

$$-2x + 4 \leq 0$$

or $x \leq 2$, which adds nothing to the problem of finding the solution since $x \leq 1$. Using the Lagrangian technique, $L = -(x - 2)^2 + 4 - \lambda(x - 1)$:

$$\frac{2L}{2x} = -2x + 4 - \lambda = 0, \quad \text{in general, } f'(x) - \lambda \frac{\partial g(x)}{\partial x} = 0 \quad \text{(C-1)}$$

$$\frac{2L}{2\lambda} = -x + 1 = 0. \quad \text{(C-2)}$$

Substituting from (C-2) into (C-1), $-2 + 4 - \lambda = 0$ or $\lambda = +2$. Positive values mean that the constraint has a cost, similar to nonzero cost of a dual variable in linear programming. The constraint $x \leq 1$ has a cost since the constraint prevents a solution $x = 2$, which is the unconstrained maximization value. Note that the sign conventions in the Lagrangian must be followed for the sign to be properly interpreted.

In summary, the *K-T* conditions for one-variable maximization

$$\max \pi = f(x)$$

$$\text{subject to } g(x) \leq 0$$

are

$$f'(x) - \lambda \frac{\partial g(x)}{\partial x} \leq 0; \quad \text{if} < \text{holds, } x = 0$$

$$g(x) \leq 0; \quad \text{if} < \text{holds, } \lambda = 0,$$

which is the same as $x = 1$ if $\lambda \geq 0$ in the problem above.

For minimization of $C = f(x)$ subject to $g(x) \geq 0$ (see Fig. C-4),

$$f'(x) - \frac{\partial g(x)}{\partial x} \geq 0; \qquad \text{if} > \text{holds}, x = 0$$

$$g(x) \geq 0; \qquad \text{if} > \text{holds}, \lambda = 0.$$

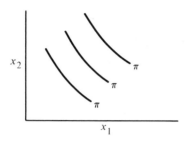

Figure C-4.

For the two-variable case (see Fig. C-5),

$$\max \pi = f(x_1, x_2)$$
$$\text{subject to } g_1(x_1, x_2) \leq 0$$
$$g_2(x_1, x_2) \leq 0$$
$$x_1, x_2 \geq 0,$$

the $K\text{-}T$ conditions are that there must be nonnegative λ_1 and λ_2 such that at the maximum (x_1^0, x_2^0)

$$\frac{\partial f}{\partial x_1} - \lambda_1 \frac{\partial g_1}{\partial x_1} - \lambda_2 \frac{\partial g_2}{\partial x_1} \leq 0; \qquad \text{if} < \text{holds}, x_1 = 0$$

$$\frac{\partial f}{\partial x_2} - \lambda_1 \frac{\partial g_1}{\partial x_2} - \lambda_2 \frac{\partial g_2}{\partial x_2} \leq 0; \qquad \text{if} < \text{holds}, x_2 = 0,$$

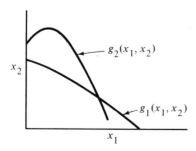

Figure C-5.

where $\partial f/\partial x_1$ is the marginal profitability of activity i, $\lambda[\partial g(x)/\partial x]$ is the imputed cost of the jth constraint, and

$$g_1(x_1^0, x_2^0) \leq 0; \qquad \text{if} < \text{holds,} \ \lambda_1 = 0$$
$$g_2(x_1^0, x_2^0) \leq 0; \qquad \text{if} < \text{holds,} \ \lambda_2 = 0.$$

Similar conditions hold for minimization except for reversal of the inequalities. Also, the conditions establish a global maximum only for concave f and g_i and a global minimum only for convex f and g_i.

F. An Example

Since the linear program discussed above is just a special case of nonlinear programming, we should be able to address it through the Kuhn-Tucker conditions. First we write the Lagrangian $L_z = 6x_1 + 9x_2 - U_1(x_1 + 6x_2 - 30) - U_2(4x_1 + 3x_2 - 36)$:

$$\frac{\partial L}{\partial x_1} = 6 - 2U_1 - 4U_2 \leq 0; \qquad \text{if} < \text{holds,} \ x_1 = 0 \qquad \text{(C-3)}$$

$$\frac{\partial L}{\partial x_2} = 9 - 6U_1 - 3U_2 \leq 0; \qquad \text{if} < \text{holds,} \ x_2 = 0 \qquad \text{(C-4)}$$

$$\frac{\partial L}{\partial U_1} = 2x_1 + 6x_2 \leq 30; \qquad \text{if} < \text{holds,} \ U_1 = 0 \qquad \text{(C-5)}$$

$$\frac{\partial L}{\partial U_2} = 4x_1 + 3x_2 \leq 36; \qquad \text{if} < \text{holds,} \ U_2' = 0. \qquad \text{(C-6)}$$

1. Assume that equality holds in (C-5) and (C-6) and solve $x_1 = \frac{8}{3}$, $x_2 = 7$.
2. Since $x_i = 0$, solve (C-3) and (C-4) as equalities $U_1 = 1 = U_2$, which is our solution—but we need to verify the assumption in 1.
3. Assume inequality in (C-5). Then $U_1 = 0$, and from (C-3) $6 - 4U_2 \leq 0$ if $<$, $x_1 = 0$, or $U_2 = \frac{3}{2}$ unless $x_1 = 0$, in which case U_2 is larger. Also, from (C-4), $9 - 3U_2 \leq 0$ if $<$, $x_2 = 0$, or $U_2 = 3$ unless $x_2 = 0$, in which case U_1 is larger. Since $U_2 = 3$ from (C-4), $x_1 = 0$ from (C-3). If $x_1 = 0$ from (C-5), $x_2 < 5$. If $x_2 < 5$ and $x_1 = 0$, (C-6) becomes an inequality and so $U_2 = 0$, but we have shown that $U_2 \geq 3$.
4. Assume inequality in (C-6). Then $U_2 = 0$, and from (C-3) $U_1 = 3$ unless $x_1 = 0$, in which case $U_1 > 3$. From (C-4) $U_1 = \frac{3}{2}$ unless $x_2 = 0$, in which case greater. Therefore x_2 must equal zero, but then $x_1 < 9$ from (C-6). If so, (C-5) will be an inequality since $2 \times 9 < 30$, and so $U_1 = 0$, but this contradicts $U_1 \geq \frac{3}{2}$.

5. Since neither (C-5) or (C-6) can be an inequality, both are equalities, as originally assumed.

Unfortunately, it is not always possible to eliminate all cases by use of the conditions because of possible nonlinear conditions and the large number of cases. Therefore the Kuhn-Tucker conditions do not provide a computational method for all problems.

References for this material are Baumol [3] and Hadley [4].

appendix D

Revised Simplex Method

A linear program is usually set up as

$$\max cx = c_1 x_1 + c_2 x_2 + \cdots + c_n x_n$$

$$\text{subject to} \quad a_{11}x_1 + a_{12}x_2 + \cdots + a_{1n}x_n = d_1$$

$$a_{21}x_{11} + a_{22}x_2 + \cdots + a_{2n}x_n = d_2 \qquad \text{or } Ax = d$$

$$a_{m1}x + a_{m2}x_2 + \cdots + a_{mn}x_n = d_n.$$

Any column a_j of A can be written as a linear combination of a set of other a_1, which form a basis B of columns of A:

$$a_j = y_1 a_1 + y_2 a_2 + \cdots = By \quad \text{or} \quad y = B^{-1}a_j.$$

For the basis, $Bx_B = d$, and so $x_B = B^{-1}d$ is a solution to the problem. If c_B is a vector of profit coefficients of the basic vectors, we define

$$z = c_B x_B.$$

We are trying to find vectors to fit into B to maximize z. The revised simplex method calculates the change in z from a new vector without calculating y. The contribution is $z_j - c_j = c_B B^{-1} a_j - c_j$. Instead of $z = \sum_i c_i x_i$, write $z - c_1 x_1 - c_2 x_2 - \cdots = 0$ as a first row of the revised simplex tableau. Then we have

$$\begin{vmatrix} 1 & -c \\ 0 & A \end{vmatrix} \begin{vmatrix} z \\ X \end{vmatrix} = \begin{vmatrix} 0 \\ d \end{vmatrix}$$

instead of $Ax = d$. A basis is now

$$\begin{vmatrix} 1 & -c_B \\ 0 & B \end{vmatrix},$$

which we denote as $\bar{B}$:

$$\bar{B}^{-1} = \begin{vmatrix} 1 & c_B B^{-1} \\ 0 & B^{-1} \end{vmatrix},$$

Therefore, instead of $y = B^{-1}a_j$, we have

$$\begin{vmatrix} c \\ y \end{vmatrix} = \begin{vmatrix} 1 & c_B B^{-1} \\ 0 & B^{-1} \end{vmatrix} \begin{vmatrix} -c \\ a_j \end{vmatrix} = \begin{vmatrix} -c + c_B B^{-1} a_j \\ B^{-1} a_j \end{vmatrix} = \begin{vmatrix} z_j - c_j \\ c \\ y \end{vmatrix}.$$

Therefore the elements of the top row of the revised simplex tableau are the evaluators which when multiplied times the new column give the contribution $z_j - c_j$ of the new column.

A reference for this material is Hadley [5].

appendix E

Introduction to Queuing

A. Introduction

Queuing phenomena occur in several production situations, such as inventory between stages of production lines, messages in information system, and breakdowns waiting for repair. In each case the *arrival* of an element or *unit* of the system finds a *facility* either occupied or empty. It may have to wait in a queue before it is *serviced*. Both the arrivals and the service times have an average rate and a distribution around that mean. Most queuing results are based on a family of distributions containing the negative exponential for service rates and the Poisson for arrival rates because these distributions have the useful property of a single parameter and are often associated with *random* events. In addition, we must be concerned with

1. Size of queue, finite or possibly infinite.
2. Queue discipline; i.e., does each arrival wait its turn—a first-in, first-out (FIFO) system—or are priorities given?
3. The number and arrangement of facilities: single, multiple, parallel, or series.
4. Arrivals may "balk" or not enter the queue if the queue is too long.

5. The system may be in equilibrium or not yet in equilibrium.

Queues can be deterministic; that is, arrival intervals and service times are constant. For example, a worker may come and use a spray gun to paint a large number of units which have accumulated at a fixed rate on an assembly line, which then moves the units to a dryer. The high capacity of the sprayer compared to the dryer makes it possible to have the worker present at the station only a short time, but in most cases, as discussed in Chap. 4, capacities of the deterministic stages would be matched so that no large queues would form. However, if the arrivals and service times are not constant, as is often the case in production systems, the queue is a realization of a stochastic process. Of course, the line between deterministic and stochastic is hard to draw in practice. Because deterministic queues are easy to handle mathematically as flows in networks with accumulation points [6], they should often be tried as a first approximation. The more difficult cases of stochastic processes, such as arrivals of men at a tool crib or breakdowns of equipment, can be handled by the methods we shall demonstrate in the following pages.

We shall start with the Poisson process because it is extremely important in queuing models and because the methodology is followed by most queuing models. Then we shall discuss the single channel queue with Poisson arrivals. Finally, we shall briefly discuss the multichannel queue and constrained queues.

B. Poisson Process

Although the Poisson distribution might be familiar to the reader, it is important in the area of queuing theory to realize which situations are characterized by Poisson processes. Therefore let us look at a process with the following properties:

1. $P_n(t)$, the probability of n items in the system af time t, depends only on the time interval, not on the initial state. In other words, we are looking at a stationary process or a process in its equilibrium.
2. The probability that the event occurs more than once in the time interval Δt is extremely small as Δt becomes small.
3. The probability that the event will occur exactly once in the time interval Δt is proportional to Δt and can be written as $\lambda \, \Delta t$.

We define a random variable n with the following properties, conforming to properties 1–3 above:

1. n remains constant when event E does not occur.

2. n increases by 1 when event E occurs.

3. n is initially zero.

Graphically, a realization of this process might be as shown in Fig. E-1. If n

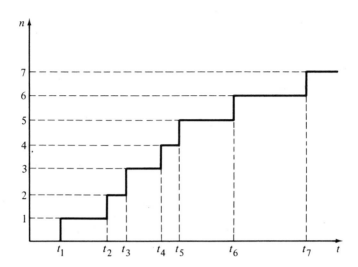

Figure E-1.

items have arrived by time t, we shall now ask what happens during the next small time interval Δt?

$$P_n(t) = \text{probability of } n \text{ items having arrived by time } t.$$

At $t + \Delta t$, for the special case $P_0(t + \Delta t) = P_0(t)(1 - \lambda \Delta t)$ starting with zero and no arrival: In general,

$$P_n(t + \Delta t) = P_n(t)(1 - \lambda \Delta t) + P_{n-1}(t)\lambda \Delta t,$$

where the last term is for $n - 1$ arrivals at t and one arrival at $t + \Delta t$. Rearranging,

$$\frac{P_n(t + \Delta t) - P_n(t)}{\Delta t} = -\lambda P_n(t) + \lambda P_{n-1}(t), \qquad n \geq 1.$$

By definition, as $\Delta t \rightarrow 0$,

$$P'_n(t) = \frac{dP_n(t)}{dt}.$$

Using the definition, we obtain

$$P_0'(t) = -\lambda P_0(t) \tag{E-1}$$

$$P_n'(t) = -\lambda P_n(t) + \lambda P_{n-1}(t). \tag{E-2}$$

We introduce the Laplace transformation or generating function of $P_n(t)$:

$$P(Z, t) = \sum_{n=0}^{\infty} P_n(t)Z^n = P_0(t) + P_1(t)Z + P_2(t)Z^2 + \cdots. \tag{E-3}$$

For example,

$$P(Z, 0) = \sum_{n=0}^{\infty} P_n(0)Z^n = P_i(0)Z^i \qquad \text{for } i = n$$

and

$$P(1, t) = 1.$$

Furthermore,

$$\frac{\partial P(Z, t)}{\partial t} = \frac{\partial}{\partial t} \sum_{n=0}^{\infty} P_n(t)Z^n = \sum_{n=0}^{n} P_n'(t)Z^n$$

$$= \lambda P(Z, t) + \sum_{n=0}^{\infty} \lambda P_{n-1}(t)Z^n$$

$$= -\lambda P(Z, t) + (\lambda P_0(t)Z + \lambda P_1(t)Z^2 + \lambda P_2(t)Z^3 + \cdots)$$

$$= \lambda Z(P_0(t)) + P_1(t)Z \cdots = \text{Eq. (E-3)}.$$

Thus

$$\frac{\partial P(Z, t)}{\partial t} - \lambda(Z - 1)P(Z, t) = 0.$$

Solution:

$$P(Z, t) = Ce^{\lambda(Z-1)t}, \qquad C = 1 \text{ for } n = 0$$

$$P_n(t) = \frac{1}{n!} \frac{\partial^n P(Z, t)}{\partial Z^n}\bigg|_{Z=0}.$$

Thus

$$P_0(t) = \frac{1}{0!}e^{-\lambda t}$$

$$P_1(t) = \frac{1}{1!}\lambda t e^{-\lambda t}$$

$$P_n(t) = \frac{(\lambda t)^n e^{-\lambda t}}{n!} \longrightarrow \text{Poisson process.}$$

Remember that for steady state

$$P_n'(t) = 0 \quad \text{or} \quad \lim_{t \to \infty} P_n(t).$$

For Poisson distributions we can obtain:

$$\text{mean } \bar{n} = \sum_{n=0}^{\infty} nP_n(t) = \lambda t$$

$$\text{variance } \sigma_n^2 = \sum_{n=0}^{\infty} (n - \bar{n})^2 P_n(t) = \lambda t.$$

Finally, we want to study the time intervals between arrivals which follow the Poisson law. Which distribution function governs the interarrival times?

Here, we want to find the probability that if an event occurred at time t, no event will occur within the next time interval—let us call it i—but that the next event occurs in the interval Δi following i:

$$f(i) = P_0(i) = \frac{(\lambda i)^0 e^{-\lambda i}}{0!} = e^{-\lambda i}$$

$$P_0(\lambda i) = e^{-\lambda \Delta i}$$

$$P(1 < x)(\Delta i) = 1 - P_0(\Delta i) = 1 - e^{-\lambda \Delta i}.$$

For $\Delta i \longrightarrow 0$,

$$P'(1 \leq x)(\Delta i) = \frac{1 - e^{-\lambda \Delta i}}{\Delta i} = \lambda$$

$$f(i)\, di = e^{-\lambda i} \lambda \, di = \lambda e^{-\lambda \Delta i},$$

and the density function becomes

$$P_0(i) = \lambda e^{-\lambda i},$$

which is the exponential distribution with

$$\text{mean } \bar{i} = \frac{1}{\lambda}$$

$$\text{variance } \sigma^2 = \frac{1}{\lambda^2}.$$

Hence our conclusion is that the interarrival times of the Poisson process are exponentially distributed.

Let us now assume that $\mu \, \Delta t$ is the probability of completing the service of 1 unit during Δt. The probability of *not* terminating a service is then $1 - \mu \, \Delta t$. If $P(t)$ is the probability that we have not finished service of that unit by time t, we obtain

$$P(t + \Delta t) = (1 - \mu \, \Delta t)P(t)$$

$$\frac{dP(t)}{dt} = \lim_{\Delta t \to 0} \frac{P(t + \Delta t) - P(t)}{\Delta t} = -\mu P(t).$$

The differential equation has the solution

$$P(t) = ce^{-\mu t}$$

with

$$\int_0^\infty ce^{-\mu t} = 1.$$

Hence

$$c = \mu$$

and

$$P(t) = \mu e^{-\mu t}.$$

Thus the service is described by the negative exponential distribution with the density $\mu e^{-\mu t}$.

The equivalence of Poisson arrival rates and exponential interarrival times is important in queuing models.

C. A Single-Channel Model

The simplest case is the infinite-length, FIFO, single-facility queue with Poisson arrivals and negative exponential service times without balking. Chapter 4 uses the following result for this case at equilibrium:

$$P(n) = \rho^n(1 - \rho)$$

for the probability of n elements in the system when arrivals are at rate λ and service times have mean μ and $\rho = \lambda/\mu$. This result can be obtained from the assumptions by examining the possible states, setting up the differential equations for the transitions, and solving for equilibrium values as follows.

The probability $P_n(t + \Delta t)$ that n elements are in the queue at time $t + \Delta t$ can be expressed as the sum of the following four independent compound probabilities:

1. The probability that
   a. n units are in the system at time t, $P_n(t)$.
   b. There is no arrival during time interval Δt, $1 - \lambda \, \Delta t$.
   c. No service is completed during interval Δt, $1 - \mu \, \Delta t$.
2. a. $n + 1$ units in system at t, $P_{n+1}(t)$.
   b. No arrival during Δt, $1 - \lambda \, \Delta t$.
   c. One service completed in Δt, $\mu \, \Delta t$.
3. a. $n - 1$ units in system at t, $P_{n-1}(t)$.
   b. One arrival during Δt, $\lambda \, \Delta t$.
   c. No service during Δt, $1 - \mu \, \Delta t$.

4. a. N units in system at t, $P_n(t)$.
   b. One arrival during Δt, $\lambda \Delta t$.
   c. One service during Δt, $\mu \Delta t$.

This system is described by the sum of following independent possibilities:

1. $P_n(t)[1 - \lambda \Delta t][1 - \mu \Delta t] = P_n(t)[1 - \lambda \Delta t] + k_1(\Delta t)^2$.
2. $P_{n+1}(t)[1 - \lambda \Delta t][\mu \Delta t] = P_{n+1}(t)\mu \Delta t + k_2(\Delta t)^2$.
3. $P_{n-1}(t)[\lambda \Delta t][1 - \lambda \Delta t] = P_{n-1}(t)\lambda \Delta t + k_3(\Delta t)^2$.
4. $P_n(t)[\lambda \Delta t][\mu \Delta t] = k_4(\Delta t)^2$.

$$P_n(t + \Delta t) = P_n(t)[1 - \lambda \Delta t - \mu \Delta t] + P_{n+1}(t)\mu \Delta t$$
$$+ P_{n-1}(t)\lambda \Delta t + \sum_{i=1}^{4} k_i(\Delta t)^2$$

$$\frac{P_n(t + \Delta t) - P_n(t)}{\Delta t} = \lambda P_{n-1}(t)\mu P_{n+1}(t) - (\lambda + \mu)P_n(t)$$
$$+ \sum_{i=1}^{4} k_i(\Delta t).$$

As $\Delta t \longrightarrow 0$,

$$\frac{d}{dt}P_n(t) = \lambda P_{n-1}(t) + \mu P_{n+1}(t) - (\lambda + \mu)P_n(t), \qquad n > 0. \qquad \text{(E-4)}$$

To these equations we have to add conditions for $n = 0$ at $t + \Delta t$. The probability that there is no unit in the system at $t + \Delta t$ is equal to the sum of two independent probabilities:

1. The product of probability that
   a. No unit in system at t, $P_0(t)$.
   b. No arrival during Δt, $1 - \lambda \Delta t$.
2. The product of the probabilities that
   a. One unit in system at t, $P(t)$.
   b. No arrival during Δt, $1 - \lambda \Delta t$.
   c. One service finishes during Δt, $\mu \Delta t$.

$P_0(t + \Delta t)$ is then equal to the sum of the following two expressions:

$$P_0(t)(1 - \lambda \Delta t)$$
$$P_1(t)[1 - \lambda \Delta t][\mu \Delta t] = P_1(t)\mu \Delta t + k(\Delta t)^2$$

for $P_0(t)$,

$$P_0(t + \Delta t) = P_0(t)[1 - \lambda \Delta t] + P_1(t)\mu \Delta t + k(\Delta t)^2$$
$$\frac{P_0(t + \Delta t) - P_0(t)}{\Delta t} = -\lambda P_0(t) + \mu P_1(t) + k(\Delta t).$$

As $\Delta t \to 0$,

$$\frac{d}{dt} P_0(t) = -\lambda P_0(t) + \mu P_1(t). \tag{E-5}$$

D. Steady-State, Permanent, or Stationary Systems

We are mainly interested in the steady-state condition of our system. As we know, the state probabilities in the steady state are independent of time. We obtain these probabilities by differentiating our system equalities with respect to time t. Differentiating (E-1) and (E-2), we get

$$\lambda P_{n-1}(t) + \mu P_{n+1}(t) - (\lambda + \mu)P_n(t) = 0, \qquad n > 0 \tag{E-1a}$$

$$-\lambda P_0(t)\mu P_1(t) = 0. \tag{E-2a}$$

(Remember, $\lambda/\mu < 1$, $\sum_{i=0}^{n} P_i = 1$.) Now, by recurrence,

$$P_0 = P_0$$

$$P_1 = \left(\frac{\lambda}{\mu}\right) P_0$$

$$P_2 = \left(\frac{\lambda}{\mu}\right)^2 P_0$$

$$P_3 = \left(\frac{\lambda}{\mu}\right)^3 P_0$$

$$\vdots$$

$$P_n = \left(\frac{\lambda}{\mu}\right)^n P_0. \tag{E-3a}$$

Since $\sum_{n=0}^{\infty} P_n = 1$, we have

$$P_0 \sum_{n=0}^{\infty} \left(\frac{\lambda}{\mu}\right)^n = 1$$

$$P_0 \frac{1}{1 - (\lambda/\mu)} = 1$$

$$P_0 = 1 - \frac{\lambda}{\mu}.$$

Substituting P_0 into (E-3a),

$$P_n = \left(\frac{\lambda}{\mu}\right)^n \left(1 - \frac{1}{\mu}\right) = \rho^n(1 - \rho)$$

with $\rho = \lambda/\mu$ and $0 < \rho < 1$.

Once we know the probability of n units being in the system as above, we can obtain the average number in the system and the average waiting time in the queue.

The average number in the system is $\bar{q}$:

$$\bar{q} = \sum_{n=0}^{\infty} nP(n) = \sum_{n=0}^{\infty} n\rho^n(1 - \rho)$$
$$= (1 - \rho)[\rho + 2\rho^2 + 3\rho^3 + \cdots]$$
$$= \rho(1 - \rho)[1 + 2\rho + 3\rho^2 + \cdots]$$
$$= \rho(1 - \rho)\frac{d}{d\rho}(\rho + \rho^2 + \rho^3 + \cdots)$$
$$= \rho(1 - \rho)\frac{d}{d\rho}\left(\frac{1}{1 - \rho}\right) \qquad \text{for } \rho < 1$$
$$= \rho(1 - \rho)\frac{1}{(1 - \rho)^2} = \frac{\rho}{1 - \rho}.$$

If $\bar{q}$ is the average number in the system, the average number in the queue, $\bar{w}$, can be obtained from the same process except that we use

$$w = q_0 - 1,$$

and so

$$\bar{w} = \sum_{n=0}^{\infty} (n - 1)P(n)$$
$$= \frac{\rho^2}{1 - \rho} \qquad \text{or note that } \bar{w} + \rho = \bar{q}.$$

The average time in the system, t, can be obtained from the average number in the system. Suppose that $\bar{q}$ is in the system and that on the average arrivals have come at the rate of λ per time period. If 4 units are in the system and units arrive at 4 per hour, then certainly the time to pass through the system must be 1 hour, or

$$\dot{t} = \frac{\bar{q}}{\lambda} = \frac{\rho}{1 - \rho}\frac{1}{\lambda} = \frac{1}{\mu(1 - \rho)}.$$

If the Poisson arrival assumption is maintained but *any* distribution of service times is allowed, the Khintchine-Polloczek formula can be derived for the average number in the queue waiting for service:

$$\bar{w} = \frac{\rho^2}{2(1 - \rho)}\left(1 + \left(\frac{\sigma}{\bar{s}}\right)^2\right),$$

where σ = standard deviation of service time
$\bar{s}$ = mean service time.

Figures E-2 and E-3 give the mean number in the queue and the mean waiting time in the queue for a single-service queue with Poisson arrivals and a variety of service distributions. Note that for exponentially distributed service times, $\sigma = \bar{s}$, and so the formula reduces to

$$\bar{w} = \frac{\rho^2}{1 - \rho},$$

as shown earlier.

Figure E-4 shows the probability that the number of units in the system will exceed various values. This table can be used for design of inventory space, as discussed in Chap. 4.

Figure E-5 shows the standard deviation in waiting time for arrival rates, which are approximately Erlang, as indicated by the ratio of $(\sigma/\bar{s})^2$. See Chap. 9 for the Erlang distribution.

Figure E-6 gives a first estimate of the effect on the variance of the time in the queue of priorities or different rules for selection of the jobs waiting in the queue other than FIFO. If selection is *not* based on service time, the mean times for *all* jobs are not changed, but the time for the high-priority jobs are reduced [7].

Often there are parallel facilities in queuing situations. Although it is often better to design one facility with adequate capacity, Chaps. 2 and 4 noted several reasons why this may not be possible, and we shall find another in this section. It is often impossible to combine several persons into a single high-capacity station, say for tool crib checkout, and so multiple facilities are required. We can model this situation as long as the choice of facility or channel by the units being serviced is made in a reasonable way, such as

1. Random unless some channels are empty.
2. Shortest queue.
3. FIFO to the total system.

E. A Multichannel Model

Suppose that there are M identical facilities with service time at $\bar{s}$ for each and that n is the total arrival rate:

$$\rho = \frac{\lambda}{\mu} = \frac{n\bar{s}}{M}.$$

Each channel acts independently. If we have Poisson arrivals and exponential service times, the probability of n units in the system is

$$P(n) = \frac{(M\rho)^n}{n!} P(0) \quad \text{or} \quad \tilde{N}(n)P(0),$$

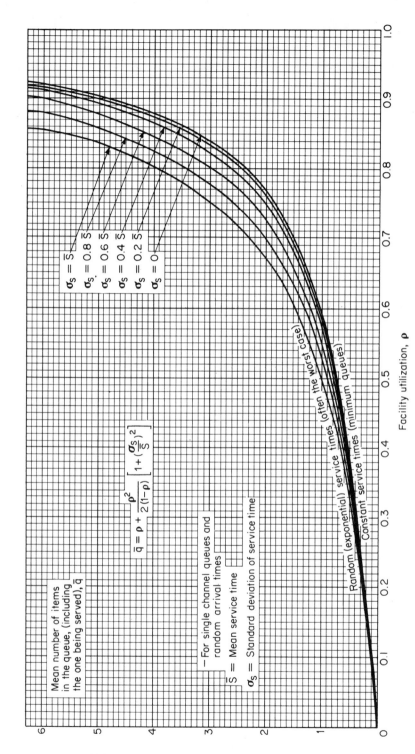

Figure E-2. Queue sizes with single-server queues.

Source: J. Martin, Design of Real-Time Computer Systems, Prentice-Hall, Inc., Englewood Cliffs, N.J., 1967, p. 411. Courtesy of Prentice-Hall, Inc.

The following labels appear within the figure:

Mean number of items in the queue, (including the one being served), $\bar{q}$

$\sigma_S = \bar{S}$
$\sigma_S = 0.8\ \bar{S}$
$\sigma_S = 0.6\ \bar{S}$
$\sigma_S = 0.4\ \bar{S}$
$\sigma_S = 0.2\ \bar{S}$
$\sigma_S = 0$

$$\bar{q} = \rho + \frac{\rho^2}{2(1-\rho)}\left[1+\left(\frac{\sigma_S}{\bar{S}}\right)^2\right]$$

For single channel queues and random arrival times

$\bar{S}$ = Mean service time

σ_S = Standard deviation of service time

Random (exponential) service times (often the worst case)

Constant service times (minimum queues)

Facility utilization, ρ

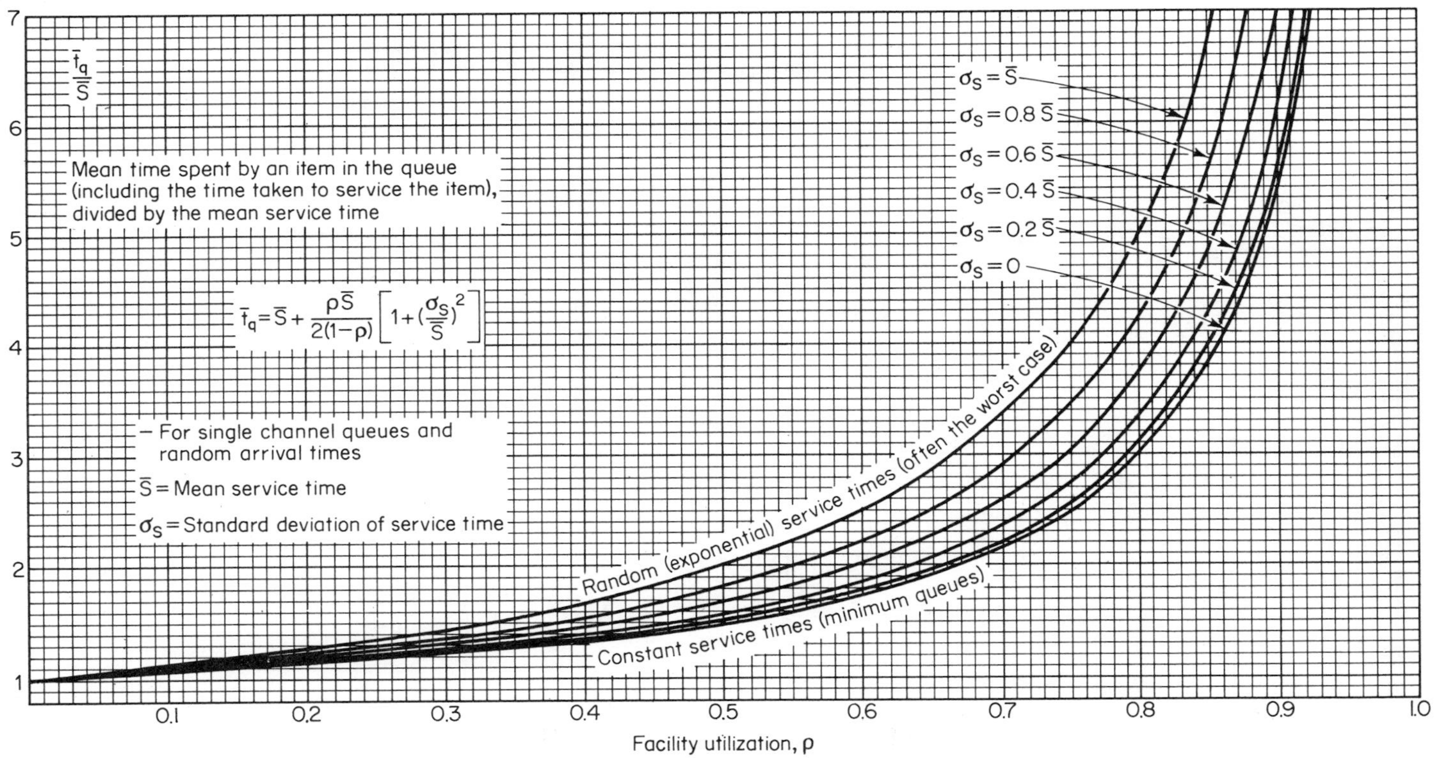
7
6
5
4
3
2
1
$\frac{\bar{t}_q}{\bar{S}}$
Mean time spent by an item in the queue (including the time taken to service the item), divided by the mean service time
$\bar{t}_q = \bar{S} + \frac{\rho \bar{S}}{2(1-\rho)} \left[1 + \left(\frac{\sigma_S}{\bar{S}}\right)^2 \right]$
– For single channel queues and random arrival times
$\bar{S}$ = Mean service time
σ_S = Standard deviation of service time
$\sigma_S = \bar{S}$
$\sigma_S = 0.8\,\bar{S}$
$\sigma_S = 0.6\,\bar{S}$
$\sigma_S = 0.4\,\bar{S}$
$\sigma_S = 0.2\,\bar{S}$
$\sigma_S = 0$
Random (exponential) service times (often the worst case)
Constant service times (minimum queues)
0.1
0.2
0.3
0.4
0.5
0.6
0.7
0.8
0.9
1.0
Facility utilization, ρ

Figure E-3. Queuing times with single-server queues.

Source: J. Martin, Design of Real-Time Computer Systems, *Prentice-Hall, Inc., Englewood Cliffs, N.J., 1967, p. 412. Courtesy of Prentice-Hall, Inc.*

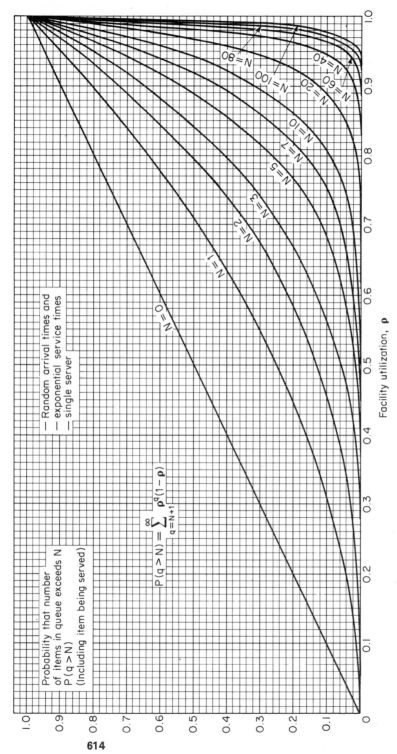

$$P(q > N) = \sum_{q=N+1}^{\infty} \rho^q (1 - \rho)$$

Facility utilization, ρ

Figure E-4. Probability of exceeding certain queue sizes in a single-server queue.

Source: J. Martin, Design of Real-Time Computer Systems, Prentice-Hall, Inc., Englewood Cliffs, N.J., 1967, p. 417. Courtesy of Prentice-Hall, Inc.

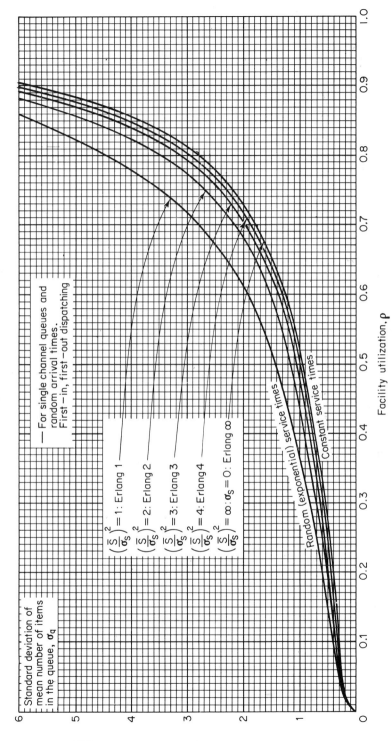

Figure E-5. Standard deviation of queue sizes in a single-server queue.

Source: J. Martin, Design of Real-Time Computer Systems, Prentice-Hall, Inc., Englewood Cliffs, N.J., 1967, p. 413. Courtesy of Prentice-Hall, Inc.

615

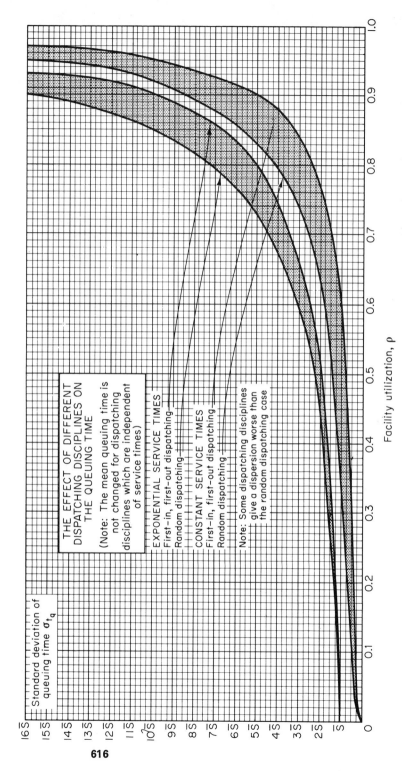

Figure E-6. The effect of different dispatching disciplines on queuing time.

Source: J. Martin, Design of Real-Time Computer Systems, Prentice-Hall, Inc., Englewood Cliffs, N.J., 1967, p. 415. Courtesy of Prentice-Hall, Inc.

The following labels appear within the chart:

Facility utilization, ρ (horizontal axis: 0, 0.1, 0.2, 0.3, 0.4, 0.5, 0.6, 0.7, 0.8, 0.9, 1.0)

Standard deviation of queuing time σ_{t_q} (vertical axis: $\bar{S}$, 2$\bar{S}$, 3$\bar{S}$, 4$\bar{S}$, 5$\bar{S}$, 6$\bar{S}$, 7$\bar{S}$, 8$\bar{S}$, 9$\bar{S}$, 10$\bar{S}$, 11$\bar{S}$, 12$\bar{S}$, 13$\bar{S}$, 14$\bar{S}$, 15$\bar{S}$, 16$\bar{S}$)

THE EFFECT OF DIFFERENT
DISPATCHING DISCIPLINES ON
THE QUEUING TIME

(Note: The mean queuing time is
not changed for dispatching
disciplines which are independent
of service times)

EXPONENTIAL SERVICE TIMES
First-in, first-out dispatching
Random dispatching

CONSTANT SERVICE TIMES
First-in, first-out dispatching
Random dispatching

Note: Some dispatching disciplines
give a dispersion worse than
the random dispatching case

616

where $\tilde{N}(n) = (M\rho)^n/n!$, and

$$P(0) = \frac{1}{\sum_{n=0}^{M-1} \tilde{N}(n) + [(M\rho)^M/(1-\rho)M!]}.$$

The average number of units in the system, $\bar{q}$, is

$$\bar{q} = B\frac{\rho}{1-\rho} + M\rho,$$

where B is similar to $P(0)$; i.e.,

$$B = \frac{1-C}{1-\rho C},$$

where

$$C = \frac{\sum_{n=1}^{M-1} \tilde{N}(n)}{\sum_{n=1}^{M} \tilde{N}(n)}.$$

Luckily, Figures E-7 and E-8 give the mean number in the system and the mean waiting time for these systems, and so computation of these terms is rarely necessary.

F. Example of Multichannel Queues

Suppose that you have the choice of installing a one-channel facility with $\mu = 10$ operations per hour with a negative exponential distribution versus five channels with $\mu = 2$ operations each per hour for the same cost. The arrival rate is Poisson-distributed with a mean of 5 units per hour, i.e., $\lambda = 5$. Which would you choose?

For the multichannel case,

$$\rho = \frac{n\bar{s}}{M} = \frac{5 \times \frac{1}{2}}{5} = .5 \text{ with } \lambda = 5$$

t = mean time in system, 31 minutes from Table E-7

$\bar{q}$ = mean number in system, 2.5 from Table E-6

$\bar{w}$ = mean number in queue, ~ 0

$\dfrac{\bar{w}}{\lambda}$ = mean time in queue, ~ 0 minutes.

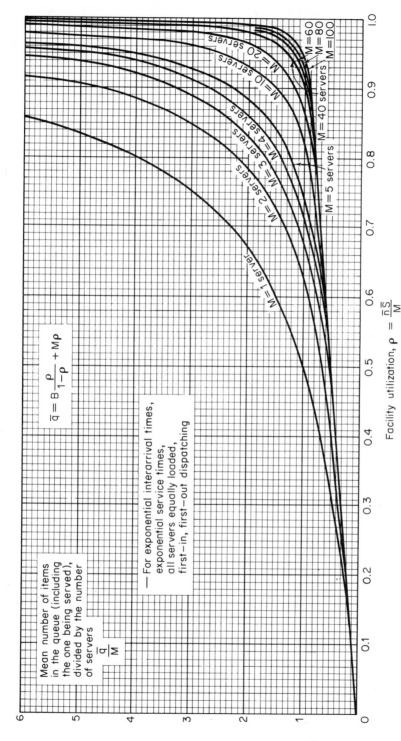

Figure E-7. Sizes of queues in a multiserver queuing system.

Source: J. Martin, Design of Real-Time Computer Systems, Prentice-Hall, Inc., Englewood Cliffs, N.J., 1967, p. 424. Courtesy of Prentice-Hall, Inc.

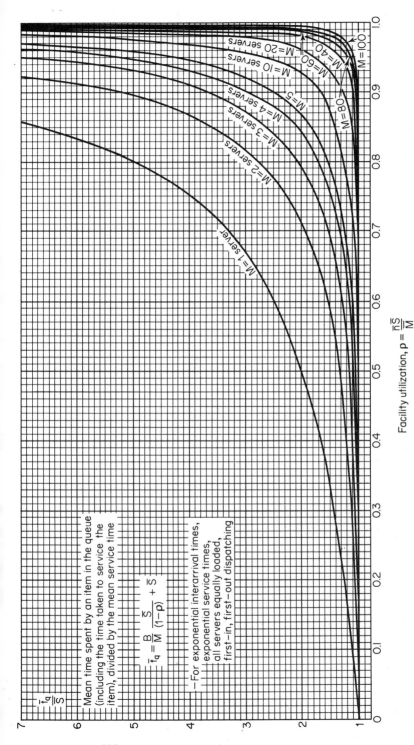

Figure E-8. Queuing times for multiserver queues.

Source: J. Martin, Design of Real-Time Computer Systems, *Prentice-Hall, Inc., Englewood Cliffs, N.J., 1967, p. 425. Courtesy of Prentice-Hall, Inc.*

For the single-channel case,

$$\rho = \frac{\lambda}{\mu} = \frac{5}{10} = .5$$

$t =$ mean time in system $= \dfrac{1}{\mu(1 - \rho)} = \dfrac{1}{10 \times .5} = \dfrac{1}{5} = 12$ minutes

$\bar{q} =$ mean number in system $= \rho + \dfrac{\rho^2}{1 - \rho} = \dfrac{\rho}{1 - \rho} = 1$

mean time in queue $= 6$ minutes

$\bar{w} =$ mean number in queue $= .5.$

Now suppose that $\lambda = 9$, so that $\rho = \frac{9}{10} = .9$. For the multichannel case,

$t =$ mean time in the system $= 2.5 \times 30$ minutes $= 75$ minutes

$\bar{q} =$ mean number in the system $= 2.3 \times 5 = 11.5$

$\bar{w} =$ mean number in the queue $= \bar{q} - M\rho = 11.5 - 4.5 = 7$

mean time in the queue $= \dfrac{\bar{w}}{\lambda} = \dfrac{7}{10} = .7$ hour $= 42$ minutes.

For the single-channel case, with $\lambda = 9$

$t =$ mean time in system $= \dfrac{1}{\mu(1 - \rho)} = \dfrac{1}{10 \times .1} = 1$ hour

$\bar{q} =$ mean number in system $= \dfrac{\rho}{1 - \rho} = \dfrac{.9}{.1} = 9$

$\bar{w} =$ mean number in queue $= 8.1$

mean time in queue $= \dfrac{\bar{w}}{\lambda} = \dfrac{8.1}{9} = .9$ hour $= 54$ minutes.

The calculation of $\bar{q}$ for $\rho = .9$ is

$$\bar{q} = B \frac{\rho}{1 - \rho} + M\rho$$
$$= 9B + 4.5$$
$$B = \frac{1 - C}{1 - \rho C},$$

where

$$\tilde{N}(n) = \frac{(M_\rho)^n}{n!}$$

and

$$C = \frac{\sum\limits_{n=0}^{M-1} N(n)}{\sum\limits_{n=0}^{M} \tilde{N}(n)}.$$

Then

$$B = \frac{1 - \{D/[D + (5^5 \times .9^5/120)]\}}{1 - \rho C},$$

where $D = 5^0 \times .9^0 + 5 \times .9^1 + [(25 \times .9^2)/2] + [(625 \times .9^3)/6] + [(3125 \times .9^4)/24]$,

$$B = \frac{1 - [(1 + 4.5 + 10.125 + 15.1875 + 16.825)/(47.6875 + 15.375)]}{1 - \rho C}$$

$$= \frac{1 - .755}{1 - .9 \times .755}$$

$$= \frac{.245}{.3205} = .765$$

$\bar{q} = 6.86 + 4.5 = 11.4 \qquad$ versus 11.5 by Table E-6.

It should be noted that the increase in capacity of the single-channel system must come from reduction of the service time of each unit, not merely in simultaneously processing several units, such as in a multispindle drill. The model developed would hold only for a higher-speed drill, not a multiprocessing facility.

The results of this example are very interesting. What choice should be made between the two alternative methods, single or multiple channels, if the costs and total capacities are equal? Kaufman [8] says

> *It is always wise, given the same overall rate and the same cost, to use the largest possible number of channels.*

It is not clear that this holds for our case or in general. Kaufman did not consider the total time in the system but only the time in the queue and the number in the queue.

As discussed in Chap. 8, in production systems one of the most important criteria is to reduce the in-process inventories. This was accomplished in Chap. 8 by reducing the process time for each unit. By designing queuing facilities to minimize the time in the system, the processing time and the in-process times will be minimized. By this criterion, the single, high-speed facility is definitely superior to the multichannel facility with equal cost and equal capacity. In our example the single facility was 25 and 250% faster, as indicated by mean time in the system. In production systems where the units are inanimate and have no ability to balk, single facilities are better unless reliability is a problem, as discussed in Chap. 4.

On the other hand, if the units are people, the primary disadvantage of the queue is that the people may avoid queuing at all if they see no facility vacant or have to wait a long time in the queue itself rather than considering the total time in the system. The multiple facilities will tend to have an open facility more often and to have a shorter queue in front of each server even though time in the system is longer. If the housewife becomes upset at having to wait while three others check out, she may prefer a situation where she gets into a checkout facility sooner even if it takes quite a while to complete the check out. In general, if the units are not people, the single facility is better. If humans are involved, careful consideration of the relative real and psychological costs of minutes in the queue versus minutes in the system is necessary.

If the length of the queue is limited by the extent of the facility so that there is a maximum queue size, the previously derived model is not adequate because it assumes that infinite queue length is possible, although infrequent. If the maximum size is small, the results are considerably different. One example is the so-called machine interference problem discussed in Chap. 9 but also pertinent to Chaps. 2 and 4. A worker tends N machines each of which can break down or require attention at negative exponentially distributed intervals. The total number of breakdowns is proportional to the number of machines not in the maintenance queue, i.e., "running" or "alive." The model is called the birth and death process for obvious reasons. We can obtain

$$P(n) = \frac{N!\,p^n}{(N-n)!}P(0),$$

where

$$P(0) = \frac{1}{1 + \sum\limits_{n=1}^{N}[N!\,p^n/(N-n)!]}.$$

Example: Suppose that an operator tends $N = 6$ machines. The arrival rate of breakdowns is 1 per hour per machine running and each adjustment takes 1 minute, and so $p = .1$. The probability of no machines running is

$$P(0) = \left[1 + 6!\left(\frac{.1}{5!} + \frac{.1^2}{4!} + \frac{.1^3}{3!} + \frac{.1^3}{2!} + \frac{.1^5}{1!} + \frac{.1^6}{0!}\right)\right]^{-1} = .484$$

$$P(6) = 6!(.1)^6 \times .484 = .0026$$

$$P(3) = 6 \times 5 \times 4 \times .1^3 \times .484 = .058.$$

REFERENCES

1. R. G. Brown, *Smoothing, Forecasting and Prediction*, Prentice-Hall, Englewood Cliffs, N.J., 1962.

2. Won M. Chow, "Adaptive Control of the Exponential Smoothing Constraint," *Industrial Engineering*, 13, No. 5 (Sept.–Oct. 1965).

3. William J. Baumol, *Economic Theory and Analysis*, Prentice-Hall, Englewood Cliffs, N.J., 1971.

4. G. HADLEY, *Nonlinear and Dynamic Programming*, Addison-Wesley, Reading, Mass., 1964.

5. G. HADLEY, *Linear Programming*, Addison-Wesley, Reading, Mass., 1962.

6. G. F. NEWELL, *Applications of Queueing Theory*, Chapman & Hall, London, 1971, Chap. 2.

7. JAMES MARTIN, *Design of Real-Time Computer Systems*, Prentice-Hall, Englewood Cliffs, N.J., 1967, p. 394.

8. A. KAUFMAN, *Methods and Models of Operations Research*, Prentice-Hall, Englewood Cliffs, N.J., 1963, p. 101.

appendix F

Financial Tables[†]

---

†W. J. Fabrycky and Paul E. Torgersen, *Operations Economy: Industrial Applications of Operations Research*, Prentice-Hall, Inc., Englewood Cliffs, N.J., 1966, pp. 460–468.

Table F-1   10% Insert Factors for Annual Compounding

n	Single Payment		Equal-Payment Series			
	Compound-Amount Factor	Present-Worth Factor	Compound-Amount Factor	Sinking-Fund Factor	Present-Worth Factor	Capital-Recovery Factor
	SP_{i-n} ( )	PS_{i-n} ( )	SR_{i-n} ( )	RS_{i-n} ( )	PR_{i-n} ( )	RP_{i-n} ( )
1	1.100	0.90909	1.000	1.00000	0.90909	1.10000
2	1.210	0.82645	2.100	0.47619	1.73554	0.57619
3	1.331	0.75131	3.310	0.30211	2.48685	0.40211
4	1.464	0.68301	4.641	0.21547	3.16987	0.31547
5	1.611	0.62092	6.105	0.16380	3.79079	0.26380
6	1.772	0.56447	7.716	0.12961	4.35526	0.22961
7	1.949	0.51316	9.487	0.10541	4.86842	0.20541
8	2.144	0.46651	11.436	0.08744	5.33493	0.18744
9	2.358	0.42410	13.579	0.07364	5.75902	0.17364
10	2.594	0.38554	15.937	0.06275	6.14457	0.16275
11	2.853	0.35049	18.531	0.05396	6.49506	0.15396
12	3.138	0.31863	21.384	0.04676	6.81369	0.14676
13	3.452	0.28966	24.523	0.04078	7.10336	0.14078
14	3.797	0.26333	27.975	0.03575	7.36669	0.13575
15	4.177	0.23939	31.772	0.03147	7.60608	0.13147
16	4.595	0.21763	35.950	0.02782	7.82371	0.12782
17	5.054	0.19784	40.545	0.02466	8.02155	0.12466
18	5.560	0.17986	45.599	0.02193	8.20141	0.12193
19	6.116	0.16351	51.159	0.01955	8.36492	0.11955
20	6.727	0.14864	57.275	0.01746	8.51356	0.11746
21	7.400	0.13513	64.002	0.01562	8.64869	0.11562
22	8.140	0.12285	71.403	0.01401	8.77154	0.11401
23	8.954	0.11168	79.543	0.01257	8.88322	0.11257
24	9.850	0.10153	88.497	0.01130	8.98474	0.11130
25	10.835	0.09230	98.347	0.01017	9.07704	0.11017
26	11.918	0.08391	109.182	0.00916	9.16095	0.10916
27	13.110	0.07628	121.100	0.00826	9.23722	0.10826
28	14.421	0.06934	134.210	0.00745	9.30657	0.10745
29	15.863	0.06304	148.631	0.00673	9.36961	0.10673
30	17.449	0.05731	164.494	0.00608	9.42691	0.10608
35	28.102	0.03558	271.024	0.00369	9.64416	0.10369
40	45.259	0.02209	442.593	0.00226	9.77905	0.10226
45	72.890	0.01372	718.905	0.00139	9.86281	0.10139
50	117.391	0.00852	1163.908	0.00086	9.91481	0.10086
55	189.059	0.00529	1880.591	0.00053	9.94711	0.10053
60	304.482	0.00328	3034.816	0.00033	9.96716	0.10033
70	789.747	0.00127	7887.469	0.00013	9.98734	0.10013
80	2048.400	0.00049	20474.000	0.00005	9.99512	0.10005
90	5313.022	0.00019	53120.222	0.00002	9.99812	0.10002
100	13780.611	0.00007	137796.110	0.00001	9.99927	0.10001

Table F-2 9% Interest Factors for Annual Compounding

	Single Payment		Equal-Payment Series			
n	Compound-Amount Factor	Present-Worth Factor	Compound-Amount Factor	Sinking-Fund Factor	Present-Worth Factor	Capital-Recovery Factor
	SP_{i-n} ( )	PS_{i-n} ( )	SR_{i-n} ( )	RS_{i-n} ( )	PR_{i-n} ( )	RP_{i-n} ( )
1	1.090	0.91743	1.000	1.00000	0.91743	1.09000
2	1.188	0.84168	2.090	0.47847	1.75911	0.56847
3	1.295	0.77218	3.278	0.30505	2.53129	0.39505
4	1.412	0.70843	4.573	0.21867	3.23972	0.30867
5	1.539	0.64993	5.985	0.16709	3.88965	0.25709
6	1.677	0.59627	7.523	0.13292	4.48592	0.22292
7	1.828	0.54703	9.200	0.10869	5.03295	0.19869
8	1.993	0.50187	11.028	0.09067	5.53482	0.18067
9	2.172	0.46043	13.021	0.07680	5.99525	0.16880
10	2.367	0.42241	15.193	0.06582	6.41766	0.15582
11	2.580	0.38753	17.560	0.05695	6.80519	0.14695
12	2.813	0.35553	20.141	0.04965	7.16072	0.13965
13	3.066	0.32618	22.953	0.04357	7.48690	0.13357
14	3.342	0.29925	26.019	0.03843	7.78615	0.12843
15	3.642	0.27454	29.361	0.03406	8.06069	0.12406
16	3.970	0.25187	33.003	0.03030	8.31256	0.12030
17	4.328	0.23107	36.974	0.02705	8.54363	0.11705
18	4.717	0.21199	41.301	0.02421	8.75562	0.11421
19	5.142	0.19449	46.018	0.02173	8.95011	0.11173
20	5.604	0.17843	51.160	0.01955	9.12855	0.10955
21	6.109	0.16370	56.765	0.01762	9.29224	0.10762
22	6.659	0.15018	62.873	0.01590	9.44243	0.10590
23	7.258	0.13778	69.532	0.01438	9.58021	0.10438
24	7.911	0.12640	76.790	0.01302	9.70661	0.10302
25	8.623	0.11597	84.701	0.01181	9.82258	0.10181
26	9.399	0.10639	93.324	0.01072	9.92897	0.10072
27	10.245	0.09761	102.723	0.00973	10.02658	0.09973
28	11.167	0.08955	112.968	0.00885	10.11613	0.09885
29	12.172	0.08215	124.135	0.00806	10.19828	0.09806
30	13.268	0.07537	136.308	0.00734	10.27365	0.09734
35	20.414	0.04899	215.711	0.00464	10.56682	0.09464
40	31.409	0.03184	337.882	0.00296	10.75736	0.09296
45	48.327	0.02069	525.859	0.00190	10.88120	0.09190
50	74.358	0.01345	815.084	0.00123	10.96168	0.09123
55	114.408	0.00874	1260.092	0.00079	11.01399	0.09079
60	176.031	0.00568	1944.792	0.00051	11.04799	0.09051
70	416.730	0.00240	4619.223	0.00022	11.08445	0.09022
80	986.552	0.00101	10950.573	0.00009	11.09985	0.09009
90	2335.526	0.00043	25939.182	0.00004	11.10635	0.09004
100	5529.041	0.00018	61422.674	0.00002	11.10910	0.09002

Table F-3 8% Interest Factors for Annual Compounding

n	Single Payment		Equal-Payment Series			
	Compound-Amount Factor	Present-Worth Factor	Compound-Amount Factor	Sinking-Fund Factor	Present-Worth Factor	Capital-Recovery Factor
	SP_{i-n} ( )	PS_{i-n} ( )	SR_{i-n} ( )	RS_{i-n} ( )	PR_{i-n} ( )	RP_{i-n} ( )
1	1.080	0.92593	1.000	1.00000	0.92593	1.08000
2	1.166	0.85734	2.080	0.48077	1.78326	0.56077
3	1.260	0.79383	3.246	0.30803	2.57710	0.38803
4	1.360	0.73503	4.506	0.22192	3.31213	0.30192
5	1.469	0.68058	5.867	0.17046	3.99271	0.25046
6	1.587	0.63017	7.336	0.13632	4.62288	0.21632
7	1.714	0.58349	8.923	0.11207	5.20637	0.19207
8	1.851	0.54027	10.637	0.09401	5.74664	0.17401
9	1.999	0.50025	12.488	0.08008	6.24689	0.16008
10	2.159	0.46319	14.487	0.06903	6.71008	0.14903
11	2.332	0.42888	16.645	0.06008	7.13896	0.14008
12	2.518	0.39711	18.977	0.05270	7.53608	0.13270
13	2.720	0.36770	21.495	0.04652	7.90378	0.12652
14	2.937	0.34046	24.215	0.04130	8.24424	0.12130
15	3.172	0.31524	27.152	0.03683	8.55948	0.11683
16	3.426	0.29189	30.324	0.03298	8.85137	0.11298
17	3.700	0.27027	33.750	0.02963	9.12164	0.10963
18	3.996	0.25025	37.450	0.02670	9.37189	0.10670
19	4.316	0.23171	41.446	0.02413	9.60360	0.10413
20	4.661	0.21455	45.762	0.02185	9.81815	0.10185
21	5.034	0.19866	50.423	0.01983	10.01680	0.09983
22	5.437	0.18394	55.457	0.01803	10.20074	0.09803
23	5.871	0.17032	60.893	0.01642	10.37106	0.09642
24	6.341	0.15770	66.765	0.01498	10.52876	0.09498
25	6.848	0.14602	73.106	0.01368	10.67478	0.09368
26	7.396	0.13520	79.954	0.01251	10.80998	0.09251
27	7.988	0.12519	87.351	0.01445	10.93516	0.09145
28	8.627	0.11591	95.339	0.01049	11.05108	0.09049
29	9.317	0.10733	103.966	0.00962	11.15841	0.08962
30	10.063	0.09938	113.283	0.00883	11.25778	0.08883
35	14.785	0.06763	172.317	0.00580	11.65457	0.08580
40	21.725	0.04603	259.057	0.00386	11.92461	0.08386
45	31.920	0.03133	386.506	0.00259	12.10840	0.08259
50	46.902	0.02132	573.770	0.00174	12.23348	0.08174
55	68.914	0.01451	848.923	0.00118	12.31861	0.08118
60	101.257	0.00988	1253.213	0.00080	12.37655	0.08080
70	218.606	0.00457	2720.080	0.00037	12.44282	0.08037
80	471.955	0.00212	5886.935	0.00017	12.47351	0.08017
90	1018.915	0.00098	12723.937	0.00008	12.48773	0.08008
100	2199.761	0.00045	27484.515	0.00004	12.49432	0.08004

Table F-4 7% Interest Factors for Annual Compounding

n	Single Payment		Equal-Payment Series			
	Compound-Amount Factor	Present-Worth Factor	Compound-Amount Factor	Sinking-Fund Factor	Present-Worth Factor	Capital-Recovery Factor
	SP $_{i-n}$ ( )	PS $_{i-n}$ ( )	SR $_{i-n}$ ( )	RS $_{i-n}$ ( )	PR $_{i-n}$ ( )	RP $_{i-n}$ ( )
1	1.070	0.93458	1.000	1.00000	0.93458	1.07000
2	1.145	0.87344	2.070	0.48309	1.80802	0.55309
3	1.225	0.81630	3.215	0.31105	2.62432	0.38105
4	1.311	0.76290	4.440	0.22523	3.38721	0.29523
5	1.403	0.71299	5.751	0.17389	4.10020	0.24389
6	1.501	0.66634	7.153	0.13980	4.76654	0.20980
7	1.606	0.62275	8.654	0.11555	5.38929	0.18555
8	1.718	0.58201	10.260	0.09747	5.97130	0.16747
9	1.838	0.54393	11.978	0.08349	6.51523	0.15349
10	1.967	0.50835	13.816	0.07238	7.02358	0.14238
11	2.105	0.47509	15.784	0.06336	7.49867	0.13336
12	2.252	0.44401	17.888	0.05590	7.94269	0.12590
13	2.410	0.41496	20.141	0.04965	8.35765	0.11965
14	2.579	0.38782	22.550	0.04434	8.74547	0.11434
15	2.759	0.36245	25.129	0.03979	9.10791	0.10979
16	2.952	0.33873	27.888	0.03586	9.44665	0.10586
17	3.159	0.31657	30.840	0.03243	9.76322	0.10243
18	3.380	0.29586	33.999	0.02941	10.05909	0.09941
19	3.617	0.27651	37.379	0.02675	10.33559	0.09675
20	3.870	0.25842	40.995	0.02439	10.59401	0.09439
21	4.141	0.24151	44.865	0.02229	10.83553	0.09229
22	4.430	0.22571	49.006	0.02041	11.06124	0.09041
23	4.741	0.21095	53.436	0.01871	11.27219	0.08871
24	5.072	0.19715	58.177	0.01719	11.46933	0.08719
25	5.427	0.18425	63.249	0.01581	11.65358	0.08581
26	5.807	0.17220	68.676	0.01456	11.82578	0.08456
27	6.214	0.16093	74.484	0.01343	11.98671	0.08343
28	6.649	0.15040	80.698	0.01239	12.13711	0.08239
29	7.114	0.14056	87.347	0.01145	12.27767	0.08145
30	7.612	0.13137	94.461	0.01059	12.40904	0.08059
35	10.677	0.09366	138.237	0.00723	12.94767	0.07723
40	14.974	0.06678	199.635	0.00501	13.33171	0.07501
45	21.002	0.04761	285.749	0.00350	13.60552	0.07350
50	29.457	0.03395	406.529	0.00246	13.80075	0.07246
55	41.315	0.02420	575.929	0.00174	13.93994	0.07174
60	57.946	0.01726	813.520	0.00123	14.03918	0.07123
70	113.989	0.00877	1614.134	0.00062	14.16039	0.07062
80	224.234	0.00446	3189.062	0.00031	14.22201	0.07031
90	441.103	0.00227	6287.185	0.00016	14.25333	0.07016
100	867.716	0.00115	12381.661	0.00008	14.26925	0.07008

Table F-5   6% Interest Factors for Annual Compounding

	Single Payment		Equal-Payment Series			
n	Compound-Amount Factor	Present-Worth Factor	Compound-Amount Factor	Sinking-Fund Factor	Present-Worth Factor	Capital-Recovery Factor
	SP $_{i-n}$ ( )	PS $_{i-n}$ ( )	SR $_{i-n}$ ( )	RS $_{i-n}$ ( )	PR $_{i-n}$ ( )	RP $_{i-n}$ ( )
1	1.060	0.94340	1.000	1.00000	0.94340	1.06000
2	1.124	0.89000	2.060	0.48544	1.83339	0.54544
3	1.191	0.83962	3.184	0.31411	2.67301	0.37411
4	1.262	0.79209	4.375	0.22859	3.46510	0.28859
5	1.338	0.74726	5.637	0.17740	4.21236	0.23740
6	1.419	0.70496	6.975	0.14336	4.91732	0.20336
7	1.504	0.66506	8.394	0.11914	5.58238	0.17914
8	1.594	0.62741	9.897	0.10104	6.20979	0.16104
9	1.689	0.59190	11.491	0.08702	6.80169	0.14702
10	1.791	0.55839	13.181	0.07587	7.36009	0.13587
11	1.898	0.52679	14.972	0.06679	7.88687	0.12679
12	2.012	0.49697	16.870	0.05928	8.38384	0.11928
13	2.133	0.46884	18.882	0.05296	8.85268	0.11296
14	2.261	0.44230	21.015	0.04758	9.29498	0.10758
15	2.397	0.41727	23.276	0.04296	9.71225	0.10296
16	2.540	0.39365	25.673	0.03895	10.10590	0.09895
17	2.693	0.37136	28.213	0.03544	10.47726	0.09544
18	2.854	0.35034	30.906	0.03236	10.82760	0.09236
19	3.026	0.33051	33.760	0.02962	11.15812	0.08962
20	3.207	0.31180	36.786	0.02718	11.46992	0.08718
21	3.400	0.29416	39.993	0.02500	11.76408	0.08500
22	3.604	0.27751	43.392	0.02305	12.04158	0.08305
23	3.820	0.26180	46.996	0.02128	12.30338	0.08128
24	4.049	0.24698	50.816	0.01968	12.55036	0.07968
25	4.292	0.23300	54.865	0.01823	12.78336	0.07823
26	4.549	0.21981	59.196	0.01690	13.00317	0.07690
27	4.822	0.20737	63.706	0.01570	13.21053	0.07570
28	5.112	0.19563	68.528	0.01459	13.40616	0.07459
29	5.418	0.18456	73.640	0.01358	13.59072	0.07358
30	5.743	0.17411	79.058	0.01265	13.76483	0.07265
35	7.686	0.13011	111.435	0.00897	14.49825	0.06897
40	10.286	0.09722	154.762	0.00646	15.04630	0.06646
45	13.765	0.07265	212.744	0.00470	15.45583	0.06470
50	18.420	0.05429	290.336	0.00344	15.76186	0.06344
55	24.650	0.04057	394.172	0.00254	15.99054	0.06254
60	32.988	0.03031	533.128	0.00188	16.16143	0.06188
70	59.076	0.01693	967.932	0.00103	16.38454	0.06103
80	105.796	0.00945	1746.600	0.00057	16.50913	0.06057
90	189.465	0.00528	3141.075	0.00032	16.57870	0.06032
100	339.302	0.00295	5638.369	0.00018	16.61755	0.06018

Table F-6   5% Interest Factors for Annual Compounding

	Single Payment		Equal-Payment Series			
n	Compound-Amount Factor	Present-Worth Factor	Compound-Amount Factor	Sinking-Fund Factor	Present-Worth Factor	Capital-Recovery Factor
	SP_{i-n} ( )	PS_{i-n} ( )	SR_{i-n} ( )	RS_{i-n} ( )	PR_{i-n} ( )	RP_{i-n} ( )
1	1.050	0.95238	1.000	1.00000	0.95238	1.05000
2	1.103	0.90703	2.050	0.48780	1.85941	0.53780
3	1.158	0.86384	3.153	0.31721	2.72325	0.36721
4	1.216	0.82270	4.310	0.23201	3.54595	0.28201
5	1.276	0.78353	5.526	0.18097	4.32948	0.23097
6	1.340	0.74622	6.802	0.14702	5.07569	0.19702
7	1.407	0.71068	8.142	0.12282	5.78637	0.17282
8	1.477	0.67684	9.549	0.10742	6.46321	0.15472
9	1.551	0.64461	11.027	0.09069	7.10782	0.14069
10	1.629	0.61391	12.578	0.07950	7.72174	0.12950
11	1.710	0.58468	14.207	0.07039	8.30641	0.12039
12	1.796	0.55684	15.917	0.06283	8.86325	0.11283
13	1.886	0.53032	17.713	0.05646	9.39357	0.10646
14	1.980	0.50507	19.599	0.05102	9.89864	0.10102
15	2.079	0.48102	21.579	0.04634	10.37966	0.09634
16	2.183	0.45811	23.657	0.04227	10.83777	0.09227
17	2.292	0.43630	25.840	0.03870	11.27407	0.08870
18	2.407	0.41552	28.132	0.03555	11.68959	0.08555
19	2.527	0.39573	30.539	0.03275	12.08532	0.08275
20	2.653	0.37689	33.066	0.03024	12.46221	0.08024
21	2.786	0.35894	35.719	0.02800	12.82115	0.07800
22	2.925	0.34185	38.505	0.02597	13.16300	0.07597
23	3.072	0.32557	41.430	0.02414	13.48857	0.07414
24	3.225	0.31007	44.502	0.02247	13.79864	0.07247
25	3.386	0.29530	47.727	0.02095	14.09394	0.07095
26	3.556	0.28124	51.113	0.01956	14.37519	0.06956
27	3.733	0.26785	54.669	0.01829	14.64303	0.06829
28	3.920	0.25509	58.403	0.01712	14.89813	0.06712
29	4.116	0.24295	62.323	0.01605	15.14107	0.06605
30	4.322	0.23138	66.439	0.01505	15.37245	0.06505
35	5.516	0.18129	90.320	0.01107	16.37419	0.06107
40	7.040	0.14205	120.800	0.00828	17.15909	0.05828
45	8.985	0.11130	159.700	0.00626	17.77407	0.05626
50	11.467	0.08720	209.348	0.00478	18.25593	0.05478
55	14.636	0.06833	272.713	0.00367	18.63347	0.05367
60	18.679	0.05354	353.584	0.00283	18.92929	0.05283
70	30.426	0.03287	588.529	0.00170	19.34268	0.05170
80	49.561	0.02018	971.229	0.00103	19.59646	0.05103
90	80.730	0.01239	1594.608	0.00063	19.75226	0.05063
100	131.501	0.00760	2610.026	0.00038	19.84791	0.05038

Table F-7 4% Interest Factors for Annual Compounding

	Single Payment		Equal-Payment Series			
	Compound-Amount Factor	Present-Worth Factor	Compound-Amount Factor	Sinking-Fund Factor	Present-Worth Factor	Capital-Recovery Factor
n	SP_{i-n} ( )	PS_{i-n} ( )	SR_{i-n} ( )	RS_{i-n} ( )	PR_{i-n} ( )	RP_{i-n} ( )
1	1.040	0.96154	1.000	1.00000	0.96154	1.04000
2	1.082	0.92456	2.040	0.49020	1.88609	0.53020
3	1.125	0.88900	3.122	0.32035	2.77509	0.36035
4	1.170	0.85480	4.246	0.23549	3.62990	0.27549
5	1.217	0.82193	5.416	0.18463	4.45182	0.22463
6	1.265	0.79031	6.633	0.15076	5.24214	0.19076
7	1.316	0.75992	7.898	0.12661	6.00205	0.16661
8	1.369	0.73069	9.214	0.10853	6.73275	0.14853
9	1.423	0.70259	10.583	0.09449	7.43533	0.13449
10	1.480	0.67556	12.006	0.08329	8.11090	0.12329
11	1.539	0.64958	13.486	0.07415	8.76048	0.11415
12	1.601	0.62460	15.026	0.06655	9.38507	0.10655
13	1.665	0.60057	16.627	0.06014	9.98565	0.10014
14	1.732	0.57748	18.292	0.05467	10.56312	0.09467
15	1.801	0.55526	20.024	0.04994	11.11839	0.08994
16	1.873	0.53391	21.825	0.04582	11.65230	0.08582
17	1.948	0.51337	23.698	0.04220	12.16567	0.08220
18	2.026	0.49363	25.645	0.03899	12.65930	0.07899
19	2.107	0.47464	27.671	0.03614	13.13394	0.07614
20	2.191	0.45639	29.778	0.03358	13.59033	0.07358
21	2.279	0.43883	31.969	0.03128	14.02916	0.07128
22	2.370	0.42196	34.248	0.02920	14.45112	0.06920
23	2.465	0.40573	36.618	0.02731	14.85684	0.06731
24	2.563	0.39012	39.083	0.02559	15.24696	0.06559
25	2.666	0.37512	41.646	0.02401	15.62208	0.06401
26	2.772	0.36069	44.312	0.02257	15.98277	0.06257
27	2.883	0.34682	47.084	0.02124	16.32959	0.06124
28	2.999	0.33348	49.968	0.02001	16.66306	0.06001
29	3.119	0.32065	52.966	0.01888	16.98372	0.05888
30	3.243	0.30832	56.085	0.01783	17.29203	0.05783
35	3.946	0.25342	73.652	0.01358	18.66461	0.05358
40	4.801	0.20829	95.026	0.01052	19.79277	0.05052
45	5.841	0.17120	121.029	0.00826	20.72004	0.04826
50	7.107	0.14071	152.667	0.00655	21.48218	0.04655
55	8.646	0.11566	191.159	0.00523	22.10861	0.04523
60	10.520	0.09506	237.991	0.00420	22.62349	0.04420
70	15.572	0.06422	364.291	0.00275	23.39452	0.04275
80	23.050	0.04338	551.245	0.00181	23.91539	0.04181
90	34.119	0.02931	827.984	0.00121	24.26728	0.04121
100	50.505	0.01980	1237.624	0.00081	24.50500	0.04081

Table F-8 3% Interest Factors for Annual Compounding

	Single Payment		Equal-Payment Series			
n	Compound-Amount Factor	Present-Worth Factor	Compound-Amount Factor	Sinking-Fund Factor	Present-Worth Factor	Capital-Recovery Factor
	SP $_{i-n}$ ( )	PS $_{i-n}$ ( )	SR $_{i-n}$ ( )	RS $_{i-n}$ ( )	PR $_{i-n}$ ( )	RP $_{i-n}$ ( )
1	1.030	0.97087	1.000	1.00000	0.97087	1.03000
2	1.061	0.94260	2.030	0.49261	1.91347	0.52261
3	1.093	0.91514	3.091	0.32353	2.82861	0.35353
4	1.126	0.88849	4.184	0.23903	3.71710	0.26903
5	1.159	0.86261	5.309	0.18835	4.57971	0.21835
6	1.194	0.83748	6.468	0.15460	5.41719	0.18460
7	1.230	0.81309	7.662	0.13051	6.23028	0.16051
8	1.267	0.78941	8.892	0.11246	7.01969	0.14246
9	1.305	0.76642	10.159	0.09843	7.78611	0.12843
10	1.344	0.74409	11.464	0.08723	8.53020	0.11723
11	1.384	0.72242	12.808	0.07808	9.25263	0.10808
12	1.426	0.70138	14.192	0.07046	9.95401	0.10046
13	1.469	0.68095	15.618	0.06403	10.63496	0.09403
14	1.513	0.66112	17.086	0.05853	11.29608	0.08853
15	1.558	0.64186	18.599	0.05377	11.93794	0.08377
16	1.605	0.62317	20.157	0.04961	12.56111	0.07961
17	1.653	0.60502	21.762	0.04595	13.16612	0.07595
18	1.702	0.58739	23.414	0.04271	13.75352	0.07271
19	1.754	0.57029	25.117	0.03981	14.32380	0.06981
20	1.806	0.55368	26.870	0.03722	14.87748	0.06722
21	1.860	0.53755	28.677	0.03487	15.41503	0.06487
22	1.916	0.52189	30.537	0.03275	15.93692	0.06275
23	1.974	0.50669	32.453	0.03081	16.44361	0.06081
24	2.033	0.49193	34.426	0.02905	16.93555	0.05905
25	2.094	0.47761	36.459	0.02743	17.41315	0.05743
26	2.157	0.46369	38.553	0.02594	17.87685	0.05594
27	2.221	0.45019	40.710	0.02456	18.32704	0.05456
28	2.288	0.43708	42.931	0.02329	18.76411	0.05329
29	2.357	0.42435	45.219	0.02211	19.18846	0.05211
30	2.427	0.41199	47.575	0.02102	19.60045	0.05102
35	2.814	0.35538	60.462	0.01654	21.48722	0.04654
40	3.262	0.30656	75.401	0.01326	23.11478	0.04326
45	3.782	0.26444	92.720	0.01079	24.51872	0.04079
50	4.384	0.22811	112.797	0.00887	25.72977	0.03887
55	5.082	0.19677	136.072	0.00735	26.77443	0.03735
60	5.892	0.16973	163.054	0.00613	27.67557	0.03613
70	7.918	0.12630	230.594	0.00434	29.12342	0.03434
80	10.641	0.09398	321.363	0.00311	30.20077	0.03311
90	14.300	0.06993	443.349	0.00226	31.00241	0.03226
100	19.219	0.05203	607.288	0.00165	31.59891	0.03165

Table F-9 2% Interest Factors for Annual Compounding

n	Single Payment		Equal-Payment Series			
	Compound- Amount Factor	Present- Worth Factor	Compound- Amount Factor	Sinking- Fund Factor	Present- Worth Factor	Capital- Recovery Factor
	SP $_{i-n}$ ( )	PS $_{i-n}$ ( )	SR $_{i-n}$ ( )	RS $_{i-n}$ ( )	PR $_{i-n}$ ( )	RP $_{i-n}$ ( )
1	1.020	0.98039	1.000	1.00000	0.98039	1.02000
2	1.040	0.96117	2.020	0.49505	1.94156	0.51505
3	1.061	0.94232	3.060	0.32675	2.88388	0.34675
4	1.082	0.92385	4.122	0.24262	3.80773	0.26262
5	1.104	0.90573	5.204	0.19216	4.71346	0.21216
6	1.126	0.88797	6.308	0.15853	5.60143	0.17853
7	1.149	0.87056	7.434	0.13451	6.47199	0.15451
8	1.172	0.85349	8.583	0.11651	7.32548	0.13651
9	1.195	0.83676	9.755	0.10252	8.16224	0.12252
10	1.219	0.82035	10.950	0.09133	8.98258	0.11133
11	1.243	0.80426	12.169	0.08218	9.78685	0.10218
12	1.268	0.78849	13.412	0.07456	10.57534	0.09456
13	1.294	0.77303	14.680	0.06812	11.34837	0.08812
14	1.319	0.75788	15.974	0.06260	12.10625	0.08260
15	1.346	0.74301	17.293	0.05783	12.84926	0.07783
16	1.373	0.72845	18.639	0.05365	13.57771	0.07365
17	1.400	0.71416	20.012	0.04997	14.29187	0.06997
18	1.428	0.70016	21.412	0.04670	14.99203	0.06670
19	1.457	0.68643	22.841	0.04378	15.67846	0.06378
20	1.486	0.67297	24.297	0.04116	16.35143	0.06116
21	1.516	0.65978	25.783	0.03878	17.01121	0.05878
22	1.546	0.64684	27.299	0.03663	17.65805	0.05663
23	1.577	0.63416	28.845	0.03467	18.29220	0.05467
24	1.608	0.62172	30.422	0.03287	18.91392	0.05287
25	1.641	0.60953	32.030	0.03122	19.52346	0.05122
26	1.673	0.59758	33.671	0.02970	20.12104	0.04970
27	1.707	0.58586	35.344	0.02829	20.70690	0.04829
28	1.741	0.57437	37.051	0.02699	21.28127	0.04699
29	1.776	0.56311	38.792	0.02578	21.84438	0.04578
30	1.811	0.55207	40.568	0.02465	22.39646	0.04465
35	2.000	0.50003	49.994	0.02000	24.99862	0.04000
40	2.208	0.45289	60.402	0.01656	27.35548	0.03656
45	2.438	0.41020	71.893	0.01391	29.49016	0.03391
50	2.692	0.37153	84.579	0.01182	31.42361	0.03182
55	2.972	0.33650	98.587	0.01014	33.17479	0.03014
60	3.281	0.30478	114.052	0.00877	34.76088	0.02877
70	4.000	0.25003	149.978	0.00667	37.49862	0.02667
80	4.875	0.20511	193.772	0.00516	39.74451	0.02516
90	5.943	0.16826	247.157	0.00405	41.58693	0.02405
100	7.245	0.13803	312.232	0.00320	43.09835	0.02320

appendix G

Statistical Tables†

Table G-1   Cumulative Normal Probabilities

Z	0.09	0.08	0.07	0.06	0.05	0.04	0.03	0.02	0.01	0.00
−3.5	0.00017	0.00017	0.00018	0.00019	0.00019	0.00020	0.00021	0.00022	0.00022	0.00023
−3.4	0.00024	0.00025	0.00026	0.00027	0.00028	0.00029	0.00030	0.00031	0.00033	0.00034
−3.3	0.00035	0.00036	0.00038	0.00039	0.00040	0.00042	0.00043	0.00045	0.00047	0.00048
−3.2	0.00050	0.00052	0.00054	0.00056	0.00058	0.00060	0.00062	0.00064	0.00066	0.00069
−3.1	0.00071	0.00074	0.00076	0.00079	0.00082	0.00085	0.00087	0.00090	0.00094	0.00097
−3.0	0.00100	0.00104	0.00107	0.00111	0.00114	0.00118	0.00122	0.00126	0.00131	0.00135
−2.9	0.0014	0.0014	0.0015	0.0015	0.0016	0.0016	0.0017	0.0017	0.0018	0.0019
−2.8	0.0019	0.0020	0.0021	0.0021	0.0022	0.0023	0.0023	0.0024	0.0025	0.0026
−2.7	0.0026	0.0027	0.0028	0.0029	0.0030	0.0031	0.0032	0.0033	0.0034	0.0035
−2.6	0.0036	0.0037	0.0038	0.0039	0.0040	0.0041	0.0043	0.0044	0.0045	0.0047
−2.5	0.0048	0.0049	0.0051	0.0052	0.0054	0.0055	0.0057	0.0059	0.0060	0.0062
−2.4	0.0064	0.0066	0.0068	0.0069	0.0071	0.0073	0.0075	0.0078	0.0080	0.0082
−2.3	0.0084	0.0087	0.0089	0.0091	0.0094	0.0096	0.0099	0.0102	0.0104	0.0107
−2.2	0.0110	0.0113	0.0116	0.0119	0.0122	0.0125	0.0129	0.0132	0.0136	0.0139
−2.1	0.0143	0.0146	0.0150	0.0154	0.0158	0.0162	0.0166	0.0170	0.0174	0.0179
−2.0	0.0183	0.0188	0.0192	0.0197	0.0202	0.0207	0.0212	0.0217	0.0222	0.0228
−1.9	0.0233	0.0239	0.0244	0.0250	0.0256	0.0262	0.0268	0.0274	0.0281	0.0287
−1.8	0.0294	0.0301	0.0307	0.0314	0.0322	0.0329	0.0336	0.0344	0.0351	0.0359
−1.7	0.0367	0.0375	0.0384	0.0392	0.0401	0.0409	0.0418	0.0427	0.0436	0.0446
−1.6	0.0455	0.0465	0.0475	0.0485	0.0495	0.0505	0.0516	0.0526	0.0537	0.0548

†W. J. Fabrycky and Paul E. Torgersen, *Operations Economy: Industrial Applications of Operations Research*, Prentice-Hall, Inc., Englewood Cliffs, N.J., 1966, pp. 449–452.

Table G-1   Cumulative Normal Probabilities (Continued)

Z	0.09	0.08	0.07	0.06	0.05	0.04	0.03	0.02	0.01	0.00
−1.5	0.0559	0.0571	0.0582	0.0594	0.0606	0.0618	0.0630	0.0643	0.0655	0.0668
−1.4	0.0681	0.0694	0.0708	0.0721	0.0735	0.0749	0.0764	0.0778	0.0793	0.0808
−1.3	0.0823	0.0838	0.0853	0.0869	0.0885	0.0901	0.0918	0.0934	0.0951	0.0968
−1.2	0.0985	0.1003	0.1020	0.1038	0.1057	0.1075	0.1093	0.1112	0.1131	0.1151
−1.1	0.1170	0.1190	0.1210	0.1230	0.1251	0.1271	0.1292	0.1314	0.1335	0.1357
−1.0	0.1379	0.1401	0.1423	0.1446	0.1469	0.1492	0.1515	0.1539	0.1562	0.1587
−0.9	0.1611	0.1635	0.1660	0.1685	0.1711	0.1736	0.1762	0.1788	0.1814	0.1841
−0.8	0.1867	0.1894	0.1922	0.1949	0.1977	0.2005	0.2033	0.2061	0.2090	0.2119
−0.7	0.2148	0.2177	0.2207	0.2236	0.2266	0.2297	0.2327	0.2358	0.2389	0.2420
−0.6	0.2451	0.2483	0.2514	0.2546	0.2578	0.2611	0.2643	0.2676	0.2709	0.2743
−0.5	0.2776	0.2810	0.2843	0.2877	0.2912	0.2946	0.2981	0.3015	0.3050	0.3085
−0.4	0.3121	0.3156	0.3192	0.3228	0.3264	0.3300	0.3336	0.3372	0.3409	0.3446
−0.3	0.3483	0.3520	0.3557	0.3594	0.3632	0.3669	0.3707	0.3745	0.3783	0.3821
−0.2	0.3859	0.3897	0.3936	0.3974	0.4013	0.4052	0.4090	0.4129	0.4168	0.4207
−0.1	0.4247	0.4286	0.4325	0.4364	0.4404	0.4443	0.4483	0.4522	0.4562	0.4602
−0.0	0.4641	0.4681	0.4721	0.4761	0.4801	0.4840	0.4880	0.4920	0.4960	0.5000

Z	0.00	0.01	0.02	0.03	0.04	0.05	0.06	0.07	0.08	0.09
+0.0	0.5000	0.5040	0.5080	0.5120	0.5160	0.5199	0.5239	0.5279	0.5319	0.5359
+0.1	0.5398	0.5438	0.5478	0.5517	0.5557	0.5596	0.5636	0.5675	0.5714	0.5753
+0.2	0.5793	0.5832	0.5871	0.5910	0.5948	0.5987	0.6026	0.6064	0.6103	0.6141
+0.3	0.6179	0.6217	0.6255	0.6293	0.6331	0.6368	0.6406	0.6443	0.6480	0.6517
+0.4	0.6554	0.6591	0.6628	0.6664	0.6700	0.6736	0.6772	0.6808	0.6844	0.6879
+0.5	0.6915	0.6950	0.6985	0.7019	0.7054	0.7088	0.7123	0.7157	0.7190	0.7224
+0.6	0.7257	0.7291	0.7324	0.7357	0.7389	0.7422	0.7454	0.7486	0.7517	0.7549
+0.7	0.7580	0.7611	0.7642	0.7673	0.7704	0.7734	0.7764	0.7794	0.7823	0.7852
+0.8	0.7881	0.7910	0.7939	0.7967	0.7995	0.8023	0.8051	0.8079	0.8106	0.8133
+0.9	0.8159	0.8186	0.8212	0.8238	0.8264	0.8289	0.8315	0.8340	0.8365	0.8389
+1.0	0.8413	0.8438	0.8461	0.8485	0.8508	0.8531	0.8554	0.8577	0.8599	0.8621
+1.1	0.8643	0.8665	0.8686	0.8708	0.8729	0.8749	0.8770	0.8790	0.8810	0.8830
+1.2	0.8849	0.8869	0.8888	0.8907	0.8925	0.8944	0.8962	0.8980	0.8997	0.9015
+1.3	0.9032	0.9049	0.9066	0.9082	0.9099	0.9115	0.9131	0.9147	0.9162	0.9177
+1.4	0.9192	0.9207	0.9222	0.9236	0.9251	0.9265	0.9279	0.9292	0.9306	0.9319
+1.5	0.9332	0.9345	0.9357	0.9370	0.9382	0.9394	0.9406	0.9418	0.9429	0.9441
+1.6	0.9452	0.9463	0.9474	0.9484	0.9495	0.9505	0.9515	0.9525	0.9535	0.9545
+1.7	0.9554	0.9564	0.9573	0.9582	0.9591	0.9599	0.9608	0.9616	0.9625	0.9633
+1.8	0.9641	0.9649	0.9656	0.9644	0.9671	0.9678	0.9686	0.9686	0.9699	0.9706
+1.9	0.9713	0.9719	0.9726	0.9732	0.9738	0.9744	0.9750	0.9756	0.9761	0.9767
+2.0	0.9773	0.9778	0.9783	0.9788	0.9793	0.9798	0.9803	0.9808	0.9812	0.9817
+2.1	0.9821	0.9826	0.9830	0.9834	0.9838	0.9842	0.9846	0.9850	0.9854	0.9857
+2.2	0.9861	0.9864	0.9868	0.9871	0.9875	0.9878	0.9881	0.9884	0.9887	0.9890
+2.3	0.9893	0.9896	0.9898	0.9901	0.9904	0.9906	0.9909	0.9911	0.9913	0.9916
+2.4	0.9918	0.9920	0.9922	0.9925	0.9927	0.9929	0.9931	0.9931	0.9934	0.9936
+2.5	0.9938	0.9940	0.9941	0.9943	0.9945	0.9946	0.9948	0.9949	0.9951	0.9952
+2.6	0.9953	0.9955	0.9956	0.9957	0.9959	0.9960	0.9961	0.9962	0.9963	0.9964
+2.7	0.9965	0.9966	0.9967	0.9968	0.9969	0.9970	0.9971	0.9972	0.9973	0.9974
+2.8	0.9974	0.9975	0.9976	0.9977	0.9977	0.9978	0.9979	0.9979	0.9980	0.9981
+2.9	0.9981	0.9982	0.9982	0.9983	0.9984	0.9984	0.9985	0.9985	0.9986	0.9986
+3.0	0.99865	0.99869	0.99874	0.99878	0.99882	0.99886	0.99889	0.99893	0.99896	0.99900
+3.1	0.99903	0.99906	0.99910	0.99913	0.99915	0.99918	0.99921	0.99924	0.99926	0.99929
+3.2	0.99931	0.99934	0.99936	0.99938	0.99940	0.99942	0.99944	0.99946	0.99948	0.99950
+3.3	0.99952	0.99953	0.99955	0.99957	0.99958	0.99960	0.99961	0.99962	0.99964	0.99965
+3.4	0.99966	0.99967	0.99969	0.99970	0.99971	0.99972	0.99973	0.99974	0.99975	0.99976
+3.5	0.99977	0.99978	0.99978	0.99979	0.99980	0.99981	0.99981	0.99982	0.99983	0.99983

Table G-2   Cumulative Poisson Probabilities × 1,000

μ \ x	0	1	2	3	4	5	6	7	8	9	10	11	12	13	14
0.1	905	995	1,000												
0.2	819	982	999	1,000											
0.3	741	963	996	1,000											
0.4	670	938	992	999	1,000										
0.5	607	910	986	998	1,000										
0.6	549	878	977	997	1,000										
0.7	497	844	966	994	999	1,000									
0.8	449	809	953	991	999	1,000									
0.9	407	772	937	987	998	1,000									
1.0	368	736	920	981	996	999	1,000								
1.1	333	699	900	974	995	999	1,000								
1.2	301	663	879	966	992	998	1,000								
1.3	273	627	857	957	989	998	1,000								
1.4	247	592	833	946	986	997	999	1,000							
1.5	223	558	809	934	981	996	999	1,000							
1.6	202	525	783	921	976	994	999	1,000							
1.7	183	493	757	907	970	992	998	1,000							
1.8	165	463	731	891	964	990	997	999	1,000						
1.9	150	434	704	875	956	987	997	999	1,000						
2.0	135	406	677	857	947	983	995	999	1,000						
2.2	111	355	623	819	928	975	993	998	1,000						
2.4	091	308	570	779	904	964	988	997	999	1,000					
2.6	074	267	518	736	877	951	983	995	999	1,000					

Table G-2 Cumulative Poisson Probabilities × 1,000 (Continued)

x \ μ	0	1	2	3	4	5	6	7	8	9	10	11	12	13	14
2.8	061	231	469	692	848	935	976	992	998	999	1,000				
3.0	050	199	423	647	815	916	966	988	996	999	1,000				
3.2	041	171	380	603	781	895	955	983	994	998	1,000				
3.4	033	147	340	558	744	871	942	977	992	997	999	1,000			
3.6	027	126	303	515	706	844	927	969	988	996	999	1,000			
3.8	022	107	269	473	668	816	909	960	984	994	998	999	1,000		
4.0	018	092	238	433	629	785	889	949	979	992	997	999	1,000		
4.2	015	078	210	395	590	753	867	936	972	989	996	999	1,000		
4.4	012	066	185	359	551	720	844	921	964	985	994	998	999	1,000	
4.6	010	056	163	326	513	686	818	905	955	980	992	997	999	1,000	
4.8	008	048	143	294	476	651	791	887	944	975	990	996	998	999	1,000
5	007	040	125	265	440	616	762	867	932	968	986	995	998	999	1,000
6	002	017	062	151	285	446	606	744	847	916	957	980	991	996	999
7	001	007	030	082	173	301	450	599	729	830	901	947	973	987	994
8	000	003	014	042	100	191	313	453	593	717	816	888	936	966	983
9	000	001	006	021	055	116	207	324	456	587	706	803	876	926	959
10		000	003	010	029	067	130	220	333	458	583	697	792	864	917
11		000	001	005	015	038	079	143	232	341	460	579	689	781	854
12		000	001	002	008	020	046	090	155	242	347	462	576	682	772
13			000	001	004	011	026	054	100	166	252	353	463	573	675
14				000	002	006	014	032	062	109	176	260	358	464	570
15				000	001	003	008	018	037	070	118	185	268	363	466

Table G-2 Cumulative Poisson Probabilities × 1,000 (Continued)

x \ μ	15	16	17	18	19	20	21	22	23	24	25	26	27	28	29
7	998	999	1,000												
8	992	996	998	999	1,000										
9	978	989	995	998	999	1,000									
10	951	973	986	993	997	998	999	1,000							
11	907	944	968	982	991	995	998	999	1,000						
12	844	899	937	963	979	988	994	997	999	999	1,000				
13	764	835	890	930	957	975	986	992	996	998	999	1,000			
14	669	756	827	883	923	952	971	983	991	995	997	999	999	1,000	
15	568	664	749	819	875	917	947	967	981	989	994	997	998	999	1,000

x \ μ	0	1	2	3	4	5	6	7	8	9	10	11	12	13	14
16					000	001	004	010	022	043	077	127	193	275	368
17					000	001	002	005	013	026	049	085	135	201	281
18						000	001	003	015	015	030	055	092	143	208
19						000	001	002	004	009	018	035	061	098	150
20							000	001	002	005	011	021	039	066	105
21								000	001	003	006	013	025	043	072
22								000	001	002	004	008	015	028	048
23									000	001	002	004	009	017	031
24										000	001	003	005	011	020

Table G-2 Cumulative Poisson Probabilities × 1,000 (Continued)

x \ μ	15	16	17	18	19	20	21	22	23	24	25	26	27	28	29
16	467	566	659	742	812	868	911	942	963	978	987	993	996	998	999
17	371	468	564	655	736	805	861	905	937	959	975	985	991	995	997
18	287	375	469	562	651	731	799	855	899	932	955	972	983	990	994
19	215	292	378	469	561	647	725	793	849	893	927	951	969	980	988
20	157	221	297	381	470	559	644	721	787	843	888	922	948	966	978
21	111	163	227	302	384	471	558	640	716	782	838	883	917	944	963
22	077	117	169	232	306	387	472	556	637	712	777	832	877	913	940
23	052	082	123	175	238	310	389	472	555	635	708	772	827	873	908
24	034	056	087	128	180	243	314	392	473	554	632	704	768	823	868

x \ μ	30	31	32	33	34	35	36	37	38	39	40	41	42	43	44
16	999	1,000													
17	999	999	1,000												
18	997	998	999	1,000											
19	993	996	998	999	999	1,000									
20	987	992	995	997	998	999	1,000								
21	976	985	991	994	996	999	999	1,000							
22	959	973	983	989	994	996	998	999	999	1,000					
23	936	956	971	981	988	993	996	997	999	999	1,000				
24	904	932	953	969	979	987	992	995	997	998	999	999	1,000		

Index